Selected Epigrams of Martial

SELECTED
EPIGRAMS
of
MARTIAL

*Edited, with an
Introduction and Notes, by*

Edwin Post

Norman : University of Oklahoma Press

Library of Congress Catalog Card Number: 67-15577

Reprinted 1967 by the University of Oklahoma Press, Publishing Division of the University, Norman, from the edition originally published 1908 by Ginn and Company.

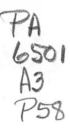

PREFACE

This volume is offered to the public with the belief that the selections herein found are sufficient in number and variety to illustrate fully the epigram as a form of literature and to afford valuable collateral information to those interested in Roman private life. However, in selecting the epigrams a wider interest in the subject matter has been continually kept in mind and the text has been so annotated as to make the book serviceable in an ordinary reading course.

To mention all the places in which preceding editors have been of help to me in the preparation of the commentary would smack of pedantry. I may, however, be allowed to say that my own annotations were originally worked out without reference to any other commentary. Subsequently most of the scholars who have devoted study to Martial, mediæval and modern, were consulted, and attempt has been made, in introduction and commentary, to credit the proper sources with all that did not fairly appear to be common property. The text as edited by Mr. J. D. Duff for Professor Postgate's Corpus, as well as M. Gaston Boissier's monograph on Martial, I did not have in time for any use in preparing my manuscript. It goes without saying that in common with all recent students of Martial I have a large debt to pay to Professor Lindsay for his work upon the text. The numbers of the epigrams found in this book have been made to conform to those in his (Oxford) text edition.

My hearty thanks are due to Dr. Emory B. Lease of the College of the City of New York for suggestions concerning the meters, and to Mr. Nathan Wilbur Helm, now Instructor in the Phillips Exeter Academy, for repeated assistance rendered while he was an Instructor at Princeton University. No less am I appreciative of the painstaking and intelligent work of the proofreaders of the Athenæum Press. Lastly, but still before all others, my thanks are due to Professor Charles Knapp of Barnard College, Columbia University, who, serving as General Editor at the request of Professors Peck and Smith, subjected every part of my manuscript to the most careful examination, bringing to the editing of the book the results of his special study of Martial, thus adding materially to the value of the work, not to speak of his interest and pains shown in seeing the book through the press.

I shall be grateful to any who may be so good as to call my attention to errors.

E. P.

CONTENTS

INTRODUCTION

I. MARTIAL: HIS LIFE AND WRITINGS

1. It is a fact at once striking and suggestive that very few of the great representatives of Latin literature were born and bred in Rome ; they came from the Italian towns and country districts, nay, in many cases, from the outlying provinces. Of these provinces Spain furnished more than her share of the men who gave distinction to the literature of Rome. M. Annaeus Seneca, the rhetorician, L. Annaeus Seneca, the philosopher, his more brilliant son, and Lucan, nephew of the latter, were all born at Corduba, Quintilian at Calagurris, Martial at Bilbilis. These writers, with others of lesser note, such as Columella and Pomponius Mela, almost constitute a Spanish school of Latin literature.

2. Martial was born at Bilbilis Augusta[1], a municipium in Hispania Tarraconensis on the road from Emerita to Caesaraugusta. The town was picturesquely situated on a high hill, at the base of which flowed the river Salo[2]. The wild scenery of his birthplace made a lasting impression upon the poet, and in after years he wrote of it with pride and longing. The splendor and charm of the imperial city were to him no match for the simple beauty of the home scenes, the praises of which he is not ashamed to sing. He even glories in the more practical advantages of the place, as the seat of a considerable trade

[1] Cf. 1. 61. 12 ; 10. 13. 1–2 ; 12. 18. 7–9. For our knowledge of Martial's life we have to rely chiefly on the poet's own writings.

[2] 10. 103. 1–2 ; 10. 104. 6. Cf. also Anicius Paulinus, bishop of Nola in the fifth century, Carm. 10. 223 *Bilbilim acutis pendentem scopulis.* For *Bilbilim*, however, the Vienna Corpus here reads *Birbilim*.

in iron and of the manufacture of weapons, for the hardening of which the cold waters of the Salo were believed to be especially fitted[1].

3. Martial was born on the first day of March[2]. In 10. 24 he informs us that he is fifty-seven years old. Since that book was written between 95 and 98 (**13**) he was born between 38 and 41[3].

4. Martial was certainly of humble extraction[4], but he was probably *ingenuus*, free-born. It is hardly likely that he could have obtained the citizenship for others (**8**), had he not possessed it himself. Rader[5] is probably right in assuming that, had he been a freedman, he would have mentioned his *patronus*.

5. The poet's full name was M. Valerius Martialis. Some have supposed that he derived this name, not from his father, but from some benefactor; others have suggested that he assumed the name Valerius out of love for Valerius Catullus (**34**), and that he borrowed the name Martialis from that of his birth-month[6].

6. His parents, (Valerius) Fronto and Flacilla[7], appear to have been dead when he came to Rome. They had had the

---

[1] 1. 49. 3-4 *videbis altam, Liciniane, Bilbilin, equis et armis nobilem*; 1. 49. 11 *brevi Salone, qui ferrum gelat*; 4. 55. 11-15 *saevo Bilbilin optimam metallo, quae vincit Chalybasque Noricosque, et ferro Plateam suo sonantem, quam fluctu tenui, sed inquieto armorum Salo temperator ambit.*

[2] 9. 52; 10. 24. 1-2 *natales mihi Martiae Kalendae, lux formosior omnibus Kalendis*; 10. 92. 10 *Martem mearum principem Kalendarum.*

[3] Unless otherwise stated, all dates in this book are dates A.D.

[4] 10. 96. 4.

[5] For this and similar citations see the Bibliography, pp. xlvii–li.

[6] Some late Mss. give him the agnomen *Cocus*. This may have been a nickname derived from his *Xenia* and *Apophoreta*; it is more likely, however, that it arose from a false reading in Aelius Lampridius (Alex. Severus 38) which the *editio princeps* made current for a time, though some think it originated in a misunderstanding of 6. 61. 7-8 *quam multi tineas pascunt blattasque diserti et redimunt soli carmina docta coci!* See Scriverius, Animadversiones to Book I Praefatio, the notes on the same *praefatio* in Schneidewin (*editio maior*), and Brandt.

[7] 5. 34; Brandt 11-12.

disposition and the means to give their son training in grammar and rhetoric [1]; whether this training was secured at Bilbilis or at some larger town, such as Caesaraugusta, cannot be determined. Perhaps the success attained at Rome by so many of their countrymen inspired the parents with an ambition to see their son equally successful there.

7. Later, probably in 64 [2], he came to Rome to seek his fortune [3]; he was then between twenty-three and twenty-six years of age. At Rome, the center of wealth, fashion, and power, he spent the best thirty-four years of his life. The sight of " the city of marble ", with its cosmopolitan street throngs, its *horti* inclosing the palaces of the rich, its *fora* and *porticus* flanked by noble trees, the temples of the gods and public buildings of every sort reflecting the sunlight from a thousand burnished roofs, must have moved profoundly the young provincial. The kaleidoscopic life of the imperial city Martial came to know thoroughly, both in its lighter and in its darker aspects. The epigrams reflect perfectly the Rome of Nero, Vespasian, Titus, and Domitian.

8. To Titus and Domitian he owed what little preferment came to him. Although a bachelor, he received the *ius trium liberorum* [4], i.e. the privileges and immunities that accrued to the father of three children, and the rank of *tribunus militum* (the *tribunatus semestris*) [5], which carried with it the rights of an *eques*. Though Martial became most expert as a court flatterer, his years of faithful subservience appear to have profited him but little. An occasional invitation to a state

[1] 9. 73. 7 *at me litterulas stulti docuere parentes.*

[2] Martial makes no reference to the burning of the city in 64; we may infer that he did not reach Rome until after that catastrophe.

[3] Brandt, 18, thinks he came to practice law.

[4] 3. 95. 5–6 *praemia laudato tribuit mihi Caesar uterque   natorumque dedit iura paterna trium*; 9. 97. 5–6.

[5] 3. 95. 9–10 *vidit me Roma tribunum   et sedeo qua te suscitat Oceanus*; 5. 13. 2; 12. 29. 2. On the *tribunatus semestris* see e.g. Marq.-Wissowa Staatsv. 2. 368.

dinner would afford but small compensation for the failure of the emperor (Domitian) to grant the trifling favors which the poet begged, such as his request for permission to tap the Marcian aqueduct for his town house[1] or his appeals for money[2]. Evidently, though the emperor might appreciate the poet's wit and *ioci*[3], he took good care that they should not come at too high a price. The citizenship that Martial obtained for several persons cost the emperor nothing, but may have helped to replenish the poet's purse.

The poet's flattery was lavished not only on the emperor, but on the court favorites and on the freedmen of the imperial house[4]. The names of the infamous Crispinus, of Euphemus, Earinus, Parthenius, and the like occur all too frequently in the epigrams.

9. Though we know but little of the life of Martial for some years after he came to Rome, it is probable that he wrote poetry. It is possible that he " had passed middle life and stood at the beginning of his fortieth year before he wrote what has come down to us "[5], but that " he wrote nothing under Nero, nor under Galba, Otho, Vitellius, Vespasian "[6], is hardly likely[7]. But poetry, even though published, could not keep the wolf from the door. When Martial came to Rome, some of the most influential and distinguished families there were of Spanish origin. It is probable that he was soon made welcome at their palaces, especially at those of L. Annaeus Seneca (1), Annaeus Mela, and Iunius Pollio[8]. It can hardly be doubted that the influence of Seneca made him a *cliens* of C. Calpurnius Piso. But any satisfaction or advantage these powerful friends brought to him was short-lived, for the so-called conspiracy of Piso in 65 ruined these great houses and resulted in the death of all the Senecas and of Piso. Though the fate of these men

---

[1] 9. 18.   [2] 6. 10.   [3] 4. 27; 5. 6; 6. 64. 14; 7. 12. 1–2.   [4] 9. 79.
[5] Schanz, Geschichte der römischen Litteratur², § 413.   [6] Tyrrell 288.
[7] Friedländer SG. 3. 386. See I. 113.   [8] 4. 40; 12. 36. 8–9.

must have shocked the young provincial, and perhaps dashed to the ground his hopes of good things to come, it did not, so far as we know, inspire him to seek a more independent means of livelihood than that open to the *cliens*, though Sellar[1] suggests that Quintilian and others had advised him to practice law[2]. He may have made a half-hearted attempt[3]; if so, he had small success. His dislike of the profession is clear[4].

10. For thirty-four years he lived at Rome the precarious life of a hanger-on. He is a chronic beggar. Yet by a shrewdness amounting to art and an ingenuity of statement unparalleled he almost succeeds in making begging attractive, or at least respectable. No beggar could be more polite or veil by more courtly words a mendicancy from which a more self-respecting man would have shrunk with horror. Well might his reader at times believe that Thalia as an inspiring cause had surrendered her place to Egestas. Yet, despite his numerous friends and the many *patroni* to whom he paid court, he dragged on a hand-to-mouth existence. The extravagance that had characterized Nero's reign was checked by the death of the representatives of some of the richest houses and of Nero himself. Vespasian was comparatively economical; the new families that came to the fore then took their cue from the Palatine. Under Domitian the danger of exciting the cupidity of the informers (*delatores*) prevented a display that might have been encouraged by a happier era[5]. To the poet of Domitian's day the times of Nero must have seemed like a Golden Age.

One piece of property at least Martial owned, a small estate near Nomentum in the Sabine country, scantily provided with wood, water, or shelter, the gift, it would seem, of Seneca; if it did not afford him anything to eat, it provided him with a place of occasional refuge from the burdens of a client's life

[1] P. xii.
[2] Sellar infers this from the tone of certain epigrams : see 2. 90; 1. 17; 2. 30.   [3] 8. 17.   [4] 5. 20. 6; 12. 68. 3.   [5] Friedländer SG. 3. 442.

and the noise of the town. This place he owned as early as the year 84[1].

11. In the city he had grown old in a garret up three flights[2], though the discomforts of an *insula* on the Quirinalis were perhaps offset somewhat by the outlook over the trees that bordered the Porticus Agrippae[3]. The house on the Quirinalis mentioned in 9. 18[4] probably afforded him ampler accommodations during the later years of his stay in Rome[5], but could not in any appreciable degree have lessened the pinch of poverty or the discomforts of the daily round. He seems to be ever in need, — now of a new toga, now of tile for a house[6], now of a *lacerna*. If 7. 16 is to be taken seriously, he must at times have been sorely reduced. His poverty so embittered him that, when he compares his own lot with that of those whom he thinks less deserving, he is ready to blame his parents for the education they had afforded him. That he refers to a slave or two[7] may but emphasize his poverty, though at a later period, toward the end of his sojourn in Rome, he had a span of mules[8].

12. About 87 or 88 he retired from the city to Gallia To-gata (Cisalpine Gaul), as if he would make it his permanent home[9]. In 3. 4 he hints at two reasons for this step, namely, weariness of the social round (*officium*) and the difficulty of eking out a living. He seems to have lived at Forum Cornelii[10] and to have visited places of interest within reach, especially Altinum[11] and Ravenna[12]. But we find him soon back in Rome, although he appears to dream of a return to the north at some subsequent time[13].

[1] Friedländer SG. 3. 445. See also 2. 38; 7. 36; 9. 18; 9. 60; 9. 97. 7; 10. 48. 19; 10. 58. 9–10; 10. 61; 10. 94; 12. 57.   [2] 1. 117.

[3] 1. 108. 3–4.

[4] The ninth book was written not later than 94.

[5] 9. 18. 2; 9. 97. 8; 10. 58. 10; Hülsen *Rhein. Mus.* 49. 396.

[6] 7. 36.   [8] 8. 61. 7.   [10] 3. 4. 4.   [12] 3. 56; 3. 57.
[7] 5. 34; 5. 37.   [9] 3. 4.   [11] 4. 25.   [13] 4. 25.

13. Prior to this time he had won an enviable position as an author. In 80 he had published the booklet called in the manuscripts *Epigrammaton Liber,* but commonly known as *Liber Spectaculorum,* because it was written to commemorate the spectacles incident to the dedication of the Flavian Amphitheater (the Colosseum) in 80. These little poems set Rome to talking and made the reading public eager for more from the same hand. Martial was so flattered by their favorable reception that he was emboldened to send an author's copy to the emperor himself:

> Da veniam subitis: non displicuisse meretur,
> festinat, Caesar, qui placuisse tibi[1].

Friedländer and Gilbert, however, think that some of the pieces may have been added in a second edition. Next appeared the two books of *epigrammata,* in the literal sense of the term epigram[2], that is, epigrammatic inscriptions to accompany presents such as the Romans sent to friends at the Saturnalia. These appeared in 84 or 85 as *Xenia* and *Apophoreta*; they were later appended to the other poems as Books XIII and XIV. Although not worthy of comparison with his later creations, they seem to have won for Martial a definite literary standing[3]; thereafter he published in regular sequence the several books. Books I and II were apparently given to the world together, in 85 or, more probably, in 86[4].

Internal evidence[5] shows that Book III was published in 87 or 88 at Forum Cornelii[6]; Book IV in the latter part of 88; Book V about a year later; Book VI in 90; Book VII in 92; Book VIII about the middle of 93; Book IX about a year later. Of Book X there were two editions; of these the first appeared in 95, the second in 98, after the accession of Trajan. Meanwhile Book XI had been written for the Saturnalia of 96.

[1] Liber Spectaculorum 31.   [2] See §§ 21; 26.   [3] 1. 1; 2. 6.
[4] Friedländer, Einleitung, 53; Dau 8 ff.; Stobbe, *Philologus,* 26. 62.
[5] Friedländer, Einleitung, 53 ff.   [6] See § 12.

There is reason to think that, after Nerva came to the throne, Martial realized that, because of its obscenity, he could not send an author's copy of Book XI to the emperor, and that he therefore made an anthology out of Books X and XI[1]. It will be noticed that the several books from III to XI appeared quite regularly. But Rome waited until 101, or, more probably, until 102, for Book XII; by that time Martial had left the city forever. No complete edition of the poet's works appeared until after his death.

14. Martial spent in all thirty-four years at Rome[2]. In 98 he returned to his native Bilbilis. What moved him to depart we can only surmise. Did he feel that his rôle of polite beggar had been played to a finish? Did love of native land and the desire to be forever emancipated from the poor client's life, with a longing for quietude and rest, prove stronger than the motives which, when he was younger, had been masterful[3]? His means were always limited, despite the possession of the estate at Nomentum[4] and of a modest town house. With these narrow resources he could not but contrast with longing the rude plenty of his far-away home[5]. Besides, as he grew older, he felt more and more the burden of his social duties. Possibly insomnia[6] or illness that warned him that the end might not be far off[7] helped to a final decision. Some have thought that the new régime[8] which was realized under Trajan, if not under Nerva, made it clear to Martial that the chances for a livelihood were now less for a man who must live by his wits. But Martial had lived for a long time without much imperial favor, and, despite the ups and downs incident to a hand-to-mouth existence, the balance was on the profit side of the account[9]. Perhaps no one motive was uppermost in his mind.

[1] See Schanz § 414.
[2] 10. 103. 7; 10. 104. 10; 12. 31. 7.
[3] 1. 49; 4. 55; 10. 96. 1.
[4] See § 10.   [5] 2. 48.
[6] 10. 74; 12. 57; 12. 68; 14. 125.
[7] 6. 70.
[8] 10. 72; 11. 7
[9] 12. 34.

In Rome he had never ceased to long for the home of his youth[1], for the ease of life there, its freedom from restraint, its comparative abundance[2]. He left Rome apparently without regret. His little property could not have brought him much, for Pliny[3] tells us that he himself furnished the means to defray the expenses of the homeward journey.

15. Whether Martial had any prospect of a livelihood in Spain before he left Rome we know not. In Bilbilis, however, he found in a certain Marcella a patroness and a friend. To her he owed the gift of an estate well provided with the things his estate at Nomentum (10) had lacked[4]; this made him comfortable, if not independent. Other friends seem to have contributed to his comfort at this time, at least to some extent[5]. There is no proof that Marcella was his wife or his mistress[6]. Martial always speaks of her with profound respect; she appears to have been a woman of great charm and culture[7], in whose society he could forget what he had lost in Rome.

For some time the poet seems to have enjoyed himself to the full in Bilbilis, if we may judge from the epigrams addressed to his old friend Juvenal (16; 19)[8]. But the novelty soon wore off. To the cosmopolitan crowds of Rome, its immense and splendid structures, the games of the circus, the contests of the amphitheater, the libraries and the *recitationes* and the many other incentives to the intellectual life that the imperial city afforded, the provinciality and barrenness of life in the little town on the Salo must have presented a painful contrast. The preface to Book XII voices the new discontent, which is echoed in the subsequent epigrams. This regret perhaps affected his health and hastened his death, for it is evident that he did not live long after the completion of Book XII.

[1] 10. 13; 10. 96; 10. 103; 10. 104. [2] 1. 49; 4. 55; 12. 18.
[3] Ep. 3. 21. 2. [4] 12. 31. [5] See e.g. 12. 3.
[6] Such passages as 2. 92; 3. 92; 4. 24; 11. 43; 11. 104 do not warrant the belief that Martial had a wife at Rome. [7] 12. 21. [8] 12. 18.

" He seems to have outlived his enjoyments, ambitions, and hopes "[1]. He died not later than 104; the letter in which Pliny[2] refers to his death cannot have been written after that year[3].

16. Having thus given a general survey of Martial's life, we may now consider certain matters in detail. First, let us note the people to whom Martial paid court in Rome or with whom he associated there. They constitute a motley company indeed; among them, besides those already mentioned, were scholars, lawyers, senators, men in public life, freedmen, spies (*delatores*), soldiers, and nobodies. With most of the literary men of the town the poet was acquainted, if not on terms of intimacy. During the latter half of the first century Roman literature still had worthy representatives, if not those of the first class. Lucan's *Pharsalia* must have been well-nigh finished, though not yet published, when Martial reached Rome, if indeed, in the shape in which we have it, it was published before the death of its author. Likewise the work of Seneca the philosopher was practically ended, for he, with Lucan, perished within a few months after Martial reached Rome[4]. Silius Italicus, consul in 68[5], and Statius were the fashionable writers of the epos; the latter distinguished himself also in lyric poetry. Tacitus was to win for himself a great name as a historian and Juvenal was to attain like eminence in satire. Pliny the Elder had still about fifteen years of work to do. Quintilian lived until within a year or two of Martial's final departure from Rome.

17. Among a multitude of lesser literary lights may be mentioned Stertinius Avitus, the poet, *consul suffectus* in 92, who signally honored Martial[6], L. Arruntius Stella, the poet,

---

[1] Tyrrell 288.   [2] Plin. Ep. 3. 21.

[3] Brandt, 37, thinks his death could not have happened before 100 or 101.   [4] See § 9.   [5] 4. 14.

[6] Cf. Praefatio to Book IX; 10. 96.

consul in 101 or 102[1], Sex. Iulius Frontinus, the distinguished
engineer, who was thrice consul[2] and author of the well-known
works *De aquis urbis Romae* and *Strategematica*. Martial
seems to have been on very friendly terms with his countryman Decianus, from Emerita. Book II is dedicated to him,
and in 1. 61 he is deemed worthy of mention with Vergil,
Catullus, Livy, Ovid, Seneca, etc. To these are to be added
Canius Rufus, a witty poet from Cadiz[3], Licinianus, the
pleader, a fellow-townsman of Martial[4], and another Spaniard
from Bilbilis, Maternus the jurist[5].

18. There is, however, reason to believe that Martial was
not on the best of terms with all of his literary contemporaries.
For example, Martial never mentions Statius, nor does Statius
mention Martial. This at first sight seems strange, since they
had many mutual friends and touched repeatedly on the same
themes. Cf. M. 6. 21 with S. 1. 2, M. 6. 28 with S. 2. 1,
M. 6. 42 with S. 1. 5, M. 7. 21; 7. 22; 7. 23 with S. 2. 7,
M. 7. 40 with S. 3. 3, M. 9. 12; 9. 13; 9. 16; 9. 17; 9. 36
with S. 3. 4, M. 9. 43; 9. 44 with S. 4. 6[6]. Yet it is easy to
see that Martial can have had little sympathy with the literary
ideals of Statius. Martial worked a vein almost wholly new,
his product was light and up-to-date; Statius dreamed of producing a great epic. To Juvenal and to Martial both, with
their contempt of the long-winded epics which were the terror
of the unhappy folk whose social relations virtually compelled
them to listen to them at the *recitationes*, the ambition of
Statius must have seemed puerile. All this explains the ill-
concealed antipathy of Martial and Juvenal to Statius.

[1] 1. 61. 4; 7. 36; 10. 48. 5; 11. 52. 15.
[2] 10. 48. 20; 10. 58.
[3] 1. 61. 9; 10. 48. 5.
[4] 1. 49. 3; 1. 61. 11.
[5] 1. 96; 2. 74; 10. 37. 1–4.
[6] The references to Statius are to his Silvae. See further Friedländer
SG. 3. 450; Vollmer, Statius, 20, N. 3.

19. Of Martial's intimacy with Juvenal there can be hardly a doubt. Between satirist and epigrammatist there was evidently a fellow-feeling. The close parallelism between the satires of Juvenal and the epigrams of Martial has been repeatedly remarked and discussed[1].

20. Other patrons of the poet, especially during his last years at Rome, were Cocceius Nerva, subsequently emperor[2]; the brothers Domitius Tullus and Lucanus, whose riches may have recommended them to Martial[3]; M. Aquilius Regulus[4], famous as an orator and infamous as a *delator*; L. Licinius Sura[5], thrice consul, who influenced Nerva to make Trajan his successor and had much to do with placing Hadrian on the throne; L. Appius Maximus Norbanus[6] and M. Antonius Primus[7], of Gaul, distinguished generals both; Atedius Melior, the exquisite[8]. Martial's friendship with these men may have been merely formal; he may well, however, have been on more intimate terms with Aulus Pudens[9], who is often mentioned by his praenomen Aulus, as he was with Q. Ovidius, who lived near his estate at Nomentum[10], and with Iulius Martialis[11]. Much that Martial wrote had a personal sting; such writing inevitably gave offense and made enemies. These apparently gave him trouble from time to time, though that they seriously interfered with his attempts to ingratiate himself with the persons to whom he paid court may well be doubted.

II. MARTIAL AS POET

21. Scholars agree that Martial wrote epigrams. But what is an epigram? The basic Greek word, ἐπίγραμμα, means an

---

[1] See Friedländer in Bursian's *Jahresbericht*, 72. 191 (1892); H. Nettleship, *Journal of Philology*, 16. 41 ff. (1888) = Lectures and Essays, Second Series, 117 ff.; H. L. Wilson *A. J. P.* 19. 193 ff.

[2] 5. 28. 4; 8. 70; 9. 26.   [3] 1. 36.   [4] 1. 12.   [5] 7. 47.   [6] 9. 84.   [7] 10. 23.
[8] 2. 69; 4. 54. 8; 6. 28.   [9] 1. 31; 12. 51.   [10] 1. 105; 9. 52; 13. 119.
[11] 1. 15; 4. 64; 5. 20; 7. 17; 9. 97; 10. 47; 12. 34.

inscription, something written upon an object of interest. The modern lexicographer says: "In a restricted sense, [an epigram is] a short poem or piece in verse, which has only one subject and finishes by a witty or ingenious turn of thought; hence, in a general sense, an interesting thought represented happily in a few words, whether verse or prose; a pointed or antithetical saying"[1].

22. What relation does this modern definition bear to the basic Greek word? Lack of appreciation of literary form or crass ignorance has at various times applied the term epigram to almost every kind of short poem; yet we cannot reduce all real epigrams to a single category. The truth seems to be that the term "epigram," even when correctly employed, has not been used at all periods for the same thing.

Originally, in the Greek sense, the epigram was an epigraphic poem or composition in verse, an inscription upon some monument or work of art, explanatory or descriptive of it, or commemorative of some person or event. Extreme simplicity and stylistic purity characterize this species of epigram[2]. Of this earliest form, in which the poems dealt with real persons or were addressed to real persons or were actual inscriptions, Simonides of Ceos is the greatest representative. Take for example his epigram on the seer Megistias[3]:

> Μνῆμα τόδε κλεινοῖο Μεγιστία, ὅν ποτε Μῆδοι
> Σπερχειὸν ποταμὸν κτεῖναν ἀμειψάμενοι,
> μάντιος, ὅς τότε κῆρας ἐπερχομένας σάφα εἰδὼς
> οὐκ ἔτλη Σπάρτης ἡγεμόνας προλιπεῖν.

23. During the brilliant period of Greek culture which succeeded the dissolution of Alexander's empire and which, because

---

[1] Century Dictionary.   [2] See Mahaffy I. 193.
[3] For the text see Bergk-Hiller, Anthologia Lyrica (1897), p. 251, No. 79. The epigram has been thus translated by John Stirling:

> Of famed Megistias here behold the tomb:
>   Him on this side Spercheus slew the Medes,
> A seer who well foresaw his coming doom,
>   But would not lose his share in Sparta's deeds.

its center was Alexandria, has been called the Alexandrian epoch, the epigram received marked attention. "Besides the new treatment of old forms, there were three kinds of poetry, first developed or perfected at Alexandria, which have special interest for us from the great celebrity they gained when imported into Rome. They are the didactic poem, the erotic elegy, and the epigram "[1]. Epigrams were now composed not only on real but on purely imaginary subjects. The satirical and the erotic elements were added during this period. Brilliancy of style took the place of purity, and the simplicity of Simonides gave way to rivalry which aimed ever to produce something new. Leonidas of Tarentum, apparently a contemporary of Pyrrhus of Epirus, is perhaps the best exponent of this style. An example of his work is his epigram on a certain Crethon :

> Αὐτὰ ἐπὶ Κρήθωνος ἐγὼ λίθος οὔνομα κείνου
> δηλοῦσα, Κρήθων δ' ἐγχθόνιος σποδιά,
> ὁ πρὶν καὶ Γύγῃ παρισεύμενος ὄλβον, ὁ τὸ πρὶν
> βουπάμων, ὁ πρὶν πλούσιος αἰπολίοις,
> ὁ πρὶν — τί πλείω μυθεῦμ' ἔτι; πᾶσι μακαρτός,
> φεῦ, γαίης ὅσσης ὅσσον ἔχει μόριον[2].

24. A further development is seen in the epigrams of Meleager of Gadara, a Syrian by birth, who flourished about 90 B.C. Here the erotic element has full play. Extreme elegance and imaginative power truly oriental characterize his diction. Of him Mr. Symonds says[3]: "His poetry has the sweetness of

---

[1] Cruttwell 218.

[2] See Stadtmüller, Anthologia Graeca (1899), 2. 515. The following translation appears in Bland's Collections, 138:

> I am the tomb of Crethon: here you read
> His name; himself is numbered with the dead,
> Who once had wealth, not less than Gyges' gold,
> Who once was rich in stable, stall, and fold,
> Who once was blest above all living men
> With lands — how narrow now! so ample then!

[3] The Greek Poets, 2. 321. Symonds's whole chapter on "The Anthology", 2. 281–344, is of importance to the student of the epigram. See also Mackail, Select Epigrams of the Greek Anthology[2], Introduction.

the rose, the rapture and full-throated melody of the nightingale ". Compare for example his epigram on Zenophilas[1]:

> Εὕδεις, Ζηνοφίλα, τρυφερὸν θάλος· εἴθ᾽ ἐπὶ σοὶ νῦν
> ἄπτερος εἰσήειν ὕπνος ἐπὶ βλεφάροις,
> ὡς ἐπὶ σοὶ μηδ᾽ οὗτος, ὁ καὶ Διὸς ὄμματα θέλγων,
> φοιτήσαι, κάτεχον δ᾽ αὐτὸς ἐγώ σε μόνος.

25. From these comparatively simple forms great variety was developed. In later days the ancients themselves recognized the mixed character of the epigram. Pliny the younger, speaking of the poems he had composed in his leisure hours, remarks[2]: *unum illud praedicendum videtur, cogitare me has nugas inscribere hendecasyllabos, qui titulus sola metri lege constringitur. Proinde, sive epigrammata sive idyllia sive eclogas sive, ut multi, poematia seu quod aliud vocare malueris, licebit voces, ego tantum hendecasyllabos praesto.*

26. Epigrams will then, for practical purposes, fall into the following classes : (1) true epigrams, or superscriptions of the epigraphic form, such as might be put upon a building, a tomb, or a work of art (we shall find such in Martial) ; (2) short erotic poems ; (3) society verses, poems due to special occasions, etc. — indeed, any short poem expressing a single striking idea ; (4) the short poem, generally satirical in character, having what we call a " point ".

It is the fourth class that allies the epigram so closely in common estimation with satire. Indeed, some refuse to regard as epigrams poems of any other sort. But, provided the form is preserved, the epigram may be elegy (compare the monumental inscription), satirical thrust, " a *bon mot* set off with a couple of rhymes ", or an erotic effusion.

[1] See Stadtmüller (1894) 1. 150; Mackail 1. xlii (p. 114). The epigram is translated thus in Bland's Collections, 224 :

> Thou sleep'st, soft silken flower! Would I were Sleep,
> For ever on those lids my watch to keep !
> So should I have thee all mine own — nor he,
> Who seals Jove's wakeful eyes, my rival be.

[2] Ep. 4. 14. 8.

27. But what are the essentials of this literary form? Certainly not mere brevity, for not all short poems, even on subjects such as have been mentioned above, are epigrams. Lessing[1], attempting to show how the literary epigram took form from the inscription, for example, on a tomb, calls attention to the fact that the monument and the inscription have a common object, to excite and to gratify the interest of the beholder. The two, he argues, are thus parts of a whole; the interest attracted by the monument is but introductory to interest in the inscription. The epigram, he continues, in the later or literary sense has two parts: first, a part which is intended to awaken interest or curiosity by description or personal allusion; secondly, the conclusion, the part that satisfies our curiosity, often by some unexpected turn. This last is known as the "point". There is no literary canon to determine the relative length of these two parts of the epigram, any more than there is a rule to prescribe the relation between the length of the inscription upon a building and the size or character of the structure itself. Naturally, the inscription must in mere size bear but slight relation to the monument; so the point must be concisely made, however long the introduction may have been. This point must also be well made; it must be clear; otherwise, the epigram will be no better than other poor wit.

28. In view of the imitative tendency so markedly present in the earliest literary attempts of the Romans, it would be strange if we should fail to see in the first epigrams written at Rome more or less dependence on Greek epigrammatic models. The simple epitaphs of Naevius, Plautus, and Pacuvius[2] seem to be essentially Greek, and remind us of Simonides (**22**),

---

[1] Ueber das Epigram, ix. 3 ff.

[2] See Aulus Gellius 1. 24; he styles them *epigrammata*. For our purposes it is unnecessary to determine whether these epitaphs were actually written by Naevius, Plautus, and Pacuvius or not.

or even of Callimachus, who was more in sympathy with the earlier writers than with his contemporaries. Callimachus has been truly called in some respects "the finished master" of Greek epigram; his share in molding Roman literature was great. From Ennius to Varro [1] Romans tried their hands at simple epigrammatic verse-writing, following closely these early models. Yet before Martial's time there were representatives of the erotic and society epigram, especially in the last century of the Republic. Of these writers of epigrams [2] Catullus (87–54 B.C.) was by far the most gifted. But Catullus's epigrams were mainly erotic in type. Therein he is to be compared not so much with his countrymen as with the Greek writers of Alexandria, who influenced more or less most of the great Roman poets of the late Republic and the early Empire. Indeed, we do not ordinarily think of Catullus as an epigrammatist at all, though it is entirely reasonable to characterize many of his pieces as epigrams and though Martial acknowledged him to be his own model and master (34).

29. It was, however, reserved for a later generation to produce the perfect master of the epigram, who saw in it not merely love poem or elegiac trifle, but all of which the epigram was capable, and accordingly was able to fix forever the character of this particular literary form. " Martial is the most finished master of the epigram, as we understand it. . . . The harmless plays on words, sudden surprises, and neat turns of expression, which had satisfied the Greek and earlier Latin epigrammatists, were by no means stimulating enough for the *blasé* taste of Martial's day. The age cried for *point*, and with point Martial supplies it to the full extent of its demand. His pungency is sometimes wonderful ; the whole flavour of many a sparkling little poem is pressed into one envenomed word, like

---

[1] Cf. here especially Varro's *Imagines*.
[2] Teuffel § 31.

the scorpion's tail whose last joint is a sting "[1]. Stephenson says[2]: " He knew what his age was capable of in poetry and what he himself was capable of, and he rigidly adhered to his last. In a time of almost universal self-ignorance on this subject, in a time when every poetaster wrote an epic, when poetic composition was an accomplishment that 'no gentleman could be without', when men would beg, borrow, buy, or steal verses rather than confess an inability to produce them, . . . it shows a rare self-restraint in Martial that he stuck to what he knew he could do, in spite of the invitations of friends and the sneers of enemies (1. 107 ; 9. 50) ". Merivale, in his review of the literature of this period, remarks[3] : " The epigram is the crowning result of this elaborate terseness of diction, and this lucid perception of the aim in view. The verses of Martial are the quintessence of the Flavian poetry. . . . The careful felicity of Horace is reproduced in Martial under the form which most aptly befits the later age in which he flourished. The lyrics of the Augustan period are characteristically represented by the epigrams of the Flavian ".

Martial not only made the epigram in the sense in which we understand that term, but he successfully challenges comparison with the greatest epigrammatists of all literatures. He is preëminently the master of the epigram, in its every variety. He could write an inscriptional epigram which could serve as a real epitaph (21), or a verbal caricature, or a bit of satire whose point needs no interpreter.

30. No one has drawn with so faithful a pencil the everyday life of the Mistress of the World. Nowhere else can the student who would really know at first-hand how the Romans lived learn so much, especially of the seamy and darker side of Roman life. In his pages we see the gladiators in the arena or the hawker as he sells boiled pease to a circle of idlers in the streets. Before us stalks the man who has won wealth by

---

[1] Cruttwell 432.   [2] P. xix.   [3] 8. 81.

poisoning a succession of wives. At one moment the reader is transported to the seaside villa or to a city *triclinium* where the poor *cliens* is insulted with the meanest of fare while the *rex* himself feasts on the fat of the land and the best the sea can yield ; at another moment we visit the bazaar, and, as we watch the shopper, are made to realize that his modern successor is not more up to date than was the man of the first century, who, though he has no intention to purchase, examines the finest wares and inquires the price of every article. In the theater the man with the face of brass insists on having the seat to which he has no right, until he is forced out by the usher. We catch a glimpse of the ladies' man as he whispers in a fair girl's ear, or sings the latest Egyptian ditty, or whistles the airs of Cadiz. We brush against the exquisite who, with every lock on his head in its particular place and with the last hair extracted from his chin, is in an agony lest his neighbor's elbow shall rub his newly whitened toga. Thus there passes before us an endless panorama of legacy-hunters, dinner-seekers, adventurers, beauties, dandies, poets, upstarts, — in a word, the men and women, good and bad, who made the Rome of Martial's day.

31. Martial has a variety that appears to be endless. He can weep over the death of a slave girl, or put in the pillory the parvenu who gets sick that he may show off his expensive bedclothes to the acquaintances who come to visit him. For his friends the poet has an affection that is sincere, for his enemies a whip of scorpions. The fact that Martial simply paints life as he saw it without attempting to preach or moralize, as the avowed satirist must do, makes his pictures of society and of life the more reliable. Although the colors of the picture are sometimes lurid or very black, we do not question its truth. Martial not only knew the Rome which he describes, but he understood human nature and in particular the people among whom he moved. Although worldly wisdom

is not so much in evidence in his pages as in those of Horace, we cannot deny that he has such wisdom. Martial, further, has brilliancy and delicacy of touch, wit far surpassing that displayed by any of his contemporaries, and originality that amounts almost to genius. Even when he seems to borrow, as from the Greek Lucillius, he has made the material his own by a different use or has surpassed his original [1].

32. Unfortunately, however, there is much truth in the charges of grossness and obscenity often brought against Martial, though, after all, of the whole body of epigrams, aggregating 1500 or more, four fifths are wholly unobjectionable. Martial himself warns the chaste and the young not to read certain of his poems, at the same time insisting that, although his verses are sometimes obscene, his life was not bad [2]. Yet, though he may have been somewhat excused by his contemporaries on the ground that grossness of speech was common and that the best of men occasionally wrote and spoke in a way that in our day would exclude them from decent society, nothing can serve to render the more objectionable pieces tolerable to the modern reader. That these pictures are terribly realistic and truly representative of actual life may enhance their value for the moralist, but such realism makes the pieces involved lose in literary value. Martial's motive was probably to amuse a constituency that liked to be amused in that way; he seems to have given his readers what they wanted. He cannot plead, as Juvenal might have pleaded, a righteous indignation as justification for his license of speech.

33. As already suggested, Martial possessed hard common sense, fertility of expression, wit, and ingenuity, qualities which stood him in good stead in his writing of epigrams. Yet he was a careful student of his predecessors among the Latin poets. On Greek models he seems to have depended less.

---

[1] Friedländer, Einleitung, 19.
[2] See below, § 37.

Sellar [1] calls attention to the fact " that while among the various presents for which he has written inscriptions there are copies of Virgil, Propertius, Livy, Sallust, Ovid, Tibullus, Lucan, Catullus, and Calvus, there is mention only of two Greek books — Homer and the Thais of Menander. . . . In one epigram (5. 10), in which he gives instances of the greatest Greek and the greatest Roman genius, the names which he specifies are Homer and Menander, Virgil and Ovid ". The quotation of a few Greek proverbs and the use of current Latinized Greek words [2] and references to Greek stories that were common literary property [3] prove no extended acquaintance with Greek models [4]. It is perfectly clear that Martial belonged to the new school of Roman poets [5] and also that he drank inspiration from more than one fountain. Though he does not seem to have borrowed from Silius and Lucan [6], there is abundant evidence that he knew Domitius Marsus and the Priapeia [7], Calvus, Pedo Albinovanus, Cornelius Lentulus Gaetulicus [8], and the Augustan poets Tibullus, Propertius [9], Horace [10], and especially Vergil [11], who, as the many references to him show, is to Martial a very corypheus among poets. To Ovid Martial owed much [12]. Ovid's salaciousness and the perfection to which he had brought the elegiac distich commended him to

[1] Introduction xxxi.

[2] See e.g. I. 27. 7; 2. 43. 1; 5. 38. 3.

[3] See e.g. I. 53. 7; 4. 49; 5. 39. 9; 5. 49. 11; 10. 35; 11. 84. 9.

[4] See Stephani, passim.   [6] Zingerle, II, passim.

[5] 11. 90.   [7] Wagner 35–42.

[8] Cf. the mention of Gaetulicus in the Praefatio to Book I. Pliny, Ep. 5. 3. 5, in defending himself against those who criticised him for writing light verse, pleads the good company of an array of poets, among whom are Calvus and Gaetulicus.

[9] Wagner 25–35.

[10] Wagner 17–25. Martial 10. 68. 1 seems to be an echo of Horace C. 1. 7. 1–2; cf. also Martial 1. 15. 12 with C. 1. 11. 8, Martial 8. 18. 6 with C. 4. 2. 1–4. See Keller and Holder on Horace Ep. 1. 20. 12 (cf. Martial 6. 61. 7) and on Ars Poetica 342 (cf. Martial 1. 25. 2–4).

[11] Wagner 3–17.   [12] Zingerle, passim.

Martial. Still, Martial was influenced more by Ovid's hexameters than by his pentameters. It is impossible to say just how far Martial intentionally or unconsciously imitated Ovid, but the reality of an imitation that embraces more than two hundred counts [1] cannot be questioned. This imitation has to do not only with meter, but with phraseology and turns of expression.

34. But, if Martial owed much to Ovid, to Catullus he owed more [2]. In his praise he cannot say too much. If only he can be named with his great exemplar as a worthy second, he is content. Cf. for example 10. 78. 14–16 :

> sic inter veteres legar poetas
> nec multos mihi praeferas priores,
> uno sed tibi sim minor Catullo.

In 10. 103. 4–6, writing of Bilbilis, he says :

> nam decus et nomen famaque vestra sumus,
> nec sua plus debet tenui Verona Catullo
> meque velit dici non minus illa suum.

That Martial had enthroned Catullus as his favorite author and as such had studied him profoundly and thought it an honor to imitate him there can be no doubt. Catullus's pre-eminence in the use of hendecasyllabic verse was as marked as Ovid's in the mastery of the elegiac distich. Naturally, then, it is in this form of verse and in the choliambic that Martial's tendency to follow Catullus is most marked. But, aside from this, Martial recognizes the older poet as his master when he imitates him in words, phrases, and expressions [3].

35. But, though he derived inspiration from such masters of his art as Ovid and Catullus, Martial has merits of style that are

---

[1] Friedländer, Einleitung, 25.   [2] Paukstadt, passim.

[3] For a detailed exhibit of the various kinds of imitation — for example, the repetition of the first word of a poem at the very end, as the last word of the piece, the position of words, the tendency to begin or to end verses immediately succeeding one another with the same word — see Paukstadt.

independent enough. He can express himself to the point, with absolute clearness and without waste of words. When he says[1]

> a nostris procul est omnis vesica libellis
> musa nec insano syrmate nostra tumet,

he tells the plain truth and expresses his contempt for the prevailing false rhetoric of his time, a style that tore passion to tatters, and by bombast and bathos and all the tricks of the rhetorician aimed to win the applause of the crowds that thronged the *recitationes*. We must not, however, shut our eyes to outright blunders in matters of fact and a certain carelessness of expression that occurs too frequently in the poems[2].

III. MARTIAL THE MAN

36. Of Martial we have no " counterfeit presentment ", though he gives us almost a pen picture of himself in 10. 65 by contrast with a Greek exquisite.

His virtues were offset by faults that were great and terribly patent. Though we need not assume with Teuffel[3] that he was weak in character, it is impossible to excuse and not easy to explain his servile flattery, his grossness and obscenity. When he has no purpose to serve he is perfectly frank and sincere ; when he is thinking of the emperor or his minions he is a consummate lickspittle and time-serving hypocrite. He seems never to be aware that in his attempts to win imperial favor he is himself a conspicuous example of the hypocrisy which he condemned in others. To Martial Domitian is the *dominus et deus* that the imperial despot claimed to be, a patriot[4], Father of his Country, a great warrior, and the embodiment of the virtues !

[1] 4. 49. 7.

[2] See e.g. 8. 18. 5; 12. 94. 5; Gilbert, Quaestiones Criticae, 3; Friedländer, Einleitung, 20.   [3] § 322.

[4] Cf. 5. 19. 5–6 *pulchrior et maior quo sub duce Martia Roma?   sub quo libertas principe tanta fuit?*

Still, abject flattery was, in Martial's day, so common as to
have become conventional. To persons wont to address the
emperor as *dominus et deus* the words must soon have become
little more than empty sound. Martial is no more fulsome
than many of his literary contemporaries, for example, Statius.
It was hardly to be expected that a poor man like Martial,
who could recall men who had paid for independence of spirit
with their lives, should act otherwise toward the despot than
did his literary contemporaries. In such an age as Domitian's
reign[1] men are apt to think that the living dog is better than
the dead lion. Most readers will agree that the judgment of
Professor Tyrrell is fair[2]: " It is customary to represent Martial
as the most debased of flatterers, who licked the feet of the
living Domitian and spat on his corse. This view is not altogether wrong. . . . He undoubtedly exaggerates habitually
anything good that may be found in the living Domitian, and
studiously conceals his faults; but that he insulted the dead
emperor is not true. What are his allusions to Domitian after
his death? He writes to Nerva: *sub principe duro temporibusque malis ausus es esse bonus.* This and a few other equally
moderate utterances[3] are the grounds on which the indict-
ment rests ". In passing judgment we must not forget that
the only hope Martial had of winning anything from the court

[1] An age vividly characterized by Tacitus, Agricola, 3: *Quid si per
quindecim annos, grande mortalis aevi spatium, multi fortuitis casibus,
promptissimus quisque saevitia principis interciderunt, pauci, ut sic di-
xerim, non modo aliorum, sed etiam nostri superstites sumus, exemptis e
media vita tot annis, quibus iuvenes ad senectutem, senes prope ad ipsos
exactae aetatis terminos per silentium venimus?*

[2] P. 285.

[3] See 12. 6; cf. such mild expressions as appear in 12. 15. 8–10 *omnes
cum Iove nunc sumus beati; at nuper — pudet, ah pudet fateri — omnes
cum Iove pauperes eramus.* For a more severe judgment of Martial cf.
Lecky, History of European Morals, 1. 204: " The flattery which he
[Lucan] bestowed upon Nero in his *Pharsalia* ranks with the epigrams
of Martial as probably the extreme limits of sycophancy to which Roman
literature descended ".

was to do what was done by every one else who had an end
to gain there.

37. The charge of grossness is the more serious charge and
one that the modern critic is the more disposed to press. See
above, **32.** Still, we must in all fairness judge the men of ancient days not by modern Christian standards but by the highest requirements of the civilization of which they are a part.
If we measure Martial by this test, something may be said in
explanation, if not in palliation, of his offense. He lived in
an age in which the standard of private morals had reached
low-water mark, in a period hardly to be paralleled in historic
times for personal impurity and worship of the bestial passions
by the so-called better classes of society. What better was to
be expected when the emperors set the pace? Indeed, Martial
claims for his epigrams no more than the indulgence allowed
at the Saturnalia and the festival of Flora[1], and would have
his readers expressly understand that, though his poetry might
sometimes be licentious, his life had no part in the wantonness that he depicts[2]. Unless this claim were at least relatively true, it is hard to understand how his society could have
been agreeable to Quintilian and Juvenal. His ambition would
seem to have been to amuse a public that wanted to be amused
in its own way, since he knew that to a certain extent his bread
and raiment depended upon it. A better man, at least in our
days, would starve rather than play such a part.

38. But the case of Martial is not wholly defensive. Though
he was not a great man or a moralist, or a man of strong character or one possessed of the finest feelings, he had good
qualities that commended him to his contemporaries and made
him popular. The younger Pliny, a fine specimen of the Roman

[1] Cf. the Praefatio to Book I (*epigrammata illis scribuntur qui solent
spectare Florales*) with 3. 69 and 11. 6.

[2] 1. 4. 8. In 9. 28. 5–6, in making Latinus say *sed nihil a nostro sumpsit
mea vita theatro et sola tantum scaenicus arte feror*, Martial may well
have been thinking of himself.

gentleman, was Martial's friend and has testified to his sincerity. In Ep. 3. 21 Pliny says: *erat homo ingeniosus, acutus, acer, et qui plurimum in scribendo et salis haberet et fellis nec candoris minus. Prosecutus eram viatico secedentem: dederam hoc amicitiae, dederam etiam versiculis quos de me composuit. . . . Meritone eum, qui haec*[1] *de me scripsit, et tunc dimisi amicissime et nunc ut amicissimum defunctum esse doleo? Dedit enim mihi quantum maximum potuit, daturus amplius, si potuisset.* Martial repeatedly claims that in all that he writes he is perfectly sincere and that he does not use his pen to strike at individuals because of any personal grudge[2]. Indeed, to such an extent does he carry the use of fictitious names that certain names are apparently used by him as typical of classes or peculiar kinds of persons; so Ligurinus denotes one who "reads" in public, Fidentinus a plagiarist, Selius a parasite[3]. He was evidently a good friend; he was appreciative of what his friends did for him[4]. "Living in an artificial age he was perfectly natural"[5]. He was willing to be himself[6] at a time when nearly every man professed to be everything except what he really was. Though the pedant, the pretender, and the parvenu pushed themselves to the fore, Martial could despise them and hold them up to ridicule, and at the same time live plainly and without affectation. He loved children, even children of servile condition; Simcox[7] remarks that "he stands almost alone in Roman literature in his appreciation of mere girlhood". He could mourn the untimely death of children in words of the tenderest pity[8]. The splendid wickedness of Rome never so dazzled him that he forgot the old life and the

---

[1] An epigram written by Martial in Pliny's honor (cf. above, *versiculis quos de me composuit*); Pliny had just quoted it in part.

[2] Cf. e.g. 10. 33. 9–10 *hunc servare modum nostri novere libelli,   parcere personis, dicere de vitiis.*

[3] See further Friedländer, Einleitung, 21–24.

[4] Cf. e.g. 1. 15.   [5] Sellar, p. xxvii.   [6] 10. 47. 12.   [7] 2. 112.

[8] 5. 34; 5. 37; 10. 61.

scenery of his Spanish Bilbilis. He knows virtue when he sees it, and cordially recognizes it in man or woman. He can laud a good woman, like Arria[1], or a good man, like Thrasea[2].

IV. MARTIAL'S FAME

39. Caricature, whether pictorial or verbal, appeals to the multitude and finds a ready response ; people enjoy seeing others in the pillory. Martial therefore was popular. Further, this popularity was not merely local, nor was his fame only posthumous. If we may trust what he tells us in 1. 1, Martial had won his literary spurs at a comparatively early time. Unless this epigram was composed later and prefixed to the poems when the latter were subsequently collected and published, this reputation must have been based on the *Liber Spectaculorum*, the *Xenia*, and the *Apophoreta*, productions that would hardly in themselves, it would seem, justify this claim, or else on poems which, despite their excellence, Martial at a later time was willing to let perish[3]. Be this as it may, it is certain that Martial had a world-wide constituency. Not only in Rome[4], but in the outlying provinces, e.g. on the Danube[5], in Britain, in Vienna on the Rhone[6], men read the epigrams[7].

40. Furthermore the judgment of Martial's contemporaries was ratified by posterity. Sober-headed men, such as Pliny the Younger, did indeed doubt the poet's immortality; in the letter already cited[8] Pliny, referring to the compliment Martial had paid him in his verse (**38**), says : *Dedit enim mihi quantum maximum potuit, daturus amplius, si potuisset. Tametsi quid homini potest dari maius quam gloria et laus et aeternitas? At non erunt aeterna quae scripsit: non erunt*

[1] 1. 13.
[2] 1. 8. 1; 4. 54. 7. See also 4. 13; 11. 53.
[3] See 1. 113; § 13.
[4] 5. 16; 6. 60.
[5] 11. 3.
[6] 7. 88.
[7] See also 5. 13. 3; 6. 82; 8. 3. 3; 8. 61. 3; 9. 84. 5; 10. 2. 9–12.
[8] Ep. 3. 21. 6.

fortasse, ille tamen scripsit tamquam essent futura. It was, perhaps, but natural that men who had been taught and had come to believe that heavy tragedy and long-drawn-out epos were the highest types of poetry should see nothing enduring in the society verses of Martial, which were to all appearances inspired by some sudden occurrence, or were written with a view only to an immediate and passing impression. But Pliny and those who shared his opinion were mistaken. Men continued to read Martial and poets to imitate him[1].

41. It is interesting to speculate how far Martial would have succeeded had he tried his hand at some of the more serious forms of literature. When his critics blamed him for not showing what he could do in the so-called higher forms of literature, he attributed his failure to poverty and to the lack of patronage by the great and well-to-do. Yet Teuffel is perhaps right in doubting whether, in view of the narrow range of his ideas, his lack of earnestness and of any love for serious work, Martial would have done anything more worthy under circumstances more favorable.

V. MANUSCRIPTS OF MARTIAL

42. The manuscripts of Martial fall into three classes, designated for convenience by the letters A, B, and C[2]. Friedländer has shown that these three classes represent as many recensions of the text, whose differences of reading may even be due to revisions made by the poet himself for various editions of his works[3].

---

[1] Martial is not very often directly mentioned by Roman writers. We can cite only Pliny Ep. 3. 21; Aelius Spartianus, Life of Helius (i.e. Commodus), 5. 9; Aelius Lampridius, Life of Alexander Severus, 38. 1–3; Sollius Sidonius Apollinaris C. 9. 268; 23. 163. On the persistency with which men read Martial see Friedländer, Einleitung, 67 ff.

[2] This division dates from Schneidewin.

[3] See Friedländer, Einleitung, 70 ff.

43. The best Mss. are those of the A class. Their service-ableness is, however, impaired by the fact that not one of them is complete; doubtless the archetype of this class did not contain all the epigrams[1]. This archetype was written during the eighth century or at the very beginning of the ninth century[1].

Professor Lindsay characterizes this class or edition as made *in usum elegantiorum*, inasmuch as " it replaces by suitable euphemisms some of the grosser words in Martial's vocabulary, words more fit for the graffiti of Pompeii than for a Roman gentleman's library ". The chief Mss. of this class are known by the appellations R, H, and T. Of these the oldest and best is R, the Codex Leidensis (or Vossianus) 86. R and H are what Lindsay calls Anthology Mss., i.e. Mss. of excerpts not only from Martial, but from other Latin poets also. R probably dates from the ninth century; it contains in all but 272 epigrams, of which four are from the *Liber Spectaculorum*, 268 from the remaining books. It was probably at one time in the monastery of Cluny; it is now in the Leyden Library. H, the Codex Vindobonensis, is of the ninth or tenth century; because of its fragmentary character it is of relatively small value. It contains in all only fourteen epigrams: *Liber Spectaculorum* 19–30, Book I. 3–4. The Ms. was taken by Sannazaro to Naples in 1502–1503, and later to Vienna. T, the Codex Thuaneus or Colbertinus or Parisinus 8071, is a Ms. of the ninth or tenth century. It contains 846 epigrams. R, H, and T are closely related; this is shown by their common blunders in spelling and by other mistakes common to all three. For readings that are found in H the value of T is small, since T seems to be a copy of H[1].

44. The B class of Mss. is based on the recension of Torquatus Gennadius (401 A.D.), evidently one of those adherents of the old pagan culture who sought to rehabilitate it and to that end interested themselves in correcting and editing Mss[2]. The

---

[1] Lindsay Anc. Ed. M. 10.

[2] On the *subscriptiones* of Gennadius see Lindsay Anc. Ed. M. 2 ff.

best Mss. of this class are those known as L, P, Q, and f. Of these the *optimus codex*, as Professor Lindsay well styles it[1], is L, the Codex Lucensis 612, a twelfth-century Ms. on poor vellum, copied and corrected by various hands, which came into possession of the Royal Library at Berlin by purchase from a bookseller at Lucca. The supreme value of this Ms. as a representative of the Gennadius recension lies not so much in its individual excellence as in the fact that it is much older than any other Ms. of this class[2].

Next in value to L is P, the Codex Palatinus Vaticanus 1696, now in the Vatican Library. This Ms. is one of the many Codices Palatini now scattered that were once in the library of the Elector Palatine at Heidelberg[3].

45. The manuscripts of the third and most numerous family, the C class, are from an archetype by no means as good as those of the A and B classes; that archetype was made in the eighth or the ninth century in early Carolingian minuscule script. Four or five of these Mss. are so much superior to the others that scholars group them by themselves, as a C^a class, to distinguish them from the inferior Mss. of the family, which are grouped together as the C^b class.

46. Of the Mss. in the C^a class the oldest and best is E, the Codex Edinburgensis, of the tenth century. This Ms., now in the Advocates' Library in Edinburgh, is written in Carolingian minuscule in several hands. It contains all of Martial except the *Liber Spectaculorum* and 10. 72–75. Codices X, A, and V also belong to this class.

---

[1] See Lindsay, *Classical Review*, 15. 309 ff., 413 ff.; Lindsay Anc. Ed. M. 61.

[2] All Mss. of this class are Renaissance copies, which are on general principles to be viewed with suspicion.

[3] The Mss. of the B class contain all the epigrams, except those of the *Liber Spectaculorum*; that book is known only from the A Mss.

VI. VERSIFICATION AND PROSODY

47. The meters used by Martial are as follows [1] :

(*a*) DACTYLIC HEXAMETER :

$$\acute{\smile} \; \overline{\smile\smile} \mid \acute{\smile} \; \overline{\smile\smile} \mid \acute{\smile} \; \overline{\smile\smile} \mid \acute{\smile} \; \overline{\smile\smile} \mid \acute{\smile} \; (\overline{\smile\smile}) \mid \acute{\smile} \; \smile$$

Except in connection with the pentameter (48) the hexameter occurs only four times in Martial : 1. 53 ; 2. 73 ; 6. 64 ; 7. 98. In this connection 6. 65 is interesting.

(*b*) *Cæsura.* — The penthemimeral cæsura (i.e. cæsura in the third foot) occurs, as was to be expected, with the greatest frequency as the chief pause in the verse ; cf. 2. 66. 7 :

> hoc salamandra notet ‖ vel saeva novacula nudet.

(*c*) Rarely we find the trithemimeral cæsura (i.e. cæsura after the third half-foot) and the hephthemimeral cæsura (i.e. cæsura after the seventh half-foot) in the same verse without the penthemimeral ; cf. 9. 100. 1 :

> denaris ‖ tribus invitas ‖ et mane togatum.

(*d*) Verses divided into four parts by the three cæsuras (trithemimeral, penthemimeral, hephthemimeral) are more frequent ; cf. 1. 53. 12 :

> stat contra ‖ dicitque ‖ tibi ‖ tua pagina "Fur es".

(*e*) The trithemimeral cæsura rarely occurs without the hephthemimeral ; but cf. 1. 15. 7 :

> exspectant ‖ curaeque ‖ catenatique labores.

(*f*) Martial agrees with Vergil and other predecessors in using quite frequently the bucolic cæsura, though he employs it far less often than does Juvenal. In such cases the fourth foot is frequently a spondee ; cf. 1. 13. 3 :

> "si qua fides vulnus quod feci ‖ non dolet" inquit.

---

[1] For an elaborate discussion of Martial's versification see Friedländer, Einleitung, 26–50.

(*g*) *Spondaic verses*. — Martial uses the spondee in the fifth place in all only fourteen times and for the most part in proper names. In such cases a quadrisyllabic word regularly ends the verse and the fourth foot is a dactyl. Cf. e.g. Liber Spectaculorum 1. 5 ; 2. 38. 1 ; 4. 79. 1 ; 5. 64. 5 ; 8. 56. 23 ; 9. 59. 9.

(*h*) *Elision*. — Martial uses elision moderately ; he elides both before long and short vowels, but restricts elision to four or five places in the verse. According to Birt [1] Martial has about 120 cases of elision in 3358 hexameters.

(*i*) *Diæresis*. — Diæresis (i.e. the simultaneous ending of word and foot) at every foot was in general regarded as a blemish to be avoided. Yet Martial shows a few examples ; cf. e.g. 12. 6. 11 [2].

48. (*a*) THE ELEGIAC DISTICH : a hexameter followed by a so-called " pentameter " (i.e. a hexameter in which a pause takes the place of the second syllable of the spondee in the third and sixth feet) :

$$\text{–}\,\overline{\cup\cup}\mid\text{–}\,\overline{\cup\cup}\mid\text{–}\,\overline{\cup\cup}\mid\text{–}\,\overline{\cup\cup}\mid\text{–}\,\widetilde{\cup\cup}\mid\text{–}\,\cup$$
$$\text{–}\,\overline{\cup\cup}\mid\text{–}\,\overline{\cup\cup}\mid\text{–}\,\wedge\mid\text{–}\,\cup\cup\mid\text{–}\,\cup\cup\mid\underline{\cup}\,\wedge$$

Martial uses the elegiac distich more frequently than any other meter ; eighty per cent of his epigrams are in that kind of verse.

(*b*) Ovid, who uses the pentameter with such vigor and perfection, generally, though not invariably, makes his pentameters end with disyllabic words. Martial, following his exemplar Catullus (**34**), frequently departs from this rule, making his pentameters close with words of one syllable (especially with forms of *esse*: cf. 1. 29. 4 ; 2. 58. 2 ; 7. 81. 2 ; 7. 90. 4 ; 12. 46. 2 ; 1. 32. 2 ends with *te*) as well as with words of three, four, five, and even six syllables. In pentameters that end with a trisyllabic word the monosyllable that in most instances immediately precedes the trisyllabic word makes for smoothness (see e.g. 2. 16. 2 ; 2. 18. 8 ; 3. 18. 2 ; 5. 9. 4 ; 10. 25. 6 ;

---

[1] In Friedländer, Einleitung, 35–38.
[2] See Lease in *Classical Review*, 11. 149–150.

13. 3. 8). Yet Martial sometimes allows a word of more than one syllable to stand next to the final trisyllabic word ; see e.g. 1. 33. 2 ; 1. 79. 4 ; 3. 63. 10 ; 6. 51. 4 [1].

(*c*) *Rhyme.* — Worthy of notice is Martial's use of rhyme, especially in the pentameter, between the ends of the hemistichs ; the rhyme occurs particularly between adjective and substantive: see e.g. 1. 2. 2 ; 1. 4. 2 ; 1. 12. 2, 8 ; 1. 33. 2. Indeed, Martial carries his love of rhyme so far as to make the rhyme not only between the halves of the pentameter but also between the parts of the preceding hexameter ; cf. e.g. Liber Spectaculorum 2. 1–2 ; 22. 1–2 ; etc.[2].

49. (*a*) PHALÆCEAN (*hendecasyllabus phalaeceus*) : a logaœdic pentapody with a dactyl in the second place :

$$\acute{\smile} \; - \; | \; \overset{\prime}{-} \smile \smile \; | \; \overset{\prime}{-} \; \smile \; | \; \overset{\prime}{-} \; \smile \; | \; \overset{\prime}{-} \; \overline{\smile}$$

This meter, said to have been invented by Sappho, was named from Phalaecus, an Alexandrian poet who used it. In the hands of Catullus it was thoroughly Latinized and popularized ; it was subsequently employed by Petronius, Martial, and others. In Martial it ranks next to the elegiac distich in frequency, although it occurs in only about fifteen per cent of the epigrams. The scheme of the verse, as used by Martial, is regular ; a spondee is always found in the first foot. Cf. 1. 41. 1 :

$$\acute{u}rba \; | \; n\acute{u}s \; tibi \; | \; Ca\acute{e}ci \; | \; l\acute{i} \; vi \; | \; d\acute{e}ris$$

and the following from Tennyson :

$$L\acute{o}ok, \; I \; | \; c\acute{o}me \; to \; the \; | \; t\acute{e}st, \; a \; | \; t\acute{i}ny \; | \; p\acute{o}em$$
$$\acute{A}ll \; com \; | \; p\acute{o}sed \; in \; a \; | \; m\acute{e}tre \; | \; \acute{o}f \; Ca \; | \; t\acute{u}llus.$$

[1] For a good discussion of the "pentameter" see Goodell, Chapters on Greek Metric, 30–42.

[2] On rhyme in Latin poetry see e.g. W. Grimm, Zur Geschichte des Reims, in *Philologische und historische Abhandlungen der königlichen Akademie der Wissenschaften zu Berlin* for 1851, pp. 627–715; H. T. Johnstone, Rhymes and Assonances in the Aeneid, *Classical Review,* 10. 9–13; Wölfflin, *Archiv,* 3. 443 ff.

(*b*) *Cæsura.* — Though not consistently used, the penthemimeral cæsura is quite common.

(*c*) *Elision* is as rare as *apheresis* is common.

(*d*) *Diæresis* at every foot of the verse, though not of great frequency, is commoner than is generally supposed [1]; see e.g. 4. 30. 5; 5. 20. 9; 5. 24. 15; 6. 17. 3; 8. 76. 7; 10. 72. 4; 12. 18. 14; 12. 34. 5.

50. IAMBIC TRIMETER or IAMBIC SENARIUS (six iambi or three iambic dipodies):

The last foot must be an iambus; the penthemimeral cæsura is the cæsura commonly used. It seems likely, despite some ancient authorities, that the ictus upon the first thesis of each dipody was stronger than that upon the second thesis of the dipody [2]. The resolutions of the iambus and the spondee are, it will be seen, like those allowed in the choliambic (**52**). In 11. 59. 1 an anapest occurs in the fifth foot.

51. THE IAMBIC DIMETER or IAMBIC QUATERNARIUS (four iambi or two iambic dipodies):

It will be observed that in both the dimeter and the trimeter (**50**) spondees are found generally, if at all, in the odd feet; the tribrach is found in the second foot (3. 14. 4; 1. 61. 8, 10); the dactyl is practically restricted to the first foot (1. 61. 10;

---

[1] Cf. Lease, *Classical Review*, 11. 149–150.

[2] For the ancient authorities see Christ, *Metrik der Griechen und Römer*, 68–70. Since Bentley's time it has been the fashion to hold that the ictus on the first, third, and fifth feet was heavier than that on the remaining feet; in all modern editions the ictus, if marked at all in the iambic trimeter and similar verse, is marked on that principle.

11. 59. 4). In 1. 61. 10 a tribrach follows the dactyl. In 3. 14 ; 11. 59 the iambic trimeter and the iambic dimeter are combined.

52. (*a*) THE CHOLIAMBUS or SCAZON or VERSUS HIPPONAC-TEUS (an iambic trimeter (**50**), in which a trochee takes the place of the iambus in the last foot) :

$$
\begin{array}{ccc}
\text{Ƨ} \ \underline{\prime} \quad \cup \ \underline{\quad} & \text{Ƨ} \ \underline{\prime} \quad \cup \ \underline{\quad} & \cup \underline{\prime} \quad \underline{\prime} \cup \\
\cup \ \check{\cup} \ \cup \quad \cup \ \cup \ \cup & \cup \ \check{\cup} \ \cup \quad \cup \ \cup \ \cup & \\
> \ \check{\cup} \ \cup & > \ \check{\cup} \ \cup & \\
\underline{\cup\cup} \ \underline{\prime} & &
\end{array}
$$

(*b*) The names *choliambus* ('lame iambus', 'halting iambus') and *scazon* ('hobbler') were given to the verse because of its halting effect, produced by the trochee in the last foot. Before Martial's time it had been used at Rome by Varro and Catullus. The scheme given above shows both the pure scazon and the substitutions of tribrach, dactyl, and anapest, all of which, except the tribrach, occur only in the odd feet, i.e. in the first and third feet. The tribrach is found most frequently in the second foot ; the anapest is restricted to the first foot and is rare even there. In 1. 89. 5 the anapest in the first foot is followed by a tribrach, as in 3. 22. 2 ; 3. 58. 3. In 3. 58. 32 we have two consecutive tribrachs. In 1. 10. 2 the dactyl is found in the first foot. In 3. 58. 29 ; 12. 57. 28 a tribrach is followed by a dactyl. The spondee does not occur in the fifth foot.

It is to be noted that the fifth foot is regularly an iambus, and that the choliambus cannot end with a monosyllable, except *est.* Cf. 1. 10. 3.

It will be seen that the choliambus is seldom pure in Martial. For examples of pure choliambi see 1. 113. 4 ; 2. 57. 6 ; 3. 58. 44 ; 10. 30. 4. In one epigram (1. 61) we have the choliambus and the iambic dimeter (**51**) combined.

(*c*) *Cæsura.*—The penthemimeral cæsura is the most common ; it is frequently followed by a monosyllable. Examples of the cæsura in the fourth foot (remarkably rare) are to be seen in 5. 14. 8 ; 5. 37. 13, 24 ; 8. 44. 3.

(*d*) *Elision*, which is only moderately used, occurs most frequently in the second foot.

53. THE IONIC A MAIORE or SOTADEAN meter is found in Martial, but does not occur in any of the epigrams in this book.

54. (*a*) *Diastole.* — Occasionally Martial lengthens a short syllable for the sake of the meter, as in 10. 89. 1 *tuūs* ; 12. 31. 9 *Nausicaā* ; 14. 187. 2 *Glycerā*. Cf. also 7. 44. 1 *tuūs* ; 14. 77. 2 *plorabāt*. The lengthening occurs either in the accented part of the foot (thesis) or at the end of the first half of the pentameter [1].

(*b*) Occasionally when a word occurs twice in the same verse Martial varies its quantity ; cf. 2. 18. 1 *captŏ* . . . *captō* ; 2. 36. 2 *nolō* . . . *nolŏ*.

(*c*) Final *o* is sometimes regarded as short, e.g. 2. 18. 5 *anteambulŏ* ; 1. 47. 1, 2 *vispillŏ*, etc. This is especially observable in iambic words and is not uncommon in words of three or more syllables, especially in words ending in *-io*. Cf. e.g. 5. 20. 8 *gestatiŏ* ; 11. 45. 5 *suspiciŏ* ; 12. 48. 11 *commissatiŏ* ; 13. 97. 1 *lalisiŏ*. Such words, as commonly measured in Vergil's time, ended in a cretic ($\_ \cup \_$), and so were impossible in hexameter verse [2].

---

[1] Here, too, we really have a thesis ; cf. the definition of the pentameter in § 48 (*a*). For *Glycerā* and *Nausicaā* see A. 44.

[2] The early writers of hexameter verse have final *o* short only in iambic words, such as *cito, modo* ; we may think here of the Law of Breves Breviantes, which plays so large a rôle in Plautus and Terence (see Lindsay, Latin Language, 201–202 ; GL. 716 ; L. 129). The Augustan poets have final *o* short also in cretic words (e.g. *Pollio*), which thus become dactyls. Poets of the Silver Age freely shorten any final *o*, except in inflectional forms of the second declension.

VII. ORTHOGRAPHY

55. It chanced that the period of Martial's literary activity at Rome, that is, the time from Nero to Trajan, was the period when Latin spelling was most fixed. Consequently, it would seem to be easy to determine on a priori grounds the orthography that Martial would use, especially when we add to this the testimony of the inscriptions and the most trustworthy manuscripts. Still, this is not so easy as it would appear to be, for, as has been said [1], "When a poem is, like the Epigram, confined to the narrow compass of a couplet, or a quatrain, or an octave, one may be sure that not merely every word but every syllable would be chosen with deliberation. Unless the manuscript evidence is patently and utterly unreliable, the idea of setting it wholly aside and adopting a featureless uniformity of spelling cannot be entertained for one moment". Accordingly, I have sought, where possible, to follow in a given case the spelling which, according to the available testimony, the poet seems to have used. Where there is a choice between two relatively good spellings, that orthography has generally been followed which seemed to have the best manuscript authority. Where there is practical agreement among the manuscripts, their readings have been followed, except where that course would result in a spelling manifestly not in use at the time in question.

56. (*a*) In the case of compound words the practice with respect to the assimilation of the preposition varies; sometimes the principles laid down by Brambach [2] prevail, sometimes other considerations obtain [3].

(*b*) In nouns and adjectives we should expect on a priori grounds to find the endings -*vus* and -*vum* rather than the older

---

[1] W. M. Lindsay, The Orthography of Martial's Epigrams, *Journal of Philology*, 29. 24.

[2] Hülfsbüchlein für lateinische Rechtschreibung, § 20. 1.

[3] Lindsay (as cited in N. 1), 37.

-vos and *-vom*. In fact, we should as a rule expect *u* instead of *o* after *v*, i.e. we should look for *vulgus, vulnus, vultus, vult, mavult*, etc., instead of *volgus, volnus, voltus, volt, mavolt*, etc. But we know that almost to the end of the first century A.D. certain earlier spellings were used side by side with the later orthography. Hence we meet with such forms as *divom, servos, volgus, volnus, volt*.

(*c*) In the genitive singular of the second declension of nouns, Martial seems to have consistently contracted the *-ii* at the end [1].

(*d*) In the accusative plural of the third declension the form in *-es* is used along with that in *-is*.

(*e*) In the numeral adverbs the manuscripts indicate that Martial did not always follow the established usage, which was, with exceptions, to write the words derived from the indefinite numerals *tot* and *quot* in *-iens*, e.g. *totiens* and *quotiens*, but to spell the words derived from the cardinals in *-ies*, e.g. *quinquies, sexies, decies*.

(*f*) Our Mss. seem to imply that Martial sometimes wrote *quu*, sometimes *cu*. We have such forms as *aequum, relicum, cocus, persecuntur*, if we may trust good manuscripts [2].

(*g*) That Martial's use of the aspirated consonants varied is quite clear from the manuscripts. We find such diversity as *thermae, sulphur*, along with *coturnus, coclea* (and *cochlea*), etc.

(*h*) Likewise the manuscripts cannot be depended upon to give us the correct reading where the vowels or diphthongs *ae, oe*, and *e* are involved [3].

---

[1] M. Haupt, Opuscula, 3. 584; Brambach § 14.

[2] It is, however, probable that *quu* was never actually in use among the Romans; see the "Report on Latin Orthography" submitted by a Committee of the American Philological Association, and printed in the Proceedings of that Association for 1896 (Volume 27, p. xxiii).

[3] For a fuller discussion of these questions see Gilbert in the Introduction to his edition of Martial, and his contribution to the Introduction of Friedländer's edition, 108–119; Lindsay, *Journal of Philology*, 29. 24 ff.

VIII. BIBLIOGRAPHY

(With abbreviations used in this book)

A. J. P. = *American Journal of Philology.*

Abbott = F. F. Abbott, History of Roman Political Institutions. Boston, 1901.

Amos = A. Amos, Martial and the Moderns. Cambridge, 1858.

Anthol. Lat. = F. Bücheler and A. Riese, Anthologia Latina. Leipzig, 1895.

B. and L. = R. T. Bridge and E. D. C. Lake, Select Epigrams of Martial : Books VII–XII (edited with English notes). Oxford, 1906.

Bähr. F. P. R. = A. Bährens, Fragmenta Poetarum Romanorum. Leipzig, 1886.

Bähr. P. L. M. = A. Bährens, Poetae Latini Minores. Leipzig, 1879.

Baumeister = A. Baumeister, Denkmäler des klassischen Altertums. München-Leipzig, 1889.

Beck. = W. A. Becker (and H. Göll), Gallus, oder Römische Scenen aus der Zeit Augusts [3]. Berlin, 1880–1882.

Birt = Th. Birt, Das antike Buchwesen. Berlin, 1882.

Birt, Buchrolle = Th. Birt, Die Buchrolle in der Kunst. Leipzig, 1907.

Blümner = Hugo Blümner, Die gewerbliche Thätigkeit der Völker des klassischen Altertums. Leipzig, 1869.

Brandt = A. Brandt, De Martialis poetae vita et scriptis ad annorum computationem dispositis. Berlin, 1853.

C.I.L. = Corpus Inscriptionum Latinarum.

Cannegieter = H. Cannegieter, De mutata Romanorum nominum sub principibus ratione. Utrecht, 1758.

Carm. Epigr. = F. Bücheler, Carmina Epigraphica. Leipzig, 1895.

Comparetti = D. Comparetti, Vergil in the Middle Ages. London, 1895.

Coning. Misc. Writ. = J. Conington, Miscellaneous Writings. London, 1880.

Cooper = F. T. Cooper, Word Formation in the Roman Sermo Plebeius. New York, 1895.

Cruttwell = C. T. Cruttwell, History of Roman Literature. New York, 1899.

Danysz = A. Danysz, De scriptorum imprimis poetarum Romanorum studiis Catullianis. Posen, 1876.

Dau = A. Dau, De M. Valerii Martialis libellorum ratione temporibusque. Pars I. Rostock, 1887.

Domit. = Domitius Calderinus (and G. Merula), Martialis. Venice, 1510 (the annotations of Domitius are found also in the Paris Variorum of 1617).

Fried. = L. Friedländer, M. Valerii Martialis epigrammaton libri mit erklärenden Anmerkungen. 2 volumes, Leipzig, 1886.

Fried. Rec. loc. Mart. = L. Friedländer, Recensio locorum in Martialis XIV epigrammaton libris corruptorum. Königsberg, 1878.

Fried. SG. = L. Friedländer, Darstellungen aus der Sittengeschichte Roms [6]. Leipzig, 1888–1890.

Giese = P. Giese, De personis a Martiale commemoratis. Greifswald, 1872.

Giese Krit. Bemerk. = P. Giese, Kritische Bermerkungen zu Martial. Danzig, 1885.

Gilbert Q. C. = W. Gilbert, Ad Martialem quaestiones criticae. Dresden, 1883.

Guttmann = O. Guttmann, Observationum in Marcum Valerium Martialem particulae quinque. Breslau, 1866.

Hehn = Victor Hehn (and O. Schrader), Kulturpflanzen und Hausthiere, etc. Berlin, 1894.

Heraldus = Desiderii Heraldi animadversiones ad lib. XII epig. M. Valerii Martialis (in Paris Variorum of 1617).

Hill, Handbook = C. F. Hill, Handbook of Greek and Roman Coins. London, 1899.

Hülsen-Jordan = Volume 1, part 3, of Jordan Top., written by Ch. Hülsen. Berlin, 1907.

Hultsch = F. Hultsch, Griechische und Römische Metrologie [2]. Berlin, 1882.

Jordan Top. = H. Jordan, Topographie der Stadt Rom in Alterthum. Berlin, 1871–1885 (Volume I, part 3, has been written by Ch. Hülsen. Berlin, 1907).

K. and H. Form. urb. Rom. = H. Kiepert and Ch. Hülsen, Formae urbis Romae antiquae. Berlin, 1896.

Klein = Jos. Klein, Fasti Consulares. Leipzig, 1881.

Lanciani Anc. R. = R. Lanciani, Ancient Rome in the Light of Recent Discoveries. Boston, 1889.

Lanciani P. and Chr. R. = R. Lanciani, Pagan and Christian Rome. Boston, 1893.

Lindsay = W. M. Lindsay, M. Valerii Martialis epigrammata (text only). Oxford, 1902.

Lindsay Anc. Ed. M. = W. M. Lindsay, The Ancient Editions of Martial. Oxford, 1903.

Lindsay L. L. = W. M. Lindsay, The Latin Language. Oxford, 1894.

Madv. Adv. Crit. = I. N. Madvig, Adversaria Critica ad scriptores Latinos. The Hague, 1873.

Mahaffy = J. P. Mahaffy, History of Classical Greek Literature. New York, 1880.

Marc. = Th. Marcilius, M. Valerii Martialis epigrammata in Caesaris amphitheatrum et venationes. Paris, 1601.

Marq. = J. Marquardt (and A. Mau), Das Privatleben der Römer [2]. Leipzig, 1886.

Marq.-Wissowa = J. Marquardt (and G. Wissowa), Römische Staatsverwaltung [2]. Leipzig, 1884.

Mau-Kelsey = A. Mau and Francis Kelsey, Pompeii: its Life and Art [2]. New York, 1902.

Merula: see Domit.

Mommsen Staats. = Th. Mommsen, Römisches Staatsrecht [3]. Leipzig, 1887.

Müller Die Tracht. d. R. = A. Müller, Die Trachten der Römer und Römerinnen nach Ovid und Martial. Hannover, 1868.

Müller Hdb. = I. Müller (et al.), Handbuch der klassischen Altertumswissenschaft. Nördlingen, 1886 ff.

Nissen = H. Nissen, Pompeianische Studien. Leipzig, 1877.

Orelli-Henz. = I. C. Orelli (and W. Henzen), Inscriptionum Latinarum selectarum amplissima collectio. 3 volumes, Zürich, 1828 ff.

Otto = A. Otto, Die Sprichwörter . . . der Römer. Leipzig, 1890.

P. and S. = F. A. Paley and W. H. Stone, M. Valerii Martialis epigrammata selecta (with English notes). London, 1888.

Paris Variorum = M. Valerii Martialis epigrammatum libri XV cum variorum virorum commentariis, notis, etc. Paris, 1617.

Paukstadt = R. Paukstadt, De Martiale Catulli imitatore. Halle, 1876.

Pauly-Wiss. = Paulys Real-Encyclopädie (revised by G. Wissowa). Stuttgart, 1894 ff.

Platner = S. B. Platner, The Topography and Monuments of Ancient Rome. Boston, 1904.

Preller-Jordan = L. Preller (and H. Jordan), Römische Mythologie³. Berlin, 1881.

Rader = M. Rader, M. Valerii Martialis epigrammata. Mayence, 1627.

Ramirez = L. Ramirez de Prado, M. Valerii Martialis epigrammaton libri XV. Paris, 1607.

Renn = E. Renn, Die Griechische Eigennamen bei Martial. Landshut, 1888.

Roscher Lex. = W. H. Roscher, Ausführliches Lexicon der Griechischen und Römischen Mythologie. Leipzig, 1884 ff.

Saintsbury = G. Saintsbury, A History of Criticism and Literary Taste (Volume I deals with Classical and Mediæval Criticism). New York, 1904.

Schanz = M. Schanz, Geschichte der Römischen Litteratur (in Müller's Handbuch, Volume 8; Part I is in the third edition, 1907, the rest in the second edition, 1899–1901).

Schn¹. = F. G. Schneidewin, M. Valerii Martialis epigrammaton libri. 2 volumes, Grimma, 1842.

Schn². = F. G. Schneidewin, M. Valerii Martialis epigrammaton libri. Leipzig, 1881.

Schneider = A. Schneider, Das alte Rom. Leipzig, 1896.

Schreiber-Anderson = Th. Schreiber (and W. C. F. Anderson), Atlas of Classical Antiquity. London, 1895.

Schrevelius = C. Schrevelius, M. Valerii Martialis epigrammata cum notis variorum. Leyden, 1670.

Scriv. = P. Scriverius, M. Valerius Martialis. Leyden, 1619.

Sellar = W. Y. Sellar and G. G. Ramsay, Extracts from Martial. Edinburgh, 1884.

Simcox = G. A. Simcox, A History of Latin Literature. New York, 1883.

Smith D. of A. = Wm. Smith, Dictionary of Antiquities[3]. London, 1890–1891.

Soed. = H. Soeding, De infinitivi apud Martialem usurpatione. Marburg, 1891.

Spiegel = P. G. Spiegel, Zur Characteristik des Epigrammatikers M. Valerius Martialis. I, Innsbruck, 1891 ; II, 1892.

Stephani = A. Stephani, De Martiale verborum novatore. Pars Prior. Breslau, 1888.

Stephenson = H. M. Stephenson, Selected Epigrams of Martial (edited with notes). London, 1880.

Teuffel = W. S. Teuffel (and L. Schwabe), History of Roman Literature (fifth edition translated from the German by Warr). London, 1891–1892.

Tyrrell = R. Y. Tyrrell, Latin Poetry. Boston, 1895.

Van Stockum = G. J. M. Van Stockum, De Martialis vita ac scriptis commentatio. The Hague, 1884.

Wagner = E. Wagner, De M. Valerio Martiale poetarum Augusteae aetatis imitatore. Königsberg, 1880.

Wilkins = A. S. Wilkins, Roman Education. Cambridge, 1905.

Wilm. = C. Wilmanns, Exempla inscriptionum Latinarum. Berlin, 1873.

Zingerle = A. Zingerle, Martial's Ovid-Studien. Innsbruck, 1877.

M. VALERI MARTIALIS

EPIGRAMMATA SELECTA

LIBER EPIGRAMMATON

I

Barbara pyramidum sileat miracula Memphis,
    Assyrius iactet nec Babylona labor,
nec Triviae templo molles laudentur Iones ;
    dissimulet deum cornibus ara frequens,

I. On this book, often called
Liber Spectaculorum, see § 13. In
this epigram M. declares that the
Colosseum surpasses the so-called
seven wonders of the world. As
given by Hyginus Fab. 223, these
wonders were the Temple of Diana
at Ephesus; the Mausoleum, or
tomb of Mausolus, ruler of Caria,
377–353 B.C., erected at Halicar-
nassus by Artemisia his widow;
the Colossus at Rhodes, a brazen
statue of the Sun-God; the statue
of Jupiter at Olympia, by Phidias;
the palace of Cyrus at Ecbatana;
the walls of Babylon; the Egyptian
pyramids. — Meter: § 48.

1. **Barbara,** *barbaric, outland-
ish.* Join with *Memphis*; cf. 8. 36.
2 *iam tacet Eoum barbara Memphis opus* ; Luc. 8. 542. The Greek
contempt for aliens, implied in
βάρβαρος, the Romans entertained
for the peoples of the East and
often for the Greeks themselves :
cf. e.g. Iuv. 3. 58–125. Besides,

the adjective here contrasts Memphis with *domina Roma* (1. 3. 3 N.),
implied in 7–8.

2. **Assyrius :** see App. — **iactet :** in 8. 28. 17 Babylon is styled
superba. — **nec** is often used in
poetry for *neve* (*neu*) or *et ne*; cf.
3, 5. Note its position ; in all kinds
of Latin verse metrical considerations often force the postpone-
ment of the conjunction.

3. **Triviae :** the Ephesian Artemis, whose priests were eunuchs
(cf. *molles*). — **templo :** *ob* or *propter templum* would be more classical; see A. 404, b ; GL. 408, N. 6.
Cf. 2. 66. 4 *saevis . . . comis* ; 7. 17.
9 *munere . . . parvo.* — **molles,**
luxurious; cf. Prop. 1. 6. 31 *mollis
Ionia.* Ionian effeminacy was no-
torious at least as early as the days
of Herodotus.

4. Plutarch twice speaks of the
altar made by the four-year-old
Apollo from the horns of animals
slain by Diana as one of the seven

5   aëre nec vacuo pendentia Mausolea
       laudibus immodicis Cares in astra ferant:
    omnis Caesareo cedit labor amphitheatro,
       unum pro cunctis fama loquetur opus.

29

Cum traheret Priscus, traheret certamina Verus
    esset et aequalis Mars utriusque diu,
    missio saepe viris magno clamore petita est,

wonders; Ov. Her. 21. 99 speaks
of it as one of the marvels of
Delos.—dissimulet . . . frequens,
let the altar of the many horns dis-
guise (conceal) the (its) god, i.e. let
the altar say no more of the tale
that a god built it (for in comparison with the Colosseum, a human
creation, it seems unworthy of a
god's hands). *simulo* = 'pretend',
dissimulo = 'dissemble', 'cloak',
'cover up (facts)'; hence *dissimulet*
here = *sileat*, 1, *nec iactet*, 2, *nec . . .*
ferant, 5–6. Cf. Ov. Her. 4. 55–56
Iuppiter Europen . . . dilexit, tauro
dissimulante deum. See App.

5–6. Plin. N. H. 36. 31 says of
the Mausoleum: *in summo est*
quadriga marmorea, quam fecit
Pythis. Haec adiecta CXXXX
pedum altitudine totum opus inclu-
dit. See Baumeister 893 ff. The
quadriga mirrored against the sky
might well be spoken of as *aëre*
vacuo pendens. But Roman poets
are fond of applying *pendens* to the
roofs of houses or of caves, to
bridges, etc. — Mausolea: see
§ 47, g. Fragments of this Mausoleum have been brought to the
British Museum, and an attempt
has been made to restore the whole.
—laudibus . . . ferant: *laudibus*
ferre or, more often, *laudibus*
efferre = 'laud', 'extol'.

7–8. These verses justify the
exhortations in 1–6. — Caesareo,
imperial. The Colosseum was the
work of the Flavian emperors;
earlier amphitheaters had been
built by private individuals.

8. fama, *the talk of men.* We
might, however, read *Fama.* — 1–6
constitute the first part of the epigram (§ 27); the 'point' is found
in 7–8.

29. Gladiators were generally
matched in pairs. It was ordinarily expected that the fight would
be to a finish, i.e. until one of
the combatants, by dropping his
weapon and raising his hand, if
able to do so, begged for mercy.
The conditions of the combat (*lex*,
4–5) were announced before the
fight began. In this fight Priscus
and Verus were so evenly matched
that neither could gain the mastery. Hence neither appealed for
missio, i.e. for mercy and discharge
from further service for that day.
— Meter: § 48.

1. traheret, *was protracting.*

2. et: this word is found out
of its logical place about 60 times
in M.; see Fried. on I. 26. 8, and
note on *nec*, Lib. Spect. 1. 2. —
Mars = *certamen* (metonymy).

3. missio . . . petita est: the
decision lay theoretically wholly

sed Caesar legi paruit ipse suae :
5   — lex erat ad digitum posita concurrere parma —
quod licuit, lances donaque saepe dedit.
Inventus tamen est finis discriminis aeque :
pugnavere pares, subcubuere pares.
Misit utrique rudes et palmas Caesar utrique :
10   hoc pretium virtus ingeniosa tulit.
Contigit hoc nullo nisi te sub principe, Caesar :
cum duo pugnarent, victor uterque fuit.

with the *editor muneris*, in this case the *princeps* himself (11), but the editor frequently merely registered the popular will; see Iuv. 3. 34–37. For the sign used by the people in extending mercy to a beaten gladiator, see Post A. J. P. 13. 213 ff. — **viris** (dat.): the great gladiators were heroes in the eyes of the crowd, as were the jockeys of the circus (*aurigae, agitatores*).

4. Caesar: the emperor; cf. *Caesareo*, 'imperial', Lib. Spect. 1.7.

5. ad digitum . . . parma: since *posita* must here = *deposita* (see on 1. 4. 2), *parma*, though it has no Ms. support (see App.), seems right, as against the Ms. *palma*. The terms of this fight were *concurrere ad digitum sublatum*, i.e. to fight until the vanquished man, dropping his shield, raised his finger (arm) in token of submission (see Introd.). In prose the vs. might run thus: *lex erat concurrere* (or *ut concurrerent*) *dum alteruter deposita parma digitum tolleret.* — **parma**: the small round shield. Evidently one or both of these combatants was a Thraex; see Fried. SG. 2.531–532.

6. lances . . . dedit: i.e. to the combatants. — **lances donaque**: i.e. *lances* heaped with *dona*, probably of money; cf. Iuv. 6. 204; Suet. Claud. 21. The *lances* were

in themselves valuable gifts. On the emoluments of popular gladiators see Fried. SG. 2. 371.

7. Inventus . . . finis: see 9.

8. subcubuere, *gave way*, i.e. to the command of the emperor to stop fighting (9–10).

9. rudes et palmas: to the gladiator, when he received his permanent *missio*, was given a *rudis*, a sort of wooden sword or foil, as a sign that his fighting days were over; cf. Hor. Ep. 1. 1. 2 and editors there. *Donari rude* was also used figuratively of discharge or exemption from any task; cf. e.g. Ov. Tr. 4. 8. 23–24. A palm branch was given to the gladiator who was victorious in a given contest; cf. Cic. Rosc. Amer. 6. 17 *plurimarum palmarum gladiator.*

10. ingeniosa, *intelligent*; *virtus* such as that of Priscus and Verus is more than mere courage backed by brute force and skill of hand.

11. nullo = *nullo alio.* — **principe**: not 'prince'. The word is a mild term, used to avoid the hated word *rex*; it describes the emperor as embodying in himself, by vote of the senate, the united powers of the state. See Abbott §§ 325 ; 400 ff.; E. G. Sihler in Gildersleeve Studies 77 ff. *Leader* may serve as a translation.

LIBER I

1

Hic est quem legis ille, quem requiris,
toto notus in orbe Martialis
argutis epigrammaton libellis,
cui, lector studiose, quod dedisti
5   viventi decus atque sentienti,
rari post cineres habent poetae.

1. The poet expresses his appreciation of the fame that has come to him during his life and thanks his admirers.— Meter: § 49.

1-2. Hic est: cf. Pers. 1. 28 *at pulchrum est digito monstrari et dicier "Hic est!"*—**ille ... Martialis:** cf. Cic. Tusc. 5. 36. 103 *Demosthenes, qui illo susurro delectari se dicebat aquam ferentis mulierculae, ut mos in Graecia est, insusurrantisque alteri "Hic est ille Demosthenes".* *Ille,* as often, = 'the well-known'. — **quem requiris:** i.e. 'whom you cannot do without'. See § 39. — **toto ... Martialis:** naturally, for Latin was the official language of the world. Even before M.'s time Roman poets expected to be read in the farthest corners of the earth; cf. 5. 13. 2–4; 7. 17. 9–10; 8. 61. 3, etc.; Ov. Tr. 4. 10. 127–128 *cumque ego praeponam multos mihi, non minor illis dicor et in toto plurimus orbe legor*; Am. 1. 15. 13 *toto cantabitur orbe*; Hor. C. 2. 20. 17–20.

3. argutis, *bright, witty, pointed.* The word is used properly of physical objects, then, in transferred sense, of the intellect; cf. the history of 'bright'.—**epigrammaton:** Greek form of gen. plural.

—**libellis:** M.'s epigrams were first given to the world separately or in small collections (§ 13); hence the diminutive. Cf. 1. 3. 2 *parve liber.* Further, books of poetry were as a rule much smaller than those of prose; see Birt 23. 1; 290 ff. M. wrote 1. 1; 1. 2 to introduce epigrams written long before, perhaps on the second publication of Books I–VII; see Dau 77; 81. — Note position of *argutis . . . libellis.* In all Latin poetry adjective and noun often stand thus at beginning and end of the vs.; so often in M.: cf. Lib. Spect. 1. 1; 1. 1. 6; 1. 3. 1, 11; 1. 4. 7; 1. 6. 2, 4; etc. So often too in Catullus, M.'s exemplar (§ 34).

4-5. quod ... sentienti: cf. 3. 95. 7–8 *ore legor multo notumque per oppida nomen non exspectato dat mihi fama rogo*; Ov. Tr. 4. 10. 121–122 *tu mihi, quod rarum est, vivo sublime dedisti nomen, ab exsequiis quod dare fama solet.*

6. post cineres: cf. 1. 25. 8; 5. 10. 1–2; 5. 13. 4 N. For other expressions of the idea of 4–6 cf. 8. 69; 11. 90; Ov. Pont. 4. 16. 2–3 *non solet ingeniis summa nocere dies famaque post cineres maior venit*; Hor. Ep. 2. 1. 15–22; Prop.

4

2

Qui tecum cupis esse meos ubicumque libellos
    et comites longae quaeris habere viae,
hos eme, quos artat brevibus membrana tabellis :
    scrinia da magnis, me manus una capit.
5 Ne tamen ignores ubi sim venalis et erres
    urbe vagus tota, me duce certus eris :
libertum docti Lucensis quaere Secundum
    limina post Pacis Palladiumque Forum.

3. 1. 21-24; Tac. Ann. 2. 88; Agr.
1. 1; D. 18; Sen. Ep. 114. 13;
Plin. Ep. 6. 21. 1. The thought
occurs too in Greek literature; cf.
e.g. Soph. Ajax 961-965.
   2. M. advertises a handy volume of his epigrams. Such a volume could hardly be a papyrus
roll (*volumen*); it was rather a
parchment book (*codex*). See on
3-4. Parchment (*membrana* : prop.
'the skin of an animal') made a
better writing surface than papyrus; it could be utilized on both
sides. For other pocket editions
cf. 14. 184 (Homer); 186 (Vergil);
190 (Livy); Birt 57 ff.—Meter: §48.
   1. ubicumque = *ubique*; for
the thought cf. 1. 1. 2 N.—libellos : here a dim. of affection. Cf.
also 1. 1. 3 N.
   2. M. is addressing those who
are looking for handy volumes
with which to beguile the tedium
of a long journey. — comites :
pred. acc.; cf. 14. 188; Pub. Syr.
104 *comes facundus in via pro vehi-
culo est.* — longae . . . viae : see
§ 48, c. — habere : *quaero* + inf. (in
poetry as old as Lucr.) is frequent
in M.; cf. 1. 33. 3; 11. 84. 1; etc.
   3. hos (*libellos*) prob. refers
only to Books I-II, published in
85 or 86; § 13. — artat . . . tabellis : the use of parchment (cf.
Introd.) enabled the copyist to

compress so much within small
pages that the reader might well
imagine he held *codicilli* or *pugillares membranei* (cf. *manus una
capit*, 4; 14. 190. 1). — tabellis =
foliis, paginis ; cf. *prima tabella*,
14. 186. 2. *tabellis* is instr. abl. with
artat.
   4. scrinia shows that the contrast is between books of parchment (*codices*) and *volumina* of
papyrus (see Introd.); for the latter the *scrinia* and oval *capsae*
were used, the rolls being stuck in
them ends down. See 14. 37.
Introd. — me repeats the thought
of 3; for the figure cf. 14. 190.
   6. urbe . . . tota implies that
all the book-trade was not in the
Argiletum (see on 8) and that these
codicilli were not easily picked up.
   7. docti Lucensis : unknown
to us, though evidently well known
in Rome. — Secundum : besides
Secundus M. had several publishers, possibly because the *libri epigrammaton* were published at
various times and in different
styles. He mentions Pollius (1.
113. 5), Atrectus (1. 117. 13-14),
and Tryphon (4. 72. 2; 13. 3. 4). On
the book-trade in Rome see Marq.
826; Beck. 2. 445 ff.; Birt 353 ff.;
357 ff.; Lanciani Anc. R. 182.
   8. limina . . . Pacis : the entrance to the Temple of Peace;

3

Argiletanas mavis habitare tabernas,
cum tibi, parve liber, scrinia nostra vacent.
Nescis, heu, nescis dominae fastidia Romae :
crede mihi, nimium Martia turba sapit.

Pacis = templi Pacis. The Forum
Pacis (Forum Vespasiani), lying
behind (i.e. north of) the Basilica Aemilia, was the easternmost
of the imperial *fora*, all of which
lay north of the Forum Magnum
(Forum Romanum). In this forum
was a magnificent Temple of
Peace, dedicated in 75 to commemorate the triumph of Rome
over the Jews. See Platner 265.
—**Palladium** . . . **Forum**: a poetic
designation of the Forum Nervae.
This plot was nicknamed Forum
Transitorium or Forum Pervium
because, being comparatively narrow, it was little more than a thoroughfare lying between the Forum
Pacis on the east and the older
fora, those of Caesar and Augustus, on the west. It was begun by
Domitian and finished by Nerva,
in 98. It contained a temple of
Minerva (Pallas); hence the name
Forum Palladium. See Platner
266–268. Cf. 4. 53. 1–2 *intra penetralia nostrae Pallados et templi
limina . . . novi.* — The chief booksellers' quarter in Rome was the
Argiletum, an important street
which ran out of the north side of
the Forum Romanum, and, passing
between the Curia and the Basilica
Aemilia, gave access to the Subura
and the whole eastern section of
the city. Domitian and Nerva converted this street into the Forum
Nervae (Palladium) ; see Platner
170; 266. See also 1.3.1; 1.117.9–10.
3. A prefatory epigram (cf. 1. 1;
1. 2), addressed to his book, which

is represented as a bird anxious to
leave the parent nest. Horace, in
Ep. 1. 20. 20–21, had similarly addressed his book ; Ovid in the
opening of his *Tristia* thus bids
farewell to his work : *parve, nec
invideo, sine me, liber, ibis in urbem.*
Cf. 3. 2, with notes. — Meter : § 48.
    1. Argiletanas : see on 1. 2. 8.
For position of adjective and noun
see on 1. 1. 3. — **habitare tabernas** implies a permanent change
of abode : ' You thirst for fame
and prefer the applause of men to
the quiet discipline of home '.
    2. parve liber : a collection
only of Books I–II ; see on *libellos*,
1. 2. 1. — **scrinia . . . vacent :** i.e.
' there is plenty of room for you
at home ' ; the pl. *scrinia* adds to
the force of the verb. See 1. 2. 4 N.
    3. dominae . . . Romae, *Rome,
mistress of the world*; cf. 10. 103. 9
*moenia . . . dominae pulcherrima
Romae* ; 12. 21. 9–10 *tu desiderium
dominae mihi mitius urbis esse
iubes* ; Hor. C. 4. 14. 43–44 *o tutela
praesens Italiae dominaequeRomae*;
Ep. 1. 7. 44 *regia Roma.* — **fastidia,**
niceness, i.e. hypercriticism; for the
plural see A. 100, c ; GL. 204, N. 5 ;
L. 1109.
    4. nimium . . . sapit explains
fastidia (3) : ' knows too much, little
book, for you to escape the conse-
quences of your temerity '. — **Martia turba** alludes to the legendary
descent of the Romans, through
Romulus, from Mars. The whole
verse is contemptuous : as if a
mob of soldiers could exercise fair

5   Maiores nusquam rhonchi : iuvenesque senesque
     et pueri nasum rhinocerotis habent.
     Audieris cum grande sophos, dum basia iactas,
     ibis ab excusso missus in astra sago.

literary criticism! Cf. 5. 19. 5 *pulchrior et maior quo sub duce Martia
Roma*, though the tone there is
different.

5-6. These verses explain *fastidia* (3); everybody is a would-be
critic; age has not learned wisdom
nor youth modesty; literature is
nothing if not satirical and epigrammatic. — **nusquam** = *nusquam alibi*, i.e. nowhere else than
in Rome; see on *nullo*, Lib. Spect.
29. 11. M. is thinking especially
of the *recitationes* which flourished
from the time of Asinius Pollio
under Augustus to Hadrian; see
Fried. SG. 3. 419 ff.; Mayor on
Iuv. 3. 9. — **rhonchi:** prop. said
of snoring (cf. ῥέγκος, ῥέγχος): cf.
3. 82. 30 *silentium rhonchis praestare iussi*, 'we are bidden to keep
still while our host snores'; then
said of a croaking frog; here used
metaphorically of the outward
manifestations of the hearers at
the recitations, *sneers*; cf. 4. 86. 7;
Apoll. Sidon. C. 3. 8 *nec nos
rhonchisono   rhinocerote notat*.
Note the onomatopoeia. — **iuvenesque senesque** occurs in 7. 71.
5; 9. 7. 9; Ov. M. 8. 526. — **nasum
rhinocerotis:** cf. *naso adunco aliquem suspendere* (e.g. Hor. S.
1. 6. 5), 'turn up the nose at';
1. 41. 18; 12. 37. 1 *nasutus nimium
cupis videri*; 13. 2. 1-3; Hor. S.
2. 8. 64; Pers. 1. 40-41 *"rides", ait,
"et nimis uncis naribus indulges"*;
1. 118; Otto s.v. *Nasus. Rhinocerotis* seems· to imply that the display of contempt was both extreme
and chronic. Even the applause is
hypocritical; see 7-8. The whole

expression appears to have become
proverbial; cf. Apoll. Sidon. C. 9.
342-343 *rugato Cato tertius labello
narem rhinoceroticam minetur.*
For public interest in the rhinoce-
ros see 14. 52; 14. 53; Lib. Spect.
9; 22; Iuv. 7. 130.

7. grande, *loud* (prop. *strong*),
is also ironical, *lusty*. — **sophos**
(=σοφῶς), *bravo! good! hear, hear!*
Cf. 3. 46. 8; 6. 48. 1; Petr. 40 *sophos
universi clamamus.* Similar excla-
mations were *sapienter, recte,* εὖγε,
μεγάλως, *bene, perbene, praeclare,
belle, optume, festive, lepide, nil
supra.* In 2. 27. 3 we have *effecte!
graviter! cito! nequiter! euge!
beate!* Appreciation was expressed
in still other ways; see 10. 10. 9-10.
— **basia iactas,** *you are throwing
kisses,* a custom current in M.'s
time in recognition of favors bestowed or as a mark of honor;
here the kisses are in acknowl-
edgment of the kisses thrown by
the audience or of their *sophos.*
Iuv. 4. 117-118 characterizes Veiento as *dignus Aricinos qui mendicaret ad axes blandaque devexae
iactaret basia raedae*; cf. Phaedr.
5. 7. 28 *in plausus consurrectum
est; iactat basia tibicen: gratulari
fautores putat. Basium* as a substitute for *suavium* was made popular in literature by Catullus. See
12. 29. 4 N.

8. ibis, *go you will,* but as you
little expect, i.e. *ab . . . missus . . .
sago.* — **ab . . . sago:** in Roman
camps the tiro was hazed by being
tossed in a blanket extemporized
out of a soldier's thick cloak; cf.
Suet. Oth. 2. The thought is: 'At

Sed tu, ne totiens domini patiare lituras
10   neve notet lusus tristis harundo tuos,
aetherias, lascive, cupis volitare per auras :
i, fuge ; sed poteras tutior esse domi.

4

Contigeris nostros, Caesar, si forte libellos,

the very moment when you are congratulating yourself on success, your pretended admirers are sneering at you, and the immortality which you fancy you have already won is fictitious'. — **excusso** = *distento*, i.e. shaken out and pulled taut.

9. **totiens . . . lituras**: the *liber* thinks of the author as a slave-master (*dominus*) from whom it longs to escape, without realizing that in so doing it will but fall into the hands of a *domina* (3) more heartless.—**lituras**: note the etymology and original meaning; here, as *harundo* shows, papyrus was used. Cf. 4. 10. 7–8; 7. 17. 7–8.

10. **notet**: *notare* (cf. *nota*) came to mean 'brand', and so 'censure'; it is here ironical ('mar') for 'correct'; cf. 7. 17. 7–8.— **lusus**: cf. *lascive*, 11, with note.— **tristis harundo**, *a harsh and over-critical pen. Harundo* = *calamus scriptorius*, which was imported from Egypt (Plin. N. H. 16. 157); cf. 14. 209. 2 *inoffensa curret harundo via.*

11. **aetherias . . . per auras**: in contrast to the dark *scrinia* (2). — **lascive**: primarily *sportive, playful* (cf. Hor. S. 1. 3. 133 *vellunt tibi barbam lascivi pueri*); here, perhaps, there is a secondary reference to the wanton character of some of the epigrams; cf. 1. 4. 8 *lasciva pagina.* Further, in Hor. Ep. 1. 20, which M. had in mind

throughout, Horace compares his book, which is now eager to leave him, to a slave ready to turn wanton; cf. *fuge* (12). M. thinks of his book as all too ready to become a (*servus*) *fugitivus.* — **cupis volitare,** *you are anxious to try your wings*, i.e. to get out into the world of letters.

12. **i, fuge** : note the asyndeton ; for other examples with *i* cf. 10. 20. 4; 10. 96. 13. The combination of *i* + another imv. is regularly emotional, often sarcastic ; cf. Lease A. J. P. 19. 59–69. — **poteras . . . esse,** *you might have been*; see A. 517, c; GL. 254, Rem. 1 ; 597, Rem. 3; L. 1495–1496. Note the tense; with *i, fuge* M. set the book (bird) free. — **domi** : i.e. in the *scrinia* (2).

4. Another prefatory epigram, a carefully worded appeal to Domitian, as *censor morum*, to overlook the 'playful' epigrams of this collection. ' If by chance my poems fall into your hands, do not criticise them with the stern look proper enough for the master of the world when he is exercising his imperial functions, but receive my pleasantries as you would the jibes of the crowd were you celebrating a triumph', etc. Cf. the Praefatio to Book I.— Meter: § 48.

1. **Contigeris** is more diplomatic than *perlegeris* would be ; cf. 10. 64. 1–2 *contigeris regina meos si Polla libellos, non tetrica nostros*

terrarum dominum pone supercilium.
Consuevere iocos vestri quoque ferre triumphi
materiam dictis nec pudet esse ducem.
5   Qua Thymelen spectas derisoremque Latinum,

excipe fronte iocos. — **forte** : of course M. saw to it that a copy of his book reached Domitian, but he is too much of a courtier to assume that Domitian will read it. — **libellos** : here dim. of (mock) depreciation ; contrast 1. 2. 1 N.

2. terrarum = *orbis terrarum* ; the Latin poets seem to prefer the single word when it is in the gen. with *dominus* ; cf. 7. 5. 5 *terrarum dominum* ; 8. 2. 6 *terrarum domino deoque rerum* (both passages refer to Domitian) ; Ov. Pont. 2. 8. 26 ; Luc. 8. 208.— **pone** = *depone* ; see on Lib. Spect. 29. 5. The simple verb is often thus used for the compound in poetry and in Silver Latin. See H. L. Wilson, Gildersleeve Studies, 49 ff. ; Trans. Amer. Phil. Ass. 31. 202–222. — **supercilium**, *nod, will, sternness* ; cf. 1. 24. 2 *cuius et ipse times triste supercilium* ; Apoll. Sidon. C. 15. 189 *nunc Stoica tandem pone supercilia.* The vs. is an echo of the court talk ; cf. 10. 64. 1–2, cited on 1. It reminds one of the famous description in Hom. Il. 1. 528–530 of Jupiter's nod that shook Olympus, which inspired, it is said, Phidias's statue of Jupiter at Olympia (cf. Lib. Spect. 1. Introd.).

3–8. 'You and other great conquerors have learned to accept gracefully, without loss of dignity, the jibes of the crowd'. — **Consuevere** and the pl. **triumphi**, by implying that Domitian had become habituated to triumphs, continue the flattery of 2. The custom of bantering (or lauding) the *imperator* at a triumph was very old ;

cf. 7. 8. 7–10 *festa coronatus ludet convicia miles, inter laurigeros cum comes ibit equos ; fas audire iocos levioraque carmina, Caesar, et tibi, si lusus ipse triumphus amat* ; Suet. Iul. 49 ; 51 ; etc. ; Marq.-Wissowa 2. 588. 2. — **vestri**, *of you emperors in general*, is more diplomatic, because less personal, than *tui* would have been ; Domitian's triumphs had not been preceded by substantial military successes. — **quoque** : i.e. as well as those of generals not *principes.*

4. materiam dictis, *a subject for jibes* ; cf. Petr. 109 *Eumolpus et ipse vino solutus dicta voluit in calvos stigmososque iaculari* ; Ov. Tr. 2. 70 *et se materiam carminis esse iuvat* (Iuppiter). Other constructions appear in Iuv. 10. 47 *materiam risus* ; Cic. De Or. 2. 59. 239 *satis bella materies ad iocandum.*—**ducem**: *dux* frequently = *imperator* in M. and contemporary poets. Iuv. 4. 145 applies *dux magnus* specially to Domitian.

5. Qua : sc. *fronte.*— **Thymelen** : a stage name (cf. θυμέλη ; see § 38 ; Fried. SG. 2. 626) of a celebrated *mima*, or pantomimic danseuse. Thymele and Latinus, an equally famous *mimus*, court favorites both, are often mentioned together ; cf. e.g. Iuv. 1. 36 *trepido Thymele summissa Latino.* Suet. Dom. 15 represents Latinus as retailing to Domitian the gossip of the town as they dined together. For Thymele's acting see Iuv. 6. 66 ; 8. 107 ; for Latinus see 13. 2. 3 ; 2. 72. 3 ; 3. 86. 3. — **spectas** : *spectare* is often used of looking

illa fronte, precor, carmina nostra legas :
innocuos censura potest permittere lusus ;
lasciva est nobis pagina, vita proba.

9

Bellus homo et magnus vis idem, Cotta, videri :
sed qui bellus homo est, Cotta, pusillus homo est.

on at *ludi, triumphi*, etc.; cf. 5. 14.
7 ; 5. 19. 3 *quando magis dignos
licuit spectare triumphos ?* 4. 2. 1–2
*spectabat modo solus inter omnes
nigris munus Horatius lacernis*;
Hor. A. P. 189–190; S. 2. 8. 79. —
derisorem, *clown, buffoon*.

6. fronte, *brow, expression* ; cf.
supercilium in 2 ; 10. 64. 1, cited
on 1 ; 7. 12. 1–2 *sic me fronte legat
dominus, Faustine, serena excipiat-
que meos qua solet aure iocos.*

7. innocuos, *harmless* ; M.
would be careful, knowing that
Domitian, as censor, had sought
to bring to book authors of libels
and to restrain the license of actors. Cf. § 38 ; 3. 99. 3 ; 5. 15. 2
*et queritur laesus carmine nemo
meo*; 7. 12. 9 *ludimus innocui* ;
10. 5, with notes. — **censura**: see
Introd. On the censorship, the
tribunicia potestas, and the *imperium* the imperial power was
largely built up. M. is asserting
that nothing in his epigrams calls
for Domitian's notice.

8. lasciva, *playful*; see on *lascive*, 1. 3. 11. Cf. Ovid's *iocosa*,
cited below. — **proba**, *clean, honorable* ; the chiasmus adds to the
antithesis with *lasciva*. Cf. Ov. Tr.
2. 353–354 *crede mihi, distant
mores a carmine nostro: vita vere-
cunda est, Musa iocosa mea.* In 9.
28. 5–6 M. makes Latinus say : *sed
nihil a nostro sumpsit mea vita theatro et sola tantum scaenicus arte

feror. Perhaps the example of
Ovid's *lascivia* had not been lost
on M.; § 33.

9. 'To call a *bellus homo* a man
of worth is a contradiction in
terms'. — Meter: § 48.

1. bellus: dim. of *benus = bonus* (*benulus, benlus, bellus*); perhaps at first, as applied to men, a
slang word. *bellus homo =* 'dandy',
'rake', 'ladies' man', etc.; Plin. Ep.
4. 25. 3 uses the phrase of a senator who took advantage of a secret
vote in the senate to write obscene
nonsense on his ballot ; Catull. 78
applies *bellus* to dissolute persons.
In Plaut. Cap. 956–957 the runaway
slave Stalagmus says : *fui ego bellus, lepidus ; bonus vir numquam
neque frugi bonae neque ero.* Cf. also
12. 39, with notes ; 10. 46. 1–2 *omnia
vis belle, Matho, dicere ; dic aliquando et bene.*— **et** = *et tamen*, as very
often in M. — **Cotta**: unknown ;
perhaps a fictitious name (§ 38).

2. pusillus: dim. of *pusus =
puer* ; cf. *pusio.* A *bellus homo* is no
man at all, or at least a man that
lacks manliness; cf. 3. 63. 14 *res pertricosa est, Cotile, bellus homo*; 12. 39.
2 *res est putida bellus* (*homo*) *et Sabellus.* Cf. also 3. 62. 8 *animus pusillus* ; 9. 50. 1 *ingenium pusillum.*

10. Before M.'s time legacy-
hunting (*captatio*) had become a
profession at Rome. Latin literature contains many allusions, humorous (see e.g. Hor. S. 2. 5) and

10

Petit Gemellus nuptias Maronillae
et cupit et instat et precatur et donat.
Adeone pulchra est ? Immo foedius nil est.
Quid ergo in illa petitur et placet ? Tussit.

12

Itur ad Herculei gelidas qua Tiburis arces

otherwise, to these *captatores*, who sought in every way to ingratiate themselves with people well-to-do, but without natural heirs. Plin. Ep. 2. 20 charges Regulus (see I. 12. Introd.) with such *captatio*; Iuv. 10. 201–202, describing the disgust excited by a man in his dotage, says : *usque adeo gravis uxori natisque sibique ut captatori moveat fastidia Cosso.* Cf. 6. 63; 5. 39; Fried. SG. I. 414 ff.— Meter : § 52.

1. **Gemellus**: see App.— **Maronillae**: objective genitive.

2. **cupit . . . donat**: his almost despairing earnestness is brought out by the series of verbs that amounts to a climax : 'Yea, he craves it, he is hot upon its trail with entreaties and with presents'.

3. **Adeone**: i.e. as to warrant such persistency in face of opposition. — **Immo**: regularly corrective. — **foedius**, *uglier*, *more loathsome.* — **nil**: more emphatic than *nemo.* Had M. said *nemo*, he would be comparing (contrasting) Maronilla only with all other women; by writing *nil* he contrasts her with all other things in the world. So often at all periods. Further, the Romans often prefer a negative sentence with a comparative such as we have here to a positive sentence with a superlative (*foedissimum rerum omnium est*).

4. **ergo** often betrays strong feeling; cf. e.g. Hor. C. I. 24. 5; Iuv. I. 3.—**Tussit,** *she has a* (*bad*) *cough.* Cf. 2. 26. 1–4 *quod querulum spirat, quod acerbum Naevia tussit inque tuos mittit sputa subinde sinus, iam te rem factam, Bithynice, credis habere ? erras : blanditur Naevia, non moritur*; 5. 39. 5–6; Hor. S. 2. 5. 106–109. *Tussit* is a παρὰ προσδοκίαν jest, of the sort common in satire, e.g. in Aristophanes; cf. Iuv. I. 74 *probitas laudatur et — alget!*

12. In praise of M. Aquilius Regulus, famous as a lawyer and infamous as a *delator* (under Domitian) and *captator* (see I. 10. Introd.). His narrow escape from the fall of a colonnade stirs M. to flattery. Cf. I. 82. M. probably had a mercenary motive, for Regulus was his patron; see § 20; 7. 16. Regulus probably felt well repaid for his patronage of M., for the poet praises him as a man of piety, wisdom, and genius (I. 111; 5. 63), an eloquent lawyer (2. 74; 5. 28; 6. 38) worthy of comparison with Cicero (4. 16), etc. The odious picture drawn of him by Plin. Ep. I. 5 ; 2. 20 and Tac. Hist. 4. 42 is probably truer to life, at least for his earlier years. See Merrill on Plin. Ep. I. 5. 1. — Meter : § 48.

1. **Herculei . . . arces**: see App. The fame of the splendid

canaque sulphureis Albula fumat aquis,
rura nemusque sacrum dilectaque iugera Musis
signat vicina quartus ab urbe lapis.

5   Hic rudis aestivas praestabat porticus umbras,

temple of Hercules at Tibur was wide-spread; see Burn, Rome and the Campagna, 397. Cf. Priap. 7 5. 8–9 *tutela Rhodos est beata Solis, Gades Herculis umidumque Tibur*; Prop. 4. 7. 81–82. *Herculeum* is as much a stock epithet of Tibur as are *umidum, udum, supinum*. With *Herculei . . . arces* cf. 4. 57. 9–10; 4. 62. 1 *Tibur in Herculeum migravit nigra Lycoris*.— **gelidas**, *cool*, because the town lay on high ground; cf. 4. 64. 32; Iuv. 3. 190 *gelida Praeneste*; Hor. C. 3. 4. 22 *frigidum Praeneste*.— **qua**, *where*. The villa of Regulus was near the Via Tiburtina and the Albula (2). — **arces**: Hor. S. 2. 6. 16 uses *arx* with reference to his Sabine farm as a place of refuge from the city.

2. sulphureis . . . aquis: the sulphur springs known as Albula or Aquae Albulae (modern Acque Albule or Solfatara), referred to by Strabo as τὰ Ἀλβουλα ὕδατα, lay near Tibur, a little north of the Via Tiburtina. The name was doubtless due to the whitish hue of the water (cf. *cana*); the malodorous sulphur vapor of the springs suggested *fumat*. For the rhyme see § 48, c; cf. *biiugis . . . equis*, 8. — **aquis**, *medicinal springs, baths*. The villa of Regulus lay between the Aquae and Rome, near enough to the city to be convenient of access and still near the mountains and the fashionable locality of the Albula. The baths at the Albulae have been in use again since 1879.

3. rura: this word is used in both numbers of a country estate with its acres, gardens, and buildings; cf. Cic. Rosc. Amer. 46. 133

habet animi causa rus amoenum et suburbanum; Hor. Epod. 2. 3 *paterna rura bobus exercet suis*. — **sacrum**: as the haunt of the Muses. — **iugera**: freely, 'acres'.

4. signat, *marks the situation of*. — **quartus . . . lapis**, *only the fourth milestone*; *lapis* is frequently used for the more exact *miliarium*. Distances were reckoned from the city gates; see Middleton, Remains of Ancient Rome, 2. 538; I. 264. M. cannot exactly locate the villa, because it lay off the road; in 7. 31 he calls this estate *rus marmore tertio notatum*. Cf. 3. 20. 17–18 *an rure Tulli fruitur atque Lucani? an Pollionis dulce (rus) currit ad quartum (lapidem)?*

5. rudis, *rough, rustic*; originally plainly built, it had now become old (cf. 7). But there is a play on words; the portico is boorish, dead to the feeling for Regulus that everything on the estate should have shared with the Muses. One or more porticoes or colonnades (*porticus*) were essential parts of a country establishment. Sometimes, as here, the portico served as a *gestatio* for use in hot or wet weather; cf. 12. 50. 3 (in a description of a villa with baths, hippodrome, etc.) *at tibi centenis stat porticus alta columnis*; Iuv. 7. 178–179 *balnea sescentis (emuntur) et pluris porticus in qua gestetur dominus quotiens pluit*; 4. 5–6. Cf. also Pliny's descriptions of his villa at Laurentum and that in Tuscany, Ep. 2. 17; 5. 6.— **aestivas . . . umbras**: cf. Petr. 131 *nobilis aestivas platanus diffuderat umbras*.

heu quam paene novum porticus ausa nefas !
nam subito conlapsa ruit, cum mole sub illa
　　gestatus biiugis Regulus esset equis.
Nimirum timuit nostras Fortuna querelas,
10　　quae par tam magnae non erat invidiae.
Nunc et damna iuvant ; sunt ipsa pericula tanti :
　　stantia non poterant tecta probare deos.

13

Casta suo gladium cum traderet Arria Paeto,

6. quam paene . . . nefas: cf.
6. 58. 3 *o quam paene tibi Stygias
ego raptus ad undas*; Hor. C. 2.
13. 21–22 *quam paene furvae regna
Proserpinae . . . vidimus. Nefas*
emphasizes the flattery.

7. subito . . . cum: Regulus
had just driven from beneath the
portico when it fell ; *cum = after.*
Cf. 1. 82. 5–6.— **conlapsa ruit:**
cf. Iuv. 8. 77 *conlapsa ruant subduc-
tis tecta columnis.* — **mole:** *moles*
is used of something massive, especially if built of stone or brick (concrete faced with brick); cf. Hor. C.
3. 29. 10 (of Maecenas's great Esquiline palace) *molem propinquam
nubibus arduis* (*desere*); 2. 15. 1–2.

8. gestatus . . . esset: *gestare*
often = to 'take the air', 'ride',
'drive', 'sail', etc., for pleasure ;
cf. 12. 17. 3 N.

9–10. 'Even fickle Fortune
would not risk the odium certain
to be incurred by snatching away
such a man as Regulus'. Cf. 7.
47. 7; Stat. Silv. 3. 5. 41–42 *su-
perique potentes invidiam timuere
tuam.*

11–12. 'This material loss and
the risk to Regulus are not without compensations. We know
now that there are gods who care
for mankind and that they have

Regulus under their special providence '.— **et,** *even. Et* and *ipsa*
here equal each other. — **tanti** =
tanti quanti constarunt, 'all they
cost', in distress to Regulus's
friends ; cf. 5. 22. 12. — **stantia** =
a protasis, or *dum stabant.* — **probare:** prop. 'put to the test';
hence, in this context, *commend,
indorse.* For the thought cf. 1. 82.
10–11 ; 2. 91. 2 *sospite quo* (= *Caesare*) *magnos credimus esse deos.*

13. Caecina Paetus espoused
the cause of Camillus Scriboni-
nus, who took up arms against
Claudius. He was arrested, taken
to Rome, and condemned to death.
His wife Arria (mother of the
Arria who was married to P. Clodius Thrasea Paetus) advised him
to commit suicide rather than in-
cur the disgrace of execution, and
set him an example of courage : cf.
Plin. Ep. 3. 16. 6 *praeclarum quidem illud eiusdem, ferrum strin-
gere, perfodere pectus, extrahere
pugionem, porrigere marito, addere
vocem immortalem ac paene divi-
nam: Paete, non dolet.* Fried. thinks
M. had in mind some work of art
which portrayed Arria's act. —
Meter : § 48.

1. Casta: emphatic by position,
that model of purity. — **suo,** *her*

quem de visceribus strinxerat ipsa suis,
"Si qua fides, vulnus quod feci non dolet", inquit,
"sed quod tu facies, hoc mihi, Paete, dolet".

15

O mihi post nullos, Iuli, memorande sodales,
    si quid longa fides canaque iura valent,
bis iam paene tibi consul tricensimus instat,
    et numerat paucos vix tua vita dies.
5   Non bene distuleris videas quod posse negari,
    et solum hoc ducas, quod fuit, esse tuum.

well-beloved; cf. the use of *suus* in superscriptions of letters, and that of *meus* in the familiar *mi fili*. — **gladium** here = *sicam, pugionem*; cf. Plin. above.

2. strinxerat: as if from its scabbard; cf. Plin. above. See App.

3. Si qua fides = *si quid mihi credis*, or *crede mihi*.

4. facies is a prediction and so more effective than an exhortation in imv. or subjunctive; Arria is sure that Paetus's courage will match her own. See App.—**dolet**: there is a partial play on words; *dolet* is used in 3 of physical pain, in 4 of pain of soul.

15. "'I'll live to-morrow', will a wise man say? To-morrow is too late: then live to-day" (Hay). This epigram is addressed to Iulius Martialis, for many years a very intimate friend of M. (cf. 12. 34. 1–2; § 20). This friendship inspired several beautiful epigrams, esp. 4. 64; 7. 17; 10. 47; 5. 20; 11. 80. — Meter: § 48.

1. memorande, *worthy of remembrance and mention*; freely, 'whom I ought to honor'. —

sodales, *boon companions, close friends*; cf. Ov. Tr. 1. 5. 1 *o mihi post ullos numquam memorande sodales.* See § 33.

2. fides: freely, 'faithful friendship'; prop. mutual confidence growing out of long friendship. — **canaque iura**, *and its hoar rights*, 'friendship's claims grown gray with age' (Steph.). *Cana* is more expressive than *vetusta* would have been; cf. Verg. A. 1. 292 *cana Fides*.

3. consul almost = *annus*; cf. 8. 45. 4 *amphora centeno consule facta minor* (i.e. wine made less by the evaporation of 100 years). — **tricensimus**: see 12. 34. 1–2.

4. et = *et tamen.* — **paucos ... dies**: 'your real life has been short, because you have not learned how to live'. — **vita**: i.e. as a time for enjoyment. See on 11–12; cf. also 6. 70. 15; 8. 77. 7–8.

5–6. bene, *wisely.*— **distuleris ... ducas**: subjunctives, because M. courteously uses the generalizing second person sing.; see A. 518, a; GL. 595, Rem. 3. — **ducas** = *existimes.* — **quod fuit**: i.e. the past.

Exspectant curaeque catenatique labores,
   gaudia non remanent, sed fugitiva volant.
Haec utraque manu conplexuque adsere toto :
10   saepe fluunt imo sic quoque lapsa sinu.
Non est, crede mihi, sapientis dicere " Vivam " :
   sera nimis vita est crastina : vive hodie.

7. **Exspectant,** *wait for*, to get you in their power. — **catenati:** freely, 'in one long line' (join with both nouns : the daily round of toil is like an endless chain), or perhaps, rather, 'close to one another', as slaves are in a chain-gang, with the intimation that Iulius himself is enslaved to them; cf. Aus. Idyll. 15. 13–14 *adflictat fortuna viros per bella, per aequor, irasque insidiasque catenatosque labores.* M. often predicates of conditions, attributes, acts, etc. what can properly be predicated only of the persons concerned (metonymy, transferred epithet): cf. 3. 46. 1 *operam togatam* ; 3. 58. 24 *albo otio* ; 10. 13. 4 *praetextata amicitia.* The usage is common in all Latin poets. For the caesura see § 47, e.

8. **gaudia . . . volant:** 'joys take wings; they are veritable birds of passage; trouble waits for us, joys never!' Cf. 7. 47. 11.

9–10. The figurative allusion to slaves in 7–8 (cf. *catenati, fugitiva*) prob. suggested the metaphor of 9. *Adserere manu in libertatem* = 'to declare a slave free in the process of *manumissio*'; in this a lictor, acting as *adsertor libertatis*, held a rod called *festuca* or *vindicta* in one hand and laid the other hand on the slave. *Aliquid adserere* came to mean 'appropriate' or 'claim' something for one's self. M. hints that to control *gaudia fugitiva* one hand and a formal legal process

will not suffice; even when embraced by both arms they often escape, as the skillful wrestler will baffle his antagonist by slipping downward from his embrace (10). — **utraque manu:** cf. Curt. 7. 8. 24 *proinde Fortunam tuam pressis manibus tene : lubrica est nec invita teneri potest.* — **imo . . . sinu:** *sinus* often, as here, denotes the loose folds of the toga where it crosses the breast; these folds were used as a sort of pocket. Hence by an easy shift *sinu* here = 'embrace', *complexu*; cf. 3. 5. 7–8 *est illi coniunx quae te manibusque sinuque excipiet.* Translate, 'from the firmest embrace '.

11. **Non . . . Vivam :** the man who understands the true philosophy of living will use the present rather than the future tense of *vivo*. For the gen. *sapientis* see A. 343, c; GL. 366; L. 1237.

12. **vive hodie:** the Epicurean doctrine, ' Let us eat, drink, and be merry, for to-morrow we die ', had large acceptation; cf. 2. 59. 3–4 ; 5. 20 ; 5. 58, esp. 1, 7, 8 ; 7. 47. 11. For the use of *vive*, 'get out of life all it has to give ', cf. *vita*, 4 N.; Verg. (?) Cop. 37–38 *pereat qui crastina curat ! mors aurem vellens "Vivite" ait "Venio";* Hor. C. 3. 29. 41–43 *ille potens sui laetusque deget, cui licet in diem dixisse "Vixi";* Catull. 5. 1 ; Varr. ap. Non. 56; Sen. Brev. Vit. 8. — The elision near the end of the pentameter is harsh and rare; cf. 7. 73. 6.

16

Sunt bona, sunt quaedam mediocria, sunt mala plura
    quae legis hic : aliter non fit, Avite, liber.

20

Dic mihi, quis furor est ? turba spectante vocata
    solus boletos, Caeciliane, voras.
Quid dignum tanto tibi ventre gulaque precabor ?
    boletum qualem Claudius edit edas.

16. M. jestingly warns his friend L. Stertinius Avitus (§ 16) not to expect perfection in his book, but to let the good pieces offset the bad. Cf. 7. 81 ; 7. 90. Of Stertinius, whose name occurs in a municipal inscription of Ostia (Orelli-Henz. 6446), M. says in the Praefatio to Book IX : *ad Stertinium clarissimum virum scripsimus, qui imaginem meam ponere in bibliotheca sua voluit.* — Meter: § 48.

2. Avite : for metrical reasons M. very often puts the name of the person to whom he is writing in the second half of the pentameter, in the voc.; cf. e.g. 1. 20. 2 ; 4. 26. 2, 4 ; 7. 88. 10 ; 10. 57. 2. See Fried. Einl. 30. On M.'s preference for certain words in the second half of the pentameter see Zingerle 13 ff.

20. Caecilianus is the type of the selfish *patronus* who occasionally, against his will, discharges his obligations to his *clientes* by inviting them to a so-called banquet (*cena publica, cena popularis*), at which the guests are put off with inferior food and wines, while the *patronus* and a few intimates enjoy the best of everything. Cf. 3. 60 : 4. 68 ; Iuv. 5 ; Plin. Ep. 2. 6 ; Fried. SG. 1, 386. — Meter: § 48.

1. quis furor est, *surely you must be crazy*; cf. 2. 80. 2 ; Tib. 1. 10. 33 *quis furor est atram bellis arcessere mortem?* — **turba :** Caecilianus does not invite a select few, but a veritable crowd. — **spectante :** the crowd is there after all only to look on ; cf. 1. 4. 5 N.; 1. 43. 11. The spectacle here is the array of fine viands set before Caecilianus himself. — **vocata,** *invited,* as guests ; sarcastic here, as in 1. 43. 1 ; 3. 60. 1.

2. solus : cf. Iuv. 1. 94–95 *quis fercula septem secreto cenavit avus?* — **boletos :** the Romans recognized various kinds of *fungi,* as *fungi pratenses, fungi suilli, tubera, boleti* ; see Plin. N. H. 22. 96 ; Beck. 3. 359 ff. Cf. Iuv. 5. 146–148 *vilibus ancipites fungi ponentur amicis, boletus domino, sed* ('and in fact') *quales Claudius edit ante illum uxoris, post quem nihil amplius edit* (see on 4). — **Caeciliane :** for position see on 1. 16. 2.

3. dignum : freely, 'fit punishment for'. — **gula :** prop. 'throat', then *gluttony* ; cf. 5. 70. 5 *o quanta est gula, centiens comesse*; 3. 22. 5 N.; Iuv. 1. 140-141 *quanta est gula quae sibi totos ponit apros.*

4. qualem . . . edit : i.e. 'such as will kill you'; cf. Iuv. 5. 146–148, cited on 2. — **Claudius :** the

25

Ede·tuos tandem populo, Faustine, libellos
    et cultum docto pectore profer opus,
quod nec Cecropiae damnent Pandionis arces
    nec sileant nostri praetereantque senes.
5   Ante fores stantem dubitas admittere Famam
    teque piget curae praemia ferre tuae?
Post te victurae per te quoque vivere chartae
    incipiant: cineri gloria sera venit.

emperor. His wife Agrippina used a *boletus* to poison him: see Suet. Claud. 44; Tac. Ann. 12. 66–67; Iuv. 6. 620 ff.

25. M. urges Faustinus, a wealthy friend, to publish his poetry while he can enjoy the praise of his contemporaries. For a like suggestion cf. Plin. Ep. 2. 10. Possibly Faustinus allowed natural diffidence or mayhap love of ease to choke his ambition; on his villas see 3. 58; 4. 57. He was probably one of those who, having under the empire no political career, wrote for amusement or for the *recitatio.* — Meter: § 48.

1. **tandem**: a compliment; M. has waited long.

2. **cultum**, *worked over, refined, polished* (cf. 1. 3. 9–10). — **docto pectore**: join with *cultum* rather than with *profer*. *Doctus* is said of one learned in Greek as well as Latin literature, and so is used especially of poets; cf. 10. 76. 6; 1. 61. 1; etc. *Docto pectore* thus = 'with the soul of a true poet'; cf. 9. 77. 3–4 *et multa dulci, multa sublimi refert, sed cuncta docto pectore.*

3–4. 'Your poems need not fear the critics, Greek or Latin'. — **Cecropiae . . . arces**: Cecrops was the fabulous founder of

Athens; Pandion was a king of Athens, so tradition said. Cf. 1. 39. 3 *si quis Cecropiae madidus Latiaeque Minervae*; Lucr. 6. 1143 *populo Pandionis = Atheniensibus.* — **nostri . . . senes**: i.e. those in Rome whose judgment is worth having; he ignores the *iuvenes* and the *pueri* of 1. 3. 5–6. — **praetereant,** *slight*; cf. Hor. A. P. 342 *celsi praetereunt austera poemata Ramnes.*

5–6. 'Are you so apathetic that you refuse admittance to Fame when she knocks, or after all the care bestowed on your poems do you hesitate to accept distinction as your reward?' Cf. Suet. Galb. 4 *sumpta virili toga somniavit Fortunam dicentem stare se ante fores defessam et, nisi ocius reciperetur, cuicumque obvio praedae futuram.* — **curae**: cf. 1. 45. 1 *edita ne brevibus pereat mihi cura libellis*; 1. 66. 5.

7–8. 'Your posthumous immortality may be sure, but you should yourself enjoy your fame now'. — **victurae . . . chartae**: cf. 11. 3. 7; 8. 73. 4. *Charta* is prop. 'a leaf of Egyptian papyrus'; here, as often in M., it = *pagina, liber, writing(s)*; cf. also Catull. 1. 5–6 *ausus es unus Italorum omne aevum tribus explicare chartis*;

27

Hesterna tibi nocte dixeramus,
quincunces puto post decem peractos,
cenares hodie, Procille, mecum.
Tu factam tibi rem statim putasti
5   et non sobria verba subnotasti
exemplo nimium periculoso :
μισῶ μνάμονα συμπόταν, Procille.

Hor. C. 4. 8. 21 *si chartae sileant
quod bene feceris.* — **vivere** : cf. 8 ;
I. 15. 11–12. — **gloria** is often used
of literary reputation, especially in
the writings of the Empire ; cf. 5.
10. 12 *si post fata venit gloria, non
propero* ; 10. 103. 3 ; Plin. Ep. 3.
9. 8 ; Prop. 4. 10. 3 *magnum iter
ascendo, sed dat mihi gloria vires.*
— **sera,** *too late* ; cf. 1. 1. 4–6, with
notes.

27. The point lies in the play
on the proverb in 7 : 'I positively
hate a table-companion who cannot forget' (what may have been
said at dinner). Cf. the promise
of Hor. Ep. 1. 5. 24–25 that at his
dinner party *ne fidos inter amicos
sit qui dicta foras eliminet.* Procillus, unknown to us, is some hanger-
on, or else the name masks some
real person ; § 38. The word may
be specially coined, to express contempt, from πρὸ + κίλλος = *asinus,*
a frequent term of abuse.— Meter :
§ 49.

1. nocte : during the *comissatio,* which followed the *cena*
proper. — **dixeramus** : perhaps
epistolary plpf. (A. 479 ; GL. 252),
but probably rather a simple plpf.
preceding in time the perfects of
4–5.

2. quincunces : a *quincunx*
was five twelfths of any whole (*as,
libra, iugerum,* etc.). Here it is five
twelfths of the *sextarius* (which

itself was one sixth of a *congius,*
3.283 liters), and = five *cyathi.* See
Marq. 335 ; Hultsch 118, Sect. 5 ;
704 Tab. XI. Cf. 2. 1. 9 ; 11. 36. 7
*quincunces et sex cyathos bessemque
bibamus.* Hor. S. 1. 1. 74 speaks
of a *sextarius vini* as a fair amount
to be taken at a meal.— **puto** :
M. doesn't know what he said ; cf.
non sobria verba (5). For the ŏ see
§ 54, c. — **peractos** = *exhaustos,
finished, drunk off.* In prose
we should have *postquam decem
quincunces peracti sunt.* The *anno
urbis conditae* construction after a
prep. belongs mainly to poetry and
to Livy.

4. factam ... rem : 'you assumed at once that the thing was
(as good as) done so far as you
were concerned, and that you were
sure of another dinner' ; 'you took
it as *un fait accompli*' (P. and S.).
Cf. 2. 26. 3 *iam te rem factam ...
credis habere ?* 6. 61. 1 *rem factam
Pompullus habet.* Cf. the phrase
dictum factum, 'no sooner said
than done', e.g. in Ter. Heau. 904
dictum factum huc abiit Clitipho.

5. subnotasti : 'you lost no
time in jotting down my invitation'.
Procillus had foreseen the very
thing that had happened, that M.
would forget.

6–7. exemplo, *precedent* ; cf.
Iuv. 13. 1 *exemplo quodcumque
malo committitur.* The precedent

29

Fama refert nostros te, Fidentine, libellos
　non aliter populo quam recitare tuos.
Si mea vis dici, gratis tibi carmina mittam :
　si dici tua vis, hoc eme, ne mea sint.

32

Non amo te, Sabidi, nec possum dicere quare :
　hoc tantum possum dicere : non amo te.

set by Procillus will be (1) dangerous to men's pocket-books, if every invitation given as this was is to count at full value, (2) dangerous to life itself, mayhap, if guests take notes of conversations. There was good reason for the popularity of the Greek proverb in 7 under emperors who fostered the *delatores*. See also on 10. 48. 21–22.

29. M. puts Fidentinus, a chronic offender, in the pillory for plagiarism; cf. 1. 38; 1. 53; 1. 72; § 37 fin. M.'s popularity seems to have made him a prey to others also : cf. 12. 63. 12–13 *nil est deterius latrone nudo : nil securius est malo poeta*; 1. 66; 2. 20. In 10. 102 he speaks of one *qui scribit nihil et tamen poeta est*. The passion for recitations may well have increased the temptation to plagiarism. — Meter : § 48.

1. **Fama**, *Rumor*.
2. **recitare** : see 1. 3. 5 N.

3–4. 'If, when reading my epigrams, you are willing to give me due credit for them, then *gratis tibi* (*mea*) *carmina mittam*. If you will not give me credit, let me at least get some cash from them '. — **hoc** : i.e. full title to ownership, with consequent right to use as one's own. Ancient notions of

literary ownership differed in some respects from those current to-day; cf. the fashion of the Sophists of writing speeches for other men to deliver. Cf. 2. 20; 12. 63. 6–7 *dic vestro, rogo, sit pudor poetae, nec gratis recitet meos libellos*; 1. 66. 13–14. The lack of copyright laws made plagiarism easier. — For the ending of the pentameter see § 48, b. — See App.

32. Cf. the following vss. written by Thomas Brown (1663–1704) on Dr. John Fell, Dean of Christ Church, Oxford, about 1670: " I do not like thee, Dr. Fell, The reason why I cannot tell; But this I know and know full well, I do not like thee, Dr. Fell ". In Thomas Forde's *Virtus Rediviva* (1661) we have : " I love thee not, Nell, But why I can't tell; Yet this I know well, I love thee not, Nell". — Meter : § 48.

1. **Non amo** = *odi* (litotes). For the *ŏ* here and in 2, cf. *puto*, 1. 27. 2 N. With the poem cf. Catull. 85 *odi et amo. Quare id faciam fortasse requiris; nescio, sed fieri sentio et excrucior.* See Paukstadt 4; 19. — **quare** : sc. *non te amem.* The subjv. is seldom omitted save when other subjunctives in the same const. are expressed in the sentence.

33

Amissum non flet, cum sola est, Gellia patrem,
    si quis adest, iussae prosiliunt lacrimae.
Non luget quisquis laudari, Gellia, quaerit,
    ille dolet vere, qui sine teste dolet.

38

Quem recitas meus est, o Fidentine, libellus,
    sed, male cum recitas, incipit esse tuus.

41

Urbanus tibi, Caecili, videris.

33. Real versus crocodile tears. — Meter: § 48.

1. non flet: either because she had been made happy by the wealth his death had brought her, or because now she can live with less restraint. — **patrem**: for acc. with verbs of emotion see A. 388; GL. 330, N. 2; L. 1139.

2. iussae: weeping as a fine art is very ancient; cf. Ter. Eu. 67–69; Ov. Am. 1. 8. 83 *quin etiam discant oculi lacrimare coacti*; Iuv. 6. 273–275; 13. 131–133 *nemo dolorem fingit in hoc casu* (i.e. when friends die), *vestem diducere summam contentus, vexare oculos umore coacto*. — **lacrimae**: for the rhyme see § 48, c.

3. laudari: i.e. for filial regard (*pietas*).

4. dolet, *feels pain*, i.e. experiences the true inner feeling of grief; *luget* (3) and *luctus* are used of grief manifested by outward signs, such as tears, mourning garb, etc. — **sine teste**: cf. *sola*, 1.

38. 'Bad reading will spoil a good epigram'. Cf. 1. 29. — Meter: § 48.

1–2. Cf. Aus. Ep. 14. 14–15 *haec quoque ne nostrum possint urgere pudorem, tu recita: et vere poterunt tua dicta videri*.

41. M., deriding Caecilius, a *parasitus* (*scurra, ardelio, nugator*), distinguishes *urbanitas* and *vernilitas* (*scurrilitas*). Cf. Quint. 6. 3. 17 *urbanitas . . . qua quidem significari video sermonem praeferentem in verbis et sono et usu proprium quendam gustum urbis et sumptam ex conversatione doctorum tacitam eruditionem, denique cui contraria sit rusticitas*. M. implies that the *vernilitas* of Caecilius has not even the merit of honest *rusticitas* (cf. 10. 101. 4, cited on 16). — Meter: § 49.

1. Urbanus, *polished, refined*, in manner or in speech; hence sometimes = *facetus, iocosus, lepidus, argutus*. Cf. εὐτράπελος, ἀστεῖος. Cf. Domitius Marsus ap. Quint. 6. 3. 105 *urbanus homo erit cuius multa bene dicta responsaque erunt, et qui in sermonibus, circulis, conviviis . . . omni denique loco ridicule commodeque dicet*; Cic. Off. 1. 29. 104 *duplex omnino est iocandi*

Non es, crede mihi. Quid ergo? verna,
hoc quod transtiberinus ambulator,
qui pallentia sulphurata fractis
5   permutat vitreis, quod otiosae
vendit qui madidum cicer coronae,

genus: unum inliberale, petulans, flagitiosum, obscenum, alterum elegans, urbanum, ingeniosum, facetum. — **Caecili**: prob. the *impurus* of 2. 72.

2. Quid ergo (*es*)? *what then are you?* — **verna** here = *scurra*. Slaves born in the master's house (*vernae*) were much better treated than other slaves; Plutarch, Cato Cens. 20, declares that Cato's wife did not think it beneath her to suckle the children of *vernae*. Hence they became spoiled and assumed special liberty in speech and action; *vernilia dicta* thus = *scurrilia dicta*. See Beck. 2. 131 ff.; Marq. 166–167. Hence *vernilitas* often = 'pertness', as well as 'cringing servility'; cf. Hor. S. 2. 6. 65–67 *ante Larem proprium vescor vernasque procaces pasco libatis dapibus*; Tib. 1. 5. 25. Many *vernae* were pets; cf. Petr. 66 *nam si aliquid muneris meo vernulae non tulero, habebo convicium*. Such slaves were often trained as jesters and buffoons, and as favorites easily secured manumission.

3. hoc (*es*) . . . **ambulator**: 'you're no gentleman, but rather what the street peddler is', etc. The Regio Transtiberina, on the west bank of the Tiber, was an unsavory district, largely given up to Jews, peddlers, and representatives of the trades which were not tolerated on the eastern bank (e.g. tanning). In 6. 93. 4 M. mentions among malodorous objects *detracta cani Transtiberina cutis*; see also Iuv. 14. 200 ff. Yet on the hills of this district were some fine estates: 4. 64; 1. 108. 1–2.

4–6. qui . . . vitreis: it is uncertain whether the *sulphurata* were bits of sulphur to be used as cement, or tinder, i.e. bits of wood tipped with sulphur (Morgan, Harv. Stud. 1. 42–43; Smith D. of A. s.v. *Igniaria*). The broken glass vessels taken in exchange would be repaired with sulphur and sold again; cf. 12. 57. 14; 10. 3. 2–4 *foeda linguae probra circulatricis, quae sulphurato nolit empta ramento Vatiniorum proxeneta fractorum*; Iuv. 5. 47–48 (*calicem*) *quassatum et rupto poscentem sulpura vitro* (cf. the scholiast there: *solent sulpure calices fractos sive calvariolas conponere*); Stat. Silv. 1. 6. 73–74. On the use of sulphur as an ingredient in cement see Plin. N. H. 36. 199; Ency. Brit. 22. 635. — **pallentia**: the Romans, being dark complexioned, turned sallow rather than pale; hence *pallens, pallidus* often = 'yellow'. — **fractis . . . vitreis**: proverbial for anything worthless or of small value (cf. Petr. 10); here, perhaps, trumpery in general, not merely glass. For the const. see A. 417, b; GL. 404, N. 1; L. 1389. See also on 9. 22. 11–12. — **otiosae . . . coronae**: *corona* is often used of a crowd of people, e.g. in the streets, the theater, the circus, or the camp; *otiosae* points to a crowd of idlers on the streets, or to people at some spectacle. When refreshments were not served at the *ludi* by the *editor*,

> quod custos dominusque viperarum,
> quod viles pueri salariorum,
> quod fumantia qui tomacla raucus
> 10 circumfert tepidis cocus popinis,
> quod non optimus urbicus poeta,

peddlers might be in demand there. Cf. 2. 86. 11, cited on 11 ; Hor. Ep. 1. 18 53 *scis quo clamore coronae proelia sustineas campestria* ; Ov. M. 13. 1–2 *consedere duces et vulgi stante corona surgit ad hos ... Aiax.* — **madidum cicer**: boiled pease, or some kind of pea-soup sold hot, common food of the poor; cf. 1. 103. 10; 5. 78. 21 ; Hor. S. 1. 6. 114–115 *inde domum me ad porri et ciceris refero laganique catinum.* Pease were also sold parched or roasted ; cf. Hor. A. P. 249. Singulars like *cicer* are often used in collective sense; cf. examples above ; Hor. C. 1. 4. 10 *flore terrae quem ferunt solutae.* See App.

7. 'Caecilius is a loathsome fakir (*circulator*), a charmer of venomous serpents'. Such fakirs were Orientals or came from the country districts of Italy, esp. from the mountainous districts east of Rome. The ancient crowds were very like the modern in their appreciation of fakirs, jugglers, rope-dancers, sword-eaters, etc.; cf. Ap. M. 1. 4 *Athenis ... ante Poecilen porticum circulatorem aspexi equestrem spatham praeacutam mucrone infesto devorasse ac mox eundem invitamento exiguae stipis venatoriam lanceam ... in ima viscera condidisse.* See also the Prologues to the Hecyra of Terence.

8. **pueri** = *servi.* — **salariorum**: dealers in salt or in salt fish ; cf. 4. 86. 9. In C.I.L. 6. 1152 we have mention of a *corpus salariorum*, though at a much later

time. See Marq. 469, N. 3. *Salarius* may be from the *sermo plebeius* ; see Cooper 73 (§ 18); cf. *helciarius*, 4. 64. 22 ; *locarius*, 5. 24. 9.

9. **fumantia . . . tomacla**, *steaming sausages.* The contracted form *tomaclum* represents the street cry. — **raucus**, *hoarse*, from crying his wares ; cf. Sen. Ep. 56. 2 *omnes popinarum institores, mercem sua quadam et insignita modulatione vendentes. Raucus circumfert* involves juxtaposition of effect and cause.

10. **circumfert ... popinis**: that the *popinae* were not simply drinking-places is very clear from Plaut. Poen. 835 *bibitur, estur quasi in popina* ; Iuv. 11. 81 *qui meminit calidae sapiat quid vulva popinae.* They were frequented by the lowest classes, and were mean and filthy ; cf. 7. 61. 8 *nigra popina* ; Iuv. 8. 171–176; Hor. S. 2. 4. 62 *immundis ... popinis* ; Ep. 1. 14. 21 *uncta popina.* The law at one time forbade keepers of *popinae* to serve cooked meat to wine drinkers, but they were hard to regulate. — **popinis** is prob. a dat. of interest, 'for the use of', etc., or a dat. of limit of motion, the const. so common in Vergil.

11. **non ... poeta**: a commonplace poet whose reputation is confined to the town ; prob. a streetsinger who, after the manner of southern Europe, dealt in improvisations, and would make noise enough to gather a crowd; cf. 2. 86. 11 *scribat carmina circulis Palaemon, me raris iuvat auribus placere,*

12 quod de Gadibus improbus magister.
14 Quare desine iam tibi videri
15 quod soli tibi, Caecili, videris,
qui Gabbam salibus tuis et ipsum
posses vincere Tettium Caballum.
Non cuicumque datum est habere nasum :
ludit qui stolida procacitate
20· non est Tettius ille, sed caballus.

12. magister: the owner of the Gaditanae; see 1. 61. 9; 5. 78. 26 *de Gadibus inprobis puellae*; Iuv. 11. 162; Stat. Silv. 1. 6. 71.

14. iam, *at last*; prop. 'by this time'; *tandem* is similarly used to give a tone of urgent appeal. — **videri**: emphasized by the repetition in *videris*, 15.

16–17. qui...posses: we should say, 'a man competent to surpass'. — **Gabbam**: a court fool of Augustus; cf. 10.101. 1–4 *Elysio redeat si forte remissus ab agro ille suo felix Caesare Gabba vetus, qui Capitolinum pariter Gabbamque iocantes audierit, dicet "Rustice Gabba, tace"*; Fried. SG. 1. 152. — **salibus**, *witticisms,* = *dictis*; cf. 3. 99. 3; 3. 20. 9 *lepore tinctos Attico sales narrat*; Hor. A. P. 270–271; Iuv. 9. 10–11 *conviva ioco mordente facetus et salibus vehemens intra pomeria natis*. Cf. 'Attic Salt'. — **posses**: for the mood and the tense see A. 516, f; GL. 596, 2; L. 2089. Our translation of this const. is misleading; here we should say, 'competent to surpass (had you lived in their day)'. Whenever a const. which, when the reference is to the future, remote or near, requires the pres. subj. is applied to the past, the pres. subj. is regularly changed to the impf. subj., e.g. in deliberative questions (cf. *quid facerem ?* with

quid faciam ?) and the potential subj. (cf. *haud facile discerneres* with *haud facile discernas*). — **Tettium Caballum**: unknown to us, though M. thinks of him as a greater *scurra* than Gabba (note *ipsum*). *Caballus* may have been a nickname.

18. 'Power of proper appreciation is rare (*you* certainly lack it)'. Cf. 1. 3. 6. — **cuicumque** = *cuivis, cuilibet*; see on *ubicumque*, 1. 2. 1. — **datum est habere**: cf. Prop. 3. 1. 14 *non datur ad Musas currere lata via*.

19. ludit, *pokes fun at, makes game of* (others); cf. 3. 99. 3. — **stolida procacitate** denotes stupid impudence, boldness meet only for a fool; cf. 2. 41. 17; Tac. Hist. 3. 62 *natus erat Valens Anagniae equestri familia, procax moribus neque absurdus ingenio, ni famam urbanitatis per lasciviam peteret*.

20. caballus = καβάλλης, *nag, pack-horse, cob*; cf. Petr. 134 *debilis, lassus, tamquam caballus in clivo*. The word is sometimes used ironically or jestingly for a nobler animal; Iuv. 3. 118 applies it to Pegasus. Here *caballus* is a play on *Caballum*, 17. The thought is 'You are but a reflection of Tettius's worse half, of the four-footed rather than of the two-legged *caballus*'.

42

Coniugis audisset fatum cum Porcia Bruti
    et subtracta sibi quaereret arma dolor,
"Nondum scitis" ait "mortem non posse negari?
    credideram fatis hoc docuisse patrem".
5 Dixit et ardentis avido bibit ore favillas.
    "I nunc et ferrum, turba molesta, nega".

43

Bis tibi triceni fuimus, Mancine, vocati
    et positum est nobis nil here praeter aprum,

42. A somewhat rhetorical glorification of the suicide of Porcia, wife of M. Iunius Brutus, the tyrannicide. Fried. thinks the epigram was prompted by some work of art representing the event. Cf. I. 13. Introd. Cf.Val. Max. 4. 6. 5 *quae* ⟨*Porcia*⟩, *cum apud Philippos victum et interemptum virum tuum Brutum cognosses, quia ferrum non dabatur, ardentes ore carbones haurire non dubitasti, muliebri spiritu virilem patris exitum imitata.* The *ardentes carbones* are prob. an invention of the Republicans; it is more likely that she inhaled the fumes of burning charcoal. Cf., however, Shakespeare, Jul. Caes. 4. 3 "With this she fell distract, And, her attendants absent, swallow'd fire". — Meter: § 48.

    1. fatum: M. often uses this word as equivalent to *mors*.

    2. subtracta: cf. Val. Max., cited in Introd. — **sibi:** join with *subtracta*; it refers to Porcia, the main subject of discourse. In prose this vs. would run *et subtracta arma quaereret dolens.*

    3. negari: i.e. every one has the right and the ability to destroy himself.

    4. "I thought my father amply had imprest This simple truth

upon each Roman breast" (Lamb).
    — **fatis** = *morte sua*; cf. note on I. Cato Uticensis, father of Porcia, committed suicide at Utica, near Carthage, after the battle of Thapsus in 46 B.C., rather than survive Caesar's triumph; cf. I. 78. 9; Plut. Cato Min.; Sen. Ep. 24. 6 ff.

    5. avido bibit ore: she drinks as if it were a refreshing draught. The juxtaposition of *ardentis* and *avido* is most effective.

    6. I nunc ... nega: Porcia's last words. *I nunc et* + an imv. commonly has derisive sense; cf. Lib. Spect. 23. 6 *i nunc et lentas corripe, turba, moras*; 8. 63. 3 *i nunc et dubita vates an diligat ipsos*; Lease A. J. P. 19. 59. See also on *i, fuge,* I. 3. 12. — **ferrum** =*ensem*.

    43. An official dinner (cf. I. 20. Introd.; Iuv. 5), at which M. was one of the guests (!). — Meter: § 48.

    1. Bis ... triceni ... vocati: cf. *turba spectante vocata,* I. 20. I N. — **triceni:** often used indefinitely of a large host (so *sescenti, mille*); cf. II. 35. 1; II. 65. I *sescenti cenant a te, Iustine, vocati*; Hor. C. 3. 4. 79–80 *amatorem trecentae Pirithoum cohibent catenae.*

    2. positum est: *ponere* often = 'serve up at table'; cf. 3. 60. 8;

non quae de tardis servantur vitibus uvae
dulcibus aut certant quae melimela favis,
5   non pira quae longa pendent religata genesta
aut imitata brevis Punica grana rosas,
rustica lactantis nec misit Sassina metas
nec de Picenis venit oliva cadis :

7. 79. 4 ; Hor. S. 2. 2. 23 *posito pavone*. — nil ... praeter aprum : a boar might be the *pièce de résistance* of a *cena*, but it could not of itself make even a decent country dinner ; much less would it suffice by itself where city style was presumed. For boars served whole cf. Plin. N. H. 8. 210 ; Iuv. 1. 140–141 ; Petr. 49. — here : mostly post-Augustan for *heri* ; see Quint. 1. 4. 7.

3–8. The delicacies mentioned might have been expected at the *mensae secundae*, some of them even during the *promulsis* (*gustus, gustatio*). But here there was no *promulsis* at all. See Beck. 3. 325 ff. ; Marq. 323 ff.

3. non : sc. *positae sunt*. — uvae : here not raisins, but grapes that ripened on the vines after the regular vintage. They were much prized, as dainties out of season ; cf. 3. 58. 8–9 ; Iuv. 11. 71–72 (at a *cena*) *et servatae parte anni, quales fuerant in vitibus, uvae* (the scholiast explains as = *uvae quas suspensas servavimus*).

4. certant : i.e. in sweetness. — melimela, *honey apples, sweet apples*, μελίμηλα ; cf. Plin. N. H. 15.51 *mustea* (*mala*) ... *quae nunc melimela dicuntur a sapore melleo* ; Varr. R. R. 1. 59. 1 (*mala*) *quae antea mustea vocabant, nunc melimela appellant*. But Hehn, 242, thinks of a quince jam or marmalade. — favis : i.e. when filled with honey ; for the poetical dat. see A. 413, b, N. ; GL. 346, N. 6 ;

L. 1186. The juxtaposition *melimela favis* helps syntax and sense.

5. pira ... genesta : broomplant was made into cords by which pears picked before maturity were suspended for slow ripening ; such pears become very juicy.

6. imitata : freely, 'that resemble'. — brevis ... rosas : *brevis* is a stock epithet of *rosa* (see e.g. Hor. C. 2. 3. 13–14) ; hence *brevis* here is not to be referred at all to *Punica grana*, though Plin. N. H. 16. 241 says : *brevissima vita est Punicis* (cf. 17. 95 *cito occidunt ... ficus, Punica, prunus*, etc.). — Punica grana = *Punica mala, pomegranates*. The red pulp inclosing the seeds was the part of the fruit most esteemed ; this pulp has a pleasant acid taste. Served in slices it would more or less resemble small roses. Cf. 7. 20. 10 *Punicorum pauca grana malorum* ; Petr. 31 *Syriaca pruna cum granis Punici mali* ; Ov. Pont. 4. 15. 7–8.

7. rustica ... Sassina : the Apennine mountain pastures about Sassina (Sarsina) were famous for sheep and cheese ; cf. Plin. N. H. 11.241 ; Sil.8.461–462. Sarsina was the birthplace of Plautus.—lactantis ... metas : small cone-shaped cheeses ; cf. 3. 58. 35. — nec : for position see on Lib. Spect. 1. 2.

8. 'Picenum, though famous for olives (cf. 11. 52. 11 ; 5. 78. 19–20), did not produce a single specimen for that dinner !' Olives were shipped in bottles, jars (*cadi*), or osier baskets (7. 53. 5).

nudus aper, sed et hic minimus qualisque necari

10   a non armato pumilione potest.

Et nihil inde datum est; tantum spectavimus omnes:

ponere aprum nobis sic et harena solet.

Ponatur tibi nullus aper post talia facta,

sed tu ponaris cui Charidemus apro.

47

Nuper erat medicus, nunc est vispillo Diaulus:

quod vispillo facit, fecerat et medicus.

9. nudus, *mere, only*; the boar was served alone, without the accompaniments requisite to a proper dinner. — **sed et**: *sed* and *sed et* are used, chiefly in Silver Latin, where we should say 'and that too', 'aye, and', i.e. they seem to us to have lost their adversative force; cf. I. 117. 7 *scalis habito tribus sed altis*; 2. 41. 7; 6. 70. 5; 7. 54. 3; 12. 18. 22; Iuv. 5. 147 (*ponetur*) *boletus domino, sed quales Claudius edit*. The adversative force is, however, commonly discoverable. The idiom arises by condensation from the familiar *non modo sed etiam* phrases. For *sed et hic* Cicero would prob. have said *et is quidem. Et = etiam* often enough, in poetry, Livy, etc.

11. Et = *et tamen.* — **nihil . . . datum est**: cf. 3. 12. 1-2 *unguentum, fateor, bonum dedisti convivis here, sed nihil scidisti.* — **tantum spectavimus**: it was a *spectaculum*, not a *cena*; cf. *turba spectante vocata*, 1. 20. 1 N. Far different was the old-fashioned frugality; cf. Hor. S. 2. 2. 89–92 *rancidum aprum antiqui laudabant, non quia nasus illis nullus erat, sed, credo, hac mente, quod hospes tardius adveniens vitiatum commodius quam integrum edax dominus consumeret.*

12. ponere: there is a play on the meaning in 2, 13. — **sic**: it is as easy to eat the boar in the one case as in the other. — **et =** *etiam, ipsa, too*; see on 9.

14. ponaris: further play on *ponere*. 'May no boar be served to you, but may you be served to the boar', etc. Cf. 2. 14. 18; 1. 20. 4. — **cui Charidemus** (*positus est*): Charidemus's death in the arena had prob. involved the enacting of some mythological or (quasi-) historical scene; cf. 8. 30; 10. 25; Lib. Spect. 7. For such horrid displays the Romans had a morbid passion. — **apro**: neatly placed to go with both clauses of the verse.

47. 'Diaulus, the quack (1. 30), has found his proper level; he has turned corpse-carrier. He has changed his trade, but not his occupation, for he still puts people underground'. For denunciations of medical charletans cf. 6. 53; 8. 74 *Hoplomachus nunc es, fueras ophthalmicus ante; fecisti medicus quod facis hoplomachus*; Iuv. 10. 221. See Marq. 779; Fried. SG. 1. 339. — Meter: § 48.

1-2. vispillo: derivatives in *-o, -onis*, were common in archaic Latin, but "were largely abandoned to the *sermo plebeius*. Here

53

Una est in nostris tua, Fidentine, libellis
pagina, sed certa domini signata figura,
quae tua traducit manifesto carmina furto.
Sic interpositus villo contaminat uncto
5   urbica Lingonicus Tyrianthina bardocucullus,
sic Arretinae violant crystallina testae,

they survived and flourished, chiefly as comic or vulgar expressions of abuse" (Cooper 54 ff.). — **et,** *also*; cf. I. 43. 9 N.

53. Cf. closely I. 29; I. 38. I. 52 is kindred in theme. — Meter : § 47.

I. est...tua: 'You wrote one page to enable you to publish something as your own'. Cf. 2. 20; 10. 100. I *quid, stulte, nostris versibus tuos misces?* Note juxtaposition in *nostris tua*.

2. certa...figura: 'that page is as surely yours as if it were actually stamped with your portrait'. For portraits of authors in books see 14. 186. Introd. — **certa,** *unmistakable.* — **domini:** contemptuous; Fidentinus is owner, not author, of the book.

3. traducit, *exposes to ridicule*; cf. 6. 77. 5–6 *rideris multoque magis traduceris, Afer, quam nudus medio si spatiere foro*; Iuv. 8. 17. Cf. Eng. 'traduce'. This sense, common in Silver Latin, is perhaps derived from the public exposure of condemned criminals, or from the parading of prisoners in triumphs. — **manifesto ... furto:** instr. abl.; we should say, more fully, 'by convicting you of', etc.

4 ff. 'Your page is as incongruous in my book as a greasy weather garment over Tyrian purple (5), or earthenware on a table beside the rarest vessels (6),

or a raven among swans (7–8), or a magpie among nightingales (9–10)'.

4–5. Sic ... bardocucullus: the *cucullus* was a hood which could be attached to the *paenula* (I. 103. 5–6 N.) or the *lacerna*, to be drawn over the head in bad weather, or to conceal the face; cf. 5. 14. 6; 10. 76. 8–9; Blümner 137 ff. The *bardocucullus*, prob. made of wool with the nap (*villus*) uncut, was cheap and of foreign origin. — **villo . . . uncto:** see App. The shaggy nap of an outer garment would soon become soiled; perhaps, however, the *cucullus* was oiled to help it shed rain. — **Lingonicus:** i.e. made among the Lingones, a people of Gaul; cf. 14. 128. I *Gallia Santonico vestit te bardocucullo*; Iuv. 8. 145. — **Tyrianthina:** an adj. used as noun; cf. τυριάνθινος. The reference is to purple (crimson) and violet-hued garments of a peculiar shade which resulted from dipping the cloth first in the violet (ἴανθος), then in the Tyrian purple; see Beck. 3. 298 ff.; Fried. SG. 3. 72. — **bardocucullus:** see above. Perhaps the term was applied at times to the whole outdoor garment as worn by the working classes, esp. in the country (contrast *urbica,* 5); see Beck. 3. 223.

6. Arretinae ... testae: Arretium in Etruria was famous for

sic niger in ripis errat cum forte Caystri
inter Ledaeos ridetur corvus olores,
sic ubi multisona fervet sacer Atthide lucus,
10   inproba Cecropias offendit pica querelas.
Indice non opus est nostris nec iudice libris :
stat contra dicitque tibi tua pagina "Fur es".

red-glazed pottery; cf. 14. 98. 1 *Arretina nimis ne spernas vasa monemus*; Plin. N. H. 35. 160; Beck. 2. 371–372. — **violant**, *spoil the beauty of*; cf. 10. 66. 3; Iuv. 3. 19–20 *viridi si margine cluderet undas herba nec ingenuum violarent marmora tofum.* — **crystallina** (*vasa*): vessels of pure white, transparent glass, or of rock crystal; cf. 8. 77. 5 *candida nigrescant vetulo crystalla Falerno*; Sen. Ben. 7. 9. 3 *video istic crystallina quorum accendit fragilitas pretium*; Beck. 2. 382.

7–8. The Roman poets imitated Homer (Il. 2. 461) in praising the birds (geese or swans) that gathered about the Caystros, a river which flows into the sea at Ephesus; cf. e.g. Verg. G. 1. 383 ff. Hence *Caystrius ales = cycnus, olor.* — **forte**: the *corvus* is an intruder. — **Ledaeos . . . olores**: *olor* is poetical for *cycnus*; *Ledaeos* alludes to the myth which represents Jupiter as visiting Leda under the guise of a swan. — **corvus**, subject of both clauses in 7–8, is postponed to make an effective juxtaposition of contrasts. In Latin poetry in general, however, the joint subject of two clauses often stands in the second clause.

9. **multisona**: the variety of the nightingale's tone is well known. — **fervet**: cf. 2. 64. 7 *fora litibus omnia fervent.* — **Atthide** = *luscinia* (metonymy). *Atthis*,

prop. an Athenian woman, here denotes Philomela, daughter of Pandion (1. 25. 3 N.), who was changed into a nightingale; see the classical dictionaries, s.v. *Tereus.*

10. **inproba . . . pica**: cf. Verg. G. 1. 388 *tum cornix plena pluviam vocat improba voce*; 1. 119 *improbus anser. Improbus* is freely used of persons and things that transcend due bounds. — **Cecropias**: see on 1. 25. 3. — **querelas**: i.e. of Philomela for her own fate and that of Itys.

11. 'There is but one Martial in Rome and his literary individuality is well known'. — **Indice**, *title.* The title of a papyrus roll was inscribed on a narrow strip of parchment, which was attached to the upper edge (*frons*: see on 1. 66. 10) of the roll; see Birt, Buchrolle, 237–239; 247, Abb. 159. Cf. 3. 2. 11. — **nostris . . . libris**: in sharp contrast to *tua pagina*, 12. — **nec iudice**: 'nor do I have to go to court to prove my claim'.

12. **stat contra**: 'that page stands between you and escape'. Cf. Iuv. 3. 290 (the street bully at night) *stat contra starique iubet*; Pers. 5. 96 *stat contra ratio et secretam garrit in aurem.* — **tibi**, (*even*) *to yourself*, as to all the world besides. — **Fur es**: for the meter see § 47, d.

61. An expression of M.'s love for his native Spain; see §§ 1; 14. 'You, Licinianus, and I shall make

61

Verona docti syllabas amat vatis,
Marone felix Mantua est,
censetur Aponi Livio suo tellus
Stellaque nec Flacco minus,
5   Apollodoro plaudit imbrifer Nilus,

Bilbilis as famous in literary history as is Verona, or Mantua, or Corduba'. It is significant that he does not include Rome; see § 1. — Meter: §§ 52; 51.

1. **Verona . . . vatis:** Catullus was born at Verona about 87 B.C. Cf. 14. 195. 1–2; Ov. Am. 3. 15. 7–8 *Mantua Vergilio gaudet, Verona Catullo; Paelignae dicar gloria gentis ego.* For other references to Catullus see e.g. 4. 14. 13; 6. 34. 7; § 34. — **docti:** a standing epithet of poets in general (see on 1. 25. 2) and of Catullus in particular; here it is given to him, probably, because he made fashionable at Rome the hendecasyllabic meter (*syllabas*); cf. 7. 99. 7; 8. 73. 8; Ov. Am. 3. 9. 62 *docte Catulle.* See Ellis, Commentary on Catullus, XXVI ff. — **vatis:** Catullus is more than a mere versifier, he is a truly inspired poet. See Munro and Merrill on Lucr. 1. 102.

2. **Marone:** P. Vergilius Maro. For M. and Vergil see § 33; cf. also 14. 195, with notes; 14. 186, with notes; 4. 14. 14; 11. 48; 1. 107. 3–4; 8. 55; 12. 3. 1; 7. 63. 5–6. Mantua did indeed owe its fame to the fact that Vergil was born in a neighboring *pagus* (Andes).

3–4. 'Men measure the fame of Patavium by that of Livy, of Stella, of Flaccus'. — **censetur** = *laudatur, is considered worthy of mention and esteem*; cf. 8. 6. 9; 9. 16. 5 *felix, quae tali censetur munere tellus*; Iust. 9. 2. 9 *Scythas virtute animi et duritia corporis, non opibus censeri*; Iuv. 8. 2, and elsewhere in Silver Latin. Strictly, the word means 'to be rated', and the abl. used with it is one of price or value. — **Aponi . . . tellus:** cf. 6. 42. 4. The medicinal hot spring Aponus or Aponi Fons (Aquae Patavinae) was not exactly at Patavium (modern Padua), as Vergil and Statius picture it, but six miles distant. See App. — **Livio:** the famous historian, T. Livius; see 14. 190. For the syntax see above, on *censetur*; the abl. might also be regarded as causal; see then Lib. Spect. 1. 3 N.—**Stella:** L. Arruntius Stella (§ 17), esteemed by M. as patron, friend, and poet; cf. 1. 7; 5. 59. 2 *Stella diserte*; 12. 2. 11 *Stella facundus.* He was a friend of Statius also, who dedicates to him Book I of the Silvae. He was born at Naples; he celebrated with *ludi* the conclusion of Domitian's Sarmatian War and was consul in 101. — **Flacco:** unknown, if we agree with the later editors that he is not Valerius Flaccus, author of the Argonautica. The phrase *Antenorei spes et alumne laris*, used of him in 1. 76. 2, suggests that at Patavium he was honored as a man of ability.

5. **Apollodoro:** Fried. thinks this Apollodorus may have been an Alexandrian who came to Rome to enter the contest in Greek poetry or eloquence at the Agon Capitolinus of 86; see Fried. SG.

Nasone Paeligni sonant,
duosque Senecas unicumque Lucanum
facunda loquitur Corduba,
gaudent iocosae Canio suo Gades,
10   Emerita Deciano meo :
te, Liciniane, gloriabitur nostra.
nec me tacebit Bilbilis.

2. 630 ff.; 3. 425. Others think of
a Greek comic poet of Carystus
in Euboea, contemporary with Menander (see on 14. 187). If this
view is right, M. has erred about
Apollodorus's birthplace (see on
8. 18. 5). — imbrifer Nilus refers
to the annual overflow of the Nile.
    6. Nasone = *Nasonis nomine*.
P. Ovidius Naso, the poet, was born
at Sulmo in the Ager Paelignus;
cf. 2. 41. 2; 8. 73. 9; 3. 38. 10; § 33.
— sonant = *resonant*.
    7. duos . . . Senecas: see
§§ 1; 9; 16. — unicum, *unique,
peerless*. M. ranks Lucan high
(7. 21), despite the difference of
opinion that obtained concerning
him; cf. 14. 194; Quint. 10. 1. 90;
Stat. Silv. 2. 7; Tac. D. 20. 6. —
Lucanum: M. Annaeus Lucanus
(39–65), author of the Pharsalia;
see §§ 1; 16. Lucan was a son of
Annaeus Mela, brother of the
younger Seneca. For the syntax
see on *loquitur*, 8.
    8. facunda, *eloquent*, in the writ-
ings and the speeches of famous
men whose birthplace it was. The
word is used primarily of orators
and lawyers, but often too of poets.
— loquitur = *celebrat*. For this
trans. use of *loquor*, 'speak of',
cf. 8. 55. 21; 9. 3. 11 *quid loquar
Alciden Phoebumque*. So *dico* in
poetry; cf. e.g. Hor. C. 3. 30. 10–14
dicar, qua violens obstrepit Aufidus,
etc. The const. with *loquor* occurs

once only in Cicero's speeches and
once only in his philosophical
works; *loqui de* is the ordinary
use. — Corduba: cf. 9. 61. 1–2. —
For meter here and in 10 see § 51.
    9. gaudent . . . Gades: to
Cadiz the fashionable world went
for dancing girls (cf. 1. 41. 12 N.)
and voluptuous songs (*Gaditana*,
3. 63. 5). — Canio: Canius Rufus
wrote poetry of the lighter sort;
he distinguished himself as time-
killer and giggler (3. 20; § 17).
    10. Emerita = Emerita Au-
gusta (modern Merida), a great
city of Lusitanian Spain whose extensive remains have won for it
the title of 'the Rome of Spain'. —
Deciano: Decianus was a Stoic,
"who, however, knew how to
couple his philosophy with cau-
tion" (Teuffel § 329). M. addressed Book II to him; cf. 2. 5.
    11–12. Liciniane: when Li-
cinianus set out for Spain, M.
addressed to him 1. 49. Cf. there
1 ff. *vir Celtiberis non tacende
gentibus nostraeque laus Hispaniae,
videbis altam, Liciniane, Bilbilin*.
— nostra . . . Bilbilis: cf. 10. 103.
4–6 (addressed to his fellow-
townsmen) *nam decus et nomen
famaque vestra sumus nec sua plus
debet tenui Verona Catullo meque
velit dici non minus (quam Catul-
lum) illa suum*. For Bilbilis see
§ 2. — nec me tacebit: cf. *non
tacende*, 1. 49. 1, cited on 11. M.'s

66

Erras, meorum fur avare librorum,
fieri poetam posse qui putas tanti
scriptura quanti constet et tomus vilis:
non sex paratur aut decem sophos nummis.
5 Secreta quaere carmina et rudes curas,
quas novit unus scrinioque signatas
custodit ipse virginis pater chartae,

modest claim is made more beautiful by contrast with the stronger terms used by him of the other persons mentioned. 11–12 are of great value in helping to fix the interpretation of Hor. C. 3. 30. 10–14; on those vss. see Knapp Proc. Amer. Phil. Ass. 25 (1894), pp. xxvii–xxx, and Class. Rev. 17. 156–158.

66. M. humorously offers to sell to a plagiarist of his poems (perhaps the offender of 1. 29; 1. 38; 1. 53) an unpublished poem and guarantees silence about the transaction. On books and their publication see Birt, passim; Marq. 799 ff.; Beck. 2. 425 ff.; Lanciani Anc. R. 183 ff. — Meter: § 52.

3. scriptura, *copying, labor of copying.* — **tomus:** prop. a cut, cutting, piece (cf. τόμος), e.g. of papyrus; then a roll of papyrus in its unwritten state; finally a completed volume, *scroll*; cf. Eng. 'tome'. Cf. M. Aurel. ap. Front. Ep. 2. 10 *feci . . . excerpta ex libris sexaginta in quinque tomis*; Beck. 2. 440. The outlay for paper and for copying is after all the smallest part of the cost of a book.

4. sex . . . nummis: *nummus* commonly = *nummus sestertius, sesterce.* M. is speaking here only of Book I (Fried.). According to 13. 3. 3 that book could be bought

for two sesterces. In 1. 117. 17 there is reference to a more costly edition. Birt, 209, thinks the papyrus here cost six sesterces, the copying ten. On the cost of books at Rome see Fried. SG. 3. 417 ff.; Birt 82 ff. — **sophos:** see 1. 3. 7 N.

5–6. 'Look for somebody who has unfinished poems under lock and key and bargain for some of them'. — **rudes:** the author may be more willing to part with poems to which he has not put the finishing touches. In 7. 95. 8 *rudis* is used of a girl too young for a lover; cf. *virginis . . . chartae,* 7. — **curas:** cf. 1. 25. 6. — **unus:** i.e. one only; explained by *ipse . . . chartae,* 7. — **scrinio:** see 1. 2. 4 N. — **signatas:** store chambers, chests, etc., were often sealed up. M. has his eye on Horace's words to his book, Ep. 1. 20. 3 *odisti clavis et grata sigilla pudico;* see on 7 and on 1. 2 passim.

7. custodit . . . chartae: the author of the still unpublished work watches it with care akin to that exercised by a father over his virgin daughter. — **virginis:** used adjectively; cf. Eng. 'virgin soil'; *anus* in 1. 39. 2 *(amicos) quales prisca fides famaque novit anus.* — **chartae:** often used of anything written on papyrus, here of a poem; cf. 1. 25. 7–8 N.; 10. 20. 17.

quae trita duro non inhorruit mento :
mutare dominum non potest liber notus.

10   Sed pumicata fronte si quis est nondum
nec umbilicis cultus atque membrana,
mercare : tales habeo, nec sciet quisquam.
Aliena quisquis recitat et petit famam
non emere librum, sed silentium debet.

8. **quae . . . mento:** the allusion is twofold: (1) to a virgin who has never been affrighted by contact with a man's face; (2) to the fresh papyrus, unsoiled by use. One who, after reading, sought to roll up a scroll held one end of it taut under his chin, while with his hands he rolled up the rest; cf. 10. 93. 5–6 *ut rosa delectat metitur quae pollice primo, sic nova nec mento sordida charta iuvat*; Birt, Buchrolle, 116–118.

9. **mutare dominum:** cf. 1. 52. 6–7 *et, cum se dominum vocabit ille, dicas esse meos manuque missos.* — **notus:** contrast *secreta . . . carmina*, 5.

10–11. 'If you can find a book that has not been published, buy that'. — **pumicata fronte:** the ends (*frontes*) of the scroll were carefully cut and then rubbed smooth with pumice-stone; cf. 1. 117. 16; 3. 2. 8; 8. 72. 1–2 *nondum murice cultus asperoque morsu pumicis aridi politus*; Ov. Tr. 1. 1. 11 *nec fragili geminae poliantur pumice frontes*; 3. 1. 13 *quod neque sum cedro flavus nec pumice levis*; Hor. Ep. 1. 20. 2 (*liber*) *pumice mundus*; Catull. 1. 2; 22. 8; Tib. 3. 1. 9–12; Beck. 2. 437; Birt, Buchrolle, 236. — **umbilicis:** according to the view commonly held the pl. *umbilici* denoted the projecting ends or knobs, colored or gilded, attached to the cylinder (*umbili-*

cus) to which the right end of the scroll was attached and on which the scroll was rolled; cf. 8. 61. 4–5 *nec umbilicis quod decorus et cedro spargor per omnes Roma quas tenet gentes*; 3. 2. 9; 4. 89. 1–2 *libelle, iam pervenimus usque ad umbilicos*; 11. 107. 1–2 *explicitum nobis usque ad sua cornua librum . . . refers*; Beck. 2. 436. But Birt, Buchrolle, 228–235, holds that the *umbilicus* was not fastened to the roll and that it did not project beyond the *frontes*; it was merely inserted in the roll and was removable at will. When one unwound a scroll as he read, he could shift the *umbilicus* to form a center for the part read as he wound this up loosely. The use of two *umbilici* began in Domitian's time. Before the reading began both were within the roll; as the reading progressed one was allowed to remain in the roll, the other was inserted in the part read. — **membrana,** *parchment*; this was tougher than papyrus and was used as a cover for the papyrus volume. It was generally highly colored (purple or yellow); cf. 8. 72. 1 *murice cultus*; 1. 117. 16; 3. 2. 10; Catull. 22. 7 *rubra membrana.*

12. **mercare:** cf. 1. 29. 4; 2. 20.

14. **silentium:** cf. Introd.

70. The early morning call (*salutatio*) was one of the most onerous forms of the *officium* exacted from the clients by the patron.

70

Vade salutatum pro me, liber : ire iuberis
    ad Proculi nitidos, officiose, lares.
Quaeris iter ? dicam.   Vicinum Castora canae
    transibis Vestae virgineamque domum ;
5   inde Sacro veneranda petes Palatia Clivo,

It is the subject of frequent and bitter complaint by M. and his contemporaries; see 5. 22; 9. 100; 10. 74; 12. 29; Iuv. 3. 239 ff.; 5. 19 ff.; 5. 76 ff.; Fried. SG. 1. 382 ff.; 1. 403 ff.; Beck. 2. 194 ff. Here M. sends a book in his stead, and in excusing his past neglect delicately compliments Proculus. The identity of Proculus is uncertain;' see Hübner on C.I.L. 2. 2349. — Meter: § 48.

1. **Vade salutatum**: sc. *Proculum*; cf. Ov. Tr. 3. 7. 1 *vade salutatum . . . Perillam*; 1. 1. 15 *vade, liber, verbisque meis loca grata saluta*. — **ire iuberis** may hint at a request by Proculus for a copy of Book I.

2. **nitidos . . . lares**, *elegant palace*. *Lares* stands here primarily for the well-ordered house (the wooden or silver images of the Lares were kept polished); yet, inasmuch as the Lares stood, at least originally, in the atrium, the word may here = *atrium, salutationem*. Cf. *atria*, 12. — **officiose**: the *officium* of the poet, prob. neglected in the past, is now to be amply discharged by the book.

3–4. **Quaeris iter ?** is a substitute for a protasis; cf. 1. 79. 2 N.; 3. 4. 5; 3. 46. 5; 9. 18. 7. — **iter**: the route would be from M.'s dwelling on the Collis Quirinalis to the palace of Proculus on the Palatine. Ov. Tr. 3. 1. 19–30 should be compared. The book is to go across the imperial *fora*, through the

Forum Romanum, along the Sacra Via, past the temple of Vesta and the Regia, through the Sacer Clivus to the Palatine. — **Castora** = *Templum Castoris·* note the Greek form of the acc. singular. This temple, the Aedes Vestae, and the Atrium Vestae, the residence of the Vestals (4), stood on the south side of the Forum Romanum; the Aedes Vestae and the Atrium Vestae lay just east of the Templum Castoris. See Hülsen-Carter, The Roman Forum, 151 ff.; 191–205. — **canae . . . Vestae:** the Italian worship of Vesta was very ancient and stood in a closer relation to the Romans than did much of their adopted mythology and religion; cf. Verg. A. 5. 744 *canae penetralia Vestae*. See on *cana . . . iura*, 1. 15. 2.

5. **Sacro . . . Clivo:** instr. abl., *by (traversing) the Sacer Clivus*. The Sacer Clivus was the section of the Sacra Via which extended from the old forum to the Arch of Titus on the Velia; see Hülsen-Carter 225–227. — **veneranda:** perhaps a piece of flattery for Domitian's benefit, though not without thought of the Palatine as the seat of the original settlement at Rome. — **Palatia:** *Palatium* at first meant Mons Palatinus; later, it was used of the imperial palace on the Palatine. The pl. may be a *pluralis maiestatis*, used to mark the splendor of the imperial palace. Here and in the great majority of

plurima qua summi fulget imago ducis.

Nec te detineat miri radiata colossi

quae Rhodium moles vincere gaudet opus.

Flecte vias hac qua madidi sunt tecta Lyaei

10   et Cybeles picto stat Corybante tholus.

Protinus a laeva clari tibi fronte Penates

cases in M. (though rarely else-where) the first *a* is long.

6. plurima . . . imago, *many a statue.* M. is fond of putting an adj. of quantity with a collective sing.; cf. e.g. 8. 3. 7; Ov. F. 4. 441 *plurima lecta rosa est*; Iuv. 1. 120; 14. 144; 4. 47; 3. 232; 8. 7, 58, 104. Busts and statues of the emperor (polished and gilded, if not of solid metal; cf. *fulget*) were to be seen everywhere in Rome. — **summi . . . ducis:** cf. 1. 4. 4 N.

7. Nec: see on Lib. Spect. 1. 2. — **detineat:** i.e. to look at it. — **radiata:** Vespasian had transformed the statue (see on 8) into an image of the Sun-God.

8. moles is correctly used of the immense statue of himself which Nero had erected within the limits of his Domus Aurea. It was called Colossus in rivalry of the Colossus at Rhodes, and was supposed to surpass the Seven Wonders of the World (see Lib. Spect. 1. Introd.); cf. Lib. Spect. 2. 1 *sidereus propius videt astra colossus*; 2. 77. 3. — **vincere gaudet:** a const. common, in both prose and verse, from early times; cf. 1. 93. 2; 2. 69. 3; 3. 58. 31; Soed. 16. The inf. is common too with verbs denoting painful emotion.

9. Flecte vias: here the *iter* turns sharply to the right (south) at the Arch of Titus. — **hac:** sc. *via* or *parte*. — **madidi:** *madidus* and *uvidus* are stock epithets of the Wine-God and his worshipers;

cf. Plaut. Aul. 573 *ego te hodie reddam madidum, si vivo, probe.* — **tecta Lyaei:** the site of this Palatine temple of Bacchus is unknown. Baumeister (1490) believes that it stood on the Summa Sacra Via; cf. K. and H. Form. urb. Rom. 75. Lyaeus (= Λυαῖος, the Care-Dispeller) is a frequent title of Bacchus, esp. in poetry; cf. 8. 50. 12; 10. 20. 19.

10. Cybeles . . . tholus: the location of the Templum Magnae Matris on the Palatine is in dispute. Hülsen (cf. Hülsen-Jordan 51–54) puts it on the side of the Palatine which overlooks the Circus valley; cf. Haugwitz, Der Palatin, 24–25; 125. For a different view see Richter, Topographie der Stadt Rom², 137–139. See also Platner 137–140 and Carter A. J. P. 28. 327. *Cybeles* is gen. sing., a Greek form; cf. 5. 13. 7; 9. 11. 6. *Tholus* (θόλος) prop. = *rotunda*, but here denotes the whole building (note *stat*). See App. — **picto . . . Corybante** may refer to a painting on the inside of the dome; further, *Corybante* may = *Corybantibus*, since the poets often use words which in themselves have no collective notion (e.g. *rosa*, *flos*) as collective singulars (see on *cicer*, 1. 41. 6).

11. Protinus: i.e. 'immediately after you pass the Templum Cybeles'. — **laeva:** sc. *parte*; cf. *hac*, 9. — **clari:** because of the *fronte*, 'façade'. — **tibi:** dat. of agent (so-called) with *adeundi*, to be supplied.

atriaque excelsae sunt adeunda domus.
Hanc pete : ne metuas fastus limenque superbum :
    nulla magis toto ianua poste patet,
15 nec propior quam Phoebus amet doctaeque sorores.
    Si dicet "Quare non tamen ipse venit ? "
sic licet excuses " Quia, qualiacunque leguntur
    ista, salutator scribere non potuit ".

72

Nostris versibus esse te poetam,
Fidentine, putas cupisque credi ?
Sic dentata sibi videtur Aegle

— **Penates:** sc. *Proculi*; see on *lares*, 2.

12. atria: the patron received his clients in his atrium; see on *lares*, 2. — **adeunda:** cf. Hor. Epod. 2. 7–8 *superba civium potentiorum limina.* The phrase involves a transferred epithet; see on 1. 15. 7.

13. ne metuas: this visit is a new experience for the book, which has been accustomed only to M.'s plain surroundings. — **limen . . . superbum:** cf. Hor. Epod. 2. 7–8 *superba civium potentiorum limina.* The phrase involves a transferred epithet; see on 1. 15. 7.

14. nulla . . . patet: cf. Ov. F. 1. 280 *tota patet dempta ianua nostra sera* ('bar'). — **poste:** one of the two door-posts; in great houses they were made of fine marble. In the poets the pl. *postes* often = the door proper, *fores, valvae*; so too sometimes in the sing., as here; Luc. 5. 531–532 *tum poste recluso dux ait.*

15. propior = adv., *more intimately.* — **quam:** rel. pronoun; with *nec* sc. *ulla domus est.* — **doctae . . . sorores:** the Muses, so often mentioned with Apollo, when

the latter is thought of as patron of literature and music; cf. 11. 93. 2 *hoc Musis et tibi, Phoebe, placet?* 12. 11. 4; 2. 22. 1 *o Phoebe novemque sorores.*

17–18. For the thought cf. 10. 58, esp. 12; 1. 108. 10 *mane tibi pro me dicet "Haveto" liber.* — **sic licet excuses,** *you may say this in excuse. Licet* is always (some 54 times) in M. used with the subjv.; see Lease Class. Rev. 12. 301. — **ista:** freely, 'that lies before you'; the book is speaking to Proculus of M.; cf. 1. 40. 1 *non legis ista libenter.* — **salutator:** disguised protasis, = *si Martialis ipse te salutatum venisset.* For *salutator* used of the professional hanger-on, who never neglects the *salutatio*, see 10. 10. 2; 10. 74. 2.

72. Cf. 1. 29, with notes. — Meter: § 49.

3. Sic: i.e. by appropriating, through purchase or otherwise, what naturally belongs to others. — **dentata:** cf. Catull. 39. 12 *Lanuvinus ater atque dentatus.* Dentatus was the cognomen of M'. Curius,

emptis ossibus Indicoque cornu,
5   sic, quae nigrior est cadente moro,
cerussata sibi placet Lycoris.
Hac et tu ratione qua poeta es,
calvus cum fueris, eris comatus.

75

Dimidium donare Lino quam credere totum
qui mavolt mavolt perdere dimidium.

76

O mihi curarum pretium non vile mearum,
Flacce, Antenorei spes et alumne laris,

4. emptis: cf. 5. 43, with notes;
12. 23. 1–2 *dentibus atque comis —
nec te pudet — uteris emptis; quid
facies oculo, Laelia? non emitur.* —
cornu: the tusk (*dens*) of the elephant, ivory; cf. 2. 43. 9; 9. 37. 3.

5. cadente: i.e. when fully
ripe; cf. 8. 64. 7 *sit moro coma nigrior caduco*; Plin. N. H. 15. 97.

6. cerussata: white lead (*cerussa*) was used by women to
whiten the skin; cf. 2. 41. 12; 7. 25. 2;
Ov. Med. Fac. 73–74 *nec cerussa
tibi... desit*; Beck. 3. 164 ff.; Marq.
786 ff. — sibi placet: cf. 4. 59. 5;
Iuv. 10. 41–42 *sibi consul ne placeat.*
At this time blond complexions
were fashionable. — Lycoris: cf.
4. 62. 1 *nigra Lycoris*; 7. 13. 2 *fusca
Lycoris.*

8. calvus: the Romans were
extremely sensitive on the score of
baldness (they commonly did not
wear hats); cf. 6. 57; 6. 74. 1–2;
12. 23; C.I.L. 1. 685 (= Ephem.
Epigr. 6. 64) *L. Antoni Calve peristi*
(a taunt on a leaden bullet thrown
at the siege of Perusia, 41 B.C.);
Suet. Iul. 45; Dom. 18. Iuv. 4. 38
calls Domitian a *calvus Nero!*

75. The shrewd creditor versus the bad debtor. — Meter: § 48.

1–2. donare, *to give outright.* —
credere, *to lend.* — mavolt: for
spelling see § 56.

76. Law versus literature as a
means of support. Since there
were no copyright laws, and since
men of letters were in large part
born in humble circumstances, the
patronage of the well-to-do had
long been a necessity before Juvenal wrote 7. 1–7. Cf. 1. 107; 8. 55;
Tac. D. 8; Fried. SG. 3. 429 ff.
Martial, thinking probably of his
own experience as a hanger-on,
seeks to persuade Flaccus (see
1. 61. 4 N.) to abandon literature
and to practice law. — Meter: § 48.

1. curarum ... non vile: i.e.
'whose friendship has been ample
return for all my pains'. In Ov. Her.
17 (18). 163–165 Leander says: *his
(= meis bracchiis) ego cum dixi
"Pretium non vile laboris, iam
dominae vobis colla tenenda dabo",
protinus illa valent.*

2. Antenorei ... laris: Patavium, which, according to tradition,
was founded after the fall of Troy

Pierios differ cantusque chorosque sororum ;
　aes dabit ex istis nulla puella tibi.
5　Quid petis a Phoebo ? nummos habet arca Minervae ;
　haec sapit, haec omnes fenerat una deos.
　Quid possunt hederae Bacchi dare ? Pallados arbor

by Antenor, a Trojan refugee; see
Verg. A. 1. 242–249; Liv. 1. 1.—
alumne: he was born and bred
there.— **laris:** the new home
where Antenor set up his *lar*; cf.
1. 70. 2 N.

3. Pierios, *poetic*; Mt. Pierus
in Thessaly and Mt. Helicon in
Boeotia were sacred to the Muses.
— **differ:** for the small returns of
literature cf. 9. 73. 7–9 *at me litterulas stulti docuere parentes: . . .
frange leves calamos et scinde,
Thalia, libellos*; Iuv. 7. 26–29 *aut
clude et positos tinea pertunde libellos. Frange miser calamos vigila-
taque proelia dele, qui facis in parva
sublimia carmina cella, ut dignus
venias hederis et imagine macra.—
choros . . . sororum: see App.
Cf. 7. 69. 8 *quamvis Pierio sit bene
nota choro*; Ov. Pont. 1. 5. 57–58
*vos, ut recitata probentur carmina,
Pieriis invigilate choris.*— **sororum:** cf. 1. 70. 15.

4. aes = *pecuniam*; for the
thought cf. 11. 3. 1–6; 3. 38.— **nulla
puella** often stands at the beginning of the second half of the pentameter; cf. e.g. 4. 71. 2; 7. 29. 4;
9. 39. 4; 14. 205. 2; Tib. 4. 2. 24.
For *ex . . . puella* M. might have
said *ex istis puellis nulla.*

5. Phoebo: see 1. 70. 15 N.—
nummos = *aes*, 4; see on 1. 66. 4.
— **arca,** *money-chest, strong box*;
cf. 2. 44. 9 *et quadrans mihi nullus
est in arca*; 2. 30. 4 N.; Iuv. 1. 89–
90; Catull. 24. 10 *nec servum tamen
ille habet neque arcam.*— **Minervae:** patroness of the practical
(remunerative) arts and trades, in

opposition to Apollo and Bacchus,
who favored literature and the fine
arts; hence she patronized forensic
orators (10. 20. 14). M. may be
attempting a compliment to Domitian, who claimed to be the especial favorite, if not the son, of
Minerva; see Preller-Jordan 1. 297.

6. haec sapit: perhaps a proverbial phrase; Minerva is worldly
wisdom personified. See Phaedr.
3. 17.— **fenerat:** *fenero* is used
absolutely in 1. 85. 4; Petr. 76 *su-
stuli me de negotiatione et coepi per
libertos fenerare.* Schr. and Fried.
hold that *deos* is used figuratively
for *deorum munera*, and that *fenerat = bestows*, i.e. 'Minerva has at
her disposal all that the gods together have'. Fried. thinks that
the const. *fenerare aliquem* (i.e.
acc. of the person to whom money
is lent) is inadmissible, but surely,
since M. is in a humorous mood
(3, 4, 9), this const. is no harsher
than Schrevelius's explanation.
The thought then is: 'Minerva is
so much richer than all the other
gods that she lends money to them,
and gets her interest, too!' Yet
the const. is without parallel.
Rather take *fenerat* as = *puts out
at interest*; we speak of a millionaire as able to buy and sell his
neighbors. The const. is then
simple. For still another interpretation see Coning. Misc. Writ.
1. 430. Köstlin's *inter una deos*
(see App.) is an attractive reading.

7. Quid . . . dare ? ivy is not
fruit-bearing (remunerative). The
ivy was sacred to Bacchus and,

inclinat varias pondere nigra comas.

Praeter aquas Helicon et serta lyrasque dearum

10   nil habet et magnum, sed perinane, sophos.

Quid tibi cum Cirrha ? quid cum Permesside nuda ?

Romanum propius divitiusque Forum est.

Illic aera sonant : at circum pulpita nostra

since the Wine-God was supposed to give inspiration, was the poet's crown; see on 3. Cf. Verg. E. 7. 25 *pastores, hedera crescentem ornate poetam*; Hor. C. I. I. 29–30 *me doctarum hederae praemia frontium dis miscent superis.* There were ivy-crowned busts and medallions of poets in the Palatine Library. Cf. *serta,* 9. — **Pallados arbor:** the olive, whose fruit and oil could be turned into money.

8. inclinat, *makes . . . bend,* with the weight of fruit. — **varias . . . comas:** the leaves are deep green on the upper side, hoary on the lower. — **pondere:** primarily of the fruit, secondarily of the money bestowed by Minerva on lawyers (Köstlin). — **nigra** is used of the tree laden with ripened fruit.

9. aquas, *springs,* named Aganippe and Hippocrene. On the proverbial poverty of poets cf. 10. 76; Ov. Tr. 4. 10. 21–22 *saepe pater dixit "Studium quid inutile temptas? Maeonides* (Homer) *nullas ipse reliquit opes";* Petr. 82; Fried. SG. 3. 429 ff.; 3. 491. — **Helicon** stands here for the poetic art, the pursuit of literature; cf. *Cirrha . . . Permesside,* 11.

10. et joins *magnum . . . sophos* to the three accusatives in 9. — **magnum . . . sophos,** *bravos loud, yes, but valueless.* — **perinane:** adjectives compounded with *per-,* though they probably originated in the *sermo plebeius,* became semiclassic and "belonged rather to the

easy tone of the *sermo cotidianus* of the upper classes" (Cooper § 63). — **sophos:** cf. I. 3. 7 N.; I. 66. 4; I. 49. 37 *mereatur alius grande et insanum sophos.*

11. Cirrha, the old harbor of Delphi, and Permessis, a river rising on Helicon, shared with Delphi and Helicon the favor of Apollo and the Muses; cf. Iuv. 13. 79 *Cirrhaei . . . vatis* (Apollo); Stat. Theb. 3. 106–107 *Cirrhaeaque virgo* (Pythia). — **Permesside:** the nymph of the river; see on *Helicon,* 9. Cf. 8. 70. 3–4 *cum siccare sacram largo Permessida posset* (Nerva) *ore.* — **nuda,** *mere, simple,* i. e. unremunerative. The adj. belongs with *Cirrha* too.

12. Romanum . . . Forum: the great court of the Centumviri met to try civil cases in the Basilica Iulia on the south side of the Forum Romanum. — **divitius:** cf. 2. 30. 5; I. 17. 1–2 *cogit me Titus actitare causas et dicit mihi saepe "Magna res est".* Brandt thinks M. came to Rome to practice law; § 7.

13. aera: cf. *aes,* 4. — **pulpita:** at the recitations (see I. 3. 5 N.) the reader stood while making his introductory remarks, explanations, or excuses; he then sat on a cushioned chair (*cathedra*) on a raised platform (*pulpitum*). Some commentators, perhaps with better reason, explain *steriles cathedras* of the chairs of the audience. In Iuv. 7. 45–57 *cathedrae* are hired for a recitation for the part of the

et steriles cathedras basia sola crepant.

79

Semper agis causas et res agis, Attale, semper ;
　est, non est quod agas : Attale, semper agis.
Si res et causae desunt, agis, Attale, mulas.
　Attale, ne quod agas desit, agas animam.

room immediately in front of the reader (*orchestra*); behind these are benches propped up for the occasion (*anabathra*).

14. basia: see 1. 3. 7 N.—**basia sola:** 'kisses, but no cash'. There is a play in *crepant*, since that verb is at times used of the jingle of money; cf. 12. 36. 3; 5. 19. 14 *qui crepet aureolos forsitan unus erit.* Cf. *sonant*, 13.

79. By a succession of plays on *agere* M. satirizes a jack of all trades, who, though always busy, accomplished nothing. The thought seems to be: 'Attalus, you are always acting, yet you are after all only a player rather than a true actor in the drama of life'. Attalus's name stamps him as an Oriental, prob. a freedman. Cf. 2. 7. 8; 4. 78. 9–10; Phaedr. 2. 5. 1–4 *est ardelionum* ('busybodies') *quaedam natio, trepide occursans, occupata in otio, gratis anhelans, multa agendo nihil agens, sibi molesta et aliis odiosissima.* The repetition of the name helps to mark M.'s contempt; cf. Paukstadt 27. — Meter: § 48.

1. agis causas, *you try cases*, i.e. play the lawyer.—**res agis:** i.e. 'you do anything and everything', 'you try your hand at business'. Note the chiasmus.

2. est, non est: it is possible, perhaps, to supply *si*, or *sive . . . sive.* But it may be doubted whether there is any ellipsis in such cases; the writer makes an assertion, with-

out throwing it into the conditional form; that statement takes the place of a genuine protasis. Questions and commands also, in Latin as in English, often thus supplant protases: cf. note on 1. 70. 3 *quaeris iter?*

4. agas animam: i.e. 'make way with yourself'. — For the meter see § 48, b.

85. M. here expresses the general contempt for *praecones*. They were of the lowest social rank and were debarred from the higher municipal offices. In 5. 56. 10–11 M. says to a man who is seeking a calling for his son : *si duri puer ingeni videtur, praeconem facias vel architectum.* Yet they made large fortunes; see 6. 8; Iuv. 3. 33, 157; Fried. SG. 1. 312–314.

Marius was selling because of financial embarrassment, but of course wished the auctioneer to conceal this fact. The latter was, however, so unskillful that he prompted the natural question of some bystander (5). Upset by this, the *praeco* had no answer ready, and stupidly extemporized the damaging joke *servos . . . locum*; the flat ending (*non . . . locum*; we should expect some strong expression) marks his embarrassment and makes for this interpretation. Some editors, however, hold that the plot was in fact unhealthy, and that the auctioneer in his perturbation revealed what he should

85

Venderet excultos colles cum praeco facetus
  atque suburbani iugera pulchra soli,
" Errat " ait " si quis Mario putat esse necesse
  vendere : nil debet, fenerat immo magis ".
5 " Quae ratio est igitur ? " " Servos ibi perdidit omnes
  et pecus et fructus ; non amat inde locum ".
Quis faceret pretium nisi qui sua perdere vellet
  omnia ? Sic Mario noxius haeret ager.

88

Alcime, quem raptum domino crescentibus annis
  Lavicana levi caespite velat humus,

have kept to himself. — Meter: § 48.

1–2. colles: the hills in Rome and near the city were much in demand for villa sites. *Excultos... suburbani* and *pulchra* are "all intended to indicate a kind of property that a man would not part with if he could help it" (Steph.). — **facetus:** ironical. — **pulchra:** cf. 1. 116. 2 *culti iugera pulchra soli*; 11. 29. 6 *dabo Setini iugera culta soli*; Tib. 1. 1. 2.

4. nil debet: a blunt lie. — **fenerat... magis,** *nay, he rather lends money at interest*; see on *fenerat*, 1. 76. 6. — **immo** is regularly corrective; it removes a doubt or misunderstanding or heightens a previous statement. Cf. 1. 10. 3 N.

5–6. ratio: sc. *vendendi* or *cur vendat.* — **Servos ... fructus:** this *praeco* had not taken to heart Cic. Off. 3. 13. 55 *quid vero est stultius quam venditorem eius rei quam vendat vitia narrare? quid autem tam absurdum quam si domini iussu ita praeco praedicet "Domum pestilentem vendo"?* — **fructus:** no slaves were left to gather the crop,

or perhaps the place was so pestilential that even the fruit would not mature.

7. faceret pretium: cf. *digitum tollere, digito liceri*; see 9. 59. 20.

8. noxius here = (1) *pestilential* and (2) *troublesome, hard to get rid of.*

88. On Alcimus, a favorite slave of M., who had died young. The rich had long built splendid family mausolea along the great roads leading from Rome. The tombs along the Via Appia were the most famous, though the sites along the Via Latina and the Via Flaminia were decidedly fashionable; cf. 11. 13; 6. 28. 5; Iuv. 1. 170–171. Alcimus's burial-place lay near the Via Lavicana (Labicana), which, leaving Rome at the Porta Esquilina, ran southeast through Lavicum (Labicum), which lay between Tusculum and Praeneste. Along this road ground was relatively cheap. — Meter: § 48.

1. domino: dative.

2. levi: sepulchral inscriptions often show S. T. T. L., which = *sit tibi terra levis*; cf. 5. 34. 9 N.

accipe non Pario nutantia pondera saxo,
   quae cineri vanus dat ruitura labor,
5 sed faciles buxos et opacas palmitis umbras
   quaeque virent lacrimis roscida prata meis.
Accipe, care puer, nostri monimenta doloris:
   hic tibi perpetuo tempore vivet honor.
Cum mihi supremos Lachesis perneverit annos,
10   non aliter cineres mando iacere meos.

3. accipe: the tomb, etc., were thought of as gifts likely to please the departed spirit; cf. 6. 85. 11–12 *accipe cum fletu maesti breve carmen amici atque haec apsentis tura fuisse puta.* — **Pario . . . saxo**: Paros, one of the Cyclades, was famous for its marble; cf. e.g. Hor. C. 1. 19. 5–6 *Glycerae nitor splendentis Pario marmore purius.* — **nutantia**: i.e. massive and top-heavy, as if about to fall; cf. Lib. Spect. 1. 5. Many tombs were immense structures, e. g. the pyramid of C. Cestius near the Porta Ostiensis and the tomb of Caecilia Metella on the Via Appia.

4. vanus = (1) *useless*, because of nature's destructive power, (2) *empty, hollow*, the result of fashion's rivalry, as compared with unpretentious but sincere grief. — **ruitura**: cf. e.g. 8. 3. 5–8; 10. 2. 9; Iuv. 10. 144–146 *saxis cinerum custodibus, ad quae discutienda valent sterilis mala robora fici, quandoquidem data sunt ipsis quoque fata sepulcris.*

5. faciles, *yielding, pliant*; the box was readily cut and trained by the *topiarius* into various fanciful forms and figures, a fashion that has at times prevailed since, esp. in France. As an evergreen the box may typify M.'s remembrance of the dead boy. See App. — **palmitis**: typical of the tender years of Alcimus.

6–7. lacrimis . . . doloris: cf. Ov. Tr. 3. 3. 81–82 *tu tamen extincto (mihi) feralia munera semper deque tuis lacrimis umida serta dato.* — **roscida**: poetical for *umida*; cf. 4. 18. 3 *roscida tecta* (of a dripping aqueduct). — **prata**, *grass, turf.*

8. hic . . . honor, *the honor my verse will give you.* Nature perpetuating herself in turf and tree will outlast the work of man's hands; man perpetuates himself in literature; cf. 9. 76. 9–10 *sed ne sola tamen puerum pictura loquatur, haec erit in chartis maior imago meis*; 10. 2. 9–12; Ov. Am. 1. 10. 61–62.

9. Lachesis: one of the Parcae, Disposer of Lots, who determines when the end (*per- neverit*) of each man's life has been reached; cf. 4. 54. 9–10; Iuv. 3. 27 *dum superest Lachesis quod torqueat.* — **perneverit**: most verbal compounds with *per-* belong to the early *sermo plebeius*; of 351 such forms Silver Latin supplies only forty-six; see Cooper § 71. To this number M. contributes two, *pernere, perosculari* (8. 81. 5). See App.

10. 'I need not wish for myself better resting-place than this'. — **mando** here = *iubeo*, in sense and const.; cf. Tac. Ann. 15. 2 *mandavitque Tigranen Armenia exturbare*; Sil. 13. 480–481. See A. 563, a; GL. 546, N. 3.

89

Garris in aurem semper omnibus, Cinna,
garris et illud teste quod licet turba,
rides in aurem, quereris, arguis, ploras,
cantas in aurem, iudicas, taces, clamas,
5   adeoque penitus sedit hic tibi morbus,
ut saepe in aurem, Cinna, Caesarem laudes.

93

Fabricio iunctus fido requiescit Aquinus,
qui prior Elysias gaudet adisse domos.

89. Cinna is forever whispering in his neighbor's ears, just as Canius Rufus (3. 20) and Egnatius (Catull. 39. 1–8) grin under the most incongruous circumstances. — Meter: § 52.

1. **Garris in aurem:** cf. 5. 61. 3 *nescio quid dominae teneram qui garrit in aurem*; 3. 28. 2 *garris, Nestor, in auriculam*; 3. 44. 12.

2. **garris:** see App. — **et** = *etiam, even.* — **teste . . . turba:** Cinna whispers things that might be said aloud in the presence of all men. — **licet:** sc. *tibi proloqui (dicere).*

3. 'You can't even laugh aloud as ordinary people do'.

4. **iudicas,** *give your opinions,* perhaps in ordinary life, perhaps as a *iudex* in court. — **taces:** a paradox.

5. **penitus . . . morbus:** cf. Cels. 3. 1 *longus tamen morbus cum penitus insedit . . . acuto par est.* What in most men would be a mere *culpa* is in Cinna's case a *morbus.* Catullus (see Introd.) says of Egnatius: *hunc habet morbum*; in Hor. S. 1. 6. 30 Barrus's vanity is a *morbus*; cf. Sen. Ep.

85. 10 *numquid dubium est quin vitia mentis humanae inveterata et dura, quae morbos vocamus, immoderata sint, ut avaritia, ut crudelitas, ut inpotentia, ut impietas?* — **sedit** = *insedit*; see 1. 4. 2 N.

6. **in aurem:** i.e. rather than where all men can hear you. Thus M. artfully makes his blame of Cinna serve as a compliment to the emperor (Ramirez). The meaning is twofold: (1) 'your disease is chronic, so that you cannot even shout the praises of your emperor, as other men do'; (2) 'you are a court flatterer'.

93. On a double monument that marked the resting-place of two centurions; in life friends, in death they were not divided. — Meter: § 48.

1. **iunctus:** in burial and in Elysium. — **requiescit:** i.e. from the warfare of camp and of life. There is an intimation, too, that even in Elysium Aquinus was hardly at ease without his friend. Cf. the formal *requiescat in pace.*

2. **Elysias . . . domos:** the more enjoyable, because as professional soldier he had had no earthly home; cf. 9. 51. 5; 11. 5. 6;

Ara duplex primi testatur munera pili:
plus tamen est titulo quod breviore legis:
5 " Iunctus uterque sacro laudatae foedere vitae,
famaque quod raro novit amicus erat ".

98

Litigat et podagra Diodorus, Flacce, laborat.
Sed nil patrono porrigit: haec cheragra est.

Ov. M. 14. 111–112 *Elysiasque do-*
mos et regna novissima mundi me
duce cognosces (the Sibyl is speaking). Note the tenses; Aquinus
is forever glad that his friend survived him; cf. 1. 36. 4–6 *quod pro*
fratre mori vellet uterque prior,
diceret infernas et qui prior isset
ad umbras "Vive tuo, frater, tem-
pore, vive meo". For *gaudeo* with
inf. see on 1. 70. 18.

3. **Ara:** used for any stone
mȯnument, esp. a sepulchral monument, upon which, figuratively
speaking, offerings were made to
the Di Manes. This monument
may, however, have resembled a
double altar. — **primi . . . pili:** of
the sixty centurions in the legion
the *centurio primipilus* (or *primo-*
pilus) was first in rank; he had
risen by promotion to the command of the first *centuria* of the
first cohort in the legion. He was
a member of the general's council
and had charge of the money-chest
and of the eagle of the legion.

4. **plus:** freely, 'of more interest', 'of greater significance', i.e.
than the complimentary record suggested by 3. The *ara duplex* contained at least two inscriptions: one
to the two men, which stated their
names, ages, military service, etc.,
and the shorter couplet given in
5–6. It is possible, too, that each
man's career was given separately

and that the shorter couplet was
displayed elsewhere on the stone.
— **tamen:** i.e. in spite of the full
testimony to their merits indicated
by 3.

5. **Iunctus . . . vitae:** sc. *erat*
(*alteri*) with *iunctus*; cf. 1. The *sa-*
cramentum, the military oath taken
by the troops in the name of the
emperor, was regarded as far more
binding than the *ius iurandum*
taken in legal processes; hence
sacro foedere.

6. **fama,** *the annals of fame.*
Men who are rivals for glory, esp.
military glory, are apt to be jealous
of each other.—**-que** connects *iunc-*
tus (*erat*) and *amicus erat*. — **quod**
. . . novit is in appos. with *amicus*
erat. — **amicus erat** = *uterque al-*
teri amicus erat.

98. On a stingy man whose disease, M. thinks, has been wrongly
diagnosed. — Meter: § 48.

2. **patrono,** *his lawyer.* — **por-**
rigit: a humorous substitute for
pendit, dat; M. pretends to believe
that Diodorus is crippled in his
hands too, and so is physically unable to hold out a coin. Lawyers'
fees depended largely on the gener-
osity of the clients, and so were
often small; see Iuv. 7. 105–149.
Contrast 1. 76; but that epigram
must not be taken too seriously.
A law passed in 204 B.C. made it
illegal to take any fee; Claudius

100

Mammas atque tatas habet Afra, sed ipsa tatarum
dici et mammarum maxima mamma potest.

102

Qui pinxit Venerem tuam, Lycori,
blanditus, puto, pictor est Minervae.

103

"Si dederint superi decies mihi milia centum"

repealed this but fixed the maximum fee at 10,000 *sestertii*. Plin. Ep. 6. 23. I tells us that he spoke without compensation. Quint. 12. 7. 8 declares that lawyer and client should not make a bargain beforehand, but also bids the client show his gratitude practically.

100. On a woman far from young (probably a *meretrix*: cf. Giese 5; note her foreign name), who by her baby talk would make people believe her still youthful. — Meter: § 48.

1–2. Mammas atque tatas: note the plural. She may have addressed grandparents as well as parents, or even other persons, in this way. Non. 81 quotes Varro as saying that children *cibum ac potionem buas ac pappas* (*vocant*) *et matrem mammam, patrem tatam.* As with such baby words finally became a part of the *sermo familiaris*; this is attested by the inscriptions, which so often give us pictures of common life where literature fails; cf. Orelli-Henz. 2813 *Dis M. Zetho Corinthus tata eius et Nice mamma F. V. A. Ī. D. XVI*; Abbott A. J. P. 19. 86–90. — **tatarum . . . maxima** (sc. *natu*), *the very oldest tata and mamma of them all.* Cf. 10. 39; note the alliteration.

102. M. has styled a Lycoris, perhaps this Lycoris, *cerussata* (1. 72. 6), *lusca* (3. 39. 2), *nigra* (4. 62. 1), *fusca* (7. 13. 2). She was evidently of the demi-monde; such women often lived under assumed names. A certain Lycoris was a beauty famous as the mistress of M. Antonius and of Cornelius Gallus, the brilliant but ill-starred poet. The picture referred to in the epigram may have represented Venus alone, or Venus, Minerva, and Juno together as they appeared before Paris on Mt. Ida; Lycoris herself posed as Venus. See Beck. 3. 97 ff. M. means, then, either that scant justice has been done to Venus's charms or that the painter has failed to appreciate the beauty of Lycoris herself. — Meter: § 49.

1–2. 'Your painter, who has flattered Minerva at Venus's expense, was not so appreciative a judge as Paris'. Cf. 5. 40. 1–2 *pinxisti Venerem, colis, Artemidore, Minervam, et miraris opus displicuisse tuum?*

103. 'One's knowledge of how to live well is frequently in inverse proportion to his means; Scaevola's meanness grew apace with his riches'. — Meter: § 48.

1. decies . . . centum: 1,000.-000 *sestertii* was the senatorial census, 400,000 the equestrian. With

dicebas nondum, Scaevola, iustus eques,
"qualiter o vivam, quam large quamque beate!"
Riserunt faciles et tribuere dei.

5　Sordidior multo post hoc toga, paenula peior,
calceus est sarta terque quaterque cute,
deque decem plures semper servantur olivae
explicat et cenas unica mensa duas,

milia sc. *sestertium*, the older (not contracted) gen. pl. of *sestertius*. The Romans reckoned large sums of money regularly in terms of the *sestertius*; commonly, too, *milia sestertium* is omitted wholly from the expressions for such sums.

2. dicebas: mark the tense, *you used to say.* — **iustus,** *full, regular, true, legal*; cf. *matrimonium iustum, uxor iusta*, etc.; 4. 67. 3–4 *dicebatque suis haec tantum desse trecentis, ut posset domino plaudere iustus eques.*

3. beate: i.e. as a real *beatus* or *rex* (= *dives*; see on 2. 18. 5).

4. Riserunt: the gods knew what the outcome would be and so with a chuckle granted his prayer. We may also take *riserunt* as = *arriserunt*; see on 1. 4. 2. — **faciles,** *compliant*; used frequently of the gods who answer prayer; cf. 12. 6. 10; Iuv. 10. 7–8 *evertēre domos totas . . . di faciles*; Hor. S. 1. 1. 22; Luc. 1. 510 *o faciles deos.*

5. Sordidior . . . toga: the toga, being of white wool, must be cleansed frequently by the *fullo*. For the general picture in 5–6 cf. Hor. S. 1. 3. 30–32; Ep. 1. 1. 94–97; Iuv. 3. 147–151.—**paenula:** a cloak of shaggy felt (*gausapa*) or leather, used by the well-to-do as a weather garment over the toga, by the poor and slaves as the ordinary outside garment, if anything at all was worn over the tunic. Scaevola seems to

have been too mean to think of a *lacerna*. See Beck. 3. 215 ff.; Marq. 564; Müller Die Tracht. d. R. 34.

6. calceus: as necessary as the toga was to formal out-of-doors dress; *soleae* or *crepidae* were worn in the house. See Marq. 588 ff.; Beck. 3. 227 ff. — **sarta . . . cute:** cf. 12. 29. 9; see on *sordidior . . . toga*, 5.

7–9. Meanness dominates Scaevola's dinners from the beginning (*promulsis, gustus*) to the *comissatio* at the end.

7. plures . . . olivae: olives were regularly served at the *promulsis*, which preceded the *fercula* of the *cena* proper; here only ten in all are served, yet more than half are carefully saved for another time; Scaevola will not eat them himself or leave them for the slaves. Cf. Iuv. 14. 126–133; contrast 3. 58. 42–43.

8. explicat . . . duas prob. refers to the *cena* proper as distinct from the *promulsis* (7) and the *comissatio* (9). Scaevola's avarice leads him to dispense with the *mensae secundae*. One *pièce de résistance*, if anything worthy this name were served at all, must answer for two days! Cf. 10. 48. 17. — **explicat,** *sets out*; cf. 1. 99. 9–13 *abisti in tantam miser esuritionem ut convivia sumptuosiora, toto quae semel apparas in anno, nigrae sordibus explices monetae* ('money').

et Veientani bibitur faex crassa rubelli,
10   asse cicer tepidum constat et asse Venus.
In ius, o fallax atque infitiator, eamus:
aut vive aut decies, Scaevola, redde deis.

107

Saepe mihi dicis, Luci carissime Iuli,

There is grim humor in the verb, which in itself suggests plenty. — **mensa**: here of what was put on the table, *service, serving*.

9. Veientani . . . rubelli: Veientan wine was commonplace; cf. 3. 49. 1 *Veientana mihi misces, ubi Massica potas.* In 2. 53. 3–4 M. says to Maximus: 'You can be a true freeman', *cenare foris si, Maxime, nolis, Veientana tuam si domat uva sitim.* — **faex crassa**: M. may wish to imply that Scaevola was careful to drain the amphora, though *faex* was used of wine that was thick and poor; cf. 11. 56. 7–8 *o quam magnus homo es, qui faece rubentis aceti et . . . nigro pane carere potes!* On Italian wines see Marq. 449 ff.; Beck. 3. 434 ff.

10. cicer tepidum: cf. *madidum cicer*, 1. 41. 6 N. — **constat**, *stands at, costs*, a mercantile term; cf. 13. 3. 2; 6. 88. 3 (note gen. there). — **asse**, *penny*; *as* is used in proverbial expressions, as we use 'copper', 'nickel'. — **Venus** = *meretrix*; cf. 2. 53. 7 'you can be truly free', *si plebeia Venus gemino tibi vincitur asse.*

11. In ius . . . eamus, *let us go into court*, a phrase used of going before the praetor's tribunal; in this case the criminal is answerable to the court of heaven. Cf. 12. 97. 10 *sit tandem pudor aut eamus in ius;* Iuv. 10. 87–88 *ne quis . . . pavidum in ius cervice obstricta dominum trahat.* The charge is perjury and misuse of a trust; the sentence is given in 12. — **fallax**: he belied the promise of 3. — **infitiator**: used technically of one who denies a debt, whether of the ordinary kind, or arising out of money left with him as a *depositum*; the latter sin was accounted especially heinous. Cf. Iuv. 13. 60 *si depositum non infitietur amicus;* Ter. Phor. 55–56. In Plin. Ep. 10. 96. 7 the Bithynian Christians are represented as swearing *ne fidem fallerent, ne depositum appellati abnegarent.* Scaevola received his wealth from the gods on conditions; he has failed to keep his promise and so has denied the *depositum.*

12. vive: cf. *vivam* (3) and see on 1. 15. 12. — **redde deis**: i.e. 'since you have proven false to your trust, give back to the gods what they gave you'.

107. M., while excusing himself from the undertaking of a *magnum opus* (see § 41), on the ground that leisure is indispensable for such an achievement, politely begs. On patronage of literature see 1. 76. Introd. Maecenas made it a part of state policy. It has been thought necessary almost down to our own times. For M. and such patronage see §§ 8–11; 14; 15; 36. Cf. 3. 38; 8. 55; Iuv. 7, esp. 1–12, 36–68, 105–123; Fried. SG. 3. 406 ff. — Meter: § 48.

1. carissime implies close friendship; it is used by M. again only in 9. 97. 1.

" Scribe aliquid magnum: desidiosus homo es ".
Otia da nobis, sed qualia fecerat olim
   Maecenas Flacco Vergilioque suo:
5 condere victuras temptem per saecula curas
   et nomen flammis eripuisse meum.
In steriles nolunt campos iuga ferre iuvenci:

2. desidiosus homo, *a lazy fel-low*; said playfully, but well, of one who lived by his wits; cf. 8. 3. 12.

3. Otia da nobis: i.e. 'give to us poets in general'; *nobis* is more than *mihi*, 1. The command supplants the prot. of a conditional sentence; see on 1. 70. 3; 1. 79. 2. The sense is, 'If you were to give, . . . I would try'. *Otium* is freedom from business (*negotium = nec + otium*), such leisure as is made possible by wealth; hence *otium* came to mean 'opportunity for literary work'; cf. Cic. De Or. 2. 13. 57 *otium suum consumpsit in historia scribenda;* Tusc. 5. 36. 105 *quid est enim dulcius otio litterato?* Plin. Ep. 1. 22. 11 *studiosum . . . otium.* — **sed:** see on 1. 43. 9. — **fecerat:** cf. Verg. E. 1. 6 *deus nobis haec otia fecit.* The plpf. often = aorist in the poets of the empire; cf. 2. 41. 2; 3. 52. 1; 5. 52. 4. See Guttmann 40 ff. Still, the plpf. may here be exact, 'had given leisure (before they produced their immortal works)'.

4. Maecenas: the typical patron of literature; cf. 8. 55. 5 ff.; 11. 3. 7–12; Iuv. 7. 94 *quis tibi Maecenas...erit?* — **Flacco:** Horace's obligation to Maecenas, esp. for the Sabine farm, is common knowledge. Vergil too had reason to appreciate Maecenas's favor; for Roman tradition on this point compare Donatus (= Suet.) Verg. 20 *Georgica in honorem Maecenatis edidit,* '*qui sibi mediocriter adhuc*

noto opem tulisset adversus veterani cuiusdam violentiam, a quo in altercatione litis agrariae paulum afuit quin occideretur (see, however, on 8. 55. 9–10). Horace and Vergil are, however, but examples of a wider patronage which embraced Varius, Propertius, etc. See Merivale 4. 214. — **suo:** see on 1. 13. 1.

5. condere ... curas: i.e. to write poetry; cf. Verg. E. 10. 50–51 *Chalcidico quae sunt mihi condita versu carmina.* For *cura* of carefully wrought literary work cf. 1. 25. 5–6 N.; 1. 45. 1 *edita ne brevibus pereat mihi cura libellis;* O. Crusius Rhein. Mus. 44. 449, Anm. 2. — **condere...temptem:** the inf. with *tempto* is common in Silver Latin. — **saecula:** cf. 10. 2. 11 N.

6. flammis: (1) of the funeral pyre, (2) of oblivion. For the thought cf. Hor. C. 3. 30. 6–7 *non omnis moriar multaque pars mei vitabit Libitinam.* — **eripuisse** here hardly means more than *eripere* would suggest. The pf. inf. seems often to be used without much regard to time, whether dependent on a verb, as here and in 2. 1. 9, or dependent on an adj., as in 6. 52. 4, esp. in dependence on forms of *volo, nolo, malo,* and at the beginning of the second half of the pentameter; in the latter case metrical convenience is at work. See L. 2225; Howard Harv. Stud. 1. 111–138, esp. 123.

7. steriles: cf. 1. 76. 14; Iuv. 7. 103 *quae tamen inde* (from literary

pingue solum lassat, sed iuvat ipse labor.

109

Issa est passere nequior Catulli,
Issa est purior osculo columbae,
Issa est blandior omnibus puellis,
Issa est carior Indicis lapillis,
5   Issa est deliciae catella Publi.

toil) *seges, terrae quis fructus aper-
tae?* — **iuvenci**: even brutes protest against useless toil.

8. pingue solum occurs in
Verg. G. 1. 64; cf. Luc. 6. 382 *pinguis sulcus*, a furrow drawn in rich
soil. The chiasmus emphasizes
the antithesis. — **iuvat . . . labor**:
because in such a case there is
reasonable expectation of a fair
return; hope is no less a stimulus
to the poet than to the farmer.

109. M. compliments Publius
on the likeness he had painted of
a favorite lap-dog, whom he called
Issa (but see on 18). It is possible
that the man praised in 2. 57; 10. 98
for elegance of dress and home
appointments is this Publius. —
Meter: § 49.

1. Issa: the ancient custom of
applying personal names to pets,
esp. love names and nicknames,
has long survived the Romans.
In Petr. 64 Croesus's pet puppy is
named *Margarita*, 'Pearl'. *Issa* is
from the *sermo familiaris*, for *ipsa*;
ps becomes *ss*. *Issa* = *domina*,
M'lady; see Bücheler, Petr., edit.
maior, on 63; Lindsay L. L. 79. On
Pompeian graffiti we have *Aprodite
Issa* and *Euge Issa*; see C.I.L.
4. 1589, 1590. — M. is fond of a
succession of lines with like beginning or like ending; cf. 10. 35. 1, 3;
2, 4; 11, 12. See Paukstadt 25–27.
— **passere . . . Catulli**: the spar-

row of Lesbia, Catullus's mistress,
whose praises are sung in Catull.
2; 3. M. alludes to this sparrow
also in 1. 7; 4. 14. 13–14. — **nequior**, *roguish, naughty*. So *nequitiae* stands for a wantonness that
charms in 4. 42. 4 *nequitias tellus
scit dare nulla magis*. See App.

2. osculo columbae, *the billing
of a dove*; doves were proverbially
affectionate. — **osculo**, *kiss*; dim.
of *os*. The dim. is used perhaps
of the mouth puckered (made
smaller) for a kiss; perhaps, however, the dim. is rather one of
endearment. Cf. Ov. Am. 2. 6. 56
*oscula dat cupido blanda columba
mari* ('mate').

3. blandior, *more coaxing, more
winsome.*

4. carior, *more precious.* — **Indicis lapillis**: *lapillus*, dim. of
lapis, is a general word for gems,
precious stones; cf. Ov. A. A. 3. 129
*vos quoque non caris aures onerate
lapillis*. The Orient, esp. India,
supplied the ancient world with
gems; cf. 10. 38. 4–5 *o nox omnis
et hora, quae notata est caris litoris
Indici lapillis!*

5. This vs. identifies Issa, and
satisfies the curiosity roused by
1–4. — **deliciae**, *pet*; cf. *passer,
deliciae meae puellae*, Catull. 2. 1;
3. 4. — **catella**: dim. of endearment. As a pet the dog seems to
have taken with the Romans the

Hanc tu, si queritur, loqui putabis;
sentit tristitiamque gaudiumque.
Collo nixa cubat capitque somnos,
ut suspiria nulla sentiantur,
10　et desiderio coacta ventris
gutta pallia non fefellit ulla,
sed blando pede suscitat toroque
deponi monet et rogat levari.
Castae tantus inest pudor catellae,
15　ignorat Venerem; nec invenimus
dignum tam tenera virum puella.
Hanc ne lux rapiat suprema totam,
picta Publius exprimit tabella,

part played by the cat among us.
Iuv. 6. 652–654 represents the
woman of his day as thinking more
of her puppy than of her husband.
Cf. Petr. 71 *aedificas monumentum
meum quemadmodum te iussi?
valde te rogo ut secundum pedes
statuae meae catellam ponas.* The
dog of this epigram may have been
the *catella Gallicana* of 14. 198. 1–2
*delicias parvae si vis audire catel-
lae, narranti brevis est pagina tota
mihi.* For other pets see 7. 87;
5. 37. 13; 14. 73; Merrill on Catull.
2. 1; Marq. 152, Anm. 5; Beck. 2.
148 ff. — **Publi**: for the form see
§ 56, c; Haupt Opusc. 3. 584.

6. queritur: cf. Prop. 4. 3. 55
catulae vox est mihi grata querentis.

7. tristitiam: sc. *Publi.*

8. Collo...cubat: presumably
at night.

9. ut ... sentiantur, *so gently
that*, etc.; she does not disturb
her master's repose.

10. ventris = *vesicae.*

11. pallia here = *stragula*; sc.
tori. — **fefellit**, *deceives, proves
traitor to,* an emotional substitute

for a prosaic *maculat, inquinat.*
For the gnomic pf. see A. 475;
GL. 236, N.; L. 1611.

12. suscitat: sc. *dominum*; cf.
8–9.

13. The inf. with *moneo* is not
common; Phaedr. 3. 17. 13 has inf.
with *admoneo.* Cf. note on *mando,*
1. 88. 10. — **rogat levari**: for *rogare*
with inf. cf. Ov. Her. 6. 144; Catull.
35. 10. — **levari**: sc. *toro,* or *alvi
seu vesicae onere* (Schr.).

14–15. Castae ... Venerem:
parataxis (coördination); M. might
have said *castae ... catellae ut
ignoret Venerem.*

17. lux ... suprema: sc. *vitae;
supremus* is used of the end of life
in many phrases, esp. with *dies,
tempus, hora, nox.* — **rapiat** =
abripiat; see on 1. 4. 2.

18. picta ... tabella: *tabella
(picta)* = *painting, picture*; cf. Hor.
Ep. 2. 2. 180–182 *gemmas, marmor,
ebur, Tyrrhena sigilla, tabellas ...
sunt qui non habeant, est qui non
curat habere.* — **exprimit**: this
verb is frequently used of representations in wax, clay, plaster; it is

in qua tam similem videbis Issam
20   ut sit tam similis sibi nec ipsa.
Issam denique pone cum tabella:
aut utramque putabis esse veram,
aut utramque putabis esse pictam.

113

Quaecumque lusi iuvenis et puer quondam
apinasque nostras, quas nec ipse iam novi,
male conlocare si bonas voles horas
et invidebis otio tuo, lector,
5   a Valeriano Pollio petes Quinto,
per quem perire non licet meis nugis.

used next of repoussé work; finally, it is used figuratively of portrayal in words or oil. Here it is most natural to suppose that Publius himself is painting Issa; still the verb could be used of him even if he were employing some one else as artist.

19. tam . . . Issam, *an Issa so like* (the living Issa).

20. nec here = *non*, *ne . . . quidem*, i.e. its connective force is or seems to be wholly lacking. The usage is not infrequent in early Latin; later, it occurs only sporadically, aside from a few compounds (*necopinans*, *negotium*). See GL. 442, N. 3; L. 1446; 1658; Ribbeck, Die latein. Partikeln, 24–26. Cf. 1. 113. 2; 4. 44. 8; 5. 62. 5; 5. 69. 4. Sometimes it is possible enough to see connective force in *nec*, by assuming condensation, as here from *nec altera catella nec ipsa*. See on *sed*, 1. 43. 9.

21. pone = *compone*. The vs. well shows how *componere* came to mean 'compare'.

113. Some one would seem to have asked the poet where his earlier poems could be purchased. The edition referred to may have been a reissue of pieces once published or a publication of early works not previously given to the world. See §§ 9; 39; 1. 117. Introd. — Meter: § 52.

1. Quaecumque lusi, *whatever sportive trifles I wrote*. *Ludo* is often thus used; cf. 14. 187. 1 *hac primum iuvenum lascivos lusit amores*; Hor. C. 1. 32. 1, etc. — **et puer**, *yes (and earlier still), as a lad.*

2. apinas = *nugas, gerras*; cf. 14. 1. 7 *sunt apinae tricaeque et si quid vilius istis.* The word is supposed to be derived from Apina, the name of a poor town in Apulia. — **nec ipse** = *ne ipse quidem*; see on 1. 109. 20.

3. male . . . horas, *to make a bad investment of some good time.* — **conlocare**: a common mercantile term, of putting things out on contract.

4. A pure choliambus; see § 52, b

5. Pollio: see 1. 2. 7 N.

6. per . . . nugis: i.e. he publishes my youthful trifles and keeps

117

Occurris quotiens, Luperce, nobis,
" Vis mittam puerum " subinde dicis,
" cui tradas epigrammaton libellum,
lectum quem tibi protinus remittam ? "
5 Non est quod puerum, Luperce, vexes.
Longum est, si velit ad Pirum venire,
et scalis habito tribus, sed altis.
Quod quaeris propius petas licebit.

them from dying a natural death. — nugis: cf. note on *apinas*, 2. M. uses this word repeatedly of his epigrams; cf. 2. 1. 6; 4. 10. 4; 8. 3. 11; etc.; Catull. 1. 3–4 *namque tu solebas meas esse aliquid putare nugas*; and other authors.

117. Cf. 4. 72. M. humorously urges a man who was always begging the loan of a copy of the epigrams to go to the Argiletum (see on 1. 2. 8) and buy a copy. M.'s motive could hardly have been a mercenary one if, as most authorities hold, no royalty was paid to authors; see Fried. SG. 3. 429; Marq. 828; Beck. 2. 450 ff. For a different view see Putnam, Authors and their Public in Ancient Times, 188; 203 ff. At any rate M. seems to have looked for remuneration mainly to sources other than his publishers, esp. to friends or to the emperor; on patronage see 1. 76. Introd.; 1. 107. Introd. — Meter: § 49.

2. Vis mittam: a simple deliberative subjv., *mittam*, would have sufficed. Beware of supplying *ut*; in Greek we have τί βούλει ποιῶ; beside τί ποιῶ; — We really have parataxis; *vis mittam = vis? mittam?* For the simple subjv. after *volo* see A. 563, b; GL. 546, Rem. 2; L. 1705; 1707. — **puerum**: cf.

1. 41. 8 N. — **subinde**, *repeatedly*, reënforces 1. Vss. 3–4 supply good examples of final rel. clauses.

5. M.'s (pretended) concern for the slave is of course only a studiously courteous snub. — **Non est quod**, *there is no reason why*; this formula is regularly followed by the subjunctive.

6. ad Pirum: M. dwelt at this time in lodgings on the Collis Quirinalis near the temple of Flora, by The Pear Tree; cf. 5. 22. 3–4; 6. 27. 1–2 *nam tu quoque proxima Florae incolis*. Topographical nomenclature arising in the *sermo plebeius* often becomes fixed. A bull of Pope Innocent III of the year 1199 mentions a locality *ad Pirum* on the Quirinal. See Jordan Arch. Zeitung, 1871, p. 71; Hülsen-Jordan 427, N. 94.

7. scalis . . . tribus: local abl., = *tertio tabulato*. M. was doubtless living in a lodging-house (*insula*, so called because flanked on all sides by streets). In such the poor found quarters; cf. Iuv. 3. 193–202. For high *insulae* see 7. 20; Iuv. 3. 197 ff., 269 ff.; Burn, Rome and the Campagna, p. lxxi; Smith D. of A. 1. 666. — **sed**: see on 1. 43. 9.

8. petas licebit: see on 1. 70. 17.

Argi nempe soles subire letum :

10   contra Caesaris est Forum taberna
scriptis postibus hinc et inde totis,
omnis ut cito perlegas poetas.
Illinc me pete.   Nec roges Atrectum
— hoc nomen dominus gerit tabernae — :

15   de primo dabit alterove nido

9. Argi...letum: simple tme-
sis. We need not assume that M.
recognized the old etymology, for
which cf. Verg. A. 8. 345; see the
lexicons. Note the irony; M. says:
'As a lover of literature, you surely
go every day to the Argiletum'.
He means of course that Lupercus
hardly knows where to buy a book.

10. Caesaris...Forum: since
the extent of the Argiletum is not
clearly fixed, we cannot say certainly which forum is meant. *Caesaris* without further designation
would naturally denote the reigning
emperor, Domitian, who began the
Forum Palladium; see I. 2. 8 N.

11. scriptis postibus: shops
were closed at night by shutters
and doors. In the daytime the
shutters, etc., were removed, and
the shop was wholly open to the
street; only a low counter of ma-
sonry, shaped like a carpenter's
square, then separated the interior
from the street. On either side of
the whole shop-front were the
postes (Hor. S. 1. 4. 71–72 calls
them *pilae*). These the booksellers
utilized for advertising the books
for sale within and for the display
of sample copies. See Overbeck,
Pompeii, 378; Mau-Kelsey 276–
278, esp. Fig. 131; Knapp Class.
Rev. 11. 359. The best place to
study the arrangements for closing
Roman shops is in the shops to be
seen in the eastern hemicycle of

Trajan's Forum, hidden from the
view of the ordinary visitor by
modern houses. In these shops
the stone lintel is yet in place; one
sees a groove in the *limen*, beginning at the point where the door
stopped and running to the left
postis; up this *postis* a groove runs
to the lintel; in the lintel a groove
runs to the right, directly above
that in the *limen*; this stops over
the point at which the groove begins in the threshold. In these
grooves slid the board shutters.—
hinc et inde: i.e. to right and to
left.

13. me: i.e. 'my works'; cf.
omnis...poetas, 12.—Nec roges:
'without a word from you the bookseller will hand you my poems, for
which there is such demand that
he has them ever within reach'.
—Atrectum: see on 1. 2. 7.

14. dominus: cf. Iuv. 2. 42 *ne
pudeat dominum monstrare tabernae.*

15. nido: *nidus* prop. = 'a nest',
then any small receptacle; here it
= *capsa, armarium, loculamentum,
pigeonhole*. The reference may,
however, be to shelves between
floor and ceiling; cf. 7. 17. 5. In
the shops at Pompeii one often
sees a small set of shelves arranged
like a staircase (*scala*) on one side
of the counter, evidently meant as
a repository for articles much in
demand — weights, measures, etc.

rasum pumice purpuraque cultum
denaris tibi quinque Martialem.
" Tanti non es " ais ? Sapis, Luperce.

16. On the cost of this edition see on I. 66. 10–11.

17. denaris: the denarius, the silver coin most in use, which originally = 10 *asses* (= 4.55 gr. = 18 to 20 cents), steadily decreased in weight and value, until at this time it contained only 3.41 gr., and was worth only about 12 cents. See Hultsch 269; 311. Note the form; thë contraction of *-iis* to *-is* in dat. and abl. pl. of the first two declensions is attested by inscriptions and by Mss. of various authors (including Cicero); see Neue-Wagener, Formenlehre, I. 47; I. 189–190.

18. Note the play on words. 'You are not worth so much', Lupercus said of the book and its contents; M. humorously refers it to his financial condition. — **Sapis,** *you have sense,* is (1) ironical; (2) serious, '*you are right*; I am poor, and so loath to lend my books'.

LIBER II

I

Ter centena quidem poteras epigrammata ferre :
  sed quis te ferret perlegeretque, liber ?
At nunc succincti quae sint bona disce libelli.
  Hoc primum est, brevior quod mihi charta perit ;
5 deinde, quod haec una peragit librarius hora,
  nec tantum nugis serviet ille meis ;
tertia res haec est, quod, si cui forte legeris,
  sis licet usque malus, non odiosus eris.

1. M. congratulates his book on its brevity, instancing three advantages possessed by a short book. Brevity, however, he continues, though a virtue, would not alone redeem it from faults.— Meter: § 48.

1. Ter centena: see on I. 43. I. — **poteras:** as in I. 3. 12; see note there. — **ferre,** *carry the burden of.* Book II has but 93 epigrams; Book I has 118, the highest number in any of the first twelve books.

2. ferret: a pun on *ferre,* 1. Vss. 1-2 constitute in sense a contrary-to-fact conditional sentence, *si ter centena epigrammata ferres, quis te,* etc.

3. succincti: this word is said prop. of one who has girded up his flowing garments for easy or rapid movement; it was used, then, probably, of the garments tucked up, 'shortened', so to say; then, as here, it signified *condensed, brief.*

4. brevior . . . charta, *less paper.* The papyrus strip necessary for Book II would be literally shorter than that needed for Book I. — **charta:** see I. 25. 7 N.; cf. 6. 64. 22–23 *audes praeterea quos nullus noverit in me scribere versiculos miseras et perdere chartas.*

5. haec: sc. *epigrammata.* — **una . . . hora:** hardly to be taken literally. — **peragit:** i.e. copies out; cf. Eng. 'drive through' a piece of work. — **librarius,** *copyist,* one of the skilled slaves of the publisher; see Marq. 825.

6. nec . . . serviet: i.e. 'he will not have to slave so much over my book'. — **nugis:** see on I. 113. 6.

7. si . . . legeris: the ancients systematically read aloud; works were often read aloud to them by slaves; cf. e.g. Nep. Att. 13. 3; Plin. Ep. 3. 5. 12; Norden, Antike Kunstprosa, 6.

Te conviva leget mixto quincunce, sed ante

10　　incipiat positus quam tepuisse calix.

Esse tibi tanta cautus brevitate videris?

Ei mihi, quam multis sic quoque longus eris!

5

Ne valeam, si non totis, Deciane, diebus

et tecum totis noctibus esse velim.

Sed duo sunt quae nos disiungunt milia passum:

quattuor haec fiunt, cum rediturus eam.

5　　Saepe domi non es, cum sis quoque saepe negaris:

vel tantum causis vel tibi saepe vacas.

9–10. **conviva leget:** on the amusements, intellectual and otherwise, introduced during the *comissatio* of the *cena* see Marq. 337 ff.; Beck. 3. 373 ff. — **quincunce:** see on 1. 27. 2. Wine was mixed with ice or snow (see on 5. 64. 2) or with hot water (*calda*), according to taste, age, or time of the year; cf. Beck. 3. 430; 3. 441; Marq. 332–333. *Mixto quincunce = postquam quincunx mixtus est.* — **positus:** see on 1. 43. 2. — **quam:** for position see on *nec*, Lib. Spect. 1. 2. — **tepuisse** (from *tepesco*), *to cool*; the verb more often = 'to become tepid'. Book II is so short, says M., that though the guest does not begin it until his drink has been mixed, he will have finished the book before the mixture cools off. For the tense see on *eripuisse*, 1. 107. 6. — **calix:** a kind of *poculum*.

11. **cautus,** *protected*, from unfriendly criticism.

12. **quam:** with *multis*, not with *longus*. — **sic quoque:** i.e. 'short as you are!' Cf. 1. 3.

5. 'I esteem you as a friend, Decianus; yea, I would gladly live with you, but the trials of a client

are enough to break any friendship'. For Decianus see on 1. 61.
10. — Meter: § 48.

1. **Ne valeam, si:** cf. 4. 31. 3 *ne valeam si non res est gratissima nobis.* A commoner way of expressing this idea is *dispeream si non,* etc:: cf. e.g. 1. 39. 8; 2. 69. 2. See GL. 263, 1, N. — **totis … diebus:** for the abl. of duration see A. 424, b; GL. 393, Rem. 2; L. 1355. The usage is common in phrases involving *totus* or its equivalent; cf. e.g. 4. 54. 3.

3. **passum** = *passuum*; so often. The shorter form of the gen. pl. of the fourth declension is attested by the Roman grammarians and by good Mss., even of Cicero.

5. **domi non es:** Decianus is either out of town, or a polite lie is told by his slave; cf. 5. 22. 9–10; 9. 6; and esp. Cic. De Or. 2. 68. 276. — **negaris** perhaps implies rudeness on the part of the slaves.

6. **tantum … vacas:** the excuse of the *ostiarius*. — **causis:** i.e. of his clients. Either Decianus was a *causidicus* and was preparing a case or he had time only (*tantum*)

Te tamen ut videam, duo milia non piget ire :
ut te non videam, quattuor ire piget.

7

Declamas belle, causas agis, Attice, belle,
    historias bellas, carmina bella facis,
componis belle mimos, epigrammata belle,
    bellus grammaticus, bellus es astrologus,
5   et belle cantas et saltas, Attice, belle,

for such clients as needed legal advice; to give such advice had been from very early times a duty of the patron. — **tibi**: M. charges Decianus with selfishness; the *salutatio* must have been at times little, if at all, less irksome to patron than to clients.

8. non goes closely with *videam*, and so may stand in the final clause: 'to fail to see you I'm loath to go four miles'. See A. 531, 1, N. 2; GL. 545, Rem. 2; L. 1947.

7. M. holds up to scorn the *magnus ardalio*, a jack of all trades who did everything *belle*, but nothing well. Cf. 1. 9, with notes; 3. 63. — Meter: § 48.

1. causas agis, *you plead in court*; *declamas* refers rather to practice speaking in the schools of rhetoric or in private; cf. 1. 79. 1. — **Attice**: a Greek freedman; cf. Iuv. 3. 75–80 *quemvis hominem secum attulit ad nos: grammaticus, rhetor, geometres, pictor, aliptes, augur, schoenobates, medicus, magus, omnia novit Graeculus esuriens; in caelum iusseris, ibit.*

2. carmina, *lyric poems*; cf. e.g. Hor. Ep. 2. 2. 91 *carmina compono, hic elegos.*

3. mimos: from the end of the Republic the *mimus* gradually supplanted the regular drama, main-taining its popularity down to the end of the Empire. As a literary form it had been popularized especially by D. Laberius (about 105–43 B.C.) and Publilius Syrus; the latter was at the height of his popularity about the time of his rival's death. See Teuffel § 8. — **epigrammata**: cf. 7. 8 5. 3–4.

4. grammaticus, *a philologist*, or rather, perhaps, *a litterateur*; the *grammatici* often lectured on the masterpieces of literature, esp. of poetry. See Sandys Hist. of Class. Scholarship 6–9. — **astrologus**: an interpreter of the stars, *astrologer*. The word often also = 'astronomer'; astronomy and astrology were not differentiated until the seventh century A.D. and astronomy did not rid itself of astrology until after the time of Copernicus (1473–1543). Belief in astrology, fostered by the court, was common under the Empire and seems to have been recognized in the schools. See Iuv. 6. 553 ff.; Fried. SG. 1. 132; 1. 362 ff.; 1. 508–509.

5. saltas: prob. in pantomime; cf. Hor. S. 1. 5. 63 *pastorem saltaret uti Cyclopa rogabat.* Dancing was unbecoming to a Roman gentleman: see Cic. Mur. 6. 13 *nemo enim fere saltat sobrius nisi forte insanit*; Hor. S. 2. 1. 24–25. Singing, too,

bellus es arte lyrae, bellus es arte pilae.
Nil bene cum facias, facias tamen omnia belle,
vis dicam quid sis ? magnus es ardalio.

II

Quod fronte Selium nubila vides, Rufe,
quod ambulator porticum terit seram,
lugubre quiddam quod tacet piger voltus,

was improper; see e.g. Nep. Praef. Further, to appear in any public spectacle to amuse a crowd involved loss of caste, esp. if done for pay; actors, etc., were under serious civil disabilities.

6. arte pilae: for ball-playing see Beck. 3. 171 ff.; Marq. 841 ff.; Smith D. of A. s.v. *Pila.*

7. bene . . . belle: cf. 10. 46. 1–2 *omnia vis belle, Matho, dicere. Dic aliquando et bene.*

8. vis dicam: see on *vis mittam*, 1. 117. 2.—**magnus . . . ardalio,** *a great idle busybody;* cf. Gloss. Laber. *ardelio, πολυπράγμων;* Gell. 11. 16. Plin. Ep. 1. 9 bitterly enumerates the *officia* that consume his time in Rome; the *ardalio* contentedly makes a life business of such things. Cf. 4. 78. 9–10; Phaedr. 2. 5. 1–4, cited in 1. 79. Introd.; Fried. SG. 1. 410 ff.

11. Besides the legacy-hunters (1. 10) and the *ardaliones* (2. 7) the dinner-hunters (*parasiti, scurrae, laudiceni*) formed a distinct class of professional hangers-on. Cf. Plaut. Cap. 75–77; Plin. Ep. 2. 14. 5. Of such spongers Selius is typical; cf. 2. 14; 2. 69; 2. 27 *laudantem Selium cenae cum retia tendit accipe, sive legas sive patronus agas: Effecte! graviter! cito! nequiter! euge! beate! hoc volui! Facta est iam tibi cena: tace.*—Meter: § 52.

1. Quod: freely, 'though'; lit. *as to the fact that.* See A. 572, a; GL. 525, 2, N. 3; L. 1844; 1845.—**Rufe:** see 2. 29.

2. ambulator: freely, 'by ceaseless promenading'; cf. Cato R. R. 5. 2 *vilicus ne sit ambulator.* For another use of the word cf. 1. 41. 3 N. —**porticum terit:** under the Empire the colonnades held a very important place in the life of Rome, forming a network that almost covered large portions of the city. See 2. 14. 5–10 N.; Lanciani Anc. R. 94–100.—**terit:** hyperbolical; cf. 3. 20. 10–11 *porticum terit templi an spatia carpit lentus Argonautarum?* Stat. Silv. 4. 6. 2–4 *cum patulis tererem vagus otia Saeptis iam moriente die, rapuit me cena benigni Vindicis.* —**seram:** transferred epithet; the word belongs logically with *ambulator.* It can be best rendered by 'in the last hours of the day'. Cf. 2. 14. 16, and *moriente die* in the passage just cited from Statius.

3. His countenance shows a grief too deep for utterance (*tacet*), befitting some terrible calamity.— **quiddam:** acc.; see A. 388, a; GL. 330, Rem., and N. 2; 333, 1, N. 1; L. 1139.—**piger:** characteristically dull, or, better, without its usual hopeful look. Translate: 'His face is dull and full of some voiceless agony'.

quod paene terram nasus indecens tangit,
5 quod dextra pectus pulsat et comam vellit,
non ille amici fata luget aut fratris,
uterque natus vivit et precor vivat,
salva est et uxor sarcinaeque servique,
nihil colonus vilicusque decoxit.
10 Maeroris igitur causa quae? domi cenat.

14

Nil intemptatum Selius, nil linquit inausum,
cenandum quotiens iam videt esse domi.
Currit ad Europen et te, Pauline, tuosque
laudat Achilleos, sed sine fine, pedes.
5 Si nihil Europe fecit, tum Saepta petuntur,

4–5. terram ... tangit: Selius is bowed to the earth by grief. — **indecens,** *ugly.* — **pectus pulsat:** as if at a funeral; cf. Tac. Ann. 1. 23. 1 *incendebat haec fletu et pectus atque os manibus verberans.* — **comam vellit:** a common expression of profound grief; cf. e.g. Ov. Tr. 3. 3. 51 *parce tamen lacerare genas nec scinde capillos.*

6. fata: see on 1. 42. 1.

8. et, *too, even,* implies that the loss of the wife, who is mentioned in close connection with the chattels and the slaves, would not be so serious after all. — **sarcinae:** goods and chattels; *traps* would give the right tone.

9. nihil ... decoxit, *has wasted nothing,* by neglect or wantonness. *decoquere* prop. = 'diminish (reduce) by boiling'. If done unskillfully this process involves waste; hence *decoquere* = 'waste', *se decoquere* = 'become bankrupt'.

10. domi cenat: to Selius the worst possible misfortune; he has not been invited out. Cf. 3. 50. 10;

5. 47. 1; 5. 78. 1–2 *si tristi domicenio laboras, Torani, potes esurire mecum.*

14. Cf. 2. 11, with notes. — Meter: § 48.

1. Nil ... inausum: cf. Hor. A. P. 285; Verg. A. 7. 308.

3–4. Europen: the Porticus Europae, which took its name from some work of art representing the rape of Europe by Jupiter disguised as a bull. It was in the Campus Martius, but its exact location is unknown; see Platner 356; Becker Top. R. 596; Burn Journ. of Phil. 10. 6; Baumeister 1513. — **Pauline:** unknown. For athletic exercises in the Campus Martius see e.g. Hor. C. 1. 8. — **tuos ... pedes:** Selius makes a second Achilles out of this Roman runner. In Homer Achilles is πόδας ὠκύς, ὠκύπους, and a stock type of manly beauty and strength; see Otto s.v. *Achilles.* Cf. 12. 82. 9–10. — **sed:** see on 1. 43. 9.

5. Saepta: the Saepta Iulia, built of marble, to take the place

si quid Phillyrides praestet et Aesonides.
Hinc quoque deceptus Memphitica templa frequentat
adsidet et cathedris, maesta iuvenca, tuis.
Inde petit centum pendentia tecta columnis,
10   illinc Pompei dona nemusque duplex.
Nec Fortunati spernit nec balnea Fausti,

of the primitive Ovile, or voting-place of the centuries. See Platner 327; 364–366. When there was no longer need of a popular voting-place, the Saepta was used first for *ludi* of various kinds. Later it became a fashionable shopping-place; for this purpose it was well adapted, since it consisted of a succession of arcades flanking the Via Lata. Cf. 9. 59.

6. The Porticus Argonautarum lay a little north of the Saepta, 5. It was distinguished by frescoes representing the Argonautic Expedition. — **Phillyrides**: Chiron, the famous Centaur, son of Saturn and the nymph Phillyra. As tutor of Jason he might have a place in the frescoes. — **Aesonides**: Jason, son of Aeson, leader of the Argonauts.

7. **Memphitica templa** = *Aegyptia templa*, the temple of Isis and Serapis in the Campus Martius, west of the Saepta; Platner 339–340. — **frequentat**: he makes one of the throng (see on *frequens*, 5. 13. 3), or, unwilling to give up, repeatedly returns thither.

8. **adsidet,** *pays court to, hangs around*, the women, the especial devotees of Isis and Serapis (see Marq.-Wissowa 3. 78 ff.), who occupied the *cathedrae*. — **cathedris**: cf. 1. 76. 13 N.; 3. 63. 7; Marq. 726. — **maesta iuvenca**: since Isis was frequently represented with a cow's horns, and the cow was symbolic of her, she is naturally confused with the Greek Io, who was

believed to have finally regained her human shape in Egypt; indeed, Io is sometimes spoken of as wedding Osiris, husband of Isis. Cf. 8. 81. 2–4; 10. 48. 1; Ov. A. A. 1. 77 *nec fuge linigerae Memphitica templa iuvencae*. — **maesta,** if said of Isis, refers to her grief over the murder and loss of Osiris; if said of Io, it refers to her persecution by Juno.

9. **centum … columnis**: perhaps the Hecatostylon, which seems to have been a structure connected with the Porticus Pompei; Platner 354. The *porticus* itself was on the east side of the stage of the Theatrum Pompei. Cf. 3. 19. 1–2 *proxima centenis ostenditur ursa columnis, exornant fictae qua platanona ferae*. — **pendentia**: see on Lib. Spect. 1. 5.

10. **Pompei dona**: presumably the Porticus Pompei rather than the Theatrum Pompei. — **nemus … duplex**: evidently a part of the *porticus* or contiguous to it. An inside double row of trees may have extended down the length of the *porticus* or have led up to it; Platner 353. The portico is commonly called *Pompeia umbra*: cf. 11. 47. 3 *cur nec Pompeia lentus spatiatur in umbra*; Ov. A. A. 1. 67; Prop. 4. 8. 75–76.

11–12. **spernit**: these were inferior baths; yet Selius visits them all. — **balnea**: baths managed by private individuals; they did not necessarily differ in kind from the

nec Grylli tenebras Aeoliamque Lupi,
nam thermis iterumque iterumque iterumque lavatur.
Omnia cum fecit, sed renuente deo,
15   lotus ad Europes tepidae buxeta recurrit,
si quis ibi serum carpat amicus iter.
Per te perque tuam, vector lascive, puellam,
ad cenam Selium tu, rogo, taure, voca.

16

Zoilus aegrotat : faciunt hanc stragula febrem ;

great public *thermae*, of which there were at this time three in Rome. — **Grylli tenebras**: cf. 1. 59. 3 *redde Lupi nobis tenebrosaque balnea Grylli*. *Tenebrae* is used elsewhere for a dark, forbidding place; cf. Iuv. 3. 225; Prop. 3. 15. 17. — **Aeoliam . . . Lupi**: humorous; Lupus's baths were draughty, a veritable cave of the winds. But *Aeolia* may have been a popular name of these baths, based on a picture of Aeolus's cave which served as a sign-board (Fried.).

13. See App. — **thermis** = *balnea*, 11 ; local abl., or, perhaps, instr. abl. In the latter case sc. *aquis*.

14. **Omnia . . . fecit**: i.e. has left no stone unturned; cf. Petr. 115 *quae ergo dementia est omnia facere, ne quid de nobis relinquat sepultura?* — **renuente deo**: i.e. in vain; cf. Tib. 1. 5. 19–20 *at mihi felicem vitam, si salva fuisses, fingebam demens, sed renuente deo.*

15. **lotus**: freely, 'from the baths'. — **tepidae**: warmed by the rays of the (winter) sun; cf. 3. 20. 12–14 *an delicatae sole rursus Europae inter tepentes post meridiem buxos sedet?* — **buxeta**: cf. 3. 20. 13, cited on *tepidae* above; Plin. Ep. 5. 6. 16 *ante porticum xystus in*

plurimas species distinctus concisusque buxo.

16. **serum . . . iter**: see on *seram*, 2. 11. 2.

17. **vector lascive**: Jupiter, seen in the fresco as the bull who carried off Europe.

18. **ad cenam . . . voca**: 'invite him to yourself (in the arena) and, tossing him, make an end of him'. M. means that a good way to rid Rome of such a nuisance would be to make a dummy (*pila*) of him and throw that to a bull in the amphitheater. For this sport cf. Lib. Spect. 22. 6 *iactat ut inpositas taurus in astra pilas*; 2. 43. 5. — **rogo**: for the paratactic use cf. e.g. 2. 80. 2.

16. M. repeatedly mentions Zoilus as a parvenu, vile, vulgar, rich, vain. In 5. 79 he makes Zoilus change his dinner-robe eleven times during a single dinner. Cf. 2. 19; 2. 58; 11. 92. The name may be fictitious; § 38. — Meter: § 48.

1. **aegrotat**: ironical; Zoilus's sickness is feigned. — **stragula**, *coverlets* laid upon the mattress (*torus, culcita*), which in turn rested on straps (*fasciae, institae, lora*); cf. *pallia*, 1. 109. 11 N.; 14. 147. 1 *stragula purpureis lucent villosa tapetis*; Beck. 2. 330 ff.

si fuerit sanus, coccina quid facient ?

quid torus a Nilo, quid Sidone tinctus olenti ?

ostendit stultas quid nisi morbus opes ?

5   quid tibi cum medicis ? dimitte Machaonas omnis:

vis fieri sanus ? stragula sume mea.

18

Capto tuam, pudet heu, sed capto, Maxime, cenam,

tu captas aliam : iam sumus ergo pares.

Mane salutatum venio, tu diceris isse

ante salutatum : iam sumus ergo pares.

5   Sum comes ipse tuus tumidique anteambulo regis,

---

2. **sanus**, *well*; cf. 6. 84. 1–2 *octaphoro sanus portatur, Avite, Philippus. Hunc tu si sanum credis, Avite, furis*; Iuv. 6. 235–236 *tunc corpore sano advocat Archigenen* (a physician) *onerosaque pallia iactat.* — **coccina** = the *stragula*; cf. 2. 43. 8. — **quid facient?** = *nil facient*; they would not be seen at all by ordinary visitors to the house.

3. **torus a Nilo**: Damascus in Syria and Antinopolis in Egypt were famous for the manufacture of mattresses and pillows. — **Sidōne** = *purpura, murice* (metonymy). Tyre and Sidon were especially famous for purple dye; cf. 11. 1. 2 (*liber*) *cultus Sidone non cotidiana* (see on 3. 2. 10). So *Tyros* is used in 2. 29. 3; 6. 11. 7. — **olenti**: Tyrian purple emitted a peculiar odor, which was especially pronounced in the case of the finer cloths, because these were repeatedly dipped in the dye; cf. 1. 49. 32 *olidaeque vestes murice*; 4. 4. 6 *bis murice vellus inquinatum.*

5. **Machaonas** = *medicos*; Machaon was a son of Aesculapius.

6. **fieri sanus** involves a play on the two senses of *sanus, well* and

rational. — **stragula . . . mea**: they are so mean that Zoilus would never be tempted to repeat his trick.

18. 'My condition as *cliens* is hard enough; I decline to be *cliens* to a *cliens*'. — Meter: § 48.

1. **Capto . . . cenam**: the client hoped to be invited occasionally to a *cena popularis* (cf. 1. 20; 1. 43). M. humorously classes himself with the legacy-hunters (2. 11; 2. 14) though his game is small. See Marq. 204 ff.; Petr. 3 (*adulatores*) *. . . cenas divitum captant.* — For the meter see § 54, b.

2. **captas aliam**: though a *patronus* to M. and others, Maximus was in turn a *cliens* to others above him; cf. 10. 10; Iuv. 1. 95–111; 3. 126–130. — **ergo**: M. and Iuv. are prone to this use of *ergo*; cf. e.g. Iuv. 3. 104 *non sumus ergo pares.*

3. **Mane salutatum**: see 1. 70. Introd.; 1. 55. 6 *et matutinum portat ineptus "Have"*; 4. 8. 1; Iuv. 5. 19–23; 3. 126–130; Hor. S. 1. 1. 9–10; Knapp A. J. P. 18. 329. — **diceris**: sc. by the *ostiarius*; cf. 2. 5. 5–8.

5. **comes**: it flattered the pride of the patron to have his clients

tu comes alterius : iam sumus ergo pares.
Esse sat est servum, iam nolo vicarius esse :
qui rex est, regem, Maxime, non habeat.

19

Felicem fieri credis me, Zoile, cena ?
felicem cena, Zoile, deinde tua ?
debet Aricino conviva recumbere clivo,
quem tua felicem, Zoile, cena facit.

20

Carmina Paulus emit, recitat sua carmina Paulus,

attend him to the forum, etc.; cf.
9. 22. 10; Iuv. 7. 141–143; 10. 44–
46 *hinc praecedentia longi agminis
officia et niveos ad frena Quirites
defossa in loculos quos sportula fecit
amicos. Comes* may, however, be
used here of the single companion
who walked on the left, or unprotected, side of the great man; cf.
9. 100. 3 (*me iubes*) *haerere tuo lateri, praecedere sellam.*—**tumidi...
regis:** the patron was styled *dominus* and *rex* (perhaps originally in
this sense slang terms of the *sermo
familiaris*); cf. 4. 40. 9 *serum est
'lium mihi quaerere regem*; Iuv.
1. 136 *rex horum vacuis ... toris tantum ipse iacebit.* In comedy *rex* is
used of the patron of the parasites.
— **anteambulo:** for -ŏ see § 54, c.
7. servum repeats the idea of
tumidi ... regis, 5; the *anteambulones* proper were slaves. — **vicarius:** an under-slave controlled or
owned by another slave (*ordina-
rius*); cf. Hor. S. 2. 7. 79–80 *sive
vicarius est qui servo paret, uti mos
vester ait, seu conservus*; Beck. 2.
133 ff.
8. non habeat: this form (instead of *ne habeat*) is not uncommon in Silver Latin, both in prose

and verse. Cf. note on *nec*, Lib.
Spect. 1. 2; L. 1547.
19. See Introd. to 2. 11; 2. 16.
— Meter: § 48.
2. deinde: freely, 'further',
'nay, more'. Strictly, the sense is:
'after holding the view suggested
in 1'.
3–4. debet ... facit: i.e. 'he
ought to turn beggar, for only a
beggar would enjoy your dinner'.
— **Aricino ... clivo:** beggars took
advantage of the fact that vehicles
found it hard to climb the ascent of
the Via Appia near Aricia, sixteen
miles south of Rome; many visitors came to the shrine of Diana at
Lake Nemi, three miles distant.
Cf. 12. 32. 10 *migrare clivum cre-
deres Aricinum*; Iuv. 4. 116–118
*caecus adulator ... dignus Aricinos
qui mendicaret ad axes blandaque
devexae iactaret basia raedae.*—
conviva: pred. nom. — **recumbere:** ironical; the beggar, possibly feigning inability to walk, lies
on the hill, as a guest lies on the
lectus tricliniaris.
20. On Paulus's title to his Carmina. Cf. 1. 29; 12. 47.—Meter: § 48.
1. Carmina ... emit: i.e.
he buys a copy of M.'s Carmina;

nam quod emas possis iure vocare tuum.

29

Rufe, vides illum subsellia prima terentem,
cuius et hinc lucet sardonychata manus
quaeque Tyron totiens epotavere lacernae
et toga non tactas vincere iussa nives,

perhaps M. himself, perhaps his booksellers (see on 1. 2. 7) sold it. See 2. 7. 2 N.; Fried. SG. 3. 460–461. — **sua**: they are legally, if not morally, his; cf. 6. 12. 1–2 *iurat capillos esse quos emit suos Fabulla; numquid, Paule, peierat?* Sen. Ben. 7. 6. 1.

29. The decay of the old families was the opportunity for the freedmen; see Fried. SG. 1. 392 ff. Court favor and immense wealth gave them entrance to the best society. They were only too anxious to hide whatever might recall their former servile condition. If as slaves they had been branded in a conspicuous place, recourse was had to surgical aid to remove these marks (*stigmata*), or, if that failed, 'beauty plasters' (*splenia*, 9) were worn. The parvenu of this epigram was doubtless typical of the *libertinus* of the day, proud, forward, dressed in extremest fashion, and jealous of his rights. — Meter: § 48.

1. It would be possible to print 1–9 as a question. — **subsellia prima**: i.e. the place reserved for the highest class (senators). See 5. 14, with the notes. — **terentem** marks the uneasiness of one claiming privileges that did not belong to him, or else his desire to attract attention by frequent changes of attitude.

2. et hinc: i.e. 'even from where we are sitting'; freely, 'even at this distance'. M., who had the rights of an *eques* (§ 8), was prob. with Rufus in one of the fourteen rows back of the senatorial places in the orchestra, but well across the theater from the parvenu, wherever the latter may have been sitting. — **sardonychata manus:** great extravagance in rings was common; rings set with the sardonyx were at this time much esteemed. *Sardonychatus* seems to have originated in the *sermo plebeius*; see Cooper 320.

3. Tyron: see on 2. 16. 3. — **totiens epotavere:** for *totiens* see on *olenti*, 2. 16. 3. For the hyperbole in *epotavere* cf. Iuv. 10. 176 *credimus . . . epota (esse) . . . flumina Medo prandente.* — **lacernae:** sc. *lucent.* The *lacerna* was often worn over the toga, sometimes in place of it; when of a brilliant hue it relieved the plain white of the toga. The pl. may be *pluralis maiestatis*; perhaps, however, the man wore several *lacernae.* See Beck. 3. 218 ff.

4. toga . . . nives: the toga had to be worn on formal occasions (e.g. in the law courts, at the *salutatio*, in the theater and the circus) and good form required that it be kept white (see on 1. 103. 5); cf. 5. 37. 6; Iuv. 10. 44–45 *hinc praecedentia longi agminis officia et niveos ad frena Quirites.* For the discomfort incident to wearing the toga see on 3. 63. 10; 10. 47. 5. — **non tactas**

5   cuius olet toto pinguis coma Marcelliano
    et splendent volso bracchia trita pilo,
non hesterna sedet lunata lingula planta,
   coccina non laesum pingit aluta pedem,
et numerosa linunt stellantem splenia frontem.
10   Ignoras quid sit? splenia tolle: leges.

30

Mutua viginti sestertia forte rogabam,

... nives: cf. Ov. Pont. 2. 5. 37–38 *tua pectora lacte et non calcata candidiora nive.* See on 5. 37. 6; 12. 82. 7.

5. olet ... Marcelliano: perfume and pomade were much used by the dandy of M.'s time; cf. 6. 55. — **Marcelliano:** sc. *theatro.* The ruins of the Theater of Marcellus stand at the southern end of the Campus Martius, between the Capitoline and the Tiber; see Schneider, Plate IX, 7. Note the synizesis. See App.

6. volso ... pilo: the cause of *splendent* (cf. 2. 36. 2); *pilo* is collective singular. Removal of hair was sometimes effected by extraction (cf. 3. 63. 6; 9. 27. 4), but the use of depilatories was common.

7. non hesterna = *hodierna*, brand-new. — **lunata ... planta:** *planta* prop. = 'foot', then *shoe* (metonymy); cf. Sil. 6. 212 *quadrupedem planta* (= *calcare*) *fodiens.* An ivory crescent was worn on the *calceus patricius* (see on 8); it rested on the ankle and so was called by the Greeks ἐπισφύριον. Since it served as an ornament and to mark the rank of the wearer, we may conclude that it was on the front of the shoe; see Marq. 589 ff. — **lingula,** *shoe-latchet.*

8. coccina ... aluta: M. seems to be thinking of the *calceus*

patricius or *mulleus*, a shoe of red leather, which came up high at the back of the foot; it was provided with little hooks (*malleoli*), under or around which the black *corrigiae* ('laces') were wound. Cf. Marq. 589; Mommsen Staats. 3. 888; Müller Die Tracht. d. R. 35 ff.; Smith D. of A. 1. 334. — **pingit** = *ornat*, adorns, without pinching (*non laesum pedem*). — **aluta:** fine leather, prepared by being treated with alum, and dyed red (with *coccum*, the oak gall of the scarlet oak). See Smith D. of A. s.v. *Coriarius.*

9. numerosa ... frontem: so many are the beauty plasters on his face (he had been often branded; see Introd.) that his face reminds one of the starry firmament; his whole forehead is one daub (*linunt*).—**splenia:** cf. 8. 33. 22 *talia lunata splenia fronte sedent*; 10. 22. 1 *cur spleniato saepe prodeam mento.*

10. quid sit, *what it means,* i.e. why he wears these plasters. — **tolle:** see on 1. 70. 3 *quaeris iter?* — **leges:** sc. *FUR* or *FUG.* (= *fugitivus*).

30. 'Advice is cheap—and unwelcome, when it is an excuse for meanness'. — Meter: § 48.

1. Mutua: pred. acc.; cf. 6. 20. 1 *mutua te centum sestertia, Phoebe,*

quae vel donanti non grave munus erat,
quippe rogabatur felixque vetusque sodalis
et cuius laxas arca flagellat opes.

5   Is mihi "Dives eris, si causas egeris" inquit.
Quod peto da, Gai: non peto consilium.

36

Flectere te nolim, sed nec turbare capillos;
splendida sit nolo, sordida nolo cutis;
nec tibi mitrarum nec sit tibi barba reorum:

rogavi. The word is used especially of loans without interest. —
viginti sestertia = 20,000 *sestertii.*
Distinguish *sestertium* and *sestertius* ; the former is a sum of money
(1000 *sestertii*), the latter a coin;
see on 1. 103. 1; Harper's Latin
Dictionary, s.v. *sestertius*, B, 3, c.

2. vel donanti, *even if he were
presenting it.*

3. quippe = *nam, enim.* — **rogabatur,** etc., *the man to whom I
was appealing was,* etc. See App.

4. arca: see on 1. 76. 5. —**laxas
. . . opes**: the chest is so full that
when one tries to shut down the
cover it 'flogs' the coins; cf. 5. 13. 6;
3. 41. 2 *ex opibus tantis quas gravis
arca premit*; Stat. Silv. 2. 2. 150–
151 *non·tibi sepositas infelix stran-
gulat arca divitias. Laxas* = *roomy,
spreading,* and so *ample*; the vs. =
'whose wealth is so ample that
(the cover of) his strong box fairly
beats it'.

5. si causas egeris: cf. 1. 17.
1–2 *cogit me Titus actitare causas
et dicit mihi saepe "Magna res est"*;
1. 76. 11–12.

6. Gai: dissyllabic; cf. 10. 17. 1;
F. D. Allen Harv. Stud. 2. 75. —
consilium, *advice.*

36. 'True manliness is not so
much a matter of clothes and body

as of soul and spirit'. — Meter:
§ 48.

1. Flectere, *curl,* with *pecten* or
calamistrum; 'I would not have
you be a woman or a dandy'. Cf.
3. 63. 3; Spart. Had. 26 *statura fuit
procerus, forma comptus, flexo ad
pectinem capillo.* — **nolim**: contrast *nolo*, 2; M. becomes more
emphatic as he goes along. — **nec,**
also . . . not. There is a fusion of
nec flectere te nec turbare velim and
(*aut*) *flectere te aut turbare nolim.*
— **turbare capillos**: i.e. in order to
look like a rustic or a man of the
olden time. Cf. Hor. C. 1. 12. 41
incomptis Curium capillis; Ov.
A. A. 2. 169 *me memini iratum dominae turbasse capillos.*

2. splendida: cf. 2. 29. 6. —
nolŏ . . . nolŏ: on the quantity see
§ 54, b. — **sordida**: i.e. neglected.

3. nec . . . nec: see on Lib.
Spect. 1. 2. — **mitrarum**: prop.
'turbans', 'headbands', used by
Orientals, women, effeminate men,
and the emasculated priests of Cybele (*Galli*); here the word denotes
those who wear the *mitra*, persons
who, like the Galli, had naturally
little or no beard, or who, like the
dandies, used depilatories (see on
2. 29. 6) and affected such marks
of effeminacy as the *mitra*. See

nolo virum nimium, Pannyche, nolo parum.

5   Nunc sunt crura pilis et sunt tibi pectora saetis

horrida, sed mens est, Pannyche, volsa tibi.

38

Quid mihi reddat ager quaeris, Line, Nomentanus ?

Hoc mihi reddit ager: te, Line, non video.

41

" Ride si sapis, o puella, ride "

Paelignus, puto, dixerat poeta :

sed non dixerat omnibus puellis.

Verum ut dixerit omnibus puellis,

5   non dixit tibi : tu puella non es,

et tres sunt tibi, Maximina, dentes,

Marq.-Wissowa 3. 368, N. 6. —
barba reorum: during the late
Republic and early Empire men
in mourning or under accusation
allowed the beard to grow; see
Marq. 600.

4. virum nimium: i.e. *horri-
dum* (Domit.). — **parum** (*virum*):
i.e. effeminate.

5. pilis: with *horrida*. — **saetis,** *bristles*; cf. 6. 56. 1 *quod tibi
crura rigent saetis et pectora villis*;
Sil. 5. 441 *et villosa feris horrebant
pectora saetis.*

6. mens est . . . volsa: outward signs of rugged virtue do not
make a man; to be a man one
needs a manly soul. Render, 'your
soul gives no token of manliness'.
For *volsa* see on 2. 29. 6.

38. M. sets forth one advantage of his Nomentanum (§ 10).
In 7. 95 a Linus is mentioned as a
very effusive person. — Meter: § 48.

1. On the spondaic verse see
§ 47, g.

41. 'Maximina, though old
enough to have lost her teeth,
would like to pass for a simper-
ing miss'. Cf. 1. 100. — Meter:
§ 49.

1. Ride . . . ride: possibly from
some lost hendecasyllabic poem of
Ovid, though M. may have had
in mind A. A. 3. 279 ff., or A. A. 3.
512–513. — **si sapis:** i.e. ' if you
wish to win or please a lover'.

2. Paelignus . . . poeta: see
on 1. 61. 6. — **dixerat:** for the tense
see on 1. 107. 3.

3–4. non . . . omnibus puellis:
he spoke only to the beautiful or
to those who still had their teeth.
For similar verses in sequence see
10. 35. In this Paukstadt (25 ff.)
sees the influence of Catullus. See
also on 1. 109. 1. — **ut dixerit:**
concessive, 'granting that', etc.;
see A. 527, a; GL. 608; L. 1963.

6. tres: i.e. only three; cf. 1.
72. 3; 3. 93. 1–2 *cum tibi trecenti
consules, Vetustilla, et tres capilli*

sed plane piceique buxeique.
Quare si speculo mihique credis,
debes non aliter timere risum
10   quam ventum Spanius manumque Priscus,
quam cretata timet Fabulla nimbum,
cerussata timet Sabella solem.
Voltus indue tu magis severos
quam coniunx Priami nurusque maior.
15   Mimos ridiculi Philistionis
et convivia nequiora vita
et quidquid lepida procacitate
laxat perspicuo labella risu.
Te maestae decet adsidere matri

---

quattuorque sint dentes. — **Maxi-mina** suggests *maxima natu*; cf., then, 1. 100, esp. 2. See § 38 for fictitious names in M.

7. sed: as in 1. 43. 9. — **picei ... buxei:** black and yellow respectively.

8. speculo: the mirror was commonly of polished metal, not of glass; see Marq. 689; 758.

10. Spanius: some dandy who fears that the wind may disarrange his hair, carefully combed or curled. Perhaps Spanius was half bald (see on 1. 72. 8). Fried. thinks the name was coined from σπάνιος; see also Crusius Rhein. Mus. 44. 455. — **Priscus** shrinks from the touch of others, lest his toga or *lacerna* be soiled or disarranged; cf. 3. 63. 10.

11. cretata ... Fabulla: cf. 8. 33. 17 *crassior in facie vetulae stat creta Fabullae*; Petr. 23 *inter rugas malarum tantum erat cretae, ut putares detectum parietem nimbo laborare.* Whiteness of skin (*candor*) and blond hair were fashionable at this time. On the means used by women to enhance their

beauty see Marq. 786 ff.; Beck. 3. 163 ff.

12. cerussata ... solem: *cerussa*, because of the white lead it contained, would be changed in color by a bright sun; see 1. 72. 5–6 N.; 7. 25. 2.

14. coniunx Priami: Hecuba, who, acc. to tradition, suffered bitterly in captivity after the fall of Troy. Cf. Ov. M. 13. 542–544 (*Hecuba*) *interdum torvos sustollit ad aethera vultus, nunc positi* ('dead') *spectat vultum, nunc vulnera nati* (Polydorus). — **nurus ... maior:** Andromache, wife of Hector; her vicissitudes after the fall of Troy were sad enough.

15. Mimos ... Philistionis: Philistion, a mime-writer of the Augustan age, seems to have come from Magnesia or Nicaea and to have written in Greek; see Teuffel § 254. 6. For the *mimi* see on 2. 7. 3.

16. vita: imperative.

19. adsidere: used technically of attendance on persons ill or in distress; cf. Hor. S. 1. 1. 80–81 *si ... alius casus lecto te adfixit, habes qui*

20 lugentique virum piumve fratrem,
   et tantum tragicis vacare Musis.
   At tu iudicium secuta nostrum
   plora, si sapis, o puella, plora.

43

Κοινὰ φίλων haec sunt, haec sunt tua, Candide, κοινά,
   quae tu magnilocus nocte dieque sonas :
te Lacedaemonio velat toga lota Galaeso
   vel quam seposito de grege Parma dedit,
5 at me, quae passa est furias et cornua tauri,
   noluerit dici quam pila prima suam.

adsideat, fomenta paret. — **matri** :
like Hecuba.

20. lugenti ... virum, *one who
is mourning*, etc., e.g. Andromache.
— **pium** : because of his *pietas* he
merits the grief felt at his taking off.

21. tantum, *only.* — **tragicis
... Musis** : rather than for the
mimi (15). — **vacare**, *have leisure.*

22. iudicium ... nostrum :
'my advice is for you better than
Ovid's'.

43. On a man whose benevolence began and ended in quoting
proverbs. — Meter : § 48.

1. Κοινὰ φίλων : cf. Eur. Orest.
735 κοινὰ γὰρ τὰ τῶν φίλων; Ter.
Ad. 804; Cic. Off. 1. 16. 51 *in Grae-
corum proverbio est amicorum esse
communia omnia*; Otto s.v. *Amicus.*
For M.'s use of Greek see § 33.—
haec : the conduct mentioned in
3-14. — **haec ... κοινά** is ironical.
haec ... haec ... tua are the emphatic words of the vs.— **Candide** :
cf. 2. 24. 5-6 (*Fortuna*) *dat tibi divitias : ecquid sunt ista deorum ? das
partem ? multum est ? Candide, das
aliquid ?*

2. magnilocus ... sonas : 'in
pompous fashion you unceasingly

refer to your (intended) benevolence'.

**3. Lacedaemonio ... Ga-
laeso** : the river Galaesus flowed
into the Gulf of Tarentum; its waters, in which sheep were washed,
were supposed to contribute to the
fineness of the fleece; cf. 12. 63. 3
(*Corduba*) *albi quae superas oves
Galaesi*; 4. 28. 3 *et lotam tepido
togam Galaeso*; and esp. Hor. C.
2. 6. 10–12; Blümner 122; Beck.
3. 281 ff. Tarentum was said to
have been colonized from Sparta,
by Phalanthus; cf. 5. 37. 2.

4. seposito, *select*, i.e. kept
apart from common stock. —
Parma : wool produced by the
flocks of Parma in Gallia Cisalpina was highly esteemed; cf. 5.
13. 8; 14. 155. 1–2 *velleribus primis Apulia, Parma secundis nobilis ; Altinum tertia laudat ovis.*
See Blümner 99.

5–6. me : sc. *toga velat.* — **quae
... tauri** : hyperbolical; M.'s toga
is as torn as a *pila* (6) tossed by a
bull. For this *pila* see on 2. 14. 18;
Fried. SG. 2. 404. — **prima** : the
animal would be apt to handle this
more roughly than those exposed

Misit Agenoreas Cadmi tibi terra lacernas :
non vendes nummis coccina nostra tribus.
Tu Libycos Indis suspendis dentibus orbes,
10   fulcitur testa fagina mensa mihi.
Inmodici tibi flava tegunt chrysendeta mulli :
concolor in nostra, cammare, lance rubes.
Grex tuus Iliaco poterat certare cinaedo,

to him after he had somewhat
spent his rage.

7. Agenoreas, *Phoenician*
(Tyrian); Agenor was king of
Phoenicia and father of Cadmus.
Cadmus founded Thebes. Cf. 10.
17. 7. — **lacernas**: see on 2. 29. 3.

8. coccina: garments dyed with
coccum; M.'s garments are inferior
both in texture and in dye. See
2. 29. 8.

9. Libycos . . . orbes: round
tables of citrus-wood or maple
(*mensae citreae, mensae acernae*)
were at this time more fashionable
than the old rectangular *mensae*.
The largest and most beautifully
marked (made of the tubers and
roots of the citrus) came from the
Mt. Atlas region of Mauretania.
Cicero gave 500,000 *sestertii* for
one; the price rose as high as
1,400,000 *sestertii*; see Plin. N. H.
13. 92; Fried. SG. 3. 113 ff.; Marq.
306 ff. Cf. Luc. 10. 144–145 *dentibus
hic niveis sectos Atlantide silva im-
posuere orbes.* — **Indis . . . dentibus**: see on *Indico . . . cornu*,
1. 72. 4. — **suspendis**: the slabs
forming such tables rested sometimes on a single column of ivory
(*monopodium*), sometimes on three
or four ivory tusks which served
as legs; cf. 9. 22. 5; 10. 98. 6 (*vis
spectem*) *aut citrum vetus Indi-
cosque dentes?*

10. fulcitur testa: M. has but
one table; contrast the pl. in 9.

This, because of a broken leg, is
propped up by a piece of earthenware. Cf. Ov. M. 8. 661–662 *mensae
sed erat pes tertius impar: testa
parem fecit.* Perhaps, however,
M. means that for him an earthenware vessel served as *monopodium*!

11. Inmodici . . . mulli: the
mullet was a great delicacy, and,
when it grew to more than normal
size (Plin. N. H. 9. 64 *binas . . .
libras ponderis raro admodum ex-
superant*) brought enormous prices
(from 5000 to 8000 *sestertii*); cf.
Beck. 3. 332. The *mulli* served to
Candidus completely cover the
dish. Cf. 10. 31. 1–4; 3. 45. 5; Iuv.
4. 15–16 *mullum sex milibus emit,
aequantem sane paribus sestertia
libris.* — **flava . . . chrysendeta**:
silver plate inlaid with gold or
having gold edges (cf. χρυσένδε-
τος). Cf. 11. 29. 7 *accipe vina,
domum, pueros, chrysendeta, mensas*; 14. 97. The huge red mullets
are served on a white and yellow
dish.

12. concolor: i.e. of like color
with the *lanx*, which was prob.
made of red earthenware. — **cammare**, *crab*, a mean dish; in Iuv.
5. 84–92 the client gets a *cammarus*,
the *dominus* a mullet.

13. Grex: often of a band of
slaves; here of the table attendants; cf. 8. 50. 18. — **Iliaco . . .
cinaedo**: Trojan Ganymedes, who

at mihi succurrit pro Ganymēde manus.

15   Ex opibus tantis veteri fidoque sodali
das nihil et dicis, Candide, κοινὰ φίλων?

57

Hic quem videtis gressibus vagis lentum,
amethystinatus media qui secat Saepta,
quem non lacernis Publius meus vincit,
non ipse Cordus alpha paenulatorum,
5   quem grex togatus sequitur et capillatus
recensque sella linteisque lorisque,

supplanted Hebe as Jupiter's cup-
bearer; cf. 3. 39. 1 *Iliaco similem
puerum . . . ministro.*
   14. mihi . . . manus: 'my own
hand serves as my Ganymedes';
cf. Iuv. 5. 52–60.
   15. sodali: more than *clienti*;
see on 1. 15. 1; cf. 2. 30. 3.
   16. et = *et tamen.*
   57. On a mán who, though he
was really poor, sacrificed everything to make an appearance. He
may be a dinner-hunter (see 2. 11;
2. 14) who, having failed to get an
invitation, must raise the wind at
a pawnshop. — Meter: § 52.
   1. quem . . . lentum, *whom you
see moving slowly about with aim-
less footsteps.*
   2. amethystinatus: his costly
lacerna was of amethyst hue (violet-
blue or purple); cf. 1. 96. 6–7 *qui
coccinatos non putat viros esse ame-
thystinasque mulierum vocat vestes*;
Iuv. 7. 136. See on *Tyrianthina*, 1.
53. 5; Marq. 508. For the adj. itself
see Cooper § 34; cf. *coccinatos*, 1. 96.
6.—**media . . . Saepta:** see on 2. 14.
   5.—**secat** perhaps suggests difficulty or slowness of movement
because of the press. But cf. the
familiar *secare viam*, τέμνειν ὁδόν.

   4. Cordus: cf. 5. 26. 1; 5. 23.
8. He is perhaps the man whom
Juvenal mentions in 1. 2; 3. 208.—
alpha paenulatorum: Cordus was
'A No. 1' among the exquisites
whose specialty was the *paenula*
(see on 1. 103. 5). The Greeks
used the letters of the alphabet
instead of numbers; hence *alpha*
= *primus.*
   5. grex togatus: i.e. the company of clients, attired in togas
(see on 2. 29. 4). *Grex* is frequently
used with a certain tinge of contempt for the clients, as for slaves
and actors; cf. 2. 43. 13 N.; Iuv.
1. 46–47 *cum populum gregibus
comitum premit hic spoliator pupilli.*
See Fried. SG. 1. 379 ff. — **capillatus** (*grex*): young slaves (pages),
whose hair, by fashion's decree,
was allowed to grow long; cf. Petr.
70 *pueri capillati attulerunt unguentum in argentea pelve.*
   6. recens: freshly upholstered
with brand-new curtains (*vela*; cf.
linteis) and straps; by the straps
the litter (*lectica, sella*) hung from
the carrying poles (*asseres*). Sedan
chairs are repeatedly mentioned in
the literature of the Empire; see
Beck. 3. 6 ff.; Marq. 736 ff.

oppigneravit modo modo ad Cladi mensam
vix octo nummis anulum, unde cenaret.

58

Pexatus pulchre rides mea, Zoile, trita.
Sunt haec trita quidem, Zoile, sed mea sunt.

66

Unus de toto peccaverat orbe comarum
anulus, incerta non bene fixus acu.
Hoc facinus Lalage speculo, quo viderat, ulta est,
et cecidit saevis icta Plecusa comis.

7. **oppigneravit**, *pledged, pawned.*

8. **vix . . . nummis**, *for barely eight sestertii,* is surely hyperbolical; M. is seeking to emphasize how meanly the man lives when removed from the public eye.

58. Cf. 2. 16; 2. 19. — Meter: § 48.

1. **Pexatus**: Zoilus wears a *toga pexa*, i.e. a toga with nap carefully combed; M.'s toga is *trita*, 'smooth from long use', 'threadbare'; cf. 2. 44. 1 *emi seu puerum togamve pexam*; Hor. Ep. 1. 1. 95–96 *si forte subucula pexae trita subest tunicae . . . rides.* On the word *pexatus* see Cooper § 34.

2. **quidem**, *yes, I grant you*; *quidem* is often thus used, at all periods, both in prose and verse, to make a concession which is at once offset by a phrase with *sed, tamen,* or *autem.* — **sed mea sunt**: Zoilus did not pay his tailor. — On the pentameter ending see § 48, b.

66. The condition of the slave, hard enough at best, was aggravated when a slave-girl was unfortunate enough to be lady's maid to a high-strung, fastidious beauty. See

Fried. SG. 1. 480; Beck. 2. 173 ff. Cf. Iuv. 6. 487–496; Ov. A. A. 3. 239–242. — Meter: § 48.

1–2. **Unus . . . anulus**: the elaborate styles of hair-dressing fashionable under the Empire are attested by works of art and literary evidence; see e.g. Tert. De Cultu Fem. 2. 7. Lalage's hair was done up in a high ball-shaped mass (*orbis*: cf. Iuv. 6. 496), composed of separate ringlets (*anuli*) kept in place by hair-pins or bodkins (*acus crinales*). — **Unus**, *only one,* which could presumably be replaced quickly. — **peccaverat**: hyperbolical; the curl shares the slave's guilt (*facinus,* 3).

3. **Lalage**: Hor. C. 1. 22. 23 had used this name; cf. λαλαγή, 'prattle', 'babbling'. — **speculo**: of metal (see on 2. 41. 8) and so no mean weapon. — **quo viderat**: in works of art the Roman woman is sometimes represented as holding in her hand a mirror in which she is watching the operations of her hair-dresser. See App. — **viderat**: sc. *facinus.*

4. **saevis . . . comis**: for case see on *templo,* Lib. Spect. 1. 3.

5   Desine iam, Lalage, tristes ornare capillos,
      tangat et insanum nulla puella caput.
    Hoc salamandra notet vel saeva novacula nudet,
      ut digna speculo fiat imago tua.

69

    Invitum cenare foris te, Classice, dicis :
      si non mentiris, Classice, dispeream.
    Ipse quoque ad cenam gaudebat Apicius ire :
      cum cenaret, erat tristior ille, domi.
5   Si tamen invitus vadis, cur, Classice, vadis ?
      "Cogor" ais : verum est ; cogitur et Selius.
    En rogat ad cenam Melior te, Classice, rectam.

Saevis is a transferred epithet; cf. *peccaverat*, 1 N.; *tristes...capillos*, 5. — **Plecusa**: the slave hair-dresser (*ornatrix*); cf. Ov. A. A. 3. 239. With the name cf. *plecto*, πλέκω.

7. **Hoc**: sc. *caput.* — **salamandra notet**: cf. Plin. N. H. 10. 188 *eiusdem* (i.e. the *salamandra*) *sanie . . . quacumque parte corporis humani contacta toti defluunt pili*; Petr. 107 *quae salamandra supercilia tua exussit?* — **notet**, *mark, brand,* and so *disgrace,* by making hideous (i.e. bald); see on 1. 3. 10.

8. **ut . . . tua**: 'that your image may be as savage as the mirror itself'; see 3-4. — **digna**: the final syllable is lengthened by the two consonants at the beginning of the next word; cf. *Romana,* 5. 69. 3. See A. 603, f, N. 1; GL. 703, Rem. 1; L. Müller, De Re Metrica, 390.

69. 'Classicus is another Selius'. Cf. 2. 11. — Meter: § 48.

2. **si non . . . dispeream**: see on 2. 5. 1; cf. Hor. S. 1. 9. 47-48 *dispeream ni summosses omnis*; Catull. 92. 2.

3. **Apicius**: in the early Empire M. Gavius Apicius became prover-

bial for all extravagances relating to the culinary art; cf. e.g. Iuv. 11. 2-3; 4. 22-23; Plin. N. H. 10. 133. Even in the fourth century Aelius Lampridius wrote that Elagabalus *comedit saepius ad imitationem Apicii,* and *cenas vero et Vitellii et Apicii vicit.* Many stories were current of him. See Fried. SG. 3. 18; Sen. Ep. 95. 42; Otto s.v. *Apicius.*

4. **tristior**, *rather dismal.*

6. **Cogor**: by the demands of etiquette or friendship. — **cogitur**: by hunger or meanness; a play on words. Cf. Ter. And. 658 *scio: tu coactus tua voluntate es.*

7. **cenam . . . rectam**: a regular, formal dinner; cf. 7. 20. 2 (*Santra*) *rectam vocatus cum cucurrit ad cenam*; 8. 49. 10 *promissa est nobis sportula, recta data est*; Suet. Dom. 7 *sportulas publicas sustulit, revocata rectarum cenarum consuetudine*; Beck. 2. 204. — **Melior**: Atedius Melior, a friend of M. and Statius, apparently famous for elegance of life and as a litterateur; cf. § 20; Stat. Silv. 2. 3; and the dedication of Book II.

Grandia verba ubi sunt ? si vir es, ecce, nega.

71

Candidius nihil est te, Caeciliane.　Notavi :
　si quando ex nostris disticha pauca lego,
protinus aut Marsi recitas aut scripta Catulli.
　Hoc mihi das, tanquam deteriora legas,
5　ut conlata magis placeant mea ?　Credimus istud :
　malo tamen recites, Caeciliane, tua.

77

Cosconi, qui longa putas epigrammata nostra,
　utilis unguendis axibus esse potes.
Hac tu credideris longum ratione colosson
　et puerum Bruti dixeris esse brevem.

8. **si vir es**: cf Ov. F. 6. 594 *si vir es, i, dictas exige dotis opes!* Hor. Epod. 1 5. 12 *si quid in Flacco viri est.* — **nega**: cf. Iuv. 14. 134 *invitatus ad haec aliquis de ponte* (i.e. a beggar) *negabit*.

71. On one who, though he praised M., was really jealous of the poet. — Meter: § 48.

1. **Candidius**, *more sincere, fairer*; ironical. Contrast *niger*, 'spiteful'. — **nihil**: see on 1. 10. 3. — **Notavi**: sc. *candorem tuum*, out of *candidius . . . te.* For *notare = animadvertere* cf. 5. 49. 7; Petr., very often, e.g. 29 *notavi etiam in porticu gregem cursorum.* It is possible also to put a comma after *notavi*, and then to regard 1–3 as paratactic, for *notavi, si . . . lego, protinus aut Marsi te recitare aut scripta Catulli.*

2. **lego**: evidently not at a formal *recitatio*, but at a dinner or the like.

3. **Marsi**: Domitius Marsus, a famous poet of the Augustan age.

In the Praefatio to Book I M. mentions together Marsus and Catullus. Cf. 2. 77. 5; 7. 99. 7.

4. **Hoc . . . das**, *are you in acting thus doing me a favor?* — **tanquam . . . legas** is subordinate to the *ut*-clause in 5.

5. **Credimus istud**: ironical.

6. 'If you h6nestly wish me to shine by contrast, read your own distichs'.

77. 'A foot-rule is not a proper measure for literary productions'. Cf. 6. 65. — Meter: § 48.

1. **Cosconi**: a Cosconius is ironically praised in 3. 69.

2. **utilis . . . potes**: i.e. 'you are a failure as a critic of literature; your proper sphere is menial work in a stable'. The expression has a proverbial ring; cf. Otto s.v. *Axis*.

3. **ratione**, *theory, principle, canon*. — **colosson**: see 1. 70. 7–8 N.

4. **puerum Bruti**: a statue of a boy by Strongylion, greatly admired by Brutus the Tyrannicide; cf. 9. 50. 5; 14. 171; Plin. N. H. 34. 82

5 Disce quod ignoras : Marsi doctique Pedonis
     saepe duplex unum pagina tractat opus.
   Non sunt longa quibus nihil est quod demere possis,
     sed tu, Cosconi, disticha longa facis.

80

Hostem cum fugeret, se Fannius ipse peremit :
   hic, rogo, non furor est, ne moriare, mori ?

88

Nil recitas et vis, Mamerce, poeta videri.
   Quidquid vis esto, dummodo nil recites.

90

Quintiliane, vagae moderator summe iuventae,

*idem (Strongylion) fecit puerum
quem amando Brutus Philippiensis
cognomine suo inlustravit.*

5. Marsi: see on 2. 71. 3.—
docti . . . Pedonis: C. Pedo Albinovanus, a poet of the Augustan
age, intimate friend of Ovid, complimented by Seneca as a conversationalist; mentioned by Quint.
10. 1. 90. For *docti* see on 1. 25. 2.
   6. duplex . . . pagina = *duae
paginae* of prose. — **opus:** prop.
'creation', here *epigram*.
   7. longa suggests both *long* and
tedious. Cf. Plin. Ep. 5. 6. 42–43
*primum ego officium scriptoris existimo ut titulum suum legat atque
identidem interroget se quid coeperit scribere sciatque, si materiae
immoratur, non esse longum, longissimum, si aliquid arcessit atque
attrahit. Vides quot versibus Homerus, quot Vergilius arma, hic
Aeneae, Achillis ille, describat:
brevis tamen uterque est, quia facit
quod instituit.*

8. tu . . . facis: i.e. 'compared
with the two *pages* of Marsus and
Pedo your two *verses* are tedious'.
   80. Meter: § 48.
   2. rogo: as in 2. 14. 18.—**furor:**
cf. 1. 20. 1; Sen. Ep. 24. 23 *his adicias
et illud licet, tantam hominum inprudentiam esse, immo dementiam,
ut quidam timore mortis cogantur
ad mortem.*
   88. Meter: § 48.
   1. et, *and yet,* i.e. without running the gauntlet of public criticism.
   2. 'The public will put up with
any claim on your part, provided
you do not inflict yourself upon
it'.
   90. A reply to a rebuke by
Quintilian; Quintilian had said,
'Why waste your time on verses?'
— Meter: § 48.
   1. Quintiliane: M. Fabius
Quintilianus, the most famous rhetorician of his time (about 35–97),
author of the Institutio Oratoria.

gloria Romanae, Quintiliane, togae,
vivere quod propero pauper nec inutilis annis,
da veniam : properat vivere nemo satis.
5   Differat hoc patrios optat qui vincere census
atriaque inmodicis artat imaginibus.
Me focus et nigros non indignantia fumos
tecta iuvant et fons vivus et herba rudis.

His birthplace, Calagurris, in Hispania Tarraconensis, was not far from Bilbilis; he was doubtless intimate enough with M. to justify him in rebuking the poet for idleness or fast living. — **vagae . . . iuventae:** the rising generation, which distinguished itself by excess in living as well as by a false literary style. *Vagus* here = *unstable*; in 4. 14. 7 it is used of the freedom of the Saturnalia. — **moderator summe:** for over twenty years Quintilian waged vigorous combat with the tendency of his age to false and meretricious style, esp. with Seneca; cf. Quint. 10. 1. 125 ff. *Summe* may allude to the illustrious character of Quintilian's clientage; Pliny the Younger and children of the imperial house were among his pupils, perhaps also Tacitus.

2. gloria . . . togae: either 'first among civilians' or 'glory of the Roman bar'. Quintilian practiced as a lawyer, though he was better known as a teacher. *Togati* often = *advocati* (see on 2. 29. 4). Cf. Aus. Commemoratio Professorum 1. 2 *alter rhetoricae Quintiliane togae.*

3–4. vivere . . . vivere: cf. 1. 15. 4, 11 N.; 1. 103. 12. — **pauper . . . annis:** 'though poor (and so having reason to work) and not yet disabled by years (and so with power to work if I would)'.

5. hoc: enjoyment, *vita*, as understood by M. — **census,** *property*; prop. 'ratings'.

6. atria . . . imaginibus: cf. 5. 20. 5–7. The atrium had become a show-place, crowded frequently not with the wax *imagines* of real ancestors, for rich men when *libertini* had no *maiores*, but with counterfeit presentments of almost anybody whose image the owner of a fine house chose to set up. See Beck. 1. 37. — **artat,** *crowds, crams*; prop. 'narrows', 'contracts'; the crowding of many objects into a given space seems to contract that space.

7. Me: 'I, whose wants are simple, can afford to enjoy life'. Cf. 10. 47 throughout. — **focus:** a real hearth in the old-fashioned atrium of M.'s house; this is clear from the allusion to the smoke; because of the fine marbles and paneled ceilings fires on a true hearth were unknown in the atria of the rich.

8. fons vivus: a spring of natural water, as distinct from water brought into a house by pipes. M. is perhaps thinking of his Nomentanum (§ 10) with its plain house and natural charms, though elsewhere (9. 18) he declares that this estate was none too well supplied with water. — **rudis :** *uncultivated, natural;* cf. Iuv. 3. 18–20.

Sit mihi verna satur, sit non doctissima coniunx,
10   sit nox cum somno, sit sine lite dies.

9. **verna satur:** 'all I ask is a single house-born slave, who, because he is well fed, is not likely to run away'; cf. 3. 58. 22, 43–44; Paulus Nolanus C. 4. 15 *verna satur . . . morigera coniunx.* — **non doctissima coniunx:** if M. is to have a wife at all, she is not to be a high-strung, fashionable dame, nor is she to be a blue-stocking; cf. 11. 19. 1 *quaeris cur nolim te ducere, Galla? Diserta es*; Iuv. 6. 434–456; Fried. SG. 1. 492 ff.

10. 'I want a life of peace, by day and night'. M. evidently liked to sleep; cf. 9. 68. 9–10; 10. 47. 9–11. — **sine lite dies:** cf. 5. 20. 6;

10. 47. 5. — Note carefully the metrical treatment of *sit* in these two verses. When a word is repeated in the same verse or in adjacent verses in the same or in similar forms the Roman poets incline to vary the metrical treatment (cf. § 54, b), unless some special purpose (rhetorical or logical emphasis, assonance, or the like) is to be won by repeating the word with the same metrical treatment. Here we have variation in 9, identity in 10; proper emphasis is thus given to *sit*, the important word of the prayer ('let me have', etc.).

LIBER III

2

Cuius vis fieri, libelle, munus?
festina tibi vindicem parare,
ne nigram cito raptus in culinam
cordylas madida tegas papyro
5 vel turis piperisve sis cucullus.
Faustini fugis in sinum? sapisti.
Cedro nunc licet ambules perunctus

2. For the author's address to his book cf. e.g. 1. 3, with notes; 2. 1; Ov. Tr. 1. 1; Stat. Silv. 4. 4. — Meter: § 49.

1. Cuius ... munus = *cui vis, libelle, donari?* Cf. Catull. 1. 1 *cui dono lepidum novum libellum?* — **munus**, *gift*, but with the further suggestion that reception of the book would impose an obligation to defend it from criticism.

2. vindicem = *patronum, defensorem*; cf. 1. 53. 11.

3–5. ne ... cucullus: 'unless you have some patron to sound your praises you will soon become waste paper for cooks and grocers'. — **nigram**: *sooty, grimy.*— **cordylas**, *tunny-fries,* which were salted and smoked. After the *cordyla* was a year old, it was known as a *thynnus.* — **madida ... papyro** involves juxtaposition of effect and cause, 'wrap till your leaves are all wet'. For this use of scrolls cf. 4. 86. 8–10; 3. 50. 9–10; 13. 1. 1–3; Hor. Ep. 2. 1. 269–270; Pers. 1. 42–43 *cedro digna ... nec scombros metuentia carmina nec tus.*— **papyro**:

parchment had not yet come into general use for books. — **cucullus**: here a conical bag or screw, of paper, resembling more or less the pointed cowl or hood (see on 1. 53. 4–5); such screws grocers extemporized out of wrapping-paper before ready-made bags came into use.

6. Faustini: cf. 1. 25. M. mentions him often, and sent to him Book IV (see 4. 10). He was apparently rich; his villas are mentioned in 3. 58; 4. 57. The poet may intend some of these presentation copies as a polite hint to his friends to remember him substantially.— **in sinum**: i.e. for protection, as if Faustinus were a second Maecenas; cf. 1. 15. 10 N.; 3. 5. 7–8 *est illi coniunx quae te manibus sinuque excipiet.*— **sapisti**: cf. 1. 117. 18 N.; 9. 10. 1–2.

7–11. For the papyrus roll see on 1. 53. 11; 1. 66. 10–11.

7. Cedro ... perunctus: cf. 5. 6. 14–15; 14. 37, with notes; Pers. 1. 42, cited on 4 (the scholiast there says: *mos apud veteres erat ut*

77

et frontis gemino decens honore
pictis luxurieris umbilicis,
10   et te purpura delicata velet,
et cocco rubeat superbus index.
Illo vindice nec Probum timeto.

4

Romam vade, liber : si, veneris unde, requiret,
Aemiliae dices de regione viae.
Si quibus in terris, qua simus in urbe, rogabit,
Corneli referas me licet esse Foro.
5   Cur absim, quaeret, breviter tu multa fatere :
"Non poterat vanae taedia ferre togae".

---

chartae, in quibus nobilia carmina scribebantur, oleo cedrino inungerentur, quod et diu durabiles faceret et a tineis conservaret); Ov. Tr. 3. 1. 13; Hor. A. P. 331–332 *speramus carmina fingi posse linenda cedro et levi servanda cupresso?* — **ambules:** the book is now a traveler; in 1. 3. 11 it was a bird.

8. frontis ... honore: cf. Ov. Tr. 1. 1. 11 *nec fragili geminae poliantur pumice frontes*; 1. 66. 10–11 N. *Frontis* is gen. sing.; the thought might be more simply expressed by *frontibus* (*duobus*) *decens* or *ornatus*.

10. purpura: the color of the parchment cover of the book.

11. cocco ... index: cf. 1. 53. 11 N.; Ov. Tr. 1. 1. 7 *nec titulus minio nec cedro charta notetur*; Catull. 22. 7; Tib. 3. 1. 9.

12. nec Probum = *ne Probum quidem*; see on 1. 109. 20. M. Valerius Probus of Berytus was the most distinguished critic of his time; see Rhein. Mus. 26. 488; 27. 63. Contrary to the usual custom of the grammarians he does not seem to have been a teacher. M.'s

language implies that Probus was still alive.

4. For the general theme, the meager returns of a literary life, cf. 1. 76; 5. 56. For M.'s sojourn at Forum Corneli see § 12. — Meter: § 48.

1. Romam vade: cf. Ov. Tr. 1. 1. 15–19 *vade, liber, verbisque meis loca grata saluta . . . si quis qui quid agam forte requirat erit, vivere me dices.* — **requiret:** sc. *Roma* as subject.

2. Aemiliae . . . viae: i.e. the region traversed by the Via Aemilia. This road ran from Ariminum on the Adriatic via Placentia, Bononia, and Forum Corneli (modern Imola). It was a continuation of the Via Flaminia.

4. referas, *reply.* — **Foro:** abl.; *Corneli . . . Foro* is clearer than *Corneli Fori* (loc.) would have been.

5. quaeret: see on 1. 70. 3; 1. 79. 2; cf. 3. 46. 5.

6. vanae: because it brings no substantial returns. — **taedia ... togae:** the nuisance of the daily *salutatio*; cf. note on 2. 29. 4.

"Quando venit?" dicet: tu respondeto: "Poeta
exierat: veniet, cum citharoedus erit".

7

Centum miselli iam valete quadrantes,
anteambulonis congiarium lassi,
quos dividebat balneator elixus.

8. **citharoedus** (κιθαρῳδός): a
player on the cithara or lyre, who
added a vocal accompaniment.
Popular musicians made vast fortunes. Cf. M.'s advice about a
boy's education, 5. 56; Iuv. 7. 175–
177; Fried. SG. 3. 354; 3. 359 ff.

7. M. complains because a 'dinner' is now given in place of the
money *sportula*. Under the Empire the patron was expected to
repay his clients by a dole of food
or of money known as a *sportula*.
In theory the *sportula* was a basket of victuals given in lieu of the
old-fashioned invitation to a *cena
recta* (2. 69. 7); when clients became numerous such a *cena* was
seldom given. The money dole
was 100 *quadrantes* = 25 *asses* =
6¼ *sestertii*. Under Domitian, however, the *cena recta* was again in
fashion; see Suet. Dom. 7. Meanness and false economy, however,
characterized the new order of
things, to judge from the cheap
menu and the poor service that
marked such *cenae rectae*; cf 1. 20.
1; 3. 60. 1. A daily *cena* would not
enable the client to shift for himself as the dole in hard cash did
(see 3. 14; 3. 30. 1–4 *sportula nulla
datur; gratis conviva recumbis: dic
mihi, quid Romae, Gargiliane, facis?
unde tibi togula est et fuscae pensio
cellae? unde datur quadrans? unde
vir es Chiones?*). In a word, many
of the clients could not live without the 100 *quadrantes*. The new

arrangement did not last long, for
there is no reference to it beyond
this book; in Book IV the money
dole is mentioned. — Meter: § 52.

1. **Centum...quadrantes**: cf.
6. 88. 3–4; Iuv. 1. 120–121 *densissima centum quadrantes lectica
petit*.

2. **anteambulonis . . . lassi**:
see on 2. 18. 5; 10. 74. 3. — **congiarium**: prop. a gift of the measure
of a *congius* (see on *quincunces . . .
peractos*, 1. 27. 2); here = *praemium, merces*. The word is really
an adj.; sc. *donum.* — **lassi**: i.e.
tired out by forcing a passage for
the *lectica* or *sella* of his patron.
The clients attended their patron
from early morning till he reached
his home or the bath after business hours. Cf. 3. 36. 3–6 *horridus
ut primo semper te mane salutem
per mediumque trahat me tua
sella lutum, lassus ut in thermas
decuma vel serius hora te sequar
Agrippae*; 10. 70. 13–14; Iuv. 1.
132–134.

3. **quos . . . elixus**: a difficult
passage; *balneator* is variously interpreted. There was no uniform
practice concerning the time and
place of paying the *sportula*. Here,
we may suppose, the distribution
was made at some bathing establishment. It must have been in
many cases convenient for the patron to pay off his clients before
he bathed, that he might bathe at
leisure and be rid of them for the

Quid cogitatis, o fames amicorum ?
5   regis superbi sportulae recesserunt.
"Nihil stropharum est : iam salarium dandum est ".

12

Unguentum, fateor, bonum dedisti
convivis here, sed nihil scidisti.
Res salsa est bene olere et esurire :
qui non cenat et unguitur, Fabulle,
5   hic vere mihi mortuus videtur.

day. The *balneator* is one of the slaves of the patron who came to the *thermae* to serve him in the bath and to act as *dispensator* (Fried.). — elixus, *parboiled*, in the heated *thermae*. The word suggests also the discomfort of the clients, and so reënforces *miselli*, 1, *lassi*, 2.

4. Quid cogitatis: addressed to the clients at the bath. — **fames amicorum** = *famelici amici* (Fried.); cf. 3. 14. 1.

5. regis: see on 2. 18. 5.

6. Nihil ... est: the answer to 4; 'we can see through that', 'no slippery trick here'; a figure borrowed from the *palaestra*, where the wrestlers smeared their naked bodies with oil. Cf. στροφή, a twist, a sudden turn by a wrestler to deceive his antagonist, generally used in the plural. — **salarium ... est**: the point lies in the humorous suggestion of what was altogether beyond expectation of realization. — **salarium**, *pension, fixed annual salary*.

12. 'Dinner-guests, who are richly anointed but get nothing to eat, are like dead folk'. The host here seems to have been ambitious to distinguish himself, but in a wrong way, as if a modern host

were to lavish money on flowers, but set a mean table. See 1. 20. Introd. — Meter: § 49.

1. Unguentum: perfumes and flowers belonged to the *comissatio*; see Beck. 3. 451. Cf. 10. 20. 18–20; Hor. C. 2. 11. 13–17; Iuv. 11. 120 ff. — **fateor**: this verb is often used paratactically in M.; cf. e.g. 5. 13. 1.

2. nihil scidisti: cf. 1. 43. 11. — **scidisti** = *carpsisti*; *scissor* = 'carver', as e.g. in Petr. 36. We have here a hyperbole, or, as some old editors think, the *pièce de résistance* of the dinner was a mere show-piece.

3. Res salsa, *droll business*; cf. Catull. 12. 4–5 (to one who stole the *mappae* of fellow-guests) *hoc salsum esse putas? fugit te, inepte! quamvis sordida res ei invenusta est.*

4. Fabulle: cf. 11. 35.

5. mortuus videtur: on the extravagant use of perfumes at funerals see Fried. SG. 3. 127; cf. Iuv. 4. 108–109 *et matutino sudans Crispinus amomo quantum vix redolent duo funera.* The poet may further hint that Fabullus's feast might make a decent *silicernium* or *epulum funebre* but not a dinner for living men. Indeed Iuv. 5. 85

14

Romam petebat esuritor Tuccius
   profectus ex Hispania ;
occurrit illi sportularum fabula :
   a ponte rediit Mulvio.

15

Plus credit nemo tota quam Cordus in urbe.
"Cum sit tam pauper, quomodo ?" Caecus amat.

18

Perfrixisse tuas questa est praefatio fauces :
  cum te excusaris, Maxime, quid recitas ?

so characterizes such a dinner: *po-nitur exigua feralis cena patella.*

14. Cf. 3. 7, with notes. Spain contributed its share to the steady movement of provincials into Rome; see § 1.— Meter: §§ 50–51.

1–2. Romam . . . Hispania: both emphatic by position. — **esu-ritor:** from the *sermo plebeius*; see Cooper § 17.

4. ponte . . . Mulvio: several miles north of Rome; by it the Via Flaminia, the great northern road from Rome to Ariminum, crossed the Tiber; cf. Cic. Cat. 3. 2. 5–6. See also on 3. 4. 4.

15. A jibe at Cordus's credulity. — Meter: § 48.

1. credit: M. plays on various meanings of *credere*: 'give credit', 'trust in a financial way', 'confide (trust) in one'. — **Cordus:** perhaps the Cordus of 2. 57.

2. quomodo: sc. *plus credit . . . urbe* (cf. 1). We may also supply *dicis* (sc. *istud*), a colloquial usage seen e.g. in Roman comedy, as in

colloquial Greek and familiar English. — **Caecus amat,** *he's blindly in love, he loves with his eyes shut,* for the charms in which Cordus believes are imaginary. Cf. 8. 51. 1–2 *formosam sane, sed caecus diligit Asper ; plus ergo, ut res est, quam videt Asper amat*; Hor. S. 1. 3. 38–40 *amatorem . . . amicae turpia decipiunt caecum vitia aut etiam ipsa haec delectant.*

18. A jeer at the excuses of a *recitator.* Cf. 4. 41 ; 6. 41.— Meter: § 48.

1. Perfrixisse . . . fauces : the *recitatio* made a great demand upon the throat; see Pers. 1. 13–18; Fried. SG. 3. 421. — **praefatio:** M. hints that Maximus was lying to win the indulgence of the audience. Cf. Tac. D. 20 *quis nunc feret oratorem de infirmitate valetudinis suae praefantem ? qualia sunt omnia fere principia Corvini.*

2. cum te excusaris: a pun ; *excusare* = (1) 'plead a thing as an excuse' (cf. 1. 70. 17), (2) 'excuse a person from a task'.

22

Dederas, Apici, bis trecenties ventri,
sed adhuc supererat centies tibi laxum.
Hoc tu gravatus, ut famem et sitim ferres,
summa venenum potione perduxti.
5 Nihil est, Apici, tibi gulosius factum.

25

Si temperari balneum cupis fervens,
Faustine, quod vix Iulianus intraret,
roga lavetur rhetorem Sabineium :
Neronianas hic refrigerat thermas.

---

22. High living run mad. On Apicius see on 2. 69. 3; cf. Sen. Cons. Helv. 10. 8 (*Apicius*) *qui in ea urbe ex qua aliquando philosophi velut corruptores iuventutis abire iussi sunt scientiam popinae professus disciplina sua saeculum infecit.* — Meter: § 52.

1. **bis trecenties** = *sescenties centena milia sestertium*, 60,000,000 *sestertii*; see on 1. 103. 1. M. is prob. speaking in round numbers; see on 1. 43. 1.

2. **centies . . . laxum**: a full 10,000,000 *sestertii*; cf. *laxas . . . opes*, 2. 30. 4 N.

3. **Hoc**: i.e. the sum left to you; ablative. — **famem et sitim**: anything less than downright profusion was to Apicius only another name for slow starvation. — **ferres** = *auferres, get rid of*, by rendering impossible; see on *pone*, 1. 4. 2. But the rendering 'bear', 'endure', gives still better point. If *ferre* is read (see App.), *hoc* is acc.; render 'loath to endure this as but (*ut*) starvation and thirst'; *gravari* with inf. occurs in Cicero and Caesar.

4. **summa** = *ultima, suprema*

(see on 1. 109. 17), as well as *greatest*; this *potio* was his greatest distinction. — **perduxti** = *epotasti, quaffed.* See App.

5. **gulosius**, *more gluttonous*; cf. 7. 20. 1 *nihil est miserius neque gulosius Santra.* See on 1. 20. 3.

25. On Sabineius, most frigid of speakers. See on 2. 7. 1. — Meter: § 52.

1-2. **temperari** almost = *refrigerari*; cf. 10. 48. 3. — **Faustine**: cf. 1. 25. — **quod . . . intraret**, (*even so hot*) *that Julianus would*, etc.

3. **lavetur** has middle force, = *se lavet*, though slaves in fact rendered the bather much assistance. *Rogare* with simple subjv. is common in M.; see Soed. 11. See also on 2. 14. 18.

4. **Neronianas . . . thermas**: for these baths see 10. 48. 4; 7. 34. 4–5 *quid Nerone peius ? quid thermis melius Neronianis ?* — **refrigerat** is of course hyperbolic. For recitations at the baths see e.g. 3. 44. 13 N.; Hor. S. 1. 4. 74–76; Lanciani Anc. R. 90.

35. On a splendid piece of metal work. — Meter: § 49.

35

Artis Phidiacae toreuma clarum
pisces aspicis : adde aquam, natabunt.

38

Quae te causa trahit vel quae fiducia Romam,
    Sexte ? quid aut speras aut petis inde ? refer.
" Causas " inquis " agam Cicerone disertior ipso
    atque erit in triplici par mihi nemo foro ".
5 Egit Atestinus causas et Civis — utrumque
    noras — , sed neutri pensio tota fuit.

1. **Phidiacae**: see on *tóreuma*, below.—**toreuma** (τόρευμα): work in relief, *opus caelatum, opus asperum*, in contrast to *argentum purum* or *argentum lēve*; see Beck. 2. 373 ff.; Smith D. of A. s.v. *Caelatura*. Cf. 4. 39. 4 N.; 8. 6. 15; Plin. N. H. 34. 54 (*Phidias*) *primus artem toreuticen aperuisse atque demonstrasse merito iudicatur*. Phidias was the great Athenian artist of the age of Pericles. An example of his skill was the chryselephantine statue of Athena in the Parthenon. See on 4. 39. 4. We need not suppose that M. really believed that this piece was actually from the hand of Phidias; the Romans liked to brag about the antiquity of their plate, etc.: cf. e.g. 8. 6; Hor. S. 1. 3. 90–91 *catillum Euandri manibus tritum*. Render 'fish wrought by Phidias's skillful hands', or 'fish wrought by hands skillful as Phidias's own '.

2. **adde . . . natabunt**: the fish are highly lifelike; cf. 3. 40. 1–2 *inserta phialae Mentoris manu ducta lacerta vivit et timetur argentum*; 8. 50. 1–2, 9–10. For the form of the sentence see on 1. 70. 3; 1. 79. 2.

38. 'Rome is no place for a good man'. Cf. Iuv. 7, esp. 1–12, 53–70, 105–123; 3. 21–57, 74–125. — Meter: § 48.

1–2. **Quae . . . inde**: Sextus lacks the good sense of Tuccius (3. 14). Cf. 4. 5. 1–2 *vir bonus et pauper linguaque et pectore vērus, quid tibi vis, urbem qui, Fabiane, petis ? —* **refer** = (*mihi*) *responde*.

3–4. **Causas . . . foro**: cf. 1. 76, esp. 12, N. — **triplici . . . foro**: the Forum Romanum, the Forum Caesaris, east of the Capitoline, built by Julius Caesar, and the Forum Augusti, still further east. These three *fora* are often referred to together; cf. e.g. 7. 65. 1–2; Stat. Silv. 4. 9. 15; Sen. Ira 2. 9. 4; Ov. Tr. 3. 12. 24. The Forum Transitorium (see on 1. 2. 8) was not finished till ten years after this epigram was published. In prose we should have *tribus foris* (cf. note on *duplex . . . pagina*, 2. 77. 6).

5–6. **Atestinus . . . Civis**: unknown to us. — **neutri . . . fuit**: they could not make ends meet, much less get rich.— **pensio**, *house rent*; cf. 3. 30. 3 *fuscae pensio cellae*; 7. 92. 5. — **fuit** seems to imply that

"Si nihil hinc veniet, pangentur carmina nobis :
    audieris, dices esse Maronis opus ".

Insanis : omnes gelidis quicumque lacernis

10   sunt ibi Nasones Vergiliosque vides.

"Atria magna colam ".   Vix tres aut quattuor ista
    res aluit, pallet cetera turba fame.

"Quid faciam ? suade : nam certum est vivere Romae".
    Si bonus es, casu vivere, Sexte, potes.

43

Mentiris iuvenem tinctis, Laetine, capillis,
    tam subito corvus, qui modo cycnus eras.

they had by this time found some-thing more remunerative or had left Rome. On the practice of law at Rome at this time see 1. 76. Introd.; 1. 98. 2 N.; Iuv. 7. 112–121, 141–145.

7–8. pangentur . . . nobis: 'I'll try my luck as poet'; *pangere* = *componere*. — **audieris:** cf. 3. 4. 5 N. — **Maronis:** cf. *Marone*, 1. 61. 2 N. In 10 as in 1. 61. 6 Ovid is mentioned by his cognomen.

9–10. gelidis: i.e. thin and threadbare; cf. 6. 50. 2 (*Telesinus*) *errabat gelida sordidus in togula*; 7. 92. 7. — **ibi:** i.e. at Rome; M. was writing in Cisalpine Gaul. See 3. 4. 1 N.

11–12. Atria . . . colam: 'I'll become a client to a millionaire'. The *salutatio* was held in the atrium; cf. 5. 20. 5; 9. 100. 1–2; Iuv. 7. 91–92 *tu nobilium magna atria curas?* — **colam:** cf. 10. 96. 13; 12. 68. 1–2 *matutine cliens, urbis mihi causa relictae, atria, si sapias, ambitiosa colas.* — **res:** i.e. toadying to the rich. — **pallet . . . fame:** cf. 1. 59. 1–2 *dat Baiana mihi quadrantes sportula centum. Inter delicias quid facit ista fames?*

13. certum est (*mihi*), *I'm resolved.*

14. Si bonus es: i.e. 'if you are an all-round scoundrel, you may live well at Rome', but, as Rader quaintly remarks, "*si vir bonus es, fortean te venti pascent Romae*". — **casu,** *by chance, by your wits,* or (with regard to the other, more common meaning of the word) *miserably, from hand to mouth.* The point lies in the abrupt change of thought, the apodosis failing to show how a good man could do anything at Rome.

43. On an aged dandy.—Meter: § 48.

1. Mentiris = *callide simulas;* cf. 6. 57. 1; Tib. 1. 8. 42–44 *Heu sero revocatur . . . iuventa cum vetus infecit cana senecta caput. Tum studium formae est: coma tum mutatur, ut annos dissimulet viridi cortice tincta nucis.* — **iuvenem:** one in the prime of manhood. — **tinctis,** *dyed.*

2. corvus . . . cycnus: apparently proverbial; cf. 1. 53. 7–8.

3. Non omnes: 'you may deceive your fellow-citizens, but death is none the less to be reckoned

Non omnes fallis ; scit te Proserpina canum :
personam capiti detrahet illa tuo.

44

Occurrit tibi nemo quod libenter,
quod, quacumque venis, fuga est et ingens
circa te, Ligurine, solitudo,
quid sit scire cupis ?   Nimis poeta es.
5   Hoc valde vitium periculosum est.
Non tigris catulis citata raptis,
non dipsas medio perusta sole,
nec sic scorpios improbus timetur,
nam tantos, rogo, quis ferat labores ?
10   Et stanti legis et legis sedenti.
12   In thermas fugio : sonas ad aurem.

with '.—**Proserpina**: as the priest clipped the forelock of the victim as a preliminary sacrifice, so Proserpina was supposed to cut a lock from the head of the dying man or woman (Verg. A. 4. 698), who was thought of as a *victima Orci* (Hor. C. 2. 3. 24).

4. personam: prop. 'a player's mask'; here used figuratively, *pretense*; cf. Lucr. 3. 58 *eripitur persona, manet res* ('reality').

44. The literary bore was much in evidence in Rome (Iuv. 1. 17). M. here shows how the itch for writing may make a nuisance of a man otherwise amiable. Cf. 3. 45; 3. 50; 1. 29. Introd. — Meter: § 49.

1. quod: see on 2. 11. 1; for position see on *nec*, Lib. Spect. 1. 2.

4. quid sit, *what it means.*

6. tigris . . . raptis: cf. Iuv. 6. 270 *tunc gravis illa viro, tunc orba tigride peior*; Plin. N. H. 8. 66. The Romans at this time saw the tiger in the *venationes*; see 8. 26. — **citata**: i.e. when in full rush for the hunter.

7. dipsas (cf. δίψάς): a venomous African serpent, so called, says the scholiast on Luc. 9. 718, *quod percussos* ('its victims') *siti mori faciat.* — **medio . . . sole**: i.e. parched by the tropical heat; cf. Luc. 9. 718 *torrida dipsas*; 9. 754 *dipsas . . . terris adiuta perustis.* The heat adds to the poisonous power of the snake.

9. tantos . . . labores: i.e. 'as you seek to inflict on people'. — **rogo**: paratactic; see on 2. 14. 18; 3. 25. 3.

10. Note the chiasmus.

12. In thermas fugio: cf. 3. 25. 4 N.; Petr. 92 *nam et dum lavor, ait, paene vapulavi, quia conatus sum circa solium sedentibus carmen recitare, et postquam de balneo tanquam de theatro eiectus sum.* — **sonas ad aurem**: cf. 3. 63. 8; 1. 89.

Piscinam peto : non licet natare.
Ad cenam propero : tenes euntem.
15 Ad cenam venio : fugas sedentem.
Lassus dormio : suscitas iacentem.
Vis quantum facias mali videre ?
Vir iustus, probus, innocens timeris.

45

Fugerit an Phoebus mensas cenamque Thyestae
  ignoro : fugimus nos, Ligurine, tuam.
Illa quidem lauta est dapibusque instructa superbis,
  sed nihil omnino te recitante placet.
5 Nolo mihi ponas rhombos mullumve bilibrem,
  nec volo boletos, ostrea nolo : tace.

13. **Piscinam** here seems to mean *baptisterium, swimming-pool*, into which M. plunges hoping to escape. — **non ... natare**: Ligurinus follows him or sits on the edge and reads to him. On the *o* of *peto* and *dormio* (16) see § 54, c.

14. **tenes** (*me*) **euntem**: 'you almost forcibly detain me, and, failing in that, you go too!'

15. The much abused custom of reading poetry at dinner, esp. during the *comissatio*, gave Ligurinus an excuse for his action. M., in 5. 78. 25, as an inducement to a friend to accept an invitation to dinner, promises: *nec crassum dominus leget volumen*; cf. 11. 52.

16. — **fugas sedentem**: until the signal was given to recline on the dinner-couches the guests sat. M. means: 'You put me to flight before I have a chance to take my place on the *lectus*; I forego my dinner rather than endure your verses'.

16. **iacentem**: note the climax: *euntem ... sedentem ... iacentem.* The assonance at the beginning and the end of these vss. adds greatly to the effect; cf. 4. 43. 5–8; 10. 35. 11–12.

18. The point is made in the last word; instead of *timeris* we expect *coleris* or *diligeris*.

45. 'Fine as Ligurinus's dinners are, his verses rob them of all charm'. Cf. 3. 44; 3. 50. — Meter: § 48.

1. **cenam . . . Thyestae**: Atreus, brother of Thyestes, served to Thyestes the latter's own sons.

3. **Illa**: the dinner of Ligurinus. — **dapibus** of itself marks the meal as rich and sumptuous; cf. *lauta* and *superbis*.

5–6. 'Spare our ears; we shall contentedly forego your delicacies'. Cf. 6. 48. — **ponas**: see 1. 43. 2 N. *Nolo . . . ponas* is the negative of the construction seen in *vis mittam*, 1. 117. 2; see note there. — **rhombos**: cf. 3. 60. 6; Hor. S. 1. 2. 115–116 *num esuriens fastidis omnia praeter pavonem rhombumque?* 2. 2. 95–96. — **mullum . . . bilibrem**: see on 2. 43. 11. — **boletos**: see 1. 20. 2 N. — **ostrea**: the oyster was

46

Exigis a nobis operam sine fine togatam.
Non eo, libertum sed tibi mitto meum.
"Non est" inquis "idem". Multo plus esse probabo :
vix ego lecticam subsequar, ille feret ;
5 in turbam incideris, cunctos umbone repellet :
invalidum est nobis ingenuumque latus ;
quidlibet in causa narraveris, ipse tacebo,
at tibi tergeminum mugiet ille sophos ;

much esteemed by the Romans; Plin. N. H. 32. 59 calls it *palma mensarum.* Cf. 12. 17. 4; 7. 78. 3–4 *sumen, aprum, leporem, boletos, ostrea, mullos mittis*; Iuv. 4. 139–143; Beck. 3. 338 ff.; Fried. SG. 3. 57. — **tace**: abrupt, yet withal a polite intimation that M. wishes no more invitations to dinner, unless Ligurinus's silence is a part of the menu. Cf. 5. 78. 25, cited on 3. 44. 15; 11. 52. 16–18.

46. A facetious epigram in which M. virtually takes leave of a patron, Candidus (see 2. 43, with notes), who had protested against the poet's attempt to excuse himself from the client's *officium* by sending a representative in his stead. See 1. 70, with notes. — Meter: § 48.

1. Exigis: a strong expression; the verb is used of collecting taxes, debts, etc. Cf. *exactor*, 'tax-gatherer'. — **operam . . . togatam**: cf. 10. 82. 2 *mane vel a media nocte togatus ero*; 2. 29. 4 N. For the transferred epithet see on 1. 15. 7.

3. probabo, *I'll prove* (to you); cf. 9. 50. 1 *ingenium mihi, Gaure, probas sic esse pusillum*; Soed. 31.

4. lecticam: see 2. 57. 6 N. — **subsequar**: cf. 10. 10. 7; 3. 36. 3–6 *ut . . . per medium . . . trahat me tua sella lutum, lassus ut in thermas . . . te sequar Agrippae.*

5. in . . . incideris: i.e. when on foot. The great man was not always carried. For the form of the vs. see on 3. 4. 5. — **cunctos . . . repellet**: scant respect was shown to common folk by the rich or their slaves and retainers. See App. — **umbone** prob. = *cubito* or *corpore*; the *umbo* of the shield was sometimes used to repel a foe, etc.; cf. Tac. Ann. 4. 51 *miles contra deturbare telis, pellere umbonibus. Umbone* may, however, denote the curbing of the street, and so stand for the roadway itself; if so, it is abl. of separation. See Class. Rev. 7. 203; cf. Stat. Silv. 4. 3. 47. On crowds in the streets of Rome see Iuv. 3. 243–248.

6. invalidum . . . latus: for that duty a stout set of ribs is necessary. — **ingenuum**: a fine play on words; prop. 'free-born', then 'such as a gentleman should have', then 'weak', 'delicate', since gentlemen are not inured to hardship as slaves are. 'Some things clients are expected to do are beneath a gentleman!' Cf. 10. 47. 6; Ov. Tr. 1. 5. 71–72 *illi corpus erat durum patiensque laborum, invalidae vires ingenuaeque mihi.*

7–8. quidlibet . . . sophos: 'good form and self-respect preclude my playing the rôle of a

lis erit, ingenti faciet convicia voce,

10   esse pudor vetuit fortia verba mihi.

"Ergo nihil nobis" inquis "praestabis amicus?"

Quidquid libertus, Candide, non poterit.

50

Haec tibi, non alia, est ad cenam causa vocandi,

versiculos recites ut, Ligurine, tuos.

Deposui soleas, adfertur protinus ingens

inter lactucas oxygarumque liber:

claqueur. But my *libertus*, not sparing his lungs, would ring the changes on applause'. See Plin. Ep. 2. 14. 4–10. — **narraveris,** *chatter, babble*; cf. 3. 63. 13; 8. 17. 3; Petr. 44 *narratis quod nec ad caelum nec ad terram pertinet.* Professor Shorey, on Hor. C. 3. 19. 3, calls this use "colloquial, almost slangy, like French 'Qu'est-ce que tu chantes?'" — **tergemi-num** = *maximum.* — **sophos:** see 1. 3. 7 N.; 1. 76. 10.

9. lis: here· *personal wrangle.* — **faciet convicia** = *conviciabitur*; cf. Ov. Am. 3. 3. 41 *quid queror et toto facio convicia caelo?*

10. No gentleman could afford to bawl out on the streets. Cf. Plaut. Most. 6–7 *quid tibi, malum, hic ante aedis clamitatiost? an ruri censes te esse?* — **fortia** = *magna, grandia, loud.*

11. Candidus politely asks M. if he is going to give up his patron.

12. Quidquid . . . poterit: sc. *ego amicus praestabo*; the emphasis is on *amicus.* 'As your friend (i.e. if I receive a friend's treatment from you) I'll do what only a gentleman (6) and a friend can do'.

50. Cf. 3. 45. Introd.; 3. 44; 6. 43; 11. 52. 16 N.; Pers. 1. 30–31 *ecce inter pocula quaerunt Romulidae*

saturi quid dia poemata narrent; Fried. SG. 1. 433 ff. — Meter: § 48.

2. versiculos: dim. of contempt. — **recites:** if Ligurinus ate anything, it is improbable that he himself acted as *recitator.* It is more likely that, as usual, recourse was had to skilled slaves (*anagno-stae, lectores*).

3. Deposui soleas: for the sake of greater ease or to avoid soiling the elegant *stragula* (2. 16. 1 N.), sandals, which had been taken by the guests to the house of the host for use indoors, were removed when the guests took their places on the couches; so *poscere soleas* comes to mean 'rise from dinner'. For the *soleae* see also on 1. 103. 6.— **adfertur:** a slave forthwith brings in the *ingens liber*; he does not even wait till the *promulsis*, during which the *lactuca* and the *oxygarum* were served (4), is over.

4. oxygarum (ὀξύγαρον): one of several varieties of caviare (*garum*), a condiment prepared with fish (generally *scomber*) and vinegar.

5. perlegitur: note the force of the prep.; Ligurinus does not spare his guests.—**fercula,** *courses. Ferculum* prop. denotes that on which something is carried, e.g.

5　alter perlegitur, dum fercula prima morantur :
　　　tertius est neque adhuc mensa secunda venit :
　et quartum recitas et quintum denique librum ;
　　　putidus est, totiens si mihi ponis aprum.
　Quod si non scombris scelerata poemata donas,
10　　　cenabis solus iam, Ligurine, domi.

52

Empta domus fuerat tibi, Tongiliane, ducentis :
　　　abstulit hanc nimium casus in urbe frequens.
Conlatum est deciens. Rogo, non potes ipse videri

a tray, then that which is carried on the tray, e.g. food ; then a course. *Prima* distinguishes the courses proper, the main part of the dinner, from the *mensae secundae*, the dessert. — morantur : we get the best effect by supposing that the service is purposely slow, to give time for the reading. The verb is then emotional ; even the *fercula* are in the plot to harass the guests.

6. The dessert was called *mensa secunda* or *mensae secundae*, because it differed in kind from the *fercula* that went before. It consisted of *bellaria*, fruits, nuts, pastry, etc. There would naturally be a pause before the *mensae secundae*; cf. Petr. 68 *interposito deinde spatio, cum secundas mensas Trimalchio iussisset adferri, sustulerunt servi omnes mensas et alias adtulerunt.*

7. quartum . . . librum : see App.

8. 'We have grown tired of having your poetry as the *caput cenae*, just as, though we all appreciate a boar, we should dislike to have it served to us four or five times at a single dinner'.

9. scombris . . . donas : cf. 3. 2. 3–5 N.

52. On Tongilianus's way of increasing his property. — Meter : § 48.

1. fuerat : the tense is correct ; the purchase preceded the loss, 2, and the contributions, 3. *Fui, fueram, fuero*, etc., are often used for *sum, eram, ero*, etc., in forming the compound tenses of the passive, in early Latin, in Silver Latin, and in the *sermo plebeius.* — ducentis : sc. *milibus sestertium* (see on I. 103. 1), 200,000 *sestertii*. At this price the *domus* must have been a plain house. Cf. I. 117. 7 N.

2. nimium . . . frequens : even after the Augustan age, despite the activity of the night watch (*vigiles*), Rome suffered greatly from fires ; cf. e.g. Iuv. 3. 197–222. The loss fell heavily on persons of moderate means, because fire-insurance associations were unknown to the Romans. See Fried. SG. I. 31 ff.; Lanciani Anc. R. 218 ff. — casus, *misfortune*, explained by *incendisse*, 4.

3. Conlatum est (*tibi*) : i.e. by friends. — deciens : ten times his loss ! — potes . . . videri : i.e. are not people excusable if they suspect?

incendisse tuam, Tongiliane, domum ?

58

Baiana nostri villa, Basse, Faustini
non otiosis ordinata myrtetis
viduaque platano tonsilique buxeto

4. incendisse ... domum: i.e.
in order to get a far better one.
Cf. the modern trick of defrauding
fire-insurance companies by firing
buildings. See Iuv. 3. 212–222
(note the similar phraseology) *si
magna Asturici cecidit domus . . .
tum gemimus casus urbis, tunc
odimus ignem. Ardet adhuc et
iam accurrit qui marmora donet,
conferat inpensas; hic nuda et
candida signa, hic aliquid praeclarum Euphranoris et Polycliti, hic
Asianorum vetera ornamenta deorum, hic libros dabit et forulos
mediamque Minervam, hic modium
argenti. Meliora ac plura reponit
Persicus orborum lautissimus et
merito iam suspectus tamquam ipse
suas incenderit aedes;* Liv. 38. 60. 9
*collata ea pecunia a cognatis ami-
cisque et clientibus est L. Scipioni,
ut, si acciperet eam, locupletior
aliquanto esset quam ante calami-
tatem fuerat* (he had been condemned for *peculatus*).

58. The ordinary Roman did
not resort to the sea-shore or to
the mountains to farm, nor could
he boast of a *rus in urbe*, as Sparsus
could (12. 57. 20 ff.). Faustinus
could well afford to gratify his
fancy here, for he had other villas
which more rigidly corresponded
to the prevailing fashions in such
matters, e.g. one near Tibur (4. 57).
Moreover, M. doubtless felt the
need of utilizing to the full his own
little Nomentanum (2. 38), and it
was pleasant to have so distinguished an exemplar as Faustinus.

The vivid description suggests personal acquaintance.— Meter: § 52.
  1. Baiana ... villa: Baiae
maintained for over 500 years its
preëminence as the most popular
pleasure resort of the ancient world.
Here were displayed the utmost
splendor of building and extravagance of living. See Fried. SG.
2. 118 ff. — **nostri . . . Faustini:**
in 4. 10 Faustinus is *carus amicus*;
M. sent him Books III–IV of the
epigrams (see 3. 2; 4. 10), which
Faustinus, as a poet (1. 25), doubtless had the taste to appreciate.
  2. otiosis, *idle* and so *unprofit-
able,* i.e. bearing no fruit. — **ordinata:** join with *villa,* 1. 'Faustinus's
villa is not set out with . . . and
does not', etc. For the sort of
villa Faustinus does not have at
Baiae see Hor. C. 2. 15. 1–10.—
myrtetis: Hor. Ep. 1. 15. 5 mentions the *myrteta* of Baiae.
  3. vidua ... platano: the Romans thought of trees as (1) profitable, because they produced fruit,
or because they afforded suitable
support for the vine, or (2) as
affording shade or pleasure to the
eye. Hence the vine is spoken of
as wedded to trees like the elm,
which, because its foliage was not
very dense, made a good support
for the vine; trees which could not
be so utilized, e.g. the myrtle and
the plane, are spoken of as wid-
owed (*vidua*) or unwedded (*caelebs*)
or barren (*sterilis*). Cf. e.g. Hor. C.
4. 5. 30 *vitem viduas ducit ad ar-
bores;* 2. 15. 4–5 *platanusque caelebs*

ingrata lati spatia detinet campi,
5   sed rure vero barbaroque laetatur.
Hic farta premitur angulo Ceres omni
et multa fragrat testa senibus autumnis ;
hic post Novembres imminente iam bruma
seras putator horridus refert uvas.
10   Truces in alta valle mugiunt tauri
vitulusque inermi fronte prurit in pugnam.

evincet ulmos; Verg. G. 2. 70; Iuv.
8. 78. As a shade-tree the oriental
plane-tree was a great favorite, because of its broad leaves (cf. Tennyson, "broad-leafed platan"). The
myrtle and the plane were sometimes planted in stately rows. See
Fried. SG. 2. 192; Hehn 287 ff. —
tonsili . . . buxeto: cf. Plin. N. H.
12. 13 *primus C. Matius . . . divi
Augusti amicus invenit nemora ton-
silia*; see 1. 88. 5 N.; Hehn 224 ff.
On the word *buxetum* see Cooper
§ 20. — For the meter see § 52, b.
    4. ingrata, *thankless, unappre-
ciative,* i.e. unproductive; cf. 10.
47. 4. — **detinet:** i.e. from profitable tillage; 'appropriates absolutely to itself'.
    5. In sharp contrast to artificial,
man-made landscapes this estate
shows the true country, wild and
rustic (*barbaro*). Cf. 10. 92. 3-4 *has
tibi gemellas, barbari decus luci,
commendo pinus.*
    6. farta premitur, *is packed
down and pressed close.*
    7. multa . . . testa: cf. *plurima
. . . imago,* 1. 70. 6 N. *Testa* = *amphora, cadus*; cf. 1. 53. 6 N. —
senibus autumnis, *old vintages.
Senibus* is here an adj.; cf. *fama
anus,* 1. 39. 2; 6. 27. 8 *amphora
anus.* For *autumnus* = 'fruits of
autumn' (metonymy) cf. 2. 46. 2
cum breve Sicaniae ver (i.e. the new
flowers) *populantur apes.*

    8. post Novembres: in De-
cember, when the vintage is over,
but before it becomes too inclem-
ent or cold to prune the vines. —
imminente . . . bruma: the work
may have been put off till just
before the solstice (recall the etymology of *bruma*); cf. 1. 49. 19–20
*at cum December canus et bruma
impotens Aquilone rauco mugiet.*
    9. seras . . . uvas: the *putator*
(*vinitor*) picks the grapes which, because they were unripe at vintage
time, had then been left unplucked;
cf. 1. 43. 3 N. Even in December
this villa is fruitful! — **putator:** it
is instructive to trace the process
by which *puto,* which fundamentally means 'cut' (cf. *amputo*), came
to mean 'think'.—**horridus,** *rough,
true son of the soil.*
    10. Truces . . . tauri: cf. Hor.
Epod. 2. 11–12 *aut in reducta valle
mugientium   prospectat   errantis
greges. Truces* = *fiery, spirited.*
    11. vitulus . . . pugnam: the
good blood of the sires (cf. *truces
. . . tauri*) shows itself before the
horns have had time to grow
(*inermi fronte*). — **inermi fronte:**
abl. abs., *though its forehead,* etc.,
or abl. of characteristic, *hornless.*
— **prurit in pugnam:** cf. Eng.
'itch for a fight'; Hor. C. 3. 13. 3–5
*haedo cui frons turgida cornibus
primis et venerem et proelia de-
stinat.*

Vagatur omnis turba sordidae chortis,
argutus anser gemmeique pavones
nomenque debet quae rubentibus pinnis
15   et picta perdix Numidicaeque guttatae
et impiorum phasiana Colchorum ;
Rhodias superbi feminas premunt galli,

12. **sordidae**, *lowly*; not necessarily 'filthy'. M. is fond of using
this adj. of outdoor things; cf.
10. 96. 4 N.; 12. 57. 2 *larem* . . .
villae sordidum (said of the Nomentanum).

13 ff. The list evidences the
utility of the place; the members
of the *turba* are all edible or at least
fit to adorn a fashionable table.

13. **argutus**, *clear-sounding*,
shrill; so often of the cry of a
bird and of the human voice. Cf.
9. 54. 8 *arguto passere vernat ager*.
The ancients liked shrill sounds.
Used of mental qualities the word
means 'sly', 'sagacious'. The epithet may have become proverbial
in this latter sense of geese, because geese were believed to have
saved the Capitol from the Gauls.
Fundamentally the word means
'bright' in the physical sense. —
anser: collective singular. —
gemmei . . . **pavones**, *spangled
peafowl*. The peafowl, though
long esteemed as a show-bird (cf.
1 Kings 10. 22; 2 Chron. 9. 21),
did not become a table dish until
a comparatively late time. The
caprice of fashion enabled it to
keep this place; its flesh is not
comparable with that of many
other fowls far less in demand.
See 13. 70. Introd.; 13. 70. 2 N.;
Hehn 342 ff. With *gemmei* cf. 13.
70. 1 *gemmantis* . . . *alas* (*pavonis*);
Phaedr. 3. 18. 7–8 *nitor smaragdi
collo praefulget tuo pictisque plumis
gemmeam caudam explicas*.

14. **nomen** . . . **quae** (*avis*): the
phoenicopterus, flamingo, esteemed
for its plumage, as was the *pavo*.
—**rubentibus pinnis**: cf. φοινικό-
πτερος. Bon vivants ate only the
tongue and brains of this bird. Cf.
13. 71. 1–2 *dat mihi pinna rubens
nomen, sed lingua gulosis nostra
sapit*.

15. **picta perdix**, *the spotted
partridge*; cf. 13. 65. 1 *ponitur Ausoniis avis haec rarissima mensis*.
— **Numidicae** . . . **guttatae**,
guinea-hens; cf. Col. 8. 2. 2 *Afri-
cana est, quam plerique Numidicam
dicunt, meleagridi similis, nisi quod
rutilam galeam et cristam capite
gerit, quae utraque sunt in mele-
agride caerulea*; Hehn 353–354.—
guttatae, *spotted*. On this word
see Cooper § 53, p. 233.

16. **impiorum** . . . **Colchorum**:
the legends of the Argonautic
expedition, esp. such as concerned
Medea, gave to the Colchians a
reputation for dealing in poison
and the black art generally; cf. e.g.
Hor. C. 2. 13. 8 *ille venena Colcha
. . . tractavit*. — **phasiana** (*avis*),
the pheasant, named by the ancients
from the river Phasis, in Colchis,
the original home of the bird; cf.
13. 72; Iuv. 11. 139 *Scythicae vo-
lucres*.

17. **Rhodias** . . . **feminas**: a
breed of hens and cocks that came
originally from Rhodes was much
prized, the hens for size, the cocks
for spirit. — **premunt** = *calcant*,
tread.

sonantque turres plausibus columbarum,
gemit hinc palumbus, inde cereus turtur.
20 Avidi secuntur vilicae sinum porci
matremque plenam mollis agnus expectat.
Cingunt serenum lactei focum vernae
et larga festos lucet ad lares silva.

18. turres: pigeons make their homes by preference in the very tops of buildings; see Ov. Tr. 1. 9. 7–8 *aspicis ut veniant ad candida tecta columbae, aspiciat nullas sordida turris aves?* — **plausibus columbarum** describes the noise made by the flapping of their wings; *gemit* (19) describes their cooing. *Columba* denotes the genus; *palumbus* and *turtur* (19) give two species; see Hehn 335 ff.

19. gemit = *queritur*; cf. Hor. Epod. 2. 26 *queruntur in silvis aves*; Verg. E. 1. 57–58 *nec tamen interea raucae, tua cura, palumbes, nec gemere aeria cessabit turtur ab ulmo*; Tennyson, "the moan of doves in immemorial elms". — **cereus**: i.e. fat and sleek, like wax to the sight, though there may be thought also of the plumage as soft to the touch. Still, the reference may be to color, *yellow*; cf. 13. 5. 1 *cerea ... ficedula*; Verg. E. 2. 53 *cerea pruna*. See also on *aureus ... turtur*, 3. 60. 7.

20. sinum: see on 1. 15. 10.

21. matrem ... expectat: the lamb shut up at home waits for the return of the mother from the fields. — **matrem ... plenam**: freely, 'the rich stores of its mother's milk'; *plenam mollis* is an effective juxtaposition. — **expectat**: i.e. shows by its bleating that it is waiting for (its mother).

22-23. The scene shifts within doors, to the atrium of the villa. Here was the *focus* (see on 2. 90. 7),

near which stood the images of the Lares (see on 1. 70. 2); there sacrifices were made to the Lares. In the olden days everywhere, in later times in the country still, the house life centered there.

22. Cingunt serenum... focum: cf. Hor. Epod. 2. 65–66 *positosque* (at supper) *vernas ... circum renidentis Lares*; S. 2. 6. 65–67. In our passage, probably (cf. 23), some special occasion is thought of, such as the Laralia or the *dies natalis* of the head of the house; at such times the Lares were specially crowned. See Preller-Jordan 2. 107; Marq.-Wissowa 3. 127–128. — **serenum** has regard not only to the good cheer of the fire, but to the well-kept condition of the hearth. See App. — **lactei**: either *white-skinned*, i.e. not tanned by exposure or outdoor labor, or, better, *nursing*, *sucking*; cf. γαλαθηνοί. — **vernae**: see on 1. 41. 2; 2. 90. 9.

23. larga ... silva: the whole forest is drawn upon; there is no lack of fuel. Cf. 12. 18. 19–20; 1. 49. 27 *vicina in ipsum silva descendet focum.* — **festos ... ad lares**: see on 22, and on *lucet* below. The epithet, however, seems conventional and may merely serve to mark the general sense of contentment in the house; it was like a continual holiday there! — **lucet**: the polished Lares would be especially resplendent in the firelight.

Non segnis albo pallet otio caupo,
25   nec perdit oleum lubricus palaestrita,
sed tendit avidis rete subdolum turdis
tremulave captum linea trahit piscem
aut inpeditam cassibus refert dammam.
Exercet hilares facilis hortus urbanos,
30   et paedagogo non iubente lascivi
parere gaudent vilico capillati,

24. On this estate everybody busies himself! The Roman whose land touched a highway was apt to follow Varro's advice, R. R. 1. 2. 23 *si ager (est) secundum viam et opportunus viatoribus locus, aedificandae tabernae devorsoriae.* See Fried. SG. 2. 41; Beck. 3. 35. Our *caupo* not only took charge of the *taberna*, which in such a place would hardly demand all his time, but did something outdoors that put the color in his cheeks. — **albo,** *whitening, pale-making*; transferred epithet. Cf. 1. 55. 14 *vivat et urbanis albus in officiis*; Fried. SG. 1. 37 ff.

25. perdit oleum: i.e. lose (spend vainly) his time; cf. Iuv. 7. 99 *perit hic plus temporis atque olei* (said of the historians, who get nothing from their books). See on 13. 1. 3. — **lubricus:** i.e. with oil, which was smeared on the naked bodies of the wrestlers. — **palaestrita:** every great *domus* (sometimes too the *villa*) had its *gymnasium* or *palaestra.* This *palaestrita* had come from town with the *familia urbana* and, finding his occupation largely gone, had taken to the useful diversions of 26–28.

26. tendit . . . turdis: cf. Hor. Epod. 2. 33–34 *aut amite levi rara tendit retia, turdis edacibus dolos.*

27. tremula . . . piscem: cf. 1. 55. 9 *et (cui licet) piscem tremula salientem ducere saeta*; Ov. M. 3.

586–587; 8. 217. *Tremula = quivering.* — **linea** = *saeta,* seen in 10. 30. 16; 1. 55. 9, cited above.

28. cassibus: from *casses*; cf. *rete, plaga.* — **refert:** sc. *domum,* as a proof of his skill. — **dammam:** to the Romans, who did not eat beef and were surfeited with swine's flesh, venison must have been a delicacy. Cf. 13. 94. 2 N.; 1. 49. 23–24 *ibi inligatas mollibus dammas plagis mactabis*; Iuv. 11. 120 ff. See 13. 94. Introd.

29. Editors differ concerning the interpretation of this vs., esp. of *hilares . . . urbanos.* — **Exercet,** *keeps busy.* — **hilares . . . urbanos:** best taken of the *familia urbana,* of whom some were regularly brought from town to equip the villa, when the master made a sojourn in the country. — **facilis,** *easy to work*; render, 'the garden provides easy work for', etc. — On the meter see § 52, b.

30. paedagogo . . . iubente: i.e. without being driven to such work, though the *paedagogus* lets up somewhat with the tasks of the *paedagogium,* or slave school, in which *vernae* were trained to skilled services. On such *paedagogia* see Marq. 157–158; Beck. 2. 145 ff.

31. parere . . . vilico: i.e. do whatever the farm-steward might bid them do. — **capillati:** sc. *pueri* = *servi,* and see 2. 57. 5 N.

et delicatus opere fruitur eunuchus.
Nec venit inanis rusticus salutator :
fert ille ceris cana cum suis mella
35 metamque lactis Sassinatis ; de silva
somniculosos ille porrigit glires,
hic vagientem matris hispidae fetum,
alius coactos non amare capones.
Et dona matrum vimine offerunt texto
40 grandes proborum virgines colonorum.
Facto vocatur laetus opere vicinus

32. delicatus, *effeminate.* For the meter see § 52, b.

33–44. Faustinus is on friendly terms with the neighboring *coloni.* The *coloni* bring to him simple gifts; he entertains them in his turn.

33. inanis, *empty-handed.* In Rome clients not only came *inanes,* but also expected the *sportula.* We need not infer that Faustinus maintained a daily *salutatio* of the city sort.

34. ceris ... cum suis: honey in the comb could not be adulterated. — **cana:** *light yellow,* almost *white.*

35–36. metam ... Sassinatis: see I. 43. 7 N. The reference may, however, be to cheeses made on the farm of the giver; *metae Sassinates* was perhaps a trade term for cheeses of a peculiar shape and color. See App. — **de silva ... glires:** cf. Plin. N. H. 16. 18 *fagum muribus gratissimum est, et ideo animalis eius una proventus ; glires quoque saginat.* — somniculosos: cf. 13. 59; Non. 119 *Laberius in Aquis Caldis : et iam hic me optimus somnus premit, ut premitur glis.* — **porrigit:** freely, 'proffers'. — **glires:** dormice were accounted a

delicacy; cf. Petr. 31 *ponticuli etiam ferruminati sustinebant glires melle ac papavere sparsos.*

37. hic: sc. *porrigit, fert.* — **vagientem . . . fetum,** *bleating kid;* the kid bleats because taken from the mother; cf. 7. 31. 3 *et fetum. querulae rudem capellae.*

38. coactos non amare = *castratos.*

39–40. The wives of the *coloni* pay their respects indirectly, perhaps to the wife of Faustinus. The simplicity and purity of the country are contrasted with the corruption of the metropolis. — **vimine . . . texto,** *in a basket of osiers.* — **grandes,** *well-grown, sturdy.*

41. vocatur = *adhibetur,* i.e. *ad cenam* ; cf. I. 20. I N.; I. 43. I. — **laetus:** i.e. satisfied because work is over, and anticipating the feast.

42–44. In contrast to what is all too common at a *cena publica* in the city, Faustinus spares no expense to make this dinner fine; besides, it is served to be eaten (*nec . . . servat . . . dapes;* contrast I. 103. 7; 10. 48. 17). Further, the delicacies are not alone for the host and a few particular friends,

nec avara servat crastinas dapes mensa ;
vescuntur omnes ebrioque non novit
satur minister invidere convivae.

45 At tu sub urbe possides famem mundam
et turre ab alta prospicis meras laurus,
furem Priapo non timente securus,
et vinitorem farre pascis urbano
pictamque portas otiosus ad villam

50 holus, ova, pullos, poma, caseum, mustum.
Rus hoc vocari debet, an domus longe ?

but all, even the slaves, are well treated (43; contrast e.g. 3. 60).

42. crastinas : proleptic; freely, 'until tomorrow', 'for another dinner'. — **dapes :** cf. 3. 45. 3 N.

43-44. novit . . . invidere : for the const. cf. 7. 25. 8; 8. 18. 6; 10. 2. 12. — **satur minister :** the slaves who serve the dinner have so much to eat from what is left by their betters that they do not envy the guests their wine; cf. 2. 90. 9.

45. tu : Bassus, who had not chickens enough to keep him in eggs (3. 47. 14) or garden enough to raise the commonest vegetables, much less grain for his slaves. — **sub urbe :** cf. 3. 47 throughout. — **famem mundam,** *elegant starvation,* i.e. an estate where neatness and order obtain everywhere but there is nothing to eat. Cf. *pictam . . . villam,* 49.

46. turre ab alta : the rich liked to rear high palaces; cf. e.g. Hor. C. 1. 4. 13-14 *pauperum tabernas regumque turres.* Faustinus had his *turres,* but he had something else too. — **meras laurus,** *nothing but laurels.* The outlook is agreeable, yes, but the *laurus* is to be classed with the trees of 2-3.

47. furem . . . securus : 'marauders will not prey on your gardens, Bassus, for no thief cares for bay leaves'. Cf. 10. 94, esp. 3-4. — **Priapo :** Priapus was the protector of gardens, vineyards, and country life in general. His statue, generally a rough red-stained Hermes of wood, was set up in gardens and served as a scarecrow for destructive birds. Cf. Verg. G. 4. 110-111 *et custos furum atque avium cum falce saligna Hellespontiaci servet tutela Priapi;* Hor. S. 1. 8. 1 ff.; Ov. F. 1. 415.

48. vinitorem : cf. *putator,* 9. — **pascis :** *pasco* is prop. used of feeding beasts. — **urbano,** *brought from town!*

49. pictam . . . villam : a mere show-place, such as one might see in a (Pompeian) wall-painting. — **otiosus :** freely, 'idly', or 'you idler'. The word contrasts the laziness and ineffectiveness of Bassus's 'farming' with the busy scenes of Faustinus's estate, where, without feeling any sense of strain, all work and make everything yield a profit.

51. Rus . . . domus longe : a country villa (cf. 1. 12. 3; 4. 64. 25) or a town house in the country.

60

Cum vocer ad cenam non iam venalis ut ante,
  cur mihi non eadem, quae tibi, cena datur ?
Ostrea tu sumis stagno saturata Lucrino,
  sugitur inciso mitulus ore mihi :
5 sunt tibi boleti, fungos ego sumo suillos :
  res tibi cum rhombo est, at mihi cum sparulo :
aureus inmodicis turtur te clunibus implet,
  ponitur in cavea mortua pica mihi.

— **longe**: i.e. far from where it naturally belongs. *Longe* seems to belong closely with *domus*, but prob. M. had *est* more or less definitely in mind. We have an adv. with a noun usually only (1) when the noun easily suggests a verb, as Verg. A. 1. 21 *populum late regem* (cf. *regnantem*), and (2) when the adv. is closely associated with an adj. and a noun, as Verg. A. 1. 13–14 *Carthago, Italiam contra Tiberinaque longe ostia*; Liv. 21.8. 5 *tres deinceps turres*; Iuv. 3. 34 *quondam hi cornicines*.

60. Rader wittily remarks that M. here "*queritur etiam in recta cena non recte cenari*". Cf. 1. 20, with notes; 1. 43; 3. 7.— Meter: § 48.

1. vocer = *adhibear*; cf. 1. 20. 1 N.— **ad cenam**: sc. *rectam*; see 2. 69. 7 N.— **non . . . venalis**: i.e. not one whose company is weighed in the balance against so much hard cash, but one who is supposed to come as a friend. Cf. 3. 30. 1 *sportula nulla datur; gratis conviva recumbis.* — **ut ante**: i.e. as when we received the money dole.

3. Ostrea . . . Lucrino: cf. 3. 45. 6; 5. 37. 3; 6. 11. 5. The Lucrine oyster was in such repute that oysters were transplanted from other less favored localities to be fattened there. — **stagno**: after

the construction of the Julian Harbor there could have been little tide from the Mediterranean in the Lacus Lucrinus; cf. 3. 20. 20 *piger Lucrino nauculatur in stagno ?*

4. sugitur: the apology for oysters served to M. had been only half opened; he could only suck the juice from the shell, and in trying to do this he cut his mouth. *Inciso . . . ore* may, however, mean 'having cut a hole therein'. — **mitulus**: the common edible mussel.

5. boleti: see 1. 20. 2 N.—**fungos . . . suillos**: an inferior kind; cf. Iuv. 5. 146–148 *vilibus ancipites fungi ponentur amicis, boletus domino.*

6–8. Note striving for variety in *te . . . implet, ponitur . . . mihi*; so, less markedly, in 3–5. — **rhombo**: see 3. 45. 5 N. — **sparulo**: a fish unknown to us, but clearly inferior to the *rhombus*; cf. Ov. Hal. 106 *et super aurata sparulus cervice refulgens.* — **aureus . . . turtur**: cf. 3. 58. 19 N. *Aureus* may = *very fine, first-rate*, or may refer to the color of the flesh when cooked. — **inmodicis . . . clunibus**: the bird was very fat in the parts that appear to have been most esteemed; cf. Plin. N. H. 10. 140 *postea culinarum artes, ut clunes spectentur*

Cur sine te ceno, cum tecum, Pontice, cenem ?
10   sportula quod non est prosit : edamus idem.

61

Esse nihil dicis quidquid petis, inprobe Cinna :
si nil, Cinna, petis, nil tibi, Cinna, nego.

63

Cotile, bellus homo es : dicunt hoc, Cotile, multi.
Audio : sed quid sit dic mihi bellus homo ?
" Bellus homo est, flexos qui digerit ordine crines,
balsama qui semper, cinnama semper olet,
5   cantica qui Nili, qui Gaditana susurrat,

(i.e. by the guests at table). — in
. . . pica : M. assumes that the
magpie was found dead in its cage,
for the *pica* was not kept to be
eaten, and as a pleasure bird would
not be wantonly killed.

9. Pontice : cf. 4. 85. 1–2 *nos
bibimus vitro, tu murra, Pontice.
Quare ? prodat perspicuus ne duo
vina calix*; 9. 19.

10. sportula . . . est : the subj.
of *prosit*; see 3. 7, with notes. —
quod : see 2. 11. 1 N. — prosit : sc.
mihi or *clientibus*. — idem : cf.
eadem . . . cena, 2.

61. M. gives Cinna, who had
apparently resented his indiffer-
ence (cf. *inprobe Cinna*), just what
Cinna asks for, i.e. *nil*. — Meter :
§ 48.

1. quidquid petis : subj. of
esse.

63. Cf. 1. 9; 2. 7; Fried. SG. 1.
431–432. — Meter : § 48.

1. Cotile : prob. coined from
κοτίλος, 'prattling', 'babbling'.

2. Audio : i.e. everywhere.

3. Cotilus answers, 3–12; M.
makes him utterlycondemn himself

(cf. 13–14). — flexos . . . crines :
i.e. curled on a *calamistrum*, curl-
ing-iron; cf. 10. 65. 6; 2. 36. 1. The
fact that the Roman gentleman ordinarily did not wear a hat encouraged the fop in extravagant care
of his hair. — ordine : abl. of manner, *carefully, elaborately*; cf. Ov.
Am. 1. 11. 1–2 *colligere incertos et
in ordine ponere crines docta*.

4. Another mark of effeminacy
unconsciously acknowledged by
Cotilus. Cf. 2. 12. 3–4 *hoc mihi
suspectum est, quod oles bene, Postume, semper ; Postume, non bene
olet qui bene semper olet*. — cinnama : cf. 4. 13. 3.

5. cantica . . . Nili : obscene
ditties from Alexandria or, more
probably, from Canopus; see Fried.
SG. 3. 335 ff.; 3. 345 ff. Canopus,
which was connected with Alexandria by a pleasure canal, was noto-
rious for vice; cf. Fried. SG. 2.
159. — Gaditana : sc. *cantica* or
carmina; cf. 1. 41. 12 N; 1. 61.
9 N. — susurrat, *hums*; note the
onomatopœia. Cf. *sibilare*, Eng.
'hiss', 'buzz', and like words.

qui movet in varios bracchia volsa modos,
    inter femineas tota qui luce cathedras
        desidet atque aliqua semper in aure sonat,
    qui legit hinc illinc missas scribitque tabellas,
10   pallia vicini qui refugit cubiti,
    qui scit quam quis amet, qui per convivia currit,
        Hirpini veteres qui bene novit avos ".

6. in ... modos: i.e. in changing attitudes called for by the varying musical measures (*modi*). *In = in accordance* (*harmony*) *with, to keep time with.* In this sense *ad* is commoner. For the Roman attitude toward dancing see on 2. 7. 5. *Saltare, saltatio,* included movements also with arms or hands; cf. Ov. A. A. 1. 595 (advice to a lover) *si vox est, canta; si mollia bracchia, salta*; 2. 305 *bracchia saltantis, vocem mirare canentis.* — **bracchia volsa:** see on 2. 29. 6.

7. inter femineas ... cathedras: e.g. at the recitations; cf. 1. 76. 13 N. The upholstered reclining *cathedra* was essentially a woman's chair; cf. Hor. S. 1. 10. 90–91 *Demetri, teque Tigelli, discipularum inter iubeo plorare cathedras*; Beck. 2. 348 ff.; Marq. 726 ff. — **tota ... luce:** from morning to night; for the abl. cf. 7. 65. 3 *viginti litigat annis*; 2. 5. 1 N.

8. desidet, *lounges idly away*; cf. Sen. Ep. 7. 2 *nihil vero tam damnosum bonis moribus quam in aliquo spectaculo desidere*; Iust. 21. 5. 4 *non contentus ... conspici in popinis lupanaribusque, sed totis diebus desidere.* — **in aure sonat:** i.e. half privately, confidentially; cf. 1. 89. 4. — **sonat =** *garrit*; cf. Prop. 1. 12. 6 *dulcis in aure sonat.*

9. The *bellus homo* receives billets-doux (*tabellas*: sc. *amatorias*) from every quarter, and is in demand at banquets, 11; cf. Ov. A. A. 1. 383 *dum (illa) dat recipitque tabellas.*

10. See 2. 41. 10 N. — **pallia:** one of the foreign types of dress that from the end of the Republic tended to take the place of the cumbersome toga. — **refugit,** *avoids, shrinks from.* For the trisyllabic verse-ending see § 48, b.

11. The *bellus homo* knows all the town gossip, and is a professional diner-out. Juvenal's typical town woman was also a gad-about: cf. 6. 402–404 *haec eadem novit quid toto fiat in orbe, quid Seres, quid Thraces agant, secreta novercae et pueri, quis amet, quis diripiatur adulter.*

12. The *bellus homo* has at his tongue's end the pedigrees of the favorite race-horses. See Fried. SG. 2. 333 ff.; Marq.-Wissowa 3. 511 ff.; Lanciani Anc. R. 213 ff. — **Hirpini:** Hirpinus (named doubtless from his birthplace, the country of the Hirpini, a well-known stock-raising region in southern Samnium) was a famous horse. He won the first prize 131 times; his grandsire Aquilo won first place 130 times, second place 88 times. Cf. Iuv. 8. 57 ff. *nempe volucrem sic laudamus ecum, facili cui plurima palma fervet et exultat rauco victoria circo; ... sed venale pecus Coryphaei posteritas et Hirpini, si rara iugo victoria sedit.*

Quid narras ? hoc est, hoc est homo, Cotile, bellus ?
res pertricosa est, Cotile, bellus homo.

99

Irasci nostro non debes, cerdo, libello :
ars tua, non vita, est carmine laesa meo.
Innocuos permitte sales : cur ludere nobis
non liceat, licuit si iugulare tibi ?

13. Quid narras? M. interrupts abruptly. For *narras* see 3. 46. 7 N. — **hoc . . . est**: the repetition marks M.'s surprise and disgust.

14. res pertricosa: pred. nom.; placed first for emphasis, and that the epigram may end with the three words with which it begins. With *pertricosa* cf. *tricae*, and note on *apinas*, 1. 113. 2. For *per-* see on *perinane*, 1. 76. 10; Cooper § 31, p. 129.

99. The word *cerdo* (cf. the name Κέρδων) seems to have been not only a common noun, but to have been used as a contemptuous soubriquet for those engaged in small trade and handicrafts, those whom Cic. Flac. 7. 17 calls *sutores et zonarii* (see Duff on Iuv. 8. 182). The *cerdo* here ridiculed may be the man satirized in 3. 16; 3. 59 *sutor cerdo dedit tibi, culta Bononia, munus, fullo dedit Mutinae: nunc ubi copa dabit?* We may suppose that he resented these epigrams; M. now, under the mask of an apology, makes matters worse. — Meter : § 48.

1. libello, *pasquinade, lampoon*; cf. Suet. Aug. 55 *etiam sparsos de se in curia famosos libellos nec expavit.*

2. ars tua: i.e. 'your *ars sutoria* and your *ars gladiatoria,* along with the new rôle you are trying to play in society'. — **non . . . meo**: 'my thrusts are harmless, which is more than I can say for yours'; cf. note on *iugulare,* 4. — **carmine laesa meo**: cf. 3. 97. 2 (*Chione*) *carmine laesa meo est. Laedere* is thus repeatedly used of hurting with libelous or satirical verses.

3. Innocuos: cf. 1. 4. 7; 7. 12. 9 *ludimus innocui.* — **sales**: cf. 1. 41. 16 N. — **ludere nobis**: i.e. 'why may not we (I and those who with me enjoy the fun) have a *ludus* on our own account, as you have your *munus*? Surely a man who kills other men ought not to think himself mortally hurt when I make game of him'. For *ludere* cf. 1. 41. 19; 1. 113. 1.

4. iugulare: the *cerdo* did this as *editor spectaculorum*; cf. 3. 59, cited in Introd.; Lib. Spect. 29, with notes.

LIBER IV

8

Prima salutantes atque altera conterit hora,
exercet raucos tertia causidicos,
in quintam varios extendit Roma labores,
sexta quies lassis, septima finis erit,
5   sufficit in nonam nitidis octava palaestris,

8. Addressed to Euphemus, with a presentation copy of Book IV for Domitian. To us the interest of the epigram lies in M.'s account of the routine of the Roman day. The *dies civilis* began at midnight and was twenty-four hours long; the *dies naturalis* extended from sunrise to sunset. With the introduction of sun-dials (*solaria horologia*) about 250 B.C. it became possible to divide the day into hours; these dials were, however, useless when the sun was obscured. Water-clocks (*clepsydrae*: see on 6. 35. 1) subsequently came into use and fixed the division into *horae*. These *horae*, though of equal length at any given time of the year, were not *horae* of sixty minutes; they were much longer in summer than in winter. See Marq. 250 ff.; Beck. 2. 406 ff. — Meter: § 48.

   1. Prima...hora: for the early hour of the *salutatio* cf. 2. 18. 3 N.; 10. 58. 11–12. — **conterit,** *uses up, wastes*; cf. Cic. De Or. 1. 58. 249 *cum in causis et in negotiis et in foro conteramur.* The word well expresses M.'s disgust with the *officium*; see 1. 70.

   2. raucos is proleptic, *till they are hoarse*; it gives the effect of *exercet*; cf. Hor. S. 1. 4. 65–66 *Sulcius acer ambulat et Caprius rauci male cumque libellis* ('their indictments'); Iuv. 8. 59 *exultat rauco victoria circo.*

   3. in quintam: i.e. to the end of the fifth hour, to midday.

   4. quies lassis: with the sixth hour came cessation from work and then luncheon (*prandium, merenda*); in olden times this was the main meal, but later, when the formal *cena* became the main meal, this was a sort of second breakfast. See Beck. 3. 319 ff.; Marq. 266 ff. — **septima . . . erit:** the seventh hour was devoted to winding up the day's work; cf. Hor. Ep. 1. 7. 46–48 *strenuus et fortis causisque Philippus agendis clarus ab officiis octavam circiter horam dum redit.*

   5. Ordinarily the eighth hour was devoted to physical exercise and to the bath; cf. 10. 48. 1. After the great *thermae* were erected (see 2. 14. 11–12 N.), with ample apartments for the *palaestra* and for games of every sort, it became

imperat extructos frangere nona toros :
hora libellorum decima est, Eupheme, meorum,
temperat ambrosias cum tua cura dapes
et bonus aetherio laxatur nectare Caesar
10   ingentique tenet pocula parca manu.

fashionable to bathe there rather than at home, and exercise and the bath proper became virtually parts of one thing. — nitidis ... palaestris: the *palaestra* was prop. a place for wrestling, then the exercise itself; cf. note on *palaestrita*, 3. 58. 25. — nitidis: i.e. with oil; cf. 3. 58. 25 N.

6. imperat . . . nona (*hora*): with regard to the dinner-hour custom is law. In the best prose only the pass. inf. is used with *impero*. See Soed. 13. — extructos . . . toros: the bolsters, piled high on the *lectus*, which was in itself a mere framework. See 2. 16. 1 N. Cf. Verg. A. 11. 66 *exstructosque toros obtentu frondis inumbrant.* — frangere: i.e. to disturb the perfect order and smoothness of the *lecti*, by taking their places on them (*accumbere, discumbere*); cf. 2. 59. 3 *frange toros, pete vina, rosas cape, tinguere nardo.*

7. hora ... meorum: i.e. 'the tenth hour is the most favorable time for bringing my new book to the attention of the emperor'. Euphemus is not to force the book upon the emperor's attention during the formal *fercula*, but to wait until the coming of the *mensae secundae* affords opportunity or the *comissatio* puts the tyrant in good humor. — **Eupheme:** a Greek freedman, *tricliniarches* or chief steward of the emperor, holding a position of importance and trust, esp. if he served also as the *praegustator*. The *tricliniarches* would seem to have remained on duty in

the *triclinium* during the whole dinner; cf. Petr. 22 *iam et tricliniarches experrectus lucernis occidentibus oleum infuderat.* Here he may have introduced a reader (*anagnostes*) as an entertainer (*acroama*) to read from the new book (see 3. 50. 2 N.) and thus excite the interest of the emperor.

8. temperat: i.e. so plans and arranges as to have a dinner perfectly proportioned in all its parts. — ambrosias . . . dapes: if Domitian were not yet in his own estimation a god, he was soon to be, and he must, according to M. and like flatterers, dine like a god; cf. 5. 8. 1; 10. 72; 8. 39. 1–4 *qui Palatinae caperet convivia mensae ambrosiasque dapes non erat ante locus; hic haurire decet sacrum, Germanice, nectar, et Ganymedea pocula mixta manu*; Mommsen Staats. 2. 759, N. 3. — cura, *anxiety to please, watchful care.*

9. bonus . . . Caesar: for M.'s flattery of Domitian see §§ 8–9; 36. — aetherio . . . nectare: cf. notes on 8; Hor. C. 3. 3. 11–12 *quos inter Augustus recumbens purpureo bibet ore nectar.* — laxatur, *unbends,* i.e. throws off the cares of state; cf. *animum laxare.*

10. ingenti . . . manu: i.e. with the hand that rules the world. — parca, *sparing, temperate*; cf. Suet. Dom. 21 *prandebatque ad satietatem ut non temere super cenam praeter Matianum malum et modicam in ampulla potiunculam sumeret.*

Tunc admitte iocos : gressu timet ire licenti
ad matutinum nostra Thalia Iovem.

10

Dum novus est nec adhuc rasa mihi fronte libellus,
　　pagina dum tangi non bene sicca timet,
i puer et caro perfer leve munus amico,
　　qui meruit nugas primus habere meas.
5　Curre, sed instructus : comitetur Punica librum
　　spongea : muneribus convenit illa meis ;
non possunt nostros multae, Faustine, liturae
　　emendare iocos : una litura potest.

11–12. Tunc admitte iocos:
see end of notes on 5; cf. 10. 20. 19–
21.—**gressu . . . Iovem**: as *censor
morum* Domitian might for appearance's sake pose as the guardian
of public virtue; see 1. 4, with notes.
—**ire**: i.e. to pay her respects to.
For inf. with *timet* cf. 4. 10. 2;
Tib. 1. 4. 21 *nec iurare time*; Soed.
15.—**licenti**, *bold, wanton.* — **matutinum**: i.e. when busied with
serious duties (cf. 1–3 above), and
so not ready for lighter things such
as *ioci.* — **nostra Thalia**: Thalia
was the Muse of lighter poetry,
esp. comedy; cf. 7. 17. 4; 9. 26. 8;
10. 20. 3. — **Iovem**: Domitian; cf.
Stat. Silv. 1. 6. 25–26 *ducat nubila
Iuppiter per orbem et latis pluvias
minetur agris dum nostri Iovis hi
ferantur imbres* (i.e. presents).

10. To the Faustinus of 1. 25
M. sends the new book. Perhaps
M. and Faustinus were friendly
critics of each other's work. —
Meter: § 48.

1. rasa . . . fronte: cf. 1. 66. 10 N.

2. tangi . . . timet: cf. *timet
ire*, 4. 8. 11 N. — **non bene sicca**:
the ink (*atramentum*) used by the
Romans was made of soot and gum;

hence before it dried thoroughly
it could be easily removed by
sponge and water.

3. i . . . et: here without the
derisive force noted on 1. 42. 6. —
leve munus: a gift insignificant in
size and trifling, light, in subject-
matter.

4. meruit . . . meas: because
of his friendship and critical acumen. — **meruit . . . habere**: cf. 5.
22. 1 N. — **nugas**: cf. 1. 113. 6 N.

5. instructus: i.e. properly
equipped; the slave is to have not
merely the book, but also a *Punica
spongea*, to erase the writing if need
be. Cf. Suet. Cal. 20 (*ferunt*) *eos
. . . scripta sua spongea linguave
delere iussos, nisi ferulis obiurgari
aut flumine proximo mergi maluissent.*

7–8. liturae: cf. 1. 3. 9 N. —
emendare, *remove the faults* (*mendae*) *of.*

14. M. wrote this epigram, it
would seem, to accompany a copy
of his poems which he sent to Silius
Italicus as a present at the·Saturnalia (see on 6). Ti. Catius Silius
Italicus, who was born about 25,
is better known to us as author of

14

Sili, Castalidum decus sororum,
qui periuria barbari furoris
ingenti premis ore perfidosque
astus Hannibalis levisque Poenos
5   magnis cedere cogis Africanis,
paulum seposita severitate,

the Punica, a long epic poem on
the Second Punic War, than as a
rich lawyer, a centumvir, and an
art critic. Yet it was only after
he had amassed wealth and had
attained consular rank that he
withdrew from public life and devoted himself to literature. Beside
other villas (one of which had been
Cicero's) he had a Neapolitanum,
and Friedländer thinks that M.
made his acquaintance during the
summer of 88, which M. seems to
have spent near Naples; cf. 3. 58.
Naturally Silius took Vergil as his
model. He carried his esteem of
Vergil almost to the point of worship, the more so, doubtless, after
he had come into possession of the
ground on which stood the tomb
of Vergil; cf. 11. 48; Plin. Ep. 3. 7.
8. At the age of seventy-five, because he was suffering from an in-
curable malady, he starved himself
to death. Cf. 7. 63. —Meter: § 49.

1. **Castalidum . . . sororum:**
in M.'s flattery Silius is the glory
not merely of the Italian Camenae
but of the nine Muses, daughters
of Zeus and Mnemosyne, to whom,
as to Apollo, the Fons Castalia on
Mount Parnassus was sacred; cf.
7. 12. 10 *per genium Famae Castali-
umque gregem*; Apoll. Sidon. C.
1. 9 *Castalidum chorus.*

2–5. qui . . . Africanis: i.e. in
the Punica; in this poem, naturally,
the Scipios were national heroes.

2. **periuria . . . furoris:** Carthaginian patriotism is *furor* in a
Roman's eyes; cf. 6. 19. 6 *et periuria Punici furoris*; Sil. 1. 79 (*Ha-
milcar*) *sollers nutrire furores.* To
the Romans Hannibal is always
periurus, perfidus; cf. Hor. C. 4. 4.
49 *perfidus Hannibal*; Liv. 21. 4. 9
tantas viri (= *Hannibalis*) *virtutes
ingentia vitia aequabant, . . . perfi-
dia plus quam Punica*; Stat. Silv.
4. 6. 77–78 *semper atrox dextra per-
iuroque ense superbus Hannibal*;
perfidos . . . astus Hannibalis, 3–4
below, with note. *Punica fides* was
proverbial.— **barbari**: see on Lib.
Spect. 1. 1.

3–4. ingenti . . . ore, *with
mighty utterance.* — **premis** = *op-
primis, overwhelm*, i.e. set forth in
words of proper scorn; M. is paying a tribute to the realistic character of Silius's poem. — **perfidos
. . . Hannibalis:** see on 2. *Perfidus* cannot be justly applied to
Hannibal. It flattered Roman
pride, however, to regard everything Carthaginian as naturally
bad, and everything Roman as naturally good; cf. Val. Max. 5. 1.
Ext. 6 *si quidem illos Punico astu
decepit, Romana mansuetudine ho-
noravit.* See App.— **levis,** *fickle,
false*, to treaties, etc.; cf. Hor. C.
3. 9. 22 *tu levior cortice.*

6. **paulum:** i.e. during the
brief period of the Saturnalia.
The festival of Saturnus, which

dum blanda vagus alea December
incertis sonat hinc et hinc fritillis
et ludit tropa nequiore talo,
10　　nostris otia commoda Camenis,
nec torva lege fronte, sed remissa
lascivis madidos iocis libellos.

occurred in December, after the harvest and the vintage (cf. etymology
of Saturnus), was a time of general
merrymaking and good-natured
license. Business was suspended;
the courts adjourned; schools
closed; presents were exchanged;
slaves enjoyed unusual liberties;
the legal prohibition of gambling
was suspended. The toga was laid
aside and men appeared in the
parti-colored *synthesis* with conical
caps (*pillei*): these were worn by
newly emancipated slaves. See
Marq.-Wissowa 3. 586 ff.; Preller-
Jordan 2. 15 ff.

　　7. blanda ... alea: so alluring
and seductive was gambling that
men repeatedly defied the law (see
on 6; cf. Hor. C. 3. 24. 58 *vetita
legibus alea*); cf. 4. 66. 15; 5. 84.
2–4 (*iam*) *blando male proditus fritillo, arcana modo raptus e popina,
aedilem rogat udus aleator. Blanda
... alea* is causal abl. with *vagus*;
'unrestrained, by reason of the al-
lurements of the gaming-table' will
give the sense. — **vagus**: a transferred epithet; it prop. applies to
the people who in December under
the charms of the gaming-table forget all restraint; see on 1. 15. 7.

　　8. incertis, *hazardous*.— **sonat**: cf. Apoll. Sidon. Ep. 2. 9. 4
*frequens crepitantium fritillorum
tesserarumque strepitus audieba-
tur.* — **hinc et hinc**: cf. 10. 83. 1;
12. 34. 5; 12. 57. 7.

　　9. ludit ... talo: see App. —
ludit, *deceives, deludes* the player;

cf. Hor. C. 3. 4. 5–6 *auditis an me
ludit amabilis insania?*— **tropa** (cf.
τρόπα): a game played by throwing
dice or nuts from a fixed distance
into a hole in the ground or into a
jar; in it *tali* were used, not *tesserae*.
See Poll. Onom. 9. 193; Marq. 840.
In Harper's Latin Dictionary *tropa*
is wrongly regarded as an adverb.
The *tali* (ἀστράγαλοι) were originally made out of the ankle-bones
of animals; they were oblong, with
rounded ends. The *tesserae* were
cubes, marked as dice are marked
to-day. The value of a throw of
the *tesserae* depended on the sum
of the points marked on the *up-
turned* faces; that of the *tali* depended on the faces on which the
tali rested after the throw (specific
values were assigned by the rules
of the game to the various possible combinations). See Fried. SG.
1. 423 ff.; Marq. 847 ff.— **nequiore**:
because the throw from the hand
gave more chance for cheating than
was afforded when the *tesserae* or
tali were thrown from a dice-box.

　　10. commoda: an imv., *lend*.—
Camenis: Camena frequently =
Μοῦσα, then it = 'poem', 'poetry'.
Cf. 12. 94. 5; 7. 68. 1 *meas Camenas*.

　　11. nec ... fronte repeats *seposita severitate*, 6; cf. Hor. Ep. 1.
19. 12–13 *si quis voltu torvo ferus
... simulet ... Catonem.*

　　12. madidos, *overflowing with,
steeped in*; cf. 1. 39. 3–4 *si quis
Cecropiae madidus Latiaeque Minervae artibus.*

Sic forsan tener ausus est Catullus
magno mittere Passerem Maroni.

15

Mille tibi nummos hesterna luce roganti
  in sex aut septem, Caeciliane, dies
"Non habeo" dixi : sed tu causatus amici
  adventum lancem paucaque vasa rogas.
5 Stultus es ? an stultum me credis, amice ? negavi
  mille tibi nummos : milia quinque dabo ?

13. forsan: M. may well be cautious, since Catullus seems to have died in 54 B.C., when Vergil was but sixteen years old. Further, Catullus's Passer (see on 14) was written probably as early as 60 B.C. — **tener . . . Catullus:** cf. 7. 14. 3–4 *teneri ploravit amica Catulli Lesbia, nequitiis passeris orba sui. Tener* seems to have been a favorite epithet of writers of erotic verse; cf. Ov. A. A. 3. 333 *et teneri possis carmen legisse Properti*; Rem. Am. 757 *teneros ne tange poetas.* Love is the 'tender passion'.

14. magno . . . Maroni: M. delicately flatters Silius, by comparing him with Vergil. For the comparison of himself with Catullus see § 34. As *Sili* begins the epigram, so *Maroni* ends it; cf. 11. 48; 11. 52. For M.'s laudation of Vergil see on 3. 38. 8. — **Passerem:** for the two poems see on 1. 109. 1. They constitute the first real pieces in our present collection of Catullus's poems; Carmen 1 is dedicatory. M. himself may use *Passerem* for one or both of these pieces as typical of all Catullus's work (Paukstadt 5–6), or it may have been the fashion generally so to refer to them; the modern writer often names his volume of tales or

verse from the first piece in the book. See also on 8. 55. 19.

15. This epigram pokes fun at a thick-headed fellow who asks M., in effect, for a loan of 5000 *sestertii*, though M. had the day before declined to accommodate him with 1000 *sestertii.* — Meter : § 48.

1. nummos: see 1. 66. 4 N.

2. in: freely 'for'; properly 'against'. — **Caeciliane:** if this Caecilianus is the man mentioned in 1. 20, he was a skinflint and a glutton.

3. Non habeo: not necessarily more than a polite refusal, which the dull Caecilianus interprets literally. — **causatus,** *having set up as excuse.* The verb belongs to poetry and Silver Latin; Cicero does not use it.

4. lancem . . . rogas: apparently for use at a dinner in honor of the coming friend.

5. Stultus . . . amice? 'You are either a fool who can't understand a plain answer (3), or a knave, minded to trick me out of my plate'. — **amice:** ironical.

6. milia quinque: i.e. the value of *lanx* and *vasa.* On the cost of such luxuries see Fried. SG. 3. 112 ff. — **dabo:** i.e. 'I might as well give them outright as to lend them to you'.

18

Qua vicina pluit Vipsanis porta columnis
　　et madet adsiduo lubricus imbre lapis,
in iugulum pueri qui roscida tecta subibat
　　decidit hiberno praegravis unda gelu,
5　cumque peregisset miseri crudelia fata,
　　tabuit in calido volnere mucro tener.
Quid non saeva sibi voluit Fortuna licere ?
　　aut ubi non mors est, si iugulatis, aquae ?

18. The climate of Italy has undergone marked change; the incident described here could not occur today. This does not, however, supply reason for discrediting this pathetic story. For the thought, esp. in 7–8, cf. Hor. C. 2. 13. 13–14 *quod quisque vitet numquam homini satis cautum est in horas.* — Meter: § 48.

1. Qua... columnis: the reference is to the Porticus Vipsania, which stood in the Campus Martius; it lay on one side of the Campus Agrippae, and extended northwards from the Aqua Virgo along the Via Lata; see Platner 455. The *porta* was an archway spanning a highway, one of the supports of the Aqua Virgo, the aqueduct built to supply the Thermae Agrippae. This aqueduct, after it reached Rome, was carried on arches from the Pincian Hill down into the Campus Martius. See Platner 98–99; Burn Journ. of Phil. 10. 6; Baumeister 1514.—**pluit:** the aqueduct channel leaked. —**Vipsanis:** for the form see on 1. 117. 17.

2. madet ... lubricus, *is wet and slippery.* With *pluit ... porta ... imbre* (1–2) cf. Iuv. 3. 11 *substitit ad veteres arcus madidumque Capenam (portam),* said of the gate in the old Servian Wall wet with the drip from the Rivus Herculaneus, a branch of the Aqua Marcia.

3. in ... pueri: the boy apparently kept looking up at the icicles as he approached, thus exposing his throat. *Roscida* is hardly a successful epithet if M. meant it as an attempt to deprive the death of its horror. Cf. 1. 88. 6 N.

4. unda: forceful substitute for *stiria* (cf. *stilla*), the common word for icicle (cf. 7. 37. 5).

5. peregisset ... fata: cf. 5. 37. 15–16.

6. mucro: prop. point of sword or dagger, then *dagger, sword.* The metaphor is effective. So too is the epithet *tener;* this *mucro* is at once deadly and yielding. *Mucro tener* involves oxymoron.

8. iugulatis is to be taken literally, *cut throats.* 'Who is safe anywhere, if water, naturally soft and fluid, becomes like steel, if water, that, when it causes death at all, does so by suffocation, takes to cutting throats as does the armed assassin'.

26. Postumus, one of those patrons who paid with no definite regularity (Beck. 2. 207), had apparently resented M.'s long-continued neglect of the *officium* (see 1. 70, with notes). M. virtually bids him a long farewell. — Meter: § 48.

26

Quod te mane domi toto non vidimus anno,
    vis dicam quantum, Postume, perdiderim?
tricenos, puto, bis, vicenos ter, puto, nummos.
    Ignosces: togulam, Postume, pluris emo.

30

Baiano procul a lacu, monemus,
piscator, fuge, ne nocens recedas:
sacris piscibus hae natantur undae,

1–2. **mane . . . non vidimus**: i.e. 'I have not in a whole year presented myself at your *salutatio*'. — **toto . . . anno**: for const. see on 2. 5. 1. — **Postume**: for position see on 1. 16. 2.

3. **tricenos . . . nummos**: 'I may on two occasions have lost 30 *sestertii*, and thrice I may have missed 20'. The loss for the year was thus 120 *sestertii*. By this time there had been a return to the money *sportula*; see 3. 7, with notes; 6. 88. Note that more than the 100 *quadrantes* might be given, esp. if the dole was not a daily one; cf. 9. 100; 10. 27.

4. **Ignosces**: i.e. 'for my plain speaking and my severance of our old relations'. — **togulam . . . emo**: 'your dole will not even pay for a toga, and a scanty one at that, much less help me to get food and drink'. *Togulam* is dim. of contempt. The client watched his *sportula* account closely; cf. Iuv. 1. 117–120 *sed cum summus honor finito computet anno, sportula quid referat, quantum rationibus addat, quid facient comites quibus hinc toga, calceus hinc est et panis fumusque domi?*

30. From the end of the Republic fish-ponds and game-preserves (*piscinae, stagna, vivaria*) were essential to the typical villa. See e.g. Varr. R. R. 3. 3. 10; Plin. N. H. 9. 170; Hor. C. 2. 15. 2–4; Macr. Sat. 3. 15. 6. M. had doubtless seen a fish-pond on the estate of Domitian near Baiae, where he may have heard the story told here, or one that gave rise to it. He makes use of it as an excuse for again playing court flatterer (4. 27 is addressed to Domitian). — Meter: § 49.

1–2. **Baiano . . . lacu**: the *piscina* is compared with the Lucrine Lake itself, unless Domitian actually laid claim to the fish of the Lucrine also. — **monemus . . . fuge**: for examples of such parataxis (instead of *monere ut* or *ne*) see Soed. 12. — **piscator**: any hypothetical poacher; M. is sounding a general warning. — **ne . . . recedas**: a final clause: 'that you may not go away a guilty thing'. M. might have put his thought affirmatively, *ut purus recedas*; cf. 14. — **nocens** = *sacrilegus, damnatus*; cf. *impius*, 8. M. talks as if Domitian were a god and his estate a temple; see on 4. 8. 9 ff. Cf. *sacris*, 3; *sacrilegos . . . hamos*, 12.

3. **sacris**: see preceding note. Through the deification of the

qui norunt dominum manumque lambunt

5   illam, qua nihil est in orbe maius :

quid quod nomen habent et ad magistri

vocem quisque sui venit citatus ?

Hoc quondam Libys impius profundo,

dum praedam calamo tremente ducit,

10 raptis luminibus repente caecus

captum non potuit videre piscem,

et nunc sacrilegos perosus hamos

Baianos sedet ad lacus rogator.

At tu, dum potes, innocens recede

15 iactis simplicibus cibis in undas

et pisces venerare delicatos.

---

emperor *sacer* often virtually = *imperial*; cf. e.g. Lib. Spect. 24. 2 *cui lux prima sacri muneris ista fuit.* — natantur : cf. Ov. Tr. 5. 2. 25–26 *quot piscibus unda natatur, . . . tot premor adversis.* In 14. 196. 2 we have the active used with accusative.

4. norunt : cf. 10. 30. 21–24. — dominum : Domitian. — manum . . . lambunt : they expect him to feed them; cf. Plin. N. H. 32. 16. *e manu vescuntur pisces in pluribus quidem Caesaris villis.*

5. qua . . . maius : cf. 4. 8. 10 *ingenti . . . manu.* — For the meter see § 49, d.

6 ff. Amos may be correct in thinking that Domitian had put out the eyes of some one who had been caught fishing in his *piscina*. M., however, represents the cruelty of the tyrant as an act of providence.

6–7. ad magistri . . . citatus : cf. Plin. N. H. 10. 193 *pisces . . . audire . . . palam est, utpote cum plausu congregari feros* ('the creatures') *ad cibum adsuetudine in*

quibusdam vivariis spectetur, et in piscinis Caesaris genera piscium ad nomen venire, quosdamque singulos. — citatus : cf. 10. 30. 23. Vss. 6–7 may be freely rendered, 'nay, more, they have', etc.

8. impius : see on *nocens*, 2. — profundo : cf. 10. 37. 15 *illic piscoso modo vix educta (lina) profundo.*

9. calamo tremente : cf. 3. 58. 27 N.; 10. 30. 16 ; 1. 55. 9.

10. luminibus : the use of *lumen* in the sense of 'the light of the eye', 'the eye', is mostly poetical : cf., however, Cic. Tusc. 5. 39. 114 *Democritus luminibus amissis alba scilicet discernere et atra non poterat.* The ancients often charged loss of sight to the gods as a punishment for iniquity.

13. rogator = *mendicus*; cf. 10. 5. 4.

14. innocens recede : cf. *ne nocens recedas* (2), with note.

15. simplicibus : i.e. casting in only harmless food, instead of *sacrilegi hami* and bait.

16. pisces venerare : because they are the property of a divine

32

Et latet et lucet Phaethontide condita gutta,
    ut videatur apis nectare clusa suo.
Dignum tantorum pretium tulit illa laborum :
    credibile est ipsam sic voluisse mori.

39

Argenti genus omne conparasti,
    et solus veteres Myronos artes,

personage. — **delicatos,** *dainty,
delicate, petted*; cf. 10. 30. 22, and
deliciae, 'pet'.

32. The tears shed by the sisters of Phaethon (Phaethontides,
Heliades) for their brother's fate
were supposed to have become
amber drops when the women were
metamorphosed into poplars. Cf.
Hyg. Fab. 154; Ov. M. 2. 340 ff.
— Meter : § 48.

1. Et latet et lucet : 'hides
itself and at the same time dis-
closes itself'; cf. Aus. Mosel. 66–
67 *lucetque latetque calculus* (at the
bottom of a spring). — **condita,**
confined, buried. — **gutta :** cf. 6.
15. 2 ; 4. 59. 2.

2. apis : cf. 4. 59 ; 6. 15. 1–4
*dum Phaethontea formica vagatur
in umbra, implicuit tenuem sucina
gutta feram ; sic modo quae fuerat
vita contempta manente, funeribus
facta est nunc pretiosa suis.* — **nectare . . . suo :** the bee in the amber
drop looked as if inclosed in a
portion of its own honey; *nectar*
is used not merely of the drink of
the gods but of other delicious or
precious liquid or semi-liquid sub-
stances. Cf. Verg. G. 4. 163–164
*aliae (apes) purissima mella stipant
et liquido distendunt nectare cellas.*
— **clusa :** cf. Tac. Ger. 45 *sucum
tamen arborum esse intellegas, quia*

*terrena quaedam atque etiam volu-
cria animalia plerumque inter-
lucent, quae implicata umore mox
durescente materia cluduntur* ; Plin.
N. H. 37. 43.

3. Dignum . . . pretium : an
ample return for a life of industry ;
it is a positive distinction to win
such a sepulcher.

39. If this Charinus is the
wretch of 1. 77, as we can hardly
doubt, the point (made in 9–10) is
the more evident. M., while throwing doubt on Charinus's honesty as
an art collector, takes occasion to
press home the old charge of
moral turpitude. Meter : § 49.

Vss. 1–8 recite Charinus's claims;
his collection embraces all kinds
of plate, and is the only genuine
collection in Rome ! M., however,
in order not to spoil his point,
mentions in detail only the *genus
caelatum* (see 3. 35. 1 N.).

1. Argenti, *plate*; cf. 8. 71. 1–2
*quattuor argenti libras mihi tempore
brumae misisti ante annos, Postu-
miane, decem* ; 7. 86. 7 N.

2–5. solus . . . habes : note the
ironical repetition of *solus.* Cf.
the claim made in 8. 6. Passion
for collecting plate and works of
art became a fad at Rome, in
which the supreme motive was
love of display; see on 3. 35. 1.

solus Praxitelus manum Scopaeque,
solus Phidiaci toreuma caeli,
5　solus Mentoreos habes labores,
nec desunt tibi vera Gratiana,

To supply the demand for antique works of art 'originals' were manufactured; see Fried. SG. 2. 176 ff.; 3. 308 ff.; Beck. 1. 41 ff.

2. veteres . . . artes, *old* (and therefore genuine) *masterpieces* (*creations*) *of Myron. Artes* is used here of the results of skill (metonymy); cf. Hor. C. 4. 8. 5–8 *artium quas aut Parrhasius protulit aut Scopas, hic saxo, liquidis ille coloribus*; Stat. Silv. 1. 3. 47 *vidi artes veterumque manus.* Cf. the use of *labores*, 5. If genuine, these articles of virtu were about five hundred years old, for Myron flourished in the fifth century B.C. He ranked among the greatest artists, as sculptor, statuary, and engraver. He excelled in the delineation of animals; much of his work was in bronze. His most famous creations were the statue of a cow and the Discobolus, both in marble. Cf. 8. 50. 1; Iuv. 8. 102–104 *et cum Parrhasii tabulis signisque Myronis Phidiacum vivebat ebur, nec non Polycliti multus ubique labor, rarae sine Mentore mensae*; Fried. SG. 3. 310.

3. Praxitelus : Greek form of genitive. Praxiteles, one of the most famous Greek sculptors and workers in bronze, was born at Athens about 400 B.C. As Phidias was the head of the earlier Attic school, so Praxiteles and Scopas represent the later. Praxiteles's most famous piece was the Venus of Cnidos. His Hermes was also famous and is yet extant, at Olympia in Greece. Cf. Priap. 10. 2–4 *non me Praxiteles Scopasve fecit, nec sum Phidiaca manu politus,*

sed lignum rude vilicus dolavit. — **manum,** *handiwork,* used esp. of finishing touches by artist or writer; so χείρ. Cf. Verg. A. 1. 455–456 *artificumque manus intra se operumque laborem miratur* ; Petr. 83 *Zeuxidos manus*; Stat. Silv. 1. 3. 47, cited on 2. — **Scopae :** Scopas of Paros — architect, statuary, sculptor of the fourth century B.C. See on *Praxitelus* above.

4. Phidiaci . . . caeli : see on 2 ; cf. 3. 35. 1 N. Phidias, the greatest sculptor and statuary of the Greeks, was born about 490 B.C. His friendship with Pericles made him a sort of art director in the erection of the greatest structures at Athens, Elis, and Olympia. — **toreuma:** see on 3. 35. 1. Cf. Plin. N. H. 34. 56 *hic* (*Polyclitus*) *consumasse hanc scientiam iudicatur et toreuticen sic erudisse, ut Phidias aperuisse.* — **caeli:** the chisel or burin of the engraver (*caelator*) or sculptor; cf. 10. 87. 15–16 *mirator veterum senex avorum donet Phidiaci toreuma caeli.*

5. Mentoreos . . . labores: Mentor, who lived in the fourth century B.C., seems to have been the greatest of the *caelatores*; cf. e.g. 8. 51. 1–2 ; 9. 59. 16; Fried. SG. 3. 311–312. — **labores** either denotes the results of his separate endeavors (metonymy; see on *artes*, 2) or is a *pluralis maiestatis.*

6. vera Gratiana (*vasa*) : silverware, apparently Italian, named from the maker or from some one who had popularized it. Plin. N. H. 33. 139, writing of the whims of fashion, says: *nunc Furniana, nunc*

nec quae Callaico linuntur auro,
nec mensis anaglypta de paternis.
Argentum tamen inter omne miror
10   quare non habeas, Charine, purum.

41

Quid recitaturus circumdas vellera collo ?
conveniunt nostris auribus ista magis.

Clodiana, nunc Gratiana . . . nunc anaglypta asperitatemque exciso circa linearum picturas quaerimus. See Marq. 695.

7. quae . . . auro: i.e. the *chrysendeta*; see on 2. 43. 11. — **Callaico . . . auro,** *Spanish gold*; the Callaici (Gallaeci) inhabited Gallaecia in Hispania Tarraconensis. Cf. 14. 95. 1–2 (on a *phiala aurea caelata*) *quamvis Callaico rubeam generosa metallo, glorior arte magis, nam Myos iste labor*; 10. 16. 3. — **linuntur,** *are inlaid, are lined.*

8. anaglypta (*vasa*) = ἀνάγλυπτα, ἀνάγλυφα, i.e. silver vessels ornamented in bas-relief; see Plin. N. H. 33. 139, cited on 6; note on *toreuma,* 3. 35. 1; Iuv. 14. 62 *hic leve argentum, vasa aspera tergeat alter.* — **paternis:** they are heirlooms.

9–10. Since Charinus had *argenti genus omne* (1), he of course had the kind technically known as *argentum purum* (see on 3. 35. 1). M., however, hints that after all none of his ware is *purum,* i.e. 'pure', 'clean'; all has been defiled by the touch of Charinus, a *homo impurus.* See Introd. M. may be hinting, too, that the claims made by Charinus for the genuineness of his plate would not bear investigation.

41. On a reader who appeared before the public with a woolen cloth (*focale*) about his throat. — Meter: § 48.

1. Quid . . . collo? men sometimes wore such *focalia* as a piece of affectation or effeminacy; cf. Hor. S. 2. 3. 254–255. In 12. 89 Charinus on pretense of earache wraps a cloth about his head: *quod lana caput alligas . . . non aures tibi, sed dolent capilli.* If this man is actually hoarse, his croaking will offend the audience (2); elegance of presentation constituted no small part of the successful recitation. For pretenses at recitations see 3. 18, with notes.

2. ista: contemptuous, as often. M. alludes not only to the possible physical disability of the man, but to the feebleness of his poetry. Cf. 14. 137. 1–2 *si recitaturus dedero tibi forte libellum, hoc focale tuas adserat auriculas.* — In *vellera collo* (sc. *tuo*) *nostris auribus ista* the chiasmus emphasizes the double contrast.

44. A picture of Vesuvius before and after the famous eruption of 79. This eruption destroyed Stabiae, Pompeii, and Herculaneum, and made a waste of the Vesuvian slope, which up to that time had been famous for fertility. In 63 an earthquake had given warning that the normal quiet of the mountain was at an end. See Plin. Ep. 6. 16; 6. 20; Dio Cass. 66. 21–23; Mau-Kelsey 19–24. — Meter: § 48.

44

Hic est pampineis viridis modo Vesbius umbris :
　　presserat hic madidos nobilis uva lacus,
haec iuga quam Nysae colles plus Bacchus amavit,
　　hoc nuper Satyri monte dedere choros,
5　haec Veneris sedes, Lacedaemone gratior illi,
　　hic locus Herculeo nomine clarus erat.
Cuncta iacent flammis et tristi mersa favilla
　　nec superi vellent hoc licuisse sibi.

47

Encaustus Phaethon tabula tibi pictus in hac est :

1. **pampineis . . . umbris**: cf.
Verg. (?) Cop. 31 *pampinea . . .
umbra*; Flor. I. 11. 16. 5 *hic* (in
Campania) *amici vitibus montes
Gaurus, Falernus, Massicus, et
pulcherrimus omnium Vesuvius,
Aetnaei ignis imitator.* — **modo**:
hardly ten years had elapsed since
the eruption. — **Vesbius**: this form
and *Vesvius* seem to belong to the
sermo familiaris.

2. **presserat**: a strong word, =
oppresserat, had overwhelmed, i.e.
had filled to overflowing; see on
I. 4. 2. — **madidos**: proleptic, *till
they were filled full.* — **nobilis uva**:
cf. 5. 78. 19 *succurrent tibi nobiles
olivae.* — **lacus**: vats into which
the grape juice flowed as it came
from the press; cf. Cato R. R. 25
*in dolia picata vel in lacum vina-
rium picatum.*

3. **Nysae colles**: Nysa (Nyssa)
was the name of many places in
Asia Minor and the Islands famous
for the growth of the vine, or associated with Bacchus myths.

4. **Satyri**: connected with Bac-
chic worship as satellites of the god.

5. **haec . . . sedes** refers to
Pompeii in particular; Venus was

the patron goddess of that town.
See Mau-Kelsey 266; 344. — **Lacedaemone**: Cythera, where Venus
was believed to have first touched
land after rising from the foam of
the sea, was off the southern coast
of Lacedaemon.

6. **locus . . . erat** refers to Herculaneum, which was reputed to
have been founded by Hercules
when he was on his way back from
Spain after stealing the oxen of
Geryones (see on 5. 49. 11).

7. **tristi**, *dismal*; a transferred
epithet, since the sense is rather
sorrow-causing.

8. **nec**: as in 1. 109. 20; see note
there. — **superi**: the gods, even
Vulcan himself, might well lament
such a display of power. — **licuisse
sibi**: cf. 4. 18. 7 N.; 7. 21. 4; Anthol.
Lat. 2. 1362. 6 *hoc quoque non vellet mors licuisse sibi.*

47. 'Why burn Phaethon a
second time?' — For an allusion
to the story of Phaethon see 4. 32.
— Meter: § 48.

1. **Encaustus** (ἔγκαυστος),
burned in, encaustic. In encaustic
work the colors were burned in
with the help of a medium of melted

quid tibi vis, dipyrum qui Phaethonta facis?

49

Nescit, crede mihi, quid sint epigrammata, Flacce,
  qui tantum lusus illa iocosque vocat.
Ille magis ludit, qui scribit prandia saevi
  Tereos aut cenam, crude Thyesta, tuam,
5   aut puero liquidas aptantem Daedalon alas,

wax mixed with oil. We know less about it than about any other kind of painting practiced in ancient times; see Smith D. of A. 2. 392 ff.; Middleton, Remains of Ancient Rome, 1. 97.

2. dipyrum, *twice exposed to fire*; cf. δίπυρος.

49. Epigram versus epos (and tragedy); a defense of epigram as a serious form of literature. Epigram deals with real life, epos with that which is legendary and imaginary. Cf. 10. 4; see § 33.—Meter: § 48.

1. crede mihi: i.e. 'I am serious in this judgment; the prevailing opinion is due to ignorance'. Cf. § 18, on the relation of M. to Statius; also § 40. — **Flacce:** it is uncertain how far we can identify persons of this name in M.

2. tantum, *only*. — **lusus:** cf. 1. 113. 1 N.; Tac. D. 10 *epigrammatum lusus.* — **iocos:** cf. 1.4. 3 N.

3–4. Ille . . . qui: M. may be thinking of Statius; see Introd. M. may have resented some words in Statius's Praefatio to Book II of the Silvae (addressed to Atedius Melior) : *scis a me leves libellos quasi epigrammatis loco scriptos* (cf. Praefatio to Book IV of the Silvae). Statius was engaged on the Thebais between 80 and 92 ; some parts of the poem had doubtless been heard at recitations. For

M.'s general thought cf. 8. 3; 9. 50. 1–4 *ingenium mihi, Gaure, probas sic esse pusillum, carmina quod faciam quae brevitate placent. Confiteor: sed tu, bis senis grandia libris qui scribis Priami proelia, magnus homo es?* 5. 53. 1–4 *Colchida quid scribis, quid scribis, amice, Thyesten? quo tibi vel Nioben, Basse, vel Andromachen? materia est, mihi crede, tuis aptissima chartis Deucalion vel, si non placet hic, Phaethon;* Iuv. 1. 2–14.— **prandia . . . Tereos** : see on *Atthide,* 1. 53. 9. Note acc. in *prandia*; the best prose commonly shows abl. with *de* after *scribo,* but cf. Liv. 21. 1. 1 *licet mihi praefari . . . bellum me scripturum.*—**crude Thyesta:** see 3. 45. 1 N. *Crudus* prop. = 'bloody', then 'merciless', *crudelis*; it is used with special reference to such cannibalistic practices as this. Cf. Ov. Her. 9. 67–68 *crudi Diomedis imago, efferus humana qui dape pavit equas.*

5. puero: Icarus. The story was not only a favorite with the epic writers (cf. e.g. Iuv. 1. 52), but was acted in a realistic way.— **liquidas,** *melting, molten,* is proleptic, and refers to the melting of the wax by the sun's rays (Schrev.) or to the ultimate fate of Icarus when he fell into the sea. In any case the adj. points out how worthless was Icarus's support.

pascentem Siculas aut Polyphemon oves.

A nostris procul est omnis vesica libellis

Musa nec insano syrmate nostra tumet.

" Illa tamen laudant omnes, mirantur, adorant ".

10   Confiteor : laudant illa, sed ista legunt.

54

O cui Tarpeias licuit contingere quercus

et meritas prima cingere fronde comas,

6. pascentem . . . Polyphemon: M. seems to have in mind Vergil's picture of the Cyclops; cf. A. 3. 655–659 *summo cum monte videmus ipsum inter pecudes vasta se mole moventem pastorem Polyphemum*, etc.

7. A . . . libellis : not an extravagant claim, when we consider the current exaggerated taste in epos and tragedy. — **vesica :** prop. 'bladder'; here used figuratively for *bombast, fustian.* See § 35.

8. Musa . . . nostra : cf. *nostra Thalia*, 4. 8. 12 N. — **insano syrmate :** the *syrma* (σύρμα) was the long trailing robe of the tragic actor, assumed, as was the high boot (*cothurnus*), to magnify his height; cf. Iuv. 8. 228–229 *ante pedes Domiti longum tu pone Thyestae syrma vel Antigonae personam vel Melanippae.* Used figuratively the word denotes tragedy or the fine frenzy appropriate to tragedy. Cf. 12. 94. 3–4 ; Iuv. 15. 30–31.

9. Flaccus's rejoinder. — **Illa :** epos and tragedy. Mark the climax in the verbs.

10. ista legunt : a higher tribute than mere mouth praise, which demands a minimum of time and pains, " with of course the implied and very sound criticism that it is not so easy to write what shall be easy to read " (Saintsbury 1. 260).

— **ista,** *what lies before you* (a meaning common in M.; cf. 1. 70. 18 N.), i.e. 'my epigrams', or, if *ista* is contemptuous (cf. 4. 41. 2 N.), *what you decry.*

54. The poet advises Collinus, as true disciple of Epicurus, to make the most of life; literary fame cannot stay the hand of fate for a single day. — Meter : § 48.

1. Tarpeias= *Capitolinas.* The Mons Tarpeius was but a part of the Mons Capitolinus. It was in honor of Iuppiter Capitolinus that Domitian instituted the *quinquennale certamen* or *agon Capitolinus.* Cf. 9. 3. 8 *quid pro Tarpeiae frondis honore (tibi solvere) potest ?* 9. 40. 1–2 *Tarpeias Diodorus ad coronas Romam cum peteret Pharo relicta.* — **quercus :** the victors received chaplets of oak leaves ; cf. 4. 1. 6 ; Iuv. 6. 387–388. Hence *quercus = querceas coronas.*

2. meritas (from *mereor*) : i.e. that have fairly earned the poet's crown ; render by *deserving,* or by *deservedly.* — **prima . . . fronde:** cf. Verg. A. 8. 274 *cingite fronde comas. Prima* may mean that Collinus won a prize for Latin poetry at the first Agon Capitolinus, held in 86, or it may mean the highest of all the prizes given in that year. See Fried. SG. 3. 426,

si sapis, utaris totis, Colline, diebus
    extremumque tibi semper adesse putes.
5 Lanificas nulli tres exorare puellas
    contigit : observant quem statuere diem.
Divitior Crispo, Thrasea constantior ipso
    lautior et nitido sis Meliore licet,
nil adicit penso Lachesis fusosque sororum
10   explicat et semper de tribus una secat.

3. sapis: cf. 1. 15. 11 N.; Hor. C.
1. 11. 6–7 *sapias, vina liques, et
spatio brevi spem longam reseces.*
—**totis . . . diebus:** ' lose no moment of a single day ; enjoy every
one '. For the sentiment cf. 1. 15 ;
5. 20 ; 7. 47.

4. extremum (*diem*) = *diem
supremum*; see on 1. 109. 17. Cf.
10. 47. 13 ; Hor. Ep. 1. 4. 13 *omnem
crede diem tibi diluxisse supremum*;
Petr. 99 *ego sic semper et ubique
vixi, ut ultimam quamque lucem
tanquam non redituram consume-
rem* ; Sen. Ep. 93. 6.

5. Lanificas . . . puellas: the
Parcae, Clotho, Lachesis, and
Atropos, represented, both in literature and in art, as spinning and
cutting off the thread of life; cf.
6. 58. 7–8 *si mihi lanificae ducunt
non pulla sorores stamina* ; Iuv. 12.
64–66. —**exorare,** *to prevail on,* i.e.
to lengthen life. *Exorare puellas*
recalls Ovid's *exorare puellam,*
which ends a hexameter in A. A.
1. 37 ; F. 4. 111 ; see Zingerle 23.

7. Divitior Crispo: Vibius Crispus, as orator and spy (*delator*) under Domitian, became enormously
rich and held many high offices.
He was consul twice, *curator aqua-
rum,* and proconsul of Africa. His
wealth is variously estimated at
from 200 to 300 million *sestertii.*
See 12. 36. 8–9; Tac. H. 2. 10 ;
Suet. Dom. 3 ; and esp. Iuv. 4.

81–93. — **Thrasea** : P. Thrasea
Paetus, one of the noblest Stoics
of his time, opposed the despotism
of Nero, and was put to death by
Nero in 66. Cf. e.g. 1. 8. 1–2 ; Tac.
Ann. 16. 21. See also 1. 13, with
notes; § 38 fin.

8. lautior . . . Meliore: see
2. 69. 7 N.—*lautior, more elegant.*
—**nitido:** because of oil or clear
complexion, *well-kept, sleek.* In
Stat. Silv. 2. 3. 1–2 Melior is *nitidus.*— **licet,** *although* ; logically
the first word of 7–8. See on 1.
70. 17.

9. penso: *pensum* prop. = a
given quantity of wool weighed
out (cf. *pendere*) to a slave for a
day's spinning, then a spinner's
task. Here it denotes the parcel
of wool allotted to a given man's
life. Cf. 10. 44. 5–6 *gaudia tu differs,
at non et stamina differt Atropos
atque omnis scribitur hora tibi*;
Sen. Herc. Fur. 181–182. — **Lachesis:** see 1. 88. 9 N.—**fusos,**
spindles.

10. explicat, *unrolls, unwinds.*
—**de tribus una:** Atropos; cf.
9. 76. 6–7 *invidit de tribus una soror
et festinatis incidit stamina pensis.*
—**secat:** see App.

57. M., who has been sojourn-
ing at Baiae or in the neighborhood, compares Baiae and Tibur,
the two popular resorts. — Meter:
§ 48.

57

Dum nos blanda tenent lascivi stagna Lucrini
　　et quae pumiceis fontibus antra calent,
tu colis Argei regnum, Faustine, coloni,
　　quo te bis decimus ducit ab urbe lapis.
5　Horrida sed fervent Nemeaei pectora monstri
　　nec satis est Baias igne calere suo ;
ergo sacri fontes et litora grata valete,
　　Nympharum pariter Nereïdumque domus.

1. **blanda**, *charming, seductive*; cf. Stat. Silv. 3. 5. 96 *sive vaporiferas, blandissima litora, Baias.* — **lascivi . . . Lucrini**: see 3. 60. 3 N. During the season Baiae was a scene of festivity and of almost unbridled license; cf. e.g. Prop. 1. 11. 27; Sen. Ep. 51. 3.

2. **quae . . . calent**: the whole region is volcanic. The hot mineral springs which gush from the tufa rocks at various points seem first to have made the place famous as a health resort. — **pumiceis**: i.e. that issue from the porous rocks. *Pumex* is used of soft porous rock in general. — **antra**: either natural or artificially made in furtherance of the medical treatment given at the springs. Since the poet was there so late in the year (5) it would appear that he was taking the waters for some malady. Cf. Stat. Silv. 3. 1. 144–145 *ipsae pumiceis virides Nereides antris exiliunt ultro.*

3. **colis . . . coloni**: Faustinus (1. 25; 3. 58) doubtless had a villa near Tibur, where he was at this writing, enjoying the coolness of the hill. — **Argei . . . coloni**: tradition declared that Tibur was founded by Tiburnus, Coras, and Catillus, sons of Catillus, who was himself son of the Argive prophet

Amphiaraus; cf. e.g. Hor. C. 2. 6. 5 *Tibur Argeo positum colono.* See App.

4. **bis decimus . . . lapis**: see 1. 12. 3–4 N.

5. **Horrida**, *shaggy.* — **fervent . . . monstri**: the Nemean lion after it was slain by Hercules was placed in the zodiac as the sign Leo. In the breast of Leo is Regulus, an especially brilliant star; cf. Plin. N. H. 18. 271 *regia in pectore Leonis stella*; Hor. C. 3. 29. 19–20 *et stella vesani Leonis (furit*), *sole dies referente siccos.* — **monstri**: sprung from Typhon and Echidna.

6. **satis est . . . calere**: for const. cf. 11. 41. 8 *te satis est nobis adnumerare pecus.* — **igne** = *calore.* — **suo**: the southern latitude, not to speak of the heat of the sulphur baths, made Baiae warm long before August.

7. **sacri**: in ancient poetry all springs are sacred, because, as Servius says on Verg. E. 1. 52, *omnibus aquis nymphae sunt praesidentes.* Cf. 8. Besides, these springs were prob. sacred to Aesculapius. — **litora grata**: no coast in the Roman world was so charming as that around the Bay of Naples.

8. **Nympharum . . . domus** refers to *sacri fontes*, **Nereïdum . . . domus** to the *litora grata.*

Herculeos colles gelida vos vincite bruma,
10   nunc Tiburtinis cedite frigoribus.

59

Flentibus Heliadum ramis dum vipera repit,
fluxit in opstantem sucina gutta feram,
quae, dum miratur pingui se rore teneri,
concreto riguit vincta repente gelu.
5   Ne tibi regali placeas, Cleopatra, sepulcro,
vipera si tumulo nobiliore iacet.

9. Herculeos ... bruma: i.e. 'as a winter resort you surpass Tibur'. For Tibur and Hercules see 1. 12. 1 N. — **vincite**: the so-called permissive use of the imv.; the sense is, 'for all I care you may surpass Tibur in the depth of winter'. For a like use of the fut. ind. cf. 5. 42. 1 N.; Hor. C. 1. 7. 1; Smith's edition of Horace's Odes, Introd. § 79. — **bruma**: see 3. 58. 8 N.

10. Tiburtinis ... frigoribus, *the cool days at Tibur.* By contrast with Baiae Tibur reminds one of the winter's cold, for which *frigus* is often used; cf. 1. 12. 1 *gelidas ... arces*; 5. 34. 5; 7. 65. 1; Hor. S. 2. 6. 45 *matutina parum cautos iam frigora mordent.*

59. Cf. 4. 32, with notes. *Vipera* (1) can hardly be taken literally; some small creeping thing more or less resembling a *vipera* may have been caught as described, or may have been artificially inclosed in a substance resembling amber. — Meter: § 48.

1. Flentibus ... ramis: see on 4. 32. 1; cf. Stat. Silv. 5. 3. 85–86 *cunctos Heliadum ramos lacrimosaque germina.*

2. fluxit ... feram: cf. 6. 15. 2, cited on 4. 32. 2. — **opstantem**: i.e. as it blocked the way of the

drop. — **feram** is justified by *vipera*; render by *creature*.

3. miratur ... teneri: *miror* with inf. occurs in Cicero. — **rore** = *umore, aqua.* Amber, though viscid, is clear like *ros* or *nectar.* Cf. *nectare* = 'amber', 4. 32. 2.

4. concreto, *thickened, hardening.* *Concretus* is one of many deponent pf. participles of intr. verbs; cf. *adultus, cautus, coalitus, cretus. Coniurati, conspirati,* 'conspirators', belong here. — **gelu**: here the thickening of the amber through atmospheric influence.

5. Ne ... placeas, *do not pride yourself*; cf. 1. 72. 6; 5. 57. 1 *cum voco te dominum, noli tibi, Cinna, placere.* — **regali ... sepulcro**: for case see on *templo,* Lib. Spect. 1. 3. Cleopatra finally shut herself up with her treasures in a splendid structure — which seems to have been intended for a mausoleum — and made away with herself there, in order that she might not be taken to Rome to adorn Augustus's triumph. — **Cleopatra**: her career was cut off as abruptly as was the life of the *vipera.* M. may have thought of her here because of the story that she died by the bite of an asp; see Suet. Aug. 17, with Schuckburgh's note,

64

Iuli iugera pauca Martialis
hortis Hesperidum beatiora
longo Ianiculi iugo recumbunt :
lati collibus eminent recessus,
5　et planus modico tumore vertex
caelo perfruitur sereniore
et curvas nebula tegente valles
solus luce nitet peculiari :
puris leniter admoventur astris
10　celsae culmina delicata villae.
Hinc septem dominos videre montis

64. A description of the estate of Iulius Martialis on the Ianiculum. Cf. 1. 15. — Meter : § 49.

1. iugera pauca : cf. 31.

2. hortis Hesperidum : these gardens were variously located, sometimes on an island in the ocean on the western verge of the world, sometimes in northern Africa near Mt. Atlas (because the Hesperides were accounted daughters of Atlas) or near Cyrene.

3. longo . . . iugo : the Ianiculum is a long ridge or succession of summits on the west bank of the Tiber. For estates on the hills of Rome see on 1. 85. 2. — **recumbunt** reflects the quiet retirement of the site, esp. as viewed from a distance.

4. lati . . . recessus : i.e. broad, level stretches that run far back stand out in sharp relief on the several hills or summits of the ridge. *Collibus* is ablative. — **eminent** : freely, 'are conspicuous'; lit. 'stand out from'. See App.

5. planus . . . vertex : the summit was level or almost level. — **modico tumore** : abl. of char-

acteristic, *gently swelling*. A prose writer would say, more exactly, *planus vel potius modico tumore.*

6. perfruitur, *enjoys in an exceptional degree* (*per-*).

7. curvas, *winding.* — **nebula tegente,** *though the mist,* etc.

8. solus : see App.—**peculiari,** *peculiarly its own.*

9-10. puris . . . villae : the roofs and gables of the house, itself on the top of the *iugum*, rise one above the other in fairy-like fashion till, as seen from below or against a distant sky, they seem to pierce the clouds. — **puris** : above the fog and smoke of the neighboring town ; cf. 8. 14. 3-4 *specularia puros admittunt soles et sine faece diem.* — **admoventur astris** : cf. Lib. Spect. 2. 1 *hic ubi sidereus propius videt astra colossus* ; Ov. M. 1. 316 *mons ibi verticibus petit arduus astra duobus.* — **delicata** : cf. 7. 17. 1 *ruris bibliotheca delicati* (of this same *rus*). Render by *graceful, fairy-like, dainty.*

11. Hinc : the villa must have been on the northern point of the Ianiculum to command this

et totam licet aestimare Romam,
Albanos quoque Tusculosque colles
et quodcumque iacet sub urbe frigus,
15   Fidenas veteres brevesque Rubras,
et quod virgineo cruore gaudet
Annae pomiferum nemus Perennae.
Illinc Flaminiae Salariaeque
gestator patet essedo tacente,

bird's-eye view of Rome and the country beyond. — **septem . . . montis**: just what hills M. meant we cannot say. The list commonly given in modern books — Capitolinus, Palatinus, Aventinus, Caelius, Esquilinus, Viminalis, Quirinalis, i.e. the hills of the Servian city — is not given in any ancient author. The first enumeration of seven hills dates from the time of Constantine. The phrase *septem montes* seems to have arisen from Septimontium, name of an ancient festival in Rome, for which see e.g. Platner 39–41; Burn, Rome and the Campagna, 37. — **dominos**, *that rule the world*; cf. Prop. 3. 11. 57 *septem urbs alta iugis toto quae praesidet orbi; dominae . . . Romae*, 1. 3. 3 N.

12. aestimare: i.e. to measure with the eye.

13. Tusculos . . . colles: Tusculum (modern Frascati) lay on a spur of the Alban mountains, about ten miles southeast of Rome, just north of Mt. Algidus, which may be referred to here.

14. quodcumque . . . frigus: esp. Tibur; cf. 4. 57. 10 N. — **sub**, *near*, not 'below' (for these places all lay higher than Rome). — **frigus**, *cool spot*; concrete for abstract.

15. Fidenas veteres: Fidenae lay high, between the Tiber and the Anio, on the Via Salaria, about five miles northeast of Rome. At this time it was a broken-down place; cf. Hor. Ep. 1. 11. 7–8; Iuv. 10. 100. — **breves . . . Rubras**: *Rubra saxa* or *ad Rubras* was a small town on the Via Flaminia about nine miles from Rome; the reddish color of the tufa rock gave the place its name.

16–17. The Romans themselves had no clear notion of the origin of the festival of Anna Perenna, which was celebrated on the Ides of March, apparently in an orchard near the first milestone on the Via Flaminia. It was the occasion for unbridled license of tongue and action. See Ov. F. 3. 523 ff., 675–676, 695; Preller-Jordan 1. 343 ff.; Roscher Lex. See App.

18. Flaminiae Salariaeque: sc. *viae*. For the Via Flaminia, named from C. Flaminius, who fell at Trasumenus, see on 3. 14. 4. The Via Salaria left Rome at the Porta Collina and ran through the Sabine country and Picenum to the Adriatic.

19. gestator: here *rider*, not 'bearer'. See on 3. 14. 1. — **patet . . . tacente**, *is in full view though one does not hear the car*; cf. 10. 6. 6 (*quando erit*) *tota . . . Flaminia Roma videnda via?* The *essedum* was a vehicle that more or less resembled the British or Belgic war

20 ne blando rota sit molesta somno,
  quem nec rumpere nauticum celeuma
  nec clamor valet helciariorum,
  cum sit tam prope Mulvius sacrumque
  lapsae per Tiberim volent carinae.
25 Hoc rus, seu potius domus vocanda est,
  commendat dominus : tuam putabis,
  tam non invida tamque liberalis,
  tam comi patet hospitalitate :

chariot of the same name, apparently in having but two wheels and no top; see Fried. SG. 2. 36 ff.; Beck. 3. 15. Cf. the modern trade and fancy names given to vehicles, e.g. ' victoria ', ' brougham '.

20. ne . . . somno: the final clause is very effective; what is really the effect or result of the distance it ascribes to the *essedum* as its deliberate purpose. — **blando . . . somno**: i.e. of people in the villa. — **rota . . . molesta**: cf. Hor. Ep. 1. 17. 7 *si te pulvis strepitusque rotarum* (in Rome) *laedit*.

21–22. rumpere: cf. 14. 125. 1 *si matutinos facile est tibi rumpere somnos*; Iuv. 6. 415–416 *nam si latratibus alti rumpuntur somni*. With *rumpere . . . valet* cf. 8. 32. 6. The const. is common in poetry, but very rare in Cicero and Caesar. — **celeuma** (κέλευμα): the call of the κελευστής or fugleman, who gives the stroke to the rowers. There was much shipping on the Tiber in ancient days; see Lanciani Anc. R. 235 ff. — **clamor . . . helciariorum**: the cries of the bargemen who towed (cf. ἕλκειν, ἕλκιον) the ships or lighters against the river from Ostia. Cf. Apoll. Sidon. Ep. 2. 10. 4–6 *curvorum hinc chorus helciariorum respon- santibus alleluia ripis ad Christum*

levat amnicum celeuma. Helciarius belongs to the *sermo plebeius*; see on *salariorum*, 1. 41. 8.

23–24. cum, *although*. — **Mulvius** (*pons*): see on 3. 14. 4. The noises here referred to were due to the passing of vehicles across the bridge at night and of boats beneath it, and the disturbance created by beggars, etc., but esp. to the fact that under the Empire the people were accustomed to congregate there for nocturnal merrymaking; cf. Tac. Ann. 13. 47. — **sacrum . . . Tiberim**: see on *sacri fontes*, 4. 57. 7. As the spring had its nymph, the river had its god. Cf. Liv. 2. 10. 11 *tum Cocles " Tiberine pater", ait, "te sancte precor, haec arma et hunc militem propitio flumine accipias".* — **lapsae**: freely, 'gliding'.

25. Hoc rus: with its villa; cf. 1. 12. 3 N. — **domus**: regularly of the city mansion; here *palace*. Cf. 3. 58. 51 N.

26–28. commendat dominus: the charm of the host adds to the other attractions. — **tuam putabis . . . hospitalitate**: a good example of parataxis. Far less forceful would be *tam non invida . . . hospitalitate ut tuam (domum esse) putes*. — **liberalis**, *gracious, hospitable*; sc. *domus (est)*.

credas Alcinoi pios Penates
30 aut facti modo divitis Molorchi.
Vos nunc omnia parva qui putatis
centeno gelidum ligone Tibur
vel Praeneste domate pendulamque
uni dedite Setiam colono,
35 dum me iudice praeferantur istis
Iuli iugera pauca Martialis.

68

Invitas centum quadrantibus et bene cenas :

29. Alcinoi . . . Penates: i.e. the house of Alcinous, king of the Phaeacians, who royally entertained Ulysses. See Od. 7–12.

30. facti . . . Molorchi: i.e. of a Molorchus who had not only the kindly spirit of the original Molorchus, but wealth as well. Molorchus of Cleonae dwelt in or near the Nemean Forest and, though in poor circumstances, entertained Hercules when the latter was hunting the Nemean lion. Cf. 9. 43. 12–13; Stat. Silv. 3. 1. 29.

31. omnia . . . putatis, *you who find no acreage large enough.* — **parva:** pred. accusative.

32. centeno . . . ligone: i.e. with a hundred slaves, each with his hoe. Note the sing. of the distributive adjective, a poetic usage; cf. Iuv. 1. 64–65 *cum iam sexta cervice feratur . . . cathedra.* See App. on 16. — **gelidum . . . Tibur:** cf. 4. 57. 10 N.

33–34. Praeneste: modern Palestrina, one of the oldest towns of Latium; it lay on the edge of the Apennines, about twenty-three miles east of Rome. The roses and the nuts of the region were highly esteemed. — **domate:** poets and

prose writers both often speak of the farmer, etc., as 'taming' the soil or the woods. — **pendulam . . . Setiam:** Setia from its lofty position on the Volscian mountains, in Latium, overlooked the Pomptine Marshes; as seen from a distance by the traveler on the Via Appia it must have seemed to hang from the mountain-side. Cf. *pendentia Mausolea,* Lib. Spect. 1. 5 N. Setian wine ranked among the best; cf. 4. 69. 1; 10. 74. 10–11; 13. 112. 1 *pendula Pomptinos quae spectat Setia' campos.* — **uni . . . colono:** i.e. 'make one vast estate, if you will, out of all Setia'.

36. Iuli . . . Martialis: cf. 1. M. imitates Catullus in thus ending a poem with a verse like the first verse; cf. 2. 41; 7. 17; Paukstadt 34.

68. Sextus was one of those who, when they invited their clients to a dinner, ate and drank the best themselves, but treated the clients shabbily. Cf. 1. 20; 1. 43; 3. 7; etc. — Meter: § 48.

1. Invitas . . . quadrantibus: i.e. 'you invite to a dinner so poor that the daily dole (100 *quadrantes*) would pay for it'. *Centum quadrantibus* is instr. abl. (= an abl.

ut cenem invitor, Sexte, an ut invideam ?

69

Tu Setina quidem semper vel Massica ponis,
　Papyle, sed rumor tam bona vina negat :
diceris hac factus caelebs quater esse lagona :
　nec puto nec credo, Papyle, nec sitio.

75

O felix animo, felix, Nigrina, marito
　atque inter Latias gloria prima nurus,

of price) with *invitas, you entertain.*
— **et** = *et tamen.*

2. Cf. 12. 29. 13–16.

69. On Papylus's wines. —
Meter: § 48.

1. **Setina** (*vina*): cf. 4. 64. 34 N.
For the pl. (*vina*) see A. 100, b;
GL. 204, NN. 5–6; L. 1108. After
the supply of Caecuban failed, the
wine of Setia held first place; cf.
8. 51. 19 N.; 10. 74. 10–11; 13. 112;
Iuv. 10. 25–27 *sed nulla aconita
bibuntur fictilibus: tunc illa time,
cum pocula sumes gemmata et lato
Setinum ardebit in auro*; 5. 33–37;
Beck. 3. 434 ff.; Marq. 449 ff. —
Massica: the Mons Massicus lay
near the sea and divided Latium
from Campania; the Ager Falernus
was contiguous to it, in Campania.
Horace mentions this wine several
times; cf. C. 2. 7. 21; 3. 21. 5; Verg.
G. 2. 143. — **ponis**: see 1. 43. 2 N.

2. **rumor**, *Madame Rumor,
town talk.* — **tam bona** (*poni*): i.e.
as many people suppose. *Bona* =
(1) *good, of fine bouquet,* (2) *harmless.* People believe that there is
poison in Papylus's cups. Poisoning
was a common way of committing
murder in ancient times, since it
was not possible to prove scien-
tifically that poison had been

administered. There was a permanent *quaestio de sicariis et veneficis*
at Rome as early as Sulla's time.
Cf. 8. 43; Iuv. 1. 69–72.

3. **diceris**: i.e. 'rumor says that
four of your wives in succession
drank poison mixed with your fine
wines'. — **caelebs**: used of a wid-
ower (*viduus*) as well as of a bachelor. — **lagona**: a long-necked,
wide-mouthed, big-bellied jar or jug
of Spanish earthenware that seems
to have been placed at times upon
the table, at times to have served
for storage, as did the *amphora.*

4. **nec sitio** virtually negatives
nec . . . credo, which was said ironically. This *nec* = *et tamen non,* i.e.
the vs. = *quamquam non puto vina
tua non bona esse, ea bibere tamen
nolo.*

75. 'Nigrina, wife of Antistius
Rusticus, surpassed in conjugal
devotion the storied Euadne and
Alcestis'. In 9. 30 we learn that
she carried the bones of her husband from Cappadocia, where he
had died, to Rome. — Meter: § 48.

1. **animo** = *indole.*

2. **Latias** = *Romanas.* — **nurus**: prop. 'daughters-in-law'; the
poets, however, often use the word
of young married women. Cf. e.g.

te patrios miscere iuvat cum coniuge census,
gaudentem socio participique viro.

5   Arserit Euhadne flammis iniecta mariti
nec minor Alcestin fama sub astra ferat :
tu melius : certo meruisti pignore vitae,
ut tibi non esset morte probandus amor.

Ov. M. 15. 486–487 *extinctum La-*
tiaeque nurus populusque patresque
deflevere Numam.

3. patrios ... census is the
property that Nigrina had inherited
and that was secured to her by law;
this she nevertheless shared with
her husband. By M.'s time the
emancipation of women was an
accomplished fact; women married
more and more frequently *sine con-*
ventione, in which case their property (the *dos* excepted) did not
become the property of their hus-
bands. See Fried. SG. 1. 467–468.
— **miscere** = *communicare*, or else
coniuge is briefly put for *coniugis*
censibus (= *bonis*). Such compa-
ratio compendiaria is common both
in Latin and in Greek. Latin is
capable of saying *oculus equi ele-*
phanto (= *quam elephanti oculus*)
maior est.

4. socio participique: i.e. as
companion and partner (of joys and
earthly goods). — **viro** = *marito*, 1.

5. Arserit Euhadne: cf. Hyg.
Fab. 243 *Euadne ... propter Capa-*
neum coniugem qui apud Thebas
perierat in eandem pyram se con-
iecit; Ov. A. A. 3. 21 ff. Verg. A.
6. 447 places her among the hero-
ines of the lower world. *Arserit*
may be meant to suggest not
merely Euadne's physical sacrifice,
but her passionate love. The subjv.
here is volitive (subjv. of will) with
concessive force, 'let Euadne have',
etc., = *though Euadne*, etc. — **in-**
iecta: pass., but with middle force.

6. minor, *in less measure, less*
freely.—**Alcestin**: when the oracle
declared that Admetus, king of
Pherae in Thessaly, must die unless some one should die in his
stead, his wife Alcestis offered herself. The story has been immortalized by the Alcestis of Euripides;
see also Hyg. Fab. 243.—**sub astra**
ferat: cf. Lib. Spect. 1. 6 (*nec*)
laudibus inmodicis Cares in astra
ferant; Ennod. C. 2. 12. 10 *quod*
vincens aevum nomen ad astra
ferat. The devotion of Nigrina
shines by contrast with Juvenal's
picture of marital infidelity and
heartlessness; cf. Iuv. 6. 652–
654 *spectant* (sc. women in the
theater) *subeuntem fata mariti Al-*
cestim et, similis si permutatio
detur, morte viri cupiant animam
servare catellae.

7–8. 'You need not die vicari-
ously to prove your devotion; by
your living you have gained greater
glory than they gained by their
dying'. Cf. 1. 8. 5–6 *nolo virum*
facili redemit qui sanguine famam ;
hunc volo, laudari qui sine morte
potest. — **melius:** sc. *fecisti.* —
certo, *unmistakable, genuine.* —
vitae may be regarded either as
gen. of definition or as subjective
gen.; *pignore vitae* = 'a pledge
supplied by your living'. — **ut ...**
amor: a result clause; *meruisti*
(7) = *effecisti.* We might rewrite
certo ... amor thus : *certo pignore,*
vita non morte, effecisti ut tibi esset
probandus amor.

79

Hospes eras nostri semper, Matho, Tiburtini.
Hoc emis; imposui: rus tibi vendo tuum.

86

Si vis auribus Atticis probari,
exhortor moneoque te, libelle,
ut docto placeas Apollinari.
Nil exactius eruditiusque est,
5 sed nec candidius benigniusque:
si te pectore, si tenebit ore,
nec rhonchos metues maligniorum,
nec scombris tunicas dabis molestas;

79. M. intimates that Matho, who has so frequently and for so long spunged upon him at his villa, might well assume that it belonged to him. In Roman law possession of property for a given time gave legal title to it.— Meter: § 48.

1. nostri . . . Tiburtini: sc. *praedi.* M. must refer to his Nomentanum (2. 38 N.), which may have been midway between Nomentum and Tibur.

2. emis: prob. ironical. 'Better buy the place outright; and yet, if I were to sell it to you, that would be a cheat, for it is yours already'. — **imposui,** *I have cheated you,* in charging you anything for it. Cf. 3. 57. 1 *callidus imposuit nuper mihi copo Ravennae.* — **rus:** see App.

86. Cf. 1. 3; 3. 2. — Meter: § 49.

1. auribus Atticis: ears of people most critical, who recognize only the highest standards. As Athens represented the high-water mark of everything Greek, *Atticus* came to mean 'preëminent',

'learned', 'critical'; cf. 3. 20. 9 *lepore tinctos Attico sales narrat?* Cic. Or. 7. 23 (*Demosthenes*) *quo ne Athenas quidem ipsas magis credo fuisse Atticas.*

3. docto: cf. 1. 25. 2 N.— **Apollinari:** apparently Domitius Apollinaris,*consul designatus* in 97. Cf. 7. 89; 10. 30.

4. Nil: see on 1. 10. 3.

5. candidius, *fairer* (in judgment); cf. 8. 28. 15–16 *sed licet haec primis nivibus sint aemula dona, non sunt Parthenio candidiora suo.*

6. pectore . . . tenebit: i.e. 'shall appreciate you'. — **tenebit ore:** i.e. 'shall talk favorably about you'.

7. rhonchos: cf. 1. 3. 5. N.

8. scombris . . . molestas: cf. 3. 2. 4 N.; 3. 50. 9. The term *tunica molesta,* 'shirt of pain' (Duff), a tunic or shirt smeared with pitch in which criminals were burned (cf. 10. 25. 5–6; Iuv. 1. 155–157) is here humorously applied to the paper in which the fish are wrapped. Cf. 13. 1. 1.

si damnaverit, ad salariorum
10   curras scrinia protinus licebit,
inversa pueris arande charta.

9. salariorum: cf. I. 41. 8 N.

10. scrinia: see I. 2. 4 N. Here the *scrinia* are boxes in which the dealers in salt fish (9) and school-masters keep their scrap-paper (see on 11). With *ad . . . scrinia* cf Catull. 14. 17–18 *ad librario-rum curram scrinia.*

11. inversa . . . charta: papy-rus (see I. 25. 7–8 ; note on *charta*, I. 66. 7) was prepared to carry writing on but one side. The un-used side often served as scrap-paper or as wrapping-paper; cf. 8. 62 I *scribit in aversa Picens epi-grammata charta*; Iuv. I. 4–6; Plin. Ep. 3. 5. 17. — **pueris**: either clerks of the tradesmen, who com-puted accounts on the reverse side, or schoolboys, who wrote exercises thereon. See Marq. 815, NN. 3–4, for mention of an Egyptian papy-rus now in Leyden which has a child's school exercises on the un-used side. — **arande** = *scribende*, but with ironical force, to mark the rough service to which the papyrus will be put. *Aro*, 'write', is rare, but Cicero, Pliny the Younger, and Suetonius use *exaro* in this sense. Note the case ; strictly we should have the nom., to agree with the subject of *curras*, but since 1–10 are directly addressed to the book, the voc. is natural enough ; it is, besides, far more effective.

LIBER V

8

Edictum domini deique nostri
quo subsellia certiora fiunt
et puros eques ordines recepit
dum laudat modo Phasis in theatro,
5   Phasis purpureis rubens lacernis,
et iactat tumido superbus ore
"Tandem commodius licet sedere,
nunc est reddita dignitas equestris,

8. At Rome in the theater people sat in classes; the senators sat in the orchestra, the knights (*equites*) in the first fourteen rows (*gradus*, *subsellia*) back of the senators, the populace back of the knights. This privilege of the knights dates at least from the Lex Roscia, carried through by L. Roscius Otho, *tribunus plebis* in 67 B.C. The law was naturally unpopular, since it unseated many persons who had occupied desirable seats on equal terms with the knights. Hence persistent attempts were made to circumvent it; Phasis is a representative of a large class. At various times attempts were made to give new force to the old enactment, e.g. by the Lex Iulia of Augustus (Suet. Aug. 44) and by the edict which Domitian as *censor morum* issued in 89 or at the end of 88 (Suet. Dom. 8). Allusions to the whole matter are numerous; cf. e.g. 5. 14 ; 5. 27. 3–4 *bis septena tibi non sunt subsellia tanti ut sedeas viso pallidus Oceano*

(a *dissignator*, 'usher'); Iuv. 3. 153 ff.; Hor. Ep. 1. 1. 62 ff. See Fried. in Marq.-Wissowa 3. 531 ff.; 3. 534 ff.— Meter : § 49.

1. **domini deique:** used here for the first time ; cf. 10. 72. 3. Domitian so styled himself, according to Suet. Dom. 13. See also 4. 8. 8 ff., with notes; Mommsen Staats. 2. 759.

3. **puros . . . ordines:** i.e. rows of seats uncontaminated by the rabble. Cf. 9. — **eques:** collective singular.

4. **Phasis:** perhaps a fictitious name (§ 38), coined to stigmatize a freedman who, as slave, had been brought from Colchis. Perhaps, however, the man's resplendent attire reminded M. of a pheasant (*phasis*). See on 3. 58. 16.

5. **purpureis . . . lacernis:** see 2. 29. 3 N.; cf. the pl. *lacernas* in 12. M. is perhaps hinting that Phasis was all clothes.

6. **tumido,** *vaunting*.

7. **commodius,** *more comfortably, more decently*; explained by 9.

turba non premimur nec inquinamur ",
10   haec et talia dum refert supinus,
illas purpureas et adrogantes
iussit surgere Leïtus lacernas.

9

Languebam : sed tu comitatus protinus ad me
venisti centum, Symmache, discipulis ;
centum me tetigere manus aquilone gelatae :
non habui febrem, Symmache, nunc habeo.

13

Sum, fateor, semperque fui, Callistrate, pauper,
sed non obscurus nec male notus eques,

10. **supinus**: i.e. lolling lazily on the comfortable equestrian seat.

12. **surgere**: i.e. to leave the equestrian seats. — **Leïtus**: a *dissignator*, mentioned repeatedly ; cf. 5. 14. 11 ; 5. 25. 1–2 *quadringenta tibi non sunt, Chaerestrate : surge, Leïtus ecce venit ; st! fuge, curre, late.*

9. M. tells how the visit of a prominent physician made him seriously ill. — Meter : § 48.

1–2. **Languebam,** *I was feeling a little dull, I was under the weather.* — **comitatus . . . discipulis**: there were no hospitals in Rome ; hence Symmachus turned M.'s bedchamber into a clinic. Symmachus seems to have had notoriety, if not fame : cf. 6. 70. 4–6. On medical practice at Rome see Fried. SG. 1. 339 ff. ; Marq. 771 ff. For the syntax cf. Verg. A. 1. 312 *ipse uno graditur comitatus Achate.*

3. **centum . . . gelatae**: every pupil felt M.'s pulse. — **aquilone gelatae**: the tramontana was blowing at the time.

4. **nunc habeo**: i.e. 'they gave me fever and ague'. For the pentameter-ending in 2 and 4 see § 48, b.

13. Callistratus was evidently a Greek, probably a freedman, perhaps an *eques* (see on 2, 6). That he was boastful and vain may be assumed from the tone of M.'s remarks. — Meter : § 48.

1. **Sum . . . pauper**: on M.'s poverty see §§ 8–11 ; 14–15 ; 36. In 10. 76 (where *Maevius* prob. is a substitute for *Martialis*) he complains that the poet freezes in an ugly garb, while the jockey shines in splendid clothes. It is altogether improbable that M. ever possessed the equestrian census (400,000 *sestertii*), though this was small enough compared with the enormous fortunes amassed by some of the freedmen, esp. such as were in favor with the emperors (see on 6). M., however, had equestrian rank ; cf. 5. 17. 2 ; 9. 49. 4 ; § 8.

2. **non . . . eques**: that the *ordo equester* had sunk very low at this time is well known ; cf. Iuv. 3. 153 ff.

sed toto legor orbe frequens et dicitur "Hic est",
   quodque cinis paucis, hoc mihi vita dedit.
5 At tua centenis incumbunt tecta columnis
   et libertinas arca flagellat opes
magnaque Niliacae servit tibi gleba Syenes
   tondet et innumeros Gallica Parma greges.
Hoc ego tuque sumus: sed quod sum non potes esse:
10   tu quod es e populo quilibet esse potest.

— **male notus** = *ignotus.* It may also mean *evilly known* (*infamis*), and contain a reference to the proverbially iniquitous means used by the freedmen (e.g. Callistratus) to enrich themselves.

3. sed . . . est: for M.'s fame see §§ 39–40. — **toto . . . orbe:** cf. 1. 1, with notes; Ov. Am. 1. 15. 8 *in toto semper ut orbe canar.* — **frequens** is prop. used of crowded places, then of persons or things that gather or are collected in numbers (e.g. *frequens senatus*). Here the use is odd, for M., in order to cling to his contrast of *ego* and *tu*, says in the pass. what he could have said more clearly in the active: *me toto orbe homines legunt frequentes.* Render by 'throngs of readers'. — **Hic est:** cf. 1. 1. 1 N.; Shakespeare, 1 Henry the Fourth, 3. 2. 47–48 "But like a comet I was wonder'd at, That men would tell their children, 'This is he'"; Otto s.v. *Digitus.*

4. quod . . . dedit: cf. 1. 1. 4–6 N.; Herrick 624 "I make no haste to have my numbers read: Seldome comes Glorie till a man be dead".

5–8. 'You are rich, yes, but obscure'.

5. tua . . . columnis: M. may be thinking of the many columns of the *peristylium* or *tecta* may = *domus* (synecdoche). In the atrium and the *peristylium*, long before

M.'s time, expensive and multicolored marbles were used. Cf. Hor. C. 2. 18. 3–5; Verg. A. 7. 170 *tectum augustum, ingens, centum sublime columnis.*

6. libertinas . . . opes: the wealth and arrogance of the freedmen were proverbial. On the rule of the freedmen see Fried. SG. 1. 392 ff.; Merivale, chap. 50. Hence *libertinas* may merely = *ingentes, immensas.* But in this context the word prob. serves rather to score Callistratus's insignificance; see on *male notus*, 2, and cf. the analysis of 5–8. — **flagellat:** cf. 2. 30. 4 N.

7. magna . . . Syenes: Rome relied largely on Egypt for its supply of grain. Syene (modern Assuan) was a Roman frontier town on the east bank of the Nile just below the Lesser Cataract. The famous syenite, which was quarried there, made the place well known. For the gen. form *Syenes* see on 1. 70. 10. — **servit tibi,** *ministers to you, yields you wealth.* — **gleba:** prop. a clod turned up by the plow; hence, virgin or rich soil, such as the Nile valley afforded in a good season.

8. tondet: sc. *tibi*; 'you know where your next toga will come from: I don't'. — **Gallica Parma:** cf. 2. 43. 4 N.

9–10. quod sum: i.e. distinguished, though poor. — **quod es:** i.e. insignificant, though rich.

14

Sedere primo solitus in gradu semper
tunc, cum liceret occupare, Nanneius
bis excitatus terque transtulit castra,
et inter ipsas paene tertius sellas
5   post Gaiumque Luciumque consedit.
Illinc cucullo prospicit caput tectus
oculoque ludos spectat indecens uno.

14. Cf. 5. 8, with notes.—
Meter: § 52.

1. primo . . . gradu: the first
of the fourteen rows of seats in
the theater assigned to the *equites*.

2. cum . . . occupare: i.e. before Domitian's edict was issued.
— **occupare:** *occupo* often = 'get
the start of (somebody or something else)'; cf. Cic. Cato M. 16. 56
*Ahala Sp. Maelium . . . occupatum
interemit.* Here it is used of getting
a seat by coming early. Render,
'when the practice was, first come,
first served'.

3. excitatus: we may perhaps
supply *e somno*, and suppose that
Nanneius pretended to be asleep
when the usher approached. —
transtulit castra: i.e. moved on.
Leïtus keeps Nanneius on the
march, as a general keeps an enemy
moving by hanging on his rear. As
used of an individual, the phrase
is prob. part of the slang of the
camp (*sermo familiaris*). Cf. Prop.
4. 8. 28 *multato volui castra movere
toro.*

4–5. inter . . . consedit is pure
hyperbole, sheer fun; all attempts
to interpret the words literally involve absolute disregard of the
known conditions and arrangements
of the Roman theater. *Sellas* apparently = ' sittings', ' sitting-places';
inter . . . sellas marks a contrast with
sedere (1), and thus makes *consedit*

(5) a bit of grim humor (*sat! took
his position!*). Formerly, Nanneius
had a full, comfortable seat; now
all he has is a place between two
seats!—**paene tertius:** more grim
humor; he was almost in line with
the other two, yet after all very far
from having seats as they had. —
post . . . Lucium: the Romans
used the names Gaius, Lucius,
Seius, and Titius as the names
John Doe and Richard Roe are
now used, esp. by lawyers. Cf. the
Digesta passim; Iuv. 4. 13–14 *nam
quod turpe bonis Titio Seioque de-
cebat Crispinum*; and the response
of the bride in the wedding ceremony *quando tu Gaius, ego Gaia.*
Here Gaius and Lucius are true
knights, fully entitled to seats in
the fourteen rows. — **-que . . .
-que:** a combination almost wholly
confined to poetry; common in M.
— **consedit** keeps up the military
figure of 3; *consido* is often used
of a general or army taking a given
position.

6. cucullo . . . tectus: he seeks
to hide his face; cf. 1. 53. 4 N. We
may suppose that there was nothing
in Nanneius's garb to attract the
usher's attention; cf. 5. 8. 5, 11.

7. oculo . . . indecens uno,
an unsightly, one-eyed creature,
gives the result of *cucullo . . . caput
tectus* (6); *oculo . . . uno* is causal
abl. — **spectat:** see 1. 4. 5 N.

Et hinc miser deiectus in viam transit
subsellioque semifultus extremo
10　et male receptus altero genu iactat
equiti sedere Leïtoque se stare.

20

Si tecum mihi, care Martialis,
securis liceat frui diebus,
si disponere tempus otiosum
et verae pariter vacare vitae,
5　nec nos atria nec domos potentum
nec litis tetricas forumque triste

8. **miser:** mock sympathy. — **deiectus:** also a military term, used of an enemy dislodged from his position. — **viam:** either one of the passages running between the blocks of seats (*cunei*), technically known as *scalae*, or, more probably, one of the *praecinctiones*. Two or three of the latter commonly ran round the theater, partly to separate the different classes of seats, partly to facilitate ingress and egress. The *viae* afforded standing room to people not having regular seats. — For the caesura see § 52, c.

9. **subsellio . . . extremo** may mean the end of a row, or, better, the last of the fourteen rows of the knights (contrast *primo . . . gradu*, 1). Nanneius clings desperately to the equestrian seats; to go further back is to be lost in the rabble. — **semi-fultus,** *only half supported.*

10. **male receptus:** freely, 'resting uncomfortably'. — **altero,** *one,* almost = *alterutro.* — **iactat,** *boasts* (cf. 5. 8. 6); with *stare,* 11, it = *asserts*; it need not imply speech.

11. **equiti:** collective singular. — **sedere:** i.e. that he has a real seat as an *eques*; cf. 1, and note on

4–5. — **Leïto:** see 5. 8. 12 N. — **stare:** as he evidently had a right to do, in the *via,* 8.

20. Cf. 1. 15, with notes. — Meter: § 49.

1–10. **Si . . . liceat . . . nosse-mus . . . essent:** M. has combined two different conditional forms: (1) *si . : . liceat . . . norimus . . . sint,* and (2) *si . . . liceret . . . nossemus . . . essent.* Fusion (confusion) of syntactical forms is common at all periods of Latin.

3. **disponere . . . otiosum:** cf. Plin. Ep. 4. 23. 1 *ex communibus amicis cognovi te, ut sapientia tua dignum est, et disponere otium et ferre.*

4. **verae . . . vitae:** cf. *vivere,* 14; notes on 1. 15. 4; 1. 103. 12; 2. 90. 3. — **pariter,** *in each other's company.*

5. **domos potentum:** houses to which clients, such as M. was, must resort at the daily levee; cf. 1. 70. 13; 12. 18. 4–5; Hor. Epod. 2. 7–8 *forumque vitat et superba civium potentiorum limina.*

6. **tetricas:** cf. 10. 20. 14 N. — **triste:** because associated with funerals, litigation, and money

nossemus nec imagines superbas,
sed gestatio, fabulae, libelli,
Campus, porticus, umbra, Virgo, thermae,
10   haec essent loca semper, hi labores
Nunc vivit necuter sibi bonosque
soles effugere atque abire sentit,
qui nobis pereunt et inputantur.
Quisquam vivere cum sciat, moratur?

22

Mane domi nisi te volui meruique videre,
sint mihi, Paule, tuae longius Esquiliae.

losses. In the forum the funeral oration (*laudatio funebris*) was pronounced; the Centumviri met in the Basilica Iulia; many of the brokers (*argentarii*) did business there. Cf. *foro abire, foro cedere*, 'become bankrupt'.

7. imagines superbas: see 2. 90. 6 N.; 3. 38. 11 N.; Sen. Ben. 3. 28. 2 *qui imagines in atrio exponunt et nomina familiae suae longo ordine ac multis stemmatum inligata flexuris in parte prima aedium collocant, non noti magis quam nobiles sunt?*

8. gestatio: a place of exercise, then the exercise taken in a *gestatio*; cf. 1. 12. 5–8. — For the *-ŏ* § 54, c. — **fabulae,** *conversation.*

9. Campus: see 2. 14. 3–4 N. — **porticus:** these colonnades were frequently flanked by rows of trees, which added to their beauty and comfort; see on 2. 11. 2; 2. 14. 3–4, 10. — **Virgo:** for this aqueduct see on 4. 18. 1. — The continuous diæresis here (§ 49, d) is most effective; it makes each item named stand out distinctly. So in 10 *semper* stands out.

10. See App.

11–12. necuter = *neuter* or *ne alteruter quidem*, neither of which is metrically admissible here. — **bonos . . . soles:** such days ought to be put to a better use. For *soles* in the sense of *dies* cf. Hor. C. 4. 5. 7–8 *gratior it dies et soles melius nitent.*

13. pereunt: cf. 10. 58. 7–8. — **et** = *et tamen.* — **inputantur:** i.e. 'are charged up to our account by the Fates, who keep the score'; cf. 10. 30. 26–27; 10. 44. 5–6 *gaudia tu differs, at non et stamina differt Atropos atque omnis scribitur* (= *inputatur*) *hora tibi.*

14. Quisquam is used chiefly in negative sentences; hence the vs. = *num quis . . . moratur.* The thought is, *Martialis, vivere nescimus, ego et tu.*

22. M. complains that his patron Paulus has treated him unfairly. — Meter: § 48.

1. Mane: at the *salutatio.* — **merui . . . videre:** *mereo* with inf. occurs also in Ov., Iuv., Quint.; cf. 4. 10. 4.

2. sint: subjv. of wish; for the structure of 1–2 cf. 2. 5. 1–2. *Sint = absint.* Down to the end of

Sed Tiburtinae sum proximus accola pilae,
　　qua videt anticum rustica Flora Iovem :
5　alta Suburani vincenda est semita Clivi
　　et numquam sicco sordida saxa gradu,
vixque datur longas mulorum rumpere mandras

the Republic the Mons Esquilinus was not a favorite place of residence. The eastern part (the Campus Esquilinus), outside of the Agger of Servius, was the place of execution and a common burial-plot where the bodies of the poor were disposed of under circumstances most revolting; see Lanciani Anc. R. 64 ff. Maecenas, the patron of Horace, bought the place, covered the burial-pits (*puticuli*) with thirty feet of earth, and laid out there the famous Horti Maecenatiani, in which he built his great palace. By M.'s time many rich people lived there. Cf. Iuv. 3. 69 ff. M. could not, for metrical reasons, use *Esquilīnus*.

3. Sed: 'but as a matter of fact I live far enough away'. — **Tiburtinae . . . pilae:** an unknown object, prob. a monument erected at a street-crossing. See Jordan Archaeol. Zeit. 4. 71 ; Baumeister 1532.

4. qua . . . Iovem : the Aedes Florae here referred to was on the northern side of the Quirinalis, prob. facing the Capitolium Vetus, which lay to the south of it. See Hülsen Rhein. Mus. 49. 407 ff.; 49. 419 ; Baumeister 1532. — **rustica Flora :** the worship of Flora was common enough in the rural districts, e.g. among the Sabini and the Marsi, before it was brought to Rome. *Rustica* may, however, refer to the temple, which, according to some, lay outside the Agger of Servius and so was in the country.

See Preller-Jordan 1. 431 ; Roscher Lex. M. at this time dwelt in lodgings on the Quirinalis (see 1. 117. 6 N.) ; later he seems to have owned a modest house there. See 9. 97. 7–8 ; Hülsen Rhein. Mus. 49. 396 ; Brandt 30.

5. alta . . . Clivi: the Clivus Suburanus led from the Subura up the Esquilinus; cf. 10. 20. 4–5. It seems to have been both steep and narrow (cf. *semita*); hence locomotion was difficult in the crowds that swarmed in and out of the Subura. — **vincenda** = *superanda*; cf. Verg. G. 3. 270 *superant montes et flumina tranant.*

6. et . . . gradu: the way is not only steep but muddy. Many of the aqueducts entered Rome by way of the Esquiline, and the dripping from countless pipes added to the mud. See Burn Journ. of Phil. 10. 2. On the press and filth of the streets see 10. 10. 7–8 ; Iuv. 3. 243–248. — **gradu:** collective sing.; the reference is to steps or stages in the steep grade of the street.

7. mandras: *mandra* (cf. μάνδρα) prop. = an inclosed space, esp. for cattle — 'pen', 'stable'; then a 'herd' or 'drove' of animals. Here the reference is to pack-animals strung out along the narrow *semita* (*longas*), blocking it. Cf. Iuv. 3. 237 *stantis convicia mandrae,* the wrangling of drivers whose pack has been brought to a stop in the streets. — **rumpere** = *perrumpere*; see on *pone,* 1. 4. 2.

quaeque trahi multo marmora fune vides.

Illud adhuc gravius, quod te post mille labores,

10   Paule, negat lasso ianitor esse domi.

Exitus hic operis vani togulaeque madentis :

vix tanti Paulum mane videre fuit.

Semper inhumanos habet officiosus amicos :

rex, nisi dormieris, non potes esse meus.

8. **trahi multo . . . fune:** i.e.
being dragged through the Subura
up the ascent; cf. Iuv. 3. 257-260.

9. **Illud . . . gravius,** *this is a
hardship still more trying. Illud*
is explained by *quod . . . domi; ille*
often thus refers to what follows.
— **adhuc:** this use of *adhuc* to
strengthen a comparative is somewhat late; cf. Iuv. 8. 36-37 *si quid
adhuc est quod fremat in terris vio-
lentius.* — **labores:** sc. *meos.*

10. **negat . . . domi:** cf. 2. 5. 5 N.;
Tib. 2. 6. 48 *haec* (i.e. his *domina*)
negat esse domi; Sen. Brev. Vit.
14. 4 *quam multi per refertum clientibus atrium prodire vitabunt et per
obscuros aedium aditus profugient?
quasi non inhumanius sit decipere
quam excludere;* Hor. Ep. 1. 5.
30-31.

11. **operis vani:** cf. 4. 26 and
many other wails of M. concerning
the unprofitableness of the *officium;*
Iuv. 5. 76-79. — **togulae:** dim., because the toga of the poor client
is scanty and threadbare; see on
4. 26. 4. — **madentis** either =
sweating (cf. *sudatrix toga,* 12. 18.
5 N.), or is to be explained by a
reference to 6.

12. **vix tanti:** cf. 1. 12. 11 N.;
2. 5. 7-8. For like const. (with inf.)
cf. 8. 69. 3-4. — **videre:** i.e. (even)
to see.

13. **officiosus,** *a man who
answers duty's call;* said of Paulus,
in part ironically, because he

wholly fails to do his duty by his
clients, in part seriously, because,
as M. intimates, though he is patron to M. and others, he is still a
client to others above him. For
this state of things cf. 2. 32. 7-8
*non bene, crede mihi, servo servitur
amico: sit liber, dominus qui volet
esse meus;* 2. 18, with notes. —
amicos: ironical; cf. Sen. Ben.
6. 33. 4 *non sunt isti amici qui
agmine magno ianuam pulsant, qui
in primas et secundas admissiones
digeruntur.*

14. **rex:** cf. 2. 18. 5 N.; 1. 112.
1-2 *cum te non nossem, dominum
regemque vocabam; nunc bene te
novi: iam mihi Priscus eris.* —
nisi dormieris: i.e. 'later (until I
can reach your house), instead of
starting forth early yourself to
dance attendance on some other
man'.

24. On a popular gladiator. In
Rome the great gladiators and
jockeys (*aurigae, agitatores*) were
in their day heroes; cf. Lib. Spect.
29. 3 N. Hermes was evidently for
a time a darling of the people. —
Meter: § 49.

1. **Hermes, Helius** (5), **Advolans** (6) are prob. stage names
(§ 38). They may, however, be
genuine slave names (gladiators
were either captives or slaves);
owners named slaves sometimes
from the places of their nativity
(cf. Afer, Syrus, etc.), sometimes

24

Hermes Martia saeculi voluptas,
Hermes omnibus eruditus armis,
Hermes et gladiator et magister,
Hermes turba sui tremorque ludi,
5　Hermes, quem timet Helius, sed unum,
Hermes, cui cadit Advolans, sed uni,
Hermes vincere nec ferire doctus,
Hermes subpositicius sibi ipse,
Hermes divitiae locariorum,

after some deity or mythological personage. — **Martia:** prop. *soldierly*; freely, 'prince of gladiators'. Cf. 2. 75. 8 *Martia non vidit maius harena nefas.* — **saeculi,** *of the age.* — The repeated omission of the verb (*est*) makes the epigram virtually a prolonged ejaculation.

2. omnibus . . . armis: most gladiators were trained to fight in some particular way (e.g. as *retiarii* or *Thraeces*; see on Lib. Spect. 29. 5) and were content to distinguish themselves therein. On the gladiatorial schools see Fried. SG. 2. 376 ff.

3. gladiator . . . magister: Hermes not only fights, but teaches others, either as a *magister* of a *ludus gladiatorius*, or as a private trainer (*lanista*).

4. turba . . . ludi: freely, 'the terror and awe of his own school'. Hermes maintains perfect discipline and the rigorous training so necessary to the making of the great gladiator. The only *turba* in Hermes's school he himself makes; the mere sight of him causes every one there to tremble. Cf. 5. 65. 5–6 *silvarumque tremor, tacita qui fraude solebat ducere nec rectas Cacus in antra boves.*

5–6. Helius . . . Advolans: star gladiators. Helius (cf. ἥλιος) is resplendent (in his armor) as the sun; Advolans flies at (cf. *advolare*) his opponent. — **sed:** true adversative conjunction; some wrongly compare *sed* in 1.43.9. The thought is: *Hermen timet Helius sed (eum) unum (timet).* Cf. 6. — **cui:** dat. of interest, 'for whom' = 'before whom'.

7. vincere . . . doctus: he is so skillful that he can render his foe *hors de combat* without giving him the fatal stroke, and so magnanimous that he prefers to do this. The inf. with ptc. or adj. is common in poetry, e.g. in Vergil's Eclogues and Horace's Odes; cf. 6. 52. 4.

8. subpositicius . . . ipse: Hermes is never worn out or wounded and so never needs a substitute, i.e. a fresh gladiator who takes the place of one killed or compelled to retire from the conflict. Cf. C.I.L. 4. 1179; Petr. 45 *tertiarius (= subpositicius) mortuus pro mortuo (erat).*

9. divitiae locariorum: i.e. a veritable fortune to speculators in seats, because, when Hermes was to appear in the arena, all Rome came. It is well-nigh certain that

10   Hermes cura laborque ludiarum,
    Hermes belligera superbus hasta,
    Hermes aequoreo minax tridente,
    Hermes casside languida timendus,
    Hermes gloria Martis universi,
15   Hermes omnia solus et ter unus.

26

Quod alpha dixi, Corde, paenulatorum
te nuper, aliqua cum iocarer in charta,

at least a part of the sittings was commonly reserved and sold; see Marq.-Wissowa 3. 492–493. *Locarii* were persons who speculated in seats by reselling places they had bought, or persons who, going early, took possession of free sittings which others were glad to buy of them. For the word see on *salariorum*, 1. 41. 8.

10. cura . . . ludiarum: Hermes is the 'anxious care' and the 'toil' of the *ludiae*, i.e. the object of their anxious care and toil; cf. Hor. C. 1. 17. 18–20 *fide Teia dices laborantes in uno Penelopen vitreamque Circen*; 1. 14. 18 *nunc desiderium curaque non levis* (said of the ship of state). The meaning of *ludia* is uncertain. The scholiast on Iuv. 6. 104 defines it as = *ludis serviens* (an *ancilla* in the service of the *ludus gladiatorius?*), *gladiatoris uxor*. It might also stand for a ballet-dancer, pantomimist (cf. *ludius*).

11. M. makes Hermes a representative of three different classes of gladiators, distinguished here, as in actual combat, by their armor; cf. 2, with note. — **belligera . . . hasta**: Hermes is now a *veles* or *Samnis*. — **superbus**: freely, 'exulting in'.

12. aequoreo . . . tridente: i.e. as *retiarius*, who sought to throw a *rete* over his foe and then kill him with a three-pronged spear, such as Neptune is represented in art as using; hence *aequoreo*. Cf. Iuv. 8. 203–206.

13. casside . . . timendus: the obscurity of this vexed passage, which is prob. corrupt, is hardly lessened by the attempts of commentators to see in *languida* a reference to the armor of an *andabata* (who, as he fought, wore a helmet that wholly covered his eyes), or to the drooping crest of a Samnite's helmet.

15. omnia solus, *all things in his single self*; cf. Ov. Her. 12. 161–162 *deseror, amissis regno patriaque, domoque, coniuge, qui nobis omnia solus erat.* — **ter unus**, *thrice unique*, as champion in three kinds of fighting (11–13). Various editors suggest that M. is thinking of τρισμέγιστος, an epithet of the god Hermes. — For the meter see § 49, d.

26. Cordus had apparently resented 2. 57. 4; M. now seeks to placate him. — Meter : § 52.

1. alpha . . . paenulatorum: see 2. 57. 4 N.

2. charta: see 1. 25. 7 N.

si forte bilem movit hic tibi versus,
dicas licebit beta me togatorum.

29

Si quando leporem mittis mihi, Gellia, dicis
" Formonsus septem, Marce, diebus eris ".
Si non derides, si verum, lux mea, narras,
edisti numquam, Gellia, tu leporem.

34

Hanc tibi, Fronto pater, genetrix Flaccilla, puellam
oscula commendo deliciasque meas,

3. bilem movit: cf. Hor. Ep.
I. 19. 19–20 *o imitatores, servum
pecus, ut mihi saepe bilem, saepe
iocum vestri movere tumultus!* Iuv.
15. 15–16 *bilem aut risum fortasse
quibusdam moverat.*

4. togatorum: men too poor
to wear the more fashionable
raiment (*paenula, lacernae*).

29. It was a popular notion
that the eating of hare would have
the effect, at least for a limited
period, of adding to one's good
looks. This view may have arisen
from the confusion of *lepus*, 'hare',
and *lepos (lepor)*, 'charm', 'grace'.
Cf. Plin. N. H. 28. 260; Ael. Lam-
prid. Alex. Sev. 38. — Meter: § 48.

1. leporem mittis: the hare
was accounted a delicacy; cf. 13.92.
1–2 *inter aves turdus, si quid me
iudice certum est, inter quadrupedes
mattea prima lepus.* In 7.20. 4–5 M.
says of a glutton *ter poscit apri
glandulas, quater lumbum, et utramque coxam leporis et duos armos.*

2. Formonsus: the earlier
spelling of *formosus.*—**Marce:** the
poet himself.

3. lux mea: ironical. For the
phrase cf. 7. 14. 7–8 *lux mea non
capitur nugis neque moribus istis*

*nec dominae pectus talia damna
movent* ; Catull. 68. 132 *lux mea se
nostrum contulit in gremium.*

34. Cf. 5. 37; 10. 61. M. com-
mends to Fronto and Flaccilla,
his parents (§ 6), now in the under-
world, the little Erotion. The child,
who had apparently been a petted
verna in M.'s house, had just died,
and had in all probability been
buried on the poet's estate. The
name Erotion means 'Little Love'.
For M.'s love of children see § 38 ;
for his possession of a slave see
§ 11. For the type of epigram here
represented see § 26 (1). Brandt,
however, thinks that M. wrote this
and other epigrams (e.g. 6. 28; 6.
52; 7. 96; 10. 61) for pay. Cf. Van
Stockum 28. In that case Fronto
and Flaccilla would be the parents
of the person for whom M. wrote
the epigram. — Meter: § 48.

1. Fronto . . . Flaccilla: parents of M.; so Fried. Einl. 11 ; Van
Stockum 7 ; Teuffel, § 322, 1. See
on *inter . . . patronos*, 7.

2. oscula . . . delicias: in app.
to *hanc . . . puellam.* For *oscula* see
on 1. 109. 2. Here it is a term of
endearment; cf. German *Küßchen.*
— **delicias:** see on 1. 109. 5.

parvola ne nigras horrescat Erotion umbras
    oraque Tartarei prodigiosa canis.
5 Inpletura fuit sextae modo frigora brumae,
    vixisset totidem ni minus illa dies.
  Inter tam veteres ludat lasciva patronos
    et nomen blaeso garriat ore meum.
  Mollia non rigidus caespes tegat ossa nec illi,
10   Terra, gravis fueris : non fuit illa tibi.

3. **parvola:** cf. 5. — **ne . . .
horrescat:** the dark specters and
monsters of Orcus, esp. Cerberus,
with his three (or more) heads and
terrific bark, would be apt to
frighten a little child.
5–6. Inpletura fuit . . . vixisset . . . ni: for the conditional
form see A. 517, d; GL. 597, Rem.
3 (a). — **sextae . . . brumae :** i.e.
she almost saw for the sixth time
the winter solstice; cf. 3. 58. 8 N.;
7. 65. 1 *te bis decumae numerantem
frigora brumae.* — **totidem** = *sex;*
join with *dies.* — **minus:** i.e. than
the number necessary to complete
the full sixth year; cf. 5. 37. 15–16;
6. 28. 7–8.
7. Inter . . . patronos marks
the contrast between the sedate
old folks and the sportive child.
The *patroni* are Fronto and Flaccilla (§ 6). *Veteres* could hardly be
used of Erotion's own parents. —
ludat lasciva: freely, 'sport and
frolic'. The natural jollity of the
child is such that even the gloom
of the lower world cannot conquer
it. On earth she had frolicked with
M. (cf. 5. 37. 17); now she must be
content with older persons. — **patronos:** in general sense, *protectors.*
8. blaeso . . . ore: the poet sees
in the girl's lisp only added charm;
cf. 10. 65. 10.
9–10. Mark the antithesis in
Mollia and **rigidus, illi** and **tibi.**

— **non . . . tegat:** note *non* (not *ne*)
with subjv. of prayer; this usage
is found but rarely in Cicero (perhaps only once), but is not infrequent in Silver Latin, occurring
even in prose, e.g. in Seneca. —
nec . . . fueris: a poetic variation
of the conventional sepulchral
S.T.T.L. = *sit tibi terra levis;* cf.
1. 88. 2 N.; 6. 52. 5; 9. 29. 11 *sit tibi
terra levis mollique tegaris harena.*
For *nec* here see on Lib. Spect. 1. 2.
On the peculiar use of the pf. subjv.
see Clement A. J. P. 21. 157. — **non
fuit:** sc. *gravis.* She was no burden
to the earth as she walked and she
gave the earth no trouble in other
ways. Cf. Anthol. Lat. (Meyer)
1349 *terraque, quae mater nunc est,
sibi sit levis, oro, namque gravis
nulli vita fuit pueri.*
37. Paetus (18) had apparently
ridiculed M. for displaying grief
for Erotion's death (see 5. 34, with
notes). M. intimates here that
Paetus's ostentatious mourning for
his dead wife is wholly assumed
for effect, perhaps even to cover
up suspicion of foul play used to
get rid of her that he might possess her wealth. Lessing ix. p. 31
is of the opinion that the point of
the epigram does not harmonize
with what leads up to it and that
this incongruous mixture of grave
and gay violates the canon of the
epigram (see § 27). — Meter: § 52.

37

Puella senibus dulcior mihi cycnis,
agna Galaesi mollior Phalantini,
concha Lucrini delicatior stagni,
cui nec lapillos praeferas Erythraeos
5   nec modo politum pecudis Indicae dentem
nivesque primas liliumque non tactum,
quae crine vicit Baetici gregis vellus
Rhenique nodos aureamque nitellam

1. **senibus . . . cycnis**: M. pictures the grace and beauty of Erotion by a series of comparisons. If *senibus = white with age, candidis,* then M. is ascribing to Erotion the brilliant whiteness of skin (*candor*) so much admired by the Romans at this time; cf. 1. 115. 2 *loto candidior puella cycno*; Verg. E. 7. 37–38 *Galatea, thymo mihi dulcior Hyblae, candidior cycnis.* But since swans were believed to have a wonderful power of song just before death (cf. 13. 77), M. may mean rather that the child had a sweet voice. *Senibus* has adj. force; see on 1. 66. 7; 3. 58. 7.

2. **agna . . . Phalantini**: cf. 2. 43. 3 N. — **agna . . . mollior**: cf. Iuv. 8. 15 *et Euganea quantumvis mollior agna,* said of a man.

3. **concha . . . stagni**: i.e. the pearl in the oyster shells taken from the Lucrine Lake. Cf. 3. 60. 3 N.

4. **cui**: Erotion was a pearl; all ocean could not show her like. — **lapillos . . . Erythraeos**: pearls from eastern seas. For *lapillos* see 1. 109. 4 N. The name Mare Erythraeum, which in later days was restricted to the Arabian and Persian Gulfs and to the sea south and east of Arabia, to Herodotus and the men of an earlier time

included also the Indian Ocean. Cf. 9. 2. 9 *splendet Erythraeis perlucida moecha lapillis*; 9. 12. 5; Stat. Silv. 4. 6. 17–18 *o bona nox! . . . nox et Erythraeis Thetidis signanda lapillis!*

5. **nec . . . dentem**: the ivory of the elephant's tusk, like the diamond, is most valuable when cut and artificially polished. — **modo**, *newly, freshly.* — **pecudis**: applied to the elephant as gregarious; *belua* marks his size and ferocity. — **dentem**: see on 1. 72. 4; 2. 43. 9. Mark the dactyl in the first and third feet.

6. **nives . . . primas**, *virgin snow*; cf. 1. 115. 3. 'Whiter than snow' has been proverbial in many literatures; cf. e.g. 12. 82. 7 N.; Ov. Pont. 2. 5. 37–38 (*pectora*) *lacte et non calcata candidiora nive*; Psalms 51. 7; Otto s.v. *Nix.* — **lilium . . . tactum**: cf. 1. 115. 3; Prop. 2. 3. 10 *lilia non domina sint magis alba mea.*

7–8. **quae . . . nitellam**: Erotion's auburn or reddish tresses rivaled in color the wool of Baetica or the hair of the maidens of the Rhineland. Wool was sometimes valued because of its native color; this varied with localities: see Beck. 3. 289. The flocks raised in the valley of the Baetis (modern

— fragravit ore, quod rosarium Paesti,
10   quod Atticarum prima mella cerarum,
     quod sucinorum rapta de manu gleba —
     cui conparatus indecens erat pavo,

Guadalquivir) had fleeces of a golden yellow that was much liked at Rome; cf. Tert. Pall. 3 *nec de ovibus dico Milesiis et Selgicis et Altinis, aut quis* (= *quibus*) *Tarentum vel Baetica cluet natura colorante.* — **Rheni ... nodos:** the yellow hair of the Germans was well known in Italy and was imported into Rome for the use of women not naturally blond, as was also Dutch pomade (*spuma Batava, caustica*), which was used to bleach the hair to the fashionable hue. Cf. 5. 68. 1–2 *Arctoa de gente comam tibi, Lesbia, misi, ut scires quanto sit tua flava magis.* Many of the German tribes had peculiar ways of arranging their hair; these may have been somewhat imitated at Rome, esp. by women. Cf. Lib. Spect. 3. 9 *crinibus in nodum torti venere* (*Romam*) *Sicambri*; Sen. Ira 3. 26. 3 *nec rufus crinis et coactus in nodum apud Germanos virum dedecet.* — **Rheni:** the name of a river often stands for that of the people living in the country watered by it (metonymy); cf. Hor. C. 3. 29. 25–28 *tu curas ... quid regnata Cyro Bactra parent Tanaisque discors* (i.e. the Scythians). — **auream ... nitellam:** Servius interprets Verg. G. 1. 181 *saepe exiguus mus* by *nitella, mus agrestis robeus.*

9–11. 'Her breath was as fragrant as roses, or honey, or amber'. M. breaks the string of relative clauses by inserting here an independent clause; 1–13, be it noted, are in app. with *Erotion*, 14. — **ore** = *breath, odore* (metonymy).—**quod ... Paesti:** sc. *fragrat.* Note that *fragro* is now construed with the

acc. (*quod*; cf. *hoc* in 3. 65. 9, cited below); the abl. is the ordinary const. with the verb (cf. *ore*). It should be noted that neuter pronouns (and adjectives) are freely used in the acc. sing., even in prose, with verbs that commonly require some other construction. — **rosarium:** there was a steady demand at Rome for roses, esp. in connection with dinners, so great a demand in fact that even the rose-farms of Paestum could not supply it, though the plants bloomed twice a year. Cf. 6. 80. 6; 12. 31. 3; Verg. G. 4. 119 *biferique rosaria Paesti*; Prop. 4. 5. 61 *vidi ego odorati victura rosaria Paesti.* — **quod ... cerarum:** i.e. 'fragrance such as honey has when first taken from combs filled by Attic bees'. — **prima** may mean *new, fresh*, such honey being more redolent than honey which has been exposed to the air, or, simply, *the very finest, prime.* Mt. Hymettus near Athens was famous for its bees and its marble; cf. 7. 88. 8 N. — **quod ... gleba:** Roman women frequently carried in their hands bits of amber or balls of glass or crystal, to cool the hands; when warmed by the hand amber gave forth a pleasant odor. Cf., then, 3. 65. 5–9 *quod myrtus, quod messor Arabs, quod sucina trita ... hoc tua ... basia fragrant*; Iuv. 6. 573; Beck. 3. 267. — **sucinorum:** see on 4. 32; 4. 59. 1. — **rapta de manu:** i.e. still warm and fragrant from contact with the hand. — **gleba,** *bit, piece*; see on 5. 13. 7.

12. cui ... pavo: cf. Ov. M. 13. 802 (Galatea) *laudato pavone*

inamabilis sciurus et frequens phoenix,
adhuc recenti tepet Erotion busto,

15 quam pessimorum lex amara fatorum
sexta peregit hieme, nec tamen tota,
nostros amores gaudiumque lususque.
Et esse tristem me meus vetat Paetus
pectusque pulsans pariter et comam vellens

20 " Deflere non te vernulae pudet mortem?
ego coniugem " inquit " extuli et tamen vivo,
notam, superbam, nobilem, locupletem ".
Quid esse nostro fortius potest Paeto?
ducentiens accepit et tamen vivit.

---

superbior. See 3. 58. 13 N. — **indecens**: cf. 5. 14. 7 N.

13. frequens phoenix: compared to Erotion, the phoenix, one
of the rarest of birds, was a common
thing. Concerning this fabulous
bird, to which tradition ascribed a
resplendent plumage, many different beliefs were current throughout the east. M. seems to have in
mind the common opinion that it
appeared in Egypt but once in five
hundred years. See Tac. Ann. 6.
28; Hdt. 2. 73. For *frequens* see
on 5. 13. 3. — For the cæsura see
§ 52, c.

14. adhuc ... busto: Erotion's
ashes are hardly yet cold. — **bu-
stum**, prop. the place where the
funeral pyre was set up, here almost
= the *pyra* itself.

16. sexta ... tota: cf. 5. 34.
5–6 N.; 10. 61. 1–2. *Sexta = only
(but) the sixth.* The abl. is tem-
poral; in prose we should have *in
sexta hieme,* etc. M. means that
Erotion *sex tantum hiemes vixit
nec eas quidem totas.*

17. nostros . . . lusus: cf. 5.
34. 2 N.

18. Et, *and yet, but.*

19. pectus . . . vellens: cf. 2.
11. 5 N. — **pariter**: sc. *mecum.* The
vs. = 'though he shows as much
grief outwardly as I'. — **-que** joins
vetat, 18, and *inquit,* 21.

20. vernulae: the dim. marks,
objectively, the contempt of Paetus
for the slave; M. makes the dim.
express, subjectively, his own affection for the child.

21. extuli: cf. 4. 24. 2. — **vivo**
= (1) *manage to live*; (2) *enjoy life.*
Cf. 1. 15. 12 N.

22. superbam: a natural epithet of a woman with blue blood
in her veins (*nobilis*) and independ-
ently rich (*locuples*); cf. 5. 35. 6
equiti superbo, nobili, locupleti. —
locupletem: the climax well marks
the mercenary basis of Paetus's
regard as contrasted with that of
M.'s affection for Erotion.

23. Quid ... Paeto: M. might
have said *nil esse nostro fortius
potest Paeto* (see on 1. 10. 3).

24. ducentiens: i.e. 20,000,000
sestertii; see on 3. 22. 1. — **et tamen vivit**: bitterly ironical play
on *et tamen vivo,* 21. Cf. 2. 65. 1–6
*Cur tristiorem cernimus Saleia-
num? "An causa levis est?" inquit.*

39

Supremas tibi triciens in anno
signanti tabulas, Charine, misi
Hyblaeis madidas thymis placentas.
Defeci: miserere iam, Charine:
5   signa rarius, aut semel fac illud
mentitur tua quod subinde tussis.
Excussi loculosque sacculumque:

"Extuli uxorem". *O grande fati
crimen! o gravem casum! illa, illa
dives mortua est Secundilla, centena
decies quae tibi dedit dotis? nollem
accidisset hoc tibi, Saleiane.* — For
the cæsura see § 52, c.

39. M., under pretense of poking fun at himself as a legacy-hunter, satirizes the class. See I. 10. Introd. To the contemporaries of the poet who knew him as a chronic beggar and hanger-on the epigram must have seemed double-pointed. — Meter: § 49.

1–2. Supremas . . . tabulas = *testamentum, last will and testament*; cf. 6. 63. 3. The will was generally written on tablets of wax (*tabulae; tabellae*). — **triciens in anno**: hyperbolic; whenever Charinus thinks he is about to die or gets out of sweet-cakes (3), he announces his intention to make a new will. — **signanti** = *obsignanti*.

3. Hyblaeis . . . placentas: the *placenta* (cf. πλακοῦς) was a small fancy sweet-cake, the essential elements of which were cheese and honey; cf. e.g. Hor. Ep. I. 10. 11 *pane egeo iam mellitis potiore placentis*. It was an appropriate present for a man racked by a cough. See II. 86. 1–3. These cakes were expensive; the region of Mt. Hybla in Sicily vied with Hymettus in producing the finest

and most costly honey. Cf. 5. 37. 10 N.; 9. 26. 4. The quality of the honey was largely due to the supply of flowers that the bees liked, esp. *thymum*: cf. Ov. Tr. 5. 13. 22 (*prius*) *careat dulci Trinacris Hybla thymo*; Verg. E. 7. 37, cited on 5. 37. 1.

4. Defeci: 'I've no more money for bait in the shape of *placentae*'. Hor. Ep. I. 4. 11 has *non deficiente crumena* of a purse that fails not.

5–6. Here the main thought comes in the middle of the epigram, with a double couplet before and after. See Paukstadt 33–34. Cf. note on 12. 24. 11. — **semel:** i.e. 'once for all die and show that your cough is not a pretense used to excite in us false hopes and thereby bring to yourself more cakes'. — **mentitur:** freely, 'lyingly suggests (promises)'. — **subinde,** *repeatedly*; see I. Other rich men had learned Charinus's trick; cf. 2. 40; Sen. Brev. Vit. 7. 7 *quot* (*dies*) *illa anus* (*abstulit*) *efferendis heredibus lassa? quot ille ad invitandam avaritiam captantium simulatus aeger?* — **tussis:** cf. I. 10. 4; 2. 26. 1–4.

7. Excussi . . . sacculum: 'I've rattled all the money-coffers at home and shaken out my purse. Result: not a copper for cakes is left!' *Loculus* sometimes denotes a receptacle for money (= *arca*),

Croeso divitior licet fuissem,
Iro pauperior forem, Charine,
10   si conchem totiens meam comesses.

42

Callidus effracta nummos fur auferet arca,
prosternet patrios impia flamma lares :
debitor usuram pariter sortemque negabit,

sometimes a coffer or case having compartments in which anything, e.g. keys, rings, jewels, may be kept. Cf. 14. 12. 1–2 *hos*(=*eburneos*) *nisi de flava loculos implere moneta non decet: argentum vilia ligna ferant*; Hor. Ep. 2. 1. 175 *gestit enim nummum in loculos demittere*; Iuv. 1. 89–90 (*loculi* versus *arca*). — **sacculum** (dim. of *saccus*, 'bag'), *purse* (*crumena*); cf. Iuv. 14. 138–139 *interea pleno cum turget sacculus ore, crescit amor nummi*; Catull. 13. 7–8 *nam tui Catulli plenus sacculus est aranearum* ('cobwebs').

8. Croeso: the Lydian monarch, whose riches became a proverb (cf. 'as rich as Croesus'), though beside modern multimillionaires Croesus would seem poor indeed; cf. e.g. 11. 5. 4; Iuv. 14. 328–329 *nec Croesi fortuna umquam nec Persica regna sufficient animo*; Catull. 115. 3–6; Otto s.v. *Croesus*. — **licet fuissem**: see on 1. 70. 17. The secondary sequence (*fuissem*) is rare, but cf. 9. 91. 3 *astra licet propius, Palatia longius essent*. Here the plpf. is correct, because M. means *etiamsi Croeso divitior fuissem*.

9. Iro pauperior: proverbial; cf. 'as poor as Lazarus'. Irus was a nickname given to Arnaeus, a poverty-stricken hanger-on at the court of Ulysses in Ithaca, who was used as a go-between by the

suitors of Penelope; cf. e.g. 6. 77. 1 *cum sis tam pauper quam nec miserabilis Iros*; Ov. Tr. 3. 7. 42 *Irus et est subito qui modo Croesus erat.* — See § 33 (p. xxix, notes 2 and 3).

10. conchem: cf. κόγχος; a sort of pea-soup made by boiling lentils with the pods, naturally a very cheap food. In Iuv. 3. 292–293 the footpad who holds up Umbricius cries insultingly *unde venis? . . . cuius aceto, cuius conche tumes?*

42. 'Riches take wings; cheat Fortune while you may, by giving to friends'. This may be more than a taking paradox, namely a polite and artful beggar's plea. — Meter: § 48.

1. effracta . . . arca: cf. Hor. Ep. 1. 17. 54 *aut cistam effractam et subducta viatica plorat.* — **auferet**: the fut. ind. here has permissive force (see on 4. 57. 9), *let the thief*, etc., *what if the thief*, etc. — **nummos** = *pecuniam*; see on 1. 66. 4. — **arca**: see on 1. 76. 5.

2. patrios, *ancestral*; because it is the old homestead its destruction will seem the more dreadful; note the juxtaposition of *patrios* and *impia*. Cf. Hor. Epod. 2. 3 *paterna rura bobus exercet suis.* — **lares**: see on 1. 70. 2.

3. debitor . . . negabit: i.e. 'the debtor will snap his fingers in your face and your investment will be a dead loss'. — **usuram**: the fee for the use of money (cf. *utor*),

non reddet sterilis semina iacta seges :
5 dispensatorem fallax spoliabit amica,
   mercibus extructas obruet unda rates ;
extra fortunam est quidquid donatur amicis :
   quas dederis, solas semper habebis opes.

43

Thais habet nigros, niveos Laecania dentes.
   Quae ratio est ? emptos haec habet, illa suos.

47

Nunquam se cenasse domi Philo iurat, et hoc est :

interest. Faenus, 'interest', is from the root which gives *femina*, and so is prop. 'breed of (barren) metal'. — **sortem**, *principal*.

4. non reddet . . . seges: the crop may utterly fail, not even paying for the seed sown. Cf. Tib. 2. 3. 61–62 *at tibi dura Ceres . . . persolvat nulla semina certa fide.*

5. dispensatorem . . . amica: the house steward may fall into the toils of a crafty sweetheart (*amica* generally = *meretrix*), who will fleece him well not only out of his own savings (*peculium*) but out of his master's money too, to which, as confidential treasurer and accountant, he has access; cf. Priap. 68. 13 *haec eadem socium tenera spoliavit amica.*

6. mercibus . . . rates: cf. Hor. C. 3. 29. 60–61 *ne Cypriae Tyriaeque merces addant avaro divitias mari.* — **unda:** note the sing.; M. writes as if one great billow is to bury the ship. Cf. Ov. Tr. 1. 2. 34 *dumque loquor, vultus obruit unda meos*; Her. 7. 78 *ignibus ereptos obruet unda deos?* M. may have consciously or unconsciously reproduced Ovid; see Zingerle 14.

7. extra fortunam est: i.e. out of Fortune's reach.

8. solas . . . opes: cf. Plaut. Mi. 673–674 *nam in mala uxore atque inimico si quid sumas* ('spend'), *sumptus est: in bono hospite atque amico quaestus est quod sumitur.*

43. Meter: § 48.

2. ratio, *explanation.* — **emptos:** cf. 1. 72. 3–4 N.; 9. 37. 3 *nec dentes aliter quam Serica nocte reponas* (i.e. lay aside when going to bed).

47. On a man who, while lying, told the truth. 2. 11 is on a similar theme. — Meter: § 48.

1. se . . . iurat: Philo, as if doubtful of his reputation for veracity, thinks it best to back his word by an oath. — **cenasse:** note the tense. Philo is taking oath to past events; hence the pf. is entirely correct. Cf. 8. 44. 12; 10. 39. 1; 11. 62. 1. The const. with pres. inf. (6. 12. 1) is quite similar. In all these cases *iurare* = *cum iure iurando adfirmare*. The common const. of *iuro*, 'promise with an oath', with fut. inf., is very different. — **hoc est :** i.e. 'it is true', 'it is as he says'.

non cenat, quotiens nemo vocavit eum.

49

Vidissem modo forte cum sedentem
solum te, Labiene, tres putavi ;
calvae me numerus tuae fefellit :
sunt illinc tibi, sunt et hinc capilli,
5　　quales vel puerum decere possunt ;
nudumst in medio caput nec ullus
in longa pilus area notatur.
Hic error tibi profuit Decembri,
tunc cum prandia misit Imperator :
10　　cum panariolis tribus redisti.

2. **non cenat**: when he is not invited out, he goes without dinner.

49. M. satirizes the greediness of Labienus. Though Labienus's head was wholly bald on top, it had an abundance of curly hair on the sides. Hence, as seen from the rear, he presented the appearance of three men in a row, a *calvus* between two *capillati*, a bald-headed man with a shorter curly-headed man on each side. M. is of course speaking hyperbolically; yet at night (see on 8) the illusion would be not impossible. Cf. 10. 83. Since Book V was addressed to the emperor (see 5. 1), who was himself bald and doubtless shared the Roman sensitiveness on the subject of baldness (see on 1. 72. 8), M. here and elsewhere seems to approach very near to the danger-line. — Meter: § 49.

1. **sedentem**: perhaps in the Amphitheatrum Flavium.

3. **calvae . . . fefellit**: 'I made a mistake concerning the number of heads your bald head numbered'. For *calva* as noun cf. 10. 83. 2.

5. **vel**, *even*; a common use, especially with adjectives.

6–7. **nudumst . . . notatur**: cf. 10. 83. 2–3; Petr. 109 *quod solum formae decus est, cecidere capilli, vernantesque comas tristis abegit hiemps. Nunc umbra nudata sua iam tempora* (temples of the head) *maerent areaque attritis ridet adulta pilis.*

8. **Decembri**: i.e. at the time of the Saturnalia, apparently in 88, when Domitian supplied refreshments to the whole people in the amphitheater by night; see Stat. Silv. 1. 6.

10. **panariolis**: baskets for bread, etc. The dim. suggests something fancy and delicate. Cf. Stat. Silv. 1. 6. 31–34 *hi panaria candidasque mappas subvectant epulasque lautiores; illi marcida vina largiuntur: Idaeos totidem putes ministros* (i.e. the cupbearers were all rivals of Ganymedes in grace).—**redisti**: the contents of the *panariola* or *sportellae* might be eaten at once or taken away. Labienus evidently took his home.

Talem Geryonem fuisse credo.
Vites censeo porticum Philippi :
si te viderit Hercules, peristi.

53

Colchida quid scribis, quid scribis, amice, Thyesten ?
quo tibi vel Nioben, Basse, vel Andromachen ?
materia est, mihi crede, tuis aptissima chartis

11. Talem ... credo: 'I believe Geryon must have looked like you'. One of the Labors of Hercules was to steal the cattle of Geryon (Geryones), a fabulous triple-bodied giant who lived on an island (Erythia) of the western sea, and to kill the monster himself. See § 33.

12. Vites censeo: M. is fond of using verbs signifying command, urge, ask, etc., with the simple subjv. (i.e. with subjv. without *ut* or *ne*). The subjv. in such cases is paratactic; cf. *moneo* + paratactic imv., 4. 30. 1–2 N. See also on 2. 14. 18; 3. 25. 3. — **porticum Philippi:** this portico lay in the southern part of the Campus Martius, just northwest of the Porticus Octaviae; it seems to have been erected around a temple of Hercules Musarum rebuilt by L. Marcius Philippus; see Platner 355.

13. si ... peristi: the temple and the porticus contained various representations of Hercules in marble and in relief. — **peristi,** *you are a dead man!* The thought is: 'If Hercules catches sight of you, he will take you for Geryon returned and will slay you forthwith'. *Peristi* is thus used frequently in comedy; the use comes, perhaps, from the *sermo plebeius.* Yet the pf. is thus employed at times most effectively in dignified style; cf. e.g. Hannibal to his troops,

Liv. 21. 43. 2 *si ... eundem* (*animum*) *mox ... habueritis, vicimus, milites.* So again Liv. 21. 44. 9.

53. M. advises a man who is determined to write on tragic or epic themes to take subjects meet for his finished work, e.g. Deucalion or Phaethon. Since these names typify destruction by water and fire respectively, M. is hinting that Bassus's poetry deserves to perish by water or by fire. — Meter: § 48.

1. Colchida: prop. 'a (the) Colchian woman' (Medea); here a tragedy in which Medea is heroine. — **Thyesten:** see on 3. 45. 1.

2. quo tibi ... Andromachen? a curious idiom, in which the dat. seems to be a dat. of interest, and the acc. to be exclamatory; see A. 397, d, N. 2; GL. 343, 1; L. 1150. Cf. Hor. Ep. 1. 5. 12 *quo mihi fortunam, si non conceditur uti?* — **quo** = *to what end;* lit. 'whither'. Render, 'Of what use to you is', etc. — **Nioben:** because Niobe, daughter of Tantalus and sister of Pelops, being mother of six boys and six girls, dared to disparage Leto (Latona), who had borne to Zeus only Apollo and Artemis, her children were slain by Apollo and Artemis and she herself was metamorphosed into stone. — **Andromachen :** wife of Hector, the son of Priam.

Deucalion vel, si non placet hic, Phaethon.

56

Cui tradas, Lupe, filium magistro
quaeris sollicitus diu rogasque.
Omnes grammaticosque rhetorasque
devites moneo : nihil sit illi
5　cum libris Ciceronis aut Maronis ;
famae Tutilium suae relinquat ;
si versus facit, abdices poetam.
Artes discere vult pecuniosas ?
fac discat citharoedus aut choraules ;
10　si duri puer ingeni videtur,
praeconem facias vel architectum.

4. Deucalion with his wife Pyrrha were.believed to have been sole survivors of the great world-flood; see e.g. Ov. M. 1. 253 ff. — **Phaethon:** see on 4. 32. 1.

56. M. seeks to dissuade Lupus (see 10.48.6) from educating his son for a literary career. The profits of a career, he urges, are in inverse proportion to its respectability. Cf. 1.76; 6.8, with notes.—Meter: § 49.

3. grammaticos ... rhetoras: see on 2. 7. 1, 4. On the unproductiveness of such careers see Iuv. 7. 215 ff., 150 ff.; Fried. SG. 1. 322 ff. — **rhetoras:** this Greek form of the acc. is somewhat rare.

4–5. devites moneo: note parataxis here and in *fac discat,* 9; see on *vites censeo,* 5. 49. 12. — **nihil . . . Maronis:** i.e. let him not devote himself to oratory or to poetry. Cicero held a place in the training of the *rhetor* similar to that held by Vergil in the school of the *grammaticus.*

6. Tutilium: a rhetorician, apparently a contemporary and

kinsman of Quintilian; cf. Quint. 3. 1. 21; Plin. Ep. 6. 32. 1. — **suae** refers to Tutilius, not to the grammatical subject; see A. 300, 2, N.; GL. 309, 2; L. 2337. The vs. = *suam Tutilius famam habeat.*

7. abdices: i.e. disinherit him; use every means to steer him into some other channel. — **poetam :** M. comically affects to think of a poet (!) as one beyond redemption.

8. This vs., whether interrogative or declarative, is the protasis to 9; see on 1. 70. 3; 1. 79. 2; 1. 107. 3; etc.

9. fac ... citharoedus in sense = *fiat citharoedus*; see on *devites moneo,* 4. — **citharoedus:** see 3. 4. 8 N. Note the nom.; we may supply *esse,* or take the nom. as in the predicate, 'make him learn as *citharoedus*', etc. — **choraules:** a flute-player (*tibicen*) who accompanied a choral dance.

10. duri ... ingeni: we should say 'thick-headed'.

11. praeconem: see 1. 85. Introd.; cf. 6. 8.

58

Cras te victurum, cras dicis, Postume, semper.
  Dic mihi, cras istud, Postume, quando venit ?
quam longest cras istud ? ubi est ? aut unde petendum ?
  numquid apud Parthos Armeniosque latet ?
5 iam cras istud habet Priami vel Nestoris annos.
  Cras istud quanti dic mihi posset emi ?
Cras vives ? hodie iam vivere, Postume, tardum est :
  ille sapit, quisquis, Postume, vixit heri.

64

Sextantes, Calliste, duos infunde Falerni,
  tu super aestivas, Alcime, solve nives,

58. The point in this epigram is made by the unexpected contrast of *heri* and *cras*. Cf. 1. 15, with notes; Pers. 5. 67–70 *sed cum lux altera venit, iam cras hesternum consumpsimus: ecce aliud cras egerit hos annos et semper paulum erit ultra.* — Meter: § 48.

1. Postume: a modern reader thinks of Hor. C. 2. 14. 1 ff. *Eheu fugaces, Postume, Postume, labuntur anni*, etc. Prob. M. did, too.

3–4. longest = *longe est*; M. is fond of using *longe* with *sum*. Parthia and Armenia stand here for the uttermost ends of the earth.

5. iam ... annos: cf. 2. 64. 1–3 *dum ... non decernis, Laure, quid esse velis, Peleos et Priami transit* (= *transiit*) *et Nestoris aetas*; 6. 70. 12–14.

7. hodie ... tardum est: cf. 1. 15. 11–12; 8. 44. 1–2 *Titulle, moneo, vive: semper hoc serum est; sub paedagogo coeperis licet, serum est.* See App.

64. 'Since death spares not emperors, it behooves us commoner folk too to remember that we must die'. Cf. 5. 58. — Meter: § 48.

1. Sextantes: see 1. 27. 2 N. — **Calliste:** Callistus and Alcimus are slaves.

2. tu ... nives: for the dilution of wine see on *quincunce*, 2. 1. 9. The wine was generally poured into the crater through a *colum* or *saccus* filled with ice or snow. Cf. 9. 22. 8; 12. 17. 6; 14. 103 (on a *colum nivarium*) *Setinos, moneo, nostra nive frange trientes*; Sen. Ep. 78. 23 *o infelicem aegrum! Quare? quia non vino nivem diluit, quia non rigorem potionis suae, quam capaci scypho miscuit, renovat fracta insuper glacie.* Cf. Petr. 31 *discubuimus pueris Alexandrinis aquam in manus nivatam infundentibus* for still greater luxury. — **super:** adv. — **aestivas:** i.e. snow kept till summer. The adj. marks the time of the year. — **solve** = *dissolve*; see note on *pone.* 1. 4. 2. — **Alcime:** see 1. 88.

pinguescat nimio madidus mihi crinis amomo
　　lassenturque rosis tempora sutilibus :
5　tam vicina iubent nos vivere Mausolea,
　　cum doceant ipsos posse perire deos.

66

Saepe salutatus nunquam prior ipse salutas :
　　sic eris aeternum, Pontiliane, vale.

3. pinguescat ... amomo:
i.e. 'let my hair drip richly with
pomade'. This pomade is to be
redolent with *amomum* (ἄμωμον),
an eastern spice-plant from the
leaves of which a fragrant perfume
was made. Cf. Stat. Silv. I. 2.
111–112 *nec pingui crinem deducere
amomo cessavit mea, nate, manus.*

4. lassentur: hyperbole; 'make
my temples ache with', etc., i.e.
supply roses without stint. See
5. 37. 9 N. Chaplets artificially
constructed of separate rose-leaves
sewed on strips of the inner bark
of the linden (*philyra*) were much
in fashion; cf. e.g. 9. 90. 6 *frontem
sutilibus ruber coronis*; Hor. C. I.
38. 2 *displicent nexae philyra coronae*; Beck. 3. 443 ff.

5. tam: with *vicina*. — Mausolea: see Lib. Spect. I. Introd.,
5–6 N. Here the reference is prob.
to the Mausoleum Augusti, built by
Augustus in 27 B.C. at the northern
end of the Campus Martius where
the Via Flaminia approached the
Tiber. It served as an imperial
sepulcher until Hadrian erected
the Mausoleum Hadriani across
the Tiber. See Platner 363–364.
— For the pl. see on I. 70. 5.

6. deos: i.e. emperors and gran-
dees; cf. Hor. S. 2. 6. 51–53 *quicumque obvius est me consulit: O
bone (nam te scire, deos quoniam
propius contingis, oportet), numquid de Dacis audisti?*

66. M. declares that, since Pon-
tilianus never honors him with a
salve or *ave*, he shall be as good as
dead to him hereafter. — Meter:
§ 48.

1. salutatus: by *salve* or *ave*.
—salutas: cf. 3. 95. 1 *nunquam
dicis "Have" sed reddis, Naevole,
semper.*

2. sic, *under these circumstances*; virtually *therefore.* —
aeternum vale: a formula used in
addressing the dead. *Aeternum*
goes with *vale*, either as adv. = *in
aeternum*, or as acc. of the thing
effected (inner object). *Aeternum
vale* together count as an adjectival
or participial phrase, pred. nom. to
eris, such as *in aeternum salutatus,*
= *mortuus.* Cf. Stat. Silv. 3. 3.
208–209 *salve supremum, senior
mitissime patrum, supremumque
vale*; Verg. A. 11. 97–98 *salve
aeternum mihi, maxime Palla,
aeternumque vale.*

69. A condemnation of Marcus
Antonius for the murder of Cicero.
In the proscriptions that followed
the formation of the so-called
Second Triumvirate, Cicero was
slain to satisfy the hatred of Antonius. This hatred dated from the
execution, in 63 B.C., of Lentulus,
the Catilinarian conspirator, who
had married Iulia, the mother of
Antonius; the feeling was intensified by Cicero's Philippic Orations.
— Meter: § 48.

69

Antoni, Phario nil obiecture Pothino
   et levius tabula quam Cicerone nocens,
quid·gladium demens Romana stringis in ora?
   hoc admisisset nec Catilina nefas.
5 Impius infando miles corrumpitur auro
   et tantis opibus vox tacet una tibi.
Quid prosunt sacrae pretiosa silentia linguae?
   incipient omnes pro Cicerone loqui.

1. **Phario** = *Aegyptio*; Pharos was an island near Alexandria upon which Ptolemy Philadelphus erected a great lighthouse. Cf. 4. 11. 4 *Phariae coniugis* (= Cleopatra) *arma*. — **nil obiecture:** because Antony's crime was worse even than Pothinus's (see next note). — **Pothino:** a eunuch, regent in place of the young king of Egypt, Ptolemy Dionysus, brother of Cleopatra. Aided by Achillas, commander of the Egyptian troops, and Theodotus, a Greek sophist, he brought about the assassination of Pompey the Great. After his defeat at Pharsalus in 48 B.C. Pompey set out for Egypt, hoping to find refuge there with the young king, but just as he stepped ashore near Alexandria he was murdered.

2. **levius:** adv., modifying *nocens*, 'less deeply guilty'.—**tabula:** sc. *proscriptorum*, the proscription list; cf. Iuv. 2. 28 *tabulam Sullae*. — **Cicerone:** i.e. the murder of Cicero. For the abl. see on *templo*, Lib. Spect. 1. 3. M. means that Antony outraged the feelings of the world more by the murder of Cicero than by the death of all the rest of the proscribed.

3. **demens Romana:** juxtaposition of effect and cause. 'Barbarians murdered Pompey; you

slew a Roman'. — **Romana . . . ora:** M. writes as if all Roman eloquence had been silenced by the death of its chief representative (*ora* = *lips*); cf. Val. Max. 5. 3. 4 *ac protinus caput Romanae eloquentiae et pacis clarissimam dexteram per summum et securum otium amputavit.* — On the metrical value of the final *a* in *Romana* see on *digna*, 2. 66. 8; L. Müller, De Re Metrica, 390.

4. **nec** = *ne* . . . *quidem*; see on 1. 109. 20. — **nefas:** the murder of Cicero is classed with crimes against the gods; cf. *impius* and *infando*, 5. Note the juxtaposition in *impius infando*, and cf. *sacrae*, 7, with note.

5. **Impius . . . miles:** C. Popillius Laenas, a *tribunus militum*, who had once been defended by Cicero on a capital charge.

6. **et . . . tibi:** 'and in return for outlay prodigious a single tongue was silenced, to please you (alone)'. Laenas received 1,000,000 *sestertii*. — **tantis** = *tantis quantas pependisti*. *Tantus, talis, tot*, etc., are often used of size, quality, number, etc., with which every one is familiar; so we use 'such' and 'so' with adjectives like 'great', 'many', etc. when we might say simply 'great', 'fine', 'many', etc.

74

Pompeios iuvenes Asia atque Europa, sed ipsum
　　terra tegit Libyes, si tamen ulla tegit.
Quid mirum toto si spargitur orbe ? iacere
　　uno non poterat tanta ruina loco.

7. **sacrae**: M. speaks as if
Cicero had been deified or listed
among the heroes of earth. Cf.
3. 66. 2. — **pretiosa**: the *silentia*
cost 1,000,000 *sestertii*, yet earned
for Antony only general execration.

8. **pro Cicerone**: and so
against Antony! Cicero cannot
defend himself, but all the world is
his champion. Hence Antony will
forever hear countless tongues,
not merely *una . . . vox* (6). *Pro*
might also be taken, less effectively, as = *in place of.*

74. The extinction of the Pompeii, father and sons, under circumstances most tragic, could hardly
fail to make a deep impression,
even in an age hardened by the
horrors of repeated proscriptions.
For the death of Pompeius Magnus
himself see on 5. 69. 1. His sons
fought against Caesar at Munda
in Spain in 45 B.C., but were defeated there; Cnaeus was captured
there and put to death. Sextus, the
younger son, maintained a powerful
naval force for several years, but
was finally caught by the soldiers
of Antonius near Miletus in Asia
and killed, 35 B.C. — Meter: § 48.

1. **ipsum**: i.e. Cn. Pompeius
Magnus, the father.

2. **Libyes**: cf. *Cybeles*, 1. 70.
10 N. — **si . . . tegit**: for the language, which apparently implies a
doubt whether Pompey was really
buried, cf. P. Terentius Varro Ata-
cinus (in Anthol. Lat. 414) *marmo-
reo Licinus tumulo iacet, at Cato
parvo, Pompeius nullo*; Luc. 1. 685.

In describing Priam's end in A. 2.
557–558 Vergil perhaps had such
a view of Pompey's fate in mind.
Yet such language may merely
mean that Pompey was not fortunate enough to receive full, formal
burial; cf. Luc. 10. 380–381 *tumu-
lumque e pulvere parvo adspice, Pompeii non omnia membra tegentem.*
In point of fact Pompey's head was
cut off and his body was thrown out
on the shore; a freedman buried his
remains. With 1–2 cf. Sen. in an
epigram (see Bähr. P. L. M. XLIII.
10 = Anthol. Lat. 400) *Magne, premis Libyam, fortes tua pignera nati
Europam atque Asiam.*

3. **toto . . . orbe**: cf. Petr. 120
*tres tulerat Fortuna duces, quos
obruit omnes armorum strue di-
versa feralis Enyo. Crassum Par-
thus habet, Libyco iacet aequore
Magnus, Iulius ingratam perfudit
sanguine Romam, et quasi non posset tot tellus ferre* (i.e. bear in one
place) *sepulcra, divisit cineres.* —
spargitur: as subject supply *Pompei domus*, or, what amounts to the
same thing, *tanta ruina* (out of 4).
— **iacere**: used here, as often,
with the suggestion of 'lying in
death'; cf. the epigram cited on 4.

4. **tanta ruina**: cf. note on 3,
and an epigram ascribed to Sen.
(Anthol. Lat. 456 = Bähr. P. L. M.
XLIII. 66) *diversis iuvenes Asia
atque Europa sepulcris distinet;
infida, Magne, iaces Libya. Dis-
tribuit magnos mundo Fortuna se-
pultos, ne sine Pompeio terra sit
ulla suo.*

76

Profecit poto Mithridates saepe veneno,
    toxica ne possent saeva nocere sibi:
tu quoque cavisti cenando tam male semper
    ne posses unquam, Cinna, perire fame.

81

Semper pauper eris, si pauper es, Aemiliane:
    dantur opes nulli nunc nisi divitibus.

76. 'Hunger can have no more effect on Cinna than poison had on Mithridates the Great, king of Pontus, who, when reduced to extremities, failed in the attempt to poison himself, because he had so thoroughly accustomed himself to antidotes that the poison would not work'. See Plin. N. H. 25. 5. — Meter: § 48.

1–2. Profecit . . . ne: M. has chosen to use a purpose clause instead of the clause of result which is the usual construction with *facio* and its compounds; numerous parallels to M.'s construction may, however, be found, even in good prose.

3. semper outdoes *saepe*, 1; Cinna's preparation was more thorough even than that of Mithridates.

4. Cinna: cf. 8. 19. 1 *pauper videri Cinna vult: et est pauper.*

81. Cf. 1. 103. 3; Matthew 13. 12; Iuv. 3. 208–222. — Meter: § 48.

LIBER VI

8

Praetores duo, quattuor tribuni,
septem causidici, decem poetae
cuiusdam modo nuptias petebant
a quodam sene; non moratus ille
5   praeconi dedit Eulogo puellam.
Dic, numquid fatue, Severe, fecit?

11

Quod non sit Pylades hoc tempore, non sit Orestes

8. M. writes ostensibly on choosing a son-in-law with an eye to business (cf. Iuv. 3. 160–161 *quis gener hic placuit censu minor atque puellae sarcinulis impar?*), but really on the meager returns from certain respectable professions, especially literature. Cf. 5. 56, with notes. — Meter: § 49.

1–2. **praetores:** see App. — **duo . . . quattuor . . . septem . . . decem:** the numerical climax is suggestive. Fried. notes that the number of suitors increases in inverse proportion to the probable income that men of the given class may hope for. — **tribuni:** see 5. 13. 1 N. — **causidici:** see 1. 98. 2 N.; 4. 8. 2.

3. **cuiusdam:** sc. *puellae*; cf. *nuptias Maronillae*, 1. 10. 1 N.

5. **praeconi:** cf. 5. 56. 11 N. The *senex* (4) was sure that any and every *praeco* had wealth; he could not be sure of finding even

one wealthy man among a host of representatives of the so-called respectable professions. — **Eulogo:** a name specially coined (cf. εὖ + λόγος) as appropriate for an auctioneer who must at least not underestimate what he sells (see § 38 fin.).

6. **numquid . . . fecit:** note that M. has treated this question as independent of *dic*. This usage, easy and natural after an imv. (we may print *dic: numquid . . . fecit?*), is common in comedy. — **fatue . . . fecit:** ironical. How far Severus is to be identified with others of like name in M. is uncertain, though Silius Severus, son of Silius Italicus the poet, may be meant here. See Spiegel II 27; Fried. on 2. 6. 3.

11. 'Real friendship is based on mutual respect. Old-time friendship cannot be expected unless there is a return to old-time equality of relations'. Cf. 1. 43; 2. 43; 3. 60.

miraris ? Pylades, Marce, bibebat idem,
nec melior panis turdusve dabatur Orestae,
sed par atque eadem cena duobus erat.
5 Tu Lucrina voras, me pascit aquosa peloris :
non minus ingenua est et mihi, Marce, gula.
Te Cadmea Tyros, me pinguis Gallia vestit :
vis te purpureum, Marce, sagatus amem ?
ut praestem Pyladen, aliquis mihi praestet Oresten.
10 Hoc non fit verbis, Marce : ut ameris, ama.

The friendship of Orestes, son of Agamemnon, and Pylades was proverbial; see Otto 258. Orestes and Pylades were cousins.— Meter: § 48.

2. **idem**: i.e. that Orestes drank. Cf. notes on 1. 20; 3. 60.

5. **Lucrina**: see 3. 60. 3 N.— **aquosa peloris**: the giant mussel, prob. coarse and insipid.

6. **non minus**: sc. *quam tibi.* — **ingenua**, *genteel, delicate*; such as properly belongs to one high-born. Cf. 10. 47. 6; 12. 3. 6. — **et** = *etiam, also*, a meaning found in Plautus and Terence, in the Augustan poets, and in post-Augustan Latin.

7. **Cadmea Tyros**: Cadmus was commonly supposed to have been a Phœnician. Here Tyrian purple is meant. Cf. Prop. 3. 13. 7 *et Tyros ostrinos* (= *purpureos*) *praebet Cadmea colores.* — **pinguis Gallia**: i.e. Gallia Cisalpina; see on 2. 43. 4; 5. 13. 8. *Pingui* = *thick, coarse,* or, perhaps, *greasy.* For the latter sense we may compare Iuv. 9. 28–30 *pingues aliquando lacernas, munimenta togae, duri crassique coloris et male percussas textoris pectine Galli accipimus. Pinguis* is a transferred epithet; it describes Gallia in terms better fitted to describe the products of that district.

8. **purpureum**: i.e. when clothed in Tyrian purple. — **sagatus**, *clad in a sagum*; see 1. 3. 8 N. The *sagum* is not fit garb for a gentleman in town.

9. **ut . . . Oresten**: 'if I am expected to be a Pylades, I must have my Orestes'. — **praestem** = *reddam, praebeam.* It is not necessary to supply *me* with *praestem* or *se* with *praestet.*

10. **ut . . . ama**: proverbial; cf. Ov. A. A. 2. 107 *ut ameris, amabilis esto*; Sen. Ep. 9. 6 *Hecaton ait:* "*ego tibi monstrabo amatorium sine medicamento, sine herba, sine ullius veneficae carmine: si vis amari, ama*"; German *Liebe erwirbt Liebe,* and *Liebe wird durch Liebe erkauft.* See Otto s.v. *Amare,* 2.

17. Cinnamus, the freedman, is anxious to remove all reminders of his servile condition; hence he seeks to change his name, for a freedman's very name was calculated to betray his old condition almost as effectually as would the mark of a branding-iron. Cf. 6. 64. 26 *stigmata nec vafra delebit Cinnamus arte*; 2. 29. 9–10 N. In the case of the cognomen, which directly represented the old slave name, the change was comparatively easy and increasingly common. See Cannegieter 25 ff.; Fried. SG. 1. 200. — Meter: § 49.

17

Cinnam, Cinname, te iubes vocari.
Non est hic, rogo, Cinna, barbarismus ?
Tu si Furius ante dictus esses,
Fur ista ratione dicereris.

28

Libertus Melioris ille notus,
tota qui cecidit dolente Roma,
cari deliciae breves patroni,
hoc sub marmore Glaucias humatus
5   iuncto Flaminiae iacet sepulcro,
castus moribus, integer pudore,

1. **Cinname**: for fanciful slave names see on 5. 24. 1. If this man is the Cinnamus *qui tonsor fueras tota notissimus urbe et post hoc dominae munere factus eques* (7. 64. 1–2), he is prob. to be identified with the upstart barber in Iuv. 1. 24; 10. 225. See Mayor on Iuv. 1. 24.

3. For the diæresis see § 49, d.

4. **Fur**: a fine pun. *Fur* was branded on the forehead of a slave given to pilfering (see 2. 29. 9–10 N.); hence *fur* is a common term of abuse in comedy. *Trifur* also occurs, once, in Plautus. — **ista ratione**, *on that principle, by that plan,* i.e. by changing names in this way.

28. An epitaph-epigram (§ 26) on Glaucias, a freedman of Atedius Melior (see 2. 69. 7 N.). Cf. 6. 29. On this Glaucias Statius wrote a long poem (234 vss.): see Silv. 2. 1.

2. **tota . . . Roma**: cf. Stat. Silv. 2. 1. 175–178 *plebs cuncta nefas et praevia flerunt agmina, Flaminio quae limite Mulvius agger transvehit, immeritus flammis dum tristibus infans traditur.*

3. **deliciae**, *pet*; cf. 1. 109. 5 N.; Stat. Silv. 2. 1. 70–75 *tu domino requies portusque senectae, tu modo deliciae, dulces modo pectore curae,* etc. — **breves**: the boy, like the rose, was short-lived; cf. 1. 43. 6 N.; Hor. C. 2. 14. 22–25 *neque harum, quas colis, arborum te praeter invisas cupressos ulla brevem dominum sequetur.*

4. **humatus** = *sepultus.*

5. **iuncto Flaminiae** (*viae*): see 1. 88; 11. 13; Iuv. 1. 170–171 *illos, quorum Flaminia tegitur cinis atque Latina.* On the road itself see 3. 14. 4 N.; 4. 64. 18. The dat. is common in poetry with *iungere, miscere,* and verbs of like meaning. — **iuncto** in sense = *proximo*; the tombs generally lay very close to the *viae.*

6. **castus . . . pudore**: the boy was good, quick-witted, and handsome; cf. (on the same boy) 6. 29. 5–6 *moribus hoc* (his freedom) *formaeque datum: quis blandior illo?* Stat. Silv. 2. 1. 39–43 *hinc me forma rapit, rapit inde modestia praecox et pudor et tenero probitas maturior*

velox ingenio, decore felix.

Bis senis modo messibus peractis

vix unum puer adplicabat annum.

10   Qui fles talia, nil fleas, viator.

35

Septem clepsydras magna tibi voce petenti

arbiter invitus, Caeciliane, dedit.

At tu multa diu dicis vitreisque tepentem

ampullis potas semisupinus aquam.

aevo. O ubi (est) purpureo suffusus sanguine candor . . . et castigatae collecta modestia frontis?

7. For the chiasmus cf. 1. 4. 8; 6. 8. 1; 10. 47. 6, 8.

8–9. Bis ... annum: i.e. the child was not yet thirteen years old. Cf. Stat. Silv. 2. 1. 124–125 *Herculeos annis aequare labores coeperat adsurgens sed adhuc infantia mixta.*

8. messibus: cf. 6. 70. 1. For the dat. with *adplicabat = addebat*, see on the dat. with *iuncto*, 5.

10. Qui ... viator: for like mortuary invocations to the passer-by see 10. 61. 5–6; 7. 96. 6; C.I.L. passim. — **fles** is here trans., *weep over*; this use appears but once in Cicero, but is common everywhere in poetry and in post-Augustan prose.

35. On a tedious lawyer, who drank much water while pleading in court. — Meter: § 48.

1. Septem clepsydras: as in modern courts of justice, the time allowed to pleaders at the bar was limited. At Athens, and later at Rome, the time was measured by the clepsydra (κλεψύδρα), a kind of *horologium*, consisting of a vessel so arranged that water escaped from it slowly through one or more apertures in the bottom (cf. the modern hour-glass). Cf. 8. 7. 1–4; Plin. Ep. 2. 11. 14 *dixi horis paene*

quinque, nam duodecim clepsydris quas spatiosissimas acceperam sunt additae quattuor; Marq. 792; 798. — **magna ... voce petenti:** Caecilianus seems to have overawed the judge by his arrogant manner.

2. arbiter: prob. here used for any *iudex*, though sometimes the *arbiter* was a sort of referee in a civil suit appointed by a praetor.

3–4. At tu, etc.: 'but then you are a lengthy, aye, and a thirsty speaker'. — **multa diu:** Caecilianus has many heads to his speech and dwells long on each. — **tepentem ... aquam:** as the water flasks would prob. be filled with fresh water before the speaker began, the mention of the warm water calls attention anew to the length of the plea. — **ampullis:** long-necked vessels used for water, oil, or wine; see 14. 110; Marq. 649, Fig. 15. — **potas:** Caecilianus's energy and lengthy pleading have made him thirsty and have irritated his throat (cf. 5). To drink during a speech was bad form; cf. Quint. 11. 3. 136 *bibere aut etiam esse* (eat) *inter agendum, quod multis moris fuit et est quibusdam, ab oratore meo procul absit.* — **semisupinus:** to drink from an *ampulla*, esp. if the contents were low, one must throw his head well back.

5   Ut tandem saties vocemque sitimque, rogamus,
        iam de clepsydra, Caeciliane, bibas.

41

Qui recitat lana fauces et colla revinctus,
    hic se posse loqui, posse tacere negat.

48

Quod tam grande sophos clamat tibi turba togata,
    non tu, Pomponi, cena diserta tua est.

51

Quod convivaris sine me tam saepe, Luperce,

5–6. saties vocem: the water may temporarily afford relief to Caecilianus's throat, but to stop speaking altogether will be the surest way. By drinking up his time (at Athens ὕδωρ, which = *aqua*, came actually to denote the time represented by the outflow of the water in the clepsydra), he can kill two birds with one stone. — **rogamus . . . bibas**: for the parataxis see on 3. 25. 3; 5. 49. 12.

41. On the recitations in general see 1. 3. 5; 1. 76. 13; 3. 50. 2. With this epigram cf. 3. 18; 4. 41, with notes. — Meter: § 48.

1. lana . . . revinctus: the man seems to have worn a neck-cloth (*focale*) to protect his throat. See 3. 18, with notes. — **fauces . . . revinctus**: for the acc. with the pf. pass. ptc. cf. the poets passim.

2. se posse loqui . . . negat: i.e. because of the bad condition of his throat. — **posse tacere negat**: because of his passion for speaking.

48. 'Any *recitator* will be praised if he is known to give good dinners'. — Meter: § 48.

1. Quod: see on 2. 11. 1. — **grande sophos** seems to be an echo of the sham applause only too common at the recitations; cf. 1. 3. 7 N. Pomponius evidently wished to be accounted a littérateur. — **turba**: such applauders were dubbed *laudiceni* or σοφοκλεῖς; see 2. 11. Introd.; 1. 20. 1. The audience at the recitation wore the conventional toga. Note the triple alliteration.

2. cena refers either to the hoped-for *cena popularis* (1. 20; 1. 43) or to the *sportula* (3. 7, with notes). Cf. Petr. 10 *multo me turpior es tu hercule, qui, ut foris cenares, poetam laudasti.* On the insincerity of the hearers see Sen. Ep. 95. 2 *recitator historiam ingentem adtulit, minutissime scriptam, artissime plicatam et, magna parte perlecta,* "*Desinam*" *inquit* "*si vultis*"; *acclamatur:* "*Recita, recita*" *ab his qui illum obmutescere illic cupiunt.*

51. Lupercus seems to have invited M. to dinner only when he had reason to believe that the poet would not come. — Meter: § 48.

1. convivaris: *convivari* implies more than *cenare* would.

inveni noceam qua ratione tibi.

Irascor : licet usque voces mittasque rogesque —
"Quid facies ? " inquis.   Quid faciam ? veniam.

52

Hoc iacet in tumulo raptus puerilibus annis
    Pantagathus, domini cura dolorque sui,
vix tangente vagos ferro resecare capillos
    doctus et hirsutas excoluisse genas.
5 Sis licet, ut debes, tellus, placata levisque,
    artificis levior non potes esse manu.

2. noceam . . . tibi: i.e. 'to annoy you and so to get even with you'.

3. usque, *repeatedly, continually*; cf. 9.48.4; 12.82.12. — voces . . . roges: a climax. — voces: see 1. 20. 1 N. — mittas: i.e. send a special messenger with an urgent request. — rogesque: we may suppose that M. pauses here (aposiopesis), unable at first to think of a suitable revenge.

4. Quid facies? Lupercus breaks in, unable to bear the suspense. — veniam: the point lies in the unexpected turn in the thought; compliance, instead of the expected indignant refusal, is forthcoming. 'I will be revenged by coming', says M.

52. An epitaph on a slave barber who understood his business. Cf. 8. 52. On the *tonsores* see Beck. 3. 237 ff. — Meter: § 48.

1. Hoc . . . tumulo: a variation of the conventional *hic iacet*; cf. 6. 28. 4–5. *Tumulus* is here not merely the swelling hillock of earth and turf, but = *sepulcrum*, as in 4. 59. 6.

2. Pantagathus, *All-Good*, is apparently a nickname; cf. πανταγαθός. — domini . . . sui: half chi-

astic in order. — cura: while alive; cf. 5. 24. 10 N. — dolor: now that he is dead; see on 6. 63. 7.

3–4. vix . . . doctus: his skill was so great that one could hardly feel the blade. For barbers of a different sort see 7. 83; 11. 84. — vagos, *straggling*. — ferro = *novacula*. — resecare and excoluisse depend on *doctus*; see on 5. 24. 7; cf. Ov. M. 11. 182 *solitus longos ferro resecare capillos*. — excoluisse: cf. Tib. 1. 8. 9 *quid tibi nunc molles prodest coluisse capillos*. Note the pf. here, but the pres. in 3; the two tenses seem to denote exactly the same time. See on *eripuisse*, 1. 107. 6. *Resecuisse* would be impossible in hexameter verse.

5. tellus: vocative. For *sis . . . tellus . . . levisque* see on 5. 34. 9–10. For the syntax in *sis licet* see on *sic licet excuses*, 1. 70. 17.

6. artificis: cf. Tib. 1. 8. 12 *artificis docta subsecuisse manu?*

55. On the basis of the paradox that he who is always redolent of perfumes smells ill (cf. 2. 12) M. intimates that Coracinus uses perfumes because he is naturally offensive to delicate nostrils or has been made so by his vices. — Meter: § 49.

55

Quod semper casiaque cinnamoque
et nido niger alitis superbae
fragras plumbea Nicerotiana,
rides nos, Coracine, nil olentis :
5　　malo, quam bene olere, nil olere.

57

Mentiris fictos unguento, Phoebe, capillos
et tegitur pictis sordida calva comis ;

1. **casia ... cinnamo:** cf. 3. 63.
4 N.; Plin. N. H. 13. 18 *ergo regale
unguentum appellatum, quoniam
Parthorum regibus ita temperatur,
constat myrobalano, costo, amomo,
cinnamo, comaco ... casia,* etc.;
Beck. 3. 159 ff.

2. **nido ... superbae:** i.e.
black with ointment got from the
nest of the phoenix; cf. 9. 11. 4;
10. 16. 6; Plin. N. H. 12. 85 *cinna-
momum et casias fabulose narravit
antiquitas princepsque Herodotus
avium nidis et privatim phoenicis
... ex inviis rupibus arboribusque
decuti*; Tac. Ann. 6. 28. On the
phoenix itself see on 5. 37. 13. —
niger: cf. 12. 17. 7 *circumfusa rosis
et nigra recumbit amomo*; 12. 38. 3
crine nitens, niger unguento.

3. **fragras** here takes acc.; see
on 5. 37. 9. — **plumbea** may in
itself = *vile, worthless,* because
adulterated (see on 10. 74. 4); cf.
10. 49. 5 *plumbea vina.* In that
case sc. *unguenta* (see next note).
But this meaning does not fit the
context; the perfumes of 1–2 are
all good. It is better, then, to
supply *vasa* with *Nicerotiana* and
to see a reference to the fact that
this perfume was prepared, or at
least stored, in leaden jars; cf.
Plin. N. H. 13. 19 *sol inimicus iis
(unguentis), quam ob rem in umbra
conduntur plumbeis vasis.* *Plumbea* then = *pretiosa.* — **Nicerotiana:** Niceros and Cosmus (cf.
cosmianum) were well-known perfumers whose names stand for their
wares; cf. 9. 26. 2 N.; 12. 65. 4; 10.
38. 8; Apoll. Sidon. C. 9. 322–326
*bonos odores, nardum ac pinguia
Nicerotianis quae fragrant alaba-
stra tincta sucis, Indo cinnamon ex
rogo petitum quo Phoenix iuvenescit
occidendo.*

4. **Coracine:** perhaps a humorous coinage suggested by his
appearance; cf. *niger,* 2, and *coracinus,* 'raven-black', κοράκινος.
Fried., however, would identify him
with the wretch of 4. 43.

5. Cf. 2. 12. 3–4 *hoc mihi suspectum est, quod oles bene, Postume, semper: Postume, non bene olet
qui bene semper olet.*

57. M. ridicules Phoebus, who
was bald but by a skillful use of
pomade imitated hair. Cf. 12. 45.
— Meter: § 48.

1. **Mentiris ... capillos:** cf.
6. 74. 2–4 *calvam trifilem semitatus*
('having made paths in') *unguento
fodit ... tonsis ora laxa lentiscis,
mentitur.* For *mentiri* with acc.
see on 3. 43. 1; 5. 39. 6.

2. **pictis ... comis:** the black
ointment (6. 55. 2) had the appearance of paint. — **sordida:** dirty

tonsorem capiti non est adhibere necesse :
radere te melius spongea, Phoebe, potest.

63

Scis te captari, scis hunc qui captat avarum,
    et scis qui captat quid, Mariane, velit ;
tu tamen hunc tabulis heredem, stulte, supremis
    scribis et esse tuo vis, furiose, loco.
5 " Munera magna tamen misit ".   Sed misit in hamo ;
    et piscatorem piscis amare potest ?
hicine deflebit vero tua fata dolore ?
    si cupis ut ploret, des, Mariane, nihil.

with pomade instead of being washed clean (*nitida*); cf. 10. 83. 2, 11. — **calva**: see 5. 49. 3 N.

4. spongea: rather than by razor or shears.

63. M. ridicules the stupidity of Marianus in allowing himself to be victimized by a legacy-hunter. See 1. 10, with notes; 11. 44. — Meter: § 48.

1. avarum (*esse*), *is moved by avarice rather than by friendship*.

2. quid . . . velit: cf. 8. 27. 1–2 *munera qui tibi dat locupleti, Gaure, senique, si sapis et sentis, hoc tibi ait "Morere"*.

3. tabulis . . . supremis: cf. 5. 39. 1–2 N.; 5. 32. 1–2 *quadrantem Crispus tabulis, Faustine, supremis non dedit uxori*.

4. esse tuo . . . loco: i.e. 'to succeed to your wealth and social standing'.

5. Munera . . . misit: Marianus's rejoinder. — **Sed . . . in hamo**: the *munera* were but bait; cf. 4. 56. 3–6 *sordidius nihil est, nihil est te spurcius uno, qui potes insidias dona vocare tuas: sic avidis fallax indulget piscibus hamus,* *callida sic stultas decipit esca feras.* The figure antedates M.; cf. Hor. S. 2. 5. 23–26 *captes astutus ubique testamenta senum, neu, si vafer unus et alter insidiatorem praeroso fugerit hamo, aut spem deponas aut artem illusus omittas*; Sen. Ben. 4. 20. 3.

7. fata: cf. 1. 42. 1 N. — **dolore**: *dolor* is often used of grief for the dead; cf. 6. 52. 2.   For the thought cf. Pub. Syr. 221 *heredis fletus sub persona* (mask) *risus est*.

8. des nihil: if Marianus leaves the *captator* nothing, the latter will mourn truly, not, to be sure, at Marianus's death, but over his disappointment and his wasted efforts; cf. Iuv. 13. 134 *ploratur lacrimis amissa pecunia veris*.

70. 'An invalid's existence is no life at all.   The proper measure of life is not mere length of days, as old Cotta knows, who, though sixty-two, has never been ill and still laughs at the doctors'.   Cf. notes on 1. 15. 12 ; 1. 103. 12 ; 2. 90. 3. It has been inferred from this epigram that M. himself was at this time not well; see § 14. — Meter: § 49.

70

Sexagesima, Marciane, messis
acta est et, puto, iam secunda Cottae,
nec se taedia lectuli calentis
expertum meminit die vel uno ;
5 ostendit digitum, sed inpudicum,
Alconti Dasioque Symmachoque.
At· nostri bene conputentur anni ˙
et quantum tetricae tulere febres
aut languor gravis aut mali dolores
10 a vita meliore separentur :
infantes sumus, et senes videmur.

1. **messis** = *aestas* = *annus*;
cf. 6. 28. 8.

2. **et** joins the numeral adjectives in 1–2.— **Cottae**: so-called
dat. of agent.

3. **taedia . . . calentis**: said of
one suffering from protracted fever.
— **calentis**, *feverish*.

4. **expertum**: sc. *esse*.— **vel**:
as in 5. 49. 5. For its use with an
adj. cf. Plaut.Trin.963–964 *te tribus
verbis volo. Vel trecentis.*

5. **digitum . . . inpudicum**:
the middle finger was called *inpu-
dicus* and *infamis*, because in a certain obscene and insulting gesture
the middle finger projected from
the clenched fist; cf. Priap. 56. 1–2
*et impudicum ostendis digitum mihi
minanti*; Iuv. 10. 52–53 *cum Fortunae ipse minaci mandaret laque-
um mediumque ostenderet unguem.
Ostendere digitum (medium, infa-
mem, inpudicum)* = 'jeer at', 'make
fun of', or 'insult', according to
the context.— **sed**: cf. 1. 43. 9 N.

6. **Alconti**: a Greek surgeon
practicing in Rome; cf. 11. 84. 5.
His name seems to have typified
skillful medical practice; cf. Aus.

Epigr. 73 *medicus divis fatisque po-
tentior Alcon.*— **Dasio . . . Sym-
macho**: also *medici*. For Symmachus cf. 5. 9. 1 N. On *medici* and
chirurgi see Beck. 2. 139.

7–10. **At . . . computentur . . .
separentur**: a volitive subjunctive, serving virtually as protasis to
11; see on 1. 70. 3; 1. 79. 2.— **bene**,
fairly, rightly; explained by 8–10,
which in effect = 'by deducting
from . . . what fever', etc.— **quantum** (*temporis*) . . . **dolores** is subj.
of *separentur*, 10.— **tulere** = *abstu-
lere, have taken away*; see on 1.
4. 2.— **languor**: weakness resulting from disease; cf. 5. 9. 1 N.; Iuv.
3. 232–233 *ipsum languorem pepe-
rit cibus inperfectus.* — **dolores**:
both bodily and mental; hence both
pain and *sorrow, distress.* — **vita
meliore**: i.e. true living; cf. 15. —
separentur: see App.

11. **infantes**: i.e. as measured
by the limited health and happiness of our existence. — **et** = *and
yet, et tamen.* M. might have written *quamquam senes videmur*, or,
still more effectively, *quamvis senes
videamur.*

Aetatem Priamique Nestorisque
longam qui putat esse, Marciane,
multum decipiturque falliturque.
15   Non est vivere, sed valere vita est.

80

Ut nova dona tibi, Caesar, Nilotica tellus
miserat hibernas ambitiosa rosas ;
navita derisit Pharios Memphiticus hortos,
urbis ut intravit limina prima tuae,
5   tantus veris honos et odorae gratia Florae,
tantaque Paestani gloria ruris erat,

12. **Aetatem**, *life-span*, viewed
as a whole, without regard to the
stages of life; so often. Cf. e.g.
Cic. Tusc. 3. 25. 61 *acta aetas ho-*
neste ac splendide tantam adfert
consolationem ut, etc.— **Priami . . .**
Nestoris: cf. 5. 58. 5; Iuv. 10. 246–
247 *rex Pylius, magno si quidquam*
credis Homero, exemplum vitae fuit
a cornice secundae.
80. This epigram seems to
have been prompted by the arrival in Rome of a messenger who
brought to the emperor a present
of winter roses from Egypt, only to
find that the gift which the sender
thought so rare was deprived of its
value by an abundance of home-
grown flowers. This was due either
to an open winter (Fried. thinks it
was the winter of 89–90) or to the
increased culture of winter roses
in the greenhouses of the rich in
town. On the demand for roses in
Rome see 5. 37. 9 N. — Meter: § 48.
1. **Ut** = *tamquam* or *quasi*; *ut*
nova = *in the thought that they*
were a rarity. See Gilbert Q. C. 10.
— **Nilotica tellus** : the Nile was
almost literally Egypt; cf. *Nile*, 10;
1.61.5 N.; Luc. 9. 130 *Nilotica rura.*

2. **hibernas . . . rosas:** cf. 4.
29. 4; 13. 127; Sen. Ep. 122. 8;
Macr. Sat. 7. 5. 32. — **ambitiosa :**
i.e. eager to gratify the emperor by
something unique, something that
no other quarter could offer.
3-4. **navita :** archaic and poetical for *nauta*; the word is appropriate because the messenger had
come over seas. — **derisit :** i.e. lost
all admiration for. — **Pharios :** see
on 5. 69. 1. — **Memphiticus** =
Aegyptius; Memphis was important enough to stand for all Egypt.
Cf. 14. 38. 1 *dat chartis habiles cala-*
mos Memphitica tellus. — **hortos :**
here esp. of rose-gardens. The Roman *horti* greeted the messenger
even before he had got within the
Servian Wall; the greatest of the
parks, the Horti Pompeiani, Horti
Lucullani, Horti Sallustiani, had
been laid out beyond the Agger of
Servius. However, *limina prima*,
4, may be understood literally, for
there were many smaller, though
elegant, *horti*, within the walls.
5. **honos**, *grace, charm, beauty.*
6. **Paestani . . . ruris:** cf. 5.
37. 9 N.; 9. 60. 4; Verg. G. 1. 168 *si*
te digna manet divini gloria ruris.

sic, quacumque vagus gressumque oculosque ferebat,
    tonsilibus sertis omne rubebat iter.
At tu Romanae iussus iam cedere brumae
10   mitte tuas messes, accipe, Nile, rosas.

82

Quidam me modo, Rufe, diligenter
inspectum, velut emptor aut lanista,
cum vultu digitoque subnotasset,
" Tune es, tune " ait " ille Martialis,
5   cuius nequitias iocosque novit
aurem qui modo non habet Batavam ? "

7. **vagus:** freely, *in his wanderings*; an important word. The messenger could see roses wherever he turned; he had no need to search for them as for rarities.

8. **tonsilibus sertis:** see 5. 64. 4 N. — **omne . . . iter:** the very streets were ruddy with chaplets exposed for sale.

9. **tu Romanae:** juxtaposition. — **cedere,** *yield precedence to.* — **brumae:** perhaps used to show that even the dead of winter did not interfere with the supply of roses; cf. 3. 58. 8 N.

10. **tuas messes:** i.e. *frumentum.* Egypt and Africa fed the Roman populace. — **accipe . . . rosas:** sc. *nostras* or *a nobis,* for, says M. to the Nile, 'you cannot hope to rival ours'.

82. M. has not forgotten how to pose elegantly as a beggar. See § 10. — Meter: § 49.

1-2. **diligenter inspectum:** *inspicere* is frequently used for a close, (half) professional examination; cf. 9. 59. 3; Sen. Ep. 47. 16 *quemadmodum stultus est, qui ecum empturus non ipsum inspicit, sed stratum eius ac frenos;* Iuv. 3.

44-45 *ranarum viscera numquam inspexi* (i.e. as *augur, haruspex*). — **emptor aut lanista:** the former is the ordinary non-professional buyer, the latter buys to secure proper material for the gladiatorial school. Each would in his way exercise great care.

3. **cum . . . subnotasset:** the man eyed M. and felt him all over.

4. **tune . . . tune:** effective repetition, picturing the man's doubts of M.'s identity. — **ille:** cf. 1. 1. 1 N.

5. **nequitias:** cf. 1. 109. 1 N.; 11. 16. 7-8 *tu quoque nequitias nostri lususque libelli . . . legas;* 5. 2. 3-5 *tu, quem nequitiae procaciores delectant nimium salesque nudi, lascivos lege quattuor libellos.* — **iocos:** cf. 1. 4. 3; 4. 49. 2. — **novit:** the subj. is the antec. of *qui,* 6; everybody who has good literary taste and a critical ear knows M.

6. **aurem . . . Batavam:** the revolt of the Batavi (Hollanders) during the reign of Vitellius had not been forgotten. The Romans thought of the Batavi as brave fighters (Tac. Germ. 29) and as

Subrisi modice levique nutu
me quem dixerat esse non negavi.
" Cur ergo " inquit " habes malas lacernas ? "
10   Respondi : " quia sum malus poeta ".
Hoc ne saepius accidat poetae,
mittas, Rufe, mihi bonas lacernas.

88

Mane salutavi vero te nomine casu
nec dixi dominum, Caeciliane, meum.

manufacturers of soap; see 5. 37.
8 N.— **qui modo non habet** involves an interesting fusion of syntactical forms. M. might have said
simply, either *cuius ... novit aurem
qui non habet Batavam* (the form of
our text, minus *modo*), or *cuius nequitias iocosque quislibet novit, modo
non* (classical *dummodo ne*) *aurem
habeat Batavam*. Two points, then,
deserve especial notice : (1) *modo*
= 'only', as in the so-called clauses
of proviso with *modo* or *dummodo*,
and (2) the mood of *habet*; with
modo, 'only', the subjv. was to be
expected. The ind. became possible only when the combination
became idiomatic and its origin
was forgotten. Cf. Cic. Cat. 4.8. 16
*Servus est nemo, qui modo tolerabili
condicione sit servitutis*; Flacc. 27.
64 *quamquam quis ignorat, qui
modo umquam mediocriter res istas
scire curavit.* •

9. **Cur . . . lacernas?** better
clothes, thinks the man, should go
with distinction such as M. has
won. For such clothes cf. 2. 29.
3 N.; 2. 43. 7.

10. **malus poeta:** *poor poet*
exactly gives the play on words.
M. of course wishes Rufus to think
especially of *malus* as poverty-
stricken; cf. *malas,* 9.

11. M., becoming serious, uses
poetae without epithet, as = *true
poet*; note *bonas* in 12 and cf.
Hor. S. 1. 4. 1 *Eupolis atque Cra-
tinus Aristophanesque poetae*.

88. 'The poor client pays in
hard cash for any lapse in etiquette'.
Caecilianus was a good specimen
of the punctilious patron.—Meter:
§ 48.

1. **salutavi ... casu:** 'thought-
lessly and without intentional slight
I addressed you with *Salve, Caeciliane*'; see on 2.

2. **nec . . . meum:** good form
required the client to say *Salve,
domine*, or *Salve, rex*; M. had failed
to make it plain that he recognized
Caecilianus as his superior. Cf.
e.g. 1. 112. 1–2 *cum te non nossem,
dominum regemque vocabam: nunc
bene te novi: iam mihi Priscus eris*;
Iuv. 8. 160–161 *Idumaeae Syro-
phoenix incola portae hospitis ad-
fectu dominum regemque salutat*;
Beck. 2. 194 ff. Since *dominus*
prop. denoted a master of slaves,
its use as a term of polite address
in ordinary society spread but
slowly; Augustus (Oros. 6. 22) and
Tiberius (Suet. Tib. 27) allowed no
one to apply the term to them. See
also Suet. Aug. 53, with Peck's
note.

Quanti libertas constat mihi tanta requiris ?
centum quadrantes abstulit illa mihi.

3. libertas: see preceding note. 'I played the freeman', says M., 'when I failed to call you *dominus*; I had to pay for that freedom'. — **constat:** cf. 1. 103. 10 N. Note the mood of *constat*: the question is put directly, *requiris* being brought in unexpectedly, almost parenthetically; see on 6. 8. 6. We might put a question mark after *tanta*. — **tanta** is ironical.

4. Centum quadrantes: for the importance of the money dole to the client see 3. 7, with notes.

LIBER VII

3

Cur non mitto meos tibi, Pontiliane, libellos?
ne mihi tu mittas, Pontiliane, tuos.

16

Aera domi non sunt: superest hoc, Regule, solum
ut tua vendamus munera: numquid emis?

17

Ruris bibliotheca delicati,
vicinam videt unde lector urbem,
inter carmina sanctiora si quis
lascivae fuerit locus Thaliae,
5   hos nido licet inseras vel imo

3. In some cases, thinks M., like exchange is undesirable; at the least such exchange would work injustice. Cf. 5. 73 throughout. — Meter: § 48.

16. With characteristic adroitness M. makes the very boldness and humor of his "grotesque joke" (Spiegel) a mask behind which the beggar hides. See § 10. For Regulus see 1. 12. Introd. — Meter: § 48.

17. Written to accompany an author's copy of Books I–VII (cf. 6) sent to Iulius Martialis (cf. 1. 15, with notes) for his library. The *bibliotheca* is that of the villa described in 4. 64. — Meter: § 49.

1. Ruris . . . delicati: cf. 4. 64. 10 N. — bibliotheca: from the end of the Republic the *bibliotheca* was a regular part of the rich man's country-house. Trimalchio boasts

thus (Petr. 48): *duas bibliothecas habeo, unam Graecam, alteram Latinam.* See Beck. 2. 418 ff.; Marq. 114, esp. note 4; Lanciani Anc. R. 179 ff. Little if any reading, however, was done in the *bibliotheca* itself; it was used simply for the storage of books.

2. vicinam . . . urbem: cf. 4. 64. 11–12 N.

3. carmina sanctiora: i.e. the work of poets whose *carmina* have received a place in the sacred canon; cf. Hor. Ep. 2. 1. 54 *adeo sanctum est vetus omne poema.*

4. lascivae . . . Thaliae: see 4. 8. 11–12 N.

5. nido . . . imo: the poet's gift craves only a humble place in the library, near the floor. For *nido* see 1. 117. 15 N.; Beck. 2. 421. — vel imo: cf. *vel uno*, 6. 70. 4 N,

septem quos tibi misimus libellos
auctoris calamo sui notatos :
haec illis pretium facit litura.
At tu munere, delicata, parvo
10　quae cantaberis orbe nota toto,
pignus pectoris hoc mei tuere,
Iuli bibliotheca Martialis.

21

Haec est illa dies, quae magni conscia partus
Lucanum populis et tibi, Polla, dedit.

7. **auctoris . . . notatos:** i.e. corrected by the author himself after it had left the hands of the copyist, and so enhanced in value; cf. 1. 3. 9–10. Of badly made copies there was in antiquity much complaint. Autograph copies, too, were prized. — **calamo:** cf. 7. 11. 1–2 *cogis me calamo manuque nostra emendare meos, Pudens, libellos.*

8. **pretium . . . litura:** 'my gift has at least one claim to value: I have corrected these books myself'. For books as gifts cf. 9. 99. 6–8 *i, liber, absentis pignus amicitiae. Vilis eras, fateor, si te nunc mitteret emptor; grande tui pretium muneris auctor erit*; Hor. C. 4. 8. 11–12 *carmina possumus donare et pretium dicere muneri.*

9. **munere . . . parvo:** partly causal, partly instrumental abl. with *cantaberis*; to join the phrase with *delicata*, as some do, in the sense of 'charming because of my gift', seems hardly consistent with 5. — **delicata:** voc.; see App. Its position seems due to the effort to secure juxtaposition with *parvo*; compared with the existing charm (1–2) of the library M.'s gift is small; yet it will add to the fame of the collection.

10. **orbe . . . toto:** cf. 1. 1. 2 N. — **nota:** pred. nom. with *cantaberis*, 'will be sung to fame'.

11. **pignus pectoris:** cf. *pignus amicitiae* in 9. 99. 6, cited on 8.

21. An epigram addressed to Polla Argentaria, widow of M. Annaeus Lucanus, the brilliant but ill-starred young poet (see 1. 61. 7–8 N.). His great wealth and literary fame excited the jealousy of Nero, who sought to ruin his reputation and to clip his poetic wings. Accordingly, Lucan took part in Piso's conspiracy against Nero. For a graphic account of his enforced suicide see Tac. Ann. 15. 70. — Meter: § 48.

1–2. **haec . . . dedit:** it is the anniversary of Lucan's birthday. Cf. 7. 22; 7. 23. — **conscia:** cf. Verg. A. 4. 167–168 *fulsere ignes et conscius aether conubiis.* Render by *well aware of, witness of.* — **populis,** *the nations,* suggests that Lucan's fame was wide-spread. — **et tibi . . . dedit:** i.e. 'as your husband'. Her devotion became proverbial. See Apoll. Sidon. Ep. 2. 10. 6 *reminiscere quod saepe versum Corinna cum suo Nasone complevit, Lesbia cum Catullo . . . Argentaria cum Lucano, Cynthia cum Propertio,*

Heu! Nero crudelis nullaque invisior umbra,
  debuit hoc saltem non licuisse tibi.

25

Dulcia cum tantum scrības epigrammata semper
  et cerussata candidiora cute
nullaque mica salis nec amari fellis in illis
  gutta sit, o demens, vis tamen illa legi!
5 Nec cibus ipse iuvat morsu fraudatus aceti
  nec grata est facies cui gelasinus abest.
Infanti melimela dato fatuasque mariscas,
  nam mihi, quae novit pungere, Chia sapit.

Delia cum Tibullo. Polla seems to have befriended M. In 10. 64 he addresses her as *regina*.

3. nulla...umbra: i.e. 'hated for Lucan's as for no other's death'; *umbra* is causal ablative. For the thought cf. 5. 69. 2 *levius tabula quam Cicerone nocens*, with notes.

4. licuisse: cf. 4. 44. 8 N.; an ironical allusion to Nero's witticism (Suet. Ner. 37): *elatus inflatusque tantis velut successibus* (murders and tyrannical acts) *negavit quemquam principum scisse quid sibi liceret.* Note the tense; the pres. inf. is the regular use after all tenses of verbs of obligation, propriety, etc., but the pf. is sometimes used, by assimilation, after past tenses of such verbs. See also on *eripuisse*, 1. 107. 6.

25. Addressed to a man who wrote epigrams which, though pretty and elegant, lacked point and sting. — Meter: § 48.

2. cerussata ... cute: see 1. 72. 6 N. — **candidiora:** perhaps used here of the clear unaffected style of the writer (cf. Quint. 10. 1. 121 *tam candidum et lene et speciosum dicendi genus*), though that

sense conveys a compliment rather than the expected criticism. Probably, therefore, the sense is rather 'more pallid', and so 'more feeble-looking'. M. is then hinting that the public prefers epigrams that have piquancy and a wanton spice; 'more spotless' will render the point.

3. nulla ... salis: see 1. 41. 16 N. The figurative use of *sal, mel, fel* is common. To these words Pliny probably refers in Ep. 3. 21, cited in § 38.

5-6. Nec ... abest: dull uniformity is unattractive; one's food, for instance, needs a little spice. — **morsu:** 'bite', i.e. *pungency*; cf. *pungere*, 8. — **gelasinus:** a dimple produced by a smile; cf. γελασῖνος, from γελάω.

7. Infanti ... mariscas: sweets please only babies; adults have more discrimination. — **melimela:** see 1. 43. 4 N. — **mariscas:** figs large but inferior, well characterized by *fatuas*, 'silly', 'insipid'; cf. 11. 31. 8 *fatuas ... placentas.*

8. quae ... pungere: cf. note on *morsu*, 5. — **Chia:** sc. *ficus*; here it typifies the *epigramma mordens* (Domit.).

36

Cum pluvias madidumque Iovem perferre negaret
et rudis hibernis villa nataret aquis,
plurima quae posset subitos effundere nimbos
muneribus venit tegula missa tuis.
5 Horridus, ecce, sonat Boreae stridore December :
Stella, tegis villam, non tegis agricolam.

43

Primum est ut praestes, si quid te, Cinna, rogabo ;
illud deinde sequens, ut cito, Cinna, neges.

36. M. again acts the beggar gracefully. He suggests to his benefactor that it is a scant beneficence to protect the farm-house if the farmer is neglected. — Meter: § 48.

1. madidum . . . Iovem: i.e. bad weather. *Iuppiter* often = 'weather' (metonymy), esp. bad weather. The phrase *Iuppiter pluvius* is rare in Latin; in this passage, too, *Iovem* does not stand for the god. See Morgan Trans. Am. Phil. Ass. 32. 99. Cf. Varr. L. L. 5. 65 *ut ait Ennius: "Istic est is Iuppiter quem dico, quem Graeci vocant aerem, qui ventus est et nubes, imber postea, atque ex imbre frigus, ventus post fit, aer denuo"*; Hor. C. 1. 22. 19-20 *quod latus mundi nebulae malusque Iuppiter urget.* — **negaret:** for *negare*, 'refuse', with inf., cf. Prop. 2. 10. 13-14 *iam negat Euphrates equitem post terga tueri Parthorum*; Soed. 15.

2. rudis . . . villa: a farm-house (M.'s own) at best rough and ill-made; *rudis* may, however, picture the result of age and neglect. Cf. also *rudis . . . porticus*, 1. 12. 5 N. — **hibernis . . . aquis:** winter cold is added to the discomfort of water.

3-4. plurima . . . tegula: see on 1. 70. 6. — **subitos . . . nimbos:** i.e. even the sudden hard showers. M.'s complaint had been made, apparently, during the winter, and relief had come before the spring rains. — **effundere,** *shed.*

5. Horridus is a common epithet of winter (personified) and of bad weather; cf. 7. 95. 1 *bruma est et riget horridus December*; Verg. G. 3. 442-443 *horrida cano bruma gelu.* — **December:** M. thinks of the Saturnalia as a good time to appeal to Stella for another present.

6. Stella: L. Arruntius Stella; see 1. 61. 4 N. — **tegis:** a pun on *tegula*, 4, spite of the difference in quantity. See on 9. 6. 4. — **tegis agricolam:** i.e. with a new toga.

43. M. tells Cinna that to promise without fulfilling the promise is worse than to refuse outright. — Meter: § 48.

1. Primum, *of first importance. Primum est = maxime volo,* and so may be construed with *ut* and the subjunctive.

2. ut . . . neges: i.e. 'if you cannot comply with promptness'. Cf. 6. 20. 1-4 *mutua te centum sestertia, Phoebe, rogavi, cum mihi*

Diligo praestantem ; non odi, Cinna, negantem :
sed tu nec praestas nec cito, Cinna, negas.

47

Doctorum Licini celeberrime Sura virorum,
    cuius prisca graves lingua reduxit avos,
redderis — heu, quanto fatorum munere ! — nobis,
    gustata Lethes paene remissus aqua.
5   Perdiderant iam vota metum securaque flebat
    Tristitia et lacrimis iamque peractus eras :

dixisses "*Exigis ergo nihil?*" *Inqui-ris, dubitas, cunctaris meque diebus teque decem crucias: iam rogo, Phoebe, nega*; 6. 30.

47. M. congratulates L. Li-cinius Sura on his restoration to health after a sickness in which his life had been despaired of. Sura, who came from Hispania Tarraco-nensis, was orator, soldier, states-man, natural philosopher, thrice consul under Trajan, and a close friend of that emperor. As Ver-ginius Rufus won fame by thrice refusing the purple, Sura may be said to have distinguished himself by virtually making two emperors, Trajan and Hadrian.—Meter: § 48.

1. Doctorum ... celeberrime: Sura seems to have been a learned naturalist and philosopher; cf. Plin. Ep. 4. 30.

2. cuius . . . avos: i.e. when Sura spoke he seemed to represent the orators of a time long past and in himself to bring back the worthies of a better age, men who possessed the typical Roman *gravitas.* — **prisca . . . lingua** may have reference to quaint or archaic phraseology, but more prob. sug-gests the old-fashioned directness of speech that formed so marked a contrast to the rhetorical and

poetic prose of M.'s time, e.g. of Seneca.

3. heu belongs closely with *quanto*, 'by the mighty, ah me! by the too mighty gift of the Fates'. In his rejoicing M. shudders as he thinks how near Sura came to death; that near approach of death made the *munus Fatorum* need-lessly great.

4. Lethes: the famous river of the under-world; cf. Hor. C. 4. 7. 27-28 *nec Lethaea valet Theseus abrumpere caro vincula Pirithoo.* Had Sura tasted this river, he had forgotten all the affairs of earth, even all his friends; see Verg. A. 6. 713-715. For the form of the gen. cf. *Cybeles,* 1. 70. 10 N.; 5. 13. 7.

5-6. Perdiderant . . . metum: i.e. 'our prayers (vows) had lost the element of fear; we no longer feared that you would die, for to us you seemed already dead'. — **secura . . . Tristitia:** the Romans freely personified mere abstract qualities. M. means that the ex-pected loss was so great that Tris-titia herself shared in the general hopelessness and manifested her feelings not merely in look but by tears. — **secura,** *in calm despair* (Steph.). — **lacrimis . . . eras:**

non tulit invidiam taciti regnator Averni
　et raptas Fatis reddidit ipse colus.
Scis igitur quantas hominum mors falsa querelas
10　　moverit, et frueris posteritate tua.
Vive velut rapto fugitivaque gaudia carpe :
　perdiderit nullum vita reversa diem.

freely, *our tears had already dis-
patched you*; i.e. 'we thought you
dead and lamented accordingly'.
M. may mean that the friends of
Sura were so sure of his death
that the *conclamatio* was actually
uttered. See App.

7. invidiam: cf. 1. 12. 9–10 N.
Even Pluto, pictured ordinarily as
illacrimabilis, dared not risk the
odium that Sura's taking-off would
involve. — **taciti . . . Averni**: near
the Lacus Avernus, which lay just
back of the Lacus Lucrinus, the
poets placed the entrance to the
lower world; hence they used
Avernus in both numbers for the
infernal regions. Cf. Verg. A. 6.
126 *facilis descensus Averno*; Ov.
Am. 3. 9. 27 *hunc quoque summa
dies nigro submersit Averno.* Avernus is *tacitus* because it is ordinarily thought of as the abode of
silent specters, but there is a reference also to the mundane Avernus,
over which, said the poets, e.g.
Verg. A. 6. 237–242, the silence of
death brooded, because of the pestilential exhalations from the lake.

8. Fatis: ancient conceptions
of the Parcae were very indetermi-
nate, and the use of *Fata = Parcae*
became increasingly common from
the Augustan epoch, until the two
terms were practically synonymous.
See Preller-Jordan 2. 193–194;
Roscher Lex. s.v. *Moira.* For the
Parcae as spinners see on 1. 88. 9;
4. 54. 5. — **colūs**: prop. 'distaffs';
here = *fila* or *pensa* (see 4. 54. 9 N.).

9. Scis igitur: '*you* know what
your contemporaries really thought
of you'. — **hominum**: with *querelas.* — **falsa**: i.e. falsely reported.

10. frueris . . . tua: cf. Plin. Ep.
2. 1. 1 (Verginius Rufus) *triginta
annis gloriae suae supervixit; legit
scripta de se carmina, legit historias,
et posteritati suae interfuit.*

11. Vive . . . carpe: i.e. make
the most of this new lease of life.
— **rapto**: here a noun; cf. the idiom
rapto (ex rapto) vivere. This new
span of life is like plunder stolen
from Pluto himself, which Pluto
may at any moment seek to re-
cover; hence one who wishes to
get full use of it must use it at once.
— **fugitiva . . . gaudia**: cf. 1. 15.
8 N. — **carpe**: cf. Hor. C. 1. 11. 8
carpe diem; Ov. A. A. 3. 661 *aliae
tua gaudia carpent.*

12. perdiderit . . . diem: i.e.
a life (= chance to live) that has
been given back, when it seemed
to have gone out forever, cannot
afford to lose a single opportunity
for enjoyment. *Perdiderit* is best
taken as subjv. of command. The
pf. tense in such commands is rare;
by dwelling on the completion of
the act commanded it gives a
tone of urgency. See A. 439, N. 1;
GL. 263, 3 N.; L. 1549.

48. Another peep at a *cena
publica* (cf. 1. 20; 1. 43; etc.). A
fashionable trick is used as a cover
for downright meanness; the food
is passed around to the guests by
slaves, instead of being brought in

48

Cum mensas habeat fere trecentas,
pro mensis habet Annius ministros :
transcurrunt gabatae volantque lances.
Has vobis epulas habete, lauti :
5   nos offendimur ambulante cena.

54

Semper mane mihi de me mera somnia narras,
    quae moveant animum sollicitentque meum ;
iam prior ad faecem, sed et haec vindemia venit,

in a more formal way on the *fercula*, and the process is so hurried that the guests can do little more than taste the viands. See Beck. 3. 368 ff.; Marq. 321 ff. — Meter : § 49.

1. Cum, *although*. — **mensas**, as often = *orbes* (cf. 2. 43. 9 N.; 1. 103. 8 N.). At an earlier period the table was literally removed at the end of each course (*ferculum*); cf. the idioms *mensa prima, mensae secundae, mensas removere*, etc. It would be possible also to say that Annius did not have the dishes placed on the single table that was brought into use, but had them handed round by slaves, because he wished to save his *orbes* ; perhaps, however, he really had none ! — **trecentas** : cf. 1. 43. 1 N.

2. pro, *in place of, in lieu of.*

3. transcurrunt . . . lances : i.e. the dishes seem animated and to be on the run; they fairly fly (as borne by the attendants). — **gabatae** : apparently dishes deeper than the flat *lanx* ; cf. 11. 31. 18–19 *inplet gabatas paropsidesque et leves scutulas cavasque lances.* The etymology of the word is uncertain.

4. vobis . . . habete : cf. 2. 48. 8 *et thermas tibi habe Neronianas,*

and the formula of divorce, *res tuas tibi habeto.* — **lauti** almost = *divites, reges* (see on 2. 18. 5).

54. M. begs Nasidianus to dream no more, or to keep his dreams to himself; otherwise attempts to ward off their evil effects will utterly ruin the poet. — Meter : § 48.

1. Semper . . . narras : i.e. 'you recount to me daily at the *salutatio* nothing but your dreams of me'. In view of the constitutional superstition of the Romans, it was but natural that ominous dreams should disquiet them, and that they should seek to ward off the evils that such visions were supposed to prognosticate. M. may be speaking wholly seriously of himself (cf. then Plin. Ep. 1. 18), or he may be merely laughing at the superstition of others.

2. quae . . . meum : either 'such that they stir', etc., or 'to stir', etc., i.e. the clause may be taken either as consecutive or as final.

3. prior . . . venit : the wine of two seasons has been utterly used up in attempted propitiation. *Prior* in sense = *proximi anni.* — **sed et** see 1. 43. 9 N.

exorat noctes dum mihi saga tuas,
5   consumpsi salsasque molas et turis acervos,
decrevere greges, dum cadit agna frequens,
non porcus, non chortis aves, non ova supersunt.
Aut vigila aut dormi, Nasidiane, tibi.

59

Non cenat sine apro noster, Tite, Caecilianus:
bellum convivam Caecilianus habet.

63

Perpetui nunquam moritura volumina Sili
qui legis et Latia carmina digna toga,

4. exorat: conative present, *has been trying to appease* (exorcise); cf. Ov. Tr. 2. 22 *exorant magnos carmina saepe deos.* — **saga:** cf. 11. 49. 7–8 *amphora nunc petitur nigri cariosa Falerni expiet ut somnos garrula saga tuos.*

5. salsas . . . molas: i.e. the money expended in buying the cakes and incense (Domit.). Spelt, ground and salted, was in sacrifice sprinkled over the victim; cf. Tib. 1. 5. 13–14 *ipse procuravi ne possent saeva nocere somnia ter sancta deveneranda mola.*

6. frequens = *plurima*; see on 1. 70. 6.

7. chortis: cf. 3. 58. 12; 7. 31. 1 *raucae chortis aves et ova matrum.* — **ova:** cf. Ov. A. A. 2. 327–330 *quotiensque libebit, quae referas illi somnia laeta vide; et veniat quae lustret anus lectumque locumque praeferat et tremula sulpur et ova manu.*

8. vigila: i.e. keep awake. — **dormi . . . tibi:** i.e. 'dream about yourself'.

59. Caecilianus is one of the gluttons who prefer to partake of a formal dinner alone. See 1. 20, with notes. — Meter: § 48.

1. apro: see 1. 43. 2 N.; Iuv. 1. 94; 1. 140–141 *quanta est gula quae sibi totos ponit apros, animal propter convivia natum!*

2. bellum convivam: Caecilianus has one guest, a pig! M. insinuates that host and guest are well matched. For *bellus* see on 1. 9.

63. To a reader of Silius Italicus. Cf. 4. 14, with notes. M.'s fulsome praise of Silius in this and other epigrams may not have been wholly disinterested; Silius was rich. Plin. Ep. 3. 7. 5 says: (Silius) *scribebat carmina maiore cura quam ingenio.* — Meter: § 48.

1. Perpetui, *immortal*; cf. 6. 64. 10 (*nugas*) *quas et perpetui dignantur scrinia Sili.* — **volumina:** Silius's Punica.

2. Latia . . . toga: i.e. which may risk comparison with the greatest Latin models. *Toga* here denotes Rome and all that Rome stands for, with a special reference, of course, to matters of poetic genius and style.

Pierios tantum vati placuisse recessus
    credis et Aoniae Bacchica serta comae?
5 Sacra cothurnati non attigit ante Maronis
    implevit magni quam Ciceronis opus:
hunc miratur adhuc centum gravis hasta virorum,
    hunc loquitur grato plurimus ore cliens.
Postquam bis senis ingentem fascibus annum
10   rexerat adserto qui sacer orbe fuit,

3–4. The thought is: 'Do you fancy that he gave heed only to poetry?'— **Pierios ... recessus:** see 1. 76. 3 N.— **vati:** cf. 1. 61. 1 N. — **Aoniae ... comae:** Aonia = Boeotia; hence *deus Aonius* = Bacchus, and the *Aonides* are the Muses (cf. *Aonidum turba = Musae omnes* in 7. 22. 2). Thus *Aoniae ... comae* denotes garlands such as are worn by Bacchus and the Muses (who are often named together).— **Bacchica serta:** cf. 1. 76. 5–7; Ov. Tr. 1. 7. 2 *deme meis hederas, Bacchica serta, comis.*

5–6. Sacra ... opus: i.e. Silius did not begin to imitate Vergil in epic poetry until he had rivaled Cicero in eloquence.— **Sacra** (*carmina*): the poet, as the favorite of Bacchus, Apollo, and the Muses, is *sacer*, a kind of *Musarum sacerdos.* Cf. Hor. C. 3. 1. 1–4; 4. 9. 28 *vate sacro.* — **cothurnati:** here *lofty* (in style), not simply 'tragic'; see 8. 3. 13 N. Cf. 5. 5. 8 *grande cothurnati pone Maronis opus.* — **Maronis ... Ciceronis:** cf. 4. 14. 14; 5. 56. 5; 11. 48.

7. hunc ... virorum: the centumviral court (cf. 1. 76. 12 N.) had to do with civil cases, i.e. with questions of ownership of land, etc. As a symbol of ownership a *hasta* was set up where the centumviri met. Cf. the like use of a spear at auctions, esp. at the sale of booty

in the camp, prob. the original use; see Blackstone 2. 20. This spear came to stand for the court itself; cf. Quint. 5. 2. 1 *partibus centumviralium quae in duas hastas divisae sunt.* The vs. praises Silius for eloquence; cf. Plin. Ep. 9. 23. 1 *frequenter agenti mihi evenit ut centumviri, cum diu se intra iudicum auctoritatem gravitatemque tenuissent, omnes repente quasi victi coactique consurgerent laudarentque.* — **gravis,** *reverend,* is a transferred epithet; it pictures rather the *iudicum gravitas* (cf. Pliny above).

8. hunc ... cliens: his clients thank him from full hearts, because he wins his cases. For the syntax in *hunc loquitur* see on *loquitur,* 1. 61. 8.— **plurimus ... cliens:** see on 1. 70. 6.

9–10. Postquam ... rexerat: i.e. after the year of his consulship, 68, the year of Nero's death.— **bis senis ... fascibus:** twelve lictors with *fasces* preceded the consul in public.— **ingentem** (*annum*): explained by *adserto ... fuit*; the year was preëminently great, because then the world was freed from Nero's tyranny. — **adserto ... orbe:** for *adserere* see notes on 1. 15. 9–10. Cf. Plin. N. H. 20. 160 *Iulium Vindicem, adsertorem illum a Nerone libertatis. Adserto ... orbe* is best taken as an abl. abs., equivalent to a causal clause. Translate,

emeritos Musis et Phoebo tradidit annos
proque suo celebrat nunc Helicona foro.

73

Esquiliis domus est, domus est tibi colle Dianae,
et tua Patricius culmina Vicus habet,
hinc viduae Cybeles, illinc sacraria Vestae,
inde novum, veterem prospicis inde Iovem.

'which was hallowed by the freeing of the world'. — **sacer**: the men of a later day thought of the *annus mirabilis* (cf. 9) with something of the grateful reverence with which men of a far earlier day looked back on the Mons Sacer.

11. emeritos ... annos: freely, 'the years of his retirement'; the figure is derived from the thought of a soldier who has served out his campaigns and has retired from the public service. *Emeritos* is from *emereor*, and = *qui stipendia emeriti erant*. Cf. Ov. M. 15. 226–227 *emeritis medii quoque temporis annis labitur occiduae per iter declive senectae*; Plin. Ep. 3. 7. 6 (of Silius) *novissime ita suadentibus annis ab urbe secessit seque in Campania tenuit*. — **Musis et Phoebo**: see on 1. 70. 15; 1. 76. 5.

12. pro ... suo ... foro: Silius is devoting himself to poetry rather than to the law and public life. — **suo**, *which he had made his own*; there had been no one to dispute his preëminence as a pleader. — **celebrat**, *frequens*. The word suggests intimate and continued association, and so balances *suo*.

73. 'For a *patronus* to live everywhere is almost as bad as it is for him to live nowhere, so far as the appearance of the client at his levee is concerned. Maximus has too many town houses!' On

the numerous villas of the Romans see Fried.SG. 3. 99 ff. — Meter: §48.

1. Esquiliis: see 5. 22. 2 N. — **colle Dianae**: i.e. the Aventine, called Diana's hill because on it was the chief seat of the worship of Diana, a temple said to have been founded by Servius Tullius (Liv. 1. 45). Cf. 12. 18. 3; 6. 64. 13 *Aventinae vicinus Sura Dianae*.

2. Patricius ... Vicus: this street ran from the Subura northeast; see Platner 425.

3–4. The best effect is got by supposing that M. is mentioning four other houses of Maximus; cf. Iuv. 14. 274–275 *tu propter mille talenta et centum villas temerarius*; 1. 94–95 *quis totidem erexit villas ... avus?* Others suppose that M. is giving the outlooks commanded by the three houses of 1–2, but they find great difficulty in adjusting four outlooks to three houses, and in determining to what portions of 1–2 *hinc, illinc, inde* refer. Besides, if M. mentions only three houses in all, *ubique* in 6 is flat because too exaggerated. — **viduae**: because her beloved Attis is dead; cf. Catull. 63. — **Cybeles ... sacraria**: cf. 1. 70. 10 N. — **novum ... Iovem**: the Capitoline temple of Jupiter, rebuilt after the destructive fire of 80; cf. Suet. Dom. 5 *plurima et amplissima opera incendio absumpta restituit, in quis*

5 Dic ubi conveniam, dic qua te parte requiram :
   quisquis ubique habitat, Maxime, nusquam habitat.

79

Potavi modo consulare vinum.
Quaeris quam vetus atque liberale ?
Ipso consule conditum : sed ipse
qui ponebat erat, Severe, consul.

81

"Triginta toto mala sunt epigrammata libro ".

(= *quibus*) *et Capitolium*, *quod rursus arserat.*—**veterem ... Iovem:** the Capitolium Vetus on the Collis Quirinalis; see 5. 22. 4 N.—**prospicis:** cf. 2. 59. 2 *ex me Caesareum prospicis ecce tholum.* On the site of this villa see Hülsen Rh. Mus. 49. 408.

5. qua ... parte: sc. *urbis.*

6. Maxime: the whole epigram has a ring of reality, but the man M. has in mind cannot be identified.—**nusquam habitat:** cf. Sen. Ep. 2. 2 *nusquam est, qui ubique est;* Tert. Praes. Her. 10 *ero itaque nusquam, dum ubique convenior.*

79. M. writes humorously of the wine served at a recent dinner. He calls it *vinum consulare*, as if it were good wine, put up long before (2), but hastens to explain that the consul involved is the consul of the current year. The wine, after all, was but *vinum hornum.* — Meter: § 49.

1. consulare vinum: amphorae, esp. those containing good wines, were often marked with the names of the consuls in whose year the wine was made. Roman hosts prided themselves on having old and good wines; cf. e.g. 3. 62. 2 *sub rege Numa condita vina bibis;* Iuv.

5. 30–31 *ipse capillato diffusum consule potat calcatamque tenet bellis socialibus uvam;* Petr. 34 *allatae sunt amphorae ... quarum in cervicibus pittacia erant affixa cum hoc titulo: Falernum Opimianum annorum centum.* Vinum Opimianum, made in 121 B.C., was especially famous.

2. liberale, *generous,* such as a gentleman should drink. See 4. 64. 27 N.

3. Ipso consule: M. writes as if he were going to add *Opimio* (see on 2) or the name of some other consul whose year was famous for its vintage.—**conditum,** *stored up,* in the amphorae, which were placed in the wine-room (*apotheca*), which was so situated that the smoke from the bath furnace could play round the jars; the smoke was supposed to hasten the mellowing of the wine. See on 12. 82. 11.

4. ponebat: cf. 1. 43. 2 N.—**Severe:** see 6. 8. 6 N.

81. M. intimates, in reply to the criticisms of Lausus, that there is no good wheat without chaff. Cf. 7. 85; 7. 88. — Meter: § 48.

1. Triginta toto: juxtaposition, due surely to M. himself rather than to Lausus, for the words as

Si totidem bona sunt, Lause, bonus liber est.

83

Eutrapelus tonsor dum circuit ora Luperci
expingitque genas, altera barba subit.

85

Quod non insulse scribis tetrasticha quaedam,
disticha quod belle pauca, Sabelle, facis,
laudo, nec admiror.　Facile est epigrammata belle
scribere, sed librum scribere difficile est.

86

Ad natalĭcias dapes vocabar,

they stand would naturally mean,
'In your whole book (but, only)
thirty epigrams are bad'; M. does
not fairly state Lausus's criticism
(which ran, 'There are fully thirty
bad epigrams in your book'; Lausus, we may be sure, did not use
totus at all in his criticism), but
phrases it in such a way as at once
to remove its sting.

2. **bona:** i.e. as measured by the
tests of point, wit, variety, etc. applied to the epigram; cf. 1. 16; 7. 90.

83. On a barber who belied his
name.　Cf. 8. 52. — Meter: § 48.

1. **Eutrapelus** (cf. εὐτράπελος):
prop. 'Nimble', a man who is skillful, who can turn himself to anything; here, however, the name
is "κατ' ἀντίφρασιν fictum" (Van
Stockum 59), i.e. given on the principle of contrasts.

85. M. comments again on the
difficulty of composing an array of
epigrams all on a high level of excellence; see 7. 81, with notes. —
Meter: § 48.

1–2. **insulse:** note the etymology, and cf. 1. 41. 16 N.; 3. 99. 3.

—**tetrasticha ... disticha:**
Greece affected not only the subject-matter and the spirit, but also
the rhetorical terminology of Latin
literature. — **belle:** see on 1. 9;
2. 7.

3. **nec** = *et tamen non.* — **epigrammata:** sc. *pauca*, suggested by
quaedam, 1, *pauca*, 2.

86. M. is resentful because
Sextus omitted him from the list
of guests invited to his birthday
dinner. — Meter: § 49.

1. **natalicias dapes:** the birthday (*natalis dies*), as sacred to the
Genius, was carefully kept (cf. 7. 21,
with notes); frequently there was
a sacrifice to the Genius; cf. Iuv.
11. 83–85. Sometimes the patron
sought on this day to discharge
his social obligations en masse by
giving a *cena publica*; cf. 10. 27. 1–2.
In recognition of the day the guests
were expected to bring presents to
the host. — **dapes:** the occasion
would demand something fine; cf.
3. 45. 3 N. — **vocabar:** note the
tense: 'was invited year after year';
cf. 4.

essem cum tibi, Sexte, non amicus :

quid factum est, rogo, quid repente factum est,

post tot pignora nostra, post tot annos

5   quod sum praeteritus vetus sodalis ?

Sed causam scio : nulla venit a me

Hispani tibi libra pustulati

nec levis toga nec rudes lacernae.

Non est sportula, quae negotiatur ;

10   pascis munera, Sexte, non amicos.

Iam dices mihi "Vapulet vocator".

---

2. non amicus: much less a *sodalis* (5).

4. pignora: sc. *amicitiae.*— **nostra:** freely, *mutual. Post . . . nostra = postquam inter nos tot pignora dedimus.*

5. quod . . . praeteritus: cf. Cic. Phil. 2. 16. 41 *fratris filium praeteriit . . . , te quem numquam viderat aut certe numquam salutaverat fecit heredem.*— **vetus sodalis:** cf. 1. 15. 1 N.; 2. 30. 3.

6. venit a me: i.e. 'on your last birthday, if not on sundry like occasions'.

7. Hispani . . . pustulati: i.e. a piece of silver plate, weighing a pound. Cf. 10. 57. 1.— **pustulati:** prop. 'blistered'. See Forcellini Lex. s.v. *Pustula.* The *pustulae* presumably appeared during the process of refining or as a result of that process; if so, render *pustulati* by 'refined'. For silver as a product of Spain see Plin. N. H. 33. 96. Cf. 8. 50. 6 *niveum felix pustula vincit ebur*; Suet. Ner. 44 (Nero) *exegit ingenti fastidio et acerbitate nummum asperum, argentum pustulatum.* Since, however, *pustulati* ought to refer to the final appearance of the plate when it is sent to Sextus, the word may mean 'blistered' in the sense of *asperi*; the

Romans liked such plate. See on 3. 35. 1.

8. lēvis toga: a smooth toga, made of smooth thin cloth (cf. *toga rasa*, 2. 85. 4) or of cloth with long silky nap (*toga pexa*, 2. 58. 1). *Toga trita* (2. 58. 1), *tritae lacernae* (7. 92. 7), are different.— **rudes:** unused, and so *new.*— **lacernae:** see 2. 29. 3 N.

9. sportula: i.e. 'an actual (genuine) present', 'true entertainment'. See 1. 20. 1; 3. 7.— **quae negotiatur,** *which trades and traffics*; a hospitality bestowed for value received or to gain an expected return is no hospitality at all. Cf. 6. 48; Sen. Ben. 4. 13. 3 *non est beneficium, quod in quaestum mittitur — hoc dabo et hoc recipiam — auctio est.* Note the gender of *quae*; strictly, in such a generalizing formula we should have *quod*; the fem. is due to the attraction of the subject pron. to the gender of the pred. noun (*sportula*), the normal usage.

10. pascis . . . amicos: 'it is for presents, not for friends, that your board is spread' (Steph.). Sextus was of like mercenary mind with Clytus (8. 64), who multiplied birthdays for what was to be got out of them.

11. Iam, *by this time,* 'when I have told you plainly what I think

88

Fertur habere meos, si vera est fama, libellos
　　inter delicias pulchra Vienna suas :
me legit omnis ibi senior iuvenisque puerque
　　et coram tetrico casta puella viro.
5　Hoc ego maluerim quam si mea carmina cantent
　　qui Nilum ex ipso protinus ore bibunt,
quam meus Hispano si me Tagus impleat auro
　　pascat et Hybla meas, pascat Hymettos apes.

of such treatment'. — **dices mihi:** the excuse was probably well-worn and not invented to suit a single case. — **vocator** = *invitator*, the slave who issued the invitations. In this sense the word seems to be as technical as *nomenclator* or *dissignator*. Cf. Plin. N. H. 35. 89 *Apelles invitatus* (by the trick of a court fool) *ad cenam venit indignantique Ptolemaeo et vocatores suos ostendenti, ut diceret a quo eorum invitatus esset, adrepto carbone extincto e foculo imaginem* (of the man who played the trick) *in pariete deliniavit*; Suet. Calig. 39.

88. M. pits the opinion of the literary world about himself against that of Lausus. Cf. 7. 81. For M.'s fame see §§ 39–40. — Meter: § 48.

2. delicias: see 1. 109. 5 N. — **pulchra Vienna:** on the Rhone, in Gallia Narbonensis (modern Vienne). By this time Latin writers were read everywhere throughout the provinces (Beck. 2. 454; Marq. 827–828); cf. 5. 13. 3; 1. 1. 1–2; 10. 104; 8. 3. 4–8.

4. tetrico ... viro: as *vir* here = *maritus*, so *puella* = *uxor*, with the further suggestion that the wife is young. Cf. 10. 35. 1. M. is adroitly insisting that his epigrams are above reproach; though the husband is stern and the wife young and chaste, she openly reads M.'s books. See 1. 4, with notes.

5. Hoc ... maluerim: a compliment to Vienna. That town was a near-by rival of Lugdunum (a literary center: see Iuv. 1. 44; Suet. Calig. 20), and M. may have in mind the whole region in which the two towns lay. — **mea carmina cantent:** cf. 2. 7. 5; 3. 63. 5.

6. qui ... bibunt: the people inhabiting the ill-defined *terra incognita* lying to the south of civilized Africa, to which the name Aethiopia was applied. Cf. Lib. Spect. 3. 5 *qui prima bibit deprensi flumina Nili.*

7. meus ... Tagus: i.e. 'the stream of my native Spain'. The Tagus shared with the Pactolus, the Ganges, etc., the reputation of being gold-bearing; cf. 10. 17. 4; 10. 96. 3; 12. 2. 3; Luc. 7. 755 *quidquid Tagus expulit auri*; Iuv. 3. 55; 14. 298–299; Otto s.v. *Tagus.* — **me ... impleat:** i.e. 'were to enrich me'.

8. Hybla: see 5. 39. 3 N.; cf. Ov. Tr. 5. 6. 38 *florida quam multas Hybla tuetur apes.* — **Hymettos:** see 5. 37. 10 N.; 13. 104 *hoc tibi Thesei populatrix misit Hymetti Pallados a silvis nobile nectar apis.*

Non nihil ergo sumus nec blandae munere linguae
10   decipimur : credam iam, puto, Lause, tibi.

89

I, felix rosa, mollibusque sertis
nostri cinge comas Apollinaris,
quas tu nectere candidas, sed olim —
sic te semper amet Venus — memento.

90

Iactat inaequalem Matho me fecisse libellum :
si verum est, laudat carmina nostra Matho ;
aequales scribit libros Calvinus et Umber :
aequalis liber est, Cretice, qui malus est.

10. credam ... tibi: ironical, and so to be interpreted by contraries; M. really means that now he must believe that there are not thirty bad pieces in his book (7. 81. 1 N.). We may, however, take M. seriously, by giving full heed to the note on *triginta toto*, 7. 81. 1.

89. Domitius Apollinaris (see on 4. 86. 3) seems to have been popular. Plin. Ep. 2. 9, addressing him, says : *diligeris, coleris, frequentaris.* — Meter: § 49.

1-2. I ... -que ... cinge: see 1. 42. 6 N.; here there is, of course, no derisive force. Further, the conjunction is -*que*, not *et.* — **felix**: i.e. in being thus distinguished. — **rosa**: see 5. 37. 9 N.; 5. 64. 4 N.

3. candidas = *cum candidae factae erint.* — **sed olim**: i.e. 'but in future (= distant) days'. The two words contain a prayer that *comae candidae* will be long in coming to Apollinaris. For *olim* said of the future, a rare use, cf. Quint. 10. 1. 104 *vir saeculorum memoria dignus, qui olim nominabitur*; Verg. A. 1. 20, 234.

4. sic, *under those circumstances, in that case, then*, i.e. 'if you fulfill my commands'. With *sic ... Venus* cf. the use, common in the *sermo familiaris*, of *amare* in asseverations, e.g. *sic (ita) me Iuppiter amet (amabit)*. The rose was sacred to Venus; see Preller-Jordan 1. 433.

90. Cf. 7. 81; 7. 85. — Meter: § 48.

1. Iactat, *cries wildly, flings abroad the statement*; for *iacto* of wild utterance cf. e.g. Verg. A. 1. 102 *talia iactanti ... procella velum adversa ferit.* — **Matho**: cf. 4. 79 for possible identification. For final *ŏ* see § 54, c.

3. aequales: i.e. equally dull in all parts; successful only in maintaining a dull level of mediocrity (Saintsbury 1. 261). — **Calvinus**: see App.

92. 'Baccara is always profuse in promising help, but is never able to see when help is needed'. Cf. 2. 43. — Meter: § 48.

92

"Si quid opus fuerit, scis me non esse rogandum"
   uno bis dicis, Baccara, terque die.
Appellat rigida tristis me voce Secundus:
   audis et nescis, Baccara, quid sit opus;
5 pensio te coram petitur clareque palamque:
   audis et nescis, Baccara, quid sit opus;
esse queror gelidasque mihi tritasque lacernas:
   audis et nescis, Baccara, quid sit opus.
Hoc opus est, subito fias ut sidere mutus,
10   dicere ne possis, Baccara, "Si quid opus".

96

Conditus hic ego sum, Bassi dolor, Urbicus infans,

3. Appellat, *duns*; cf. Quint.
5. 13. 12 *heres eras et pauper et
magna pecunia appellabaris a credi-
toribus.* — **rigida tristis**: juxtaposition of cause and effect; for
tristis see on 4. 44. 7. — **Secundus**:
a money-lender; cf. 2. 44. 7 *septem
milia debeo Secundo.*
  4. et = *et tamen.*
  5. pensio: see 3. 38. 6 N. —
coram: with *te*. 'You cannot plead
ignorance, for my landlord duns
me before your very eyes and speaks
in no whisper'.
  6. audis et nescis: the repetition (cf. 8) intensifies the sar-
casm.
  7. tritas: the opposite of *rudes*,
7. 86. 8; see note there.
  9. sidere: instr. abl.; translate 'that you may of a sudden
be rendered dumb by (the influence of) some star'. Cf. 2. 7. 4 N.;
11. 85. 1 *sidere percussa est subito
tibi, Zoile, lingua*; Liv. 8. 9. 12 *ibi
haud secus quam pestifero sidere
icti pavebant.* The evil influence

was called *sideratio*, a term first
used of a blight upon vegetation,
then applied to sudden paralysis;
see Plin. N. H. 17. 222. Belief in
astrology was widespread at Rome.
  10. See App.
  96. A sepulchral epigram (§ 26);
cf. 5. 34; 6. 28; 6. 52. If M. wrote
such epigrams for money (see 5. 34.
Introd.), they may have been actually cut upon the tombs themselves.
— Meter: § 48.
  1. Conditus = *sepultus.* Cf.
an epitaph on Vergil by Palladius
(Bähr. P. L. M. 4. 133, p. 122) *conditus hic ego sum, cuius modo rustica musa per silvas, per rus venit
ad arma virum*; Verg. A. 3. 67–68.
— **Bassi**: perhaps Saleius Bassus,
the poet, of whom Quint. 10. 1. 90
says: *vehemens et poeticum ingenium Saleii Bassi fuit nec ipsum
senectute maturuit.* Tac. D. 5 calls
him *absolutissimus poeta.* — **dolor**:
see 6. 52. 2 N. — **Urbicus**: the
name indicates that the babe was
probably a *verna* or freed-child.

cui genus et nomen maxima Roma dedit.

Sex mihi de prima deerant trieteride menses,

    ruperunt tetricae cum male pensa deae.

5 Quid species, quid lingua mihi, quid profuit aetas ?

Da lacrimas tumulo, qui legis ista, meo :

sic ad Lethaeas, nisi Nestore serior, undas

    non eat, optabis quem superesse tibi.

98

Omnia, Castor, emis : sic fiet, ut omnia vendas.

2. genus . . . dedit seems to mean that the child was born in Rome. — **nomen:** Urbicus. Rome is often called simply *urbs* (*Urbs*), 'the City'. — **maxima Roma:** cf. 10. 58. 6; *dominae . . . Romae,* 1. 3. 3 N.; Prop. 4. 1. 1 *maxima Roma.*

3. trieteride (cf. τριετηρίς): the child was thirty months old. Cf. 10. 53. 3.

4. ruperunt . . . deae: the goddesses are the Parcae; see on 4. 54. 5; 7. 47. 8. — **tetricae:** cf. 4. 73. 6 *moverunt tetricas tam pia vota deas*; 7. 88. 4. — **male** = *maligne.* See App. — **pensa:** cf. 4. 54. 9 N. Verses 3–4 give a good example of *cum inversum*; see A. 546, a; GL. 581; L. 1869. Cf. 8. 3. 9.

5. species, *beauty*; cf. Curt. 7. 9. 19 *cum specie corporis aequaret Hephaestionem.* — **lingua,** *my baby voice.* — **aetas,** *my tender years.*

6. Da . . . meo: cf. 6. 28. 10 N. — **tumulo:** cf. 4. 59. 6; 6. 52. 1.

7. sic: cf. 7. 89. 4 N.—**Lethaeas . . . undas:** see 7. 47. 4 N.; Verg. (?) Cul. 214–215 *at mea manes viscera Lethaeas cogunt transnare per undas.* — **nisi . . . serior:** i.e. until he has surpassed Nestor's proverbial age. Cf. 5. 58. 5 N.; 6. 70. 12 N.; Sen. Apocol. 4 *vincunt Tithoni,*

vincunt et Nestoris annos. — **serior:** see App.

8. non eat: for *non* in wishes or commands see on 2. 18. 8. — **quem:** verses 1–6 suggest *filius* (*tuus*) as antec. to *quem*, but M. has purposely made his language vague, to give it wider scope. To the Romans there was something peculiarly sad in the death of children (even adult children) before the death of the parents. With 7–8, then, cf. e.g. Plaut. Asin. 16–19; Ter. Heau. 1030 ff.; Plin. Ep. 1. 12. 11 *decessit superstitibus suis*; 3. 7. 2; Iuv. 10. 241; Tac. Agr. 44; Cic. Cato M. 23. 84; and many passages in the inscriptions.

98. "If for mere wantonness you buy so fast, For very want you must sell all at last" (Bouquet). — Meter: § 47.

99. M. begs Crispinus to say to Domitian a good word for his book. Crispinus is the low-born Egyptian whom Juvenal so unmercifully castigates (1. 26–29) and who as a freedman at Rome played his infamous part so well. He was at first a fish-peddler, but became *princeps equitum,* and apparently for a time *praefectus praetorio,* under Domitian. See Mayor's notes on Iuv. 1. 26–29. — Meter: § 48.

99

Sic placidum videas semper, Crispine, Tonantem
　　nec te Roma minus quam tua Memphis amet :
carmina Parrhasia si nostra legentur in aula
　　— namque solent sacra Caesaris aure frui —,
5　dicere de nobis, ut lector candidus, aude :
　"Temporibus praestat non nihil iste tuis,
nec Marso nimium minor est doctoque Catullo ".
Hoc satis est : ipsi cetera mando deo.

1. Sic is explained in full by the *si*-sentence in 3–7. — **placidum:** sc. *tibi*. — **semper:** i.e. always, as at present; a timely wish at a period when men rose to favor or lost all at a tyrant's whim. — **Tonantem:** i.e. Domitian, identified with Iuppiter Tonans; cf. *sacra aure*, 4; *ipsi deo*, 8; 4. 8. 9 N.; 5. 8. 1 N.; 9. 86. 7 *aspice Tarpeium Palatinumque Tonantem*; 12. 15. 6 *haec sunt pocula quae decent Tonantem*.

2. Memphis = *Aegyptus*; see 6. 80. 3 N. Cf. *verna Canopi*, Iuv. 1. 26, said of Crispinus.

3. Parrhasia . . . aula: Domitian's palace on the Palatine. The name Parrhasia was applied to a part of Arcadia; hence — because, said tradition, the Arcadian Evander settled on the Palatine — *Parrhasius* = *Palatinus*, 'imperial'. Cf. 7. 56. 2 *Parrhasiam mira qui struis arte domum*; 12. 15. 1 *quid Parrhasia nitebat aula*; Verg. A. 11. 31 *Parrhasio Euandro*. — **aula** = *regia, palatio*; Prop. 4. 11. 5 *te licet orantem fuscae deus audiat aulae*.

4. solent: sc. *carmina nostra*. — **sacra . . . aure:** cf. 4. 30. 3 N.

5. dicere . . . aude: cf. 4. 8. 7–12, with notes. — **ut . . . candidus:** i.e. as an impartial critic. Cf. 2. 71. 1 N.

6–7. non nihil = *aliquid* = *aliquid magnum*. — **iste:** 'the man whose poems you are reading'; see on 1. 70. 18; 4. 49. 10. — **Marso:** see 2. 71. 3 N.; 2. 77. 5 N. — **nimium** = *multo*; a colloquialism. — **docto . . . Catullo:** see on 1. 61. 1; 1. 109. 1; 2. 71. 3; 4. 14. 13. For *docto* see 1. 25. 2 N.

8. cetera: i.e. 'the proper monetary or other recognition of my genius'. — **deo:** Domitian; see on *Tonantem*, 1.

LIBER VIII

3

"Quinque satis fuerant, nam sex septemve libelli
    est nimium : quid adhuc ludere, Musa, iuvat ?
sit pudor et finis : iam plus nihil addere nobis
    Fama potest : teritur noster ubique liber,
5   et cum rupta situ Messalae'saxa iacebunt
    altaque cum Licini marmora pulvis erunt,

3. M. adroitly excuses himself for writing more epigrams and for not undertaking the more serious and ambitious forms of poetry. In 1–8 he seems to reply to the Muse, who has urged him to resume his writing; in 11–22 we have her convincing rejoinder. — Meter: § 48.

2. adhuc = *etiam nunc, still, yet.* — **ludere:** see I. 41. *19*; I. 113. *1*; Sen. Epigr. 39. 2–3 (in Bähr. P. L. M. 4. p. 72) *ludere, Musa, iuvat: Musa severa, vale.* Supply *te* as subject; M. throws all responsibility on the Muse. — **Musa:** see on 9.

4. teritur . . . liber: see on I. 1. 1–2; 5. 13. 3; 7. 88. 2. *Teritur = is thumbed, is read;* cf. 11. 3. 3–4 N.; Hor. Ep. 2. 1. 91–92 *aut quid haberet quod legeret tereretque viritim publicus usus?*

5–6. 'My literary fame will outlast the splendid Mausolea of the rich!' — **rupta situ . . . iacebunt,** *shall be corroded and shall lie in ruins.* Here and in 10. 2. 9–12 (see notes) M. has his eye on Hor. C. 3. 30. 1–2 *exegi monumentum aere perennius regalique situ pyramidum altius,* but in Horace *situ* prob. means 'site'; he is thinking of

'pyramids built by the hand of kings'. — **situ:** prop. 'position' (cf. *sino, pono,* which contains *sino*), then the mold that gathers on things that lie long in one position, then *decay, corrosion,* as here. — **Messalae saxa:** the cognomen Messala (Messalla) belonged to the most distinguished family of the Gens Valeria; of that family the most celebrated member was M. Valerius Messala Corvinus, orator, poet, historian, grammarian, patron of letters, intimate friend of Tibullus (cf. Tib. 4. 1; passim), much esteemed by Horace. At Philippi he fought with the Republicans, but later sided with the Triumvirs and at Actium commanded a part of Octavianus's fleet; he was consul in 31, but soon afterward retired to private life. — **Licini:** Licinus was one of the richest of the freedmen (see 2. 29. Introd.). Julius Caesar brought him from Gaul as a slave, and made him his *dispensator.* He was emancipated probably by Caesar's will, for he is spoken of as a freedman of Augustus. Sent by Augustus in 15 B.C. to govern his

184

me tamen ora legent et secum plurimus hospes
　　ad patrias sedes carmina nostra feret ".
Finieram, cum sic respondit nona sororum,
10　　cui coma et unguento sordida vestis erat :
" Tune potes dulcis, ingrate, relinquere nugas ?
　　Dic mihi, quid melius desidiosus ages ?
an iuvat ad tragicos soccum transferre cothurnos,
　　aspera vel paribus bella tonare modis,

native Gaul, he amassed enormous wealth by plundering it; cf. Sen. Ep. 120. 19 *modo Licinum divitiis, Apicium cenis, Maecenatem deliciis provocant*; Iuv. 1. 109. His monument on the Via Salaria near the second milestone was a show-piece.

7. ora legent: cf. Ov. M. 15. 877–878 *quaque patet domitis Romana potentia terris ore legar populi*. On literature in the provinces see on 7. 88. 1.— **plurimus hospes:** see on 1. 70. 6.

8. feret: i.e. from Rome.

9. Finieram cum: an example of *cum inversum*; see on 7. 96. 3–4. — **nona sororum** merely = *one of the Muses nine*, not the ninth (last) Muse. The reference is to Thalia, the patroness of comedy and lighter poetry in general; cf. 1. 70. 15; 2. 22. 1–2 *quid mihi vobiscum est, o Phoebe novemque sorores? ecce nocet vati Musa iocosa suo*; 12. 94. 3; 4. 8. 12 N.

10. cui . . . erat: cf. Ov. Am. 3. 1. 5–7 *hic ego dum spatior tectus nemoralibus umbris, quod mea quaerebam Musa moveret opus; venit odoratos Elegeia nexa capillos.*— **sordida**, *streaming, drenched*. Thalia, as the Muse of Comedy, is appropriately described in terms often used of those who are on pleasure bent; cf. e.g. the mention of perfumes in Horace in connection with feasts.

11. Tune . . . nugas: ironical and indignant.— **dulcis:** i.e. 'which Rome loves to read and talk about'. Note the juxtaposition *dulcis ingrate*. M. fails after all to appreciate what he owes to the world for its favor (3 ff.); if he did not, he could not talk as in 1–3.

12. desidiosus: cf. 1. 107. 2 N. The vs. = *cum desidiosus sis, nil melius ages*. For the parataxis in this vs. see on *numquid . . . fecit*, 6. 8. 6.

13. an: frequently used after such a question as that in 12, to set forth an alternative which to the writer is really unthinkable. Cf. e.g. Hor. S. 1. 10. 74–75 *an tua demens vilibus in ludis dictari carmina malis?*— **soccum . . . cothurnos:** as the low-soled *soccus* worn by comic actors came to denote *comoedia* or light poetry in general (e.g. epigrams), so the high buskin (*cothurnus*) worn by tragic actors (at least in later times; see K. K. Smith in Harv. Stud. 16) came to stand for *tragoedia*. Cf. e.g. 7. 63. 5–6 N.; 12. 94. 3; Ov. Rem. Am. 375–376 *grande sonant tragici: tragicos decet ira cothurnos; usibus e mediis soccus habendus erit*; Pont. 4. 16. 29–30 *Musaque Turrani tragicis innixa cothurnis et tua cum socco Musa, Melisse, levi.*

14. aspera . . . modis: i.e. to write epic poetry in hexameter

15   praelegat ut tumidus rauca te voce magister
          oderit et grandis virgo bonusque puer ?
     Scribant ista graves nimium nimiumque severi,
          quos media miseros nocte lucerna videt.
     At tu Romano lepidos sale tinge libellos :
20   adgnoscat mores vita legatque suos.

verse. — **paribus ... modis**: hexameters, which, as contrasted with
the lines of the elegiac couplet, are
approximately equal in length. Cf.
Hor. A. P. 73–75 *res gestae regumque ducumque et tristia bella quo
scribi possent numero monstravit
Homerus: versibus impariter iunctis querimonia primum, post etiam
inclusa est voti sententia compos*;
Ov. Tr. 2. 220 *imparibus ... carmina facta modis*. — **tonare**, *to
thunder forth*. The verb is appropriately used of the epic style, but
it carries also, probably, a side
thrust at the prevailing fashion of
reading such poems at the recitations; cf. 7. 23. 1–2 *cum bella
tonanti ipse dares Latiae plectra
secunda lyrae*; Iuv. 1. 12–13 *Fron-
tonis platani convulsaque marmora
clamant semper et adsiduo ruptae
lectore columnae* (Juvenal was writing especially of tragedy and epos).
M. may be thinking of Statius: see
4. 49. 3 N.; 11. 3. 8.

15. praelegat ... magister:
'that the pompous *grammaticus*
may dictate your works till he is
hoarse'. That *magister = grammaticus* (see on 2. 7. 4) seems clear
from 16. Oral teaching, dictation,
and memory work played a greater
part in ancient teaching than in
our times. M. seems to have his
eye on Hor. S. 1. 10. 74–75, cited
on 13. On the use of the poets
in Roman schools see Fried. SG.
3. 378 ff.; Beck. 2. 101 ff.; Marq.
105 ff. — **tumidus ... magister**:

cf. 10. 104. 16, though there *magister*
has a different sense; Ov. M. 8. 396
*talia magniloquo tumidus memora-
verat ore*. — **rauca ... voce**, *till
his voice is hoarse*, is proleptic, as in
4. 8. 2; it gives the result of *praelegat*. Cf. note on *bella tonare*, 14.
Raucus seems frequently to be
contemptuous; cf. 4. 8. 2; 1. 41. 9;
7. 31. 1 *raucae chortis aves*.

16. grandis virgo: cf. 3. 58. 40.
— **bonus**: an important adj. here;
even a well-behaved boy will loathe
tragedy and epos.

18. 'Writers of such long-drawn-
out epics have to burn the midnight
oil'. M. implies that time and toil
enter more largely into such poetry
than do genius and poetic art. Cf.
Ov. Am. 3. 9. 29–30 *durat opus vatum: Troiani fama laboris tardaque
nocturno tela retexta dolo*; Iuv. 7. 99
perit hic (in the labor of historians)
plus temporis atque olei plus. —
miseros: because of tedious and
toilsome labors. — **lucerna**: prop.
'lamp', then *nocturnal labor*; cf.
Iuv. 1. 51 *haec ego non credam Ve-
nusina digna lucerna?*

19. Romano lepidos: see App.
— **lepidos sale**: the former word
may refer to the verse itself, the
latter to the spice put into it. Cf.
11. 20. 9–10 *absolvis lepidos nimirum, Auguste, libellos, qui scis Romana simplicitate loqui*. — **sale**:
see 1. 41. 16 N.

20. 'Continue to hold a mirror
up to nature and let society see
itself'. Cf. 10. 4. 7–10 *quid te vana*

Angusta cantare licet videaris avena,
　　dum tua multorum vincat avena tubas ".

5

Dum donas, Macer, anulos puellis,
desisti, Macer, anulos habere.

6

Archetypis vetuli nihil est odiosius Aucti
　— ficta Saguntino cymbia malo luto —,

*iuvant miserae ludibria chartae?
Hoc lege quod possit dicere vita
"Meum est". Non hic Centauros,
non Gorgonas Harpyiasque inve-
nies: hominem pagina nostra sapit.*
For M.'s realism see §§ 30–31.

21. Angusta . . . avena: the
shepherd's reed-pipe, an insignificant, weak instrument, compared
with the big, loud *tuba*; cf. e.g. Ov.
Tr. 5. 10. 25 *pastor iunctis pice
cantat avenis*; Verg. E. 1. 2 *silve-
strem tenui Musam meditaris
avena. Avena* here symbolizes the
simple, lowly themes of common
life, *tubas* (22) the 'lofty' subject-
matter of heroic epos and tragedy.
— **videaris:** i.e. to the uncritical
and the thoughtless. The vs. =
'let men think of you as playing
on', etc.

22. dum, *provided that.* M. has
in fact eclipsed Silius, Statius, Lucan, and Valerius Flaccus.—**tubas:**
the tuba was the trumpet used by
infantry, and so well symbolizes
heroic (epic) poetry.

5. The equites had the right to
wear the *angustus clavus* on the tunic, and the *ius anuli aurei*. Macer, however, has squandered so
much money in rings given to girls
of the demi-monde that he has
lost the equestrian census, i.e. he

has not enough left to entitle him to
wear the gold ring. — Meter: § 49.

1. puellis: cf. *amicas*, 4. 24. 1.

2. desisti . . . habere: cf. Iuv.
11. 42–43 *talibus a dominis post
cuncta novissimus exit anulus et
digito mendicat Pollio nudo.*

6. M.'s complaint is twofold:
Auctus shows bad taste in dilating
on his rare plate and in serving
poor wine. The poet insinuates
also that Auctus lies about his
plate. Cf. 3. 35. 1 N.; 4. 39, with
notes; 7. 19 (on a pretended fragment of the ship Argo); 14. 93;
Hor. S. 2. 3. 20–21 *olim nam quaerere amabam quo vafer ille pedes
lavisset Sisyphus aere*; Petr. 52. —
Meter: § 48.

1. Archetypis, *originals, antiques,* or what passed for such
(see on 4. 39. 2–5). — **vetuli,** *oldish*;
the dim. is contemptuous. Auctus
seems as old as his plate! — **odiosius,** *more of a bore.* — **Aucti:** see
App.

2. ficta . . . luto: honest earthenware is preferable to fictitious plate.
For *ficta* see on 1. 53. 6. — **Saguntino . . . luto:** Saguntine earthenware was good; cf. 14. 108. 2 *sume
Saguntino pocula facta luto*; Iuv.
5. 29, cited on 7. — **cymbia** (cf.
κυμβίον): bowls without handles,

argenti fumosa sui cum stemmata narrat
garrulus et verbis mucida vina facit :
5   " Laomedonteae fuerant haec pocula mensae :
ferret ut haec muros struxit Apollo lyra ;
hoc cratere ferox commisit proelia Rhoetus
cum Lapithis : pugna debile cernis opus ;

deep but long, bearing more or less
resemblance to a skiff.

3-4. fumosa, *smoke-begrimed*,
i.e. 'time-honored', 'genuine'. Cf.
2. 90. 7 N.; Sen. Ep. 44. 5 *non facit
nobilem atrium plenum fumosis
imaginibus*; Iuv.8.7–9 (*quis fructus*)
*posthac multa contingere virga fu-
mosos equitum cum dictatore magi-
stros, si coram Lepidis male vivitur.*
See App. — **stemmata** (cf. στέμμα),
family trees. The word prop. =
'chaplets', 'wreaths'. Here, however, it is used of pedigrees, genea-
logical charts painted on the
walls of the atria of distinguished
families; the names in these charts
were surrounded by painted garlands and were joined together in
such a way as to make clear the
interrelations of the members of
the family. The *stemmata* were
distinct from the *imagines* (2. 90.
6 N.); see Duff on Iuv. 8. 1; Len-
drum in Hermathena 6. 360. Hence
stemmata frequently = *nobility*,
high birth, as here; cf. 4. 40. 1 *atria
Pisonum stabant cum stemmate
toto*; Iuv.8. 1 *stemmata quid faciunt,
quid prodest, Pontice, longo sanguine
censeri.*—**narrat garrulus:** Auctus
talks much because after all his
plate is not genuine; he tries by a
wealth of details to carry convic-
tion. Besides, his garrulity is a
natural failing of the *vetulus* (1).
—**verbis . . . facit:** for politeness'
sake the guests must listen and
praise, without drinking (15–16).
Meanwhile the wine becomes vapid.

**5. Laomedonteae . . . men-
sae:** the cups were part of the
table service of Laomedon, father
of Priam! Elsewhere also a form
of *Laomedonteus* begins the verse
and the noun ends it; cf. Verg. G.
1. 502 *Laomedonteae . . . Troiae*;
Ov. M. 11. 196 *Laomedonteis . . .
arvis.* See Wagner 10, and note
on 1. 1. 3.—**haec:** Auctus points
to each object as he speaks; cf.
hoc, 7, *hi*, 9, *hic*, 11, *hac*, 13. Who
can doubt when the owner is so
explicit?

6. haec: identical with *haec*, 5.
According to one account Neptune
and Apollo had to build the walls
of Troy as a punishment for having
conspired with Juno against Jupiter.
—**struxit . . . lyra:** cf. Ov. Her.
16. 179–180 *Ilion adspicies firma-
taque turribus altis moenia, Phoe-
beae structa canore lyrae.*

7–8. At the wedding feast of
Pirithous, king of the Lapithae,
and Hippodamia, the chief Centaurs were guests. An attempt by
one of the Centaurs to steal the
bride led to a fierce conflict. —
hoc cratere: such a mixer would
serve a Centaur well as an extemporized weapon. Cf. Iuv. 5. 26–29
*iurgia proludunt, sed mox et pocula
torques saucius et rubra deterges
vulnera mappa, inter vos quotiens
libertorumque cohortem pugna Sa-
guntina fervet commissa lagona*;
Petr. 74 *Trimalchio contra offensus
convicio calicem in faciem Fortu-
natae immisit*; Verg. G. 2. 455–457

hi duo longaevo censentur Nestore fundi :
10   pollice de Pylio trita columba nitet ;
hic scyphus est, in quo misceri iussit amicis
largius Aeacides vividiusque merum ;
hac propinavit Bitiae pulcherrima Dido
in patera, Phrygio cum data cena viro est ".
15 Miratus fueris cum prisca toreumata multum,
in Priami calathis Astyanacta bibes.

*ille furentes Centauros leto domuit,
Rhoetumque Pholumque et magno
Hylaeum Lapithis cratere minan-
tem.* — **ferox:** cf. Luc. 6. 390 *Rhoete
ferox*; Ov.M.12.235–244. — **debile,
weakened,** i.e. dented, mutilated
(because of misuse); cf. 7. 20. 12
debilis boletus, said of a mushroom
that has been bitten. — **cernis
opus:** can any man refuse to believe what he sees? — **opus:** the
crater; cf. 3. 35. 1 N.

9. longaevo . . . Nestore: i.e.
because Nestor once owned them.
See 5. 58. 5; 6. 70. 12. — **censentur:**
see 1. 61. 3 N.; Iuv. 8. 1, cited on 3.
— **fundi,** *cups. Fundus* prop. =
'the bottom' of anything; here,
however, the part seems put for the
whole (synecdoche), the depth of the
vessel being emphasized. Auctus
professes to have the famous
drinking-cup of Nestor, which,
according to Hom. Il. 2. 622 ff.,
had two *fundi* (πυθμένες) and four
handles (οὔατα).

10. pollice . . . nitet: the same
visible proof as in 8. The thumb of
the user would rub on the *columba*
which ornamented the handle.

11. scyphus (cf. σκύφος): a big
deep tankard; no ordinary *poculum*
would serve such a hero. Cf. Sen.
Ep. 83. 23 *intemperantia bibendi et
ille Herculaneus ac fatalis scyphus
condidit* (*Alexandrum*); Hor. Epod.

9. 33 *capaciores adfer huc, puer,
scyphos.*

12. largius . . . vividius: M.
has in mind Hom. Il. 9. 201 ff. The
scyphus is a *crater* in Homer; we
seem here to have a slip on the part
of Auctus. "Perhaps M. means
a sneer at the ignorance of his
host" (Steph.). — **Aeacides:** here
Achilles.

13–14. propinavit: cf. 2. 15. 1–2
*quod nulli calicem tuum propinas,
humane facis, Horme, non superbe.*
— **Bitiae . . . patera:** cf. Verg. A.
1. 723–740 for the banquet given by
Dido to Aeneas at Carthage. Verses
737–738 explain *propinavit*; in
Greece and Rome one who would
drink another's health drank lightly
first himself and then passed the
cup to the one whom he would
honor. The other must drain the
cup. — **pulcherrima Dido:** cf.
Verg. A. 1. 496 *forma pulcherrima
Dido*; 4. 60. — **patera:** a round
saucer-like vessel (the φιάλη). —
Phrygio . . . viro: Aeneas; in
Verg. A. 4. 103 Aeneas is *Phrygio
marito.*

15. Miratus fueris: i.e. 'shall
have expressed your wonder in
words of praise'; *mirari* here =
admirari. — **prisca toreumata:**
cf. 3. 35. 1 N.

16. Priami calathis: i.e. old
enough to have been owned by

9

Solvere dodrantem nuper tibi, Quinte, volebat
lippus Hylas, luscus vult dare dimidium.
Accipe quam primum ; brevis est occasio lucri :
si fuerit caecus, nil tibi solvet Hylas.

10

Emit lacernas milibus decem Bassus
Tyrias coloris optimi : lucri fecit.
"Adeo bene emit ? " inquis.   Immo : non solvet.

Priam.— **calathis** (cf. κάλαθος): prop. vase-shaped baskets for fruit, wool, etc. But the word was used for drinking-cups of similar shape; cf. 9. 59. 15; 14. 107. 1–2 *nos* (= *calathos*) *Satyri, nos Bacchus amat, nos ebria tigris, perfusos domini lambere docta pedes*. — **Astyanacta bibes:** i.e. new (and here inferior) wine, wine as young as Astyanax, son of Hector, grandson of Priam. Such wealth and such plate demand wine of corresponding value and excellence. Cf. 10. 49. 3–5 *propinas modo conditum Sabinum et dicis mihi, Cotta, "Vis in auro?" Quisquam plumbea vina volt in auro?*

9. A fling at Hylas, who will not pay his debts. — Meter: § 48.

1. Solvere dodrantem: i.e. to pay three fourths of a sum due. *Solvere* is often used of paying debts.

2. lippus, *blear-eyed,* i.e. when he was but half blind (in one eye: see next note). The Romans often used *lippus* in derision because they thought that *lippitudo* was due to irregular living; see Kiessling on Hor. S. 1. 1. 120. — **luscus,** *one-eyed,* i.e. when he had entirely lost the sight of the eye affected.

3. brevis . . . lucri: aphoristic in ring; cf. Pub. Syr. 449 *occasio aegre offertur, facile amittitur;*

Cato Dist. 2. 26 *fronte capillata, post est occasio calva* (cf. Eng. 'take time by the forelock').

10. On Bassus's easy way of providing himself with fine clothes. — Meter: § 52.

1. lacernas: if we take the pl. literally, we shall regard Bassus as a dandy who must have a large supply of clothes with a proper range of color; see on 2. 29. 3; 2. 43. 7. The pl. may, however, be *pluralis maiestatis* (see on 1. 70. 5); in that case Bassus bought but one *lacerna.* — **milibus decem:** i.e. at 10,000 *sestertii* apiece (if the first view suggested on *lacernas* above is correct). Cf. 4. 61. 4–5 *dum fabulamur, milibus decem dixti emptas lacernas munus esse Pompullae;* Fried. SG. 3. 72 ff.; Marq. 509 ff.

2. coloris optimi: cf. 2. 29. 3 N.

— **lucri fecit:** despite the price he has made money. *Lucri* is pred. gen. of possession, 'made . . . gain's'; cf. *compendi facere,* 'shorten.'

3. Adeo bene: i.e. so shrewdly, at such a good bargain; cf. Sen. Ben. 6. 15. 4 *praeterea nihil venditori debet qui bene emit.* Contrast *male emere.*—**Immo:** see 1. 10. 3 N. — **non solvet:** his shrewdness consists not in buying well but in avoiding payment. See on 8. 9. 1.

12

Uxorem quare locupletem ducere nolim
quaeritis ? uxori nubere nolo meae.
Inferior matrona suo sit, Prisce, marito :
non aliter fiunt femina virque pares.

13

Morio dictus erat : viginti milibus emi.
Redde mihi nummos, Gargiliane : sapit.

12. M. tells his friend Terentius Priscus (see 12. 3) why he does
not marry a Roman fortune. —
Meter: § 48.

2. uxori . . . meae involves
a very fine play on *viro nubere*, the
phrase ordinarily used of a woman's
marriage; contrast *in matrimonium
ducere, uxorem ducere*, said of the
man. 'When I marry', says M., 'I
don't propose to play the woman's
part'. Cf. 10. 69. 1–2 *custodes das,
Polla, viro, non accipis ipsa: hoc
est uxorem ducere, Polla, virum*
(*uxorem* is subject). Roman comedy shows many examples of hus-
bands in subjection to richly
dowered wives; cf. e. g. Plaut. Men.
766–767; Asin., passim.

3. Inferior . . . marito: i.e.
ready to do his will, as the rich
wife of a poor man, who feels her
financial independence, is not apt
to do; cf. Ov. Her. 9. 32 *si qua
voles apte nubere, nube pari*; Iuv.
6. 460, 136–141; Hor. C. 3. 24. 19–20
nec (among the tribes of the North)
*dotata regit virum coniunx nec
nitido fidit adultero.* Several hundred years before M.'s time Anax-
andrides had written : πένης . . . τὴν
γυναῖκα πλουσίαν λαβὼν ἔχει δέ-
σποιναν, οὐ γυναῖκ' ἔτι. See Fried.
SG. 1. 468 ff.

13. Even cultured Romans had
a strange liking for fools, dwarfs,

idiots, jesters, especially if some
physical deformity was added to a
mental defect or peculiarity (cre-
tins); Suetonius takes pains to note
(Aug. 93) that Augustus did not
share this liking. They were much
in evidence at meal-times, when
they were subjected to all sorts of
insult and abuse. Cf. such words
as *scurra, nanus, fatuus, morio,* and
see Beck. 2. 148 ff. Cf. also the
court fools of mediæval times. M.
feels that he was cheated by Gar-
gilianus (a *praeco* or *mango*), because the 'fool' for whom he had
paid a large price turned out to
have good sense and was therefore
worth no more than an average
slave. M. can hardly be writing of
himself; the keeping of such fools
was a luxury, and the price named
in 1 was high. — Meter: § 48.

1. Morio (cf. μωρός), *an arrant
fool, a real idiot*; cf. Aug. Ep. 26
*quidam tantae sunt fatuitatis, ut non
multum a pecoribus differant, quos
moriones vulgo vocant.* — **viginti
milibus:** 20,000 *sestertii.* See
Marq. 173 ff.; Beck. 2. 148 ff.

2. nummos: see 1. 66. 4 N.

14. To an unnamed patron,
who took better care of his plants
and fruit-trees than of his clients.
On the *horti* of the rich see 6. 80.
3 N.; Mayor's exhaustive note on
Iuv. 1. 75. — Meter: § 48.

14

Pallida ne Cilicum timeant pomaria brumam
    mordeat et tenerum fortior aura nemus,
hibernis obiecta Notis specularia puros
    admittunt soles et sine faece diem,
5   at mihi cella datur non tota clusa fenestra,

1. **Pallida**: not inaptly used of the greenish-yellow color of growing things; cf. χλωρός and the note on 1.41.4.—**pomaria**: prop. 'fruit-gardens', 'orchards'. If the word bears this sense here, the identity of the trees in these *Cilicum . . . pomaria* is unknown. The Romans understood the use of hot-houses to which the sun was admitted through glass or mica; cf. 6. 80, with notes; 8. 68; Plin. N. H. 19. 64. Some, however, have held that the *pomaria* did not contain fruit-trees, but oriental saffron plants (*crocus*: see Hehn 255 ff.), the *Crocus sativus*, popular among the Romans because of its odor and its yellow hue, seen in the stigmas; among Orientals it vied with purple as a dye. The best came from Cilicia; cf. 3. 65. 2 *quod de Corycio* ('Cilician') *quae venit aura croco*. But *nemus*, 2, and *arboris*, 8, point rather to trees than to plants; besides, the *Crocus* is (at least to-day) very hardy. If, then, M. had the *Crocus* in mind, he was using *pomaria* loosely, and exaggerating in *nemus* and *arboris*, and was using *tenerum*, 2, ironically, representing his patron as taking particular care of a plant hardy enough to look after itself. — **brumam**: see 3. 58. 8 N.

2. **mordeat**, *nip with frost*; cf. Hor. S. 2. 6. 45 *matutina parum cautos iam frigora mordent*; Shakespeare, Hamlet 1. 4. 1, "The air bites shrewdly; it is very cold".— **tenerum**: i.e. not indigenous to Italy,

flourishing only in an Oriental clime.

3–4. **hibernis . . . Notis**: a southern exposure enabled the hot-house to profit to the fullest extent by the winter sun.—**specularia**: window-panes made of talc or mica ('isinglass', *lapis specularis*; the best came from Spain and Cappadocia) or glass (*vitrum*). They were in common use. Cf. Plin. Ep. 2. 17. 4 *egregium hae* (*porticus*) *adversus tempestates receptaculum, nam specularibus ac multo magis imminentibus tectis muniuntur*; Beck. 2. 315; Marq. 757–758. — **puros . . . soles**: cf. 4. 64. 9 N. — **sine faece**: the prep. phrase here = an adj., a usage not uncommon in Silver Latin, esp. in phrases with *sine*. — **diem** = *lucem*.

5. **cella**, *den, garret, cabinet*, a marked contrast to a house big enough for a *nemus* (2). *Cella* is always used of a small apartment, frequently of the abode of a poor man, or slave, or prostitute; cf. Eng. 'cell'; 3. 30. 3 *fuscae pensio cellae*; Iuv. 7. 28 *qui facis in parva sublimia carmina cella*. — **non . . . fenestra**: i.e. 'not only are my quarters contracted, but they are not tight at that: the one window admits cold wind'. — **non totā**, *incomplete, ill-fitted*. For the phrase *non totus* cf. 9. 68. 9; 9. 82. 5. *Non . . . fenestra* is really oxymoric; we should say, far less effectively, 'but imperfectly closed (i.e. protected) by its window'.

in qua nec Boreas ipse manere velit.

Sic habitare iubes veterem crudelis amicum ?

arboris ergo tuae tutior hospes ero.

17

Egi, Sexte, tuam pactus duo milia causam :

misisti nummos quod mihi mille, quid est ?

" Narrasti nihil " inquis " et a te perdita causa est ".

Tanto plus debes, Sexte, quod erubui.

18

Si tua, Cerrini, promas epigrammata vulgo,

6. nec: see on 1. 109. 20. — **Boreas** = *Aquilo*, the very wind that brings lowering or wet weather and cold. Cf. 7. 36. 5.

7. veterem is here used most strictly, of something that has long existed and still exists; cf. Hor. S. 2. 6. 80–81 *rusticus urbanum murem mus paupere fertur accepisse cavo, veterem vetus hospes amicum.* The position of *amicum* emphasizes M.'s question.

8. arboris: collective sing.; see 4. 64. 32 N. — **tutior:** i.e. 'in less danger of perishing than in my windy garret'. Cf. 7. 36 in full. — **hospes:** pred. nom., *as a guest.*

17. The protest of a lawyer who wanted a thousand sesterces as a relief to his feelings. For M. as a lawyer see § 9 fin. But M. need not be speaking of himself; see 8. 13. Introd. — Meter: § 48.

1. pactus duo milia: on lawyers' fees see 1. 76. Introd.; 1. 98. 2 N.; Fried. SG. 1. 327 ff.

2. nummos: cf. 1. 66. 4 N.— **quod:** see 2. 11. 1 N.; 3. 44. 1. The vs. = 'What do you mean by sending', etc.

3. Narrasti nihil: 'you made no statement of facts even, much

less did you make a plea'. This interpretation rests on the use of *narratio* as a technical term of rhetoric for a formal statement of facts; such a statement is a necessary part of a lawyer's plea. It may well be, however, that Sextus was using *narrasti* in the sense explained in the note on 3. 46. 7; if so, the sense is: 'what you said was worthless, yes, worse than worthless (*a te ... est*)'. Sextus, then, charges M. at first with leaving his case *indicta*, then with deliberately betraying it.

4. quod erubui (sc. *narrare*): i.e. 'because I was ashamed to "make a statement" of so shameless a case, and so saved you more than you would have won, had you gained your case at such a cost'.

18. Cerrinius was one of the many poetasters whose verses have long since perished. M.'s high-flown praise is not to be taken in such cases at its face value. — Meter: § 48.

1. promas ... vulgo suggests that Cerrinius has an abundant store of epigrams on which he can draw at will, as a butler or housewife draws on the supply of wine; cf. e.g. Hor. Epod. 2. 47 *et horna*

vel mecum possis vel prior ipse legi,
  sed tibi tantus inest veteris respectus amici,
    carior ut mea sit quam tua fama tibi.
5 Sic Maro nec Calabri temptavit carmina Flacci,
    Pindaricos nosset cum superare modos,
  et Vario cessit Romani laude cothurni,
    cum posset tragico fortius ore loqui.
  Aurum et opes et rura frequens donabit amicus :
10   qui velit ingenio cedere, rarus erit.

dulci vina promens dolio; Plaut. Pseud. 608 *condus promus sum, procurator peni.*

2. vel . . . legi: see App. — **vel . . . vel** is effective; it implies that the choice lies with Cerrinius himself. — **mecum:** as an equal. — **prior** (*me*): as even superior.

3. veteris . . . amici: cf. 8. 14. 7 N.

5. Maro: Vergil; cf. 1. 61. 2 N. — **Calabri . . . carmina Flacci:** i.e. Horace's lyric poetry. Horace, however, was not a Calabrian; he was born at Venusia, near the boundary between Lucania and Apulia. Hence he says (S. 2. 1. 34), perhaps with a touch of humor, *sequor hunc* (= Lucilius), *Lucanus an Apulus anceps*; cf. 12. 94. 5. M. seems strangely ignorant or careless at times in matters of fact. He gives Arpi, instead of Arpinum, as the birthplace of Cicero (4. 55). See also on 1. 61. 5; § 35 fin. For Horace see also 1. 107. 4.

6. Pindaricos . . . modos: as if to show how easily Vergil might have distanced Horace in lyric poetry, M. says that he could have eclipsed Pindar himself, with whom Horace expressly disclaimed rivalry (C. 4. 2. 1–4, 25–32). Pindar, a Greek lyric poet, of Thebes in Boeotia (about 520–450 B.C.), was

consummate master of every form of lyric poetry. — **modos:** cf. Hor. C. 4. 2. 9–12; Ep. 1. 3. 12–13 *fidibusne Latinis Thebanos aptare modos studet auspice Musa, an . . . ?*

7. Vario: L. Varius Rufus, friend of Maecenas, Vergil, and Horace, one of the literary executors of Vergil, was, at the beginning of the Augustan epoch, the greatest epic writer at Rome. He distinguished himself also in tragedy; his Thyestes, which was acted at the games held in honor of Actium and for which Augustus paid him a million sesterces, in public opinion divided with Ovid's Medea the honor of being the greatest Roman tragedy. See e.g. 8. 55. 21; 12. 3; Hor. S. 1. 10. 43; C. 1. 6; Quint. 10. 1. 98. — **laude:** abl. of specification, or, better, abl. of separation, 'yielded from', etc. — **cothurni:** cf. 8. 3. 18 N.

8. fortius: frequently used as a rhetorical term with reference to vigor of style. — **ore:** cf. Hor. C. 4. 2. 7–8 *fervet inmensusque ruit profundo Pindarus ore.*

9. frequens . . . amicus: cf. 14. 122. 1 *ante frequens, sed nunc rarus nos donat amicus.*

10. ingenio cedere: this demands a personal sacrifice, which the giving of *aurum, opes*, or *rura*

·23

Esse tibi videor saevus nimiumque gulosus,
　　qui propter cenam, Rustice, caedo cocum :
si levis ista tibi flagrorum causa videtur,
　　ex qua vis causa vapulet ergo cocus ?

24

Si quid forte petam timido gracilique libello,
　　inproba non fuerit si mea charta, dato,

does not of necessity involve. — With the epigram as a whole cf. 11. 10. 1–2 *contulit ad saturas ingentia pectora Turnus. Cur non ad Memoris carmina? Frater erat.*

23. M. explains why he beat his cook. — Meter: § 48.

1. gulosus: cf. 7. 20. 1–2 *nihil est miserius neque gulosius Santra. Rectam vocatus cum cucurrit ad cenam*, etc.; 3. 22. 5 N. See also on 1. 20. 3.

2. Rustice: perhaps a jeering epithet, rather than true name, 'you simple fool', 'you rustic, unacquainted with the ways of city folk'. — **caedo:** we get the best effect by taking this word at its fullest value, of cutting through the skin (see on *flagrum*, 3), though in practice *caedo* often bore a sense less severe, even when used of flogging. The vs. thus = 'for meting out punishment so severe for offense so trifling'.

3. levis: in sharp contrast to *flagrorum*. The *flagrum* or *flagellum* (ironical diminutive) was a cat o' nine tails, or knout, at times knotted with bits of metal or bone. Verbs like *caedere, scindere, rumpere*, and *secare* are used to describe its effect; cf. Hor. S. 1. 3. 119 *horribili . . . flagello*; 1. 2. 41–42 *ille flagellis ad mortem caesus.*

4. ex qua . . . causa: i.e. except failure to get up good dinners. M. grimly challenges Rusticus's estimate of the value of a *cena* and of the shortcomings of a cook who fails to do his duty. — **vis . . . vapulet:** for syntax see on *vis mittam*, 1. 117. 2. With the epigram as a whole cf. 3. 43. 1–4; 3. 94. 1–2 *esse negas coctum leporem poscisque flagella : mavis, Rufe, cocum scindere quam leporem*; Petr. 49.

24. 'Olympian Zeus does not resent petition, even though he must deny the request. Our mundane Jupiter should not do less'. See 4. 8. 8; 7. 99; § 8. — Meter: § 48.

1. timido: cf. 5. 6. 7–8 *admittas timidam brevemque chartam intra limina sanctioris aulae.* — **gracili:** used with *libello* in the more general sense of that word (cf. 1. 1. 3; 13. 3. 1 *in hoc gracili Xeniorum . . . libello*), though M. seems to be thinking also of *libellus* = 'petition'. Cf. 5. 6 throughout.

2. inproba: prop. 'not according to the standard'; here, according to the sense of *libello* (1), it = *lacking in literary merit*, or, *morally bad* (and so calculated to offend Domitian as *censor morum*: see 1. 4. Introd.), or, *annoying, rude, unreasonable.*

et si non dederis, Caesar, permitte rogari :
offendunt nunquam tura precesque Iovem.
5 Qui fingit sacros auro vel marmore vultus,
non facit ille deos : qui rogat, ille facit.

29

Disticha qui scribit, puto, vult brevitate placere :
quid prodest brevitas, dic mihi, si liber est ?

32

Aëra per tacitum delapsa sedentis in ipsos
fluxit Aratullae blanda columba sinus.
Luserat hoc casus, nisi inobservata maneret
permissaque sibi nollet abire fuga.

3. permitte rogari: for inf. with *permitto* see Soed. 16, for many examples; cf. e.g. 10. 30. 25.

5-6. 'The true worshiper is not the man who is content with making a graven image of his god, but the man who prays to him because he believes that the god can and will answer prayer'.

5. fingit: the verb is used primarily of what is fashioned in clay; it especially designates the work of men's hands.

29. On true brevity. 'Brevity becomes prolixity when a man who writes epigrams because the epigram is short and so more likely to be read writes a whole book of them'. Cf. 7. 85; 1. 110. 1-2 *scribere me quereris, Velox, epigrammata longa. Ipse nihil scribis: tu breviora facis.* — Meter: § 48.

1. Disticha: cf. 2. 77. 8; 2. 71. 2; 7. 85. 1 N.

2. quid ... brevitas, *of what profit is this brevity?* — **si liber est:** cf. 7. 85. 3.

32. The Roman, by nature superstitious, was prone to see something supernatural or prognostic in anything unusual, especially in connection with the flight of birds. M. would have Aratulla see in the circumstances described in this epigram an omen of her brother's return from exile in Sardinia, and in the same words veils a delicate petition to the emperor to recall him. — Meter: § 48.

1-2. Aëra ... delapsa: the dove was not driven by stress of weather to seek refuge, but came of its own accord. *Delapsa* and *fluxit* finely picture the easy, gentle (unaffrighted, voluntary) movement of the bird. — **blanda columba:** cf. 11. 104. 9 *basia me capiunt blandas imitata columbas*; Ov. Am. 2. 6. 56 *oscula dat cupido blanda columba mari* ('its mate'). The fact that Venus's own bird comes to Aratulla hints at her charms. — **sinus,** *bosom,* or, more probably, *lap* (*gremium*); see on 1. 15. 10.

3-4. Luserat ... nisi: 'this had been a mere freak of chance (as it was not), but for the fact that', etc. For the mood of *luserat*

5 Si meliora piae fas est sperare sorori
      et dominum mundi flectere vota valent,
   haec a Sardois tibi forsitan exulis oris,
      fratre reversuro, nuntia venit avis.

35

Cum sitis similes paresque vita,
uxor pessima, pessimus maritus,
miror non bene convenire vobis.

43

Effert uxores Fabius, Chrestilla maritos,

see on 5. 34. 5–6. — **hoc:** acc. of effect (inner object); see on 5. 66. 2. — **inobservata:** i.e. though not detained in any way. — **maneret . . . nollet:** M. uses the impf. to emphasize the long continuance of the bird's stay; see A. 517, a; GL. 597; L. 2092; 2094, b.

5. meliora: the pardon and return of the exiled brother.

6. dominum mundi: Domitian. See I. 4. 2 N. — **flectere:** cf. 11. 91. 12; Verg. A. 6. 376 *desine fata deum flecti sperare precando.* — **flectere . . . valent:** for constr. see on 4. 64. 21–22.

7–8. Sardois . . . oris: *oris* is used appropriately of an island. Banishment to an island (which ordinarily meant one of the very small islands), as taking one from the centers of culture and life, was looked upon as little better than a living death. Further, Sardinia was proverbially unhealthy. — **forsitan . . . venit:** in Cicero *forsitan* (= *fors sit an* = 'it would be problematical whether') naturally is construed only with the subjv.; the constr. with the ind. belongs chiefly to poetry and to post-Augustan prose. — **exulis . . . venit:** freed

from metrical restraints M. might have said *exulis fratris reversuri nuntia venit,* or, better, *exulem fratrem reversurum esse nuntia venit. Exulis* and *fratre* denote the same person. *Exulis* is obj. gen. with *nuntia;* logically, of course, the real object of *nuntia* is the idea involved in *reversuro.* — **nuntia:** pred. nom.

35. "Both man and wife as bad as bad can be: I wonder they no better should agree" (Hay). — Meter: § 49.

1. **pares . . . vita,** *well-matched in conduct;* cf. Macr. S. 7. 7. 12 *similibus enim similia gaudent;* Cic. Cato M. 3. 7 *pares autem vetere proverbio cum paribus facillime congregantur;* Otto s.v. *Par.*

2. Note the chiasmus; cf. 1. 4. 8; 6. 28. 7; 8. 43. 1.

3. **miror . . . convenire:** for the syntax see on 4. 59. 3. — **non . . . vobis,** *that you do not agree perfectly. Convenire* is impersonal; cf. Petr. 10 *intellego nobis convenire non posse.*

43. M. suggests that a sure way of ridding the world of such adepts at poisoning as Fabius and Chrestilla are will be to make them

funereamque toris quassat uterque facem.
Victores committe, Venus, quos iste manebit
exitus una duos ut Libitina ferat.

50

Quis labor in phiala? docti Myos anne Myronos?

man and wife, that they may try their skill on each other. See 4. 69; 9. 15; 9. 78 *funera post septem nupsit tibi Galla virorum, Picentine; sequi vult, puto, Galla viros.* — Meter: § 48.

1. Effert: cf. 4. 24. 2. — **Chrestilla:** fem. dim. of Chrestus (cf. χρηστός = *utilis, bonus*); the name is derisive, given κατ' ἀντίφρασιν (see on 7. 83. 1). For the chiasmus in this vs. see on 8. 35. 2.

2. funeream . . . facem: not only was a *fax* used to light the funeral pyre, but torches were carried at funerals, a survival, probably, from the time when all funerals took place at night, as did those of slaves and the poor even in M.'s time. Cf. Verg. A. 11. 142–144 *Arcades ad portas ruere et de more vetusto funereas rapuere faces; lucet via longo ordine flammarum et late discriminat agros.* — **toris:** the *lectus genialis* of both houses. Cf. Ov. M. 6. 430–431 *Eumenides tenuere faces de funere raptas, Eumenides stravere torum* (at the marriage of Progne and Tereus). We have either a dat. of interest (disadvantage), a bit of grim humor, or a free use of the local abl. (= *super toros*).

3–4. Victores committe: M. compares Fabius and Chrestilla to gladiators who have vanquished their opponents and must now fight each other to a finish. Since illicit love has been the motive of the murders committed by them, M. appropriately calls on Venus to

act as *editor spectaculorum*, in a fight *sine missione*; see Lib. Spect. 29, with notes. — **committe:** a term from the arena; cf. Iuv. 1. 162–163 *securus licet Aenean Rutulumque ferocem committas.* For the cæsura in 3 see § 52, c. — **quos . . . ferat:** the antec. of *quos* is *duos*, 4; *iste . . . exitus* is death by poisoning (cf. 1–2); in *manebit* M. turns prophet. Render, 'that two, who will surely die themselves by poison, two, I say, one bier may bear away'. For the sense given to *iste* ('that which you have in mind', or the like), see on 1. 70. 18. It is possible, also, to make *victores* the antec. of *quos*, and regard vs. 4 as a result clause explanatory of *iste*, which then virtually = *talis*. — **Libitina:** prop. goddess of funerals; see e.g. Hor. C. 3. 30. 6–7 *non omnis moriar multaque pars mei vitabit Libitinam.* Here the word = a *bier, feretrum, sandapila* (metonymy). — **ferat** = *auferat*; see on 1. 4. 2.

50. M. goes into raptures over a phiala presented to him by his friend Istantius Rufus. — Meter: § 48.

1. Quis labor (*est*): i.e. 'what artist made it?' *Cuius labor est* would have been simpler. *Labor* is very aptly used of the severe toil of the *caelator*; cf. 4. 39. 5; 14. 95, cited below. — **phiala** (φιάλη): a saucer-like drinking vessel, generally of gold or silver, like the *patera*. See 8. 6. 14; 14. 95 (on a *phiala aurea caelata*) *quamvis Callaico*

Mentoris haec manus est an, Polyclite, .tua ?
Livescit nulla caligine fusca nec odit
    exploratores nubila massa focos ;
5 vera minus flavo radiant electra metallo,
    et niveum felix pustula vincit ebur.
Materiae non cedit opus : sic alligat orbem,

rubeam generosa metallo, glorior arte magis, nam Myos iste labor.— **Myos:** Mys was a master engraver, a contemporary of Phidias and Parrhasius. — **anne:** see A. 332, c, N. 2; GL. 457, 1, N. 2. — **Myronos:** see 4. 39. 2 N.

2. **Mentoris:** see 4. 39. 5 N. — **manus:** see 4. 39. 3 N. — **Polyclite:** Polyclitus rivaled Phidias as a sculptor; cf. 9. 59. 12; 10. 89; Fried. SG. 3. 309 ff. Fried. remarks on this vs. that the names of famous artists were very freely used by the Romans, esp. in connection with works of the sort here described.

3–4. **Livescit . . . fusca** (sc. *phiala* or *massa*): the surface of the vessel is clear and undimmed; therein it differed from most of the antiques. — **nullā:** M. might have said *nec livescit ulla caligine fusca.* — **nec odit . . . focos:** it is no dun lump of metal that has to be tested to prove its genuineness or that has cause to fear such tests. In Latin, sentences containing negatives are often so much condensed that a literal rendering conveys a false impression. Here translate: 'no blackness makes it swart and tarnished; there is no cloud upon its whole mass, and it shrinks not from', etc. — **exploratores . . . focos,** *crucibles, furnaces; exploratores* is adj., *testing* (see on 1. 66. 7; 3. 58. 7; 5. 37. 1). Cf. Claud. III Cons. Hon. Praef. 11–12 *exploratores oculis qui pertulit ignes sustinuitque acie nobiliore diem.*

5. **vera . . . metallo** most naturally = 'real amber is less resplendent than the yellow metal of this *phiala*'. If this rendering is right, the *phiala* must be of gold or of the metal called *electrum*. Yet it is not likely that M. would receive a *phiala* of gold, unless it were like the unsubstantial one of 8. 33. Further, the comparison with amber lacks point unless this cup were composed of *electrum*. The basis of this metal was gold, but it resembled amber because of the silver ($\frac{1}{5}$ or more) which entered into it. So far as syntax goes, the vs. may = 'real amber shines with a luster less golden' than the luster of this cup. — **electra:** for the pl. see on 4. 69. 1.

6. **et . . . ebur:** from this it appears that silver was used somewhere on the surface of the *phiala*. — **felix pustula:** cf. 7. 86. 7 N. *Felix* apparently = an adv.; it describes the happy combination of metals.

7–8. **opus,** *workmanship*; cf. Ov. M. 2. 5 (of the palace of the Sun) *materiam superabat opus.*— **sic . . . nitet:** 'so the moon binds together her orb when at her largest she shines with all her torch'. The poets often thus speak of the moon as binding together her horns into an orb; cf. Ov. M. 7. 530–531 *iunctis explevit cornibus orbem luna.* The important word in 7–8 is *materiae*; this is illustrated at length in 9–16 by the description of the graver's

plurima cum tota lampade luna nitet.

Stat caper Aeolio Thebani vellere Phrixi

10   cultus : ab hoc mallet vecta fuisse soror ;

hunc nec Cinyphius tonsor violaverit et tu

ipse tua pasci vite, Lyaee, velis.

Terga premit pecudis geminis Amor aureus alis,

skill. It may well be, therefore, that M. has in mind the patterns with which the full moon is chased ('the man in the moon'). The *phiala*, then, is adorned as gloriously as is the moon, when, at last waxed full, she shows us the complete splendor of her decoration. — **plurima . . . luna:** cf. Ov. M. 14. 53–54 *medio cum plurimus orbe sol erat.* — **lampade:** cf. Verg. A. 4. 6 *postera Phoebea lustrabat lampade terras*; Lucr. 5. 610 *rosea sol alte lampade lucens.*

9. Stat caper: a goat was embossed on the *phiala*; cf. Iuv. 1. 76 (*criminibus debent*) *argentum vetus et stantem extra pocula caprum. Stat = exstat*; cf. Ov. M. 12. 235–236 *forte fuit iuxta signis exstantibus asper anticus crater.* The goat was an appropriate relief on a drinking cup, for, as especially destructive to the vine, it was a favorite victim on the altars of Bacchus. — **Aeolio . . . Phrixi:** the hair of this goat reminds one of the famous Golden Fleece itself. Phrixus and his sister Helle, fleeing from their stepmother Ino, were carried through the air on a ram with golden fleece. Helle fell into the sea (the Hellespont), but Phrixus made his way to Colchis; after sacrificing the ram he hung up its fleece there in the grove of Mars. The fleece was brought back to Greece by the Argonauts. Athamas, father of Phrixus, was at first king of Orchomenos in Boeotia; later he lived in Thessaly. — **Aeolio** = *Boeotio* or *Thessalo*; the Aeolians, one of the three great divisions of the Hellenic race, occupied both Boeotia and Thessaly. — **Thebani:** M. is either careless (see on 8. 18. 5), forgetting the facts of Athamas's career (see above), or he is thinking that Phrixus fled from Ino, his stepmother, who was daughter of Cadmus, the founder of Thebes.

10. ab hoc: i.e. by the goat on the *phiala* rather than by the ram of the story. — **mallet . . . fuisse:** see GL. 258; L. 1559; 2223.

11. hunc: the *caper*. — **nec:** see perhaps on 1. 109. 20. But *nec* (*neque*) . . . *-que* (*et*) is not uncommon, even in prose; cf. οὔτε . . . τέ. We might also say that M. at first thought of writing *nec . . . violaverit nec tu ipse . . . Lyaee nolis.* — **Cinyphius tonsor:** the region about the Cinyps, a stream of Libya flowing into the Mediterranean between the two Syrtes, was famous for a breed of goats from whose hair a felt or sort of hair-cloth was made which rivaled the Cilician product; cf. 7. 95. 11–13 *rigetque barba qualem forficibus metit supinis tonsor Cinyphio Cilix marito.*

12. pasci is an example of the middle voice. — **Lyaee:** see 1. 70. 9 N. — **velis**, *would be willing that, would suffer* (permit).

13. pecudis: the *caper*. — **aureus:** the epithet applied so often to Venus (*aurea*) may be bestowed

Palladia et tenero lotos ab ore sonat:
15   sic Methymnaeo gavisus Arione delphin
languida non tacitum per freta vexit onus.
Imbuat egregium digno mihi nectare munus
non grege de domini, sed tua, Ceste, manus ;
Ceste, decus mensae, misce Setina: videtur
20   ipse puer nobis, ipse sitire caper.
Det numerum cyathis Istanti littera Rufi,
auctor enim tanti muneris ille mihi :

here on her son, or the tiny figure may have been of gold. Cf. Ov. Rem. Am. 39 *movit Amor gemmatas aureus alas.* Note that *aureus* is often used in poetry of things perfect after their kind.

14. Palladia . . . lotos: Pallas's pipe; cf. Fest. 119 *Lotos: arboris genus, ex cuius materia frequenter tibiae fiebant.* Minerva was accounted the inventor of certain wind instruments; cf. Ov. F. 6. 697–698. See App.

15. Methymnaeo . . . Arione: the wonderful story of Arion, of Methymna in Lesbos, the distinguished player on the lute (*cithara*), may be read in Gell. 16. 19; Ov. F. 2. 79 ff.; etc. — **gavisus . . . delphin:** remarkable stories were told of the dolphin, giving to the creature attributes almost human.

16. languida . . . freta: Arion quieted the waters by his strains; cf. Ov. F. 2. 116 *aequoreas carmine mulcet aquas,* and the stories of Orpheus.—**non tacitum . . . onus:** the burden (Arion) was melodious. The thought of 13–16 lies primarily in 14 and in *non tacitum onus,* 16. Verses 15–16 = 'so 'twas no voiceless burden that the dolphin', etc.

17. Imbuat, *fill* (for the first time), *christen* (Steph.). *Imbuo* is often thus used of doing something

for the first time. The subj. is *manus,* 18. — **nectare:** see 4. 32. 2 N.; cf. 3. 82. 24 *Opimianum nectar.*

18. grege: see 2. 43. 13. — **de:** postpositive, for metrical convenience. This is common enough in poetry, esp. with a dissyllabic preposition. Further, *grege de domini* somewhat resembles the common prose usage by which a monosyllabic preposition stands between an adj. and a noun. — **domini:** Rufus, not M., for M. probably had no great array of slaves (*grex*). We may suppose that M. received the gift at Rufus's table.

19. decus mensae: Cestus is a very Ganymedes in beauty and skill.—**Setina:** see 4. 69. 1 N. Setia, a town of Latium, overlooked the Paludes Pomptinae. Its wine was a favorite with most of the emperors. For the pl. (sc. *vina*) see on 4. 69. 1.

20. Such nectar is enough to make even the goat and his rider look thirsty.

21–22. Det . . . Rufi: whenever a health was proposed, the number of *cyathi* must coincide with the number of letters in the name of the person honored; cf. 1. 71. 1–2; 9. 93. 3–4. — **cyathis:** see 1. 27. 2 N. — **Istanti . . . Rufi:** see App.

si Telethusa venit promissaque gaudia portat,
    servabor dominae, Rufe, triente tuo ;
25 si dubia est, septunce trahar ; si fallit amantem,
    ut iugulem curas, nomen utrumque bibam.

55

Temporibus nostris aetas cum cedat avorum
    creverit et maior cum duce Roma suo,
ingenium sacri miraris deesse Maronis
    nec quemquam tanta bella sonare tuba.

— **littera**: collective sing., used apparently for metrical convenience. — **auctor ... mihi**: M. means that the *phiala* must first be used to toast Rufus, since it was a gift from him.

23. Telethusa: M.'s *amica* (real or pretended).

24. servabor is a middle; 'I shall watch myself, I shall drink so as not to lose my head'. — **triente tuo**: instr. abl., 'by (confining myself to) the third of your name', i.e. by drinking but four *cyathi*, representing the letters of the voc. *Rufe*, necessarily used in addressing the person whose health was to be drunk.

25. si dubia est: i.e. if by her delay she makes her coming doubtful. — **septunce trahar**, *I shall be allured by*, i.e. shall be tempted to the extent of, *seven cyathi*, answering to the voc. *Istanti*. Cf. 3. 82. 29 *septunce multo deinde perditus stertit*. For this use of *trahere* cf. Verg. E. 2. 65 *trahit sua quemque voluptas*. — **fallit amantem**: cf. Ov. M. 4. 128–129 *ne fallat amantem, illa redit*.

26. iugulem curas: so we talk of 'killing (drowning) care'. — **curas**: i.e. 'my chagrin at her failure to come'.

55. M.'s theory of the making of a great literature is very simple: Vergils will spring up like mushrooms, provided Maecenases supply the seed and fructify the soil (5). Cf. 1. 76; 1. 107; 3. 38. — Meter: § 48.

1–2. Temporibus ... suo: for like flattery of Domitian see 5. 19. **1–5.** In fact, with slight exceptions, e.g. under Agricola in Britain, Rome suffered great loss in prestige and territory under Domitian. See 1. 70. 6 N. M. doubtless hoped that this flattery would bear fruit and help literature as represented by himself. — **cum**: prob. *since*; *though* will also fit the context. — **maior**: pred. nom. with *creverit*, which = *facta sit*. — **cum**: here the prep. — **suo**, *her beloved*; see on 1. 13. 1; cf. Ov. Tr. 4. 2. 66 *laetaque erit praesens cum duce turba suo*.

3. sacri: cf. 5. 69. 7 N.; 1. 12. 3 N. — **deesse**: dissyllabic, to suit the meter. Cf. 10. 48. 10; *deerunt*, 5. So *deest* becomes a monosyllable; cf. 7. 34. 6 *non deest protinus, ecce, de malignis*.

4. sonare: cf. 7. 23. 1; 8. 3. 14; Stat. Silv. 4. 2. 66–67 *cum modo Germanas acies modo Daca sonantem proelia Palladio tua me manus*

5 Sint Maecenates, non deerunt, Flacce, Marones
     Vergiliumque tibi vel tua rura dabunt.
   Iugera perdiderat miserae vicina Cremonae
     flebat et abductas Tityrus aeger oves ;
   risit Tuscus eques paupertatemque malignam
10   reppulit et celeri iussit abire fuga :

induit auro. See App. — **tuba:** see 8. 3. 22 N.

5. Maecenates: this wail over the increasing lack of patronage — a wail that grew louder and louder as the years pₐssed — had an element of sincerity. Cf. 1. 107. 3–4; 11. 3. 6–10; 12. 3; Iuv. 7. 94 ff. — **deerunt:** see on *deesse*, 3. — **Flacce:** not to be identified with certainty, but perhaps the Flaccus of 4. 49. 1; 10. 48. 5.

6. Vergilium ... dabunt: 'even your farm (i.e. your money properly bestowed) could produce a Vergil as easily as it raises corn or olives. You yourself may have honor like that of Maecenas, if you will but pay for it'. — **rura:** cf. 1. 12. 3 N.

7–8. Iugera ... oves: in 41 B.C., after the success of the Triumvirs, nearly 175,000 veterans had to be provided with land. The resultant confiscations of land embraced regions far distant from Rome and involved in ruin not only the foes of the Caesarians, such as Cremona, but in some cases their adherents, as, for example, Mantua and the surrounding region. Vergil himself was ejected from his estate, but he recovered it by grace of Octavianus. Tityrus, the shepherd of Vergil's first Eclogue, is Vergil himself, who has regained the land he had lost. — **miserae:** because of the ruin of the town and the small landholders brought about by the confiscations. — **vicina Cremonae:** M. is thinking of Verg.

E. 9. 28 *Mantua, vae, miserae nimium vicina Cremonae.* The Triumvirs meant to confiscate only the lands of Cremona, but since these were not ample enough, Mantuan territory was taken. In fact the two towns were about forty miles apart. — **Tityrus:** cf. Apoll. Sid. C. 4. 1–8. — **aeger:** cf. Verg. E. 1. 12–13 *en, ipse capellas protinus aeger ago*, said by *Meliboeus*, the shepherd who, less fortunate than Tityrus, is leaving the farm of which he has been dispossessed. M. is again inaccurate; see on 8. 18. 5.

9–10. risit ... eques: M. is again inaccurate (see on 8); Maecenas had nothing to do with the restoration of Vergil's farm (his name does not occur in the Eclogues; he was not yet a factor in the Roman state. See 1. 107. 4 N.). Vergil's benefactors at that time were Asinius Pollio, Alfenus Varus, and Octavianus. Later, however, Maecenas did much for Vergil, as he did for Horace. — **eques:** though the Tuscan ancestors of Maecenas were of very high rank (cf. Hor. C. 3. 29. 1 *Tyrrhena regum progenies*; 1. 1. 1 *Maecenas atavis edite regibus*), at Rome he never aspired to be more than an *eques*; cf. e.g. 12. 3. 2 *Maecenas, atavis regibus ortus eques*; Hor. C. 1. 20. 5 *care Maecenas eques*; 3. 16. 20 *Maecenas, equitum decus*. — **abire:** the subject is *paupertatem*, 9.

11–12. vatum ... esto: as if worry about material things were

"Accipe divitias et vatum maximus esto ;
    tu licet et nostrum " dixit "Alexin ames ".
Adstabat domini mensis pulcherrimus ille
    marmorea fundens nigra Falerna manu,
15   et libata dabat roseis carchesia labris,
    quae poterant ipsum sollicitare Iovem.
Excidit attonito pinguis Galatea poetae
    Thestylis et rubras messibus usta genas ;

the only hindrance to great literary achievement. Cf. Iuv. 7. 52–73, 94–97. — **vatum:** cf. 1. 61. 1 N. — **nostrum . . . Alexin:** Alexis is the beautiful slave boy of Vergil's second Eclogue. M. speaks as if Maecenas had given the boy to Vergil, or at least owned him and invited Vergil to share with him the society of the boy. But see notes on 9–10. Other ancient writers say the boy belonged to Pollio. Cf. 8. 73. 9–10; 6. 68. 6 *hic amor, hic nostri vatis Alexis erat.*

13. domini: Maecenas; verses 13–16 seem to explain that the gift was made while Vergil was dining with Maecenas. M. may, however, be rather describing what happened in Vergil's house after the gift; in that case *adstabat = adstare solebat.* Verses 13–16 will then give the result of 12. This view fits *dabat,* 15, better. — **pulcherrimus:** cf. Verg. 2. 1 *formosum Alexim.*

14. marmorea . . . manu: the boy was fair-skinned; *marmorea = candida;* cf. Petr. 126 (of a woman) *iam mentum, iam cervix, iam manus iam pedum candor intra auri gracile vinculum positus: Parium marmor extinxerat.* — **nigra Falerna:** Falernian wine, though fine, was at this time hardly ranked by epicures with some other kinds, e.g. Setian and Caecuban. It was darker (dark red) than some others;

cf. 9. 22. 8; 8. 77. 5 *candida nigre-scant vetulo crystalla Falerno.*

15. libata . . . labris: the favorite drinks first; the wine touched by his lips (15) seems better. — **carchesia** (cf. καρχήσιον): a splendid drinking beaker of Greek origin, somewhat narrower in the middle than at the top or the bottom. The word is generally found in the pl.; cf. e.g. Verg. A. 5. 77.

17–20. Once in possession of Alexis, Vergil forgot his country loves, chubby Galatea and sun-burned Thestylis, i.e. he abandoned bucolic poetry to write an epic, which should in its scope and fulfillment be commensurate with the glory of imperial Rome, whose origin it sought to immortalize.

17. Excidit (sc. *memoria*), *was forgotten,* a sense common in Silver Latin; cf. too Verg. A. 1. 25–26 *necdum etiam causae irarum . . . exciderant animo;* Prop. 3. 24. 20, cited below on *poetae.* The position and the tense give the force of 'forthwith forgot'. The same idea is differently expressed in 19. — **attonito,** *inspired;* cf. Verg. A. 7. 580 *attonitae Baccho matres;* Hor. C. 3. 19. 14 *attonitus vates.* — **pinguis,** *plump,* and so *coarse.* — **poetae:** dat.; cf. Prop. 3. 24. 20 *exciderant surdo tot mea vota Iovi.*

18. Thestylis: as Galatea is more chubby than the city beauty

protinus ITALIAM concepit et ARMA VIRUMQUE,

20   qui modo vix Culicem fleverat ore rudi.

Quid Varios Marsosque loquar ditataque vatum

    nomina, magnus erit quos numerare labor?

Ergo ero Vergilius, si munera Maecenatis

    des mihi? Vergilius non ero, Marsus ero.

57

Tres habuit dentes, pariter quos expuit omnes,

    ad tumulum Picens dum sedet ipse suum,

liked to be, so such tan as reddened the cheeks of Thestylis city maidens carefully avoided; cf. 5. 37. 1 N.; Hor. Epod. 2. 41–42 *perusta solibus pernicis uxor Apuli.* For *Thestylis* cf. Verg. E. 2. 10–11.

19. Italiam concepit (*animo*), *he had a vision of,* etc. *Italiam* and *Arma virumque* stand at the beginning of the second and the first verses of the Aeneid as the poem is commonly printed. Some Mss., however, put four other verses before *arma virumque,* and those verses are recognized by some ancient Roman authorities. See the editors of Vergil, e.g. Conington, and, for a recent discussion, Fitz Hugh, Proc. Amer. Phil. Ass. 34 (1903), pp. xxxii–xxxiii. The ancients were not wont to mention a given work by a set title, but referred to it in some less technical but no less direct way, as, for instance, by quoting the opening words. Cf. 14. 185. 1–2 *accipe facundi Culicem, studiose, Maronis, ne nucibus positis Arma Virumque legas.* See also on *Passerem,* 4. 14. 14.

20. vix ... **rudi:** his early inspiration scarcely sufficed to enable him to sing, in unpolished verse, the dirge of a gnat and similar lowly themes. Cf. the themes of

the Carmina Minora ascribed to Vergil. A poem called Culex is extant, but scholars are divided in opinion whether it was written by Vergil or by some one who sought to imitate his style. For a very recent and excellent discussion of this question see Mackail in Classical Review, 22. 65–73.

21. Varios: see 8. 18. 7 N. — **Marsos:** cf. 2. 71. 3; 2. 77. 5; 7. 99. 7. — **loquar:** used with acc. as in 1. 61. 8; see note there. — **ditata:** transferred epithet, for it logically modifies *vatum.* M. ends as he began; given generous patrons, we shall always have good poetry in plenty.

23–24. M. answers a hypothetical objection that his argument proves too much. — **Ergo:** see 1. 41. 2 N.

57. On an elderly man who assists, in part at least, in his own interment. — Meter: § 48.

1. Tres ... **dentes:** they were the last, too. — **pariter** ... **expuit:** as the result of a single cough; cf. Priap. 12. 1, 8–9 *Quaedam, Cumaeae soror, ut puto, Sibyllae, ... hesterna quoque luce dum precatur, dentem de tribus excreavit unum.*

2. tumulum ... **suum:** his family monument beside one of

collegitque sinu fragmenta novissima laxi
oris et adgesta contumulavit humo.
5   Ossa licet quondam defuncti non legat heres
hoc sibi iam Picens praestitit officium.

69

Miraris veteres, Vacerra, solos
nec laudas nisi mortuos poetas.
Ignoscas petimus, Vacerra: tanti
non est, ut placeam tibi, perire.

the great roads. Such tombs were often erected before the demise of the head of the family. Cf. 4. 59. 6; 6. 52. 1.

3. **collegit**: as one might for mercy's sake collect and cover unburied bones of some unfortunate who had not received proper burial. — **sinu**: i.e. of his toga; see on 1. 15. 10. Picens cherishes the *fragmenta*. A Roman reader would remember that after the body was burned on the funeral pyre the bones were carefully gathered, sometimes at least in a mourning robe; cf. Tib. 3. 2. 19 ff. — **laxi**, *loose, flabby*:

4. **adgestā . . . humo**: cf. Ov. Ib. 462 (*aut ut*) *saucius ingesta contumuleris humo.*

5. **Ossa . . . heres**: 'though his heir by and by fail to gather', etc.— **Ossa . . . legat**: cf. e.g. Suet. Aug. 100 *reliquias* (*Augusti*) *legerunt primores equestris ordinis, tunicati et discincti pedibusque nudis, ac mausoleo condiderunt.* — **quondam** is here said of the future, a rare use; cf. Verg. A. 6. 876–877 *nec Romula quondam ullo se tantum tellus iactabit alumno.* — **defuncti** (*vitā*): euphemistic for *mortui*; prop. one who has discharged the duties of life and has been mustered out, as veterans are mustered out.

6. **praestitit officium**: he has buried himself so far as his teeth are concerned. For the phrase cf. Prop. 2. 18. 14 (Aurora) *invitum et terris praestitit officium.*

69. 'Post-mortem glory, at least of some sorts, is not worth dying for'. — Meter: § 49.

1. **Miraris**: see 8. 6. 15 N. — **veteres**: used esp. of ancient writers, 'the writers of the good old days'; cf. Hor. Ep. 2. 1. 19 ff., 50–89; Quint. 9. 3. 1 *ut veteres et Cicero praecipue.* For the terms *veteres, antiqui,* etc., as applied to writers in the pages of Silver Latin, and the admiration which, beginning even in Cicero's time, was bestowed in increasing measure on the *antiqui* until in Hadrian's time the archaizing tendency became supreme, see Knapp, Studies in Honour of Henry Drisler, 126–141.

2. **nec . . . poetas**: Vacerra did not waste time on the recitations.

3. **Ignoscas petimus**: for the syntax see on 5. 49. 12.

4. **perire**: stronger than *mori*; cf. 5. 10, esp. 11–12 *vos tamen o nostri ne festinate libelli: si post fata venit gloria, non propero*; 1. 1. 4–6, with notes.

73. 'Love has ever been the poet's inspiration. Give me what Propertius and others had and I

73

Istanti, quo nec sincerior alter habetur
　　pectore nec nivea simplicitate prior,
si dare vis nostrae vires animosque Thaliae
　　et victura petis carmina, da quod amem.
5　Cynthia te vatem fecit lasciva, Properti,
　　ingenium Galli pulchra Lycoris erat,
fama est arguti Nemesis formosa Tibulli,
　　Lesbia dictavit, docte Catulle, tibi:

---

too will write worthily'. If the person here addressed is the man of 8. 50, the kindness ascribed to him there may have emboldened M. to ask for more. — Meter: § 48.

2. nivea = *candida*; see 2.71.1. — **simplicitate**: cf. 1. 39. 4 (Decianus) *vera simplicitate bonus*. — **prior**: cf. 12.44.4 *pectore non minor es, sed pietate prior*. In writing 1–2 M. may have had in mind Hor. S. 1. 5. 41–42 (Vergil and Varius) *animae qualis neque candidiores terra tulit neque quis me sit devinctior alter.*

3. nostrae . . . Thaliae: cf. 4. 8. 12 N.

4. victura: cf. 1. 25. 7; Ov. Am. 3. 1. 65 *das nostro victurum nomen amori*. — **quod amem**: i.e. some *deliciae.*

5–8. M. mentions, though not in chronological order, the greatest Roman writers of erotic elegy and the women who inspired their verses.

5. Cynthia: so Propertius calls his mistress; her true name was Hostia. (In the Latin poets such a 'nom de plume' regularly has the same metrical value as the name for which it is a substitute). She was "the mistress of his life, the directress of his inspiration" (Postgate). — **lasciva**: see App. Cf. Ov. Tr. 2. 427 *sic sua lascivo cantata*

est saepe Catullo femina cui falsum Lesbia nomen erat.

6. ingenium: cf. 8. 55. 3. — **Galli**: the ill-starred C. Cornelius Gallus was, if we may judge from ancient testimony, a worthy rival of the others here named. His love for Lycoris was the burden of the four books of erotics that we know he wrote. His work has, however, perished, unless Mackail is right in ascribing some at least of the Carmina Minora current under Vergil's name to Gallus; see Class. Rev. 22. 65–73. With 5–6 cf. 12. 3. 5–6.

7. arguti, *melodious*; cf. 6. 34. 7 *arguto Catullo*; 3. 58. 13 *argutus anser* (see note there); Hor. Ep. 2. 2.90 *qui*('how')*minus argutos vexat furor iste poetas ?* — **Nemesis** succeeded Delia as Tibullus's mistress; cf. Ov. Am. 3.9.31 *sic Nemesis longum, sic Delia nomen habebunt.*

8. Lesbia: Clodia, wife of Q. Caecilius Metellus Celer, sister of Cicero's bitter enemy, P. Clodius Pulcher. She was to Catullus "the mastering passion of his life" (Merrill). — **dictavit**: cf. Anthol. Lat. II. 937. 1 *scribenti mi dictat Amor monstratque Cupido*; Ov. Am. 2. 1. 38 *carmina purpureus quae mihi dictat Amor.* — **docte**: cf. 1. 61. 1 N.

non me Paeligni nec spernet Mantua vatem,
10   si qua Corinna mihi, si quis Alexis erit.

76

"Dic verum mihi, Marce, dic amabo;
nil est quod magis audiam libenter".
Sic et cum recitas tuos libellos
et causam quotiens agis clientis,
5   oras, Gallice, me rogasque semper.
Durum est me tibi, quod petis, negare;
vero verius ergo quid sit audi:
verum, Gallice, non libenter audis.

9. **Paeligni** and **Mantua** stand for those who appreciate good poetry. Ovid was born at Sulmo in the region of the Paeligni (1.61.6), Vergil in the neighborhood of Andes near Mantua.

10. **Corinna**: the name under which the mistress of Ovid passed. —**Alexis**: see 8. 55. 12 N.

76. M. declines to favor Gallicus with the honest criticism of his verses and legal speeches which Gallicus (dishonestly) invites. — Meter: § 49.

1. **Marce**: the praenomen was used in familiar address. Cf. 5. 63. 1–2 *"quid sentis", inquis, "de nostris, Marce, libellis?" sic me solli-*

citus, Pontice, saepe rogas.—**amabo,** *I beg of you, please, do* (lit. 'I shall love you, if', etc.). The word thus used belongs to the *sermo familiaris*; it occurs chiefly in comedy, being used there by women or in speeches addressed to women. Cf. Apoll. Sid. C. 9. 1 *dic, dic, quod peto, Magne, dic, amabo.* Perhaps M. is hinting that Gallicus is effeminate.

7. For the diæresis see § 49, d.— **vero verius,** *truer than the truth itself,* has a proverbial ring; cf. 6. 30. 6 *vis dicam tibi veriora veris?* Sen. Ep. 66. 8 *nihil invenies rectius recto, non magis quam verius vero, quam temperato temperatius;* Q. N. 2. 34. 2 *vero verius nihil est.*

LIBER IX

6

Dicere de Libycis reduci tibi gentibus, Afer,
  continuis volui quinque diebus "Have";
"Non vacat" aut "dormit" dictum est bis terque reverso:
  iam satis est: non vis, Afer, havere: vale.

10

Nubere vis Prisco: non miror, Paula; sapisti.
  ducere te non vult Priscus: et ille sapit.

11

Nomen cum violis rosisque natum,

6. 'I have wanted to congratulate you, Afer, on your safe return to Rome, but can never gain admission to your presence. If I may not say to you "How do you do?", let me say "Farewell"'. — Meter: § 48.

  1. reduci: cf. Verg. A. 1. 390–391 *namque tibi reduces socios classemque relatam nuntio.* — **Afer:** perhaps a rich freedman, who has returned to Rome after revisiting his native land.

  2. Have: the imv. serves as a noun in acc., object of *dicere*, 1.

  3. Non . . . dormit: words of the *ostiarius*; cf. 2. 5. 5 N.; 4. 8. 4 N.; 5. 22. 10. — **bis terque**, in the light of 2, must = *identidem.* — **reverso:** sc. *mihi.*

  4. havere: perhaps a pun on *Afer* is intended (spite of the difference in quantity: see on 7. 36. 6). — **vale:** cf. 5. 66. 2 N.

10. About two people who show worldly wisdom in desiring things diametrically opposed to each other. Priscus was well-to-do and apparently of high social standing; Paula is apparently the *mulier infamis* of 1. 74, etc. — Meter: § 48.

  1. Nubere: see 8. 12. 2 N. Cf. 10. 8. 1–2 *nubere Paula cupit nobis, ego ducere Paulam nolo: anus est. Vellem, si magis esset anus.*

  11. Flavius Earinus was a freedman and eunuch of Domitian, and his cup-bearer or *praegustator.* Here, as in 9. 12; 9. 13, M. plays upon his name. The play was rendered possible by the fact that *Earinus* could be referred to ἐαρινός (from ἔαρ = Latin *ver*, 'spring'). See Saintsbury 1. 263. — Meter: § 49.

  1. cum . . . natum: i.e. in spring. Cf. 9. 12. 1–2 *nomen habes teneri quod tempora nuncupat anni,*

quo pars optima nominatur anni,
Hyblam quod sapit Atticosque flores,
quod nidos olet alitis superbae,
5   nomen nectare dulcius beato,
quo mallet Cybeles puer vocari
et qui pocula temperat Tonanti,
quod si Parrhasia sones in aula,
respondent Veneres Cupidinesque,
10   nomen nobile, molle, delicatum
versu dicere non rudi volebam,
sed tu, syllaba contumax, rebellas.

cum breve Cecropiae ver populantur apes; 9. 16. 4 *nomine qui signat tempora verna suo.* — **violis rosisque**: cf. Ov. Tr. 4. 1. 57 *vere prius flores, aestu numerabis aristas.*

2. pars . . . anni: as coming into sharp contrast, both within and without doors, with winter, which was *horrida* in an especial degree to the Romans; cf. 9. 13. 2 N.; *horridus . . . December*, 7. 36. 5. See Lowell's essay, A Good Word for Winter.

3. Hyblam . . . flores: see 5. 39. 3; 5. 37. 10.

4. nidos . . . superbae: cf. 5. 37. 13; 6. 55. 2 N.

5. nectare dulcius: proverbial; cf. Apoll. Sid. C. 23. 288 *suco nectaris esse dulciorem*; Otto s.v. *Nectar.* Paukstadt, 20, sees here a reflection of Catull. 99. 2 *saviolum dulci dulcius ambrosia.* For *nectare* see 4. 32. 2 N. — **beato**: perhaps *wealthy* (*nectar* is used of the drink of gods and of the wines of the rich: see 1. 103. 3 N.), perhaps *happy*, in the sense of *causing* happiness (cf. Hor. Ep. 1. 5. 16–20).

6. Cybeles puer: Attis; cf. 7. 73. 3 N. For the form *Cybeles* cf. 1. 70. 10 N.; 5. 13. 7.

7. qui . . . Tonanti: Ganymedes; see 2. 43. 13–14. Cf. 9. 16. 6 *nec* (Earinus) *Ganymedeas mallet habere comas.* 'Attis and Ganymedes would gladly exchange names with Earinus'.

8. quod: sc. *nomen.* — **Parrhasia . . . aula**: cf. 7. 99. 3 N.; 9. 12. 8 (*Earinus, nomen*) *quod decet in sola Caesaris esse domo*; 9. 16. 3 *ille puer tota domino gratissimus aula*, also said of Earinus.

9. respondent: the ind. after *sones*, 8, is most effective. — **Veneres Cupidinesque**: another echo of Catullus. See Catull. 3. 1 *lugete, o Veneres Cupidinesque*; 13. 12 *donarunt Veneres Cupidinesque. Veneres* is *pluralis maiestatis* (see on 1. 70. 5); Venus is the incarnation of all charms and graces. See also on 11. 13. 6.

11. non rudi: i.e. polished, refined, perfect, fitting the name.

12. contumax, *stubborn, unyielding*, defying every effort to work *Ĕărĭnŭs, Ĕărĭnĕ*, into hendecasyllabic verses (both forms are impossible also in hexameters). *Syllaba* may refer to the *first* syllable of the name *Earinus* (cf. 13–15), or may be collective sing., used

Dicunt *Eiarinon* tamen poetae,
　　sed Graeci, quibus est nihil negatum
15　et quos Ἄρες Ἄρες decet sonare :
　　nobis non licet esse tam disertis,
　　qui Musas colimus severiores.

13

Si daret autumnus mihi nomen, Oporinos essem,
　　horrida si brumae sidera, Chimerinos ;
dictus ab aestivo Therinos tibi mense vocarer :
　　tempora cui nomen verna dedere quis est ?

15

Inscripsit tumulis septem scelerata virorum
　　se fecisse Chloe ; quid pote simplicius ?

of hendecasyllabic verse in general. In the latter case cf. 1. 61. 1; 10. 9. 1 *undenis pedibusque syllabisque.*

13-14. poetae . . . Graeci: the Greek poets used the form εἰαρινός, and so escaped the metrical difficulties of ἐαρινός (see on 12).

15. Ἄρες Ἄρες: cf. Hom. Il. 5. 31 Ἄρες, Ἄρες βροτολοιγέ, μιαιφόνε, τειχεσιπλῆτα, with Leaf's note. Cf. Lucil. 354-355 (Marx) *scribemus "pacem: placide; Ianum, aridum: acetum",* Ἄρες, Ἄρες *Graeci ut faciunt.* M. forgets that Roman poets handle the quantity of proper names with great freedom, esp. in names of Greek origin; cf. e.g. Verg. E. 6. 44 *clamassent, ut litus "Hylā, Hylā" omne sonaret.*

17. Musas . . . severiores: i.e. poetry more subject to rule, less disposed to lend itself to poetic license. — **severiores** = *more austere, more strait-laced.*

13. As in 9. 11, the point lies in the difficulty of putting the name of Flavius Earinus into verse. Here

Earinus is represented as speaking. — Meter: § 48.

1. Oporinos: cf. ὀπωρινός. ὀπώρα = the latter part of the summer (late July, August, and early September).

2. horrida: see 7. 36. 5 N.; 9. 11. 2 N. — sidera, *season, weather.* Cf. Amm. Marc. 27. 12. 12 *sidere flagrante brumali.* — **Chimerinos:** cf. χειμερινός. Χειμών = *hiems.*

3. Therinos: cf. θερινός. θέρος = *aestas.*

4. tempora . . . dedere: cf. 9. 11. Introd.

15. On poisoning in ancient Italy see on 4. 69. 2; 8. 43. — Meter: § 48.

1. tumulis: see 6. 52. 1 N. — virorum: see 7. 88. 4 N.

2. se fecisse: the point lies in a play on *fecisse.* In accordance with the usual form Chloe would have had cut on the monuments of the *septem viri* the words CHLOE FECIT (sc. *tumulum, monumentum*). M., perhaps, intimates that

18

Est mihi — sitque precor longum te praeside, Caesar —
   rus minimum parvi sunt et in urbe lares.
Sed de valle brevi quas det sitientibus hortis
   curva laboratas antlia tollit aquas :
5 sicca domus queritur nullo se rore foveri,
   cum mihi vicino Marcia fonte sonet.

the more appropriate ellipsis for such a poisoner would be *scelera*. But in certain contexts *feci* is almost a technical term, 'I am guilty'; cf. Iuv. 6. 638 ff. *sed clamat Pontia "Feci, confiteor, puerisque meis aconita paravi . . . facinus tamen ipsa peregi*"; 4. 12 *et tamen alter si fecisset idem*. — **simplicius**, *truer*; cf. *nivea simplicitate*, 8. 73. 2 N.

18. The poet petitions Domitian for the privilege of tapping the Aqua Marcia (without the payment of water rent) for his house in town. See §§ 8; 10. — Meter: § 48.

1. Est . . . Caesar: cf. 1. 108. 1–2 *est tibi — sitque precor multos crescatque per annos — pulchra . . . domus*. M. is praying (1) that the *rus* may long be his, (2) that Domitian may have a long reign. — **longum:** sc. *mihi*; *longum* in sense = *diu*; cf. 1. 31. 7–8 *utque tuis longum dominusque puerque fruantur muneribus*.

2. rus minimum: the Nomentanum; see 2. 38. 1 N.; 4. 79. 1. — **parvi . . . lares:** a small house will make small demand upon the great aqueduct. The chiasmus, which brings *minimum* and *parvi* together, emphasizes M.'s poverty. — **lares:** see 1. 70. 2 N.; 1. 76. 2. At this time even the plural of *lar* was used of a single house, interchangeably with *penates*; cf. 8; 9. 61. 5, 15. For M.'s city houses see § 11.

3. de valle brevi: i.e. from a spring or stream in a vale on the

Nomentanum. Iuv. 3. 226–227 *hortulus hic* (in the country) *puteusque brevis nec reste movendus in tenuis plantas facili diffunditur haustu* is similar in language, but the tone is quite different; see on 4.

4–6. 'But, though I can get water on my country estate (only, to be sure with great labor), I have none at all in my city house'. — **laboratas . . . aquas:** 'though the valley from which my water supply comes is not deep (3), serious toil is after all necessary to raise the water'. — **antlia** (cf. ἀντλία) here prob. = *tolleno*, an old-fashioned well-sweep, which would bend (*curva*) with the weight of the full bucket. — **sicca:** the city house (*domus*) is absolutely without water supply. — **rore** = *aqua*, as often in poetry; cf. Verg. A. 6. 230–231 *spargens rore levi et ramo felicis olivae lustravit . . . viros*; Hor. C. 3. 4. 61–62 (Apollo) *qui rore puro Castaliae lavit crinis solutos*. The word suggests that the supply is limited or that water is gently applied in some way. — **foveri:** often used of applying healing (prop. 'warm') remedies to the human body; then used generally as = *freshen, cheer*, etc. — **cum**, *although*. — **Marcia:** the aqueduct known as Aqua Marcia, which, because of the poor quality of the water supplied by the Anio Vetus and the inadequacy of the Aqua Appia, Q. Marcius Rex was empowered to construct in 144 B.C.

Quam dederis nostris, Auguste, penatibus undam,
    Castalis haec nobis aut Iovis imber erit.

19

Laudas balnea versibus trecentis
cenantis bene Pontici, Sabelle :
vis cenare, Sabelle, non lavari.

22

Credis ob haec me, Pastor, opes fortasse rogare
    propter quae populus crassaque turba rogat,
ut Setina meos consumat gleba ligones
    et sonet innumera compede Tuscus ager,

Its water was highly esteemed. — **fonte**: one of the many fountains which the aqueducts supplied. — **sonet**: his inability to use the water is the more exasperating in that he can hear it as it leaps or spouts.

7–8. **Quam . . . undam . . . haec**: the antec. is thus regularly incorporated in the relative clause when the relative clause precedes. — **Auguste**: regular title of the reigning emperor. — **penatibus**: see on *lares*, 2; cf. 4. 64. 29. — **undam** = *aquam*, *lympham*, a use frequent in the poets (with the suggestion of plentiful supply; contrast note on *rore*, 5); cf. 6. 42. 19–20 *quae* (the Marcia) *tam candida, tam serena lucet ut nullas ibi suspiceris undas.* — **Castalis . . . nobis**: i.e. not only because of the clearness and purity of the water, but because the material help will inspire poetic effort. M. is here referring in complimentary terms to Domitian's literary aspirations; in 5. 6. 18 he calls Domitian *dominus novem sororum.* — **Iovis imber**: cf. 5. 8. 1 N.; 8. 24.

19. 'Sabellus is a dinner-hunter'. Cf. **2. 11.** — Meter: § 49.

1. **balnea**: see 2. 14. 11–12 N. — **trecentis**: cf. 1. 43. 1 N.

22. M. professes to despise the reasons which prompt the vulgar crowd to crave wealth. His own reasons for desiring it, which are made more forceful by his abruptness (16), may be after all only a hint of what he hopes that others will do for him. — Meter: § 48.

1. **haec**: i.e. desire for landed estates, fine furniture and plate, outward display, etc., described in 3–14.

2. **populus** here = *vulgus,* those who see in wealth only means for vulgar enjoyment. Of this class the rich freedmen afforded daily a lively illustration. See App. — **crassa**, *coarse, gross, thick-headed.*

3. **Setina**: see 4. 64. 33–34 N. This word is the most important in this vs., which = 'that the soil which wears out . . . may be that of Setia itself'.— **gleba**: see 5. 13. 7 N. — **ligones** lit. = *hoes, mattocks*, but, as in 4. 64. 32, carries a secondary reference to the slaves who handle them.

4. **sonet . . . ager**: the great estates were tilled by slaves, the

5   ut Mauri Libycis centum stent dentibus orbes
          et crepet in nostris aurea lamna toris,
     nec labris nisi magna meis crystalla terantur
          et faciant nigras nostra Falerna nives,
     ut canusinatus nostro Syrus assere sudet
10   et mea sit culto sella cliente frequens,
     aestuet ut nostro madidus conviva ministro,

least reliable of whom by day worked in chain-gangs and were loaded with fetters, and at night were housed in horrible quarters (frequently underground) known as *ergastula*. — **sonet**: cf. Tib. 2. 6. 25–26 *spes etiam valida solatur compede vinctum: crura sonant ferro, sed canit inter opus.* — **innumera compede**: the slaves on the great estates (*latifundia*) were numbered by the hundred. For *innumerus* with the sing. cf. 8. 53. 2 *innumero quotiens silva leone furit*; see also on 1. 70. 6. — **compede**: cf. Ov. Pont. 1. 6. 31–32 *haec facit, ut vivat fossor quoque compede vinctus liberaque a ferro crura futura putet*; Iuv. 11. 80; Tib. 2. 6. 25, cited on *sonet* above.

5. **Mauri . . . orbes**: see on 2. 43. 9; 7. 48. 1. — **Libycis . . . dentibus**: see on 1. 72. 4; 2. 43. 9; 5. 37. 5.

6. **crepet . . . lamna**: the exposed parts of the *lectus* were veneered with expensive woods or covered with plates of gold or silver (*lamnae*) or with gold leaf (*bractea*). But this interpretation makes *crepet* difficult to explain; how could firmly fastened *lamnae* rattle? Perhaps M. means 'that gold plate may rattle over my dinner-couches (tables)'. For this use of *lamna* see Ov. F. 1. 208 *at levis argenti lammina crimen erat* (i.e. to own silver plate, thin plate, too, of little

weight, once exposed one to criticism). In this case *lamna* suggests the delicacy and value of the plate. — **toris** = *lectis*, or rather *mensis*; see 2. 16. 1, 3.

7. **nec . . . terantur** = *et nulla* (*pocula*) *nisi magna*, etc., 'that no goblet, save huge goblets of pure crystal, shall be fretted by my lips'. — **crystalla** (i.e. *pocula*): see 1. 53. 6; 10. 66. 5.

8. **nigras . . . nives**: cf. 8. 55. 14 N.; 8. 77. 5 *candida nigrescant vetulo crystalla Falerno. Nigras* is pred. accusative.

9. **canusinatus**: i.e. attired in a *paenula* (see 1. 103. 5–6 N.) of red or dark Canusian wool, the ordinary livery of *lecticarii*. The region about Canusium in Apulia produced excellent wool; cf. 14. 127; Suet. Ner. 30 *canusinatis mulionibus*. Even the slaves of the rich wear luxurious clothing. — **nostro . . . sudet**: i.e. 'sweat under my litter-poles'. For the sedan-chair (*lectica*, *sella*) see on 2. 57. 6; 3. 46. 4. — **Syrus**: Syrians and Cappadocians were much in demand as *lecticarii*, though some preferred Medes or Germans.

10. **sit . . . frequens**: i.e. accompanied by a great retinue of well-clad clients; cf. 2. 57. — **culto**, *natty*, *well-dressed*. — **frequens**, *thronged*; see on 5. 13. 3.

11–12. **aestuet . . . velis**: i.e. be able to give a great banquet where

quem permutatum nec Ganymede velis,
ut lutulenta linat Tyrias mihi mula lacernas
et Massyleum virga gubernet ecum.

15   Est nihil ex istis : superos ac sidera testor.
Ergo quid ? ut donem, Pastor, et aedificem.

the cup-bearers shall be the most beautiful (and expensive) boys the slave market can afford. Cf. the picture in 8. 55. 13–16. — **aestuet,** *fall in love with.* — **quem . . . velis:** 'whom you would decline to exchange even for Ganymedes'. — **permutatum . . . Ganymede:** verbs of exchanging (*mutare, vertere,* and compounds) take properly an acc. of the thing surrendered, an abl. of the thing taken in exchange. The abl. is instr.; the idea is that of changing one thing by means of another (substituted for it). In practice, however, either thing is put in the acc., and the other, of course, stands then in the abl. See also on 1.41. 4–5. — With **quem . . . velis** cf. 2. 43. 13; Iuv. 5. 56–57 *flos Asiae ante ipsum pretio maiore paratus quam fuit et Tulli census pugnacis et Anci.* — **nec:** see on 1. 109. 20.

13–14. The mule held much the same place as a road animal in ancient times as the horse has held in more recent days (cf. e.g. Hor. S. 1. 6. 104–105), and still plays an important rôle in classic lands, esp. in Greece. To avoid the fate mentioned here people rode much in the *gestatio*; cf. 1. 12, with notes; Iuv. 7. 178–181. — **Massyleum . . . ecum:** a horse of Numidian blood and training; cf. 10. 14. 2; 12. 24. 6. The Massyli occupied what is to-day eastern Algeria, part of ancient Numidia. The Numidians were famous horsemen, as the Romans had come to know,

esp. since Hannibal's time; Numidian slaves were much in demand as drivers and outriders. See Fried. SG. 2. 35 ff. The Massylian horses were perfectly broken, being taught to obey the whip, spur, and voice without the aid of bridle. Cf. Luc. 4. 682–683 *et gens, quae nudo residens Massylia dorso ora levi flectit frenorum nescia virga.* The ancients generally appear to have depended more on the whip than do modern horsemen. See App. — **gubernet:** sc. *mihi*, from 13.

15. sidera: see 7. 92. 9 N. — **ac:** the only occurrence of *ac* in M. On *atque* and *ac* in Juvenal and Martial see Lease, Gildersleeve Studies, 412 ff.

16. ut . . . aedificem: these words are to be interpreted in part simply, at their face value, in part as a hint to Pastor; see Introd. M. seems to be speaking somewhat bitterly; his Nomentanum and his city house were both modest; see 9. 18, with notes. The mania for building great town houses and extensive villas in the mountains and on the seashore was acute; see Fried. SG. 3. 107; 3. 58, with notes; Iuv. 14. 86–95; Sen. Ep. 89. 21; Hor. C. 3. 1. 33–37.

26. The man whose poetic ability is here lauded was afterward the emperor Nerva. Pliny, in defending himself for dabbling in verse (Ep. 5. 3. 5), after citing a number of well-known names, adds: *et si non sufficiunt exempla privata, divum Iulium, divum Augustum,*

26

Audet facundo qui carmina mittere Nervae
pallida donabit glaucina, Cosme, tibi,
Paestano violas et cana ligustra colono,
Hyblaeis apibus Corsica mella dabit :
5   sed tamen et parvae nonnulla est gratia Musae ;
appetitur posito vilis oliva lupo.
Nec tibi sit mirum, modici quod conscia vatis
iudicium metuit nostra Thalia tuum :

divum Nervam, Tiberium Caesarem (decuit poesis). See § 20. —
Meter: § 48.

1. facundo characterizes Nerva
as poet; cf. 1. 61. 8 N. It may contain an additional compliment; the
grandfather and father of Nerva
had been distinguished jurists, an
ability which Nerva himself probably shared. Cf. 8. 70. 1 quanta quies
placidi tanta est facundia Nervae.

2. pallida . . . glaucina: an oil
or perfume of some kind, made,
perhaps, from the plant called
glaucium, celandine; see Plin. N.H.
27. 83. — Cosme: one might infer
that Cosmus stood at this time at
the head of perfumers in Rome;
cf. 1. 87. 2 pastillos Cosmi luxuriosa
voras; 3. 55. 1–2; 3. 82. 26 et Cosmi-
anis ipse fusus ampullis; 6. 55. 3 N.;
11. 15. 5; 14. 59. 2; 14. 146. 1; Iuv.
8. 85–86 dignus morte perit, cenet
licet ostrea centum Gaurana et Cosmi
toto mergatur aëno. Donabit . . .
tibi thus suggests a superfluous,
senseless act, like 'carrying coals
to Newcastle'. Further, pallida
must mean that yellow (see on 1.
41. 4; 8. 14. 1) glaucina was inferior; the adj. will then play the rôle
sustained by Corsica, 4.

3. Paestano . . . colono: see
on 5. 37. 9; 6. 80. 6. — violas . . .
ligustra: not likely to be appreciated

by one who had the finest of red
roses. — cana ligustra: cf. Ov.
M. 13. 789 candidior folio nivei,
Galatea, ligustri; Verg. E. 2. 18 alba
ligustra cadunt.

4. Hyblaeis apibus: see on
5. 39. 3; 7. 88. 8. — Corsica mella:
Corsican honey was so inferior that
the bees of Hybla would despise
it; cf. 11. 42. 3–4; Ov. Am. 1. 12.
9–10; Plin. N. H. 30. 28 cum melle
Corsico, quod asperrimum habetur.

5–6. sed . . . lupo: 'but still
there is a demand for common
products; fine fish and common
relishes may go together; though
one cannot rival Nerva, he need
not maintain absolute silence'. —
et = etiam, even. — appetitur
. . . lupo: i.e. people who rave
over the lupus do not think the
less of the vilis oliva. — posito:
cf. 1. 43. 2 N. — lupo: cf. 2. 37. 4;
2. 40. 4; 10. 30. 21; 11. 49. 9 nunc
et emam grandemve lupum mullumve bilibrem.

7. tibi: Nerva. — modici . . .
vatis: to our feeling modici carries
the main part of the thought; we
should say, 'conscious of the
mediocrity of the poet'. — vatis:
Martial.

8. iudicium: critical acumen,
literary taste. — nostra Thalia:
see on 4. 8. 12; 8. 3. 9.

ipse tuas etiam veritus Nero dicitur aures,
10   lascivum iuvenis cum tibi lusit opus.

30

Cappadocum saevis Antistius occidit oris
    Rusticus.   O tristi crimine terra nocens !
Rettulit ossa sinu cari Nigrina mariti
    et questa est longas non satis esse vias,
5   cumque daret sanctam tumulis quibus invidet urnam,
    visa sibi est rapto bis viduata viro.

46

Gellius aedificat semper : modo limina ponit,
    nunc foribus claves aptat emitque seras,
nunc has, nunc illas reficit mutatque fenestras.
    Dum tantum aedificet, quidlibet ille facit,
5   oranti nummos ut dicere possit amico
    unum illud verbum Gellius " Aedifico ".

---

9. ipse . . . aures: the efforts of Nero to pass for poet and musician are well known.

10. lascivum . . . opus: cf. on I. 4. 8; 4. 14. 12. — **iuvenis,** *in the days of his youth.* Nero was but thirty-one when he died. — **lusit:** cf. I. 113. I N.; 8. 3. 2; Hor. C. 4. 9. 9 *si quid olim lusit Anacreon.*

30. See 4. 75, with notes. — Meter: § 48.

1. saevis . . . oris: cf. 6. 85. 3–4 (of another man) *impia Cappadocum tellus et numine laevo visa tibi cineres reddit et ossa patri.*

3. Rettulit . . . sinu: she assumed personal charge of the cinerary urn, carrying it as something too precious to be intrusted to another. So Agrippina, the widow of Germanicus, bore his ashes from Syria to Rome; see Tac. Ann. 2. 75.

4. longas . . . vias: it was a last mournful privilege — too soon over — to bear and guard the ashes of her dead. For the rhyme see § 48, c.

5. sanctam: because it contains the ashes of a *sanctus homo.* — **invidet:** on account of their new acquisition, her husband's ashes.

6. bis viduata: first, when he died, again, when she must finally surrender his ashes.

46. 'Gellius seeks to hide his parsimony by saying "I am building and so have no spare cash"'. On the passion for building see 9. 22. 16 N. — Meter: § 48.

1–2. modo . . . nunc: either *modo . . . modo* or *nunc . . . nunc* (3) is more regular.

4. Dum tantum = *dummodo;* cf. *tantum,* 'only', with subjv. in 10. 34. 6; 11. 84. 12.

48

Heredem cum me partis tibi, Garrice, quartae
   per tua iurares sacra caputque tuum,
credidimus — quis enim damnet sua vota libenter ? —
   et spem muneribus fovimus usque datis,
5 inter quae rari Laurentem ponderis aprum
   misimus : Aetola de Calydone putes.
At tu continuo populumque patresque vocasti ;
   ructat adhuc aprum pallida Roma meum :
ipse ego — quis credat ? — conviva nec ultimus haesi,
10   sed nec costa data est caudave missa mihi.
De quadrante tuo quid sperem, Garrice ? nulla
   de nostro nobis uncia venit apro.

48. M. humorously relates how, though he threw out his best bait as a *captator* (see 1. 10; 5. 39; 6. 63), he himself was caught.— Meter: § 48.

   1. **Heredem . . . quartae** = *heredem ex quadrante.* A sole heir was *heres ex asse*; cf. 3. 10. 5 *idem te moriens heredem ex asse reliquit.* — **me:** sc. *fore.* — **Garrice:** see App.

   3. **quis . . . vota:** i.e. what man would not give his hopes a chance ?

   4. **spem:** i.e. of a fat legacy. — **fovimus,** *nursed*; cf. 9. 18. 5 N. — **usque:** as in 6. 51. 3.

   5. **rari . . . aprum:** the flavor of the Laurentian boar was not, however, accounted as fine as that of the Umbrian and Tuscan animals. Cf. Hor. S. 2. 4. 42 *nam Laurens malus est, ulvis et harundine pinguis.* For the boar at the *cena* see 1. 43. 2 N.

   6. **Aetola . . . putes:** the animal made one think of the Calydonian boar, that ravaged Aetolia about Calydon until it was slain by Meleager. Cf. 13. 93 (*aper*) *qui Diomedeis metuendus saetiger agris*

Aetola cecidit cuspide talis erat; Iuv. 5. 114–116 *ante ipsum . . . flavi dignus ferro Meleagri spumat aper.*

   7. **populumque patresque:** as if the dinner were an imperial banquet to which the mob, as well as the élite, were bidden; cf. 8. 49. 7–8 *vescitur omnis eques tecum populusque patresque et capit ambrosias cum duce Roma dapes.*

   8. **pallida:** either because of overeating or from the disgusting but common use of emetics. See App.

   9. **ipse ego:** doubly emphatiç: ‘I, the one man of all who deserved to be invited, was left out!’ — **nec** = *ne . . . quidem*; see on 1. 109. 20. — **haesi:** sc. *lecto.* The word suggests that not even the smallest part of a couch was given to M.

   10. **nec:** as in 9. — **costa . . . cauda:** the meanest parts. Verses 9–10 = ‘Not only was I not invited, but not even a morsel was sent to me to my house’.

   11–12. **De quadrante:** see on 1. — **tuo** and **nostro** are the important words, standing in emphatic

52

Si credis mihi, Quinte, quod mereris,
natalis, Ovidi, tuas Aprilis
ut nostras amo Martias Kalendas.
Felix utraque lux diesque nobis,
5   signandi melioribus lapillis !
hic vitam tribuit, sed hic amicum.
Plus dant, Quinte, mihi tuae Kalendae.

59

In Saeptis Mamurra diu multumque vagatus,
hic ubi Roma suas aurea vexat opes,

contrast; **uncia** too is important.
The whole = 'Why should I hope
to get the whole of the promised
fourth of *your* property? You gave
me not one twelfth of *my* boar!'

52. M. declares that the birthday of his friend Q. Ovidius has
brought him more than has his
own. Q. Ovidius (§ 20) was a country neighbor of M. at Nomentum.
Fried. thinks it probable that he
and M. were clients of Seneca and
owed to him their little estates.
It is said that Ovidius voluntarily
accompanied into exile another
friend, Caesonius Maximus, who
was banished in connection with
Piso's conspiracy. See Fried. SG.
3. 443.—Meter: § 49.

1. quod mereris: freely, *as you
deserve.* Strictly, however, *quod* is
the rel. pronoun; its antec. is the
clause *natalis . . . Kalendas,* 2–3.

2. natalis: see 7. 86. 1 N.—
Aprilis: sc. *Kalendas.*

3. nostras . . . Kalendas: § 3.

4–5. Felix, *lucky,* and so worthy
of the *meliores lapilli.*—**melioribus
lapillis:** i.e. with white counters;
unlucky days were *dies atri.* The
custom of marking lucky days with
white stones or white marks (cf.

Eng. 'red-letter days') and unlucky
days with black marks was regarded as of eastern origin; it was
referred to the Scythians, the Cre-
tans, and the Thracians. Cf. e.g. 8.
45. 2; 12. 34. 5–7; Pers. 2. 1–2 *hunc,
Macrine, diem numera meliore la-
pillo qui tibi labentis apponit candidus annos;* Plin. Ep. 6. 11. 3 *o diem
laetum notandumque mihi candi-
dissimo calculo;* Tib. 1. 7. 63–64 *at
tu, natalis, multos celebrande per
annos, candidior semper candidior-
que veni;* Catull. 107. 6 *o lucem
candidiore nota;* 68. 148; Hor. C.
1. 36. 10; λευκή ψῆφος; German *Den
Tag will ich mir im Kalender rot
anstreichen.* — **signandi:** the pl. is
natural enough, since (*uterque*)
dies, 4, virtually = *ambo dies.*

6. hic . . . hic: for the more
frequent *hic . . . illic.*

7. Plus: i.e. than my own.

59. A shopping picture, whose
scene is the great bazaar, the Saepta
Iulia (see 2. 14. 5 N.). A pretended
purchaser (a man!) makes endless
trouble for the salesfolk but in the
end buys next to nothing.— Meter:
§ 48.

2. aurea: in the Saepta the
golden splendor of Rome could be

inspexit molles pueros oculisque comedit,
   non hos, quos primae prostituere casae,
5 sed quos arcanae servant tabulata catastae
   et quos non populus nec mea turba videt.
Inde satur mensas et opertos exuit orbes
   expositumque alte pingue poposcit ebur,
et testudineum mensus quater hexaclinon

seen, as it were, massed. Cf. Ov.
A. A. 3. 113–114 *nunc aurea Roma
est et domiti magnas possidet orbis
opes*; Aus. Ord. Urb. Nob. 1 *prima
urbes inter, divum domus, aurea
Roma.* — **vexat**, *harries*, i.e. subjects to grievous wear and tear at
the whim of buyers. Rome is said
to do what her sons do; see on 1.
15. 7.

3. inspexit: cf. 6. 82. 2 N.; 10.
80. 1–2 *plorat Eros, quotiens macu-
losae pocula murrae inspicit* (in the
Saepta) *aut pueros nobiliusve citrum.* — **molles**, *soft, effeminate.*
Such beautiful boys were serviceable as cup-bearers and pages (9.
22. 11–12 N.). They commanded
fabulous prices. — **oculis . . .
comedit:** cf. 1. 96. 12 *spectat oculis
devorantibus draucos.*

4. quos . . . casae: whom the
slave-pens, first seen on entering
the bazaar, exposed to the vulgar
gaze.

5. arcanae . . . catastae: the
catasta (κατάστασις) was the scaf-
fold or elevated stage on which the
slave was exposed for sale. Cf.
10. 76. 3–4. To render inspection
easier, it was sometimes made to
revolve. On this *arcana catasta*
'private sales' took place. The
catasta, if movable, was probably
made of wood. But see below, on
tabulata. — **servant**, *reserve.* —
tabulata: prop. 'planking', 'floor-
ing'; then, often, 'story' (of a

building, siege tower, etc.). Perhaps, then, the pl. *tabulata* looks to
the various stories of the building,
each of which had its *catasta*; in
that case the *primae catastae* were
on the ground floor.

6. populus almost = *vulgus*; cf.
9. 22. 2. — **mea turba:** i.e. 'common folks like myself'.

7. satur: i.e. with looking (cf.
oculis . . . comedit, 3). — **opertos
. . . orbes:** see 2. 43. 9; 7. 48. 1.
The expensive tables were covered
with *gausape* to keep them from
being scratched; cf. 14. 139. 1 *no-
bilius villosa tegant tibi lintea citrum.* — **exuit:** Mamurra has the
covers removed that he may properly inspect the tables.

8. expositum . . . ebur: he has
the ivory supports, that hung above
the tables, taken down. See 1. 72.
4 N.; 2. 43. 9; 5. 37. 5. — **alte:** the
harder they are to get down, the
better Mamurra is pleased. — **pingue:** *greasy, oily*, with the oil with
which the ivory was rubbed and
polished.

**9. testudineum . . . hexa-
clinon:** the *orbis* required a different sort of dinner couch from
that needed with the old-fashioned
rectangular *mensa.* Hence a new
style of *lectus*, called *sigma* (from
its resemblance to the Greek letter
C, Sigma) or *stibadium*, was forthcoming. The *sigma* was not restricted to three persons; cf. 10.

10   ingemuit citro non satis esse suo.
    Consuluit nares an olerent aera Corinthon
        culpavit statuas et, Polyclite, tuas,
    et turbata brevi questus crystallina vitro
        murrina signavit seposuitque decem.
15   Expendit veteres calathos et si qua fuerunt
        pocula Mentorea nobilitata manu,
    et viridis picto gemmas numeravit in auro,

48.6. The *hexaclinon* could accommodate six. That the *sigma* might in elegance match the *orbis*, it was inlaid or veneered with silver, ivory, or tortoise-shell. Cf. Dig. 32. 100. 4 *lectos testudineos pedibus inargentatos.* — **quater**: as if he could not give up the thought of buying. *Ingemuit*, 10, also marks his pretended interest.

10. ingemuit ... esse: for construction see on 1. 70. 8. — **citro =** *orbi*. See on 2. 43. 9.

11. Consuluit ... Corinthon: the manufacture of the ware known as *aes Corinthium* was even in antiquity one of the lost arts. Naturally, imitations were sold. Connoisseurs professed to identify the genuine ware by its peculiar smell. The story of the origin of this ware given in Plin. N. H. 34. 6 (cf. 34. 8 on the *tria genera*) appears fanciful. See Beck. 1. 43. — **Corinthon**: acc. of effect (inner object); see on 5. 66. 2.

12. culpavit: perhaps to air his special knowledge of art; perhaps he questions their genuineness, to get a better price. For Polyclitus see 8. 50. 2 N.

13. brevi ... vitro, *by a speck of common glass.*

14. murrina (*vasa*): vessels of *murra.* Some hold that *murra* was fluorspar, others that it was red and white agate (the most probable

view), still others argue that it was porcelain. It is clear from Plin. N. H. 33. 5 that it was a mineral substance found in the East; hence it cannot have been porcelain (which is a manufactured product). Pompey the Great first brought such vessels to Rome as part of the booty of the Mithridatic War. Enormous sums were paid for pure *murrina*; Nero paid for a *capis murrina* 1,000,000 *sestertii*. Cf. 3. 26. 2–3 *aurea solus habes, murrina solus habes, Massica solus habes et Opimi Caecuba solus*; Iuv. 7. 133 *empturus pueros, argentum, murrina, villas.* — **signavit**: i.e. he had them marked with his seal. — **decem**: an important word; he acted as if he were going to make a very elaborate purchase.

15. Expendit: i.e. he held in his hand and examined critically. — **veteres** is emphatic; age added value. Cf. 8. 6, with notes.— **calathos**: see 8. 6. 16 N. — **si qua =** *quaecumque, omnia quae.* The words imply that such cups were scarce.

16. Mentorea ... manu: see 4. 39. 5 N.

17. viridis ... gemmas: i.e. emeralds (*smaragdi*), which were in high esteem; cf. 4. 28. 4; 5. 11. 1–2; 11. 27. 10 (*me ... poscat amica*) *aut virides gemmas sardonychasve pares.* See Fried. SG. 3. 79. —

quidquid et a nivea grandius aure sonat.
Sardonychas veros mensa quaesivit in omni
20   et pretium magnis fecit iaspidibus.
Undecima lassus cum iam discederet hora,
asse duos calices emit et ipse tulit.

60

Seu tu Paestanis genita es seu Tiburis arvis,
seu rubuit tellus Tuscula flore tuo,
seu Praenestino te vilica legit in horto,

picto . . . in auro: the gold is re-splendent (*picto*) with the emeralds which adorn it. Such Oriental ornamentation came much into vogue at Rome. Cf. 14. 109; Plin. N. H. 33. 5 *turba gemmarum pota-mus et smaragdis teximus calices*; Iuv. 10. 26–27 *tunc illa* (poison) *time, cum pocula sumes gemmata.* — **numeravit:** he is bound to get the worth of *his* money.

18. quidquid . . . sonat: he counted also the big pearls or drops in a pendant such as might adorn a woman's ear. See 1. 109. 4 N.; Iuv. 6. 458–459 *cum virides gem-mas collo circumdedit et cum auribus extentis magnos commisit elenchos*; Fried. SG. 3. 81 ff. — **grandius** may be adv. with *sonat*, or adj. with *quidquid*.

19. Sardonychas: cf. 4. 28. 4; 5. 11. 1–2. — **veros:** see App. — **mensa . . . in omni:** i.e. of the sellers of gems.

20. pretium . . . fecit, *set a price on, he made an offer for*. Cf. 1. 85. 7 N. — **magnis . . . iaspi-dibus:** the size adds to the value. See 5. 11. 1; Verg. A. 4. 261 *illi* (Aeneas) *stellatus iaspide fulva ensis erat*; Iuv. 5. 43–45.

22. asse . . . emit: the point lies in the contrast. He spends one copper coin, whereas the goods he had examined or had caused to be laid aside for him were worth mil-lions of *sestertii*. He had spent a day to accomplish what might have been done in a minute or two; despite his airs he was not accom-panied by a single *pedisecus*, where-as a retinue of slaves would have been necessary to carry the numer-ous articles he had pretended to be so anxious to purchase.

60. To a rose-chaplet sent by M. to his friend Caesius Sabinus of Sassina. In 7. 97. 2 M. calls Sabinus *montanae decus Umbriae*, and then says (5–7): *instent mille licet premantque* (*eum*) *curae, no-stris carminibus tamen vacabit, nam me diligit ille.* — Meter: § 48.

1. The repeated **seu** in 1–4 shows that M. does not know where the roses that he has bought in Rome grew, and that it does not matter. — **Paestanis . . . arvis:** cf. 5. 37. 9 N. — **Tiburis:** Tibur ap-pears, however, to have been more famed for fruit than for roses.

2. tellus Tuscula: Tib. 1. 7. 57 has *Tuscula tellus*; see on *Tuscu-los . . . colles*, 4. 64. 13. — **flore:** col-lective singular; see on 1. 41. 6.

3. Praenestino . . . horto: cf. Plin. N. H. 21. 16 *genera eius* (the

seu modo Campani gloria ruris eras,

5   pulchrior ut nostro videare corona Sabino,

de Nomentano te putet esse meo.

61

In Tartesiacis domus est notissima terris,

qua dives placidum Corduba Baetin amat,

vellera nativo pallent ubi flava metallo

et linit Hesperium brattea viva pecus.

5   Aedibus in mediis totos amplexa penates

rose) *nostri fecere celeberrima Prae-nestinam et Campanam* ; 21. 20 *prae-cox* (*rosa*) *Campana est, sera Milesia, novissime tamen desinit Praene-stina.* — **vilica**: the wife of the *vili-cus* (see 2. 11. 9); cf. 10. 48. 7–8.

4. Campani . . . ruris: see Plin. N. H. 21. 16, cited on 3; 18. 111.

6. Nomentano . . . meo: see 2. 38. 1 N.

61. On a plane-tree (*Platanus orientalis*, represented in the west-ern world to-day by the *Platanus occidentalis*, the American syca-more or buttonwood) set out by Julius Caesar in the peristylium of a house at Corduba in Spain. On the plane-tree, 'the aristocratic tree' of antiquity, see Hehn 283 ff. — Meter: § 48.

1. Tartesiacis = *Hispanis*; cf. 7. 28. 3; 8. 28. 5; Sil. 13. 674 *Tar-tessia tellus*; 15. 5–6.

2. dives . . . Corduba: as a com-mercial center Corduba was sur-passed in Spain only by Gades. See 1. 61. 8–9. — **placidum . . . Baetin**: cf. 8. 28. 5–6 *an Tartesiacus, stabuli nutritor Hiberi, Baetis in Hesperia te quoque lavit ove?* In writing *placidum* M. speaks from observa-tion. — **amat**: because of its beauty and its commercial advantages.

3–4. vellera . . . pecus: the sheep of this region had wool of a golden or blond hue; cf. 5. 37. 7–8; 12. 63. 3–5 (Corduba) *albi quae superas oves Galaesi nullo murice nec cruore mendax, sed tinctis gregi-bus colore vivo*; 14. 133. — **nativo pallent . . . metallo**: the wool has the pale yellow hue that Spanish gold possesses; cf. Ov. M. 11. 110 *saxum quoque palluit auro*; Catull. 64. 100. On *pallor, pallidus*, see on 1. 41. 4; 8. 14. 1; cf. 8. 44. 10. — **linit** = *inaurat* (Rader). The sheep seem coated with gold, but the gold has life (*viva*)! There is no thin artificial gilding (*bratteae*) here such as is seen on animals in public spectacles or in temples (see Fried. SG. 2. 401–402), but nature's own genuine work. — **Hesperium**, *Spanish*; cf. 8. 78. 6 *Hesperio qui sonat orbe Tagus*.

5. aedibus in mediis: appar-ently the tree stood in the peri-stylium of the house; cf. Stat. Silv. 1. 3. 59 *quae mediis servata penatibus arbor*. — **amplexa penates**: i.e. throwing its ample shade over the whole house. Cf. Verg. A. 2. 512–514 (of Priam's palace) *aedibus in mediis . . . veterrima laurus, incum-bens arae atque umbra complexa pe-nates*; 7. 59–67 (of Latinus's palace).

stat platanus densis Caesariana comis,

hospitis invicti posuit quam dextera felix,

coepit et ex illa crescere virga manu.

Auctorem dominumque nemus sentire videtur:

10   sic viret et ramis sidera celsa petit,

dumque fugit solos nocturnum Pana per agros,

saepe sub hac latuit rustica fronde Dryas.

Saepe sub hac madidi luserunt arbore Fauni

terruit et tacitam fistula sera domum,

15   atque oluere lares comissatore Lyaeo

6. platanus: the name is derived from πλατύs, because of the broad leaves of the tree. "Der Ruhm des Platanenbaums erfüllt das ganze Alterthum" (Hehn); cf. Plin. N. H. 12. 6 *quis non iure miretur arborem umbrae gratia tantum ex alieno petitam orbe? platanus haec est.* — **densis . . . comis:** Caesar was propraetor in Further Spain in 61 B.C. If set out then, the tree was now over 150 years old.

7. hospitis: Caesar would seem to have been asked by his host to set out the tree as a reminder of his visit. — **posuit,** *set out.*

8. virga, *sprout, shoot*; cf. Ov. Rem. Am. 85–86 *quae praebet latas arbor spatiantibus umbras, quo posita est primum tempore virga fuit.*

9. Auctorem . . . videtur: i.e. whatever Caesar put hand to felt his power and responded to his touch; nature's realm, as well as his fellowmen, acknowledged him as *dominus.* — **nemus:** the tree is so large that it might almost be mistaken for a whole *nemus*; cf. Ov. M. 8. 743–744 *stabat in his ingens annoso robore quercus, una nemus.* See App.

10. ramis . . . petit: if one standing in the peristylium viewed the tree at close range this hyperbole would seem literally true.

11–14. See App.

11–12. fugit . . . Pana . . . Dryas: there was ever need for the nymphs to be on the lookout for Pan; cf. Hor. C. 3. 18. 1 *Faune, nympharum fugientum amator.* — **Pana:** the Greek Pan rather than the Roman Faunus. — **rustica . . . Dryas:** some wood nymph, e.g. Echo or Pitys, whom Pan loved. Cf. Ov. M. 8. 746 *saepe sub hac Dryades festas duxere choreas.* For the position see on 1. 53. 8.

13. madidi: see 1. 70. 9.

14. terruit: i.e. has often roused the sleeper by a music that seemed unearthly. — **fistula sera:** i.e. the strains of a Faun playing in the dead of night on the pipe of Pan (σῦριγξ); cf. Verg. E. 2. 32–33 *Pan primus calamos cera coniungere pluris instituit.*

15. atque . . . Lyaeo: 'yea, more; the God of Wine himself held his revels beneath its branches, till the whole house was fragrant with wine'. — **lares:** cf. 9. 18. 2 N. — **comissatore Lyaeo:** abl. abs., 'when Bacchus himself was the reveler'.

16. effuso . . . mero: poured out to make libations or spilled in

crevit et effuso laetior umbra mero,
hesternisque rubens deiecta est herba coronis
　　atque suas potuit dicere nemo rosas.
O dilecta deis, o magni Caesaris arbor,
20　　ne metuas ferrum sacrilegosque focos ;
perpetuos sperare licet tibi frondis honores :
　　non Pompeianae te posuere manus.

68

Quid tibi nobiscum est, ludi scelerate magister,
　　invisum pueris virginibusque caput ?

revelry. It was supposed that the *platanus* liked wine and throve the better when wine was poured about it. See the story in Macr. S. 3. 13. 3. — **laetior**: freely, *more beautifully, more luxuriantly*.

17. hesternis . . . coronis: i.e. the turf was littered (lit. bent down) with the dinner chaplets of yesterday's banquet (see 5. 64. 4 N.). — **rubens**: pred. nom., and proleptic, 'till it grew red'; the roses were flung in such profusion that the grass (*herba = gramen*) appeared red.

18. atque . . . rosas heightens the effect of *rubens*; the garlands lay mingled together in inextricable confusion.

20. ne . . . focos: 'no man will ever lay ax to your root; to make fire-wood of you would be to commit sacrilege by outraging Divus Caesar; the *focus* itself would lose its sacred character, if used to consume you'. — **ferrum** = *securim*.

21. perpetuos belongs logically with *frondis* rather than with *honores*.

22. non . . . manus = *non enim Pompeianae* (*sed Caesaris*) *te posuere manus*. Caesar was everywhere successful, Pompey's line had been

overwhelmed by failure and death. See on 9; cf. 5. 69; 5. 74.

68. To a schoolmaster whose noisy school near M.'s house on the Collis Quirinalis spoiled the poet's morning nap. On Roman teachers see Fried. SG. 1. 318 ff. — Meter : § 48.

1. Quid tibi . . . est: 'what have you to do with *us* ? why plague *us* ?' Cf. 2. 22. 1 *quid mihi vobiscum est, o Phoebe novemque sorores ?* — **ludi . . . magister**: a teacher in the elementary school (= γραμμα-τιστής), in distinction to the *grammaticus*, who taught the school next higher in rank, the school of grammar and literature. Cf. 10. 62. 1; 12. 57. 5. — **scelerate**: M.'s patience, if not his health, has been severely tried, and he curses the schoolmaster. On M.'s fondness for sleep see on 2. 90. 10.

2. invisum . . . caput: cf. 8. 3. 15–16. — **pueris virginibusque**: the rising generation, those young and teachable; cf. 3. 69. 7–8; Hor. C. 3. 1. 4 *virginibus puerisque canto.* — **caput** = *vita* = *homo*; cf. Hor. C. 1. 24. 1–2 *quis desiderio sit pudor aut modus tam cari capitis ?* on which Professor Shorey remarks: "This use of *caput* is warm with

Nondum cristati rupere silentia galli :
    murmure iam saevo verberibusque tonas.
5 Tam grave percussis incudibus aera resultant,
    causidicum medio cum faber aptat equo,
    mitior in magno clamor furit amphitheatro,
    vincenti parmae cum sua turba favet.

feeling, whether of love or hate",
and cites Shelley, Adonais 3, "Thaw
not the frost which binds so dear
a head". Κάρα and κεφαλή are similarly used.

3-4. Nondum ... galli: cf. 14.
223. 1-2 *surgite: iam vendit pueris
ientacula pistor cristataeque sonant
undique lucis aves* ; Ov. Am. 1. 13.
17-18 *tu* (Aurora) *pueros somno
fraudas tradisque magistris ut sube-
ant tenerae verbera saeva manus.*
— **murmure,** *grumbling, scolding.*
— **verberibus . . . tonas:** discipline was severe in Roman schools
and the *ferula* was often in use;
cf. 10. 62. 10 *ferulaeque tristes,
sceptra paedagogorum* ; 14. 80; Iuv.
1. 15 *et nos ergo manum ferulae
subduximus,* ' I too have gone to
school'. Hor. Ep. 2. 1. 70 has immortalized one of his teachers as
plagosus Orbilius ; Marq. 113; Wilkins 49–50. — For the early hour at
which Roman schools began cf. 9.
29. 7 *matutini cirrata caterva magistri*; 12. 57. 4–5 *negant vitam ludi
magistri mane*; Iuv. 7. 219–227
('work, teacher, work from midnight and then remit part of the fee
agreed on') *dum modo non pereat
totidem olfecisse lucernas quot stabant pueri, cum totus decolor esset
Flaccus* (Horace) *et haereret nigro
fuligo Maroni* (Vergil); Ov. Am.
1. 13. 17, cited on 3.

5. Tam grave, *so loudly.* Note
varying forms of expression in 5–6,
7–8. — **aera:** equestrian statues
(cf. 6) were ordinarily of bronze.

6. causidicum: see 1. 98. 2.—
aptat: i.e. rivets the statue of the
man to the back of the horse (cast
separately), to complete the equestrian statue. For equestrian statues
of lawyers see Iuv. 7. 124–128;
Fried. SG. 1. 327 ff.

**7. in magno . . . amphithe-
atro:** the Flavian amphitheater
had at this time been finished
about fourteen years. See Lib.
Spect. 1. — **clamor:** the noise of
cheering, applause. The *factiones*
of the theater and the amphitheater (see Fried. SG. 2. 388 ff.) were
noisy enough, though not quite so
violent and lawless as those of the
circus (10. 48. 23 N.); cf. Lib. Spect.
29. 3 *missio saepe viris magno
clamore petita est.* — **furit:** it is not
only a mob (*turba,* 8), but like an
enraged wild beast. Cf. Sil. 16. 319–
328 (describing a race in the circus)
*tollitur in caelum furiali turbine
clamor . . . hic studio furit acris
equi, furit ille magistri.*

8. parmae: for *Thraeci* (metonymy); the gladiators known as
Thraeces carried a *parma* (see
on Lib. Spect. 29. 5). Not only
individual gladiators but whole
classes of gladiators had their
special adherents. Those who
favored the Thraeces were known
as *parmularii,* those who supported
the *Samnites* and the *mirmillones*
were called *scutarii.* Though the
excesses of the *factiones* of the amphitheater never equaled those of
the circus, the spirit was the same ;

Vicini somnum — non tota nocte — rogamus,
10   nam vigilare leve est, pervigilare grave est.
Discipulos dimitte tuos : vis, garrule, quantum
    accipis ut clames, accipere ut taceas ?

81

Lector et auditor nostros probat, Aule, libellos,
    sed quidam exactos esse poeta negat.
Non nimium curo, nam cenae fercula nostrae
    malim convivis quam placuisse cocis.

88

Cum me captares, mittebas munera nobis :
    postquam cepisti, das mihi, Rufe, nihil.
Ut captum teneas, capto quoque munera mitte,
    de cavea fugiat ne male pastus aper.

cf. Quint. 2. 11. 2 *Alius* (i.e. another rhetorician) *percontanti Theodoreus an Apollodoreus esset "Ego" inquit "parmularius sum".* — **sua**: see on 5. 56. 6.

9. **non tota nocte**: see on 8. 14. 5; 2. 5. 1.

10. **pervigilare**: the emphasis is on the prefix, *throughout the livelong night.* Cf. Plaut. Amph. 314 *continuas has tris noctes pervigilavi.*

12. **clames**: derisive, *bawl* (not teach); cf. *clamor*, 7.

81. On an envious rival poet. Jealousy and petty spite seem to have had free course with the writers of antiquity. See Fried. SG. 3. 451 ff. — Meter: § 48.

1. **Lector**, the private reader, and *auditor*, the hearer at a recitation or a dinner, together typify everybody except the poet of 2. — **probat**, *approves.* — **Aule**: the use of the *praenomen* implies that M. is addressing some one with whom he is intimate (see on 8. 76. 1).

Giese, 28, identifies Aulus with Aulus Pudens. See 12. 51.

2. **quidam . . . poeta**: perhaps the *quidam* of 9. 97. 1. — **exactos**, *finished, polished*; cf. 4. 86. 4 *nil exactius eruditiusque est.* See Saintsbury 1. 263–264.

3–4. **nam . . . cocis**: 'the literary feast I serve is meant for the public (*convivis*) rather than for rival poets (*cocis*) '. M. thus insinuates that the *poeta* of 2 is *cocus* rather than true *vates.*

88. To a legacy-hunter (see 1. 10; 5. 39) who, having caught his prey, ceased to feed it. — Meter: § 48.

1. **mittebas**: note the tense; 'you were always sending presents'.

2. **postquam cepisti** (*me*): i.e. 'after you found that I had made you a legatee in my will'.

4. **de cavea . . . aper** involves a metaphor where a simile would seem to us more natural; so often

97

Rumpitur invidia quidam, carissime Iuli,
  quod me Roma legit, rumpitur invidia,
rumpitur invidia, quod turba semper in omni
  monstramur digito, rumpitur invidia,
5 rumpitur invidia, tribuit quod Caesar uterque
  ius mihi natorum, rumpitur invidia,
rumpitur invidia, quod rus mihi dulce sub urbe est
  parvaque in urbe domus, rumpitur invidia,
rumpitur invidia, quod sum iucundus amicis,

in Latin. M. means, 'lest, if you give me nothing more, I shall break away from you (i.e. erase your name from my will), as a boar when starved breaks out of his cage'. The *captator* is here, as often, represented as a hunter (more often still he is pictured as a fisherman); cf. Tac. Ann. 13. 42. 7 *Romae testamenta et orbos velut indagine eius* (Seneca) *capi*; Hor. Ep. 1. 1. 77–79 *sunt qui ... excipiant senes quos in vivaria mittant.*

97. On some jealous enemy. Cf. 9. 81. — Meter: § 48.

1. Rumpitur invidia: cf. Verg. E. 7. 25–26 *hedera crescentem ornate poetam, Arcades, invidia rumpantur ut ilia Codro*; Ter. Ad. 369 *disrumpor* (with anger or chagrin); Phaedr. 1. 24. 2–10 (the story of the frog that sought to rival the *bos*); Otto s.v. *Rumpo.* — **quidam:** see 9. 81. 2 N. — **carissime Iuli:** prob. Iulius Martialis; see 1. 15; 4. 64; note on 1. 107. 1.

2. quod ... legit: cf. 1. 1. 1–2 N.; 3. 95. 7–8; 8. 61. 1, 3–7 *livet Charinus, rumpitur, furit, plorat: ... non iam quod orbe cantor et legor toto, nec ... quod spargor per omnes Roma quas tenet gentes, sed quod sub urbe rus habemus aestivum*

vehimurque mulis non ut ante conductis.

3. turba ... in omni: i.e. on the street, at the *ludi*, etc.

4. monstramur digito: cf. Pers. 1. 28 *at pulchrum est digito monstrari et dicier "Hic est"*; Hor. C. 4. 3. 22 *quod monstror digito praetereuntium*; Plin. Ep. 9. 23. 4. See also on 1. 1. 1.

5–6. tribuit ... natorum: see § 8. The *ius trium liberorum* was frequently granted to people who had fewer than three children or had no children at all (this was M.'s case). The emperors here meant are almost certainly Titus and Domitian; the latter apparently confirmed what Titus had promised or given. Mommsen, however, Staats. 2. 888. 4, thinks the emperors were Vespasian and Titus.

7. rus ... sub urbe: the Nomentanum; see 2. 38, with notes; 9. 18. 2; 9. 60. 6; 8. 61. 6–7, cited on 2. — **dulce:** because affording a refuge from the distractions and discomforts of the town. Cf. 3. 20. 18 *an Pollionis dulce currit ad quartum?*

8. parva ... domus: see 9. 18. 2.

10   quod conviva frequens, rumpitur invidia,
rumpitur invidia, quod amamur quodque probamur :
rumpatur quisquis rumpitur invidia.

100

Denaris tribus invitas et mane togatum
    observare iubes atria, Basse, tua,
deinde haerere tuo lateri, praecedere sellam,
    ad viduas tecum plus minus ire decem.
5   Trita quidem nobis togula est vilisque vetusque :
    denaris tamen hanc non emo, Basse, tribus.

11. **probamur:** cf. 9. 81. 1.

12. **rumpatur:** a curse, = *dispereat*; cf. Prop. 1. 8. 27 *rumpantur iniqui.*

100. Another variation of the client's dirge. — Meter : § 48.

1. **Denaris tribus:** if this were promised as a daily dole, it was nearly twice as large as the normal *sportula* (100 *quadrantes*; cf. 3. 7, with notes; 4. 26. 3). Sometimes, however, clients (and others) were employed for a special service, at special fees; see Plin. Ep. 2. 14. 6 *here duo nomenclatores mei ternis denariis ad laudandum trahebantur.* For the form *denaris* cf. 1. 117. 17 N.; 4. 18. 1. — **mane togatum:** the toga must be worn by the client and he must present himself early ; cf. 2. 29. 4 N.; 1. 108. 7 *sed tibi non multum est, unum si praesto togatum.* — For the caesura see § 47, c.

2. **observare,** *keep my eyes always on, dance attendance on.*

3. **praecedere sellam :** i.e. as an *anteambulo* (cf. 3. 7. 2 N.), a duty the more galling because it was ordinarily performed by slaves. See also 2. 57. 6 N.

4. **viduas:** such women were much exposed to the arts of the legacy-hunters, esp. if childless; cf. 2. 32. 6 *respondes "Orba est, dives, anus, vidua"*; Iuv. 3. 127–130. *Vetulas* (see App.), *shriveled-up old women,* also makes excellent sense. — **plus minus . . . decem:** cf. 8. 71. 4 *venerunt plusve minusve duae* (this latter passage well illustrates the rule that the omission of *quam* after *plus, minus, longius,* and *amplius* is normally without influence on the construction).

5. **trita:** see 2. 58. 1 N. — **togula:** the dim. may imply that the toga was not voluminous enough to be fashionable, or may give an effect like 'my poor (sorry) toga'. Cf. 3. 30. 3 *unde tibi togula est et fuscae pensio cellae*; 4. 26. 4 N.; 4. 66. 3. — **vetus:** in town one ought not to wear one toga long; cf. 10. 96. 11–12 *quattuor hic* (at Rome) *aestate togae pluresve teruntur, auctumnis ibi* (in Spain) *me quattuor una tegit.* With the whole vs. cf. Ov. M. 8. 658–659 *sed et haec vilisque vetusque vestis erat.* See App.

LIBER X

2

Festinata·prior decimi mihi cura libelli
   elapsum manibus nunc revocavit opus.
Nota leges quaedam, sed lima rasa recenti ;
   pars nova maior erit : lector, utrique fave,
5   lector, opes nostrae, quem cum mihi Roma dedisset,
     " Nil tibi quod demus maius habemus " ait.
   " Pigra per hunc fugies ingratae flumina Lethes
   et meliore tui parte superstes eris.

2. On the revised edition of Book X. See § 13. — Meter: § 48.

1–2. Festinata prior: the publication had been hurried, apparently, to get the book ready for the Saturnalia of 96. *Festinata* contains the logical subject of *revocavit*; render, 'the haste which marked the publication of the earlier edition . . . recalled (i.e. made it necessary to recall)'. The syntax, then, is that seen in the familiar *anno urbis conditae*, or in *angebant . . . Sicilia Sardiniaque amissae*, Liv. 21. 1. 5. — **cura:** the work of preparation and anxiety for the success of the book; cf. 1. 25. 6 N.; 1. 66. 5. *Festinata . . . cura* is really oxymoric. — **elapsum:** the book slipped out as if by stealth, or like an escaping bird (1. 3. 11 N.); it was not *emissus*, i.e. deliberately sent out after full preparation.

3. Nota, *familiar*, because they appeared in the first edition. — **lima,** *revision*; cf. Ov. Tr. 1. 7. 30 *defuit et scriptis ultima lima meis*; Hor. A. P. 291 *limae labor*. — **rasa:** a figure suggested by the literal sense of *lima*; cf. Ov. Pont. 2. 4. 17–18 *utque meus lima rasus liber esset amici non semel admonitu facta litura tuo est.*

4. utrique (*parti*): the *nova pars* of 4, the *nota quaedam* of 3.

5. opes nostrae: in app. with *lector*: 'you, reader, are everything to me; your favor makes or mars my position'. — **quem:** the *lector*; so *hunc*, 7.

6. Nil . . . habemus: literary fame rather than wealth or preferment is the greatest gift that Rome can bestow.

7. Pigra . . . flumina: everything in the lower world lacks the activity associated with the life of earth. *Flumina* is *pluralis maiestatis.* — **Lethes:** see 7. 47. 4 N.

8. meliore . . . parte: i.e. 'your fame'; the poet's work is his true self. Cf. Hor. C. 3. 30. 6–7 *multaque pars mei vitabit Libitinam* ; Ov. Am. 1. 15. 42 *vivam, parsque mei multa superstes erit*; M. 15. 875–876 *parte tamen meliore mei super*

Marmora Messallae findit caprificus et audax
10   dimidios Crispi mulio ridet equos :
at chartis nec furta nocent et saecula prosunt,
solaque non norunt haec monumenta mori ".

5

Quisquis stolaeve purpuraeve contemptor
quos colere debet laesit impio versu,

*alta perennis astra ferar, nomenque
erit indelebile nostrum.*

9-12. See 8. 3. 5-8, with notes.

9-10. Marmora denotes the monument itself (synecdoche). — **Messallae**: see 8. 3. 5 N. — **findit . . . ridet**: the tense makes it easy to take *Messallae* and *Crispi* in a generic sense, i.e. as standing for the rich and noble in general. — **findit caprificus**: cf. Iuv. 10. 143-146 *laudis titulique cupido haesuri saxis cinerum custodibus, ad quae discutienda valent sterilis mala robora fici, quandoquidem data sunt ipsis quoque fata sepulcris.* — **audax**: the *mulio* is a rude dolt, who has no respect even for death and its tokens and fears them not. — **dimidios** = *dimidiatos, broken, mutilated*; cf. Iuv. 8. 4-5 (*quid prodest . . . ostendere*) *Curios iam dimidios umerosque minorem Corvinum et Galbam auriculis nasoque carentem.* — **Crispi**: see on *findit . . . ridet,* 9. M. was probably thinking of C. Passienus Crispus, the second husband of Agrippina, who was mother of Nero by her former husband. Cf. 12. 36. 8-9. — **equos**: part of a work of art, e.g. a *quadriga*, that surmounted the monument.

11. nec . . . et: see on 8. 50. 11. — **furta**: sneak thieves cannot appropriate to themselves what belongs to the whole world, what

every man is guarding. — **saecula,** *the ages, the generations.* See 1. 107. 5.

12. norunt . . . mori: see 8. 18. 6.

5. A denunciation of all who publish libels on the great. If the foul-mouthed poet of 10. 3 is referred to here, M. had a personal basis for his indignation in that this poet had circulated his work under M.'s name. See 10. 3. 1-6. — Meter: § 52.

1. Quisquis: here an adjective; normally the word is a substantive. — **stolae**: i.e. pure womanhood, as typified by honorable matrons; the *stola* was as characteristic of the *matrona* as was the toga of the male citizen. The courtesan had to wear a toga. — **purpurae**: men of rank and position, senators and magistrates distinguished by the purple of the *tunica laticlavia* and the *toga praetexta* respectively. Cf. 8. 8. 4 (to Janus) *purpura te felix, te colat omnis honos.*

2. laesit: at all periods *laedo* was virtually a technical term for injuring by scurrilous or libelous writing or utterance. — **impio**: freely, *ribald, licentious*; the word is really far stronger, as implying an offense against heaven. Caricaturists and libelists in verse were much in evidence under the

erret per urbem pontis exul et clivi,
interque raucos ultimus rogatores
5   oret caninas panis inprobi buccas;
illi December longus et madens bruma
clususque fornix triste frigus extendat;
vocet beatos clamitetque felices
Orciniana qui feruntur in sponda.
10   At cum supremae fila venerint horae

Empire, as early as the time of
Augustus; cf. Tac. Ann. 1. 72. 4.
Domitian had issued an edict
against lampoons (1. 4. 7 N.; Suet.
Dom. 8); this explains why M.
is so eager to prove that certain lampoons current under his
name are not really his.

3–5. With these verses cf. Ov.
Ib. 113–114 *exul, inops erres, alie-*
naque limina lustres, exiguumque
petas ore tremente cibum.

3. pontis . . . clivi: gradients
in great highways gave beggars a
favorable place to intercept and
harry travelers (cf. 2. 19. 3–4 N.).
Many bridges, owing to extreme
elevation in the center, offered two
such gradients. Cf. Iuv. 5. 8 *nulla*
crepido vacat? Nusquam pons?
(i.e. as a place to beg); Sen. Vit.
Beat. 25. 1. We have metaphor
again, not simile (see on 9. 88. 4);
M. prays that the libelous poet may
be as poor as a beggar who, exiled from the ordinary (profitable)
haunts of beggars, can only wan-
der about the town.

4. raucos: i.e. with unremitting
begging.— rogatores: cf. 4. 30. 13 N.

5. caninas . . . buccas: i.e.
mouthfuls of bread fit only for
dogs; coarse bread made of barley
was sometimes fed to dogs. Cf.
Iuv. 5. 10–11 ('why be a client')
cum possit ('one can') *honestius . . .*
sordes farris mordere canini?

6–7. 'May he not only starve,
but freeze'.

6. madens bruma: M. prays
that the bitterness of the dead of
winter may be intensified by damp-
ness and rain. See 3. 58. 8.

7. clusus matches *longus* and
madens, 6; hence this vs. = 'may
even the arches be closed against
him and so prolong', etc. The
language is hyperbolic; if even
arches are to be closed against the
man, where can he hope for shelter?— fornix: collective singular.
In such places, normally always
open, beggars could generally find
a refuge, sorry though it was; M.
prays that even this resource may
be denied to the libelous poet.—
extendat: M. prays that the torture of the libelist may be long
drawn out.

8. clamitet: sc. *eos esse.*

9. Orciniana: Cooper, § 36 a,
pp. 144 ff., holds that forms in
-*anus* belong to the *sermo plebeius.*
— sponda: prop. the framework
of a bed or couch, then a 'bed',
'couch', used by the living rather
than by the dead. Here *Orciniana*
. . . sponda = sandapila, the plain
bier, used for burying the bodies of
the poor or unfortunate.— feruntur = *efferuntur;* see 4. 24. 2; 8.
43. 1.

10. fila: of the Fates; see 4.
54. 5; 7. 96. 4.

diesque tardus, sentiat canum litem
abigatque moto noxias aves panno.
Nec finiantur morte supplicis poenae,
sed modo severi sectus Aeaci loris,
15 nunc inquieti monte Sisyphi pressus,
nunc inter undas garruli senis siccus
delasset omnis fabulas poetarum,
et cum fateri Furia iusserit verum,
prodente clamet conscientia "Scripsi".

10

Cum tu, laurigeris annum qui fascibus intras,

11. tardus: emphatic by position; 'slow may it be in coming'. — **sentiat . . . litem:** i.e. may he realize, before death releases him, that the dogs are already fighting for his body and that he will be deprived of honorable burial.

12. abigat: i.e. may he be compelled to drive away. — **noxias . . . aves:** vultures; such birds often attack the dying. — **panno,** *rags.*

13. supplicis is the noun and depends on *poenae,* but may be best rendered by an adj., *suppliant, abject.* Translate, then, 'and let not his punishment be ended even by an abject death'.

14. modo: coördinate with *nunc . . . nunc,* 15–16; see on 9. 46. 1–2. — **sectus:** cf. e.g. Hor. Epod. 4. 11 *sectus flagellis hic triumviralibus;* Iuv. 10. 316; Ov. Am. 2. 7. 22; see on 8. 23. 3. — **Aeaci:** Aeacus, Minos, and Rhadamanthus were the fabled judges of men in the lower world; cf. Iuv. 1. 9 *quas torqueat umbras Aeacus;* Ov. Ib. 187–188.

15. inquieti: in the lower world Sisyphus is ever rolling a huge stone (*monte*) up a steep incline;

cf. 5. 80. 10–11 *nam securus erit nec inquieta lassi marmora Sisyphi videbit.* On earth, as king of Corinth, Sisyphus had been notoriously wicked.

16. nunc . . . siccus: i.e. may he suffer the torments of Tantalus, condemned in the lower world to endless thirst and hunger, though he stood in water and though tempting viands were displayed before him or hung over his head. — **garruli:** he could not keep the secrets he had learned at the banquet to which he had been invited by Jupiter.

17. delasset personifies the *fabulas* and turns them into executioners; 'may he bring into play, aye, till he wearies them to exhaustion, all the punishments told of in the tales of the poets'.

19. Scripsi: sc. the libels which he attributed to others. M. writes as if the confession, wrung from the man by the Fury, were to be the severest punishment of all.

10. Another wail from the poor dependent. See 2. 18.—Meter: § 48.

1. laurigeris . . . intras: at this time the consuls took office

> mane salutator limina mille teras,
> hic ego quid faciam? quid nobis, Paule, relinquis,
>   qui de plebe Numae densaque turba sumus?
> 5 Qui me respiciet, dominum regemque vocabo?
>   hoc tu — sed quanto blandius! — ipse facis.
> Lecticam sellamve sequar? nec ferre recusas

on January 1. They were escorted from their homes by a sort of triumphal procession to the Capitol; the *fasces* (see 7. 63. 9 N.) carried by the lictors seem to have been decorated with bay or laurel, as in a true triumph. Cf. Claud. IV. Cons. Hon. 14–15 *nec te laurigeras pudeat, Gradive, secures pacata gestare manu*; Mommsen Staats. 1. 414 ff.

2. **mane salutator**: cf. 1. 70; 3. 4. 6; 4. 8. 1; 9. 100. 1. — **limina . . . teras**: for consuls and praetors who stooped to be clients cf. Iuv. 1. 99–102 *iubet a praecone vocari* (to receive the *sportula*) *ipsos Troiugenas, nam vexant limen et ipsi nobiscum: "Da praetori, da deinde tribuno"*; 1. 117–120; 3. 126–130. See also on 2. 18. 2; 5. 22. 13.— **limina mille**: hyperbole; but cf. Sen. Brev. Vit. 14. 3. — **teras**: cf. 2. 11. 2; 8. 44. 4 *sed omne limen conteris salutator*. Cf. *vexant limen*, Iuv. 1. 100, cited above.

3. **hic** = *Romae*. — **nobis**, as defined by vs. 4, is in sharp contrast to *tu*, 1, as defined there by *laurigeris . . . intras*.

4. **de plebe . . . turba**: plain Romans, poor and numberless. For metrical convenience, perhaps, M. here substitutes the name of the second king of Rome for that of Romulus; cf. Iuv. 10. 72–73 *sed quid turba Remi?* But since Numa was famed for his piety, M. may well mean by this verse, 'we, the host of pious, honest (though poor)

sons of Rome'. Cf. 5. 38. The theme of Juvenal's third Satire ('Rome is no place for a man at once poor and honest') may then be compared. Join *de plebe* with *sumus* (= *exsistimus*), not with *turba*; the prepositional phrase = an adj., *plebeii* (see on 8. 14. 3–4). — **densa . . . turba**: cf. 1. 20. 1; Iuv. 1. 120–121 *densissima centum drantes lectica petit*. Here the phrase = 'the lower classes', 'the masses', countless in number, and not worth individualizing.

5. **Qui . . . respiciet**: 'who will look condescendingly upon me', 'who will give me nothing but a patronizing glance'; cf. Iuv. 3. 184–185 *quid das ut Cossum aliquando salutes, ut te respiciat clauso Veiento labello?* — **dominum regemque**: pred. acc. The primary object of *vocabo* is (*eum*), antec. of *qui*. Cf. 2. 18. 5; 2. 68. 2 *quem regem et dominum prius vocabam*; 4. 83. 5; Iuv. 5. 137.— **vocabo**: distinguish such a question (naturally answered by *non vocabo* or the like) from a question with deliberative subj. (*vocem*, 'would you have me call . . . ?'), to which the answer would be made in terms of an imv., *voca*, or of a prohibition, *noli vocare*.

6. **sed** may be taken as in 1. 117. 7, or as true adversative conjunction.

7–8. **Lecticam . . . sequar**: see 2. 57. 6 N.; 3. 46. 4; Fried. SG. 1. 384. — **nec . . . et**: see on 8. 50. 11; 10. 2. 11; 'you are willing even

per medium pugnas et prior ire lutum.

Saepius adsurgam recitanti carmina ? tu stas

10   et pariter geminas tendis in ora manus.

Quid faciet pauper, cui non licet esse clienti ?

dimisit nostras purpura vestra togas.

13

Ducit ad auriferas quod me Salo Celtiber oras,

pendula quod patriae visere tecta libet,

to take a slave's place as bearer of the litter'. — **per medium** . . . **lutum:** cf. 12. 29. 8 ; 3. 36. 3–4 *horridus ut primo semper te mane salutem per mediumque trahat me tua sella lutum*. For mud in streets see also 7. 61.6 ; etc. — **et** . . . **ire:** see App. The vs. = 'You seek to outstrip all other bearers of litters'. For inf. with *pugnare* cf. Ov. M. 2. 822 *illa quidem pugnat recto se attollere trunco*. The verb has in these passages the sense and the constr. of *conor* in prose, of *tento*, *nitor* in poetry.

9–10. **Saepius** . . . **manus:** 'at the recitation I am equally helpless, for no one can outdo you in rising to give applause, or in throwing kisses ; you stand all the time and throw kisses with both hands'. — **adsurgam:** i.e. 'rise from my seat in (pretended) enthusiasm'. Further, to rise before another was a compliment; cf. Cic. Cato M. 18. 63 ; Plin. Ep. 6. 17. 2, cited on 10; Quint. 2. 2. 9 *minime vero permittenda pueris, ut fit apud plerosque, assurgendi exultandique in laudando licentia*. Julius Caesar gave great offense by remaining seated while receiving the senate (Suet. Iul. 78). — **recitanti:** dat. of interest, 'in compliment to', etc. — **geminas** . . . **manus:** i.e. 'you bring both hands up to your face

in blowing kisses or in applause'; cf. 1. 3. 7 N.; Iuv. 3. 104–106 (the Greekling) *semper et omni nocte dieque potest . . . iactare manus, laudare paratus*; Quint. 2. 2. 9, cited above; Plin. Ep. 6. 17. 2 *surdis mutisque similes audiebant; non labra diduxerunt; non moverunt manum, non denique adsurrexerunt.*

11. **Quid** . . . **pauper:** cf. Iuv. 1. 117–120. See on 4 above.

12. **dimisit:** an effective word, because it understates the case. M. says 'has dismissed', i.e. 'has relieved'; he means 'has ousted'. — **purpura vestra:** the *toga praetexta* (see 10. 5. 1 N.) of clients who are magistrates has taken the place of the plain white togas of common folks.

13. Who Manius, the poet's countryman, was cannot be determined; the use of the praenomen implies intimacy (see on 8. 76. 1; 9. 81. 1). See § 41. — Meter: § 48.

1–2. **Ducit** . . . **me Salo:** several epigrams in this book voice M.'s longing for his native country; cf. 10. 96; 10. 104. For the Salo see § 2. — **auriferas** . . . **oras:** cf. 12. 18. 9 *auro Bilbilis et superba ferro*. In Rome there were no *auriferae orae* for M. — **quod** . . . **quod:** cf. 2. 11. 1 N. M. says 'My going to Spain, my resolve to

tu mihi simplicibus, Mani, dilectus ab annis
    et praetextata cultus amicitia,
5 tu facis, in terris quo non est alter Hiberis
    dulcior et vero dignus amore magis.
Tecum ego vel sicci Gaetula mapalia Poeni
    et poteram Scythicas hospes amare casas.
Si tibi mens eadem, si nostri mutua cura est,
10   in quocumque loco Roma duobus erit.

16

Dotatae uxori cor harundine fixit acuta,
    sed dum ludit, Aper : ludere novit Aper.

visit home are due to you'. — **pen-dula . . . tecta:** Bilbilis was perched on an elevation above the river; § 2. Cf. note on *pendentia*, Lib. Spect. 1. 5; 1. 61. 11–12 N.; 4. 64. 33.—**patriae . . . tecta:** an additional motive for bidding farewell to Rome.

3. simplicibus . . . ab annis: i.e. 'from the time we lived the simple, provincial life of our Spanish home'.

4. praetextata: freely, *youthful, boyish*. Their friendship began early, when they wore the *toga praetexta* together.

5. in terris . . . Hiberis: i.e. in all Spain. For the pl. cf. 12. 18. 11–12 *Celtiberis haec sunt nomina crassiora terris*.

7–8. 'With you I would brave the dangers and solitude of the most barbarous regions'. For this proverbial test of friendship cf. e.g. Catull. 11. 1–12; Hor. C. 2. 6. 1–4.

7. vel: see 10. 20. 21. — **sicci . . . Poeni:** i.e. any point of Africa, as the confused allusion to the Gaetuli and the Carthaginians shows. The Romans habitually picture Africa as savage and dangerous

(by reason of its wild animals and its uncivilized tribesmen). — **sicci:** because the desert was near. — **mapalia :** these rude dwellings would afford scant comfort to men who knew the luxury of Rome. But the companionship of his friend would make M. oblivious of discomforts. Cf. Sall. Iug. 18. 8 *aedificia Numidarum agrestium, quae mapalia illi vocant, oblonga incurvis lateribus tecta quasi navium carinae sunt*.

8. poteram: see on *poteras*, 1. 3. 12.

9. si nostri . . . est (*tibi*): i.e. 'if you return my love'. Cf. Ov. M. 7. 800 *mutua cura . . . duos habebat*; F. 2. 64 *mutua cura tui*; Tib. 3. 1. 19 *illa mihi referet, si nostri mutua cura est*. — **nostri :** objective gen. with *cura*.

10. quocumque = *quovis, quolibet,* i.e. *omni*; in 1. 2. 1 *ubicumque* = *ubique*; in 1. 41. 18 *cuicunque* = *cuivis*.

16. Aper, while playing (!), shot his rich wife through the heart. — Meter : § 48.

2. Aper may involve a pun on *aper*; if so, Aper is as dangerous

17

Si donare vocas promittere nec dare, Gai,
    vincam te donis muneribusque meis.
Accipe Callaicis quidquid fodit Astur in arvis,
    aurea quidquid habet divitis unda Tagi,
5 quidquid Erythraea niger invenit Indus in alga,
    quidquid et in nidis unica servat avis,
quidquid Agenoreo Tyros inproba cogit aheno :
    quidquid habent omnes, accipe, quomodo das.

as a boar. — **ludere**: a good play on *ludit*; 'Aper is a sportsman' (B. and L.). For inf. with *novit* cf. 7. 25. 8; 10. 33. 9–10.

17. M. professes a benevolence equal to that of Gaius. — Meter: § 48.

1. Si . . . dare: *promittere nec dare* is obj. of *vocas*, *donare* is pred. acc.; 'if you call promising . . . giving'.

3. Callaicis . . . arvis: see 4. 39. 7 N. — **quidquid**: here, as in 4–8, suggestive of plenty, 'all that'. — **Astur**: the country of the Astures, in Hispania Tarraconensis. This was the richest gold-bearing district in Spain; cf. Plin. N.H. 33. 78; Sil. 1. 231 ff.

4. Tagi: see 7. 88. 7 N.

5. quidquid . . . in alga: i.e. pearls. M. may mean that pearls are so plentiful along that coast as to be found in the seaweed on the shore. But we get a closer parallelism with 3–4 and 6 by thinking rather of weeds rooted on the bottom of the sea, among which the diver gropes for the pearl-oysters. *Invenit*, which regularly implies careful search, agrees well with this picture. It may be noted that the ancient Hebrew (and, we may suppose, Phoenician) name of the Mare Erythraeum meant

'Sea of Weeds (Reeds)'; and the Greco-Roman name has by some been taken to refer to red seaweed seen through the water. — **Indus**: M. is using *Erythraea* freely; see on 5. 37. 4.

6. quidquid . . . avis: i.e. perfumes from the nest of the phoenix; see on 5. 37. 13; 6. 55. 2. — **unica . . . avis**: see 5. 37. 13 N.; Ov. Am. 2. 6. 54 *et vivax phoenix, unica semper avis*.

7. quidquid . . . aheno: i.e. the finest Tyrian dye. — **Agenoreo . . . aheno**: i.e. in Phoenician caldrons; Agenor was the reputed father of Cadmus. Cf. 2. 43. 7 N.; Sil. 7. 642 *purpura Agenoreis saturata micabat aenis*. — **inproba**, *tricky* (see on 1. 53. 10; 8. 24. 2); the Phoenicians (e.g. the Carthaginians) were from very early times accounted most deceitful. There may, however, be special reference to counterfeit dye.

20. M., addressing his Muse (cf. 3), sends through her a copy of his book to Pliny the Younger. Pliny seems to have been much pleased and to have manifested his appreciation by supplying M. with the means (*viaticum*) of returning to Spain. See § 38. Plin. 3. 21. 5 cites vss. 12–21 of this epigram. Pliny was one of the greatest lawyers of his time, and frequently pleaded

20

Nec doctum satis et parum severum,
sed non rusticulum nimis libellum
facundo mea Plinio Thalia
i, perfer : brevis est labor peractae
5   altum vincere tramitem Suburae.
Illic Orphea protinus videbis
udi vertice lubricum theatri

before the centumviri (see on 1. 76.
12; 7. 63. 7). — Meter: § 49.

1. **Nec doctum satis**: i.e. for
so great a scholar, who knows good
poetry; cf. 1. 25. 2 N. — **parum severum**: not austere enough for a
lawyer, esp. a lawyer of such strict
morality as Pliny. Pliny came from
Gallia Cisalpina; in Ep. 1. 14. 4–6
he speaks in the highest terms of
the morality of that district. Cf.
11. 16. 7–8 *tu quoque nequitias nostri lususque libelli . . ., puella, leges,
sis Patavina licet.*

2. **non . . . nimis**: the book
after all has a fair share of *urbanitas*; see 1. 41. Introd.

3. **facundo . . . Plinio**: cf. Introd.—**mea...Thalia**: cf. 4.8.12 N.

4–5. **i, perfer**: see 7. 89. 1 N. —
peractae... Suburae: the Subura
(the most important thoroughfare
between the region about the Fora
and the eastern part of the city) was
traversed before the *trames* was
entered. See 5. 22. 5 N. The path,
though steep, is soon mounted.
Render, 'it is easy, after you have
gone through the Subura, to climb
its steep path (i.e. the steep path
that leads out of it)'. —**vincere** =
superare, as in 5. 22. 5. Pliny's home
was on the Esquiline; cf. Plin. Ep. 3.
21. 5 (Martialis) *adloquitur Musam,
mandat ut domum meam Esquiliis
quaerat, adeat reverenter.*

6–7. **Illic**: i.e. on the Esquiline.
—**Orphea . . . theatri**: on the
north side of the Esquiline was a
Lacus Orphei, a fountain with a
semicircular pool (*theatri*) into
which the water fell. In or on this
fountain was a representation of
Orpheus playing, surrounded by
the entranced birds and beasts.
Jordan, Top. 2. 127, is probably correct in locating it near the churches
S. Lucia in Orfea and S. Martino
in Orfea near the Thermae Traiani.
See K. and H. Formae Urb. R. —
udi: i.e. besprinkled with the spray
of the fountain. See on *theatri* below.— **vertice**: the Orpheus figure
rose above the others. Orpheus
doubtless stood erect; the beasts,
soothed by the music, crouched
before him. — **theatri**: we may
easily see in this word two ideas
at once. M. has in mind, in part,
a semicircular pool (see above),
perhaps with steps similar to the
gradus of a theater, but he is thinking more of the beasts giving ear
to Orpheus's performance; Orpheus is *actor* or rather *musicus*,
the beasts and the eagle are *audi-
tores spectaculi in theatro.* In writing *udi* M. had in mind especially
this latter train of ideas. The vs. =
'standing, slippery with moisture,
at the top of (above) the theater-
like pool and the listening beasts'.

mirantisque feras avemque regis,
raptum quae Phryga pertulit Tonanti,
10   illic parva tui domus Pedonis
caelata est aquilae minore pinna.
Sed ne tempore non tuo disertam
pulses ebria ianuam videto :
totos dat tetricae dies Minervae,
15   dum centum studet auribus virorum
hoc quod saecula posterique possint
Arpinis quoque conparare chartis.
Seras tutior ibis ad lucernas :

8. avem . . . regis: the eagle, bird of Jupiter.

9. raptum . . . Phryga: Ganymedes; cf. 2. 43. 13.

10. Pedonis: Pedo Albinovanus; see 2. 77. 5.

11. caelata . . . pinna: i.e. 'adorned with a graven eagle whose plumage spreads less widely' (i.e. than that of the *avis regis*, 8).

12–13. non tuo: i.e. unfavorable. See 19. — **disertam . . . ianuam**: cf. *facundo . . . Plinio*, 3. — **pulses ebria ianuam**: as a drunken Bacchanal might do. — **pulses**: the Romans beat at doors with their feet; cf. Plaut. and Ter. passim; Hor. C. 1. 4. 13–14 *pallida mors aequo pulsat pede pauperum tabernas regumque turris*. — **ebria, wantonly.** The book is to go *reverenter*; cf. Plin. Ep. 3. 21. 5, cited on 4. — **videto** has the sense and the constr. of *curato*; cf. 6. 21. 4 *tu ne quid pecces, exitiose, vide*.

14. tetricae: this adj. seems to have been conventionally applied to Minerva; cf. Apoll. Sidon. C. 9. 142 *atque inter tetricae choros Minervae*. Cf. also 5. 20. 6 *litis tetricas forumque triste*. — **Minervae**: cf. 1. 76. 5 N.

15. centum . . . virorum: Pliny repeatedly mentions his practice before this court; cf. e.g. Ep. 2. 14. 1 *destringor centumviralibus causis, quae me exercent magis quam delectant*.

16. saecula: see 10. 2. 11 N.

17. Arpinis . . . chartis: i.e. the speeches of Cicero, who was born at Arpinum. Pliny did in fact use Cicero as his model; cf. Plin. Ep. 1. 5. 12 *est enim mihi cum Cicerone aemulatio nec sum contentus eloquentia saeculi nostri*. Tacitus, too, in his earlier works, esp. the Dialogus, took Cicero as his model. In this they show the influence of Quintilian; see 2. 90. 1 N.

18. Seras . . . lucernas: i.e. the closing hours of the dinner, when the wine flowed and there was a tendency to unbend, 19 (the *comissatio*). — **tutior ibis**: M. may have in mind Ov. M. 2. 137 *medio tutissimus ibis*. — **ad**: best taken simply as = *to*; it may, however, be taken as in the phrase *ad lunam*, for which cf. Iuv. 10. 21 *motae ad lunam trepidabis harundinis umbram*; Petr. 103 *notavit sibi ad lunam tonsorem intempestivo inhaerentem ministerio*.

haec hora est tua, cum furit Lyaeus,
20   cum regnat rosa, cum madent capilli :
tunc me vel rigidi legant Catones.

21

Scribere te quae vix intellegat ipse Modestus
et vix Claranus quid, rogo, Sexte, iuvat ?
Non lectore tuis opus est, sed Apolline libris :
iudice te maior Cinna Marone fuit.
5   Sic tua laudentur sane : mea carmina, Sexte,
grammaticis placeant, ut sine grammaticis.

19. haec...tua: cf. 4. 8. 7–12. For this use of *hora* cf. Sil. 12. 193 *perge, age, fer gressus; dexter deus horaque nostra est.* — **Lyaeus:** see 1. 70. 9; 8. 50. 12; 9. 61. 15.

20. cum regnat rosa: for roses at the *comissatio* see 5. 64. 4 N.; 9. 61. 17. — **madent:** i.e. with ointments (see on 3. 12. 1); cf. Petr. 65 *oneratusque aliquot coronis et unguento per frontem in oculos fluente praetorio loco se posuit* (at table).

21. tunc...Catones: even a Cato unbends at the *comissatio* and has an ear for something light and sportive. — **vel** = *etiam*. — **rigidi,** *stern, strictly moral;* cf. *severum,* 1; Sen. Ep. 11. 10 *elige itaque Catonem: si hic tibi videtur nimis rigidus, elige remissioris animi virum Laelium.* — **legant . . . Catones:** cf. Praef. to Book I; 11. 2. 1–2 *triste supercilium durique severa Catonis frons;* Sen. Ep. 97. 10 *omne tempus Clodios, non omne Catones feret;* Otto s.v. *Cato.*

21. This unknown Sextus is a type of the versifiers who imagined that obscurity of subject matter and display of erudition were proofs of inspiration. — Meter : § 48.

1–2. quae . . . Claranus: i.e. what even a professional gram-

marian can scarcely understand. Modestus is generally identified with Julius Modestus, freedman of C. Julius Hyginus, himself a freedman of Augustus. Fried., however, identifies him with Aufidius Modestus, mentioned by Plutarch as a contemporary. So Teuffel, § 282. 1. Claranus is placed by Teuffel, § 328. 4, under Domitian.

3. Apolline: i.e. an interpreter. Apollo was ἐξηγητής, interpreter and expounder of the future to men. 'Your books need some divine power to explain their meaning'.

4. maior...fuit: a proof of the assertion of 3. — **Cinna:** C. Helvius Cinna, contemporary of Catullus, wrote a long erudite poem called Smyrna(Zmyrna). Cf. Catull. 95. 1–2 *Zmyrna mei Cinnae nonam post denique messem quam coepta est nonamque edita post hiemem.* His "fancy for out-of-the-way words we can see, even in the petty wreckage of his work that time has fated to us" (Saintsbury 1. 264).

5. Sic, *on that principle* (cf. 5. 66. 2; 7. 89. 4), i.e. that obscurity affords a better title than clearness to popular appreciation.

6. ut: sc. *placeant,* a clause of result, 'in such wise, however, that

23

Iam numerat placido felix Antonius aevo
  quindecies actas Primus Olympiadas
praeteritosque dies et tutos respicit annos
  nec metuit Lethes iam propioris aquas.
5 Nulla recordanti lux est ingrata gravisque,
  nulla fuit cuius non meminisse velit.
Ampliat aetatis spatium sibi vir bonus : hoc est
  vivere bis, vita posse priore frui.

they shall please (the world)', etc.
M. means: 'I have no objection to
the recognition of scholars, provided that scholars do not have a
monopoly of appreciation; I would
have the common reader able to
enjoy my poetry because it is free
from book-learning'.—**sine grammaticis** = *sine interprete* (Domit.).

23. M. congratulates Antonius
Primus on his advanced age and
his success in life. — Meter : § 48.

1. placido felix . . . aevo,
blessed in the calm of his old age.
His earlier years had been somewhat checkered. Born at Tolosa
in Gaul, he was a man of affairs, but
utterly unscrupulous, cruel, and a
turncoat in his political and personal relations. He was banished
from Rome under Nero because of
forgery, but was restored to favor
by Galba. He then supported
Otho, and finally rendered important service to Vespasian against
Vitellius. Cf. 10. 32 ; in 10. 73 M.
thanks him for a new toga.

**2. quindecies . . . Olympi-
adas:** if *Olympiadas* is to be understood literally, Antonius would be
but 60 years old ; yet he seems to
have been much older than that in
98. Fried. therefore holds that M.
uses *Olympias* as = *lustrum*, a space
of five years. The word clearly
bears this sense in 4. 45. 4, being

interchanged there with *quinquen-
nium*, 3. In 7. 40. 6 it may perfectly
well be interpreted of a period of
four years, though the passage is
more effective if we take the word
of the longer period. In this M. perhaps follows Ovid's example; see
Pont. 4. 6. 5 *in Scythia nobis quin-
quennis Olympias acta est.* Ovid's
reckoning of a *single* Olympiad as
covering five years is quite in accord with the Greco-Roman practice of counting in both ends of a
period of time; M's use here and
in 4. 45. 4 is strange and forced.

3–4. praeteritos: join with both
annos and *dies; tutos* also modifies
both nouns, as pred. acc. Antonius
'looks back on . . . and finds them
safe'. — **tutos:** an important word,
in view of Antonius's checkered
experiences ; it suggests that the
years actually lived are safely
one's own, whereas the future is
wholly uncertain. See App. If
totos is read, the sense is 'he sur-
veys all his life and yet finds nothing to make him fear death'. *Nec*,
4, then = *et non tamen.* — **Lethes
. . . aquas:** see 7. 47. 4 ; 7. 96. 7 ;
10. 2. 7.

5–6. lux = *dies.* — **meminisse:**
for the tense see on *eripuisse*, 1.
107. 6.

7–8. Ampliat, *increases, adds to.*
— **spatium:** the span or course of

25

In matutina nuper spectatus harena
Mucius, inposuit qui sua membra focis,
si patiens durusque tibi fortisque videtur,
Abderitanae pectora plebis habes,
5   nam cum dicatur tunica praesente molesta
"Ure manum", plus est dicere "Non facio".

life (a figure from the race-course).
— **bonus** contains the logical subject; the sense is 'virtue adds
years to a man's life'. M. explains
in *hoc . . . frui*, which = *hoc enim
est*, etc. *Hoc* is explained mainly
by what follows, *vita . . . frui.*
   25. The Roman stage had become horribly realistic in its de-
generacy. "Comedy must be actual
shame, and tragedy genuine blood-
shed. . . . It was the ultimate ro-
mance of a degraded and brutal-
ized society" (Farrar, Early Days
of Christianity, 1. 69). M. writes
as if he had witnessed this stage
scene, in which a condemned criminal was compelled to enact the
story of Mucius Scaevola and actually burn off his hand in a slow
fire to save himself from the ex-
cruciating death by the *tunica molesta* (see on 4. 86. 8). 8. 30 is on
the same theme. In Lib. Spect. 7
a malefactor is torn to pieces on a
cross by a wild boar. See Fried.
SG. 2. 408–410. — Meter: § 48.
   1. matutina . . . harena: *venationes*, executions, and exhibitions
such as that described here took
place during the morning hours;
cf. 8. 67. 3. — **spectatus:** cf. 1. 4.
5 N.; 1. 43. 11; 5. 14. 7.
   2. Mucius: the unfortunate
man plays the rôle of C. Mucius
Scaevola, who, when caught in a
plot to assassinate King Porsenna,
and threatened with being burned

alive, showed his contempt of the
king's threats by thrusting his
hand in a sacrificial fire conven-
iently near, and holding it there
until it was burned off. See 1. 21;
Liv. 2. 12.
   3. patiens . . . videtur: cf. 1.
21. 5. The subj. of *videtur* is *Mucius*, 2.
   4. Abderitanae . . . habes:
i.e. 'you are as great a fool as the
veriest Abderite'. The people of
Abdera in southern Thrace were
proverbially stupid, though the
city produced several men of ability, e.g. Democritus the philosopher (see Iuv. 10. 47–50); cf. Cic.
Att.7. 7. 4 *id est* Ἀβδηριτικόν ('fool-
ish'), *nec enim senatus decrevit nec
populus iussit me imperium in Sicilia habere*; Otto s.v. *Abdera.*
   5. dicatur: the subj. is *ure
manum*; so *dicere non facio* is
subj. of *est*, 6. — **tunica . . . molesta:** i.e. as an alternative to
burning off his hand. Cf. Sen. Ep.
14. 5 *cogita hoc loco carcerem et cru-
ces et eculeos et uncum et adactum
per medium hominem qui per os
emergeret stipitem et distracta in
diversum actis curribus membra,
illam tunicam alimentis ignium et
inlitam et textam, et quicquid aliud
praeter haec commenta saevitia est.*
   6. plus, *the more heroic thing.*
— **Non facio,** 'I am not doing it',
is more effective than *non faciam*
or *facere nolo.*

27

Natali, Diodore, tuo conviva senatus
    accubat et rarus non adhibetur eques
et tua tricenos largitur sportula nummos :
    nemo tamen natum te, Diodore, putat.

30

O temperatae dulce Formiae litus,
vos, cum severi fugit oppidum Martis
et inquietas fessus exuit curas,
Apollinaris omnibus locis praefert.

27. Although Diodorus invites the best society to his birthday dinner, men refuse to forget that he was a base-born slave. On the *libertini* see 2. 29. Introd.; 5. 13. 6 N. — Meter: § 48.

1. Natali . . . tuo: see 7. 86. 1 N. — **Diodore:** the Greek name implies that he was a freedman. — **conviva:** pred. nom., in the sing. because the senate is there *en masse*.

2. rarus . . . eques: the neg. belongs very closely with the verb, 'few indeed are the knights who fail to get an invitation'. *adhibere aliquem cenae* is idiomatic.

3. tua . . . sportula here prob. denotes *apophoreta*, things given to the guests to be carried away; see 14. 37. Introd.—**tricenos . . . nummos:** if this is to be taken literally, this sportula was larger than the normal *centum quadrantes*, but smaller than the dole of *tres denarii* mentioned in 9. 100. 1 (see note there).

4. nemo . . . putat: 'people think of you precisely as if you had never seen the light at all'. Cf. Petr. 58 *ergo aut tace aut meliorem noli molestare, qui te natum non putat*; Sen. Apocol. 3 *nemo*

enim umquam illum natum putavit. In the view of Roman law slaves had no parents; hence M. means: 'you have no parents, you were never born at all; you have no right to celebrate a *dies natalis*'.

30. M. rallies his friend Domitius Apollinaris (see on 4. 86. 3 ; 7. 89) on maintaining a villa in a charming place (Formiae), to be enjoyed after all only by his slaves, while he himself slaved in town, too busy to enjoy life. — Meter: § 52.

1. O . . . litus: *Formiae* is voc. (cf. *vos*, 2); *litus* is in app. with it. Formiae lay on the coast of Latium and was easy of approach by the Via Appia; many Romans had villas there. At his villa there Cicero was murdered; see 5. 69. 5 N. The town was well sheltered, lying in a recess of the Sinus Caietanus (cf. 11–15). — **dulce . . . litus:** because of the mild climate and delightful outlook.

2. severi: Mars is the natural foe of rest and relaxation. — **oppidum** is seldom used of Rome. Fried. cites Liv. 42. 36; Varr. L. L. 6. 14.

3. inquietas fessus: juxtaposition of cause and effect.

5   Non ille sanctae dulce Tibur uxoris
     nec Tusculanos Algidosve secessus,
     Praeneste nec sic Antiumque miratur,
     non blanda Circe Dardanisve Caieta
     desiderantur, nec Marica nec Liris,
10   nec in Lucrina lota Salmacis vena.

5. sanctae . . . uxoris: Apollinaris had married a woman of Tibur, or else his wife owned a villa there. — sanctae: esteemed and beloved for her virtues. — dulce Tibur: cf. 1. 12. 1 N.; 4. 57. 10. On the beauty of Tibur (modern Tivoli) see e.g. Hare, Days Near Rome, 1. 193 ff.

6. Tusculanos . . . secessus: see 4. 64. 13 N.; Fried. SG. 2. 107 ff.— Algidos: rare as adj. except with *Mons*; cf. Ov. F. 6. 722 *in campis, Algida terra, tuis.* The poets (esp. Horace) not infrequently convert place names into adjectives, without adding the proper adjectival termination or suffix. In some of these cases, however, the adj. use may after all be the original use, and the substantival use may have arisen through ellipsis of some obvious noun; so we may suppose *Algidus Mons* to have given way to a shorter and more convenient *Algidus.* The eastern slopes of the Alban Hills, known as Mons Algidus, afforded favorite sites for villas; cf. Sil. 12. 536 *amoena Algida.*

7. Praeneste: see 4. 64. 33 N. Tibur (*Tivoli*), Tusculum (*Frascati*), and Praeneste (*Palestrina*) were the most fashionable hill resorts east of Rome; cf. Stat. Silv. 4. 4. 15–17 *hos Praeneste sacrum, nemus hos glaciale Dianae Algidus aut horrens aut Tuscula protegit umbra, Tiburis hi lucos Anienaque frigora captant*; Suet. Aug. 72; Iuv. 14.

86–90.— Antium: delightfully situated on a promontory, nearer to Rome than was Circeii or Caieta, Antium was the favorite of more than one emperor. See Fried. SG. 2. 110.

8. blanda Circe: i.e. the Circeian promontory (about midway between Antium and Caieta), named after the enchantress Circe, who, story said, had dwelt there; see Preller-Jordan 1.410. M. writes *blanda*, as if Circe were still there, or as if her charms were reflected in the loveliness of the region. For the metonymy in *Circe* cf. *Marica, Liris, Salmacis,* 9–10.— Dardanis . . . Caieta: the promontory and town of Caieta on the Sinus Caietanus were said to have derived their name from the fact that Aeneas's nurse, Caieta, was buried there; see Aen. 7. 1–2 *tu quoque litoribus nostris, Aeneia nutrix, aeternam moriens famam, Caieta, dedisti.*

9. desiderantur: i.e. so long as Apollinaris can stay at Formiae. — nec Marica nec Liris: the nymph Marica had a temple in a sacred grove not far from Minturnae near the mouth of the Liris, the river between Latium and Campania. Cf. 13. 83; Hor. C. 3. 17. 7; Preller-Jordan 1. 412.

10. in Lucrina . . . vena: 'the nymph who bathes in (= dwells in) the Lucrine waters'. Salmacis, a Carian nymph, fell in love with Hermaphroditus, who bathed in

Hic summa leni stringitur Thetis vento,
nec languet aequor, viva sed quies ponti
pictam phaselon adiuvante fert aura,
sicut puellae non amantis aestatem
15   mota salubre purpura venit frigus.
Nec saeta longo quaerit in mari praedam,
sed e cubili lectuloque iactatam
spectatus alte lineam trahit piscis.

her fountain. The waters of this fountain were supposed to be enervating; cf. Cic. Off. 1. 18. 61. M. for some reason unknown to us transfers her to the Lucrine Lake (for which see 3. 60. 3 N.; 4. 57. 1). Probably *Lucrina . . . vena* stands here for Baiae, with all its natural charms and wanton gaiety, with special emphasis on the latter. — **vena** is seldom used alone for *aqua* or *lacus*; Ov. Tr. 3. 7. 16 has *fecundae vena aquae.*

11. Hic: at Formiae. — **summa . . . Thetis,** *the surface of the sea.* Thetis, name of the daughter of Nereus and Doris, in poetry and late prose = *mare*; cf. 10. 14. 4 *et Thetis unguento palleat uncta tuo*; Verg. E. 4. 32 *temptare Thetim ratibus.*

12. nec languet aequor: there is not a dead calm, but a *viva quies*; the breeze is gentle, but still lively enough to make sailing possible. *Nec = et tamen non.*

13. pictam phaselon: a pleasure yacht (named from a fancied resemblance to the φάσηλος, or kidney bean), adapted to sailing in quiet waters. They were sometimes constructed of papyrus or baked clay, which could easily be painted; cf. Verg. G. 4. 289 *pictis phaselis*; Iuv. 15. 126–127 *vulgus, parvula fictilibus solitum dare vela phaselis.*

14. puellae: gen. with *purpura,* 15. — **aestatem,** *summer heat*; cf. Hor. C. 1. 17. 2–3 *Faunus . . . igneam defendit aestatem capellis.*

15. mota . . . purpura, *through the movement of,* etc. — **purpura:** prob. a 'fan' (*flabellum*) of peacock's feathers; such fans were much used by Roman women. Fried. interprets of a purple *palla,* 'cloak'.

16. saeta, *fish-line,* made of hair; cf. 1. 55. 9 *et piscem tremula salientem ducere saeta*; Ov. Hal. 34–35 *atque ubi praedam pendentem saetis avidus rapit.* — **longo . . . in mari:** i.e. far out at sea; *longo = longinquo.*

17–18. sed . . . piscis: he can throw his fish-line either from his *cubiculum* or from his *triclinium.* — **cubili:** see App. — **lectulo:** Plin. Ep. 9. 7. 4, describing two of his villas on the Lacus Larius, says: *ex illa possis dispicere piscantes, ex hac ipse piscari hamumque de cubiculo ac paene etiam de lectulo ut e naucula iacere.* Probably Apollinaris's villa, like many around the Bay of Naples, was extended out over the water; cf. Hor. C. 2. 18. 18; 3. 1. 33. — **spectatus alte:** either 'seen deep down in the water' or 'seen from a height'. In either case the phrase emphasizes the clearness of the water (and perhaps the size of the fish).

Si quando Nereus sentit Aeoli regnum,
20 ridet procellas tuta de suo mensa :
piscina rhombum pascit et lupos vernas,
natat ad magistrum delicata murena,
nomenculator mugilem citat notum
et adesse iussi prodeunt senes mulli.
25 Frui sed istis quando Roma permittit ?
quot Formianos inputat dies annus
negotiosis rebus urbis haerenti ?
O ianitores vilicique felices !
dominis parantur ista, serviunt vobis.

19. Si . . . regnum: i.e. when-ever a storm rages, thus prevent-ing sea-fishing. — **Nereus** (prop. name of the son of Oceanus) often = *mare*; cf. note on *Thetis* above, 11. — **Aeoli regnum:** cf. Verg. A. 1. 52 ff. *hic vasto rex Aeolus antro luctantis ventos tempestatesque so-noras imperio premit ac vinclis et carcere frenat.* — **regnum** almost = *imperium*.

20. tuta de suo, *safe (from =) by virtue of its own resources.* Apollinaris's table has a supply in-dependent of the sea (21–24).

21. piscina: here a salt-water fish-pond; such *piscinae* were a comparatively late fad. Cf. Plin. N. H. 9. 170; Macr. S. 3. 15. 6; Beck. 3. 57 ff. — **rhombum:** see 3. 45. 5 N.; 3. 60. 6. — **lupos:** see 9. 26. 6 N. — **vernas:** i.e. home-raised in the *piscina.* On the word see 1. 41. 2; 2. 90. 9; 3. 58. 22. Here it is virtually an adjective.

22. magistrum: Apollinaris. — **delicata murena:** the best sea-eels came from Sicily. With *delicata* cf. *pisces . . . delicatos*, 4. 30. 16 N.

23. nomenculator: prop. the slave whose business it was to know the names of those whom

his master was likely to meet, esp. at the *salutatio*, and to remind his master of their names (see Beck. 2. 156; 198), but here the slave who could call the fish-friends of his master by name. *Nomenclator* is the usual spelling; with the text cf. *navita* (= *nauta*), 6. 80. 3. — **mugilem . . . notum:** cf. 4. 30. 3–7, with notes.

24. senes: adj., the primary use. See also on 1.66. 7 ; 3. 58. 7 ; 5. 37. 1. The word plays the same rôle as *notum*, 23; master and fish are old friends. — **mulli:** see 2. 43. 11 N.

25. istis, *these delights.* — **per-mittit:** sc. *Apollinari.* See App.

26. Formianos . . . dies: de-lightful days spent at Formiae. — **inputat,** *charges up to the account of.* This use of *inputo* is post-Augustan; cf. Iuv. 5. 14–15 *fructus amicitiae magnae cibus : inputat hunc rex, et quamvis rarum tamen inputat.*

27. negotiosis . . . urbis: cf. e.g. Hor. S. 2. 6; Plin. Ep. 1. 9. — **haerenti:** general, 'to one who de-votes himself to'.

28. felices: because they are al-ways at Apollinaris's (*praedium*) *Formianum.*

31

Addixti servum nummis here mille ducentis,
  ut bene cenares, Calliodore, semel.
Nec bene cenasti : mullus tibi quattuor emptus
  librarum cenae pompa caputque fuit.
5 Exclamare libet : "Non est hic, inprobe, non est
  piscis : homo est ; hominem, Calliodore, comes ".

32

Haec mihi quae colitur violis pictura rosisque
  quos referat voltus, Caediciane, rogas ?
Talis erat Marcus mediis Antonius annis
  Primus : in hoc iuvenem se videt ore senex.

31. M. satirizes the gluttony of his time by an epigram on a gourmand who, to get money to buy a big mullet, sold a slave. — Meter : § 48.

1. **Addixti,** *sold. Addico* prop. = 'knock down to the highest bidder', i.e. 'sell by auction'; here and elsewhere it merely = *venumdare, vendere.* Note the (contracted) form : cf. 12. 16. 1 *addixti, Labiene, tres agellos.* — **here :** see on 1. 43. 2.

2. **Calliodore :** evidently a freedman. — **semel :** i.e. for once at least.

3. **Nec** = *et tamen non.* — **mullus :** see 2. 43. 11 N. M. means : 'All you had as the *pièce de résistance* of your dinner (!) was a fourpound mullet'.

4. **pompa caputque :** the chief dish, which the perverted and depraved taste of the time required should be striking because of rarity, size, cost, or display of the culinary art. — **pompa :** it was brought into the triclinium with great ceremony, as the wine was carried into Nasidienus's banquet in Hor. S. 2. 8. 13–15 *ut Attica virgo*

cum sacris Cereris procedit fuscus Hydaspes Caecuba vina ferens. Cf. 12. 62. 9–10 *cernis ut Ausonio similis tibi pompa macello pendeat ;* Petr. 60 *avidius ad (hanc) pompam manus porreximus ;* Knapp Class. Rev. 10. 427–428. — **caput :** cf. Cic. Tusc. 5. 34. 98 *ubi cum tyrannus cenavisset Dionysius, negavit se iure* ('broth') *illo nigro, quod cenae caput erat, delectatum.*

5. **Exclamare libet :** cf. 2. 75. 9 *exclamare libet* " *Crudelis, perfide, praedo* " . . . ; Iuv. 8. 29–30 *exclamare libet populus quod clamat Osiri invento.*

6. **homo . . . comes :** cf. Iuv. 4. 25–26 *hoc pretio squamae (emptae sunt)? potuit fortasse minoris piscator quam piscis emi.* — **comes :** from *comedo.*

32. On a picture of M. Antonius Primus. Cf. 10. 23. — Meter : § 48.

1. **Haec** (*pictura*) : subj. of *referat,* 2. — **colitur . . . rosis :** chaplets were hung about the picture.

3. **mediis . . . annis :** i.e. in his prime ; cf. *iuvenem,* 4.

4. **ore,** *likeness ;* prop. the face shown in the picture.

5   Ars utinam mores animumque effingere posset!
    pulchrior in terris nulla tabella foret.

35

Omnes Sulpiciam legant puellae
uni quae cupiunt viro placere,
omnes Sulpiciam legant mariti
uni qui cupiunt placere nuptae:
5   non haec Colchidos adserit furorem,
diri prandia nec refert Thyestae,
Scyllam, Byblida nec fuisse credit:
sed castos docet et pios amores,
lusus, delicias facetiasque.
10   Cuius carmina qui bene aestimarit

5. Ars ... posset: cf. the verses written by Ben Jonson to accompany the Droeshaut engraving of Shakespeare printed in the first folio of Shakespeare's works: "O, could he but have drawn his wit As well in brasse as he hath hit His face, the print would then surpasse All that was ever writ in brasse".

35. Sulpicia, whose wedded love is commemorated here, was a contemporary of M. and wrote erotic elegy. Cf. 10. 38. 2; Teuffel, § 323. 6, 7. — Meter: § 49.

1. puellae: for the thought cf. 7. 88. 3-4. *Puella* is used of a (young) wife in poetry and post-Augustan prose; cf. 7. 88. 4 N. See below on 3, 20.

2. uni ... placere: i.e. who are faithful to their marriage vows.

3. mariti proves clearly the sense to be ascribed to *puellae,* 1.

5. Colchidos ... furorem: she does not appropriate as her theme the lust and crimes of a

Medea. — **Colchidos:** see 5. 53. 1 N. — **adserit:** see on 1. 15. 9.

6. diri ... Thyestae: see 3. 45. 1 N.; cf. Apoll. Sidon. C. 23. 277 *sive prandia quis refert Thyestae.*

7. Scyllam ... credit: Sulpicia does not credit certain stories of impure love; much less does she deem them worthy of her song. For Byblis see Ov. M. 9. 454-455.

8. docet: Sulpicia is like a moral teacher or preacher. — **pios amores:** see App.

9. lusus: Domitius thinks of dalliance "*inter coniuges*". This sense is possible enough after *amores,* 8; *ludere* is likewise used of amorous playing. But we may rather interpret *lusus* by the nouns that follow and think then of 'frolics' in general. In any case the adjectives of 8 must be carried over into this verse. — **delicias,** *charming badinage* (Steph.). — **facetias:** wit and humor.

10-12. bene, *fairly.* — **aestimarit ... dixerit:** for the tenses

nullam dixerit esse nequiorem,
nullam dixerit esse sanctiorem ;
tales Egeriae iocos fuisse
udo crediderim Numae sub antro.

15   Hac condiscipula vel hac magistra
esses doctior et pudica, Sappho,
sed tecum pariter simulque visam
durus Sulpiciam Phaon amaret.

Frustra, namque ea nec Tonantis uxor

see A. 516, c, N.; L. 1627.—**nequi-orem**: cf. *lusus*, 9, *iocos*, 13; see 1. 109. 1 N.; 6. 82. 5 N. For the marked similarity of 11 and 12 cf. 3. 44. 14–15; 4. 43. 7–8 *iuro per Syrios tibi tumores, iuro per Berecyntios furores*; 5. 24. 5–6, etc. This usage, common in M., occurs chiefly in his hendecasyllabics, the meter Catullus made so peculiarly his own; Catullus himself was fond of such repetitions (cf. e.g. 1. 3 *Passer*, etc.). See on 2. 41. 3–4; 1. 109. 1; § 34.—**sanctio-rem**: cf. 10. 30. 5.

13. Egeriae: one of the old Italian Camenae, who was said to have assisted King Numa in establishing the religion of Rome. See Liv. 1. 19. 5; Ov. F. 3. 275. She is variously spoken of as the *coniunx* or the *amica* of Numa; one tradition declared that he met her in a *spelunca* near the Porta Capena at Rome, another made the grove of Aricia their rendezvous. See Preller-Jordan 2. 129; Roscher Lex.

14. udo: because of the water running from the spring in the cave.

15–16. 'Sappho might have learned both wisdom and good morals, had she been so fortunate as to be a schoolmate or pupil of Sulpicia'. Sappho and Alcaeus

were the chief representatives of the Æolic school of lyric poetry. Brilliant Sappho surely was; modern scholars refuse to accept the view once current which represented her as immoral.—**esses**: for tense see on *amaret*, 18.—**doctior**: see on 1. 25. 2; 1. 61. 1; etc. —**pudica**, following *doctior*, has comparative force.

17. sed: there would have been loss to Sappho to offset her gain. —**tecum . . . visam**: i.e. 'had you and Sulpicia been seen together by Phaon'.

18. durus: i.e. toward Sappho. —**amaret**: we might have had *amasset* (the protasis is in *visam*, 16), so for *esses*, 16, we might have had *fuisses*. But M. is writing as if Sappho were alive; we have in the unreal condition, then, a usage akin to that seen in the historical present. It would be possible, also, to say that we have a 'future less vivid' condition (of the *si* plus pres. subjv. type) used of the past; see on *posses*, 1. 41. 17.

19. Frustra (*amaret*): 'Phaon would have loved her in vain; nay, no god even could win her from Calenus'.—**ea**: Sulpicia.—**Tonantis**: see 10. 20. 9 N.—**Tonantis uxor**: Juno. *Uxor* and *puella* (20) are pred. nominatives.

20   nec Bacchi nec Apollinis puella
     erepto sibi viveret Caleno.

39

Consule te Bruto quod iuras, Lesbia, natam,
    mentiris.   Nata es, Lesbia, rege Numa ?
sic quoque mentiris, namque, ut tua saecula narrant,
    ficta Prometheo diceris esse luto.

43

Septima iam, Phileros, tibi conditur uxor in agro :
    plus nulli, Phileros, quam tibi, reddit ager.

20. Bacchi: join with *puella*.
— **puella** here has a different sense
from that seen in 1; render by
'lass', 'love'. We may suppose
that Jupiter is mentioned in 19 for
his majesty, which none could share
with him save by wedlock, and that
Bacchus and Apollo are named for
their youthful beauty, which was,
according to story, the undoing of
many maids who did not become
uxores of these gods.
   21. erepto . . . Caleno = a
protasis in plpf. subjunctive. — **vi-
veret:** on this same wedded life
see 10. 38. 1–3, 9–14.
   39. 'Lesbia is wrong about her
age'. — Meter: § 48.
   1. Consule . . . Bruto: i.e. in
the first year of the Republic.
   2. rege Numa: at a time far
antedating Brutus.
   3. namque: see App. — **saecula,** *generations, centuries;* nom.,
though some make it acc. See
1. 107. 5; 5. 24. 1. — **narrant,** *tell
the story.*
   4. Prometheo . . . luto: of the
many confused Prometheus myths
M. has used that which represents
Prometheus as having created man
out of clay; he thus created Pan-

dora, the first woman. On another
old woman cf. 10. 67. 1–5.
   43. 'His private burial-plot
affords Phileros his best harvest;
he has been enriched by the dowry
of seven wives, who successively
died'.   M. insinuates that the wives
died by Phileros's help. On poisoning in Rome see on 4. 69. 2; 8. 43;
9 15; cf. Iuv. 14. 220–222 *elatam
iam crede nurum, si limina vestra
mortifera cum dote subit: quibus
illa premetur per somnum digitis!*
— Meter: § 48.
   1. Septima . . . uxor: cf. 9. 15;
9. 78. 1–2 *funera post septem nupsit
tibi Galla virorum, Picentine: sequi
vult, puto, Galla viros.* — **tibi** is
both dat. of interest and dat. of
the agent (so-called). — **conditur**
= *sepelitur;* cf. 7. 96. 1 N.; Pers.
2. 14 *Nerio iam tertia conditur
uxor.*
   2. ager, *the countryside, farm
land, a (his) farm.* Roman law required that the burial-plot should
be outside the city walls. Until
wealth and luxury had made common great mausolea along the roads
leading from the city, this plot was
apt to be strictly private, on a farm;
there are many such old family

47

Vitam quae faciant beatiorem,
iucundissime Martialis, haec sunt:
res non parta labore, sed relicta,
non ingratus ager, focus perennis,
5   lis numquam, toga rara, mens quieta,
vires ingenuae, salubre corpus,

burial-plots in our own land. Cf.
I. 114. 1–4; I. 116. 1–3. On the
word *ager* see Kirk Class. Journ.
2. 81.

47. What constitutes a happy
life? — Meter: § 49.

2. Martialis: Iulius Martialis;
see on I. 15; 4. 64; 5. 20; etc.

3. res = *res familiaris, money,
wealth,* a frequent meaning, esp. in
poetry. — **relicta:** i.e. by kinsfolk
or friends; we should say *inherited.*
Cf. Hor. Epod. 2. 1 ff. *beatus ille
qui . . . paterna rura bobus exercet
suis, solutus omni faenore.* M.'s
point is made clear by Plat. Rep.
330 B–C; there Socrates declares
that those who have inherited their
wealth are generally free from the
vice of caring too much for it.
Excessive regard for wealth keeps
one from using it.

4. non ingratus: see 3. 58. 4 N.;
Cic. Cato M. 15. 51 *terra, quae numquam recusat imperium nec umquam sine usura reddit quod accepit.*
— **focus perennis** stands for an
unfailing supply of food and the fuel
necessary to cook it (metonymy);
cf. Tib. I. 1. 5–6 *me mea paupertas
vitae traducat inerti, dum meus adsiduo luceat igne focus.*

5. lis, *lawsuits,* though less formal disputes may be included; cf.
2. 90. 10. — **toga rara:** the toga
was costly in itself and in the expense of keeping it clean (1. 103.
5 N.), heavy, and in warm weather

hot. The disposition to disuse it,
by laying it off temporarily within
one's own house or in the country,
or by substituting for it in public
something lighter, like the *lacerna,*
was natural and tended to increase
(3. 63. 10 N.). Men, however, had
to wear it at the various *ludi,* and
the client was burdened with it
when he danced attendance on his
patron (2. 29. 4 N.). With the text
cf. I. 49. 31 *nusquam toga* (of life in
Spain); 10. 51. 6 *o soles, o tunicata
quies* (in the country)! 12. 18. 17;
Iuv. 3. 171–172 *pars magna Italiae
est, si verum admittimus, in qua
nemo togam sumit nisi mortuus*;
Plin. Ep. 5. 6. 45 *nulla necessitas
togae* (at his Tuscan villa). — **quieta:** i.e. free from worry.

6. ingenuae: see 6. 11. 6 N.;
Ov. Tr. I. 5. 71–72 *illi corpus erat
durum patiensque laborum: invo-
lidae vires ingenuaeque mihi.* M.
desires such strength as is needed
by a gentleman, i.e. by one who
does not depend on sheer physical
force for his livelihood. The word
may, however, = *innatae,* ἐγγενεῖς.
— **salubre corpus:** cf. Sen. Ep.
10. 4 *roga bonam mentem, bonam
valetudinem animi, deinde tunc
corporis*; Petr. 61 *omnes bonam
mentem bonamque valetudinem sibi
optarunt*; Iuv. 10. 356 *orandum est
ut sit mens sana in corpore sano.*
Note the chiasmus in this vs.; cf.
8. 2. 6; Paukstadt 31.

prudens simplicitas, pares amici,
convictus facilis, sine arte mensa,
nox non ebria, sed soluta curis,
10   non tristis torus, et tamen pudicus,
somnus, qui faciat breves tenebras :
quod sis esse velis nihilque malis ;
summum nec metuas diem nec optes.

48

Nuntiat octavam Phariae sua turba iuvencae,

7. **simplicitas**: cf. 8. 73. 2 *nivea simplicitate*; 11. 20. 10 *qui scis Romana simplicitate loqui*; 1. 39. 3–6 *si quis ... vera simplicitate bonus ... erit.* — **pares**: perhaps of equality in rank, wealth, etc., with the thought that friendship is possible only between equals; perhaps, rather, *well-matched, congenial.* For the latter sense cf. Hor. Ep. 1. 5. 25 ('come to dinner with me: I will see to it') *ut coeat par iungaturque pari*; Cic. Cato M. 3. 7 *pares autem vetere proverbio cum paribus facillime congregantur.*

8. **facilis**: because the *amici* are *pares*. — **sine arte mensa**: a plain, old-fashioned dinner, plainly served, such as 10. 48 describes.

9. **nox . . . curis**: i.e. let there be just wine enough at the *comissatio* to make us forget the burdens of life.

10. **tristis**, *prudish.*

11. **somnus . . . tenebras**: i.e. sound, unbroken sleep. See on 2. 90. 10; 9. 68. 1.

12–13. **quod sis**: pred. nom. to *esse velis.* — **sis**: subjv. because dependent on other subjunctives (attraction). — **velis . . . optes**: these four subjunctives of wish or prayer, coming as they do after a long array of nouns in app. to *haec*,

2, seem at first sight abrupt; it should be noted, however, that M.'s statement of the essentials of happiness really involves a prayer for their acquisition. We should say something like 'willingness to be what you are, absence of all desire for change, no fear of death, no craving for its coming'. — **nihil . . . malis**: cf. Iuv. 10. 356–362. See § 37. — **summum . . . diem** = *supremum diem, death*; see on 1. 109. 17. — **nec optes**: i.e. on account of life's burdens.

48. A picture of a simple dinner. Cf. 5. 78; 11. 52. See § 18. — Meter: § 48.

1. **Nuntiat**: i.e. as water-clock or sun-dial or slave-crier might; cf. 8. 67. 1 *horas quinque puer nondum tibi nuntiat*; Petr. 26. The noise of the metallic rattle (*sistrum*) used in the worship of Isis announces to the goddess that the hour for the realistic ceremony has arrived. See Preller-Jordan 2. 381. — **octavam**: sc. *horam.* — **Phariae . . . iuvencae**: see 2. 14. 7–8 N.; Ov. F. 5. 619–620 *hoc alii signum Phariam dixere iuvencam, quae bos ex homine est, ex bove facta dea.* For the Isis Pharia see Preller-Jordan 2. 374; 382; on the cow-symbol see id. 2. 375; 377; 381. 3;

et pilata redit iam subiitque cohors.
Temperat haec thermas, nimios prior hora vapores
halat et inmodico sexta Nerone calet.
5   Stella, Nepos, Cani, Cerialis, Flacce, venitis?
septem sigma capit: sex sumus; adde Lupum.
Exoneraturas ventrem mihi vilica malvas

Roscher Lex. — **turba**: the worship of Isis was very popular; the word covers priests as well as devotees. Cf. 12. 28. 19 *linigeri fugiunt calvi sistrataque turba*.

2. **pilata . . . cohors**: an obscure verse, of uncertain text and variously interpreted; see App. It is perhaps hopelessly corrupt. Fried., following Gronovius, interprets *pilata* as 'equipped with *pila*' (cf. Verg. A. 12. 121) and *pilata cohors* as a cohort of the Praetorian Guard, which has just been relieved from duty by another cohort (see Marq.-Wissowa 2. 476. 7) and on its way back to the Castra Praetoria has approached M.'s dwelling on the Quirinal. But we have no proof that the watch was regularly changed at the eighth hour; further, the change of tense and the omission of the terminus ad quem (*domum meam*, or the like) are very harsh and very unlike M.'s usually limpid style. Scaliger read *atque pilata*, and made *pilata cohors* the company of devotees of Isis with shaven heads (*pilata = depilata = calva*; see 12. 29. 19, cited on 1) returning to the temple from a religious procession. The temple of Isis in the Campus Martius would probably be visible from M.'s lodging on the Quirinal.

3. **Temperat**: i.e. from the eighth hour the water is more tempered and agreeable than at an earlier hour, prob. because that hour suited the greatest number

of bathers. On the bathing hours see Beck. 3. 152 ff.; Marq. 269 ff. — **haec**: sc. *hora*. — **thermas**: see 2. 14. 11–12 N.; 4. 8. 5. — **nimios . . . vapores**: heat too great for the ordinary bather, shown by excess of steam.

4. **inmodico . . . Nerone**: i.e. the baths of Nero (see 3. 25. 4), popular with the exquisites, and apparently heated earlier and to a higher temperature than the other thermae. For the metonymy cf. 9. 61. 15 N.; 10. 24. 11 *post hunc Nestora* (i.e. such a life as Nestor might have lived) *nec diem rogabo*.

5. **Stella**: see 1. 61. 4 N.; 7. 36. 6. — **Nepos**: a friend and city neighbor of M. — **Cani**: see 1. 61. 9 N. — **Cerialis**: Iulius Cerialis; on his poetry see 11. 52. 17–18. — **Flacce**: prob. the Flaccus of 4. 49; 8. 56; etc. — **venitis**: it is now time for dinner. The word is semi-technical; cf. 11. 52. 2; Plin. Ep. 1. 15. 1 *heus tu promittis ad cenam nec venis!* The usual hour for dinner was the ninth; see 4. 8. 6–7 N.; 11. 52. 3; Marq. 297–298.

6. **sigma**: cf. 9. 59. 9 N.; 14. 87. 1–2 *accipe lunata scriptum testudine sigma; octo capit; veniat quisquis amicus erit.* — **Lupum**: cf. 5. 56.

7. **vilica**: perhaps the wife of the *vilicus* on his Nomentanum; see 19; cf. 9. 60. 3. — Verses 7–12 tell what was served during the *gustus* (see 1. 43. 3–8 N.; 1. 103. 7–8). — **malvas**: esteemed as a

adtulit et varias, quas habet hortus, opes,
in quibus est lactuca sedens et tonsile porrum,
10   nec deest ructatrix mentha nec herba salax ;
secta coronabunt rutatos ova lacertos,
et madidum thynni de sale sumen erit.
Gustus in his ; una ponetur cenula mensa,
haedus, inhumani raptus ab ore lupi,

laxative; cf. Hor. Epod. 2. 57–58 *gravi malvae salubres corpori*; C. 1. 31. 16 *levesque malvae.*

8. varias . . . opes: in antiquity vegetables were the staple food of the poor; meat was too expensive.

9. lactuca . . . porrum: *lactuca* and *porrum* were sometimes allowed to grow before they were used; sometimes the leaves were cut off as they came up, and were used forthwith. The former sort was called *capitatus*, the latter *sectilis, sectivus, tonsilis, sessilis, sedens*; see Beck. 3. 352. Cf. 3. 47. 8 (*illic videres*) *utrumque porrum sessilesque lactucas.* — **sedens:** a picturesque epithet of the *lactuca* (*porrum*) *sectilis*; translate by *squat, dwarf.* In comparison with this the other sort of *lactuca* and *porrum* would tower high. — **tonsile porrum**, *tops of cut leek, cut-leek tops. Porrum* was a poor man's dish; cf. Hor. S. 1. 6. 114–115 *inde domum me ad porri et ciceris refero laganique catinum*; Iuv. 3. 293–294 *quis tecum sectile porrum sutor . . . comedit*; Beck. 3. 356.

10. deest: see 8. 55. 3 N. — **mentha:** cf. Plin. N. H. 19. 160 *grato mentha mensas odore percurrit in rusticis dapibus.* — **herba salax:** some spice or aphrodisiac, prob. *eruca* (or *satureia*), is meant. Cf. Ov. A. A. 2. 421–423 *candidus . . . bulbus et ex horto quae venit*

herba salax ovaque sumantur; Beck. 3. 356.

11. secta . . . ova: no rarity; cf. Iuv. 5. 84–85 *sed tibi dimidio constrictus cammarus ovo ponitur.* — **coronabunt,** *will garnish*; prop. 'will surround'; cf. 10. 62. 5; see on *coronae*, 1. 41. 5. — **rutatos . . . lacertos:** the *lacertus* was a salt-water fish of which several varieties were recognized; cf. 11. 52. 7–8; Beck. 3. 331. The rue (*ruta*) was served, perhaps, as sauce, as we serve mint sauce with lamb; perhaps the leaves were used as garnishing, as in 11. 52. 7–8.

12. madidum . . . sumen: the udder and the matrix of a young sow, esp. when the pigs had been taken away from the mother before they had sucked, were in fact accounted great delicacies, and are often found at a dinner more elaborate than this is supposed to be; cf. 7. 78. 3 *sumen, aprum, leporem, boletos, ostrea, mullos.* M.'s dinner, though simple, is fine. — **madidum .·. de sale:** the udder was spiced with a brine (*muria*) made from the *thynnus.* — **thynni:** see 3. 2. 4 N.

13. una . . . mensa: a modest feast served as a single course (*ferculum*). Note the dim. *cenula.*

14. haedus: rather than the conventional *aper.* — **inhumani . . . lupi:** i.e. the kid was not killed specially for the *cenula*; cf. Hor. Epod. 2. 60 *vel haedus ereptus*

15   et quae non egeant ferro structoris ofellae,
        et faba fabrorum prototomique rudes ;
    pullus ad haec cenisque tribus iam perna superstes
        addetur. Saturis mitia poma dabo,
    de Nomentana vinum sine faece lagona,
20   quae bis Frontino consule trima fuit.
    Accedent sine felle ioci nec mane timenda
        libertas et nil quod tacuisse velis :

lupo, with Smith's note; Prop. 4. 4. 54 *nutrit inhumanae dura papilla lupae*. Shorey on Hor. Epod. 2. 60 remarks that "there was a belief that the wolf selected the best, and that τά λυκόβρωτα were the most toothsome (Plut. Sympos. 2. 9)".

15. ferro, *knife.* — **structoris** = *scissoris*; carving had been reduced to an art; see 3. 12. 2 N.; Iuv. 5. 120–124; Beck. 3. 369 ff.; Marq. 146. — **ofellae:** small bits of meat, *cuts*; cf. 12. 48. 17. *Ofellae* were sometimes very elaborately prepared; see Apic. 7. 265. The word, a dim. of *offa*, belongs to the *sermo plebeius*; see Cooper, § 41.

16. faba: food of the poor; cf. Hor. S. 2. 6. 63–64 *o quando faba Pythagorae cognata simulque uncta satis pingui ponentur holuscula lardo?* Beck. 3. 358; Fried. SG. I. 295. — **fabrorum:** with *faba*; logically it = an adj., *simplex.* — **prototomi:** i.e. early sprouts, esp. of *caulis* and *coliculi*; cf. Col. 10. 369 *sed iam prototomos tempus decidere caules.* — **rudes:** perhaps *common, simple,* perhaps *young.*

17. cenis . . . superstes: i.e. the ham would now be served for the fourth time. Among the rich to serve the same food more than once was accounted niggardly. Cf. 1. 103. 7; 3. 58. 42; Iuv. 14. 129–133. In Petr. 41 a boar is

pilleatus, because *cum heri summa cena eum vindicasset, a convivis dimissus est itaque hodie tamquam libertus in convivium revertitur.*

18. Saturis (*vobis*): i.e. 'after you have fared well on the substantial part of the dinner'. The *mensae secundae* come now (18–20); see 3. 50. 6 N.

19. Nomentana . . . lagona: for M.'s *Nomentanum* see 2. 38; 9. 18. 2; etc.; for *lagona* see 4. 69. 3 N. M. hints that he had raised this wine himself and that therefore it has value, though in itself a common sort of wine. — **sine faece:** added as further compensation for the fact that the wine was none of the best.

20. quae . . . fuit: M. is speaking playfully (see on 7. 79. 1); it has some age, too, to recommend it. — **bis . . . consule:** *bis* replaces the normal *iterum*, a rare use. The date meant is 98 or 97; see Klein 52. Gilbert Rh. Mus. 40. 216 differs. — **trima:** see App.

21–22. Accedent in sense = *addentur.* — **nec . . . libertas:** *nec* = *et non*; *et non mane timenda* is then restrictive, as *sine felle* is with *ioci.* The thought is: 'there will be freedom of speech, yes, but not the sort that calls for repentance the day after'. M. is thinking of the dangers that beset men under rulers like Tiberius and Domitian,

de prasino conviva meus venetoque loquatur,
nec faciunt quemquam pocula nostra reum.

50

Frangat Idumaeas tristis Victoria palmas,
plange, Favor, saeva pectora nuda manu ;
mutet Honor cultus et iniquis munera flammis

when innocent remarks of a private conversation were purposely misconstrued and when traps were set to tempt men to utter words that turned out to be their death-warrants (see on 1. 27. 6–7). It is instructive to find M. talking under Nerva as if such dangers still threatened men. — tacuisse velis : see on 1. 107. 6.

23. de . . . loquatur: i.e. 'let my guests discuss harmless matters'. There were originally two *factiones circi*, i.e. two companies that provided the horses, chariots, and jockeys; these were the White (*albata*) and the Red (*russata*). To these were soon added the Green (*prasina*) and the Blue (*veneta*). Domitian added two, the Gold and the Purple. The spectators championed the various colors, showing passionate enthusiasm and hatred of rival partisans. See Gibbon, chapter 40. 2, on the great riot in Constantinople in 532. See 9. 68. 8 N.; Fried. SG. 2. 336 ff.; Marq.-Wissowa 3. 517 ff.; Lanciani Anc. R. 213–217. — **prasino... veneto:** sc. *colore*; cf. 11. 33. 1–2 *saepius ad palmam prasinus post facta Neronis pervenit et victor praemia plura refert*; 14. 131. 1–2 *si veneto prasinove faves, quid coccina sumes? ne fias ista transfuga sorte vide*; Plin. Ep. 9. 6, in full.

24. faciunt ... reum: i.e. because of what he has unwittingly said. Note shift of moods in 21–24.

50. On the death of Flavius Scorpus, a famous charioteer (*auriga, agitator*) of the circus. See Fried. SG. 2. 327; 515. In 10. 74. 5 and 11. 1. 16 Scorpus is spoken of as living; this epigram, then, was written for the second edition of Book X (see 10. 2. Introd.). Fried. thinks that Scorpus died between December 96 and the summer of 98. — Meter: § 48.

1. Frangat ... palmas: since Victory's favorite son has at last met a conqueror in death, 'let Victory mourn and lay aside all symbols of success'. — **Idumaeas ... palmas:** parts of Judaea produced fine palms; cf. Verg. G. 3. 12 *primus Idumaeas referam tibi, Mantua, palmas*. For the bestowal of the palm, symbol of victory, on the victorious charioteer cf. Iuv. 8. 57–59 *nempe volucrem sic laudamus ecum, facili cui plurima palma fervet et exultat rauco victoria circo*; Marq.-Wissowa 3. 522.

2. plange ... pectora: a common expression of grief, prob. Oriental in origin; cf. Ov. M. 6. 248–249 *aspicit Alphenor laniataque pectora plangens advolat*. For display of grief at funerals see Beck. 3. 503–504; 512 ff. — **Favor:** the applause or favor of the spectators personified; cf. Plin. Ep. 9. 6. 2 *nunc favent (spectatores) panno* (i.e. their favorite colors).

3. mutet ... cultus: i.e. put on mourning. — **munera:** pred.

mitte coronatas, Gloria maesta, comas.

5   Heu facinus! prima fraudatus, Scorpe, iuventa
occidis et nigros tam cito iungis equos.
Curribus illa tuis semper properata brevisque
cur fuit et vitae tam prope meta tuae?

53

Ille ego sum Scorpus, clamosi gloria circi,
plausus, Roma, tui deliciaeque breves,

acc.; cf. Val. Flac. 3. 312–313 *et socios lustrate rogos; date debita caesis munera, quae nostro misisset Cyzicus igni*; Suet. Iul. 83; Beck. 3. 527–528.

4. mitte . . . comas: Glory is not merely to rend her hair (*scindere comas*), but to offer it to the dead man. In *coronatas* there is an allusion to the fact that the victorious drivers received crowns.

5–6. prima . . . occidis: Scorpus died at 27 (see 10. 53. 3); cf. Ov. M. 10. 196 *laberis, Oebalide, prima fraudate iuventa*. — **nigros . . . equos**: M. writes as if Scorpus were to continue in the lower world his earthly occupations. Objects in Hades were conventionally dark-hued. Various commentators make Pluto appropriate Scorpus as his own charioteer; for Pluto's black horses cf. Ov. M. 5. 359–361.

7. illa: i.e. of the circus; join with *meta*, 8. The *metae* were sets of cone-shaped turning-posts, three in each set, at the ends of the *spina*, the low wall which ran down the race-course for about two thirds of its length, to divide it into two parts. One set marked the close of the race. — **properata**, *quickly traversed*.

8. et = *etiam*, *quoque*; it adds *vitae* to *illa*, 7. — **meta**: for the fig. use cf. Ov. Tr. 1.9 1 *detur inoffensam*

vitae tibi tangere metam; Verg. A. 10. 471–472 *etiam sua Turnum fata vocant metasque dati pervenit ad aevi*; 12. 546 *hic tibi mortis erant metae*. — **prope**: note the adv. with *fuit*. *Sum*, as meaning 'exist', was originally construed only with an adverb. Certain adverbs (*bene, male, aegre, clam, ut, sic, ita, aliter, contra, prope, procul*) are used with the verb in classical prose; in colloquial language many others are so used (see on *pulchre esse*, 12. 17. 9). — We might set a colon after 7 and supply *fuit*; this, however, would be harsh. Yet the mixture of the literal and the fig. sense of *meta* in one sentence in our interpretation is also harsh.

53. See 10. 50. Introd.—Meter: § 48.

1–2. clamosi . . . circi: cf. 10. 50. 1–2 N.; Aus. Epitaph. 33 (35). 1 *clamosi spatiosa per aequora circi*; Sen. Ep. 83. 7 *ecce Circensium obstrepit clamor; subita aliqua et universa voce feriuntur aures meae*. — **gloria . . . plausus . . . breves**: cf. 9. 28. 1–2 *dulce decus scaenae, ludorum fama, Latinus ille ego sum, plausus deliciaeque tuae*. — **plausus**: Rome had applause for no one else; cf. *Favor*, 10. 50. 4 N. — **deliciae**: see 1. 109. 5 N.; 7. 88. 2. — **breves**: cf. 10. 50. 7–8 N.; 6. 28. 3.

invida quem Lachesis raptum trieteride nona,
dum numerat palmas, credidit esse senem.

54

Mensas, Ole, bonas ponis, sed ponis opertas ;
ridiculum est : possum sic ego habere bonas.

57

Argenti libram mittebas ; facta selibra est,
sed piperis. Tanti non emo, Sexte, piper.

58

Anxuris aequorei placidos, Frontine, recessus

3. **Lachesis**: subject of both verbs in 4; cf. 1. 88. 9 N.; 4. 54. 9. — **raptum . . . nona**: i.e. he was but 27 years old. *Raptum* emphasizes the cruelty of his untimely taking-off; cf. 1. 88. 1–2 *Alcime, quem raptum domino crescentibus annis Lavicana levi caespite velat humus*; C.I.L. III. Suppl. 8376 *militia insigni raptus trieteride sexta*. — **trieteride**: see 7. 96. 3 N.

4. **numerat palmas**: see 10. 50. 1 N. According to C.I.L. 6. 2. 10048 Scorpus won 2048 victories. — **credidit . . . senem**: cf. 4. 73. 8 *seque mori post hoc credidit ille senem*. — **senem**: i.e. a fit subject for death. Cf. Consol. ad Liv. 447–449 *quid numeras annos? vixi maturior annis: acta senem faciunt: haec numeranda tibi, his aevum fuit implendum, non segnibus annis*; Curt. 9. 6. 19 *ego . . . non annos meos, sed victorias numero: si munera fortunae bene computo, diu vixi*.

54. Meter: § 48.
1. **Mensas**: see 7. 48. 1–2. — **ponis**: see 1. 43. 2 N. — **opertas**: see 9. 59. 7 N.

2. **ego**: emphatic; 'even a poor man like myself'.

57. To a *patronus*, whose present at the Saturnalia has diminished from year to year. Cf. 8. 71. — Meter: § 48.
1. **Argenti libram**: prob. a small piece of plate. — **mittebas** = *olim mittere solitus es*.
2. **sed piperis**: as in 1. 43. 9. *Facta . . . piperis = facta non modo selibra sed etiam piperis est.* — **Tanti** = *argenti libra*; M. humorously represents the current gift, *selibra piperis*, as bought by the *argenti libra* he received in other days, and so says 'I am not in the habit of buying pepper for twice its weight in silver'. Cf. 4. 26. 4; 9. 100. 6.

58. M. makes his excuses for failing to pay his respects to Frontinus (see 10. 48. 20) at Rome as he had at Anxur.— Meter: § 48.
1. **Anxuris aequorei**: Anxur was an old Volscian town, situated where the Via Appia touched the sea at the southern end of the Paludes Pomptinae. *Tarrăcīna*, its Roman name, cannot stand

et propius Baias litoreamque domum,
et quod inhumanae cancro fervente cicadae
non novere nemus flumineosque lacus
5 dum colui, doctas tecum celebrare vacabat
Pieridas : nunc nos maxima Roma terit.
Hic mihi quando dies meus est ? iactamur in alto
urbis et in sterili vita labore perit,
dura suburbani dum iugera pascimus agri
10 vicinosque tibi, sancte Quirine, lares.

in dactylic verse. — **placidos** . . .
recessus: a marked contrast to
the bustle and drive of Rome (6–8);
cf. 10. 51. 6–8 *o tunicata quies! o
nemus, o fontes solidumque madentis harenae litus et aequoreis
splendidus Anxur aquis.* — **recessus**, *retreat*; cf. *secessus*, 10. 104. 14;
Iuv. 3. 4–5 (Cumae) *ianua Baiarum
est et gratum litus amoeni secessus.*

2. propius Baias, *a nearer
Baiae*, involves a metaphor and the
use of adv. with a noun (see on 3.
58. 51). 'Anxur is a second Baiae,
aye, more than a second Baiae, for
it is nearer to Rome'. See Gilbert
Q. C. 2, N. 2. — **litoream** . . . **domum**: a seaside villa with the comforts of a town palace (*domus*).

3. inhumanae: applied to the
cicadae because their presence
always betokens heat; cf. e.g. Verg.
E. 2. 13 *sole sub ardenti resonant
arbusta cicadis.* The *cicada* (τέτ-
τιξ) is not the grasshopper, but a
hemipterous insect which lives on
trees (its American representatives
are the harvest-fly and the seven-
teen-year locust); cf. Plin. N. H.
11. 95 *cicadae non nascuntur in rari-
tate arborum . . . nec in campis nec
in frigidis aut umbrosis nemoribus.*
— **cancro fervente**: i.e. at the hot
period, when the sun is in the sign
of the zodiac called Cancer and

the *cicadae* are unusually noisy; cf.
Ov. M. 10. 126–127 *solisque vapore
concava litorei fervebant bracchia
cancri.*

4. non novere: the grove is so
cool that the *cicadae* are not found
there; see on 3. — **flumineos** . . .
lacus: prob. the canal that ran from
Forum Appi through the Paludes
Pomptinae to Anxur. In 10. 51. 10
M. says this same villa *videt hinc
puppes fluminis, inde maris. Flumen* is used elsewhere of a canal.
Horace's amusing account of experiences on this canal (S. 1. 5. 11–23)
is known to all classical readers.

5. colui = *incolui*. — **vacabat**
(*mihi*): impersonal, 'I had leisure'.

6. Pieridas: see 1. 76. 3 N. —
maxima Roma: see 1. 3. 3 N.;
7. 96. 2. — **terit**: cf. 4. 8. 1 N.

7. Hic: at Rome. — **iactamur
in alto**: 'I am storm-tossed on the
sea of city life'.

8. sterili: see 1. 76. 14 N.

9–10. See §§ 10–11. — **suburbani** . . . **agri**: see on 2. 38; 9. 18.
2; 9. 60. 6; 9. 97. 7. — **dura** . . .
iugera: see 1. 85. 2; cf. *sterili* . . .
labore, 8. — **pascimus**: i.e. 'I keep
the farm, it does not keep me'. Cf.
9. 18, with notes; 10. 96. 7. — **vici-
nos** . . . **lares**: the temple of Qui-
rinus was on the western slope of
the Collis Quirinalis and evidently

Sed non solus amat qui nocte dieque frequentat
    limina nec vatem talia damna decent.
Per veneranda mihi Musarum sacra, per omnes
    iuro deos : et non officiosus amo.

61

Hic festinata requiescit Erotion umbra,
    crimine quam fati sexta peremit hiems.
Quisquis eris nostri post me regnator agelli,
    manibus exiguis annua iusta dato :
5   sic lare perpetuo, sic turba sospite solus
    flebilis in terra sit lapis iste tua.

not far from M.'s town house. —
lares: see 1. 70. 2; 9. 18. 2 N. Lanciani, P. and Chr. Rome 192, thinks
that M. did not live in his own house
here, but "was the guest of his
wealthy relative and countryman,
Valerius Vegetus, cos. 91 A.D., whose
city residence occupied half the
site of the present building of the
Ministry of War on the Via Venti
Settembre". Cf. Hülsen Rh. Mus.
49. 396 ff.

11–12. nocte dieque: for metrical reasons this order is frequent
in verse; cf. 11. 55. 6; Iuv. 3. 105.
Nocte emphasizes the earliness of
the *salutatio.* — **vatem:** see 1. 61.
1 N.; 8. 55. 11. — **damna:** constant
attendance on patrons involves
loss of time that might be put to
profitable use; cf. 1. 70. 17–18.

13. veneranda logically belongs with *Musarum* rather than
with *sacra. Per . . . sacra* = 'by
my art that I am bound to love
above all else'.

14. et non officiosus: 'even
though I am remiss in discharging
my duty as a client'. — **officiosus:**
cf. 1. 70. 2 N.

61. On Erotion. See 5. 34;
5. 37. M.'s anxiety lest the subse-

quent owner of the Nomentanum
should neglect the tomb of Erotion
was increased by his intention to
leave Rome and return to Spain.
— Meter: § 48.

1. festinata: i.e. that overtook
her all too soon; cf. 2; 5. 34. 5–6.
— **umbra:** sc. *monumenti, tumuli*;
local ablative.

2. crimine . . . fati: cf. 11. 93.
3–4 *o scelus, o magnum facinus
crimenque deorum, non arsit pariter quod domus et dominus*; Stat.
Silv. 1. 4. 17 *nec tantum induerint
fatis nova saecula crimen.* — **sexta
. . . hiems:** see 5. 34. 5–6.

3. regnator, *master.* As *rex* =
patronus, so *regnum* = 'the (a) rich
man's estate'; cf. 12. 31. 8; 12. 57.
19. — **agelli:** dim. of affection.

4. manibus exiguis = *manibus
huius tam parvae puellae. Manes*
= 'the spirits of the good'; cf.
Preller-Jordan 2. 66; Roscher Lex.
With *exiguis* cf. *parvola,* 5. 34. 3.
— **annua iusta:** rites in honor of
the dead were celebrated on the
anniversary of the death, and at
the Parentalia (February 13–21);
see Preller-Jordan 2. 98 ff.

5–6. lare . . . sospite: abl. abs.
with causal force. — **perpetuo:** i.e.

62

Ludi magister, parce simplici turbae :
sic te frequentes audiant capillati
et delicatae diligat chorus mensae,
nec calculator nec notarius velox
5   maiore quisquam circulo coronetur.
Albae leone flammeo calent luces
tostamque fervens Iulius coquit messem :

remaining in the undisturbed possession of your family. — **turba,**
your household; cf. Iuv. 14. 166–
167 *saturabat glaebula talis patrem
ipsum turbamque casae.* — **flebilis**
= either *flendus* (freely, *cause for
tears*), or *fletus, bemoaned.* Cf. Hor.
C. 1. 24. 9. The sense is ' may no
one else in all your household die '.
Cf. 6. 28. 10.

62. An appeal to schoolmasters
to deal gently with their pupils
in summer. Cf. 9. 68. — Meter :
§ 52.

1. **Ludi magister:** see 9. 68. 1.
— **simplici,** *tender, youthful.* See
on 2.

2. **sic** = *quod si feceris;* see on
7. 89. 4. — **capillati:** boys wore
their hair long till they laid aside
the *toga praetexta.* See 2. 57. 5 ; 3.
58. 30–31 ; 9. 29. 7 *nec matutini cirrata caterva magistri.*

3. **delicatae:** transferred epithet; it would be used more properly of the children who sit at the
master's table. See on 1. 15. 7.
Perhaps, however, *delicatae* pictures the result of *te . . . diligat,*
' love you till they count your table
their heart's delight '. Cf., then,
deliciae = ' pet ', and note the juxtaposition of effect and cause.

4. **calculator:** a teacher of
arithmetic ; in reckoning, counters
(*calculi*) were moved back and

forth on a reckoning-board (*abacus*). Cf. also Isid. Orig. 10. 43 *calculator* (*est,* 'is derived') *a calculis,
id est lapillis minutis, quos antiqui
in manu tenentes numeros compo-
nebant;* Beck. 2. 101 ; Marq. 97.
— **notarius,** *a shorthand writer.*
Stenography (*notae Tironianae*),
which had been brought to a high
state of perfection by this time,
seems to have been in great demand
in the courts, in the schools, and
even in the houses of the well-to-
do; see 14. 208.

5. **circulo:** a ring of people,
here of pupils ; cf. *chorus,* 3 ; 2. 86.
11–12 *scribat carmina circulis Palaemon, me raris iuvat auribus
placere.* — **coronetur:** cf. 10. 48.
11 N.

6. **Albae . . . luces,** *cloudless
days.* With the vs. cf. 4. 57. 5 N.

7. **tostam,** *till it is parched* ;
cf. note on *delicatae,* 3. — **Iulius**
(*mensis*) : July. The months long
known as Quintilis and Sextilis
were named Iulius and Augustus
in honor of Julius Caesar and
Augustus. — **coquit:** cf. Pers. 3.
5–6 *siccas insana canicula messes
iam dudum coquit.* We might also
render this vs. by ' is positively
cooking the parched earth '.

8–10. M. is playful ; he cannot
find words strong enough to express his horror.

cirrata loris horridis Scythae pellis,
qua vapulavit Marsyas Celaenaeus,
10   ferulaeque tristes, sceptra paedagogorum,
cessent et Idus dormiant in Octobres :
aestate pueri si valent, satis discunt.

65

Cum te municipem Corinthiorum

8. cirrata ... pellis, *the Scythian's skin ringleted* (tufted) *with bristling thongs*, is grimly humorous for 'the cat-o-nine-tails of curling Scythian leather'. M. seems to be thinking of a *flagellum* ; see on 8. 23. 3. Another view is that the instrument consisted of but one lash, whose side (sides) was (were) cut into short strips which hung loose about it. When this lash had been wet, by blood, perspiration, or otherwise, these tags of leather (*loris*) would curl up (*cirrata*) and stand out stiff and hard (*horridis*) till they were wet again, and so when the scourge was first brought into use on any occasion they would have much the same effect as the loading of the *flagellum* (8. 23. 3 N.). — **Scythae** is gen. sing. masc. The Scythians were typical barbarians ; Hdt. 4. 64 describes the uses to which they put the skins which they stripped from their dead foes. M. thinks of the Scythian as fit source of the lashes with which schoolmasters flog boys (see on 9. 68. 4).

9. qua: i.e. the like of that which Apollo used to flog Marsyas, before he flayed him alive for having dared to vie with him in musical skill. — **vapulavit** : this verb is regularly pass. in sense, though always active in form. — **Celaenaeus:** Apollo and Marsyas

contended at Celaenae in Phrygia. Xenophon Anab. 1. 2. 8 mentions the flaying of Marsyas (but not the flogging).

10. ferulae: rods fashioned from the giant fennel (νάρθηξ) were used as an instrument of punishment in schools ; cf. Iuv. 1. 15 *ergo manum ferulae subduximus* ; Suet. Gramm. 9 *si quos Orbilius ferula scuticaque cecidit.* — **sceptra:** cf. Aus. Ep. 14. 1 *Ausonius, cuius ferulam nunc sceptra verentur.*

11. Idus ... in Octobres: this passage is often taken to imply that schools were regularly closed from July to October (see editors on Hor. S. 1. 6. 75) ; but no such inference concerning school practice can be drawn from a single man's appeal to the schoolmaster to give a long vacation — unless indeed it be the inference that such vacation was exceptional: else why the appeal ?

12. valent, *keep their health*.

65. M. resents the familiarity of Charmenion, a Greek fop, and threatens retaliation in kind. — Meter : § 49.

1. municipem prop. designates a citizen of a free town ; Corinth, however, was in M.'s day a *colonia*, established by Julius Caesar. The old city, which was destroyed by L. Mummius in 146 B.C., had been accounted the most luxurious and

iactes, Charmenion, negante nullo,
cur frater tibi dicor, ex Hiberis
et Celtis genitus Tagique civis ?
5 an voltu similes videmur esse ?
Tu flexa nitidus coma vagaris,
Hispanis ego contumax capillis,
levis dropace tu cotidiano,
hirsutis ego cruribus genisque ;
10 os blaesum tibi debilisque lingua est,
nobis filia fortius loquetur :
tam dispar aquilae columba non est,
nec dorcas rigido fugax leoni.
Quare desine me vocare fratrem,
15 ne te, Charmenion, vocem sororem.

effeminate city in Greece; cf. Iuv.
8. 112–113 *despicias tu forsitan in-
bellis Rhodios unctamque Corinthon.*
   2. Charmenion: doubtless a
freedman.
   3–4. Hiberis . . . genitus: cf.
1. 61. 11–12 N.; 4. 55. 8 *nos Celtis
genitos et ex Hiberis.* The Hiberi
and the Celtae are frequently mentioned together; cf. 10. 78. 9–10 *nos
Celtas, Macer, et truces Hiberos
. . . petemus.* Though the Romans
had learned to respect the Gauls
and the Spaniards for their virility
and rugged strength, they still commonly regarded them as lacking in
culture. — **Tagi:** cf. 7. 88. 7 N.;
10. 17. 4.
   5. an . . . esse: see on 8. 3.
13.
   6. flexa . . . coma: cf. *flexos
. . . crines,* 3. 63. 3 N. — **nitidus:**
cf. 3. 63. 3; 4. 54. 8. — **vagaris:** i.e.
in the porticoes, the fora, and the
Campus Martius, as a man of
leisure can. In 7 and 9 some more
general verb (*eo*) is needed.

   7. contumax capillis: *contumax* is a transferred epithet; it
prop. belongs with *capilli*, 'I with
my stubborn Spanish locks'.
   8. dropace: for depilation cf.
2. 29. 6 N.; 3. 74. 1 *psilothro faciem
levas et dropace calvam.*
   9. cruribus: cf. Iuv. 8. 114–
115 *quid resinata iuventus cruraque
totius facient tibi levia gentis?*
   10. os blaesum: cf. 5. 34. 8.
Charmenion's lisping was probably
an affectation.
   11. filia . . . loquetur: ' my
daughter (should I have one) will ',
etc. See § 15; Gilbert Q. C. 15.
See also App.
   12. aquilae columba: the king
of birds is contrasted with one of
the weakest of birds; cf. Hor. C.
4. 4. 31–32 *neque imbellem feroces
progenerant aquilae columbam ;*
German *Adler brüten keine
Schwächlinge.*
   66. On a cook whose beauty
fitted him for a higher place. Cf.
12. 64. — Meter: § 48.

66

Quis, rogo, tam durus, quis tam fuit ille superbus,
    qui iussit fieri te, Theopompe, cocum?
Hanc aliquis faciem nigra violare culina
    sustinet, has uncto polluit igne comas?
5 Quis potius cyathos aut quis crystalla tenebit?
    qua sapient melius mixta Falerna manu?
Si tam sidereos manet exitus iste ministros,
    Iuppiter utatur iam Ganymede coco.

72

Frustra, Blanditiae, venitis ad me
    adtritis miserabiles labellis:

1. **durus**, *rugged, boorish, blind
to physical graces.* — **superbus**,
arrogant, perhaps in slighting
beauty wholly, perhaps rather in
decreeing that his very cooks must
be beautiful, expensive slaves.

3-4. **nigra . . . culina:** cf. 3. 2.
3. — **violare:** cf. 1. 53. 6. — **violare
. . . sustinet:** for the constr. cf.
Iuv. 14. 127-128 *neque enim omnia
sustinet* ('brings himself to') . . .
panis consumere frusta. — **uncto**,
greasy, sooty with grease.

5-6. **cyathos:** see 1. 27. 2; 8.
50. 21. — **crystalla:** see 9. 22. 7. —
tenebit: i.e. as cup-bearer. — **qua
. . . manu:** with *mixta*. Even the
best wine can be improved by
right handling. — **Falerna:** see 4.
69. 1; 8. 55. 14.

7. **sidereos**, *beautiful, excellent, superlative*; cf. 9. 36. 10 *tantaque sidereos vix capit aula mares*;
Hor. C. 3. 9. 21–22 *sidere pulchrior
ille est*; and the name Asterie (e.g.
in Hor. C. 3. 7). — **exitus** = *eventus,
fate, lot.* — **iste:** contemptuous.

8. **utatur:** hortatory, 'let Jupiter forthwith use', etc. The thought
is, 'if you with your beauty are to

be but a cook, Jupiter ought to
degrade Ganymedes to a like position', i.e. 'you are as worthy to be
cup-bearer as is Ganymedes himself'.

72. While asserting that the
flattery which was expected by
Domitian and hence was fashionable under him is not in place
under the present régime, M. actually flatters the new emperor
(Rader). If this epigram was a
part of the first edition of Book X,
Nerva is the emperor referred to
(Stobbe Phil. 27. 637); if it was
written for the second edition of
the book, Trajan is meant (Mommsen Herm. 3. 121; Fried., Einleitung,
64). Nerva died in January 98. —
Meter: § 49.

1. **Frustra:** Van Stockum, 37–
38, holds that Book X was written
in the year in which Nerva succeeded Domitian, and sees then in
1–4 one of the chief reasons that
influenced M. to leave Rome, i.e.
the realization that his occupation
was gone. But see § 14.

2. **adtritis:** freely, *shameless,
debased*; prop. 'worn', i.e. by kissing the throne or the feet of the

dicturus dominum deumque non sum.

Iam non est locus hac in urbe vobis ;

5   ad Parthos procul ite pilleatos

et turpes humilesque supplicesque

pictorum sola basiate regum.

Non est hic dominus, sed imperator,

sed iustissimus omnium senator,

10   per quem de Stygia domo reducta est

siccis rustica Veritas capillis.

Hoc sub principe, si sapis, caveto

verbis, Roma, prioribus loquaris.

74

Iam parce lasso, Roma, gratulatori,

lasso clienti : quamdiu salutator

---

monarch after the Oriental fashion (cf. 5–7). Still, in 8. 59. 2 *sub adtrita fronte* ; 11. 27. 7 *cum perfricuit frontem posuitque pudorem* ; Iuv. 13. 241–242 *quando recepit eiectum semel adtrita de fronte ruborem ?* the thought seems to be of a face (forehead) rubbed so smooth that it cannot show shame (that shame will not cling to it, so to say).

3. **dominum deumque :** see 5. 8. 1 N.

4. For the diæresis at every foot see § 49, d.

5. **pilleatos,** *hatted,* in marked contrast to the Roman, who ordinarily wore no hat.

7. **pictorum :** a derisive term, used of Oriental kings as attired in gaudy splendor (parti-colored or embroidered garments, gold, and jewels) ; we might say 'embroidered'. — **sola :** sc. *pedum.*

8–9. **Non ... dominus :** see on 5. 8. 1. — **sed ... sed :** for double or triple *sed* or *at* thus used cf.

Hor. S. 1. 3. 32–33 ; Ov. M. 5. 17–18 ; 507–508. So occasionally in English we find repeated 'but'.

10. **per quem :** i.e. who by his actions as a senator made men believe that Veritas had actually returned to earth. — **de Stygia domo :** truth had perished from the earth, and was with the dead, beyond the Styx in Orcus.

11. **siccis . . . capillis :** i.e. Truth with all the simple, rugged virtues of the country. *siccis... capillis* prop. = 'with locks not drenched by perfumes' ; the perfumes stand for the excesses of the town (see on 2. 95. 5 ; 3. 63. 4 ; 3. 12. 1).

12–13. **caveto . . . loquaris :** for the syntax see A. 450 ; 565, N. 1 ; GL. 548, N. 3 ; L. 1711.

74. Another wail from the long-suffering client. — Meter: § 52.

1. **gratulatori** = *salutatori* ; cf. 2.

2. **quamdiu,** *how much longer,*

anteambulones et togatulos inter
centum merebor plumbeos die toto,
5 cum Scorpus una quindecim graves hora
ferventis auri victor auferat saccos ?
Non ego meorum praemium libellorum
— quid enim merentur ? — Apulos velim campos ;
non Hybla, non me spicifer capit Nilus,
10 nec quae paludes delicata Pomptinas
ex arce clivi spectat uva Setini.
Quid concupiscam quaeris ergo ? dormire.

3. **anteambulones**: cf. 2. 18.
5 N.; 10. 10. 8. — **togatulos**: note
the dim.; cf. the noun *togula* in
4. 26. 4; 11. 24. 10–11 *ut tibi tuorum
sit maior numerus togatulorum*. —
inter: for the postposition see on
8. 50. 18.

4. **centum . . . plumbeos**
(*nummos*): for the daily dole cf.
3. 7. 1 N. *Plumbeus* is prop. used
of leaden (i.e. counterfeit) coins;
then it is used of anything mean
and worthless; cf. 6. 55. 3 N.; Petr.
43 *in manu illius plumbum aurum
fiebat*. M. in his bitterness de-
nounces the dole not only as paltry, but as paid in counterfeit coins.
Plumbeos, then, is contrasted with
auri, 'pure gold', 6.

5–6. 'Compare by contrast the
enormous gains of Scorpus, the
successful *auriga*'. See 10. 50; 10.
53.—**cum**: either *since* or *although*
fits the context. — **una . . . hora**:
i.e. as the result of a single race
in the circus. — **quindecim . . .
saccos**: i.e. bags or purses of
money; *quindecim* seems to be
used indefinitely; cf. 11. 6. 12–13
*bibenti succurrent mihi quindecim
poetae*. For the gains of charioteers
cf. e.g. Iuv. 7. 113–114 *si libet, hinc
centum patrimonia causidicorum,
parte alia solum* ('estate') *russati*

pone Lacertae. — **ferventis**, *resplendent, shining*, as if fresh from
the mint. See App.

7–8. **Non . . . velim**: 'I would
not crave (ask for)'; sc. *si quis me
roget quid velim*. — **Apulos . . .
campos**: the plains of northern
Apulia afforded excellent pastur-
age in winter and spring, when the
wind called Atabulus did not blow;
on great estates in Apulia the very
finest wool was produced; cf. e.g.
2. 46. 6; 8. 28. 3.

9. **Hybla**: cf. 5. 39. 3 N.; 7. 88.
8. — **spicifer . . . Nilus**: see 1. 61.
5 N.; 6. 80. 10. Egypt was one of
the main sources of the grain supply of Rome. — **capit**, *captivates,
charms*, with visions of wealth.

10–11. **quae**: the antec. is *uva*,
11. — **delicata**: because Setian
wine was the very finest (see on
4. 64. 34; 4. 69. 1). — **ex arce clivi
. . . Setini**: cf. *pendulam Setiam*,
4. 64. 33 N. — *uva = vinea*.

12. **dormire**: almost as difficult
as money for the client to secure,
on account of the early hour of the
salutatio. Cf. 12. 57 passim; 12. 68.
5–6 *otia me somnusque iuvant,
quae magna negavit Roma mihi*.
The poor in general found it hard
to sleep in Rome, since they had
to live near the busy quarters;

76

Hoc, Fortuna, tibi videtur aequum?
civis non Syriaeve Parthiaeve
nec de Cappadocis eques catastis,
sed de plebe Remi Numaeque verna,
5　iucundus, probus, innocens amicus,
lingua doctus utraque, cuius unum est
sed magnum vitium, quod est poeta,
pullo Maevius alget in cucullo,
cocco mulio fulget Incitatus.

see e.g. 12. 57; 12. 68; Iuv. 3. 232–238.

76. 'The slave muleteer is resplendent in scarlet, while the poor poet, free-born Roman though he is, freezes in an ugly *paenula*'. Cf. 1. 76; Iuv. 7. — Meter: § 49.

2. non . . . Parthiae: i.e. no despised Oriental; see Lib. Spect. 1. 1 N.; 2. 29. Introd.; 10. 27; Fried. SG. 1. 229–233. — **Syriae:** here prob. used in its wider sense, to embrace all the region between the Mediterranean and the Tigris. The literature of the time abounds in references to Syrian slaves; many of them, when freed, became rich; indeed some of them were the richest men in the Empire. Cf. 2. 29. Introd.

3. de . . . eques catastis: i.e. now a knight, but once a slave of the poorest sort (see on 9. 59. 4–6); cf. Tib. 2. 3. 59–60 *regnum iste tenet quem saepe coegit barbara gypsatos ferre catasta pedes.*

4. de . . . verna: i.e. a knight of the people of Remus, true son of Numa; sc. *eques* with *de plebe Remi.* For *verna* see on 1. 41. 2. M., emphasizing one part of its true force, takes it as = (*verus*) *filius.* — **plebe Remi:** cf. Iuv. 10.

73 *turba Remi.* — **Numae:** see 10. 10. 4 N.

5. innocens: i.e. not *malignus.*

6. lingua . . . utraque: a common expression for Greek and Latin, as if all other languages were unworthy of consideration; cf. e.g. Hor. C. 3. 8. 5 *docte sermones* ('literature', 'lore') *utriusque linguae*; Stat. Silv. 5. 3. 90 *gemina plangat Facundia lingua.* — **doctus:** see 1. 61. 1 N.; 8. 73. 8.

8. pullo . . . cucullo: the hood of the ugly *paenula* (or of a *lacerna*); see 1. 53. 5 N. — **Maevius:** this name, prop. that of an enemy of Vergil (cf. Serv. on Verg. E. 3. 90 *Maevius et Bavius pessimi fuerunt poetae, inimici tam Horatio quam Vergilio*), became proverbial for a poetaster. Here, as in *cuius . . . poeta*, 6–7, M. is humorously giving the world's view of poets, including himself. — **alget:** for the language cf. Iuv. 1. 74 *probitas laudatur et alget.* On literature as a means of support see 1. 76; 6. 8. 2; 10. 74. 4–5; Fried. SG. 3. 429.

9. cocco: see 2. 29. 8 N. — **mulio:** if *Incitatus* is the right reading, *mulio* prob. = *muleteer*; *Incitatus* then is a slave name, possibly given κατ᾽ ἀντίφρασιν (see on 7. 83. 1),

83

Raros colligis hinc et hinc capillos
et latum nitidae, Marine, calvae
campum temporibus tegis comatis,
sed moti redeunt iubente vento
5 reddunturque sibi caputque nudum
cirris grandibus hinc et inde cingunt :
inter Spendophorum Telesphorumque
Cydae stare putabis Hermerotem.
Vis tu simplicius senem fateri,
10 ut tandem videaris unus esse ?
calvo turpius est nihil comato.

because he was so slow. But since
Incitatus was the name of a favorite
race-horse (Suet. Cal. 55), *mulio
Incitati*, a conjecture of P. Faber,
should perhaps be read; *mulio* then
= *auriga, agitator*.

83. On a bald-headed man who
brushed his hair from the sides of
his head, so as to cover as far as
possible the exposed parts. Cf.
5. 49, with notes. — Meter: § 49.

1. hinc et hinc: see 4. 14. 8 N.
2–3. latum . . . campum: cf.
5. 49. 3, 6–7; 6. 57. 2. — **nitidae:**
cf. 4. 54. 8. — **temporibus . . . comatis:** instr. abl., a grotesquely
humorous way of saying that Ma-
rinus combs the hair back from
the temples.

4. redeunt: i.e. to their proper
place, the temples.

7–8. inter . . . Hermerotem:
i.e. one will surely think that a bald
head is flanked by two heads which
nature has favored with plenty of
hair. Cf. 5. 49. 1–7. Some see a
reference to three statuettes, but the
vss. have more point if three living
men are referred to. — **Cydae . . .
Hermerotem:** prob. best taken
as = 'Hermeros, slave (freedman,

son) of Cydas', whose baldness
was well known at Rome (Fried.).
For the expression cf. Verg. A.
1. 41 *Aiacis Oilei*; 6. 36 *Deiphobe
Glauci*; Plin. Ep. 6. 16. 8 *Rectinae
Tasci* (' Rectina, wife of Tascus ');
Ter. And. 357 *huius Byrriam* (a
slave); the Didascalia to Ter. And.
modos fecit Flaccus Claudi, 'the
music was composed by Flaccus,
slave of Claudius'. The gen. is pos-
sessive; there is no ellipsis.

9. Vis tu . . . fateri: for this
use of *vis* or *vis tu* with inf. to
express an urgent command or
exhortation cf. Hor. S. 2. 6. 92, with
Bentley's note; Petr. 111 *vis tu
reviviscere? vis discusso muliebri
errore, quam diu licuerit, lucis com-
modis frui?* Iuv. 5. 74–75 *vis tu
consuetis, audax conviva, canistris
impleri panisque tui novisse colo-
rem?* Cic. Fam. 4. 5. 4 *visne tu te,
Servi, cohibere et meminisse hominem te esse natum?* — **simplicius**
= both *more naturally* and *more
frankly* (see on *nivea simplicitate*,
8. 73. 2).

11. calvo . . . comato, *a bald-
headed man with luxurious hai* .
Cf. 1. 72. 8 N.

89

Iuno labor, Polyclite, tuus et gloria felix,
    Phidiacae cuperent quam meruisse manus,
ore nitet tanto, quanto superasset in Ide
    iudice convictas non dubitante deas.
5   Iunonem, Polyclite, suam nisi frater amaret,
    Iunonem poterat frater amare tuam.

94

Non mea Massylus servat pomaria serpens
    regius Alcinoi nec mihi servit ager,

89. On the Juno of Polyclitus. For Polyclitus see 8. 50. 2 N.; cf. Iuv. 8. 103–104 *Phidiacum vivebat ebur, nec non Polycliti multus ubique labor.* — Meter: § 48.

1. **labor:** cf. 8. 50. 1 N.; Iuv. 8. 104, cited in Introd. — **labor . . . felix:** cf. 8. 53.13 *unde tuis, Libye, tam felix gloria silvis*; 9.44.2 *opus laborque felix.* — **tuūs:** for the quantity see § 54, a; cf. 7. 44. 1 *Maximus ille tuūs, Ovidi, Caesonius hic est.*

2. **Phidiacae . . . manus:** i.e. which Phidias would be proud to have made. — **manus:** cf. 4. 39. 3 N.

3–4. **ore . . . deas:** freely, 'is resplendent with such marvelous beauty that the judge on Ida's slopes would have shown no hesitation and she would have surpassed', etc.; more literally, 'with a beauty thanks to whose marvelousness the judge', etc. M. declares Polyclitus's statue superior in beauty to Juno herself. *Quanto* supplants the protasis to *superasset*, and in sense = *quantum si habuisset* (*Iuno ipsa*). — **in Ide:** Mt. Ida (Ide) in Asia Minor, the scene of the *iudicium Paridis* (Verg. A. 1. 27). — **superasset . . . deas:** i.e.

would have surpassed not only the real Juno and Minerva, who both lost in the actual *iudicium Paridis*, but also Venus, who won. — **iudice . . . non dubitante:** in the famous contest Paris hesitated long. — **convictas:** a strong word, used most frequently of convicting persons of crime or error or of refuting their claims; *superasset . . . convictas* = 'would have refuted all their claims to beauty and have surpassed'.

5. **frater:** Jupiter was brother and husband of Juno; see Verg. A. 1. 46–47.

6. **poterat:** see on *poteras*, 1. 3. 12; cf. 11. 3. 7.

94. This epigram was apparently written to be sent with a present of fruit. — Meter: § 48.

1–2. 'My fruits are not like those of the garden of the Hesperides, or those which Alcinous set before Ulysses'. — **Massylus . . . serpens:** see 4. 64. 2 N. For *Massylus* see 9. 22. 14 N.; here the word is used loosely; the Hesperides were generally located farther to the west, near Mt. Atlas. — **Alcinoi . . . ager:** see 4. 64. 29 N. Cf. Hom. Od. 7. 117 ff.; Iuv. 5. 151–152 (*poma*) *qualia perpetuus*

sed Nomentana securus germinat hortus
arbore nec furem plumbea mala timent.
5 Haec igitur media quae sunt modo nata Subura
mittimus autumni cerea poma mei.

96

Saepe loquar nimium gentes quod, Avite, remotas
miraris, Latia factus in urbe senex,
auriferumque Tagum sitiam patriumque Salonem
et repetam saturae sordida rura casae.

Phaeacum autumnus habebat, credere quae possis subrepta sororibus Afris; Verg. G. 2. 87 *pomaque et Alcinoi silvae*; Ov. Am. 1. 10. 56 *praebeat Alcinoi poma benignus ager.* — servit: cf. 5. 13. 7 N.

3–4. Nomentana logically modifies *hortus* rather than *arbore*. However, to put two adjectives with *hortus* and leave *arbore* unmodified would be inartistic, as destroying the balance of the sentence. Cf. e.g. Hor. C. 1. 9. 7–8 *deprome quadrimum Sabina . . . merum diota.* — securus: M.'s garden tempts no thieves; cf. 4; 3. 58. 47 N. — plumbea: see on 6. 55. 3; 10. 74. 4. The apples of the Hesperides were *aurea*.

5–6. 'All I can do, therefore, is to send you some apples from—the Subura'. — media . . . Subura: M.'s apples are like 'fish caught with a silver hook'. The markets of the Subura were convenient to M.'s house on the Quirinalis (cf. 5. 22. 5 N.). Cf. 7. 31. 9–12 *quidquid vilicus Umber aut colonus aut rus marmore tertio notatum aut Tusci tibi Tusculive mittunt, id tota mihi nascitur Subura.* For the phraseology cf. 12. 21. 5 *nulla nec in media certabit nata Subura.* — cerea, *ripe, mellow-looking.* For the color cf.

3. 58. 19 N.; Verg. E. 2. 53 *addam cerea pruna.*

96. M. again voices his discontent with the conditions of life in Rome and longs for his old Spanish home. L. Stertinius Avitus was consul in 92, from the Kalends of May (Klein 50); see also 1. 16; § 17; Fried. SG. 3. 443.

1. loquar . . . quod involves indirect discourse; M. is quoting Avitus. For position of *quod* ('because') see on *nec*, Lib. Spect. 1. 2. — gentes . . . remotas is explained by 3–4. For the acc. with *loqui*, 'to speak of', see on 1. 61. 8.

2. Latia . . . senex: see § 14; cf. 10. 103. 7–8 *quattuor accessit tricesima messibus aestas . . . moenia dum colimus dominae pulcherrima Romae*; 10. 104. 9–10; 12. 34. 1.

3. auriferum . . . Tagum: cf. 7. 88. 7 N.; Stat. Silv. 1. 3. 108 *limo splendente Tagus.* — sitiam is to be taken partly in its literal, partly in its figurative sense; *thirst after* gives both senses.

4. repetam: 'I am ever revisiting, in imagination and hope of return'. — saturae . . . casae: farms and houses are poor, but plenty reigns in them. Fried. remarks on 1. 49. 28 that M. often

 5 Illa placet tellus, in qua res parva beatum
        me facit et tenues luxuriantur opes :
    pascitur hic, ibi pascit ager ; tepet igne maligno
        hic focus, ingenti lumine lucet ibi ;
    hic pretiosa fames conturbatorque macellus,
10   mensa ibi divitiis ruris operta sui ;
    quattuor hic aestate togae pluresve teruntur,
        autumnis ibi me quattuor una tegit.
    I, cole nunc reges, quidquid non praestat amicus
        cum praestare tibi possit, Avite, locus.

uses *sordidus* of outdoor objects without meaning to ridicule them (see also on 3. 58. 12). The word then means merely *plain, simple*; city throngs and things are *nitida*.

5. tellus: poetic for *regio* or *terra*. Van Stockum sees here one of M.'s two chief reasons for leaving Rome. For the other see 10. 72. 1 N. — **res**: see 10. 47. 3 N. — **parva beatum**: effective juxtaposition. For *beatum* see 1. 103. 3 N.

6. tenues . . . opes: i.e. persons of small means (metonymy). *Tenuis* is often used as the opposite of *dives, locuples*; cf. Cic. Invent. 1. 25. 35 *servus sit an liber, pecuniosus an tenuis*; Hor. Ep. 1. 20. 20 *me libertino natum patre et in tenui re*.

7. pascitur hic: cf. 10. 58. 9 N. — **tepet**: freely, *is scarcely made warm*. — **maligno**, *spiteful*, i.e. 'niggardly', 'scanty'. 'Fuel is so dear I cannot get sufficient to keep warm'. Cf. Verg. A. 6. 270 *per incertam lunam sub luce maligna*.

8. focus: see on 2. 90. 7; 3. 58. 22. — **ingenti . . . ibi**: cf. 1. 49. 27 (said of Spain) *vicina in ipsum silva descendet focum*; 3. 58. 23 *larga festos lucet ad lares silva* (said of Baiae).

9. pretiosa fames: in Rome it is costly to starve to death! Cf. Iuv. 3. 166-167 (*Romae*) *magno hospitium miserabile (constat), magno servorum ventres et frugi cenula magno.* — **conturbator . . . macellus**: the market bankrupts men; cf. 7.27. 10 *conturbator aper*; *rationem* (*rationes*) *conturbare*, 'to become bankrupt'. *Conturbator* is effective ; nouns in -*tor* commonly suggest the repeated performance of an act ; *conturbator . . . macellus* thus = *macellus qui rationes conturbare solet*. — **macellus**: this masc. form is very rare; here, probably, it is due to attraction to the gender of *conturbator*.

10. operta, *buried*.

11-12. With these vss. cf. note on *toga rara*, 10. 47. 5; 4. 66. 3-4 (of the country) *Idibus et raris togula est excussa Kalendis duxit et aestates synthesis una decem.* — **autumnis . . . quattuor**: for the constr. see on 2. 5. 1.

13-14. I . . . nunc: distinctly scornful; see on 1. 3. 12.—**reges**: see 1. 103. 3 N.; 2. 18. 5; 3. 7. 5. There is a contrast between this scornful *reges* and *locus*, 14; 'in Spain a place (the very ground) gives you what in Rome patrons (!) deny'. — **praestat**; cf. 3. 46. 11.

104

I nostro comes, i, libelle, Flavo
longum per mare, sed faventis undae,
et cursu facili tuisque ventis
Hispanae pete Tarraconis arces :

5   illinc te rota tollet et citatus
altam Bilbilin et tuum Salonem
quinto forsitan essedo videbis.
Quid mandem tibi quaeris ? ut sodales
paucos, sed veteres et ante brumas

10   triginta mihi quattuorque visos
ipsa protinus a via salutes
et nostrum admoneas subinde Flavum,
iucundos mihi nec laboriosos
secessus pretio paret salubri,

---

104. By Flavus, who is about to return to Spain, M. sends one or more copies of his book to his old home friends. See § 14.— Meter: § 49.

2. longum per mare: Flavus prob. sailed from Ostia to Tarraco. — **sed . . . undae** is in effect a prayer for safe arrival; the gen. is one of characteristic.

3. tuis: i.e. favorable, auspicious; cf. 10. 20. 19; 10. 20. 12 *tempore non tuo.*

4. arces, *heights.* Tarraco lay about 750 feet above sea level. Cf. Aus. Clar. Urb. 84 *arce potens Tarraco.*

6. altam Bilbilin: see 1. 61. 11–12 N.; 10. 13. 1–2; § 2. — **Salonem:** see 1. 49. 12; 10. 13. 1; § 2.

7. quinto . . . essedo: i.e. after five days' journey, whether M. is thinking of a single car harnessed five times, or means that a new *essedum* will be hired daily; *after*

five stages will preserve the ambiguity. — **essedo:** see 4. 64. 19 N. — **forsitan:** i.e. if good time is made; for *forsitan* with ind. see on 8. 32. 7–8.

9–10. ante brumas . . . visos: see on 10. 96. 2; *triginta . . . brumis ante visos* would be the usual expression; see L. 1394. — **brumas:** see 3. 58. 8 N.; 5. 34. 5.

11. ipsa . . . a via: i.e. without delay; cf. the familiar *ex itinere oppugnare* (*adgredi*), e.g. in Caes. B. G. 1. 25. 6; 2. 6. 1; 2. 12. 2; 3. 21. 2.

12–14. admoneas . . . paret: for constr. see on 5. 56. 4.

14. secessus: prop. 'retirement', but here place of retirement, *retreat*; cf. Iuv. 3. 4–5 *ianua Baiarum est* (Cumae) *et gratum litus amoeni secessus*; Plin. Ep. 1. 3. 3, and often; Ov. Tr. 1. 1. 41 *carmina secessum scribentis et otia quaerunt.* — **salubri,** *healthful,* i.e.

15 qui pigrum faciant tuum parentem.
Haec sunt. Iam tumidus vocat magister
castigatque moras, et aura portum
laxavit melior : vale, libelle :
navem, scis, puto, non moratur unus.

moderate, reasonable; cf. Plin. Ep. 6. 30. 3 *attendimus ergo ut quam saluberrime reficiantur*; I. 24. 4 *praediolum istud quod . . . tam salubriter emerit.*

15. pigrum: i.e. able to indulge in repose because freed from the exactions of a client's life; cf. 12. 18. 10. — **parentem:** the *libellus* (1) is M.'s offspring; cf. Ov. Tr. I. 7. 35 *orba parente suo . . . volumina*; Pont. 4. 5. 29 *quidque parens ego vester agam.*

16. Haec sunt: sc. *quae tibi mando* (cf. 8). — **tumidus,** *imperious.* — **magister:** sc. *navis*; so

often. Cf. e.g. Verg. A. 5. 176 *ipse gubernaculo rector subit, ipse magister*; 1. 115.

17-18. portum . . . laxavit: i.e. has made the harbor (seem) more spacious by allowing ships to sail. The tense implies that Flavus's vessel is already late in getting under way.

19. navem . . . non moratur unus: cf. 'time and tide wait for no man'. — **scis puto:** this parenthetical use of *scio* comes from the *sermo familiaris*; cf. 12. 88. 1 *Tongilianus habet nasum, scio, non ego.* See Soed. 28.

LIBER XI

3

Non urbana mea tantum Pimpleïde gaudent
   otia nec vacuis auribus ista damus,
sed meus in Geticis ad Martia signa pruinis
   a rigido teritur centurione liber
5 dicitur et nostros cantare Britannia versus.
   Quid prodest ? Nescit sacculus ista meus.
At quam victuras poteramus pangere chartas
   quantaque Pieria proelia flare tuba,
cum pia reddiderint Augustum numina terris,
10   et Maecenatem si tibi, Roma, darent !

3. M.'s excuse for not being a greater literary light. Cf. 1. 107; 8. 3; 8. 55. — Meter: § 48.

1–2. Non urbana ... otia: i.e. not only the leisure class in Rome. — **otia:** abstract for concrete (metonymy); see 1. 107. 3 N. — **Pimpleide** = *Musa*; Pimplea (Pimpla) was a fountain sacred to the Muses. — **ista:** as in 1. 70. 18; 4. 49. 10.

3. in Geticis ... pruinis: in the camps on the northern frontiers of the empire. For *Geticis ... pruinis* cf. Iuv. 5. 50 (*aqua*) *frigidior Geticis petitur decocta pruinis*. On the early dissemination of Latin literature see on 1. 1. 2; 7. 88. 2; Beck. 2. 454; Marq. 827–828.

4. a rigido ... centurione: 'even rough centurions, chosen primarily for brute strength, thumb

my epigrams'. — **teritur:** cf. 8. 3. 4.

5. Britannia stands for the western frontiers of semi-civilization, as the land of the Getae (3) stands for the eastern.

6. sacculus: see 5. 39. 7 N.; the dim. is grimly humorous.

7. quam: with *victuras*; freely, *what immortal* ; cf. 1. 25. 7; 10. 2. 11. — **poteramus:** see on *poteras*, 1. 3. 12; cf. 10. 89. 6.

8. quanta ... tuba: M. intimates that he might have competed successfully with the great representatives of the epos, had contemporary patronage matched the patronage of Vergil's days. — **Pieria ... tuba:** cf. 10. 64. 4 *Pieria caneret cum fera bella tuba*; 8. 3. 14, with notes.

9. cum ... reddiderint, *seeing that* (since) *they have,* etc. The

274

5

Tanta tibi est recti reverentia, Caesar, et aequi
    quanta Numae fuerat : sed Numa pauper erat.
Ardua res haec est, opibus non tradere mores
    et, cum tot Croesos viceris, esse Numam.
5 Si redeant veteres, ingentia nomina, patres,
    Elysium liceat si vacuare nemus,
te colet invictus pro libertate Camillus,
    aurum Fabricius, te tribuente, volet,

clause gives the reason why M. utters the regret expressed in 10. — **reddiderint Augustum :** have restored Augustus to us in the person of Nerva. Augustus was a patron of literature, perhaps at the suggestion of Maecenas.

10. et, *also.* — **Maecenatem :** see on 8. 56; 1. 107. 4.

5. A tribute to the uprightness of the emperor Nerva. — Meter: § 48.

1. recti reverentia : cf. Luc. 9. 192 *cui non ulla fuit iusti reverentia.*

2. Numae : revered as founder of the religion of the state; see 10. 10. 4 N.; 10. 76. 4. Numa's type of morality was, according to Juvenal, at this time virtually extinct ; cf. Iuv. 3. 137–141 *da testem Romae tam sanctum quam fuit hospes numinis Idaei, procedat vel Numa vel qui servavit trepidam flagranti ex aede Minervam ; protinus ad censum, de moribus ultima fiet quaestio.* — **pauper :** i.e. free from the temptations inseparable from wealth and luxury.

3. opibus . . . mores : i.e. not to sacrifice character to (i.e. to amass) wealth. The vs. has an aphoristic ring ; cf. Sen. Vit. Beat. 26. 1 *divitiae enim apud sapientem virum in servitute sunt, apud stultum in imperio.*

4. Croesos : see 5. 39. 8 N.

5. veteres . . . patres : the worthies of the past who made Rome great.

6. Elysium . . . nemus : for the delights of Elysium see e.g. 7. 40. 4 *Elysium possidet ambo nemus;* Verg. A. 6. 673–675 *nulli certa domus; lucis habitamus opacis riparumque toros et prata recentia rivis incolimus.* — **liceat :** sc. *eis = veteribus patribus.*

7. te colet : the fut. ind., with its prophetic tone, is very effective after *si . . . redeant . . . liceat si,* 5–6. — **invictus pro libertate,** *undaunted champion of liberty.* Tradition said that when the Gauls had got possession of all Rome save the Capitol, 390 B.C., Camillus forgot his private wrongs, accepted appointment as dictator, collected an army, and defeated the Gauls. Again in 367 B.C. he forced the invading Gauls to retire. He long held place with Curius Dentatus, the Decii, and Fabricius as a national hero ; cf. e.g. Hor. C. 1. 12. 39–44.

8. aurum . . . volet : i.e. he will not spurn it as he did when Pyrrhus, king of Epirus, tried to bribe him with an offer of money, or when the Samnite ambassadors offered him a large sum (Gell. 1. 14).

te duce gaudebit Brutus, tibi Sulla cruentus
10   imperium tradet, cum positurus erit,
et te privato cum Caesare Magnus amabit
donabit totas et tibi Crassus opes.
Ipse quoque infernis revocatus Ditis ab umbris
si Cato reddatur, Caesarianus erit.

13

Quisquis Flaminiam teris, viator,
noli nobile praeterire marmor :

— **te tribuente**: i.e. ' such is your reputation for honor that Fabricius would feel certain that an offer of gold from you could not be a bribe '. Cf. Claud. Panegyr. Manl. Theod. Cos. 163–165 *nunc Brutus amaret vivere sub regno, tali succumberet aulae Fabricius, cuperent ipsi servire Catones.*

9. te ... Brutus: i.e. 'Brutus, who helped to expel Tarquin, will (would) welcome your leadership'. — **Sulla cruentus:** Sulla's merciless proscription of the defeated Marians long made his name synonymous with cruelty. Cf. Sen. Suas. 6. 3 *civilis sanguinis Sullana sitis in civitatem redit.*

10. imperium: his dictatorship. — **positurus** = *depositurus.* In 79 B.C. Sulla unexpectedly resigned his dictatorship and retired to private life. M. accommodates the mood and tense of *positurus erit* to those of *tradet* (see on *te colet*, 7).

11–12. et te ... opes: i.e. 'all the men composing the so-called First Triumvirate — Julius Caesar, Pompey the Great, and Crassus — will (would) lay aside their personal ambitions, and as private citizens give you their warm esteem'. — **amabit:** i.e. 'will love you, though they hated and fought each other'.

— **totas ... opes:** i.e. 'for you Crassus will impoverish himself'. Crassus was known as Dives, because of his enormous wealth; to that wealth he owed his place in the Triumvirate.

13. infernis ... umbris: cf. 4.16.5 *magnus ab infernis revocetur Tullius umbris.*

14. si ... reddatur ... erit: for moods see on *te colet*, 7.— **Cato:** see 1. 42. 4 N. — **Caesarianus:** i.e. a supporter of Nerva; Cato killed himself to escape the rule of Julius Caesar.

13. An epigraphic epigram (§§ 22 ; 26–27), written as if for the tomb of Paris, the very popular pantomime of Domitian's time, put to death by Domitian because of a liaison, supposed or real, with the empress Domitia. He is not to be confounded with the Paris who was put to death by Nero. Paris was probably merely his stage-name ; actors often assumed the names of distinguished predecessors. On tombs along the *viae* see 1. 88. Introd. — Meter: § 49.

1. Flaminiam: on the Via Flaminia see 3. 14. 4 N.; 4. 64. 18. The Mausoleum Augusti was quite near this road, between it and the Tiber; the tombs began immediately outside the Servian Wall

urbis deliciae salesque Nili,
ars et gratia, lusus et voluptas,
5   Romani decus et dolor theatri
atque omnes Veneres Cupidinesque
hoc sunt condita, quo Paris, sepulcro.

18

Donasti, Lupe, rus sub urbe nobis,
sed rus est mihi maius in fenestra.
Rus hoc dicere, rus potes vocare ?
in quo ruta facit nemus Dianae,

at the very foot of the Capitoline.
— **teris:** cf. 2. 11. 2; 10. 10. 2. —
viator: for such addresses see on
6. 28. 10.

3. deliciae: cf. 1. 109. 5 N.; 7.
88. 2; 10. 53. 2. — **sales . . . Nili:**
for *sales* cf. 1. 41. 16 N.; 3. 99. 3; 7.
25. 3. Paris would seem to have
been born in Egypt. The Alexan-
drians were especially noted for
obscene witticisms; cf. 1. 61. 5 N.;
3. 63. 5; 4. 42. 3–4; Quint. 1. 2. 7.

5. dolor: see on 6. 63. 7.

6. Veneres Cupidinesque:
see 9. 11. 9. The Latin poets used
the pl. of *Amor*, *Cupido*, in part at
least because Greek writers had
pluralized Ἔρως. Cf. Ov. F. 4. 1
geminorum mater Amorum; Hor.
C. 1. 19. 1 *mater saeva Cupidinum*.
For the pl. *Veneres* see Ellis on
Catull. 3. 1.

7. condita: for the gender see
A. 287. 3, 4; GL. 286. 1. The pl. is
due to the long array of subjects.
— With 3–7 cf. the epitaph of Plautus, given in Gell. 1. 24. 3: *postquam
est mortem aptus Plautus, Comoedia
luget, scaena est deserta, dein risus,
ludus, iocusque et numeri innumeri
simul omnes conlacrimarunt.*

18. On a farm that was not
worth as much as a good lunch-

eon. The epigram may well be a
jest, based on a Greek original
(Brandt 31 ; Spiegel 2. 30). —
Meter : § 49.

1. rus: see 1. 12. 3; the hyperbole throughout suggests that this
rus is purely imaginary. It is not
easy to refer it to the Nomentanum
(see § 10; note on 8. 61. 6 ; 9. 97. 7;
9. 18. 2; 10. 58. 9), as Van Stockum,
84, and others refer it. — **sub
urbe:** the *rus* is a *suburbanum*.

2. rus . . . in fenestra: i.e. in
the potted plants on the window-
ledge of his town residence; cf. Plin.
N. H. 19. 59 *iam in fenestris suis
plebs urbana imagine hortorum cotidiana oculis rura praebebant ante-
quam praefigi prospectus omnes
coegit multitudinis innumerae saeva
latrocinatio.* Iuv. 3. 270, in speaking of *rimosa et curta vasa* as falling
fenestris, may have this custom in
mind.

4. ruta: for the rue as an em-
blem of insignificance cf. Petr. 37
*quemvis ex istis . . . in rutae folium
coniciet* ; 58 *nec sursum nec deor-
sum non cresco, nisi dominum tuum
in rutae folium coniecero*; Luke 11.
42 "Ye tithe mint and rue". The
hyperbole is intensified if we suppose that M. had in mind the grove

5   argutae tegit ala quod cicadae,
    quod formica die comedit uno,
    clusae cui folium rosae corona est,
    in quo non magis invenitur herba
    quam Cosmi folium piperve crudum,
10 in quo nec cucumis iacere rectus,
    nec serpens habitare tota possit.
    Urucam male pascit hortus unam,
    consumpto moritur culix salicto,
    et talpa est mihi fossor atque arator.
15 Non boletus hiare, non mariscae
    ridere aut violae patere possunt.
    Fines mus populatur et colono
    tamquam sus Calydonius timetur,
    et sublata volantis ungue Prognes
20 in nido seges est hirundinino ;

of Diana near Aricia (see 2. 19. 3 N.).
On the worship of Diana among
country folk see Preller-Jordan 1.
312 ff.

5. argutae: cf. 3. 58. 13 N.; 8.
73. 7 N.—**cicadae:** see 10. 58. 3 N.

7. clusae . . . est: i.e. which
could be surrounded (covered) by
the leaf of a rose-bud that has not
yet opened. For this sense of *corona* see on *coronabunt*, 10. 48. 11.
It seems unnecessary to see in
corona an unknown technical sense
such as 'parterre' (Fried.; Gilbert).

9. Cosmi folium: prob. a leaf
of spikenard, from which was extracted the famous *unguentum foliatum* or *nardinum*; see 9. 26. 2
N.; Marq. 783. Cf. 14. 146. 1 *tingue
caput Cosmi folio: cervical olebit.*
See App.—**crudum:** i.e. the green
fruit, as distinct from the dried fruit
that was imported. Pepper was an
Oriental product,

10. nec . . . rectus: it must
stand on end! Perhaps, however,
M. is thinking of the vine rather
than of the fruit. The runners of
the cucumber tend to grow in
straight lines; on this *rus*, however,
they have to curve.— **rectus,** *at
full length* (or, perhaps, *straight*).

14. talpa . . . arator: i.e. a
ground mole can do all the dig-
ging and plowing of which the
rus admits.

15. mariscae: see App. Cf. 7.
25. 7.

16. ridere: i.e. to split open, as
the mouth opens when one laughs
aloud.

17–18. Fines . . . populatur:
burlesque use of military language.
— **sus Calydonius:** see 9. 48. 6 N.

**19–20. sublata . . . hirun-
dinino:** 'my whole crop can be
swept off by a swallow (whose
flight will not be disturbed by the

22   non est dimidio locus Priapo.
Vix implet cocleam peracta messis
et mustum nuce condimus picata.

25   Errasti, Lupe, littera sed una,
nam quo tempore praedium dedisti,
mallem tu mihi prandium dedisses.

35

Ignotos mihi cum voces trecentos,
quare non veniam vocatus ad te
miraris quererisque litigasque.
Solus ceno, Fabulle, non libenter.

42

Vivida cum poscas epigrammata, mortua ponis
lemmata. Quid fieri, Caeciliane, potest ?

effort) and stored within her nest'.
— **Prognes**: see 4. 49. 3 N.; 1. 70.
10 N. (on *Cybeles*). — **seges**: spe-
cifically the grain crop. This crop
is all straw and no wheat.

22. Priapo: see 3. 58. 47 N.

24. nuce: i.e. in a nutshell instead of in an amphora. The *mustum* was regularly racked off from
the vat (*dolium*), where the grape
juice had been allowed to ferment,
into amphorae. — **picata**: the
stopper of the amphora was often
sealed with pitch; M. with extravagant humor hints that, if one takes
such precautions with a nut as
one takes with the amphora, one
nut will securely hold all the wine
grown on the *rus*.

25. una, *only one*.

27. mallem . . . dedisses: for
mallem see A. 442, b; GL. 258 and
N. 1; for *dedisses* see on *vis mittam*,
1. 117. 2. The whole = *utinam tu
mihi . . . dedisses*. — **prandium**:
'when you gave me a field, I wish

you had given me a feed' (P. and S.).

35. M. objects to his loneli-
ness amid a crowd of strange
guests at a *cena popularis* (see 1.
20; 3. 58. 42). — Meter: § 49.

1. cum, *although*. — **voces**:
see 1. 20. 1 N.; 1. 43. 1 N. — **trecentos**: cf. 1. 43. 1 N.; 9. 19. 1; 11. 65. 1.

2. vocatus ad te: see App.

4. Solus: for the play on *solus*
cf. Cic. Off. 3. 1. 1 *Publium Scipi-
onem . . . dicere solitum scripsit
Cato . . . numquam se . . . minus
solum* (*esse*) *quam cum solus esset*.

42. 'No worthy poem is possible without a worthy theme'. The
epigram shows that M. wrote in
some sense "to order". Cf. 5. 34.
Introd. Perhaps 10. 47 was written
on a lemma propounded by his
friend: *quae beatiorem vitam faciunt?* — Meter: § 48.

2. lemmata (λήμματα), *themes*.
The word prop. denotes the matter, substance of a sentence, as distinct from its style, then 'theme'

Mella iubes Hyblaea tibi vel Hymettia nasci
et thyma Cecropiae Corsica ponis api!

44

Orbus es et locuples et Bruto consule natus:
esse tibi veras credis amicitias?
Sunt verae, sed quas iuvenis, quas pauper habebas:
qui novus est, mortem diligit ille tuam.

48

Silius haec magni celebrat monumenta Maronis,
iugera facundi qui Ciceronis habet.
Heredem dominumque sui tumulive larisve
non alium mallet nec Maro nec Cicero.

in general; then, since the subject (e.g. of an epigram) is indicated by its title, it = 'title'; cf. 14. 2. 3–4 *lemmata si quaeris cur sint adscripta, docebo: ut, si malueris, lemmata sola legas*; 10. 59. 1 *consumpta est uno si lemmate pagina.* — **Quid fieri:** see App.

3. Mella . . . Hyblaea: see on 5. 39. 3; 7. 88. 8; 9. 11. 3; 9. 26. 4; 10. 74. 9. — **Hymettia:** see 5. 37. 10 N.

4. et = *et tamen.* — **thyma . . . Corsica:** see 9. 26. 4 N. — **Cecropiae,** *Attic*; see 1. 25. 3 N.; Verg. G. 4. 270 *Cecropium thymum.*

44. Another warning against the *captatores.* — Meter: § 48.

1. Orbus: for attentions to *orbi (orbae)* see 1. 10; 2. 32. 5–6 *retinet nostrum Laronia servum: respondes "Orba est, dives, anus, vidua"* (i.e. 'I dare not risk offending her by trying to get your slave for you'); 1. 49. 34 *imperia viduarum*; Sen. Ad Marc. 19. 2 *in civitate nostra plus gratiae orbitas confert quam eripit.* — **Bruto consule natus:** i.e. very old; cf. 10. 39. 1 N.

4. novus (sc. *amicus*): i.e. 'acquired since you became rich'.

48. On the honor paid by Silius Italicus to the tomb of Vergil. Silius had secured and redeemed from neglect the ground near Naples hallowed by Vergil's tomb. See 4. 14. Introd.; 7. 63; 11. 50. — Meter: § 48.

1. celebrat . . . Maronis: cf. Plin. Ep. 3. 7. 8 *multum ubique* (i.e. in Silius's various villas) *. . . imaginum, quas non habebat modo verum etiam venerabatur, Vergilii ante omnes, cuius natalem religiosius quam suum celebrabat, Neapoli maxime.*

2. iugera . . . habet: which of Cicero's numerous villas had come into the possession of Silius is not clear. De Rossi thinks, with reason, that an inscription found near Tusculum proves that it was the Tusculanum; Nissen and Schmidt argue for the Arpinum, Teuffel for the Cumanum. — **iugera:** see 1. 85. 2 N.

4. non . . . Cicero: for Silius's devotion to Cicero see 7. 63. 5–6 N.

52

Cenabis belle, Iuli Cerialis, apud me ;
   condicio est melior si tibi nulla, veni.
Octavam poteris servare ; lavabimur una :
   scis quam sint Stephani balnea iuncta mihi.
5 Prima tibi dabitur ventri lactuca movendo
      utilis, et porris fila resecta suis,
   mox vetus et tenui maior cordyla lacerto,
      sed quam cum rutae frondibus ova tegant ;
   altera non deerunt tenui versata favilla,
10   et Velabrensi massa coacta foco,

52. An invitation to Iulius Ce-
realis (see 10. 48. 5) to attend a
plain dinner. Cf. 10. 48; 5. 78; Plin.
Ep. 1. 15; Hor. S. 2. 2; Ep. 1. 5. —
Meter: § 48.

1. belle: see 2. 7. 7 N.; 11. 34.
4 *cenabit belle, non habitabit Afer.*
M. has in mind Catull. 13. 1 *cenabis
bene, mi Fabulle, apud me.*

2. condicio: a broad term, like
'proposition'; here *invitation, en-
gagement.* Cf. Plaut. Cap. 179–180
(Ergasilus the parasite accepts
Hegio's invitation to dinner) *nisi
qui meliorem adferet quae mi atque amicis placeat condicio magis*;
Hor. Ep. 1. 5. 27–28 *nisi cena prior
potiorque puella Sabinum detinet
adsumam* (*eum*: i.e. 'I will add him
to our dinner-party').

3. Octavam (sc. *horam*): the
bathing hour; see 4. 8. 4–5; 3. 36.
5–6. The usual dinner hour was
the ninth; see 4. 8. 6–7; 10. 48. 1.
— **Octavam . . . servare:** i.e. 'you
can bathe at your usual time'. —
una: adv., *together.*

4. quam . . . iuncta mihi: cf.
6. 28. 5 *iuncto Flaminiae iacet sepulcro.* — **Stephani balnea:** private baths; cf. 14. 60. 2 *si clara
Stephani balnea luce petes.*

5. lactuca: see 10. 48. 9 N.

6. porris . . . suis: the green
tops of the chives (*sectile porrum*:
see on 10. 48. 9); cf. 13. 18. 1–2
(on *porri sectivi*) *fila Tarentini
graviter redolentia porri edisti quotiens, oscula clusa dato.*

7. vetus: perhaps *full grown*
(cf. *maior*), perhaps *smoked, salted.*
— **cordyla:** see 3. 2. 4 N.; 13. 1. 1.
— **lacerto:** see 10. 48. 11 N. The
lacertus is commonly part of a
plain, or even mean meal; acces-
sories (here eggs and rue) were
needed to make the fish palatable.
Cf. 12. 19. 1–2 *in thermis sumit lactucas, ova, lacertum, et cenare domi
se negat Aemilius.*

8. sed: a saving qualification.
— **quam** = *talem ut eam.* — **cum
. . . tegant:** cf. 10. 48. 11 N.

9. altera: sc. *ova.* — **deerunt:**
dissyllabic; see 8. 55. 3 N. — **tenui
. . . favilla:** i.e. eggs thoroughly
roasted in a thin bed of hot ashes;
cf. Ov. M. 8. 667 *ovaque non acri*
(i.e. not excessively hot) *leviter
versata favilla.*

10. Velabrensi . . . foco: prob.
smoked cheese (*caseus fumosus*),
for the making of which the cheese-
mongers of the Velabrum (between

et quae Picenum senserunt frigus olivae.

Haec satis in gustu. Cetera nosse cupis ?

mentiar, ut venias : pisces, conchylia, sumen

et chortis saturas atque paludis aves,

15   quae nec Stella solet rara nisi ponere cena.

Plus ego polliceor : nil recitabo tibi,

ipse tuos nobis relegas licet usque Gigantas

Rura vel aeterno proxima Vergilio.

59

Senos Charinus omnibus digitis gerit

nec nocte ponit anulos

the Palatine and the Tiber) had a well-deserved reputation. Cf. 13. 32 *non quemcumque focum nec fumum caseus omnem, sed Velàbrensem qui bibit, ille sapit.* For such cheese goat's milk was best; cf. Plin. N. H. 11. 240–241. — **coacta:** perhaps merely *manufactured* (prop. 'coagulated', 'curdled', 'solidified'), perhaps *forced*, i.e. ripened artificially (Steph.). For the former sense cf. in a way 10. 17. 7 N.; for the latter cf. 10. 36. 1 *inproba Massiliae quidquid fumaria cogunt.*

11. quae . . . olivae: such olives were not the best; cf. 7. 31. 4 *nec iam frigoribus pares* ('a match for') *olivas.* For the olives of Picenum see 1. 43. 8 N.; 9. 26. 6.

12. gustu: see on 1. 43. 3–8; 1. 103. 7–8. — **Cetera:** the *cena* proper.

13. mentiar . . . venias: 'I'll make lying promises to get you to come'. — **pisces,** by contrast with 7–8, = 'fine fish', e.g. the mullet. — **conchylia,** *oysters.* See 3. 45. 6 N. — **sumen:** see 10. 48. 12 N.

14. chortis . . . aves: i.e. domestic fowl; cf. 3. 58. 12; 9. 54. 11 *mittimus ergo tibi parvae munuscula*

chortis. — **saturas,** *fat,* is to be taken twice with *aves.* — **paludis aves:** esp. wild geese and ducks.

15. nec = *ne . . . quidem*; see on 1. 109. 20. — **Stella:** see on 1. 61. 4.

16. ego: emphatic; it implies that the promises of 13–15 are made by many. — **nil . . . tibi:** the value of this promise appears from 3. 50. 7 (see notes); 5. 78. 25 *nec crassum dominus leget volumen.*

17. licet: see on 1. 70. 17. It is possible to put a heavier stop after *tibi,* 16, and to interpret 'but you yourself may', etc. — **Gigantas:** Cerialis had written a Gigantomachia as well as an agricultural poem (*Rura,* 18), in both imitating Vergil. On Vergil's immense influence on subsequent poets see Fried. SG. 3. 454 ff.

18. aeterno . . . Vergilio: cf. 10. 26. 7 *sed datur aeterno victurum carmine nomen.*

59. On Charinus's ostentatious display of his finger-rings. On the use of rings see Beck. 3. 244 ff.; Müller Hdb. IV 2, p. 930. — Meter: §§ 50–51.

1. Charinus (cf. Χαρῖνος): prob. a Greek freedman.

nec cum lavatur. Causa quae sit quaeritis ?
Dactyliothecam non habet.

67

Nil mihi das vivus ; dicis post fata daturum :
si non es stultus, scis, Maro, quid cupiam.

80

Litus beatae Veneris aureum Baias,
Baias superbae blanda dona naturae,
ut mille laudem, Flacce, versibus Baias,
laudabo digne non satis tamen Baias.

5   Sed Martialem malo, Flacce, quam Baias ;

4. Dactyliothecam (cf. δακτυ-
λιοθήκη): cf. 14. 123 (a *dactyliotheca*
speaks) *saepe gravis digitis elabitur
anulus unctis, tuta mea fiet sed tua
gemma fide*; Plin. N. H. 37. 11. —
non habet: Charinus is too poor
to have so many rings and a jewel-
casket too.

67. M., playing the rôle of beggar, says, ' If you don't give, I shall
have to take the attitude of a *captator*'. See 1. 10. — Meter: § 48.

1. post fata = *post mortem*; i.e.
'by your last will and testament';
see on 1. 42. 1. — **daturum**: sc. *te
esse*; the omission of both subj.
and *esse* with the fut. inf. is common, esp. in Livy.

2. quid cupiam: i.e. 'your
speedy death'.

80. A somewhat obscure epigram, since it is not clear whether
Martialem, 5, denotes the poet himself or his friend Iulius Martialis
(see 1. 15, with notes; 4. 64; etc.),
and since the text is disputed in 7.
Flaccus seems to have asked M. to
come to visit him at Baiae (cf. 6).
— Meter: § 52.

1. Litus . . . aureum: cf. Iuv.
3. 4–5 *ianua Baiarum est* (Cumae)
et gratum litus amoeni secessus;
Stat. Silv. 3. 5. 96 *vaporiferas, blandissima litora, Baias*. For Baiae
in general see 3. 58. 1 N. — **Veneris**: on the Venus-cult in this
locality see C.I.L. 10. 3692. Certain ruins are still pointed out as
those of the temple of Venus at
Baiae, but the identification is uncertain. Baiae belonged to Venus,
surely, as the home of pleasure
and revels of all sorts. — **aureum**:
see 8. 50. 13 N.

2. superbae . . . naturae: as
if nature was proud of her gift to
men. — **blanda,** *alluring*; cf. 4.
57. 1; Stat. Silv. 3. 5. 96, cited on 1.

3. ut, *although*; see on 2. 41. 4.
— **Flacce**: see 4. 49. 1; 8. 55. 5;
10. 48. 5.

5. Martialem: it is far more
natural to think here of Iulius
Martialis (see Introd.) than of the
poet himself. Verses 1–5 = 'I know
how lovely Baiae is, but I prefer to
remain here with Martialis'. See
on 7.

optare utrumque pariter inprobi votum est.
Quod si deorum munere hoc tibi detur,
quid gaudiorum est Martialis et Baiae!

84

Qui nondum Stygias descendere quaerit ad umbras
tonsorem fugiat, si sapit, Antiochum.
Alba minus saevis lacerantur bracchia cultris,
cum furit ad Phrygios enthea turba modos,

6. optare . . . pariter: i.e. to wish for the society of my friend and the life at Baiae at the same time. — inprobi, *unreasonable, shameless.* The vs. = 'I am not unreasonable enough to crave both together; hence I give up Baiae'.

7. Quod . . . detur: it is clear from 5–7 that Martialis was not at Baiae. Perhaps he was in his fine villa on the Ianiculum (see 4. 64), but we have no means of deciding the point. — tibi: see App.

8. quid gaudiorum = *quantum gaudiorum, quanta gaudia.*

84. On a bad barber. Cf. 7. 83. Until about 300 B.C. the Romans did not shave; Plin. N. H. 7. 211 states that barbers came from Sicily with other Greek innovations. On the care of hair and beard see Beck. 3. 237 ff.; Marq. 597 ff. Cf. Sen. Brev. Vit. 12. 3 *quis est istorum* (the dandies) *qui non malit rem publicam suam turbari quam comam ? qui non sollicitior sit de capitis sui decore quam de salute ? qui non comptior esse malit quam honestior ?* Barbers not only shaved and cut hair, but were manicures. — Meter: § 48.

1. Stygias . . . umbras: cf. 1. 101. 5 *ne tamen ad Stygias famulus descenderet umbras*; 1. 114. 5; 12. 90. 3; 1. 36. 5 *infernas ad umbras*; 9. 29. 2 *ad infernas aquas.* See App. — descendere: cf. Verg. A.

6. 126 *facilis descensus Averno.* For *quaero* with inf. see on 1. 2. 2.

2. Antiochum: some freedman. For fancy names given to slaves see on 5. 24. 1.

3–4. lacerantur: the Bellonarii, priests of the Asiatic goddess Bellona, whose worship was introduced into Rome from Comana in Cappadocia about 100 B.C., cut their arms and thighs with knives (see Preller-Jordan 2. 386; Marq.-Wissowa 3. 76); the self-mutilation of the devotees of Cybele is well known. Cf. Sen. Vit. Beat. 26. 8 *cum aliquis secandi lacertos suos artifex bracchia atque umeros suspensa manu cruentat.* There is a fine double juxtaposition in the verse; the adjectival elements are brought together at the beginning, the substantival at the end. — ad . . . modos: the Oriental music produced by the *cornu, cymbala, tympana,* and *tibiae* is horribly discordant to western ears, and seems fit concomitant to fanatical rites. — Phrygios: the worship of Cybele (the Magna Mater) was brought to Rome from Pessinus, a town in a part of Galatia that originally belonged to Phrygia. For the orgiastic worship of Cybele see e.g. Ov. F. 4. 212–214 *aera deae comites raucaque terga movent ; cymbala pro galeis, pro scutis tympana pulsant : tibia dat Phrygios, ut*

5   mitior inplicitas Alcon secat enterocelas
      fractaque fabrili dedolat ossa manu.
   Tondeat hic inopes Cynicos et Stoica menta
      collaque pulverea nudet equina iuba ;
   hic miserum Scythica sub rupe Promethea radat :
10   carnificem nudo pectore poscet avem ;
   ad matrem fugiet Pentheus, ad Maenadas Orpheus,
      Antiochi tantum barbara tela sonent.
   Haec quaecumque meo numeratis stigmata mento,

dedit ante, modos; Ib. 453–454 *attonitusque seces ut quos Cybeleia mater incitat ad Phrygios vilia membra modos*. The Phrygian pipes (*tibiae*) were distinguished from the Lydian and the Dorian measures. — **enthea turba**: the wild mob of frenzied worshipers. Cf. 12. 57. 11 *nec turba cessat entheata Bellonae*. *Entheus* (ἔνθεος) is common in the post-Augustan poets, esp. of the Maenads and others who participate in orgiastic rites.

5. inplicitas . . . enterocelas: i.e. strangulated hernia. — **Alcon**: see 6. 70. 6 N. On Roman surgery see Fried. SG. 1. 341 ff.

6. dedolat, *chops away*, a purposely rough word to describe the removal of splinters of bone preparatory to setting or dressing.

7. Tondeat, *clip*, is in sharp contrast to *radat*, 9. Antiochus should confine himself to cutting hair; even then he should select only such mortals as can endure much. Philosophers were often bearded; cf. e.g. Hor. S. 1. 3. 133–134 *vellunt tibi barbam lascivi pueri*; Pers. 1. 133 *si Cynico barbam petulans nonaria vellat*.

9. miserum . . . radat: for the story that Prometheus was fastened to a rock of the Scythian Caucasus and torn by an eagle (vulture) cf.

e.g. the Prometheus of Aeschylus. The imperatival subjunctive clause serves as a protasis; see on 1. 70. 3; 1. 79. 2; 1. 107. 3; etc. So 12 is protasis to 11.

10. 'Prometheus will clamor for the eagle to escape Antiochus'. — **carnificem**: cf. Sil. 1. 173 *carnificaeve manus*. — **poscet**: for mood and tense see on *te colet*, 11. 5. 7.

11. ad . . . Pentheus: Pentheus will regard his mother, Agave, as more merciful than Antiochus, though she and his sisters, thinking him a beast, in their frenzy tore him to pieces, because they discovered him watching their Bacchanalian orgies. As king of Thebes he had opposed the introduction of the rites of Bacchus. — **ad . . . Orpheus**: Orpheus was torn to pieces by the Thracian women when they were engaged in a Bacchanalian orgy. — **Maenadas** (Μαινάδες, 'the raving ones'): the Thracian Bacchanals, who resented Orpheus's devotion to his dead wife Eurydice.

12. tantum = 'only', *modo*, *dum*; cf. note on *dum tantum*, 9. 46. 4. — **barbara tela**: his *novacula*; cf. *saevis . . . cultris*, 3.

14. pyctae: this word is from the Greek ; *pycta*, *pyctes* = πύκτης. The Latin word is *pugil*. The *caestus*, boxing-gloves, were well

in vetuli pyctae qualia fronte sedent,
15   non iracundis fecit gravis unguibus uxor:
       Antiochi ferrum est et scelerata manus.
       Unus de cunctis animalibus hircus habet cor:
       barbatus vivit, ne ferat Antiochum.

86

Leniat ut fauces medicus quas aspera vexat
       adsidue tussis, Parthenopaee, tibi,
mella dari nucleosque iubet dulcesque placentas
       et quidquid pueros non sinit esse truces.
5   At tu non cessas totis tussire diebus:
       non est haec tussis, Parthenopaee, gula est.

calculated to cut and bruise; a leather strap, in which plummets of lead and iron were fastened, was wrapped round and round the hands; cf. e.g. Verg. A. 5. 401–408.

15. gravis, *disagreeable* (with a hint that her physical prowess is not to be despised in a brawl).

16. est: since the logical subject, *stigmata* (13), is rather remote, the verb naturally takes the number of the pred. nominatives. — **scelerata manus:** cf. Sil. 1. 173, cited on 10.

17. cor, *judgment, sense,* a meaning common in early Latin, and seen in *cordatus* and the name Corculum; cf. 3. 27. 4 *et mihi cor non est, et tibi, Galle, pudor;* 2. 8. 5–6 *quod si non illum* (the copyist) *sed me peccasse putabis, tunc ego te credam cordis habere nihil.* See Cic. Tusc. 1. 9. 18.

86. M. insinuates that Parthenopaeus feigns illness because he likes the remedies administered. — Meter: § 48.

1. fauces: the upper throat; *gula* is the gullet. See further the note on 6.

2. Parthenopaee: the former slave name of some freedman; on fanciful slave names see on 5. 24. 1. The original Parthenopaeus was son of Meleager and Atalanta.

3. mella . . . nucleos . . . placentas: these are all things whose lubricity and sweetness would tend to allay tickling and irritation due to cold. Cf. Plin. N. H. 22. 108 (*mel est) faucibus, tonsillis, anginae omnibusque oris desideriis utilissimum.* — **placentas:** see 5. 39. 3 N. The remedies are at once palatable and substantial.

4. quidquid . . . truces: i.e. whatever keeps children in good humor; cf. Hor. S. 1. 1. 25–26 *ut pueris olim dant crustula blandi doctores, elementa velint ut discere prima.*

6. gula: 'your disease lies below the part of the throat that the doctor is treating' (see on 1). For the play on words cf. 2. 40. 8 *o stulti, febrem creditis esse? gula est.* For *gula,* 'gluttony', see on 1. 20. 3; 3. 22. 5.

91. A tender epitaph-epigram (see § 26) on Canace, a little slave girl, who seems to have died of

91

Aeolidos Canace iacet hoc tumulata sepulcro,
    ultima cui parvae septima venit hiems.
Ah scelus, ah facinus ! properas qui flere, viator,
    non licet hic vitae de brevitate queri :
5   tristius est leto leti genus : horrida vultus
    apstulit et tenero sedit in ore lues,
ipsaque crudeles ederunt oscula morbi,
    nec data sunt nigris tota labella rogis.
Si tam praecipiti fuerant ventura volatu,
10   debuerant alia fata venire via,
sed mors vocis iter properavit cludere blandae,
    ne posset duras flectere lingua deas.

92

Mentitur qui te vitiosum, Zoile, dicit :
    non vitiosus homo es, Zoile, sed vitium.

cancer of the lip. — Cf. 5. 34. —
Meter : § 48.

1. **Canace:** the Canace of leg-
end was a daughter of Aeolus. On
the name here cf. *Antiochum*, 11.
84. 2 N.; *Parthenopaee*, 11. 86. 2 N.

3. **Ah . . . facinus:** cf. 11. 93. 3
*o scelus, o magnum facinus crimen-
que deorum.* — **qui:** the antec. is
tibi, to be supplied with *licet*, 4. —
viator: cf. 11. 13. 1 N.

4. **non licet . . . queri** may
mean either 'you may not weep
because her life was short', since
her death was a mercy, or 'you may
not weep merely over the short-
ness of her life', since her life was
not merely short but full of suffering. In the one case M. says 'Weep
not at all', in the other he says
'Weep not till you know how
much there is to lament'.

5. **leto:** a poetic word, suggestive of annihilation.

6. **lues:** a wasting disease, here
prob. cancer; cf. 1. 78. 1–2 *indignas
premeret pestis cum tabida fauces
inque suos vultus serperet atra lues*;
1. 101. 6 *ureret . . . cum scelerata
lues.*

7. **oscula:** see 1. 109. 2 N.; cf.
labella, 8.

9–10. **Si . . . debuerant:** a
simple condition. — **volatu:** cf.
Eng. 'wings of fate' and like expressions. — **fata:** see 7. 47. 8 N.;
1. 42. 1 N. For position see on 1.
53. 8; 9. 61. 11–12.

11. **blandae,** *persuasive*; cf. 4.
57. 1; 8. 32. 2; 11. 80. 2.

12. **deas:** the Parcae.

92. A fling at Zoilus. See 2.
16; 2. 19; 2. 58. — Meter : § 48.

2. **non . . . vitium,** *you are
depravity personified*; cf. Iuv. 2. 34–
35 *nonne igitur iure ac merito vitia
ultima* ('bad men') *fictos contem-
nunt Scauros?*

LIBER XII

3

Quod Flacco Varioque fuit summoque Maroni
Maecenas, atavis regibus ortus eques,
gentibus et populis hoc te mihi, Prisce Terenti,
fama fuisse loquax chartaque dicet anus :
5   tu facis ingenium, tu, si quid posse videmur,
tu das ingenuae ius mihi pigritiae.

6

Contigit Ausoniae procerum mitissimus aulae

3. M. calls Priscus Terentius, his patron (see 8. 12. 3 N.), a second Maecenas. See 8. 55, with notes. — Meter: § 48.

1. **Flacco**: see 1. 107. 4 N.; 8. 18. 5. — **Vario**: cf. 8. 18. 7 N.; 8. 55. 21.—**summo**... **Maroni**: see 1. 107. 4 N.; 5. 56. 5; 11. 52. 18 *aeterno Vergilio.*

2. **Maecenas . . . eques**: cf. *Tuscus eques,* 8. 55. 9, with note. — **atavis regibus ortus**: cf. Hor. C. I. 1. 1 *Maecenas, atavis edite regibus.*

3. **gentibus et populis**: on M.'s wide-spread fame cf. 1. 1; 5. 13; 9. 97. 2; § 40. — **hoc**: pred. acc. with *fuisse.*

4. **fama . . . loquax**: cf. Lib. Spect. I. 8 *fama loquetur,* and note on *charta* below. — **charta . . . anus**: cf. Catull. 68. 46 (= 68 b. 6) *facite haec charta loquatur anus.* For *anus* as adj. (= *annosa,* 'long-lived') cf. 1. 39. 2 *quales prisca fides famaque novit anus.* Such a *charta* contains *victura carmina,* 8. 73. 4, *vividum . . . carmen,* 12. 61. 1.

5. **ingenium** (*mihi*): cf. 8. 73. 5–6 N. — **si quid . . . videmur** is more modest than *quidquid* or *quidcumque posse videmur.* Sc. *facis* with *tu . . . tu.*

6. **ingenuae**... **pigritiae** : i.e. a gentlemanly leisure; cf. sense of *ingenuus* in 10. 47. 6; 6. 11. 6.

6. M. lauds the changed conditions under the emperor Nerva. Cf. 11. 5; 8. 70. — Meter: § 48.

1. **Ausoniae . . . aulae**: see on *Parrhasia . . . aula,* 7. 99. 3. *Ausonius* often merely = *Romanus*; cf. 8. 53. 5 *in Ausonia . . . harena*; 12. 62. 9 *Ausonio macello*; 13. 65. 1 *Ausoniis mensis.* — **procerum** denotes the men who have held high positions or have glorified their country, and so is more inclusive and more complimentary than *principum* or *Caesarum* would have been. — **mitissimus**: Nerva repressed the *delatores,* lessened taxation, protected the senate, and recalled the exiles. Contrast *Sulla cruentus,* 11. 5. 9.

Nerva : licet toto nunc Helicone frui :
recta Fides, hilaris Clementia, cauta Potestas
    iam redeunt ; longi terga dedere Metus.
5   Hoc populi gentesque tuae, pia Roma, precantur :
    dux tibi sit semper talis, et iste diu.
Macte animi, quem rarus habes, morumque tuorum,
    quos Numa, quos hilaris possit habere Cato.

2. licet . . . frui: i.e. under a good emperor men of letters are encouraged to do their best ; the Muses have a fair and full chance. There is a personal compliment also to Nerva ; cf. 9. 26, with notes ; 8. 70. 7–8. See App.—**Helicone:** see 1. 76. 9 N.; 7. 63. 12.

3. **recta Fides:** that the adj. is not superfluous is shown by the familiar phrase *bona fides.* — **hilaris Clementia:** if a Nero or a Domitian ever showed clemency or mildness, it was but a freakish perversity of a nature thoroughly depraved ; Nerva's benignity was characteristically cheerful. — **cauta:** i.e. that observes due metes and bounds. — **Potestas** is legal, constitutional power ; *potentia* is personal authority, illegal or extra-constitutional. In Italian *podestà* = 'a magistrate'.

4. **longi** . . . **Metus:** M. is thinking primarily of Domitian's long reign of 15 years, 81–96 (see on this reign Tac. Agr. 3, cited in Introduction, p. xxxii, n. 1). Still, from 14, when Tiberius succeeded Augustus, till Nerva ascended the throne, with the exception of the administrations of Vespasian and Titus (69–81), Rome had had little government that made patriots happy or hopeful. *Longi = diuturni.* — **Metus:** for the pl. see 1. 15. 7 N.

5. **pia Roma:** the real object of the Roman's worship was Rome ;

his *pietas* embraced not simply *parentes* and *dei,* but *patria.* Hence temples were erected to (dea) Roma ; see Preller-Jordan 2. 353 ff.

6. **dux:** often applied to the emperor in the poetry of the Empire, in place of the more formal *princeps*; cf. 12. 11. 6. — **et iste diu** (*tibi dux sit*) : cf. Hor. C. 1. 2. 45–46 (of Augustus) *serus in caelum redeas diuque laetus inter sis populo Quirini. Iste* = Nerva ; see on 1. 70. 18.

7–8. **Macte . . . Cato:** 'all hail to a soul and to a character which are in these days rare indeed, aye, were known only in far distant times '. — **Macte animi:** cf. Stat. Silv. 5. 1. 37 *macte animi*; Theb. 2. 495 *macte animi, tantis dignus qui crederis armis. Animi* may be gen., in imitation of the gen. of source much used in Greek in connection with words (interjections) and expressions of emotion ; it may, however, be locative (*animi* is certainly locative in a number of phrases). *Macte* is more often used with the abl. ; cf. the familiar *macte virtute.* The origin and nature of *macte* itself are uncertain ; see A. 340, c, and N.; GL. 85, c; 325, Rem. 1 ; Conington on Verg. A. 9. 641. — **rarus:** cf. 10. 78. 2 *ibit rara fides amorque recti*; Iuv. 8. 27–28 *rarus civis.* — **morum** . . . **tuorum:** cf. 11. 5. 3. — **Numa** (*habuit*): see 10. 10. 4 ; 11. 5. 2. Nerva was religious.— **hilaris . . . Cato,**

Largiri, praestare, breves extendere census,
10   et dare quae faciles vix tribuere dei
nunc licet et fas est. Sed tu sub principe duro
temporibusque malis ausus es esse bonus.

10

Habet Africanus miliens, tamen captat:
Fortuna multis dat nimis, satis nulli.

11

Parthenio dic, Musa, tuo nostroque salutem,

a *Cato grown cheerful* (B. and L.);
Nerva has the uprightness and
the probity of Cato the Censor
(see 10. 20. 21) without his asper-
ity and narrowness. — hilaris =
si hilaris sit. For the real Cato
M. had little sympathy; cf. 11.2.1–6.

9–10. Largiri, praestare: to
win distinction in any way, even by
true beneficence, was dangerous
under a Domitian. Such beneficence betokened wealth; wealth
such emperors craved. Note the
four expressions for giving, rising
to a climax in 10; *largiri* and
largitio often enough, when used
alone, suggest rather bribery. —
faciles . . . dei: see 1. 103. 4 N.
vix: even from *faciles dei* money
is not always easy to get.

11. sub principe duro: esp.
Domitian. For M.'s treatment of
the dead Domitian see § 36. — For
the meter see § 47, i.

12. temporibus . . . malis:
Iuv. 4. 80 uses *temporibus diris* of
Domitian's reign of terror.

10. On a specially avaricious
captator. — Meter: § 52.

1. miliens: sc. *centena milia*
(see 3. 22. 1 N.); the amount is
100,000,000 *sestertii.*

2. Fortuna . . . nulli: proverbial; cf. German *Das Glück*

*gibt vielen zu viel, aber niemandem
genug*; Publ. Syr. 174 *Fortuna
nimium quem fovet stultum facit*;
Otto s.v. *Fortuna* 12; 13. Similar
in thought is Hor. Ep. 1. 2. 56
semper avarus eget; Sen. Ep. 94.
43 *avarus animus nullo satiatur
lucro*; Otto s.v. *Avarus.* Petronius
makes a freedman say: *nemini nil
satis est.*

11. A sort of epistolary epigram. Parthenius had been *cubi-
cularius* or high chamberlain at the
palace under Domitian. See Fried.
SG. 1. 114 ff. He helped to assassinate Domitian, but later (in 97)
met a horrible death at the hands
of the Praetorians. M. had used
his good offices to introduce Book
V to the emperor (5. 6. 1). The
brevis libellus in whose interest he
now asks Parthenius's help (7) cannot be Book XII, for that book did
not appear until after Parthenius's
death. Perhaps the reference is to
the selection from books X–XI
of which M. writes in 12. 4. The
poem accords honor to Parthenius's
literary ability, to which M. pays
tribute in several other places. —
Meter: § 48.

1. dic . . . salutem, *greet*; a
variation of the formula S.D. or
S.P.D. (= *salutem (plurimam)*

nam quis ab Aonio largius amne bibit ?

cuius Pimpleo lyra clarior exit ab antro ?

quem plus Pierio de grege Phoebus amat ?

5　et si forte — sed hoc vix est sperare — vacabit,

tradat ut ipse duci carmina nostra roga

quattuor et tantum timidumque brevemque libellum

commendet verbis " Hunc tua Roma legit".

17

Quare tam multis a te, Laetine, diebus

non abeat febris quaeris et usque gemis.

Gestatur tecum pariter pariterque lavatur ;

cenat boletos, ostrea, sumen, aprum ;

dicit) used in the headings of letters. — **tuo:** see on *suo*, I. 13. 1.

2. Aonio . . . amne: the springs of the Muses on Mt. Helicon. See I. 76. 9 N.; 7. 63. 4.

3. Pimpleo . . . antro: the Pierian grot which the Muses loved; to this, figuratively speaking, Parthenius resorted for inspiration. Cf. II. 3. 1; Catull. 105. 1 (*poeta*) *conatur Pipleum scandere montem.* — **lyra,** *lyric strains* (metonymy). — **clarior:** pred. nom. to *exit*, 'issues'. We should use an adverb.

4. Pierio de grege: see I. 76. 3; 10. 58. 5–6; cf. 9. 86. 3 *cum grege Pierio maestus Phoeboque querebar.* — **Phoebus:** as patron of art, music, etc.; see I. 70. 15; I. 76. 5; 7. 63. 11.

5. si forte . . . vacabit: a compliment, because it suggests that Parthenius had many important duties; cf. II. 1. 1. 6 (of Parthenius) *nec Musis vacat, aut suis vacaret.* **est** = *licet, is possible;* cf. II. 98. 1 *effugere non est, Flacce, basiatores.*

6. tradat . . . duci . . . roga: cf. 4. 8. 7–12. — **duci:** see 12. 6. 6 N.

7–8. quattuor . . . tantum . . . verbis, *with just four words.* — **timidum . . . libellum:** in 5. 6 M., requesting Parthenius to present Book V to Domitian, says in 7–8: *admittas timidam brevemque chartam intra limina sanctioris aulae.* — **brevem** might easily be applied to any of the separate books. *Brevem . . . libellum* gives the effect of a double diminutive.

17. To Laetinus, a high-liver, who feeds his fever so well that it will not leave him. Laetinus may be the man of 3. 43. 1. — Meter: § 48.

1. tam multis . . . diebus: for the abl. see on 2. 5. 1.

3. Gestatur: cf. 1. 12. 8 N.; Iuv. 7. 178–179 (*porticus*) *in qua gestetur dominus quotiens pluit;* Sen. Ep. 15. 6 *gestatio et corpus concutit et studio non officit : possis legere, possis dictare, possis loqui, possis audire.* — **tecum . . . pariterque :** see App. Note the chiasmus.

4. boletos: see 1. 20. 2 N.; 3. 60. 5. — **ostrea:** see 3. 45. 6 N. — **sumen:** see 10. 48. 12 N. — **aprum:** see 1. 43. 2, etc.

5   ebria Setino fit saepe et saepe Falerno
        nec nisi per niveam Caecuba potat aquam ;
    circumfusa rosis et nigra recumbit amomo
        dormit et in pluma purpureoque toro.
    Cum sit ei pulchre, cum tam bene vivat apud te,
10   ad Damam potius vis tua febris eat ?

18

Dum tu forsitan inquietus erras

5. Setino: see 4. 69. 1 N.; 8.
50. 19.— **Falerno:** see 4. 69. 1 N.;
8. 55. 14.
6. per . . . aquam: on the
cooling of wine see on 2. 1. 9–10;
5. 64. 2.— **Caecuba:** see 4. 69. 1 N.
7. circumfusa rosis: at a
dinner roses were not only used for
chaplets but were scattered about
the triclinium. See on 5. 37. 9; 5.
64. 4; 6. 80.— **nigra . . . amomo:**
see 5. 64. 3; 6. 55. 2 N.— **recumbit:** cf. 3. 50. 3; 4. 8. 6; 10. 27. 2.
8. pluma: i.e. down pillows; cf.
10. 14. 6 *dormiat in pluma nec meliore Venus*; Prop. 3. 7. 50 *fultum
(erat) pluma versicolore caput*; Iuv.
1. 158–159 *vehatur pensilibus
plumis*; 10. 360–362 *potiores Herculis aerumnas credat saevosque
labores et venere et cenis et pluma
Sardanapali.* — **toro:** *torus* is used
here for the *vestes stragulae* or
stragula laid upon it; see 2. 16.
1–3.
9. Cum sit ei pulchre: i.e.
'since your fever fares so well'.
The idiom *pulchre esse* is from the
sermo familiaris; cf. Hor. S. 2. 8.
18–19 *quis* (= *quibus*) *cenantibus
una, Fundani, pulchre fuerit tibi
nosse laboro*; Plaut. Mer. 583–584
*quin ergo imus atque obsonium
curamus, pulchre ut simus?* See
on 10. 50. 8. *Bene* (*melius*) *esse* is
far commoner: cf. e.g. Hor. S. 2. 2.

120–121 *bene erat non piscibus urbe
petitis, sed pullo atque haedo*; 2. 8.
3–4 *sic ut mihi numquam in vita
fuerit melius.* See App.
10. Damam: *Dama* seems to
be used in a half conventional way
for any slave, as Gaius stands for
any free citizen (see on 5. 14. 5);
cf. e.g. Hor. S. 1. 6. 38–39 *tune Syri,
Damae, aut Dionysi filius, audes
deicere de saxo cives aut tradere
Cadmo?* Pers. 5. 76 *hic Dama est
non tresis agaso.* — **vis . . . eat:**
see on *vis mittam*, 1. 117. 2.— **eat**
= *abeat*, 2. Danysz, 60, sees the
influence of Catullus in this similarity of the beginning and the end
of an epigram.
18. 'While you, Juvenal, are
still bearing the burden of life in
Rome, I am happy in Spain'. For
M.'s return to Spain see §§ 14–15.
Cf. 1. 49. There seems no good
reason to doubt that this Juvenal
is the famous satirist; see § 19.
Juvenal's third satire may then be
compared advantageously with this
epigram, not only because it presents Juvenal's ideal of country
life, but because it enables us to
see what M. had gained.— Meter:
§ 49.
1. Dum . . . erras: i.e. stroll
about at random, in leisurely fashion, in contrast to his definite
destinations (*limina*, 4) and his

clamosa, Iuvenalis, in Subura
aut collem dominae teris Dianae,
dum per limina te potentiorum
5   sudatrix toga ventilat vagumque
maior Caelius et minor fatigant,
me multos repetita post Decembres
accepit mea rusticumque fecit
auro Bilbilis et superba ferro.
10   Hic pigri colimus labore dulci
Boterdum Plateamque — Celtiberis

breathless hurry as client on the way
to the *salutatio*, 3–6. Juvenal was
perhaps gathering materials for his
Satires; he writes himself (1. 17–18,
45–80) as if he were on the street,
composing as he moved about.
Juvenal's first book of Satires did
not appear till 107 (Fried. SG. 3.
492), whereas this book of epigrams was published as early as
101 or 102. At this time Juvenal
may have been a pleader by necessity; cf. *facunde . . . Iuvenalis*, 7.
91. 1. — **forsitan . . . erras:** see on
8. 32. 7–8.

2. clamosa . . . Subura: the
dense population and busy trade
of the Subura made it the noisiest
part of Rome; cf. 7. 31. 9–12; 10.
20. 4–5; 10. 94. 5.

3. collem . . . Dianae: see 7.
73. 1 N. — **teris:** see 2. 11. 2 N.

4. limina . . . potentiorum:
cf. 1. 70. 13; 5. 20. 5. Translate by
'at portal after portal of the great'.

5. sudatrix toga: for references to the discomfort of wearing the toga see on 3. 4. 6; 10. 47.
5; cf. 17 below. For *sudatrix* see
Cooper, § 17, p. 69. Juvenal fans
himself with his toga, but gets no
relief; even his toga is sweating.
Contrast *algentem . . . togam*, 12.
36. 2 N.

6. maior Caelius: the Mons
Caelius proper, in distinction from
the Caeliolus, which M. designates
as Caelius Minor. It is not clear
to what portion of the Caelius the
name Caeliolus was applied. Many
great palaces stood on the Caelian,
especially after the emperors had
preëmpted the Palatine, e.g. those
of Mamurra, the Pisones, and the
Laterani.

7. multos . . . Decembres:
34 years; see § 14. In 16 M. uses
round numbers.

9. auro . . . ferro: cf. 4. 55.
11–12, 14–15; 1. 49. 3–4.

10–12. pigri: cf. 10. 104. 15 N.
— **colimus:** 'instead of dancing
attendance upon a patron (cf. *colere
atrium*, 3. 38. 11), I reverence the
wood-nymphs at Boterdum', i.e.
'I visit Boterdum for pleasure'.
Boterdum was somewhere near
Bilbilis and had a grove; it was
prob. a place of resort for the people
of the town. Cf. 1. 49. 7–8. Platea,
too, was near Bilbilis; cf. 4. 55. 8–13
*Nos Celtis genitos et ex Hiberis no-
strae nomina duriora terrae grato
non pudeat referre versu: saevo
Bilbilin optimam metallo, quae vincit Chalybasque Noricosque, et ferro
Plateam suo sonantem.* — **Celtiberis . . . terris:** cf. 1. 49. 1 *vir*

haec sunt nomina crassiora terris ;
ingenti fruor inproboque somno
quem nec tertia saepe rumpit hora,
15   et totum mihi nunc repono quidquid
ter denos vigilaveram per annos.
Ignota est toga, sed datur petenti
rupta proxima vestis a cathedra.
Surgentem focus excipit superba
20   vicini strue cultus iliceti,

Celtiberis non tacende gentibus. —
crassiora, *rougher and more
uncouth*; cf. 4. 55. 8–13, cited above
on 11; 4. 55. 21–29 *Turgontique
lacus Perusiaeque, et parvae vada
pura Tuetonissae, et sanctum Bura-
donis ilicetum, per quod vel piger
ambulat viator, et quae fortibus ex-
colit iuvencis curvae Manlius arva
Vativescae. Haec tam rustica, delicate lector, rides nomina? rideas
licebit: haec tam rustica malo quam
Butuntos.*

   13. inprobo: see on 1. 53. 10;
8. 24. 2; 11. 80. 6.

   14. nec = *ne . . . quidem*; see
on 1. 109. 20. — **rumpit:** cf. 1. 49.
35–36 *non rumpet altum pallidus
somnum reus, sed mane totum dor-
mies.* — For the diæresis see § 49, d.

   15. totum agrees with *quidquid
. . . annos* taken as a noun. On
M.'s craving for sleep when he was
in Rome see on 2. 90. 10; 9. 68. 1;
10. 47. 11; 10. 74. 12. Cf. also Hor.
S. 2. 6. 60–63 *o rus, quando ego te
adspiciam? quandoque licebit nunc
veterum libris, nunc somno et iner-
tibus horis ducere sollicitae iucunda
oblivia vitae?* For sleep in Spain
see 1. 49. 35 (cited on 14); 12. 68.
5–6. Cf. too Plin. Ep. 7. 3. 2 *quin
ergo aliquando in urbem redis? . . .
quousque vigilabis cum voles, dor-
mies quam diu voles? quousque*

calcei nusquam, toga feriata ('on a
holiday')? — **repono:** prop. used,
as here, of paying a debt.

   16. See on 7.

   17. Ignota . . . toga: see on 5.
— **petenti:** i.e. 'as I call for my
clothing upon rising in the morning'.

   18. rupta . . . cathedra: plain
tunics and broken chairs go together in the country. — **proxima
vestis** includes the *tunica* (which
was frequently worn in the country
as an outer garment) and possibly
a *lacerna* (see 2. 29. 3 N.). *Proxima
vestis* denotes, as we might say,
the first clothes that come to hand,
clothes easy to find on the *cathedra*
where they had been left at bed-
time, instead of being carefully
folded and put away by a special
slave (*vestiplica*) in a press (*prelum*),
as was done in houses of the rich
in Rome (2. 46. 3). The manners
of Bilbilis were doubtless simple,
but it is grotesque to imagine, as
some have done, apparently in all
seriousness, that M. wrapped himself in a *stragulum* or chair-cover.

   19. superba, *royal*. At Rome
the client freezes, as he hurries
through the wintry air to his patron's house.

   20. vicini . . . iliceti: i.e. good
fuel, and easy to get; cf. 1. 49. 27

21   multa vilica quem coronat olla.
24   Dispensat pueris rogatque longos
25   levis ponere vilicus capillos.
     Sic me vivere, sic iuvat perire.

21

Municipem rigidi quis te, Marcella, Salonis
   et genitam nostris quis putet esse locis ?
tam rarum, tam dulce sapis. Palatia dicent,
   audierint si te vel semel, esse suam :

vicina in ipsum silva descendet fo-
cum (at Bilbilis). — **cultus,** *graced,*
honored; M. writes as if the wood
were a sacrifice offered to the hearth
(i.e. the Lares). — *iliceti*: see on
buxeto, 3. 58. 3.
   21. vilica: see 9. 60. 3 N.; 10.
48. 7. — **coronat**: see on *corona-*
bunt, 10. 48. 11.
   24–25. Dispensat . . . vilicus:
the farm-steward himself (see 2.
11.9) portions out the food (*demen-*
sum, cibaria) to the slaves; for this
purpose on great estates and in
town palaces a special official was
provided. At Bilbilis the slaves
may eat in the atrium, a practice
common' in the more primitive
times. — **rogat . . . capillos**: the
meaning is not plain. Many modern editors supply *puerorum* with
capillos and *me* with *ponere*. But
M.'s slaves at Bilbilis cannot have
been *capillati* in the sense borne
by that word in 2. 57. 5; 3. 58. 30–31;
such slaves belong to luxurious
city life. Why then does the *vilicus*
urge M. to have their hair cut? that
they may be graduated, so to say,
into the ranks of grown-up slaves
liable to work? But to insist on
that idea is to spoil the epigram;
freedom from work, ease of living,
is its keynote. We must then sup-

ply *suos* with *capillos*; the beardless
steward (*lēvis,* 25) thinks himself
grown-up. This fits the picture
well enough; since little or no
serious work is needed, a simple
boy may be *vilicus*. It must be
confessed, however, that the ellipsis of *me* is very harsh. — **rogat**
. . . ponere: *rogat* seems to have
the force and the constr. of *iubet*
(cf. 1. 109. 13); verbs of command-
ing often take the inf. in poetry. —
ponere = *deponere*; cf. 11. 5. 10;
Iuv. 3. 186 *crinem hic deponit amati.*
   26. vivere: see 1. 15. 12 N.
   21. A tribute to Marcella, his
Spanish patroness; see § 15. —
Meter: § 48.
   1. rigidi . . . Salonis: see 10.
13. 1; 10. 96. 3; 10. 104. 6. *Rigidi*
is a transferred epithet. M. habitually represents his country as uncouth; cf. note on 10. 65. 3–4.
   3–4. tam . . . sapis: i.e. 'culture
such as yours is rare anywhere, aye,
it is to be found only in Rome'. —
rarum . . . dulce: acc. of effect
(inner object); see on 5. 66. 2. —
Palatia: i.e. Rome, as the seat of
the highest culture of the world.
For the pl. see 1. 70. 5 N.; cf. Ov.
A. A. 3. 119 *Palatia fulgent.* With
Palatia . . . suam cf. 11. 53. 1–4
(of Claudia Rufina, the British

5   nulla nec in media certabit nata Subura
        nec Capitolini collis alumna tibi,
     nec cito ridebit peregrini gloria partus,
        Romanam deceat quam magis esse nurum.
     Tu desiderium dominae mihi mitius urbis
10   esse iubes : Romam tu mihi sola facis.

24

O iucunda, covinne, solitudo,

wife of Pudens) *Claudia caeruleis cum sit Rufina Britannis edita, quam Latiae pectora gentis habet! Quale decus formae! Romanam credere matres Italides possunt, Atthides esse suam.* — **vel**, *even*; see 10. 19. 21 N. — **esse**: the subject *te* is to be got out of the *te* actually written in the verse.

5-6. nulla nec . . . nec: for this type of double neg., common enough at all periods, both in prose and in verse, see A. 327; GL. 445; L. 1661. — **in media . . . Subura**: i.e. in the very heart of Rome; cf. Iuv. 10. 155-156 "*Actum*", *inquit* (Hannibal), "*nihil est, nisi Poeno milite portas* (*Romae*) *frangimus et media vexillum pono Subura*"; Apoll. Sidon. C. 23. 235-237 *et te seu Latialiter sonantem tamquam Romulea satum Subura, seu*, etc. — **tibi**: for syntax see A. 413, b, N.; GL. 346, N. 6; L. 1186.

7-8. These vss. are obscure. If the text is sound, the best interpretation, perhaps, is that of Rader: ' not soon will any (other) maiden born outside of Rome itself, even though she is the best that foreign lands can show, smile (at her birth on her parents) better fitted to be a daughter of Rome'. In *ridebit* M. is perhaps thinking of Verg. E. 4. 60 ff., itself a difficult passage. There Vergil says to the child whose birth is to mean so much to the world, *Incipe, parve puer, risu cognoscere matrem*. See the editors there; Fowler Harv. Stud. 14. 17–35. For M. and Vergil see § 33; he knew well that his contemporaries were thoroughly conversant with Vergil's poems. Yet, after all, we may well take the vss. more simply: ' not in long ages will there be a smiling, high-born maiden of foreign birth more fit', etc. — **peregrini . . . partus** involves metonymy, 'a maid that is the fairest flower of', etc.

9-10. For the discontent visible here with his life in Spain see § 15. — **dominae . . . urbis**: see 1. 3. 3 N.; 3. 1. 5; 9. 64. 4.

24. In praise of a *covinnus*, a present from his friend Aelianus. The *covinnus* was properly a British war-chariot; here, however, it is a traveling vehicle much like the *essedum* (4. 64. 19 N.); it was two-wheeled and topless; it had but one seat and could accommodate only two persons. See Beck. 3. 18 ff.; Marq. 734. For the Roman tendency to name vehicles somewhat fancifully see on 4. 64. 19. — Meter : § 49.

1. solitudo: the *covinnus* was an unpretentious vehicle ; the traveler might drive himself, thus getting rid of any eavesdropping

carruca magis essedoque gratum
facundi mihi munus Aeliani!
Hic mecum licet, hic, Iuvate, quidquid
5   in buccam tibi venerit loquaris:
non rector Libyci niger caballi
succinctus neque cursor antecedit;
nusquam est mulio: mannuli tacebunt.
O si conscius esset hic Avitus,
10   aurem non ego tertiam timerem.
Totus quam bene sic dies abiret!

muleteer, and there was no call for display of outriders or footmen.

2. carruca . . . gratum: the *carruca* was an ambitious conveyance; it was prob. larger and heavier and more expensive even than the typical *raeda*. See 3. 62. 5; 3. 47. 13–14; Dig. 34. 2. 13(14) *carruca dormitoria* (prob. for night travel).

3. facundi . . . Aeliani: we cannot identify Aelianus; the adj. would suggest a lawyer or rhetorician. Giese and Gilbert, however, make him the author of a work on Roman military tactics (Τακτική Θεωρία). Hirschfeld, Verwaltungsgesch. 224. 29, and others think that M. had in mind Casperius Aelianus, commander of the Praetorians under Domitian and Nerva. He was apparently a fellow-countryman of M. (Fried.), for the present was evidently made in Spain.

4–5. Iuvate: some Spanish friend. — **quidquid . . . venerit**: a phrase of the *sermo familiaris,* = *quidquid venerit in mentem.* Cf. Cic. Att. 1. 12. 4 *tu velim saepe ad nos scribas: si rem nullam habebis, quod in buccam venerit scribito;* 7. 10 *tu, quaeso, crebro ad me scribe vel quod in buccam venerit.* See Otto s.v. *Bucca.*

6–7. rector . . . cursor: for African drivers and outriders see 9. 22. 14 N. *Rector = driver.* — **cursor**, *a fore-runner,* who, girded for running (*succinctus*) and often expensively and gaudily attired, preceded the carriage of the grandee (cf. the *anteambulo* of the *lectica*; see on 2. 18. 5; 3. 7. 2; 10. 74. 3); see Fried. SG. 2. 35 ff.; Marq. 150, N. 6. Cf. Iuv. 5. 52–53 *tibi pocula cursor Gaetulus dabit, aut nigri manus ossea Mauri*; Petr. 28 *hinc involutus coccina gausapa lecticae impositus est praecedentibus phaleratis cursoribus quattuor.*

8. nusquam . . . mulio: see on 1; cf. 11. 38 *mulio viginti venit modo milibus, Aule. Miraris pretium tam grave? surdus erat.* — **mannuli tacebunt**: the ponies will betray no secrets. *Mannuli* (dim. of *mannus*) were small Gallic horses or ponies prized by the well-to-do for speed and endurance; cf. Plin. Ep. 4. 2. 3 *habebat . . . mannulos multos et iunctos et solutos*; Prop. 4. 8. 15. For the word see Cooper, § 41.

9. conscius: pred. nom., *to share my secrets.* — **Avitus**: L. Stertinius Avitus; see § 17.

11. Paukstadt, 33–34, sees in this and other epigrams of M. (e.g. 5.20)

29

Sexagena teras cum limina mane senator,
　esse tibi videor desidiosus eques,
quod non a prima discurram luce per urbem
　et referam lassus basia mille domum.
5　Sed tu, purpureis ut des nova nomina fastis
　aut Numidum gentes Cappadocumve regas :

an imitation of Catullus, because the poet places the important part of his theme in the middle of the epigram (4–8) with an equal number of verses before and after the chief matter. Cf. note on 5. 39. 5–6.

29. A rejoinder to the senator who had charged M. with neglect of his duties as a client. — Meter : § 48.

1. **Sexagena :** see on 1. 43. 1 ; 3. 22. 1. — **teras . . . limina :** cf. 8. 44. 4 *sed omne limen conteris salutator.* On *teras* see 10. 10. 2 ; 11. 13. 1. — **senator :** for the attendance of the great or high-born on the *salutatio* see 10. 10. 2 N.

2. **desidiosus :** see 1. 107. 2. — **eques :** on M. as *eques* see 5. 13. 1–2 N.

3. **a prima . . . per urbem :** on the early hour of the *salutatio* see 4. 8. 1 N.; cf. 9. 92. 5–6 *Gaius a prima tremebundus luce salutat tot dominos.* — **discurram :** cf. 4. 78. 3 *discurris tota vagus urbe.*

4. **basia mille :** a poor return for a day's service at best uncomfortable (cf. 8–10). Kissing was common in ancient Rome. Not only intimate friends, but mere acquaintances were greeted in this fashion. See 11. 98 entire, esp. 1 ff. *effugere non est* ('is possible'), *Flacce, basiatores : instant, morantur, persecuntur, occurrunt et hinc et illinc, usquequaque, quacumque.* See Beck. 1. 88 ; Lanciani Anc. R. 270 ff.

5–6. **Sed tu :** sc. *teris limina.* **purpureis . . . regas :** i.e. 'that you may get a consulship and so have your name recorded in the Fasti Consulares and subsequently obtain a province with its opportunities for wealth and exercise of power'. — **purpureis . . . fastis :** the official lists of the higher magistrates, who wore the *toga praetexta* (in *purpureis,* then, we have a fine transferred epithet); cf. 11. 4. 5–6 *et qui purpureis iam tertia nomina fastis, Iane, refers Nervae* ; Apoll. Sidon. Ep. 8. 8. 3 *licet tu . . . fastos recolas purpurissatos.* — **nomina :** the pl. is strictly correct ; the free Roman had at least three names, praenomen, nomen, cognomen. — **Numidum :** Numidia was organized at first as a province called Africa Nova, but in 30 it was united with the province of Africa as a senatorial province governed by a proconsul. See Marq.-Wissowa 1. 466. This form of the gen. pl. belongs to poetry ; see Neue-Wagener, Formenlehre, 1. 34–35. The form in *-um* is older than the longer form in *-arum* ; it is in no sense a contraction of the latter. See App. — **Cappadocum :** after 70 Cappadocia and Galatia were united as a single province governed by a consular legatus ; see Marq.-Wissowa 1. 367. — **regas :** a strong verb, used to mark a rule that required more or less display of military force. See App.

at mihi, quem cogis medios abrumpere somnos
    et matutinum ferre patique lutum,
quid petitur ? rupta cum pes vagus exit aluta
10   et subitus crassae decidit imber aquae
nec venit ablatis clamatus verna lacernis,
    accedit gelidam servus ad auriculam
et " Rogat ut secum cenes Laetorius " inquit.
    Viginti nummis ? non ego : malo famem

7. **cogis:** conative present; see A. 467; GL. 227, N. 2; L. 2301. — **medios . . . somnos:** for the language cf. Ov. Am. 2. 10. 19 *at mihi saevus amor somnos abrumpat inertes*; Verg. G. 3. 530 *nec somnos abrumpit cura salubris*. For the *salutatio* as foe to sleep cf. 10. 70. 5 *non resalutantes video nocturnos amicos*; 12. 18. 12–16 N.

8. **matutinum . . . lutum:** cf. 3. 36. 3–4 *horridus ut primo semper te mane salutem per mediumque trahat me tua sella lutum*; 10. 10. 8 N. — **ferre patique:** half idiomatic; cf. Lucr. 2. 291 (*sed ne mens ipsa*) *devicta quasi hoc cogatur ferre patique*; Hor. Ep. 1. 15. 17 *rure meo possum quidvis perferre patique*.

9. **vagus exit:** the foot is no longer held snugly by the broken shoe, but, so to say, roams at will; cf. Ov. A. A. 1. 516 *nec vagus in laxa pes tibi palla natet*. M. frequently uses *vagor* and *vagus* to describe tramping about Rome; cf. 1. 2. 6; 4. 78. 3 *discurris tota vagus urbe*. — **aluta** here = *calceo*; see 2. 29. 8 N.; cf. Ov. A. A. 3. 271 *pes malus in nivea semper celetur aluta*. With *rupta . . . aluta* cf. 1. 103. 5–6; Iuv. 3. 149–150 *rupta calceus alter pelle patet*.

10. **crassae . . . aquae:** a perfect downpour; cf. Ov. Am. 3. 6. 8 (of a river) *et turpi crassas gurgite*

volvis aquas. See Zingerle 15. — **decidit:** cf. Tib. 1. 2. 30 *cum multa decidit imber aqua*.

11. **nec . . . lacernis:** the poet's *lacerna* (see 2. 29. 3 N.; 2. 43. 7) had been taken by a fine house-slave, and now, when he calls lustily for it, the slave takes his time, leaving M. unprotected in the rain. This vs. matches *rupta . . . aluta*, 9. — **verna:** see 1. 41. 2 N.; 2. 90. 9. The word might refer to M.'s own *pedisecus*; if so, see § 11.

12–13. **accedit:** i.e. 'while I am waiting for the rain to cease'. — **servus . . . inquit:** the patron does not condescend to give the invitation in person ; the invitation is thus as mean as the meal to which it bids M. See on 1. 20; 1. 43; etc. Verses 9–14 = 'when I am without good shoes, and cloak-less too, some one bids me come (forthwith) through the rain to a worthless dinner'.

14–15. **Viginti nummis:** sc. *cenem* (deliberative subjv.): 'what, dine on twenty sesterces?' Note the hyperbole; the patron will not spend twenty sesterces on the whole dinner! The sum named, if expended upon *each* guest, would provide an ample repast. — **malo . . . mereamur** (16): see on *vis mittam*, 1. 117. 2. — **quam,** *than.* — **merces:** i.e. 'the pay for our services as clients'. The commercial

15   quam sit cena mihi, tibi sit provincia merces,
          et faciamus idem nec mereamur idem.

31

Hoc nemus, hi fontes, haec textilis umbra supini
     palmitis, hoc riguae ductile flumen aquae,
prataque nec bifero cessura rosaria Paesto,
     quodque viret Iani mense nec alget holus,

word well marks the commercial character of the *amicitia* at this time, as does *mereamur*, 16.

16. nec: = *et tamen non.*— **mereamur,** *earn*; cf. *stipendium merere* (*mereri*).

31. On the home which Marcella (see 12. 21) gave to M. after his return to Spain. It must have been in marked contrast to the Nomentanum (cf. 2. 38. 1 ; 9. 18. 2; etc.), to judge from the charming description of 1–6. See § 15. — Meter: § 48.

1–2. Hoc . . . hi . . . haec . . . hoc, *yonder*; M. points to object after object. — **nemus** is more than *silvae*; the estate has woodland that affords a good place to keep stock. Cf. νέμος. — **fontes:** the estate has good natural springs, an independent water supply; contrast the situation on his Nomentanum and at his city house (9. 18). — **haec . . . palmitis:** i.e. the dense shade afforded by the interwoven shoots and leaves of the vine; the words suggest not simply a cool retreat from summer heat, but a supply of wine. Cf. Hor. C. 1. 38. — **supini palmitis:** the Romans ordinarily trained the vine about trees (3. 58. 3 N.) or over poles; the former arrangement constituted an *arbustum*, the latter a *vinea*. M. seems to have had a *vinea*; hence *supini*, *low-lying*

(prop. 'lying on its back '). This adj., however, might well describe a vineyard on a terrace or hillside; cf. Hor. C. 3. 4. 23 *Tibur supinum.* —**hoc . . . aquae,** *yonder channeled stream of fertilizing water*. M. points to some aqueduct that was tapped for purposes of irrigation; the abundant flow gives rise to the hyperbole in *flumen.* — **riguae:** active in sense; cf. Verg. G. 2. 485 *rigui . . . in vallibus amnes.* Irrigation was commonly practiced in ancient Greece and ancient Italy; see e.g. Cic. Cato M. 15. 53 *quid ego irrigationes . . . proferam, quibus fit multo terra fecundior* and F. G. Moore's note there: "The art was learned by the Romans from its past-masters, the Etruscans". — **ductile:** cf. *aquae ductus*, 'aqueduct'.

3. prata: cf. 1. 88. 6 N. — **nec** = *ne . . . quidem*; see on 1. 109. 20. — **bifero . . . Paesto:** see 5. 37. 9 N.; 6. 80. 6; 9. 60. 1. For a similar hexameter-ending cf. Verg. G. 4. 119; Prop. 4. 5. 61.

4. viret . . . alget: the winter climate of central Spain is distinctly more severe than that of Rome, but the local conditions at Bilbilis in general or on M.'s farm there in particular may have been especially favorable; it is probable, also, that M. had paid much less attention to the possibilities of winter

5   quaeque natat clusis anguilla domestica lymphis,
   quaeque gerit similes candida turris aves,
   munera sunt dominae : post septima lustra reverso
   has Marcella domos parvaque regna dedit.
   Si mihi Nausicaa patrios concederet hortos,
10   Alcinoo possem dicere " Malo meos".

vegetables at Rome than at Bilbilis; in that case he might have regarded here as a rare phenomenon what had been common enough at Rome, though he knew it not.

5. anguilla domestica, *tame eels*, kept prob. in a preserve or reservoir (*piscina*: cf. *clusis . . . lymphis*); cf. 10. 30. 21–24. For the collective sing. see 3. 58. 13; 7. 89. 1; 4. 64. 32. — **lymphis**: this word denotes clear water and suggests that the reservoir was constructed by damming a rivulet from one of the *fontes* (1). Metrical considerations precluded putting the antec. in this verse at the end, as in 4, 6.

6. gerit: i.e. gives a home to. — **similes . . . aves**: i.e. white doves. Cf. 3. 58. 18 N. With *similes* sc. *sibi = turri*. — **candida turris**: cf. Col. 8. 8 *totus autem locus et ipsae columbarum cellae poliri debent albo tectorio, quoniam eo colore praecipue delectatur hoc genus avium*; Ov. Tr. 1. 9. 7.

7. dominae: on the strength of this word some (e.g. Brandt 35; Van Stockum 39) have held that Marcella was M.'s wife; see § 15. *Domina* was indeed used by the husband in addressing his wife, but it was also used by clients of their patronesses. Cf. *dominus = patronus* (see on 2. 18. 5). All M.'s expressions concerning Marcella can easily be explained as the utterances of beneficiary concerning benefactor. — **post . . . lustra**:

see 12. 18. 15–16 N. — **reverso**: sc. *mihi*.

8. domos: see App. — **parva . . . regna**: *regna* often in poetry = *domain* (cf. note on 10. 61. 3). But the sense may rather be that M. proudly feels himself at last a true *rex*, i.e. a *dives*, a *homo beatus* (see on 2. 18. 5), even though his realm is small; cf. 4. 40. 3 *praetulimus tantis solum te, Postume, regnis*; 12. 48. 16; 12. 57. 19.

9. Nausicaa: the lovely daughter of Alcinous, king of the Phaeacians (see 4. 64. 29 N.; 10. 94. 2). In this comparison M. seems to have in mind the fruit-producing virtue of his garden; cf. Priap. 16. 3–4 (*pompa*) *qualia credibile est spatiantem rure paterno Nausicaam pleno saepe tulisse sinu*; Stat. Silv. 1. 3. 81 *quid bifera Alcinoi laudem pomaria ?* — For the final *ā* of *Nausicaa* see § 54, a; cf. 14. 187. 2 *nec Glycerā pueri, Thais amica fuit.*

34. M.'s thoughts after his return to Spain must have reverted often to Rome; see § 15 fin. In Rome he had suffered much (3), but the balance had been after all on the side of enjoyment. Of one phase of that enjoyment, the possession of friends, M. is thinking especially. The poem then means: ' Leaving Rome was worse than I thought; I didn't realize what I was going to lose by breaking the ties of my friendships at Rome. Verily, friendships are a nuisance;

34

Triginta mihi quattuorque messes
tecum, si memini, fuere, Iuli,
quarum dulcia mixta sunt amaris,
sed iucunda tamen fuere plura,
5   et si calculus omnis huc et illuc
diversus bicolorque digeratur,
vincet candida turba nigriorem.
Si vitare velis acerba quaedam
et tristes animi cavere morsus,
10   nulli te facias nimis sodalem :
gaudebis minus et minus dolebis.

36

Libras quattuor aut duas amico

they make one suffer so at parting'.
— Meter: § 49.

1. **Triginta ... messes:** see
12. 18. 16 N.   For *messis = annus*
(metonymy) cf. 6. 70. 1; 10. 103. 7
*quattuor accessit tricesima messibus
aestas.*

2. **Iuli:** for Iulius Martialis see
1. 15; 4. 64; 5. 20. 1; etc.

5-6. **si calculus ... digeratur:**
for the custom of marking days
with stones of different colors see
9. 52. 4-5 N. — **diversus bicolorque:** pred. nom., giving the result
of *huc et illuc ... digeratur;* we
may render, freely, 'in two heaps
so that the two colors show'. The
two colors are white (for the *dulcia*
and *iucunda* of 3-4), black (for the
amara of 3).— For the diæresis in
5 see § 49, d.

8-12. The second person is generalizing (we should say 'one'); in
such cases the subjv. is the usual
mood; cf. note on 1. 15. 5.

9. **animi ... morsus:** torture
of soul, due to separation, tempo-
rary or permanent.

10. **sodalem:** see 1. 15. 1 N.;
7. 86. 5; 2. 43. 15; 10. 104. 8.

11. **gaudebis minus:** i.e. 'you
(one) will lack the undeniable
pleasures of friendship'. — **minus
dolebis:** separation from persons
not *sodales* will give no pain.

36. M. reminds Labullus, a
patronus otherwise unknown, who
had perhaps boasted of his gener-
osity, that his self-congratulation
is not justified, for, measured by the
standards of the past, his generos-
ity becomes downright meanness.
— Meter: § 49.

1. **Libras:** sc. *argenti;* silver
plate was a common present, e.g.
at the Saturnalia. Cf. 2. 44. 1-2;
2. 76. 1; 7. 86. 7; 8. 71. 1-2 *quattuor
argenti libras mihi tempore brumae
misisti;* 10. 15. 7-8; 10. 57. 1-2. The
value of such plate was estimated by

algentemque togam brevemque laenam,
interdum aureolos manu crepantes
possint ducere qui duas Kalendas,
5 quod nemo, nisi tu, Labulle, donas,
non es, crede mihi, bonus. Quid ergo?
ut verum loquar, optimus malorum es.
Pisones Senecasque Memmiosque

weight; the weight was sometimes engraved on the plate itself; cf. C. I. L. 3. 1. 1769; Petr. 31 *tegebant asellum duae lances, in quarum marginibus nomen Trimalchionis inscriptum erat et argenti pondus*; Fried. SG. 3. 123–124; 163 ff. — The accusatives in 1–3 are objects of (*donat . . .*) *donas*, 5. — **quattuor . . . duas:** i.e. only four, just two.

2. **algentem . . . togam:** a toga so thin that it freezes itself! how can it keep any one warm? Cf. 4. 34. 2 *quisquis te niveam dicit habere togam*; 14. 135. 2 *cum teget algentes alba lacerna togas*; contrast *sudatrix toga*, 12. 18. 5 N. — **brevem . . . laenam:** the *laena* was a garment of the *sagum* or *lacerna* type (see 2. 29. 3 N.; 2. 43. 7), not easy to distinguish from the *lacerna*. It was heavier than the toga and seems to have been worn over it, or even over the *lacerna*, perhaps as a weather garment. Under the Empire it was used as a thick warm outer garment instead of the toga. It might be of various colors, and was held in place by a brooch or clasp at the shoulder. Cf. Iuv. 3. 282–284 *quamvis improbus annis atque mero fervens cavet hunc quem coccina laena vitari iubet et comitum longissimus ordo*; Pers. 1. 32 *circum umeros hyacinthina laena est*; Beck. 3. 221. — **brevem:** too short for style or warmth; cf. *brevis toga*, 10. 15. 7; *togula*, 4. 26. 4; etc.

3. **aureolos . . . crepantes:** cf. 5. 19. 14 *qui crepet aureolos forsitan unus erit.* The *aureus*, a gold coin equivalent to 100 *sestertii* or 25 *denarii*, corresponded to an English sovereign or to an American half-eagle. See Hultsch 308 ff.; Hill, Handbook 54. The dim. marks M.'s contempt (see on 4. 26. 4; 5. 37. 20); the noun thus plays the rôle played by the adjectives in 1–2. On the other hand *manu crepantes*, which suggests that the money was real (it rang true), plays the part filled by the nouns of 1–2. We thus get very pleasing as well as subtle variety.

4. **ducere** = *producere, protrahere*; we may, however, render by *last, endure,* as if the verb were here intransitive. Cf. 4. 66. 4 *duxit . . . aestates synthesis una decem.* The vs. is artificial; M. might have said, more simply, *quibus possis ducere duas tantum Kalendas.* See on *catenati . . . labores,* 1. 15. 7. — **Kalendas** = *menses* (synecdoche).

5. **nemo:** sc. *donat*; *quod nemo, nisi tu, Labulle, donat* is the commoner form.

6. **non . . . mihi:** cf. 1. 41. 2.

7. **ut . . . loquar,** *to speak plainly, not to mince matters.* See A. 532; GL. 545, Rem. 3; L. 1962. —**optimus . . . es:** for the thought cf. Sen. Ep. 79. 11 *nec enim bonitas est pessimis esse meliorem.*

8. **Pisones:** the Pisones, though of a plebeian gens, constituted an old and very illustrious

et Crispos mihi redde, sed priores :
10   fies protinus ultimus bonorum.
Vis cursu pedibusque gloriari ?
Tigrim vince levemque Passerinum :
nulla est gloria praeterire asellos.

39

Odi te, quia bellus es, Sabelle :
res est putida bellus et Sabellus ;

family. M. is thinking of its last great representative, C. Calpurnius Piso, after whom the great conspiracy against Nero in 65 was named; see §9; Fried. SG. 1. 249 ff.; Merivale chap. 53. This Piso was noted for his liberality; see Tac. Ann. 15. 48. There appears no reason to doubt that the liberality of the patrons had been steadily diminishing for a generation; see Fried. SG. 1. 381. — **Senecas**: see §9; 1. 61. 7 N.; 4. 40. 1–2 *atria Pisonum stabant cum stemmate toto et docti Senecae ter numeranda domus.* The three Senecas alluded to in 4. 40, as perhaps here also, were the philosopher, an older brother Junius Gallio, and a younger brother Annaeus Mela. Junius Gallio is believed to be the proconsul of Achaia before whom St. Paul appeared at Corinth (Acts 18. 12); see e.g. Teuffel, § 268. 7. To the philosopher M. probably owed his Nomentanum; see § 10.— **Memmios**: C. Memmius Regulus, consul in 63, was prob. in M.'s thoughts.

9. Crispos: see 4. 54. 7 N. With *Pisones . . . Crispos* cf. Iuv. 5. 108–111 *nemo petit (nunc) modicis quae mittebantur amicis a Seneca, quae Piso bonus, quae Cotta solebat largiri, namque et titulis et fascibus olim maior habebatur donandi gloria.* — **priores:** none of their stingy descendants, but liberal givers like to those of the good old days. For Seneca's idea of liberality cf. e.g. Ben. 2. 1. 1 *sic demus quomodo vellemus accipere, ante omnia libenter, cito, sine ulla dubitatione*; 2. 1. 2 *proximus est a negante qui dubitavit.* Publilius Syrus has *bis dat qui cito dat.*

11–13. 'Would you win true fame as a benefactor? Be willing then to outdo worthy contestants'. — **Tigrim . . . Passerinum:** famous race-horses; see 7. 7. 8–10. On the public furor over such animals see Fried. SG. 2. 335 ff. — **levem**, *light-footed, swift.* — **asellos**: dim. of contempt; see on *aureolos*, 3. For the thought cf. Hor. S. 1. 1. 90–91 *infelix operam perdas, ut si quis asellum in Campo doceat parentem currere frenis ?* M. is not thinking of the stupidity of the ass, but of his lack of speed.

39. M. jeers at Sabellus (see 7. 85; 9. 19), playing on his name. Note the similarity of verse termination, after the manner of Catullus (see on 1. 109. 1; 2. 41. 3–4). — Meter: § 49.

1. **bellus:** see 1. 9, with notes; 3. 63.

2. **putida**, *rotten, decaying*, and so *disgusting*; the word perhaps

bellum denique malo quam Sabellum.
Tabescas utinam, Sabelle, belle !

46

Difficilis facilis, iucundus acerbus es idem :
nec tecum possum vivere nec sine te.

51

Tam saepe nostrum decipi Fabullinum
miraris, Aule? semper homo bonus tiro est.

54

Crine ruber, niger ore, brevis pede, lumine laesus

suggests that Sabellus was suffering from some offensive malady, a result of excesses ; *tabescas*, 4, may point the same way (but see note there). In 3. 98 ; 6. 33 ; 12. 43, a Sabellus, perhaps the man named here, is described as filthy and licentious. — **bellus :** sc. *homo*.

3. bellum . . . Sabellum : M. works to a climax ; 'in short (*denique*) Sabellus is worse than a *bellus homo*'. One may, however, get a far better effect by seeing a play on *bellum*, 'war'; 'I prefer war with all its horrors to Sabellus'.

4. Tabescas : see on *putida*, 2. The inference there stated is of course not inevitable ; the vs. may be only a sort of informal *devotio*. — **Tabescas . . . belle** is as oxymoric as *tabes bella* would be. This view seems more effective than the other interpretation (good as that is), got by omitting the comma after *Sabelle* and taking *belle* as adjective.

46. On a testy friend. — Meter; § 48.

1. Difficilis, *captious, hard to get along with.*

2. nec tecum . . . sine te : cf. Ov. Am. 3. 11. 39 *sic ego nec sine te nec tecum vivere possum* ; Hor. C. 3. 9. 24 ('spite of your faults') *tecum vivere amem, tecum obeam libens.*

51. 'Good men are ever unsophisticated'. — Meter : § 52.

2. Aule : see 9. 81. 1. — **tiro :** a greenhorn among sharpers ; prop. a raw recruit among veterans.

54. A pen picture of Zoilus. See 2. 16 ; 2. 19 ; 2. 58. — Meter : § 48.

1. Crine ruber = *rufus*. Red hair is proper to one who had been a slave ; cf. the conventional redhaired wigs and masks worn by the actors who personated slaves in comedy (see e.g. Ter. Phorm. 51). — **niger ore** = *nigra facie, swarthy.* Perhaps M. is hinting that this *nigra facies* is but a reflection of the malignity of the inner man. Cf. Hor. S. 1. 4. 85 *hic niger est, hunc tu, Romane, caveto,* and the secondary meaning of μέλας. — **brevis pede :** one (foot =) leg is shorter than the other. As *manus* often = 'arm', so *pes* often = 'leg', or = *crus*, the lower part of the

rem magnam praestas, Zoile, si bonus es.

57

Cur saepe sicci parva rura Nomenti
laremque villae sordidum petam quaeris?
Nec cogitandi, Sparse, nec quiescendi
in urbe locus est pauperi: negant vitam
5   ludi magistri mane, nocte pistores,
aerariorum marculi die toto;

leg. — **lumine laesus** perhaps =
luscus; perhaps, however, the reference is to a disfigurement that resulted from injury, or even from
punishment inflicted on him while
he was a slave.

2. **rem . . . praestas,** *you are
a veritable miracle.* — **si . . . es:**
i.e. 'if in spite of such an exterior
you are a man of morals'.

57. 'The poor man has no adequate relief from the noises of the
town'. — Meter, § 52.

1. **sicci . . : Nomenti:** on M.'s
Nomentanum see 2. 38. 1 N.; etc.
Sicci indicates that the soil was
unproductive, for the water supply
was poor; see 9. 18. 5 N. — **parva
rura:** see 9. 18. 2; 9. 97. 7. There
was little at the Nomentanum, and
that little was but mediocre.

2. **larem . . . sordidum:** for
lar (*lares*) see 1. 70. 2 N.; 1. 76. 2;
9. 18. 2; etc. — **sordidum** logically
modifies *villae* rather than *larem*;
for its meaning see 10. 96. 4 N.

3. **cogitandi:** on the time-
stealing exactions of life in town
see Plin. Ep. 1.9; Hor. Ep. 2.2.65–
80 (the latter passage ends with *tu
me inter strepitus nocturnos atque
diurnos vis canere et contracta sequi vestigia vatum?*). — **quiescendi**
includes freedom from such noises
as preclude literary work, but primarily refers to opportunity to

sleep; cf. then 10.74. 12 N.; 12.18.
15–16 N. Plin. Ep. 9.6.1 welcomes
the Ludi Circenses only because
they attracted such crowds that the
town was quiet enough to admit of
some literary work. The extreme
narrowness of the streets and the
tendency of shopkeepers to en-
croach more and more on the highway itself added to the press and
the resulting confusion and noise;
see Fried. SG. 1. 27 ff.

4. **vitam:** i.e. such life as is
worth the living; see 1. 15. 4, 12 N.

5. **ludi magistri mane:** see
9. 68, with notes. — **mane, nocte**
together give the parts of the night
and so together balance *die toto*, 6;
we need not be troubled because
M. does not mention these parts
in proper sequence. — **pistores,**
bakers, who had then, as now, to
prepare their wares in the night.
They seem also to have cried their
wares before daylight; see 14. 223.
1–2 *surgite: iam vendit pueris ientacula pistor cristataeque sonant
undique lucis aves.* — Note the
chiasmus.

6. **aerariorum,** *brasiers, copper-
smiths.* — **marculi:** a comparatively
rare word; cf. Lucil. 1165–1166
Marx (= 1181–1182 Lachmann) *et
velut in fabrica fervens cum mar-
culus ferrum tinnitu multo cum
magnis . . . ictibus tundit.*

hinc otiosus sordidam quatit mensam
Neroniana nummularius massa,
illinc palucis malleator Hispanae
10   tritum nitenti fuste verberat saxum ;
nec turba cessat entheata Bellonae,
nec fasciato naufragus loquax trunco,

7. **otiosus,** *lounging*; he spends much of his time waiting for custom. — **sordidam,** *dirty,* whether in the literal sense, or in the figurative, *mean, paltry.*— **quatit mensam:** when business is dull, the *nummularius* (8) shakes the table and the coins, that the chink of the money may attract the attention of possible customers. The man is a money-changer (at least this is the usual sense of *nummularius*); his table is in the open air. Money-changers were frequently called *mensarii.* See Marq.-Wissowa 2. 66 ff.

8. **Neroniana . . . massa,** *with his supply of money of Nero's coinage*; *massa,* prop. 'lump', 'bar', 'ingot', is frequently used of money in quantity; cf. the etymology and uses of 'bullion'. It is probable that Nero's coinage is singled out for mention because he debased the currency. He reduced the *denarius* to $\frac{1}{96}$ lb. (3.41 gr.) of silver, the *aureus* to 7.4 gr. of gold. From Augustus's time the *aureus* had contained 7.8 gr. of gold; this again was the average weight long after Nero's time (Hultsch 311; 318; Hill, Handbook 53–54). After the old coinage had been restored, the *mensarii* were doubtless often called upon to make exchange between the debased and the better currency. The debased coinage on the table of this man is a part of the characterization of the small curb-stone broker. *Neroniana . . . massa* seems to be abl.

of char., with the usual adjectival force ('tricky', 'cheating'). P. and S., however, thinking that a money-changer could not make noise enough to interfere with sleep, interpret *nummularius* of a 'coiner', striking out coins with hammer and die. This agrees well with 9–10, and makes *Neroniana . . . massa* an easy instr. abl., but there seems no authority for taking *nummularius* as 'coiner'.

9. **palucis,** *gold-dust.* This is a Spanish word, of uncertain spelling; see Harper's Latin Lexicon s.v. *Ballux.* See App. Hultsch thinks, perhaps rightly, that this man hammered Spanish gold-dust into leaves of gold which he used for gilding. On the word see Cooper, § 17.

10. **tritum,** *worn,* i.e. by the *fustis.*— **nitenti,** i.e. bright with the particles of gold adhering to it. — **fuste,** *beetle,* of wood.

11. **entheata** = *fanatica*, an epithet applied to priests of Cybele, Isis, Serapis, and Bellona. Cf. 11. 84. 4 *furit ad Phrygios enthea turba modos,* with notes ; Iuv. 6. 511–512 *ecce furentis Bellonae matrisque deum chorus intrat.* See Preller-Jordan 2. 386. On the word see Cooper, § 80.

12. **fasciato . . . trunco:** a common street sight in antiquity was the shipwrecked sailor, real or pretended, begging alms, sometimes singing or telling his tale of woe. Such beggars often carried a piece of the wrecked vessel or a picture

a matre doctus nec rogare Iudaeus,
nec sulphuratae lippus institor mercis.
15   Numerare pigri damna quis potest somni ?
dicet quot aera verberent manus urbis,

of the wreck; cf. Pers. 1. 88–90 *men moveat (naufragus) ? . . . cantet si naufragus, assem protulerim ? cantas, cum fracta te in trabe pictum ex umero portes ?* Iuv. 14. 301–302 *mersa rate naufragus assem dum rogat et picta se tempestate tuetur*; Phaedr. 4. 22. 24–25 *ceteri tabulam suam portant rogantes victum.* Here *fasciato . . . trunco* is commonly interpreted of a picture of the shipwreck painted on a fragment of the lost vessel, wrapped in bands to protect it. But the picture would have effectiveness only because uncovered and visible to every passer-by. Besides, *truncus* is commonly used not of a fragment of anything, but of the thing from which a part is cut, e.g. of the trunk stripped of branches, not of the several branches. Further, on this view it is difficult, if not impossible, to explain the syntax of *fasciato . . . trunco.* It is better, then, to regard the phrase as an abl. of characteristic, to render by 'the wordy mariner of the swathed (bandaged) body', and to suppose that the man, feigning great bodily injury, has his body wrapped in bandages, pretending, perhaps, to have lost an arm or a leg. For a similar trick cf. 7. 39. 5–9 *quam (podagram) dum volt nimis adprobare veram et sanas linit obligatque plantas inceditque gradu laborioso . . . desit (= desiit) fingere Caelius podagram* (i.e. he became lame in very fact).

13. a . . . Iudaeus: in the Latin poets the Jew is a professional beggar or fortune-teller; see Fried. SG. 3. 617 ff. Because of prejudice

and enactments against them, esp. after the destruction of Jerusalem by Titus, they were virtually forced to beg in order to live. Cf. Iuv. 3. 13–16 *nunc sacri fontis nemus et delubra locantur Iudaeis, quorum cophinus faenumque supellex, omnis enim populo mercedem pendere iussa est arbor et eiectis mendicat silva Camenis.*

14. sulphuratae . . . mercis: see 1. 41. 4–5 N. — **institor,** *peddler*; cf. 7. 61. 1; Ov. A. A. 1. 421–422 *institor ad dominam veniet discinctus emacem, expediet merces teque sedente suas*; Hor. C. 3. 6. 30. — **lippus:** see on 8. 9. 2. Here, however, the *lippitudo* may be due to the sulphur fumes, if the *institor* mended broken glassware (see on 1. 41. 4–5).

15. pigri . . . somni: sleep such as a man enjoys who thinks that he has a right to be lazy and to live a life of inglorious ease. Cf. 12. 62. 1–2 *antiqui rex magne poli mundique prioris, sub quo pigra quies nec labor ullus erat.* The question serves as protasis to 16; '*if* any man tells . . . he will also be able to tell', etc.

16. quot . . . urbis: i.e. how many tinkling cymbals or brazen instruments are used in Rome to exorcise the evil spirits that, as men believe, have bewitched Luna. Cf. Iuv. 6. 442 ff.; Liv. 26. 5. 9; Ov. M. 4. 332 ff.; Tib. 1. 8. 21 ff.; Tac. Ann. 1. 28; etc. The din was intended to drown out the incantations by which the magicians (cf. 17) had affected the moon and so to break their spell.

cum secta Colcho Luna vapulat rhombo.
Tu, Sparse, nescis ista nec potes scire,
Petilianis delicatus in regnis,
20　cui plana summos despicit domus montes
et rus in urbe est vinitorque Romanus
— nec in Falerno colle maior autumnus —
intraque limen clausus essedo cursus,

17. Colcho . . . rhombo: i.e.
is tortured and sorely wounded by
the magician's circle or wheel. —
Colcho: because Medea, famed
for her magic skill, was a Colchian,
Colchus or *Colchicus = magicus*;
see 3. 58. 16 N. — **vapulat:** for the
meaning see on 10. 62. 9. — **rhombo**
(cf. *ῥόμβος*): cf. 9. 29. 9–10 *quae nunc
Thessalico lunam deducere rhombo
. . . sciet.* The Latin name for the
rhombus was *turbo*; cf. e.g. Hor.
Epod. 17. 7, with Smith's note. The
turbo was a small lozenge-shaped
board, to one end of which was attached a cord; it was whirled round
and round to make a loud buzz-
ing noise; the witch meanwhile
chanted her incantations. The instrument (known as a 'bull-roarer')
is still in use in this way among uncivilized peoples.

19. Petilianis . . . regnis: see
12. 31. 8 N. Though the estate of
Petilius had passed into the hands
of Sparsus, still, after a custom
which to this day has abundant
illustration, it is known by the
name of him who conferred distinction upon it by owning or inhabiting it. In Iuv. 3. 212–222 the
magna Asturici domus seems now
to be owned by a man named Persicus. The exact reference may
be to Q. Petilius Cerialis Caesius
Rufus, consul suffectus in 70 and
again in 74 (Klein 43–44), or to his
son or brother, Q. Petilius Rufus,

consul in 83 (Klein 47, N. 4). — **delicatus:** i.e. living luxuriously; see
on 4. 30. 16.

20. cui . . . domus: see 1. 117.
7 N.—**plana . . . domus:** an obscure
phrase. It seems least unsatisfac-
tory to say that the adj. carries the
main thought; the sense is then
'the levels (roof) of your house
(palace) look down on the mountain tops'; cf. then 4. 64. 10–12, with
notes.

21. rus in urbe: i.e. country
enjoyed in town; cf. 8. 68. 1–2 *qui
Corcyraei vidit pomaria regis, rus,
Entelle, tuae praeferet ille domus*;
3. 58. 45. This *rus in urbe* was
apparently as large as that of Iulius
Martialis (4. 64) was small; it had
ground enough for a large vineyard
(22) and an ample *gestatio* (23). On
the great *horti* in Rome see 6. 80.
3 N.; 3. 58. 2–4. — **Romanus =**
urbanus, in urbe ipsa. A far commoner epithet of a *vinitor* in Italy
would be *Campanus.*

22. Falerno colle: see 4. 69.
1 N.; 5. 64. 1.— **autumnus =** *vindemia, vintage*; cf. 3. 58. 7.

23. limen: i.e. of the range of
buildings or of the estate. Cf. 12.
50. 5 (on a highly ornamental mansion) *pulvereumque fugax hippo-
dromon ungula plaudit.* — **clusus:**
freely, 'private'. The other reading, *latus*, 'spacious', also yields a
good sense. See App. — **essedo:**
see 4. 64. 19 N. — **cursus:** i.e.

et in profundo somnus, et quies nullis
25   offensa linguis, nec dies nisi admissus.
Nos transeuntis risus excitat turbae,
et ad cubile est Roma. Taedio fessis
dormire quotiens libuit, imus ad villam.

67

Maiae Mercurium creastis Idus,
Augustis redit Idibus Diana,
Octobres Maro consecravit Idus :

gestatio, curriculum (hippodromos),
porticus; see on 1. 12. 5.

24. in profundo somnus: cf.
the quietude of the Ianiculum; see
4.64.18-23. Even at a distance from
the city great pains were taken to
insure easy sleep; cf. e.g. Plin. Ep.
2. 17. 22 (of a *cubiculum* in his villa
at Laurentum) *non maris murmur,
non tempestatum motus, non fulgu-
rum lumen ac ne diem quidem sentit,
nisi fenestris apertis.*

25. dies = *lux diei.* Plin. Ep.
9. 36. 1–2, writing of his life on his
Tuscan estate, says: *evigilo cum
libuit . . . clausae fenestrae manent
. . . cogito . . . notarium voco et die
admisso quae formaveram dicto.* —
admissus: freely, *with your con-
sent.*

26. excitat = *expergefacit*; cf.
Plaut. Mer. 160 *dormientis specta-
tores metuis ne ex somno excites?*
Cf. note on *excitatus*, 5. 14. 3.

28. imus ad villam: cf. Hor.
Ep. 1. 17. 6–8 *si te grata quies et
primam somnus in horam delectat,
si te pulvis strepitusque rotarum, si
laedit caupona, Ferentinum ire iu-
bebo.* — On the meter see § 52.

67. Another tribute to Vergil.
See on verses 3-4; § 33.— Meter:
§ 49.

1. Maiae . . . Idus: vocative.
— **Mercurium creastis:** i.e. for

the Romans, esp. from the time
when the first temple was dedicated
to Mercury (then revered as the
god of trade) on the Ides of May,
259 B.C.; see C.I.L. 1, p. 393; Marq.-
Wissowa 3. 367; 575. M. calls the
festival observed annually on
May 15 in honor of Mercury the
dies natalis of the god; cf. Fest. 148
*Maiis Idibus mercatorum dies festus
erat, quod eo die Mercurii aedes esset
dedicata.*

2. Augustis . . . Idibus: there
was a festival of Diana on August 13. It was a slave's holiday;
her temple on the Aventine was a
slave's sanctuary. Cf. Fest. 343
*servorum dies festus vulgo existi-
matur Idus Aug., quod eo die Ser.
Tullius, natus servus, aedem Dianae dedicaverit in Aventino.* See
Preller-Jordan 1. 316 ff.; Marq.-
Wissowa 3. 581. For the form of
the adj. *Augustis* see on *Algidos*,
10. 30. 6. — **Diana** here = 'Diana's
festival'.

3. Octobres . . . Idus: cf. Donatus (Suet.) Vita Verg. 2 *natus est Cn.
Pompeio Magno M. Licinio Crasso
primum consulibus Iduum Octo-
brium die.* — **Maro consecravit:**
cf. Comparetti 49: "Vergil was
then already (i.e. by M.'s time) the
saint of poets; and, of all the apo-
theoses of the Roman Empire, this

Idus saepe colas et has et illas,
5   qui magni celebras Maronis Idus.

80

Ne laudet dignos, laudat Callistratus omnes :
cui malus est nemo, quis bonus esse potest ?

82

Effugere in thermis et circa balnea non est
Menogenen, omni tu licet arte velis.
Captabit tepidum dextra laevaque trigonem,

deification of Vergil, though ill-defined in its origin and exaggerated in its effects, was, without doubt, the only one inspired by a really generous sentiment". Note that M. speaks as highly of Vergil as he does of Mercury and Diana.

4. saepe colas: the subject may be wholly indefinite ; still it is easy to think that M. had in mind Silius Italicus. Cf. 4. 14, with notes; 11. 48; 11. 50. — **has:** the Ides of October. — **illas:** the Ides of May and August. For the custom of honoring the memory of a great man by observing his birthday cf. 7. 21, with notes; 7. 86. 1 N.; 10. 27. 1; Iuv. 5. 36–37 (*vinum*) *quale coronati Thrasea Helvidiusque bibebant Brutorum et Cassi natalibus*; Sen. Ep. 64. 9 *quidni ego magnorum virorum et imagines habeam incitamenta animi et natales celebrem ? quidni ego illos honoris causa semper adpellem?* M.'s regard for Vergil seems to have been something deeper than the high, but conventional, esteem in which his name was held by M.'s contemporaries; cf. 3. 38. 8 ; 5. 56. 5 ; 4. 14. 14 *magno . . . Maroni*; 11. 52. 18 *aeterno . . . Vergilio*; 12. 3. 1 *summo . . . Maroni*; 14. 186. 1 *inmensum . . . Maronem* (but see note there).

80. 'Callistratus praises without discrimination'. — Meter: § 48.

1. Ne . . . dignos: 'that he may not praise the worthy *only*', 'that he may not confine his praise to the worthy' (to do that is to run risk of offending those who are not praised); sarcastically interpreted, the clause = 'that he may not praise the worthy at all'. This form of wit, which consists in a sarcastic ascription of purpose in a given act, a purpose which of course the actor never in fact entertained at all, appears elsewhere in Latin, e.g. several times in Horace.

2. quis . . . potest: sc. *ei*, a dat. of interest, 'in the eyes of him '.

82. On a persistent dinner-hunter, who resorts to the lowest means to gain his end. Cf. 2. 11; 2. 14. — Meter: § 48.

1. Effugere . . . non est: see on 12. 11. 5; cf. 11. 98. 1 *effugere non est . . . basiatores.*

2. Menogenen: doubtless a freedman. — **licet:** cf. 1. 70. 17 N.

3–4. Captabit . . . pilas: to translate this passage is easy enough, but our knowledge of Roman ways of playing ball is too limited to enable us to interpret it with certainty. On the general subject see Beck. 3. 171 ff.; Marq. 841 ff.;

inputet acceptas ut tibi saepe pilas,

Smith D. of A. 2. 421 ff.; McDaniel Trans. Am. Phil. Ass. 37. 121–134. The *trigon* (τρίγων) or *pila trigonalis* was a game played by three persons who stood in the form of an equilateral triangle. The ball used was the ordinary *pila*; each player had a ball. It would seem that a player might arbitrarily strike or throw the ball to either of the other two players (i.e. there was no necessary routine of throws); hence, since a player might be compelled at any moment to handle two or even three balls simultaneously or nearly so, to play the game well one must be as skillful with the left hand as with the right. Cf. 14. 46. 1–2 *si me (= pilam trigonalem) mobilibus scis expulsare sinistris, sum tua. Tu nescis? rustice, redde pilam.* The phrase *captabit . . . pilas* is grimly humorous; Menogenes carries his *captatio* so far that he is *captator ipsarum pilarum!* — **tepidum,** *warm,* in the sense of *warming, causing perspiration;* ball and game are described in terms of their effects (transferred epithet). The *trigon* was a very active game; hence the players stripped wholly or nearly so for the play. Cf. 4. 19. 5–9 *seu lentum ceroma teris tepidumve trigona, sive harpasta manu pulverulenta rapis, plumea seu laxi partiris pondera follis.* — **inputet . . . pilas:** the obscurity (see on 3) lies here. The vs. seems to = 'that he may charge up his many catches against you'. It is clear that Menogenes helps some player by catching balls that the player ought himself to catch, and that he charges his skill in doing this against the player, as entitling him to a dinner. According to Marq. 844 there were in the *trigon* three persons, standing

one behind each player, whose business it was to stop the balls missed and in the shortest possible time to get them back into the hands of the player, and three other persons to keep score; cf. C.I.L. 4. 1936 *Amianthus Epaphra Tertius ludant; cum Hedysto Iucundus Nolanus petat* (i.e. collect the balls missed); *numeret Citus et Acus Amiantho;* Petr. 27. In this view Menogenes is not a player at all, but a member of the second group of three; he assists one player by catching the balls that player misses. This is substantially McDaniel's view (published after the above was written; see Trans. Am. Phil. Ass. 37. 126–128); Menogenes is thus a 'chaser' or 'backstop', whose attentions it is impossible for the players to escape, particularly since such attentions, when rendered by the right person, were most helpful and welcome (as they are in tennis to-day). But it seems hardly likely that under such circumstances he would be called upon to display much skill and activity (cf. 3), unless the man he is trying to assist were a very poor player. It remains then to suppose that Menogenes is a player proper, who plays into the hands of his patron by displaying extraordinary activity and skill and thus taking, in place of the other, balls he might not be able to handle. For a hint of this view see Smith D. of A. 2. 425. But why does one who wants to escape Menogenes engage with him "in anything so voluntary as a game of ball" (McDaniel), and why should any one else enter into a game so unfairly conducted or remain therein? Finally, McDaniel (129–130) interprets the passage cited

5　colliget et referet laxum de pulvere follem,
　　et si iam lotus, iam soleatus erit;
　lintea si sumes, nive candidiora loquetur,
　　sint licet infantis sordidiora sinu;
　exiguos secto comentem dente capillos

above from C.I.L. 4. 1936 somewhat differently. — **inputet**: cf. 12.
48. 13 *inputet ipse deus nectar mihi,*
fiet acetum, 'let Jupiter charge
against me … (and) it will become',
etc. — **acceptas**, *caught, inter-
cepted*; *accipere pilam* was a technical phrase, like our 'catch a ball'.
　5. colliget … follem: another
way of playing ball, practiced apparently in an open court (cf. *de
pulvere*) with the *follis*, a large but
light ball, filled merely with air; cf.,
then, the modern basket-ball. This
light ball was struck by the fist or
palm or forearm, affording exercise
less violent than that given by the
trigon, and so adapted to the needs
of boys and older men; cf. 14. 47.
1–2 *ite procul, iuvenes; mitis mihi*
(= *folli*) *convenit aetas; folle decet
pueros ludere, folle senes.* The man
Menogenes is helping is old. —
colliget et referet, *will pick out
of the dirt and return* to the player.
Colliget … follem involves zeugma,
since *colligere … follem* is not a
natural phrase; M. is thinking
rather of *colligere pulverem*, i.e.
the vs. = *follem laxum tam arden-
ter referet ut pulverem ipsum colli-
gat.* — **laxum**: this adj. is regularly
used of the *follis* as *soft, spreading*; cf. 4. 19. 7, cited on 3; 14. 45.
1–2 (on the *pila paganica*) *haec
quae difficili turget paganica pluma
folle minus laxa est et minus arta
pila.*
　6. et si, *although.* — **iam lotus
… soleatus**: i.e. already bathed
and dressed for dinner; he will
not hesitate to risk spoiling his

best clothes. — **soleatus**: see 3. 50.
3 N.
　7. lintea … sumes: i.e. to
rub down, after exercise and bath
are both over. *Lintea* = *mantelia*
(*mantilia*), towels brought to the
bath by slaves for the master's
use; cf. Ap. M. 1. 23 *ac simul ex
promptuario oleum unctui et lintea
tersui ac cetera huic eidem usui
profer ociter et hospitem meum per-
duc ad proximas balneas*; Petr. 28
*itaque intravimus balneum … iam
Trimalchio unguento perfusus ter-
gebatur, non linteis, sed palliis ex
lana mollissima factis.* — **nive candidiora** (*esse*); cf. 4. 42. 5 *sit nive
candidior*; 5. 37. 6 N.; 7. 33. 2 *candidior prima … nive*; Catull. 80.
1–2 *quare rosea ista labella hiberna
fiant candidiora nive*; repeatedly in
Ov., e.g. Am. 3. 5. 11 *candidior nivibus.* We may supply *esse* or take
loquetur as in 1. 61. 8; 10. 96. 1 and
candidiora as pred. accusative to
ea = *lintea.*
　8. licet: as in 2. — **sinu**: the
front of an infant's outer garment;
freely, *bib.*
　9. exiguos … capillos:
'though the locks you are comb-
ing with the toothed ivory are
scanty indeed'. *Exiguos* carries
the emphasis. Note position of
the adj. and the noun at the ends
of the verse; see on *argutis …
libellis,* 1. 1. 3. — **dente**: collective
sing., = *pectine* (synecdoche). It is
possible also to take *dente* as =
'ivory'; cf. 5. 37. 5 N. In either
case *secto* = *cut, sawn.* Combs were
often made of boxwood.

10   dicet Achilleas disposuisse comas ;
        fumosae feret ipse tropin de faece lagonae,
        frontis et umorem colliget usque tuae ;
        omnia laudabit, mirabitur omnia, donec

10. **Achilleas . . . comas**: M.
may be thinking of the tradition
told e.g. by Hyg. Fab. 96 that
Thetis, mother of Achilles, to keep
him out of the Trojan War, sent
him in his early boyhood to the
court of Lycomedes king of Scy-
ros, to grow up there in female attire among the daughters of the
king. Here his hair grew long.
Cf. 5. 48. 5–6 *talis deprensus
Achilles deposuit gaudens, matre
dolente, comas.* Homer gives to
Achilles, as to the other heroes,
ξανθὴ κόμη, fair golden hair, which,
because it was in fact less familiar
to the Homeric people than dark
hair, was accounted the ideal of
youthful beauty. Again, in Homer certain of the Greeks are
καρηκομόωντες, long - haired. M.
may be thinking of all this, or of
the convention of the Greco-
Roman stage by which all fighting
men were represented as long-
haired; cf. Plaut. Mil. Glor. 61–64
*rogitabant (me mulieres) "Hicine
Achilles est ?" . . . "Immo eius frater", inquam, "est". Ibi illarum
altera "Ergo mecastor pulcher est"
inquit mihi "et liberalis: vide cae-
saries ('hair') quam decet!"* In art
Achilles is generally represented
with his helmet on, so that his hair
is for the most part concealed. In
an Attic vase-painting of the sixth
century B.C., in which Achilles and
Ajax are represented as playing a
game of backgammon(?), Achilles's
hair is abundant, hanging below the
helmet (see Schreiber-Anderson
Pl. XXXVI, Fig. 8).

11. **fumosae**: amphorae carefully pitched (see 11. 18. 24 N.) were

exposed to the smoke and heat
of the bath-room furnace, because
this process was supposed to hasten the mellowing of the wine ; cf.
7. 79. 3 N.; Ov. F. 5. 518 *promit
fumoso condita vina cado*; Hor. C.
3. 8. 9–12 *hic dies anno redeunte
festus corticem adstrictum pice di-
movebit amphorae fumum bibere
institutae consule Tullo.* — **feret
ipse**: he will do a slave's work. —
tropin de faece: the very dregs of
the dregs, the residuum at the very
bottom of the amphora, which is
compared to bilge-water in the
bottom of a ship (cf. τρόπις =
carina, 'keel'). The point of this
vs. cannot be clearly determined.
Can *feret* = *auferet* (see on 1. 4. 2),
and is the meaning that he will
carry away the dregs as if they were
a treasure (to be drunk later, as
Santra carries off food to be eaten
later: see 7. 20)? *Ipse* will then
suggest that the patron drinks the
rest. Still, *feret* may merely mean
'will endure', 'will put up with'.
— **faece**: see 1. 103. 9 N.

12. **frontis . . . tuae**: editors
generally take this verse in close
connection with 11 and suppose
that the *tropis* was rubbed on the
patron's skin or taken by him as an
emetic, with *frontis umor* as the
result. In this case Menogenes
carries the lees for another's use.
But 12 need not have any connection at all with 11 ; the vs. is most
effective if taken by itself, as a
crowning example of Menogenes's
sycophancy. — **usque**: see 9. 48.
4 N.; Menogenes can never be
moderate in his services; for him
ne quid nimis has no meaning.

perpessus dicas taedia mille "Veni!"

92

Saepe rogare soles qualis sim, Prisce, futurus,
    si fiam locuples simque repente potens.
Quemquam posse putas mores narrare futuros?
    dic mihi, si fias tu leo, qualis eris?

94

Scribebamus epos; coepisti scribere: cessi,
    aemula ne starent carmina nostra tuis;
transtulit ad tragicos se nostra Thalia cothurnos:
    aptasti longum tu quoque syrma tibi;
5   fila lyrae movi Calabris exculta Camenis:
    plectra rapis nobis, ambitiose, nova;

14. Veni: i.e. to dinner (cf. 11. 52. 2 N.); abruptly said in self-defense; we should have expected rather a curse.

92. M. answers a hypothetical question of Priscus by asking one himself. — Meter: § 48.

1. Prisce: probably Terentius Priscus (see 8. 12. 3 N.; 12. 4), despite Friedländer's objections.

4. qualis eris: for the ind. after the imv. *dic mihi*, whereas in 1 after *rogare soles* we have the subjv., see on 6. 8. 6; 6. 88. 3.

94. 'Imitation is the sincerest form of flattery, but, Tucca, it can be carried too far'. — Meter: § 48.

1. Scribebamus epos: placed at the head of the various departments of literature; so Quint. 10. 1. 46; 10. 1. 85 places epic at the head of Greek and Latin literature.

2. This vs. is not to be taken too seriously.

3. transtulit . . . cothurnos may well = 'I shifted from comedy to tragedy', i.e. 'I tried comedy,

then tragedy'; in that case he says nothing of Tucca's comedies. But *nostra Thalia* need mean no more than 'my poetic genius' (cf. 4. 8. 12; 7. 17. 4); in that case comedy is not mentioned at all here or anywhere else in the epigram, unless it is suggested by *epigrammata*, 9. For the language of this vs. see 8. 3. 13 N.; 8. 18. 7; 5. 30. 1 *Varro, Sophocleo non infitiande cothurno*; Ov. Tr. 2. 393 *impia nec tragicos tetigisset Scylla cothurnos*; Am. 1. 15. 15.

4. longum . . . syrma: see 4. 49. 8 N.

5. fila lyrae movi = *lyrica (carmina) scripsi*; lyric poetry was, in theory, written to be sung or chanted. — **Calabris . . . Camenis:** see 8. 18. 5 N. — **Camenis:** see 4. 14. 10 N.

6. plectra: the *plectrum* (cf. πλῆκτρον, πλήττω) was a quill or stick, generally of ivory or gold, used to strike (pick) the chords of the *lyra* ('lyre'); cf. e.g. Hor. C. 2. 13. 26–28 *et te sonantem plenius*

audemus saturas : Lucilius esse laboras ;

    ludo leves elegos : tu quoque ludis idem.

Quid minus esse potest? epigrammata fingere coepi :

10   hinc etiam petitur iam mea palma tibi.

Elige quid nolis — quis enim pudor omnia velle ? —

    et si quid non vis, Tucca, relinque mihi.

aureo, Alcaee, plectro dura navis, dura fugae mala, dura belli. — **rapis** = *eripis*; *rapio* and its compounds constantly suggest rude force and haste. — **nobis** may be construed with *rapis*, or with *nova*, or with both ; in any case the sense is 'you snatch the quill out of my hands before I have had time to become accustomed to its use'.

7. audemus saturas: under the Empire to write satire, at least such personal satire as Lucilius wrote, was dangerous; see Iuv. I. 151–171. *Audemus* may, however, have a very different point, i.e. it may mean that to venture another form of literature was to draw on himself once again Tucca's rivalry ; that is a danger to make any man flinch ! For *audemus* cf. Hor. A. P. 382, cited on 9, and Eng. 'venture' in similar connections.—**Lucilius:** C. Lucilius, who died in 103 B.C. The date of his birth is disputed; he was born at Suessa Aurunca. He was a member of the Scipionic circle at Rome. That he was a writer of great vigor and boldness we know both from the extant fragments of his works and from the testimony of the ancient writers themselves. He converted the miscellany or medley that had long been known as Satura into a poem of which personal invective was an essential feature. Further, he made the heroic verse (the hexameter) the vehicle of that invective ; in modern literatures the heroic verse

of a given nation has become the vehicle of its satire. Hence modern and ancient writers both regard Lucilius as the typical satirist. See e.g. Hor. S. I. 4. 1–13; 2. I. 62 ff.; Quint. 10. I. 93; Iuv. I. 165–167; Pers. I. 114. Of his thirty books of Saturae about 1400 verses remain. M. thus naturally makes Lucilius rather than Persius or his friend Juvenal the typical satirist. — **esse laboras:** for the constr. cf. e.g. 10. 3. 11 *cur ego laborem notus esse tam prave?*

8. ludo: cf. I. 113. 1; 8. 3. 2; 9. 26. 10. The verb particularly fits the erotic elegy of Ovid, Tibullus, and Propertius.

9. minus: i.e. lower in the literary scale. — **epigrammata:** for M.'s opinion of the epigram see 4. 49. — **fingere,** *compose,* a common meaning; cf. Hor. C. 4. 2. 27–32 *ego apis Matinae more modoque ... parvus carmina fingo*; A. P. 382 *qui nescit versus tamen audet fingere*; Suet. Tit. 3 (*peritissimus Titus erat*) *Latine Graececque, vel in orando vel in fingendis poematibus.*

10. mea palma: i.e. 'my fame', 'my reputation'; see 10. 50. 1; 10. 53. 4.

11. quis . . . velle: an ironical query, in sense an exclamation rather than a question; ''tis a strange modesty (i.e. 'tis no modesty at all) to wish', etc. *Pudor* prop. = 'regard for the proprieties', such respect for public opinion as restrains one from doing wrong.

[LIBER XIII]

XENIA

I

Ne toga cordylis et paenula desit olivis
aut inopem metuat sordida blatta famem,
perdite Niliacas, Musae, mea damna, papyros :
postulat ecce novos ebria bruma sales.

I. On Books XIII–XIV see § 13. They come in time between the Liber Spectaculorum and Book I of the Epigrams; they were published at the Saturnalia of 84 or 85 (perhaps one collection appeared in each of these years). The separate pieces were intended as sentiments or labels attached to gifts at the Saturnalia or to favors given to guests at dinner; they thus represent the earliest stage of the epigram (§§ 22; 26), being in theory written on the gift itself. For such a purpose they would find a ready sale. Nearly all the Xenia are for presents that cater to the needs of the inner man.— Meter: § 48.

1. Ne ... olivis: cf. 3. 2. 4–5 N.
— **cordylis:** see 3. 2. 4 N.; 11. 52. 7.
— **paenula:** see 1. 103. 5–6 N.

2. aut ... famem: cf. 14. 37. 2.
— **sordida:** the *blatta* loves dark, musty places.—Verses 1–2 perhaps mean 'That fish and olives may have clothes, though I have none, that roaches may have food, though I myself starve'.

3. perdite ... papyros: i.e. 'inspire me to fill (destroy) paper enough to satisfy these demands'.

— **perdite:** cf. 2. 1. 4; 6. 64. 22–23 *audes praeterea quos nullus noverit in me scribere versiculos miseras et perdere chartas*; Iuv. 1. 17–18 *stulta est clementia, cum tot ubique vatibus occurras, periturae parcere chartae*; 7. 99 *perit hic* (in writing history) *plus temporis atque olei plus.* In this sense *perire* is the pass. of *perdere*; the use is a reflection of the proverbial *oleum et operam perdere*; see Otto s.v. *Oleum.*
— **Niliacas ... papyros:** see 3. 2. 4, 7 N. The Nile valley was the chief source of papyrus. This was so abundant and cheap that it long held its place against parchment (*membrana*: see 1. 2. 3 N.; 1. 66. 11) as a substance on which books were written, spite of the superior advantages of parchment (see on 14. 188. 1).— **mea damna:** i.e. both in paper and in time spent in filling it, with the secondary thought that the toil after all brings no adequate return.

4. novos ... sales: i.e. a new collection of witticisms. The Saturnalia (see 4. 14. 6–7) was a season of relaxation and festivity for all classes; wine flowed freely then. Cf. 14. 1. 9 *sed quid agam*

5   Non mea magnanimo depugnat tessera talo
        senio nec nostrum cum cane quassat ebur ;
    haec mihi charta nuces, haec est mihi charta fritillus:
        alea nec damnum nec facit ista lucrum.

potius madidis, Saturne, diebus;
Stat. Silv. 1. 6. 1–7 (on the *Kalendae Decembres*) *et Phoebus pater et
severa Pallas et Musae procul ite
feriatae : Iani vos revocabimus
Kalendis,* etc.; Sen. Ep. 18. 4 *hoc
multo fortius est, ebrio ac vomitante
populo siccum ac sobrium esse* (i.e.
at the Saturnalia). — **sales:** see
1. 41. 16; 7. 25. 3.

5–6. 'My gambling stakes at
the Saturnalia will be small, mere
child's play '. On gambling at the
Saturnalia see 4. 14. 6–8 N. — **mea
. . . talo:** on *tesserae* and *tali* see 4.
14. 9 N. — **mea . . . nostrum:** such
change of number is not uncommon,
even in prose. — **magnanimo . . .
talo:** i.e. gambling that is reckless,
for high stakes. With the use of
magnanimo cf. Iuv. 1. 88–89 *alea
quando hos animos* (*habuit*) ? Note
the fine double juxtaposition ; the
adjectives are brought together at
the beginning of the verse, the
nouns at the end, as in 11. 84. 3.
See App. — **depugnat:** note the
force of the prep. For the thought
cf. Amm. Marc. 14. 6. 25 *ex turba
vero imae sortis et paupertinae . . .
nonnulli . . . pugnaciter aleis certant.* — **senio . . . ebur:** ' my dice-
box concerns itself neither with the
best nor with the worst throw ', i.e.
' I do not gamble at all '. — **senio,** *the
six-throw, the sice.* The best throw
with the *tesserae* (*iactus Venereus*
or *basilicus*) was made when three
sixes were turned up, the worst
throw (*canis, canicula, iactus dam-
nosus*) was made when three aces
(*uniones*) were turned up. Cf. e.g.
Pers. 3. 48–50 *etenim id summum,*

*quid dexter senio ferret scire, erat
in voto, damnosa canicula quantum
raderet.* — **cum cane:** *cum* with
abl. is used at times where *et* and
the proper case (here the nom.)
might be employed. In prose M.
might have said *nostrum ebur nec
senio nec canis quassat.* — **ebur:**
the ivory dice-box (see on *fritillus,* 7) or the dice themselves.

7. nuces here has a double
meaning : (1) *sport, amusement*
(children played with nuts, esp. at
the Saturnalia, which was a school
vacation ; cf. the proverb *relinquere nuces,* 'to come to man's estate '); (2) *gains,* from gambling
(among children, and in friendly
sport between older people, where
money was not risked, nuts were
often the stake). Cf. 4. 66. 15–16
*subposita est blando numquam tibi
tessera talo, alea sed parcae sola
fuere nuces* ; 14. 19. 1 *alea parva
nuces et non damnosa videtur.* See
Preller-Jordan 2. 17. — **fritillus:**
see 4. 14. 8 N. ; 5. 84. 3.

8. alea is to be taken in the
double sense of gambling and
children's play ; see on *nuces,* 7. —
damnum . . . lucrum: common
technical terms of business; cf.
Eng. 'profit' and 'loss'. See e.g.
Hor. S. 2. 2. 95–96 *grandes rhombi
patinaeque grande ferunt una cum
damno dedecus* ; Sen. Apocol. 12 fin.
*vosque in primis qui concusso magna
parastis lucra fritillo* ; Pub. Syr.
297 *lucrum sine damno alterius fieri
non potest.*

3. 'Talk about presents !
Here's a book full, and for but a
few coppers '. — Meter : § 48.

3

Omnis in hoc gracili Xeniorum turba libello
   constabit nummis quattuor empta tibi.
Quattuor est nimium? poterit constare duobus
   et faciet lucrum bibliopola Tryphon.
5 Haec licet hospitibus pro munere disticha mittas,
   si tibi tam rarus, quam mihi, nummus erit.
Addita per titulos sua nomina rebus habebis:
   praetereas, si quid non facit ad stomachum.

1. gracili: here, as often, M. appears to use a word in a double sense, as (1) *slender, slight,* physically (*gracili . . . libello* gives the effect of a double dim.), (2) *simple, unadorned* in style. For the latter sense cf. Quint. 12. 10. 66 *sed neque his tribus quasi formis* ('kinds of style') *inclusa eloquentia est, nam . . . inter gracile validumque tertium aliquid constitutum est*; Gell. 6. 14. 1–3; Hendrickson, The Origin and Meaning of the Ancient Characters of Style, A. J. P. 26. 249–290, esp. 268–276, 288–289.

2. constabit: see 1. 103. 10 N. — **nummis quattuor:** four sesterces. The price is low (see on 1. 66. 4; 1. 117. 17), but if we consider the value of slaves and remember that a large number could copy at the dictation of a single reader, there is no reason to question it.

3. poterit . . . duobus: i.e. there is an edition still cheaper. Cf. Stat. Silv. 4. 9. 7–9 *noster purpureus novusque charta et binis decoratus umbilicis praeter me mihi constitit decussis* (10 *asses:* perhaps Statius is joking).

4. et = *et tamen.* — **bibliopola Tryphon:** cf. 4. 72. 1–2 *exigis, ut donem nostros tibi, Quinte, libellos: non habeo, sed habet bibliopola Try-*

phon. Tryphon was publisher also for Quintilian; see the epistle addressed to him by Quintilian as preface to the Institutiones. See also on 1. 2. 7.

7. titulos: the lemmata or titles of the various couplets; see 11. 42. 2 N. The vs. shows that the lemmata in this book are genuine. — **rebus:** the various objects described in the book.

8. praetereas: cf. 14. 2. 3–4 *lemmata si quaeris cur sint adscripta docebo; ut, si malueris, lemmata sola legas.* — **stomachum,** *taste, liking.* Cf. Plin. Ep. 1. 24. 3 *in hoc autem agello, si modo adriserit pretium, Tranquilli mei stomachum multa sollicitant, vicinitas urbis, opportunitas viae,* etc.

70. A protest against the eating of a bird so beautiful as was the peacock. We must not take the protest too seriously, especially if we recall 13. 1. Introd.; the giver of a *pavo* would hardly question seriously the propriety of his own gift. For similar humor, frequent enough in these two books, cf. e.g. 13. 87; 13. 94. On the *pavo* see 3. 58. 13 N. In Varro's time a single egg of the *pavo* was worth five *denarii,* and a bird fifty *denarii.* Cf. Suet. Tib. 60 *militem praetorianum ob surreptum e viridiario pavonem*

70

Pavones

Miraris quotiens gemmantis explicat alas
et potes hunc saevo tradere, dure, coco?

77

Cycni

Dulcia defecta modulatur carmina lingua
cantator cycnus funeris ipse sui.

87

Murices

Sanguine de nostro tinctas, ingrate, lacernas
induis, et non est hoc satis : esca sumus.

capite puniit. That the Romans raised these birds extensively we know from Varro and Columella. See Beck. 1. 109; Mayor on Iuv. 1. 143. — Meter: § 48.

1. Miraris = *admiraris*; cf. 8. 6. 15; 8. 69. 1. — **gemmantis**: cf. *gemmei . . . pavones*, 3. 58. 13 N. — **explicat**: cf. Phaedr. 3. 18. 7–8 *nitor smaragdi collo praefulget tuo pictisque plumis gemmeam caudam explicas*; Ov. Am. 2. 6. 55 *explicat ipsa suas ales Iunonia pinnas*; Med. Fac. 33–34 *laudatas homini volucris Iunonia pinnas explicat.*

2. et = *et tamen.* — **potes**, *have you the heart?* (cf. *dure*). On the use of the peacock at dinner see 3. 58. 13 N. Hortensius the lawyer first had one served at dinner. Later, it was for a season indispensable to an up-to-date *cena*; gluttons who tired of the fleshy parts served up the brains or tongues of the birds.

77. For the song sung by the swan, esp. at its death, see on 5.37.1; cf. Ov. Her.7.1–2 *sic ubi fata vocant, udis abiectus in herbis ad vada Maeandri concinit albus olor*; Sen. Phaed. 302 *dulcior vocem moriente cycno.* — Meter: § 48.

1. defecta, *failing, dying*; note the juxtaposition, helped by alliteration, in *dulcia defecta.* — **modulatur**: cf. Verg. E. 10. 51 *carmina pastorisque Siculi modulabor avena.*

2. cantator . . . sui: the bird supplies in himself a substitute for the conventional *praeficae* and *nenia.*

87. The lament of the *murices.* —Meter: § 48.

1. Sanguine . . . nostro = *purpura* (see 2. 16. 3 N.). — **ingrate**: cf. *dure*, 13.70.2: 'instead of showing gratitude you eat us' (cf. 2). — **lacernas**: see 2. 29. 3 N.; 2. 43. 7.

2. esca sumus: the mollusk from which the purple dye was extracted was edible.

94

DAMMAE

Dente timetur aper, defendunt cornua cervum :
inbelles dammae quid nisi praeda sumus ?

126

UNGUENTUM

Unguentum heredi numquam nec vina relinquas :
ille habeat nummos, haec tibi tota dato.

94. The *damma* cannot be identified with certainty. It may have been the chamois (cf. Plin. N. H. 8. 214 on the various kinds of *caprae*: *sunt et dammae et pygargi et strepsicerotes multaque alia haud dissimilia; sed illa Alpes, haec transmarini situs mittunt*), or, perhaps, an antelope. They appeared in the *venationes* of the Empire; M. had prob. seen them there. See Fried. SG. 2.544. In 4.35.1 *dammae* fight in the arena; in 1.49.23–24 M. says they were hunted in Spain. They are mentioned here because they were good to eat; Iuv. 11.120–122 *at nunc divitibus cenandi nulla voluptas, nil rhombus, nil damma sapit, putere videntur unguenta atque rosae.* See also on 3.58.28. — Meter: § 48.

1. Dente, *tusk*; cf. 11.69.9 (on a dog killed by a boar) *fulmineo spumantis apri sum dente perempta*; Ov. M. 10.550 *fulmen habent acres in aduncis dentibus apri.* For the thought cf. Hor. S. 2.1.52–53 *dente lupus, cornu taurus petit: unde nisi intus monstratum ?*

2. inbelles: cf. Isid. Orig. 12.1. 22 *damula vocata, quod de manu effugiat: timidum animal et imbelle* (i.e. the word *damula, dammula* is derived from *de + manus* !); Hor.

C. 1. 2. 11–12 *superiecto pavidae natarunt aequore dammae.*

126. M. urges his reader to be an Epicurean (in the sense in which many Romans — e.g. Horace — understood that term) and to use up in self-enjoyment what he can, while he may. — Meter: § 48.

1. unguentum and **vina**, which suggest the *comissatio* (see on 1.27. 1; 3.12.1; 10.20.20), typify the pleasures of life. With the vs. as a whole cf. 8.77.3–8; Hor. C. 4.7. 19–20 *cuncta manus avidas fugient heredis amico quae dederis animo*; 2.3.19–20 *cedes et exstructis in altum divitiis potietur heres* ('therefore enjoy life while you may', 13–16); 2.14.25–28 *absumet heres Caecuba dignior servata centum clavibus et mero tinguet pavimentum superbo, pontificum potiore cenis* (the ode is addressed to "a man of wealth, surrounded by all the comforts . . . of life, but perhaps a trifle overcareful in the use of his means" (Smith)); Ep. 1.5.13–14 *parcus ob heredis curam nimiumque severus adsidet insano.*

2. nummos: i.e. only 'such money as you can not eat or drink or spend in any way upon yourself'.

127

Coronae roseae

Dat festinatas, Caesar, tibi bruma coronas :
quondam veris erat, nunc tua facta rosa est.

127. This piece naturally and appropriately follows 126. On the use of roses at Rome see on 5. 37. 9: 10. 20. 20; on the *coronae conviviales* (*sutiles*) see on 5. 64. 4; 9. 61. 17. — Meter: § 48.

1. festinatas, *forced*; freely, *early*. The garlands are made of roses raised under glass in hot-houses; see 8. 14. 1–4 N.; 4. 22. 5 *condita sic puro numerantur lilia vitro.* — **bruma:** on the word see 3. 58. 8; 5. 34. 5. For winter roses cf. 6. 80, with notes; Macr. S. 7. 5. 32 *nec sic admitto varietatem, ut luxum ₁ obem, ubi quaeruntur aestivae nives et hibernae rosae.*

[LIBER XIV]

APOPHORETA

37

Scrinium

Selectos nisi das mihi libellos,
admittam tineas trucesque blattas.

186

Vergilius in Membranis

Quam brevis inmensum cepit membrana Maronem!

37. On this book see 13. 1. Introd. The pieces of this book were written to accompany dinner favors (*apophoreta*) which the guests carried away in their napkins (*mappae*); for such apophoreta cf. e.g. 10. 27. 3 N.; Petr. 56; 60. — *Scrinium* commonly denotes, as here, a receptacle for books, cylindrical in shape, a larger *capsa*; cf. 1. 2. 4 N. For other book receptacles see 1. 117. 15 N. — Meter: § 49.

1. Selectos: i.e. few and choice. — **mihi:** the *scrinium* speaks; this device M. often uses in this book.

2. tineas . . . blattas: see 6. 61. 7 *quam multi tineas pascunt blattasque diserti*; Iuv. 7. 24-26 *quae componis dona Veneris . . . marito* (i.e. 'give to Vulcan to burn') *aut clude* (*in scrinio*) *et positos tinea pertunde libellos*. For the use of oil of cedar to preserve books from insects see 3. 2. 7 N. Plin. N. H. 13. 86, quoting Cassius Hemina con-

cerning some books found in the coffin of King Numa when it was dug out of the Ianiculum, says: *mirabantur alii, quomodo illi libri durare possent, ille ita rationem reddebat . . . libros citratos fuisse, propterea arbitrarier tineas non tetigisse.*

186. On a miniature or pocket edition of Vergil, a parchment codex. On these handy editions in parchment see 1. 2. 3–4, with notes. Cf. 14. 188. — Meter: § 48.

1. brevis . . . membrana: since one could write on both sides of parchment (see 1. 2. Introd.) and in a very fine hand (things not easily done well on papyrus), a small parchment book would hold much. — **inmensum,** *voluminous;* note the antithesis with *brevis.* But the word also refers to Vergil's literary greatness; see 12. 67. 3–4 N., and cf. Hor. C. 4. 2. 7–8 *inmensusque ruit profundo Pindarus ore.* The emphasis is intensified by the juxtaposition of the two adjectives.

ipsius vultus prima tabella gerit !

187

Μενάνδρου Θαΐς

Hac primum iuvenum lascivos lusit amores ;
nec Glycera pueri, Thais amica fuit.

188

CICERO IN MEMBRANIS

Si comes ista tibi fuerit membrana, putato

2. The value of the copy was further enhanced by a portrait of Vergil on the first page. Before the end of the first century portraits of popular authors were common not only in the public libraries, along with statues in marble and bronze, but in their works. M. himself enjoyed this distinction (see O. Crusius in Rh. Mus. 44. 455). See Fried. SG. 3. 239 ff. Varro produced a work called Imagines, which contained 700 such portraits; see Teuffel, § 166. 5. — **vultus**, *features, looks*; see 1. 53. 2 N.

187. On the Thais, a play of Menander. Menander, who flourished during the latter part of the fourth century B.C., was the greatest representative of the New Attic Comedy; this is attested both by his reputation among the Greeks and by the use made of his plays by Roman playwrights, esp. Afranius, Caecilius, and Terence. The play here meant was named after Thais, the Athenian *hetaera*, who was famous not only for her wit and beauty, but as having been the mistress successively of Alexander the Great and Ptolemy, king of Egypt. — Meter: § 48.

1. **Hac**: sc. *fabula* or *dramatis persona*; render by 'in this play'

or 'under the guise of this character'; instr. ablative. The gift in this case was a copy of the play. — **lusit**: see 1. 113. 1; 8. 3. 2; 9. 26. 10. — **lusit amores**: for syntax see on 5. 66. 2.

2. **nec . . . fuit**: 'and in fact not Glycera, but Thais was the love of his youth'. — **Glycera**: a name often adopted by the *hetaerae* (cf. the meaning of Γλυκέρα). A woman of this name is said to have been the mistress of Menander. — For the quantity of *Glycerā* see § 54, *a*. — **pueri**: i.e. of Menander in his youth, when he is said to have been unusually handsome. — **Thais . . . fuit**: not to be taken literally. M. rather means that Menander fell in love with the heroine of his comedy.

188. A parchment pocket edition of Cicero is recommended as a handy traveling companion. Cf. 14. 186. Introd. One could not well handle a papyrus volume in a wagon. There is nothing here to show how much of Cicero was included in the edition to which M. refers; contrast note on 14. 190. 2. Fried., however, maintains that we are to think of several volumes. — Meter: § 48.

1. **comes**: see 1, 2. 1–2 N,

carpere te longas cum Cicerone vias.

189

MONOBYBLOS PROPERTI

Cynthia, facundi carmen iuvenale Properti,
    accepit famam, nec minus ipsa dedit.

190

TITUS LIVIUS IN MEMBRANIS

Pellibus exiguis artatur Livius ingens,
    quem mea non totum bibliotheca capit.

---

2. carpere . . . vias: *carpere viam*, *carpere iter* often = *ire* with a suggestion of rapid progress; cf. e.g. Hor. S. 2. 6. 93 *carpe viam, mihi crede, comes*; Ov. M. 8. 208 *me duce carpe viam*; Verg. A. 6. 629 *sed iam age, carpe viam.* — **longas:** but rendered short by a companion so agreeable. Cf. Pub. Syr. cited on 1. 2. 1–2.

189. The Monobiblos (Μονόβιβλος) was the first book of Propertius. That book begins with the word *Cynthia*, the assumed name of Propertius's mistress (see on 8. 73. 5); the name Cynthia is given to the book in at least one Ms. of Propertius. For Roman ways of referring to books see on 4. 14. 14; 8. 55. 19. — Meter: § 48.

1–2. Cynthia . . . famam: for the thought cf. 8. 73. 5 N. *Cynthia* here suggests the woman rather than the book; she has been immortalized by Propertius's work. — — **facundi:** see on 1. 61. 8. — **accepit:** sc. *a Propertio.* — **nec . . . dedit:** sc. *Propertio.* But for his mastering passion for Cynthia, says M., Propertius would have missed immortality.

190. See 14. 186. Introd.; note on *totum*, 2. — Meter: § 48.

1. **Pellibus** shows clearly that the book is written on parchment (*membrana*). — **exiguis . . . ingens:** antithesis similar to that in *brevis inmensum* in 14. 186. 1; the antithesis is helped here, too, by word-order, though in a somewhat different way; the contrasted expressions, treated as wholes, are set at the opposite ends of the verse. — **artatur . . . ingens:** cf. 1. 2. 3 N.

2. **totum** throws light on 1, and shows that M. has in mind an epitome of Livy. We still know of at least two epitomes of Livy; recently an Oxyrhynchus papyrus has given us a fragment of an epitome not identical with that previously known. The epitome of our text may, however, well have been in several volumes; see 14. 188. Introd. The practice of making epitomes of lengthy works was well established by the Augustan age and became increasingly common later. — **capit:** note the mood; M. talks as if he had already tested the matter.

194

LUCANUS

Sunt quidam qui me dicant non esse poetam,
sed qui me vendit bibliopola putat.

195

CATULLUS

Tantum magna suo debet Verona Catullo,
quantum parva suo Mantua Vergilio.

208

NOTARIUS

Currant verba licet, manus est velocior illis :
nondum lingua suum, dextra peregit opus.

194. For Lucan see on 1. 61.
7–8 ; 7. 21. — Meter: § 48.

1. Sunt . . . poetam: *quidam*
implies that this was not the con-
sensus of critical opinion. These
quidam may have echoed an older
depreciation of Corduba as a literary center; see Fried. S.G. 3. 379–
380. See on *unicum*, 1. 61. 7.

2. putat: sc. *me esse poetam*.
'The rapid sale of my books is
proof enough of what the world in
general thinks'.

195. On Catullus see 1. 61.
1 N.; 2. 71. 3; 4. 14. 13; § 34; etc.
— Meter: § 48.

1. magna . . . Verona: Verona was great only by comparison
with *parva Mantua* (see 8. 73. 9);

Mantua can hardly be said to have
had any place in Roman history
until a comparatively late time,
except in so far as Vergil's career
made the town known as his birthplace. See 1. 61. 1–2, with notes.
— **suo,** *her beloved*; see on 1. 13. 1 ;
8. 55. 2. Cf. 10. 103. 5 *nec sua plus
debet tenui Verona Catullo* ('than
Bilbilis to me').

208. On the *notarius* see 10.
62. 4 N.; Beck. 1. 62 ff.; Marq. 826.
— Meter; § 48.

1. licet: as in 11. 52. 17. —
manus . . . illis: cf. Sen. Ep. 90. 25
*quid verborum notas, quibus quam-
vis citata excipitur oratio et celeri-
tatem linguae manus sequitur ?*

CRITICAL APPENDIX

For a brief account of the more important Mss. see Introd. §§ 42 ff. For a more complete account see the Praefatio of Professor W. M. Lindsay's critical edition of Martial in the Scriptorum Classicorum Bibliotheca Oxoniensis; Lindsay, Ancient Editions of Martial; Friedländer, Einleitung, 67–108. Only the more important variants can be cited here. For a more complete apparatus criticus see the editions of Friedländer, Lindsay, and J. D. Duff (in Postgate's Corpus Poetarum Latinorum). When the name of a modern scholar follows a reading, it is to be understood that the reading is a conjectural emendation by that scholar. To save space, where all or a majority of the best Mss. of a given class support a reading, no specific reference to separate Mss. is ordinarily given. Since Lindsay's text is the latest, its readings are given where they differ from those followed in this book. The reading given in black-face type is that of the text in this edition.

ABBREVIATIONS

a = all or some of the best Mss. of the A-class (§ 43).
b = "   "   "   "   "   "   "   "   " B-class (§ 44).
c = "   "   "   "   "   "   "   "   " C-class (§§ 45–46).
m = some inferior Mss.
A = Codex Leidensis (Vossianus) 56. See § 46.
B =   "   Leidensis 121.
C =   "   Leidensis 89.
E =   "   Edinburgensis. See § 46.
F =   "   Florentinus Mediceus.
f =   "   Florentinus (on fifteenth century paper). See § 44.
G =   "   Gudianus Wolfenbuttelensis 57.
H =   "   Vindobonensis. See § 43.
L =   "   Lucensis 612. See § 44.
Ly = Lindsay's edition.
P = Codex Palatinus Vaticanus 1696. See § 44.
Q =   "   Arundellianus 136. See § 44.
R =   "   Leidensis (Vossianus) 86. See § 43.
T =   "   Thuaneus (Colbertinus or Parisinus) 8071. See § 43.
V =   "   Vaticanus 3294. See § 46.
X =   "   Parisinus (Puteanus) 8067. See § 46.

Liber Spectaculorum

I. 2 Assyrius Alciatus *adsiduus* T Q m　　**3 Iones** Scaliger *ho-nores* T Q m　If this is read, *templo* is local abl., and *honores* will denote the temple itself, the works of art it contained, etc., thought of together as a complex honor to Trivia　　**4 deum** Q m　*deion* T　*Delon* J. F. Gronovius Ly　　**7 cedit** *cedat* Q m　　**8 loquetur** *loquatur* Q m

29. 5 parma Wagner　*possita ... palma* H　*positam ... palmam* R *palma* seems unlikely in view of *palmas* in 9 (Fried.)　　**9 utrique** (after *misit*) Scaliger　*utrisque* H　*utriusque* R　　**11 te sub** Scaliger　*tibi* H R

Book I

3. 5 rhonchi E m　*ronchi* L Q　*runt* H　　**iuvenesque senesque** a E　*iuvenisque senisque* c　Early (not later) Latin shows -*is* in nom. pl. of declension 3; see A. 73 and footnote; GL. 38, 1

10. 1 Gemellus T b　*venustus* or *gemellus venustus* c　As a coinage to represent some disguise (see on 8. 73. 5), *Venustus* (cf. *pulchra* in 3) is more probable than *Gemellus*, but the latter is better attested　　**4 peti-tur** a c　*appetitur* L Q

12. 1 Herculei gelidas b (L) c (E)　*herculeas gelidi* T　　**5 um-bras** T c　*auras* b (L)　　**10 par tam** *parta* L Q　　**12 deos** b c *deum* T

13. 1 traderet *traheret* c (E)　　**2 strinxerat** T b　*traxerat* c (E) **3 feci** *fecit* L　　**4 quod tu** T c (E)　*tu quod* b (L)

15. 1 sodales b　*sodalis* c (E)　　**5 quod** b (L)　*quae* c　　**10 fluunt** b m　*fluent* c (E)　　**12 nimis** *minis* L

25. 2 pectore *pectine* O. Mueller; see Hermes, 12. 304

27. 2 quincunces *qui nunc est* c (E)　　**3, 7 Procille** *procille* c *procelle* b (L)

29. 3 si tua vis dici L. Martens, Festgabe für W. Crecelius (Elberfeld, 1881), 27 ff.　　**4 si dici mea vis** L. Martens, ibid.　　**hoc** b c　*haec* Q m　*en* (*eme*) Schn.

41. 6 madidum *calidum* Heinsius　*tepidum* Mordtmann (cf. 1. 103. 10; 5. 78. 21)　　**11 urbicus** *Urbicus* Scriverius　　**17 posses** *possis* Scriverius 1621

42. 1 fatum *factum* T　　**4 fatis** G　*satis* T Q c (E)　Most modern editors read *fatis* (abl.); cf. *fatum*, 1. But *satis* has the support of at least two classes of Mss. Besides, the sentence profits by an adv. balancing *nondum*, 3. If, however, *sătĭs* is read, further changes are, for metrical reasons, necessary, e.g. *satis hoc edocuisse* C or *satis hoc vos docuisse* X Scriverius

43. 3 tardis *seris* Flach (cf. 3. 58. 8)   6 **grana** T   *mala* c (E)
7 **lactantis** *lactantes* T X V   *lactentes* c (E G)   **Sassina** *sasina* (*sassina*) T   *fuscina* c (E)   *fiscina* Scriverius   10 **armato** *amato* T

53. 3 **carmina** *crimina* c (E)   4 **interpositus** c   *interposito* b
(L)   **uillo** Heinsius   *uilis* b (L)   *vitio* c (E)   *vili . . . unco* Scriverius
9 **multisona** *dulcisona* Heinsius   **Atthide** *alite* T

61. 1 **syllabas** *syllabos* O. Crusius in Rh. Mus. 47. 71   3 **Aponi**
aponi b (L)   *apono* c (E)   *apona* m   5 **Apollodoro** *Apollinari* Giese
15   **plaudit** b   *gaudet* c (E)

66. 3 **constet** b (L)   *constat* c (E)   4 **sophos nummis** *nummis sophos* b (L Q)   10 **pumicata** *punicata* b (L Q)   11 **umbilicis** *umbilicus* c (E)

70. 5 **veneranda** *venerando* c (E)   10 **tholus** b c   *torus* T   13 **ne**
T b   *nec* c (E)   See on Lib. Spect. 1. 2; App. on 7. 92. 10   **limenque**
lumenque T   15 **propior** c (E)   *potior* T   **amet** *amat* b (L)
17 **sic** b   *si* c (E)   **excuses** *excusses* Ly   Forms like *caussa, divissio*
(i.e. with double *s* after a long vowel) were used by Cicero and Vergil,
but by Quintilian's time were uncommon; see Quint. 1. 7. 20

72. 3 **sibi** b   *tibi* c (E)

76. 3 **cantusque chorosque** b (L)   *cantus citharamque* c Ly
6 **omnes** *inter* Köstlin (i.e. *haec inter fenerat una deos*)   8 **varias**
varios b (L)   *vario* Schmieder   9 **dearum** *deorum* c (E)   10 **sed**
perinane c   *semper inane* b   11 **Permesside nuda** *permesside
nuda* b   *permessidis unda* c (E)   *parnaside nuda* Q   12 **propius**
proprius L   **divitiusque** *divitiumque* c (E)

88. 3 **accipe** a c   *aspice* b (L)   **Pario** *parvo* T   *Fario* (*Phario*)
E m   5 **faciles** T c   *fragiles* b (L)   7 **accipe, care** *acum pectore* T
monimenta b (L) c (E)   *monumenta* c   *momenta* T   8 **vivet** b c
vivit T   9 **perneverit** *supremus Lachesis peruenerit annus* T Q E

89. 2 **garris** m   *garrire* L E Ly   *garrire*, the better attested reading, would depend on *licet*. But the repetition *Garris . . . garris*, 1–2, is
more in M.'s manner; see on 10. 35. 11–12; 3. 44. 16   5 **adeoque** b
adeone c (E)

93. 1 **Aquinus** in lemm. of L   *amicus* b (L)   2 **adisse** c   *abisse*
b (L)   4 **plus tamen est** b   *inscriptum est* c (E)   **legis** b   *leges*
c (E)   6 **raro** *raros* b   *quos raros* Rooy

103. 4 **riserunt** *Aiserunt* archetype of the C-class (according to
Ly)   *audierunt* Heinsius   6 **est** *et* Heinsius   **terque quaterque** b
bisque quaterque c (E)   7 **semper** c (E)   *tibi nunc* b (L)   8 **cenas**
. . . duas mensas . . . duas Rooy   11 **in ius, o** *illuso* (out of *inluso*)
b (L)   *iniusto* c (E)

107. 1 **carissime** *clarissime* P

109. 1–5 **Issa** *Ipsa* P Q L B₁   4 **lapillis** *capillis* c (E)   8 **colla** *colla* b (L)   **nixa** *nexa* c (E)   13 **monet et rogat** b *rogat et monet elevari* c (E)   19–21 **Issam** *Ipsam* P Q L

117. 6 **velit** *velis* c *uaelis* E   13 **pete** *petes* c (E) The fut. ind. often enough is equivalent to an abrupt imv.; the usage belongs to colloquial style   **Atrectum** *arrectum* (through *adrectum, atrectum*) c (E) See Renn 57   17 **denaris** c *denariis* L (unmetrical)

Book II

1. 2 **perlegeretque** *perlegeretve* P₂   5 **peragit** a L Q *peraget* c (E)

5. 3 **disiungunt** a *distingunt* (or *distinguunt*) b (L) c (E)

7. 1 **Attice** *attice* a *attale* b (L) c (E)   5 **Attice** *attice* a b *attale* c (E)   6 **es arte** *et arte* b (L)   7 **facias tamen** *facis tamen* b (L) c (E) *facis attamen* Q

11. 2 **seram** c *sera* b (L) Ly prints *seram*, but thinks *sera* may be right   10 **cenat** b c *cena est* T

14. 5 **tum** c (E) *tunc* b (L)   7 **hinc** *hic* Scriverius   13 **nam thermis iterumque iterumque iterumque lavatur** b (L) *nam thermis iterumque iterumque lavatur* c (E) *nam thermis iterum ternis iterumque lavatur* Heinsius   15 **tepidae** *tepida* b (L)

18. 8 **Maxime** *maxime* a b *postume* c (E) but the lemma shows *Ad Maximum* Ly thinks that *Postume* may have been an old variant in 1, 8

20. 2 **iure vocare** R *dicere iure* c (E)

29. 1 **terentem** c (and L) *tenentem* P Q F   5 **Marcelliano** b *marcellino* G (perhaps rightly, says Ly. See Müller, De re metrica, 299) *marcelliniano* E (which perhaps arose, as Ly suggests, out of *Marin celliano*)   8 **laesum** *album* Young Class. Rev. 6. 305   **pingit** b *cingit* c (E) *stringit* Heinsius

30. 3 **felixque** a c *fidusque* b (L) The latter reading may be correct, either in the sense of '(once) faithful' or with ironical force

38. 2 **reddit** *reddet* c

41. T gives a different order, thus: 9, 10, 12, 11, 6, 7, 13–23   6 **et nam** T   13 **severos** *saevos* T   20 **lugentique** b (L) c (E) *lugentive* a   **piumve** a *piumque* b (L) c (E)

43. 2 **sonas** *sonas?* (with Κοινὰ φίλων! in 1) Duff   4 **Parma** *terra* c (E) Ly compares 2. 46. 6, though with hesitation

57. 7 **Cladi** Salmasius *gladi* b (L) *claudi* c (E)

66. 2 **incerta** *inserta* Heraldus   3 **quo** b F c   *quod* T   4 **et ceci-dit** *caeditur et* Heinsius   **saevis** *sectis* Merula ["with her hair (i.e. scalp) cut" (P. and S.)]   **Plecusa** *plecusa* or *plecussa* a c   *phlegusa* (L) or *phlecusa* b   **comis** *genis* Markland (who also read *sectis* for *sae-vis*)   6 **tangat** *tangit* T   *tangito* Heinsius   8 **tua** a b (L)   *tuo* c (E)

71. 1 **candidius** b c   *gallidius* T (a mere graphic blunder for *calli-dius*)   2 **lego** a b   *legis* c (E)   5 **istud** a c   *illud* b (L)

Book III

2. 4 **madida** c   *madidas* b (L)   5 **piperisve** b (E)   *piperisque* c (E)   11 **rubeat** *rubeas* c (E)   12 **vindice** *iudice* c (E)

4. 1 **requiret** *requirit* T   3 **rogabit** b (L)   *rogarit* T   *rogavit* c (E)   5 **absim** a c   *absit* b (L)   **quaeret, breviter** *quae breviter quaeret* E   *breviter quaeret* X B G   7 **respondeto** *responde poetae* c (E)

12. 3 **salsa** *falsa* T Q C G

22. 2 **sed** or **set** b (L)   *et* c Ly   3 **ferres** c (E)   The other Mss have *ferre*   4 **summa** *sumpta* Heinsius   **perduxti** Scriverius *duxisti* b (L)   *perduxit* c (E)   5 **nihil** b (*nichil* L)   *nullum* c (E)

25. 4 **hic** c   *is* L Ly   *si* P

38. 3 **disertior** c (E)   *disertius* b (L)   But *discretior* T   7 **pan-gentur** *tangentur* c (E)

43. 3 **fallis** a b   *falles* c (E)

44. 4 **quid** *quod* b (L) c (E)   12 **sonas ad aurem** *tenes euntem* c (E); cf. 14   13 **licet** T b   *sinis* c (E)   14 **tenes euntem** *sonas ad aurem* c (E); cf. 12   15 **fugas** *fuga* T c (E)   18 **probus** a c   *bonus* b (L)

45. 3 **illa** a c   *ista* b (*iste* L)   5 **rhombos** a b   *rhombum* c (E)

46. 5 **cunctos** *cuneos* Turnebus Heinsius Schn.[2]   7 **causa** a c *causam* b   *cena* [*coena*] Hartman Mnemos. 25. 338

50. 5 **perlegitur** b (L)   *perletor* G_1 *porrigitur* X C G_2 *perge-tor* E   6 **neque** b (P Q)   *nec* E Ly   **venit** b (P Q)   *fuit* c (E)   7 **librum** b (L P Q)   *bruma* c (E A V B_2 G)   *broma* X   βρῶμα Gilbert Q. C. 1, n. 1   *promis* Fried. Acad. Alb. Regim. 1878, I, p. 4; id. ibid. 1878, II, p. 3   *drama* and *deinde* (for *denique*) *poema* Heinsius

52. 1 **ducentis** *ducenis* Scriverius

58. 16 **phasiana** *phasianae* c (E)   21 **agnus** E A G   *annus* X *anus* B   *anius* C   22 **serenum** *perennem* Mordtmann (cf. 10. 47. 4) 26 **subdolum** c   *subdole* b (L)   35 **Sassinatis; de silva** *Sassinate de silva* Mss Ly (with ; after *silva*) This reading is possible enough; the Romans pastured their cattle largely in the woods; see e.g. Smith on

Hor. C. 1. 31. 5 *Sassinatis, de silva* Heinsius *Sassinatis ; e silva* Rooy
39 **vimine offerunt** Heinsius *vimineo ferunt* L E

60. 1 **vocer** a D *vocor* b (L) c (E)   **4 sugitur** a b *sumitur* c (E)
5 **suillos** c *pusillos* T b   **6 at** T c *et* b (L)

63. 6 **modos** c *choros* b (L) This may be the correct reading
9 **missas** *missa* c (E)

99. 3 **innocuos** b (L) c (E) *non nocuos* T   **ludere** a b *laedere* c
(see on 3. 99. 2; 10. 5. 2)   **4 liceat, licuit** b (Q) *licuit, liceat* T c (E)

BOOK IV

8. 1 **conterit** c *continet* b (L)   **6 extructos** c (E) *excelsos* b
(L), probably a gloss on *extructos*   **11 gressu timet ire** *gressu metire* P f *gressum metire* L E

14. 4 **astus** b *fastus* c (E)   **9 tropa** Brodaeus *popa* b (L) *rota*
c (E)

18. 2 **madet** *manet* c (E)

30. 1 **monemus** b *recede* (i.e. *a lacu recede*) c (E)   **13 rogator**
rogatur E

32. 3 **laborum** *malorum* b (L)

39. 3 **manum** c *manus* P Q   **6 Gratiana** *grantiana* b (L) *gra-
niana* c (E) *Grattiana* Postgate

41. 2 **ista** *illa* b (L)

44. 6 **nomine** T b *numine* c (E)

49. 1 **nescit** T *nescis* b (L)   **2 illa** b (L) c (E) *ista* T   **vocat** a c
putas b (L)

54. 2 **cingere** *tingere* (doubtless from *contingere*, 1) b   **fronde**
fronte b (L)   **5 nulli** c *nullis* b (L Q)   **10 secat** Heinsius *neget* b
negat c (E) L Ly *negat* may well after all be right; it fits well with *nil
adicit penso*, 9, and even better with *lanificas . . . contigit*, 5–6

57. 1 **lucrini** b c *neronis* T   **2 calent** *latent* b (L)   **3 Argei**
Heinsius *argio* T *argivi* b (L) *argoi* c (E)

59. 2 **gutta** a *gemma* b (L) c (E)

64. 4 **eminent** b (L) *imminent* c This text P. and S. interpret as =
"wide sweeps (reaches, or hollows) overlook the hills on the other
side of the Tiber". But this inartistically anticipates 10 ff. Further,
such a qualification of *collibus* as P. and S. suppose should be clearly
indicated by the author, not left to the reader to supply   **8 solus**
solis G Schn. This may be the correct reading   **16 virgineo cruore:**
a troublesome passage, generally regarded as corrupt. Heinsius conjectured *virgineo canore, virgineo rubore,* or *virginea cohorte,* based
on Ovid's testimony (see Commentary) to the license and immorality

connected with the festival. Precisely because of this, I believe that *vir-gineo cruore* may stand for the loss of virginity by the girls who went there. Munro's conjecture, *virgine nequiore*, which has the merit of making good sense, is further supported by the tendency of M. to use a sing. instead of the plural; cf. e.g. 1. 70. 10; 9. 22. 4; 9. 22. 10   **18 illinc** b *illic* c (E)   **19 patet** b (Q)   *iacet* c (E)   **32 centeno** c   *contento* (*contentum*) b (Q)

69. 1 **ponis** b c   *potas* T   **2 Papyle** L E   *Pamphile* Renn 58

75. 4 **participique** c (E)   *participeque* P   *participemque* L Q   *participare* T   See Gilbert Rh. Mus. 39. 518   **5 iniecta**   *inlecta* T b (L) *intecta* c (E)   **7 certo**   *certe* Q   **pignore**   *pignora* c (E)   **vitae** b c   *famam* T (cf. 6)

79. 2 **rus** b · *ius* c (E)

BOOK V

8. 3 **recepit**   *recipit* b   **5 rubens** b (L)   *ruber* c Ly

14. 4 **paene tertius**   *semitertius* Hartman Mnemos. 24. 339 **11 sedere** Scriverius   *se dedere* L Q E   **Leïtoque**   *letoque* b (L)

20. 10 **loca**   *ioca* Madv. Adv. Cr. 2. 163; cf. Fried. Burs. Jahresb. 2. 1142   **11 necuter sibi** Schn.   *neuter sibi* b (L)   *nec ut eius ibo* c (E)   **22.** 5 **Suburani**   *suburbani* L E   **7 mulorum**   *murorum* b (L) **rumpere** b   *vincere* c (E)

34. 3 **parvola (parvula) ne** a (R T) c (E X) F   *pallida nec* b (L) *paulula ne* Scriverius

37. 5 **Indicae dentem**   *indicentem* T   *indicae gentem* c (E) **12 pavo**   *pano* T b   *pavus* c (E)   **22 notam**   *noram* c (E) Schenkl, putting a period after 21, read *noram superbam* (*eam*), nobilem, *locu-pletem.*, and gave the verse to M. The passage thus treated is, however, far less effective

42. 7 **quidquid (quicquid)** b (L)   *siquid* c (E)

49. 5 **possunt** a b (L Q)   *possint* c (E)   **9 tunc** b (L) c (E) *tum* a   **11 Geryonem**   *Geryonen* Renn 66 (cf. Burs. Jahresb. 72. 185) Ly

56. 4 **devites**   *divites* b (L) c (E)   **6 Tutilium**   *utilium* c (E) **relinquat** b (L)   *relinquas* c (E)

58. 3 **longest**   *longe est* b (L)   *longe* (without *est*) c Ly (though he suggests that *longest* should perhaps be read)   **6 posset** b (L)   *possit* c **7 tardum** b (L)   *serum* c Ly   This may be the correct reading

64. 5 **tam** b   *iam* c (E)

76. 1 **poto**   *toto* b (L) c (E)

81. 2 **nulli** T   *nullis* b (Q) F c (E) Ly   *nullius* R

Book VI

8. 1 **praetores** *praecones* T   This reading would hopelessly ruin the epigram   6 **dic, numquid** *digno nequid* b (L) *dignum quid* c (E)

28. 6 **integer** c   *innocens* b (E)   8 **messibus** *mensibus* b (L)
9 **adplicabat** *applicarat* (?) Postgate

35. 3 **dicis** R b (L, corrected from *ducis*) *ducis* T

51. 4 **inquis** b   *inquit* T c (E) Ly   *inquit* is possible enough (supply *Lupercus* as subject), but is less effective than *inquis*. We may get a still better effect by setting a question-mark after *inquis*

70. 10 **separentur** Mss   *separetur* J. D. Duff

80. 8 **tonsilibus** T R b   *textilibus* c (E)   *sutilibus* Scriverius

82. 6 **Batavam** *habebat avam* F   *Boetam* Ruhnken   Cf. Gilbert Rh. Mus. 39. 520; Müller, De re metrica, 287

88. 3 **constat** T L$_1$ *constet* b (L$_2$) E

Book VII

3. 2 **ne . . . mittas** b   *nec . . . mittas* R   *nec . . . mittis* c (E)

17. 9 **delicata** c (E) Q   See Munro Jour. of Phil. 9. 219   *dedicata* b (L) See Fried. Rec. loc. Mart. 5

21. 1 **quae magni** R Q c   *magni quae* b (L) Ly

47. 5 **flebat** *flebant* Postgate   6 Ly regards this verse as corrupt; he prints † *tristitia et lacrimis iamque peractus eras* † : **Tristitia** *tristia* P Q   **et lacrimis** *tristia cum lacrimis* Scriverius   *illacrimans* Gilbert   *a lacrimis* Munro (this phrase he connects with *secura*)   *Tristitia exanimis* Zingerle   **iamque peractus** Ly thinks that *iam reparatus* may perhaps be read   8 **raptas** *ruptas* Gronovius

54. 1 **mera** E F   *mihi* B P Q   *mala* Gilbert Rh. Mus. 40. 212   *nova* Rooy   *tua* Schn.[2]

85. 3 **belle** *felle* b (L)

86. 7 **Hispani** *argenti* c (E)   8 **levis** c   *tenuis* b (L)   This reading, however, is contrary to M.'s practice of writing a spondee in the first foot of a hendecasyllabic verse; see § 49, a

88. 9 **blandae** b   *blande* L (in late times *e* often replaced *ae*) *blandi* c (E)   *magnae* T

90. 3 **Calvinus** *calvianus* T   *Cluvienus* Schn.[2] (see Philol. 3. 331)

92. 1 **scis** T c   *tibi* b (L)   2 **uno bis** T c   *bis nobis* b (L)   10 **ne** b F c   *nec* T B V   *non* E   *nec* may well enough be read; after an *affirmative* clause of purpose *nec* (not *neve*) is common enough, even in good prose. If *nec* is read, omit the comma after 9   **si quid opus** Gilbert Q. C. 1   *quid sit opus* Mss

96. 4 **male** Heinsius   *mala* Mss   7 **serior** b (L)   *serius* c (E)

Book VIII

3. 19 Romano lepidos b (L) *romanos lepidos* T *romano lepido* c (E) *romanos lepido* G **22 tubas** *tubam* c (E)

6. 1 Aucti F and the lemmata of E (AVCTI) and of T (AVTI) as well as the gloss **αὐτῷ** in E (where the text reading is *studiosius illo*) make for *Aucti* as against *Eucti* b (L) *illo* c **3 fumosa** Lipsius and most editors *furiosa* Mss Ly *cariosa* Heinsius It seems impossible to interpret *furiosa*. The note in B. and L. ("possibly 'maddening in its antiquity'") seems absurd **5 Laomedonteae** *laomedontea* c (E)

10. 3 solvet c (E X) *solvit* b (L)

14. 4 sine faece b c *sine sole* R

17. 3 narrasti *navasti* A. Palmer, Hermathena, 9. 165

18. 1 si *sic* c (E) **2 possis** *poscis* b (L) **6 nosset** b c *possit* T The reading of T may perhaps, as Ly suggests, have arisen out of an original *posset* (cf. 8)

32. 3 hoc casus *occasus* T L E **4 sibi** T c (E) F *diu* b (P Q f)

50. 7 orbem *urbem* b (L) **14 Palladia et** Heinsius *Palladius* Mss Ly The word, however, seems everywhere else to be feminine **21 Istanti** Munro *instanti* b *instantis* c (E) See App. on 8. 73. 1

55. 4 sonare *tonare* Heinsius **5 sint** b c (E) *sunt* T If *sunt* is read, see on 1. 79. 2 **21 ditataque** *dictataque* c (E) L Q *dicataque* T **23 ergo ero** b (L) c (E) *ergo ego* T

57. 1 expuit c *expulit* b (L)

73. 1 Istanti *Instani* b (L) *stant* c (E) See App. on 8. 50. 21 **5 lasciva** b (L) *lascive* c Ly (with comma after *fecit*) *pulchra* (6) and *formosa* (8) make for *lasciva*

Book IX

11. 12 rebellas b (*rebella* L) F *repugnas* c (E)

15. 1 tumulis b *tumulo* c (E)

18. 4 tollit *ducit* c (E)

22. 2 populus b (L) *vulgus* c (E) *vulgus* is probably a gloss on *populus* **3 ut Setina** *vos et ina* c (E) On the basis of the reading of c Oudendorp wrote *quo Setina* **14 massyleum** b (*mossileum virga* L) This seems a better reading than the Mss *Massyla meum*, which is kept by Ly (who thinks that the reading of b arose out of *Massylāeum = Massyla meum*); the local epithet fits *ecum* far better than it would suit *virga* **15 superos ac sidera** *superos ad sidera* c (E) *sideraque et supera* b (L)

30. 5 daret sanctam *dare sanctis* c (E)

46. 3 nunc illas R c   *aut illas* b (L)   mutatque R   *mutatve* b *mutuatve* L   On punctuation of 3–4 see J. S. Reid Class. Rev. 11. 351 and Friedländer's note on these verses

48. 1, 11 Garrice   *Gallice* c (E), but *De Garrico* is in the lemma of c 8 pallida Dousa; Heinsius   *callida* T b (Q; *calida* L) E Ly   So too B. and L., who interpret *callida Roma* as = "the Roman gourmet", thus understanding *callida* of Rome's knowledge of table-dainties; cf., then, in a way, the description of Montanus in Iuv. 3. 139–142 *nulli maior fuit usus edendi tempestate mea: Circeis nata forent an Lucrinum ad saxum Rutupinove edita fundo ostrea callebat primo deprendere morsu* (note especially *callebat* in 142). But after all *callida*, thus interpreted, does not square with the note on 5

59. 13 vitro   *nitro* b (L)   19 veros Aldus   *vero* b   *viro* c (E)

60. 6 putet   *putat* c (E)   *pudet* T

61. 1 Tartesiacis   *tarpesiacis* c (E)   9 nemus b   *suum* c (E) 11–14 The order of verses differs in the Mss.   P Q have in sequence 13, 14, 11, 12; this order Ly adopts.   E has 14, 11, 13, 12.   The order adopted in this edition is due to Munro (see Friedländer's notes on this epigram), who calls attention to the fact that in the Ovidian passage which M. evidently has in mind (M. 8. 746–748 *saepe sub hac Dryades festas duxere choreas, saepe etiam manibus nexis et ordine trunci circuiere modum*) the verses beginning with *saepe* immediately follow each other   12 latuit b   *placuit* c (E), possibly the correct reading.   The thought then is that, though the nymph fled, Pan caught up with her

68. 4 tonas T   *sonas* b (L)   *tonos* E   6 causidicum medio… equo b (P) c   *causidico medium … equum* T   *medico* L Q

81. 4 malim T c   *mallem* b (L)

88. 2 cepisti b   *coepisti* R   *desisti* c (E)

100. 4 viduas b (L)   *vetulas* c (E)   5 vetusque b (F)   *putrisque* c (E)   See Lindsay Anc. Ed. M. 20

BOOK X

2. 4 utrique c   *ubique* b (L)   11 et saecula T R   *nec saecula* b (L) c (E)   *nec saecula desunt* Burmann

5. 3 urbem b c   *urbis* T

10. 3 hic ego   *dic ego* Heinsius   5 respiciet   *respicies* c (E) 8 et b (L)   *set* c (E)   *et* may stand perfectly well after *nec*, 7 ; frequently after a negative sentence *et* and *-que* have (apparently) adversative force.   For the position of *et* see on Lib. Spect. 29. 2   ire b (L)   *isse* C Ly   *iste* c (E)   For the tense of *isse*, if read, see on *eripuisse*, 1. 107. 6

13. 3 **Mani, dilectus** b   *mansuetus* c (E)   *Mani consuetus* Schn.   Ly thinks the reading of E may have arisen out of an original *Mani consuetus*. *Consuetus*, however, is not a very happy reading; it too readily suggests the phrase *consuescere cum aliquo*, which, though used at times in an honorable sense, is more often employed *in malam partem*. *Diligo*, on the other hand, is always a noble word, denoting affection based on esteem   8 **hospes** b   *hoste* E   *hostis* X   *hos et* T

17. 7 **cogit**   *coxit* Heinsius

20. 2 **tamen** b (L)   *talia* c (E)   Ly thinks this reading may have arisen out of *Thalia* (*thalia*) in 3   **15 studet** b (L)   *vacat* c (E) *studet* is supported by the Mss of Plin. Ep. 3. 21

21. 2, 5 **Sexte**   *sexte* c (*sextae* E)   *crispe* b (L)   6 **ut** b   *et* c (E)

23. 3 **tutos** b (*tuos* L) c (E)   *totos* T

25. 3 **durusque tibi fortisque** a b   *fortisque tibi durusque* c (E)

27. 3 **et** b c   *at* T

30. 17 **cubili** b (L)   *cubiculo* c (E)   25 **permittit** b (L)   *permittis* c   Ly   With this reading *Roma* must be set off by commas

31. 1 **ducentis** T c (E)   *trecentis* b (L)   6 **comes** T c   *voras* b (L)

32. 5 **posset** b   *possis* c (E)

35. 8 **pios amores** b (L)   *probos amicos* c (E)   *probos amores* Ly **18 amaret** b   *amarit* L (corrected to *amaret*)   *amarat* c   See Gilbert Q. C. 23

39. 1 **quod** T b   *quid* c (E)   3 **namque, ut** T c   *nam qui* b (L, but without *ut*)   **narrant** T b   *narres* c (E)

47. 1 **faciant** T c (E)   *faciunt* b (L)   **beatiorem** c   *beatorum* T (Ly thinks this may have arisen out of *beatiorum*)   *iocundiorem* b (L) This reading, thinks Ly, may be due to the proximity of *iucundissime* in 2

48. 2 **redit iam subiitque cohors** Paley and Stone   This reading is given by Fried. in his text   *redit iamque subitque cohors* Mss Ly *redit iam aere iubente* (or *sonante*) *cohors* Wagner (see Fried. Rec. loc. Mart. 7)   *et pila iam*, *tereti iam subit orbe* (or *aere*) *trochus* Heinsius 3 **nimios . . . vapores** b (P)   *nimio . . . vapore* c (E)   **11 rutatos** *ructatos* T   *rutaceos* f   *roctatos* L   *roratos* P   *r . . atos* Q   **20 trima** Heinsius   See Hermes, 3. 122 (Haupt)   *prima* L E Ly   Paley and Stone, who retain *prima*, interpret it as meaning "either 'which was first laid down in the second consulship of Frontinus', or 'which was the choicest product of that year'". It is hard to see, however, how they get the first interpretation; the other gives too high praise to the wine, praise out of keeping with the spirit of the epigram (unless we suppose playful irony, and so interpret by contraries)   **21 accedent** P Q f (but *accedant* L)   *accedunt* T   **23 de prasino conviva meus venetoque**

loquatur T (see Lindsay Anc. Ed. M. 14)   *de prasino scutoque meus conviva loquatur* b (L)   This Gruter followed, except that in place of *scutoque* he conjectured *Scorpoque   de prasino conviva meus scipioque loquatur* c (E)   Ly thinks that *scipioque* in the reading of c may have arisen out of an original *Scorpoque*   **24 faciunt** T c (E)   *facient* b

50. 7 **semper**   καμπή A. Palmer, Hermathena, 9. 165 ff.

65. 11 **filia** b   *fistula* Schn.[2]   *nobis nil Laco fortius loquetur* Munro *nobis ilia fortius loquentur* Haupt Opus. 3. 562   *ilia . . . loquuntur* Gilbert

66. 4 **polluit**   *palluit* R   **igne** b   *ille* R

74. 6 **ferventis**   *flaventis* Heinsius

83. 4 **iubente**   *iuuente* c   *iuuante* C

89. 1 **labor, Polyclite, tuus**   *tuus, Polyclite, labos* Heinsius   **2 meruisse**   *peperisse* Heinsius

96. 9 **macellus** b   *macelli* c (E)

BOOK XI

3. 1 **Pimpleïde**   *pieride* b (L)   *pipeide* c (E)   **10 darent** Heinsius *daret* Mss

5. 7 **te colet** Q   *tholet* E A   *te volet* X   *tollet* V

18. 9 **Cosmi** T   *costi* c E   This may well be the correct reading; it would give far greater symmetry to the verse, in view of the Eastern origin of *piper*; both references would then be to Eastern plants **12 urucam** T c (E)   *erucam* b (*eruca* L)   **15 mariscae**   *aristae* Gilbert Rh. Mus. 40. 218   *myricae* Fr. Schoell

35. 2 **ad te** L E   *a te* m

42. 2 **quid** T F c   *qui* b (L) Ly   This is a very effective reading; translate, '(but) how can that be done?'   *Quid?* Gilbert Rh. Mus. 40. 219

52. 13 **conchylia** c (*conchilia* E)   *coloephia* b (L)   This may be corrupted from *colēpia*, 'knuckles of beef or pork'

80. 6 **inprobi** c (E)   *inprobum* b (L)   **7 tibi**   *mihi* Gilbert Q. C. 2; so too in his second edition, in the critical notes on this passage   *tamen* Munro

84. 1 **umbras** T Q   *undas* L c (E)   **2 fugiat** a b   *fugiet* c (E) **4 furit**   *fuerit* T   *fugit* c (E) and L (corrected to *furit*)   **5 mitior** b (*micior* L) c (E)   *mitius* T   **10 nudo** b c   *duro* a Ly

86. 6 **haec** a b (*hec* L)   *hoc* c (E)

91. 3 **qui** c (*quia* E)   *quid* b (L)

BOOK XII

3. 4 **dicet** c   *dicit* b (L)   **5 videmur**   *videntur* c (E)   **6 mihi** *minus* c (E)

6. 2 **toto** *tuto* Gilbert   Friedländer would compare 12. 5. 3   7 **habes** b   *habet* c (E) F   11 **nunc**   *hunc* c (E)   This wholly impossible reading arose easily out of confusion of H and N

17. 3 **tecum pariter pariterque** P Q f   *tecum pariter tecumque* T Ly   *tecum pariterque* b (L) A   *tectum pariterque* c   9 **cum sit ei pulchre** b (L)   *cum si te pulcre* c (E)   *sit tam* N   *cum recubet pulcre* T Ly

18. 1 **erras**   *eras* L Q   24 **dispensat pueris** c   *dispensant pueri* b (L)

29. 1 **sexagena** Voss   *sexaginta* Mss   6 **Numidum**   *numadum* b   *Nomadum* Schn. Ly   **regas** Heinsius   *petas* b Ly   *regas* is far the better reading   11 **ablatis**   *oblatis* Heinsius

31. 5 **lymphis** T c   *nymphis* b (L)   *nympha = aqua* is possible in poetry   8 **has . . . domos** b c   *has . . . dapes* T   *hos . . . lares* Heinsius

34. 1 **messes** b   *menses* L c (E)   3 **quarum** b   *quorum* c (E) 8 **velis** b (L) c (E)   *voles* T

57. 5 **magistri** a c   *magister* b (L)   9 **palucis** Friedländer *paludis* b (L) c (E)   *balucis* Turnebus Heinsius   22 **colle** b   *monte* c (E) 23 **clausus** c (E)   *latus* b (L) Ly

82. 4 **acceptas** b   *exceptas* c (E)   5 **laxum**   *lapsum* Q   5, 12 **colliget** G   *colligit* L E   10 **dicet**   *dices* c (E)   11 **feret**   *bibet* Hartman   **tropin** m   *propin* Mss

94. 5 **Calabris**   *calabris* T   *doctis* b (L) c (E)   9 **potest** b *potes* a c (E)   **fingere coepi** a P   *scribere coepi* L Q f   *pingere possis* c (E)   10 **palma** T   *fama* b c (E)   *forma* L

BOOK XIII

1. 5 **talo** b (L) c (E)   *telo* T Ly   This is a possible reading; gambling is often enough described in military terms (cf. e.g. Iuv. 1. 90–92 *posita . . . luditur arca. Proelia quanta illic dispensatore videbis armigero!* Cf. also *depugnat* in our text, with note

3. 4 **faciet** b c   *faciat* T Ly

77. 1 **defecta** c   *defacta* a   *deficiens* b (L)

BOOK XIV

37. 1 **selectos** T   *constrictos* b (L) c   *(constictos* E)

187. 1 **hac** a c   *haec* b E

189. 1 **iuvenale** T R c   *iuvenile* Q F   2 **nec** b c (E)   *non* T R

194. 1 **dicant** T P c   *dicunt* R Q

INDEX OF PASSAGES CITED IN
THE NOTES

The various works cited are indicated by the abbreviations used in the notes.

This index supplies material for interesting and instructive study. When all allowances have been made for personal bias of an editor for certain parts of Latin literature and for his consequently greater familiarity with such parts, the illustrative passages cited by him in his Commentary throw much light on the range of his author's interests, subject-matter, reading, etc. Thus, what is said in § 33 about the limitations of M.'s acquaintance with Greek models is fully confirmed by the very small number of passages to be found in this index from Greek authors. In like manner the passages cited from Catullus, Horace, Ovid, and Vergil illuminate §§ 33–34. How deeply interested M. was in the subjects that claimed the attention of his contemporaries is seen by the passages cited from Pliny the Younger, Petronius, Statius, and Juvenal. The passages from Juvenal light up § 19; those from Statius supplement § 18.

GENERAL INDEX

This index seeks to include the more important matters treated in the Introduction and the Notes. It is not in any sense an *index verborum*; occasionally, however, for the sake of completeness, references (inclosed in marks of parenthesis) are given to verses in which the lemma, word or phrase, occurs, though there is no discussion of the particular matter in the commentary on the verses themselves.

a final, long before *sp*, 2. 66. 8; before *str*, 5. 69. 3; *Nausicaä*, 12. 31. 9; *Glycerä*, 14. 187. 2.

abacus, in schools, 10. 62. 4.

Abdera, noted for stupidity, 10. 25. 4.

ablative, of duration, 2. 5. 1; 3. 63. 7; 4. 25. 1; 9. 68. 9; 12. 17. 1; of cause, Lib. Spect. 1. 3; with *comitatus*, 5. 9. 2.

abstract ideas and qualities personified, 7. 47. 5–6.

ac, once only in M., 9. 22. 15.

accedere = passive, 10. 48. 21.

accipere pilam, 12. 82. 4.

accusative, of exclamation, 5. 53. 2; of effect, 5. 34. 5–6; 8. 32. 3; 9. 59. 11; 12. 21. 3–4; with verbs of feeling, 1. 33. 1; with *fragrare*, 5. 37. 9; with *scribere*, 4. 49. 3–4; with *tacere*, 2. 11. 3; with *loqui*, 1. 61. 8; 7. 63. 8; 8. 55. 21; 10. 96. 1; 12. 82. 7; with pf. pass. ptc., 6. 41. 1.

Achilleae comae, 12. 82. 10.

Achillei pedes, 2. 14. 4.

Achilles, type of manly beauty, etc., in Homer, 2. 14. 4.

addicere = *vendere* or *venumdare*, 10. 31. 1; *addixti*, form, 10. 31. 1.

adhibere, 'invite' (to dinner), 10. 27. 2.

adhuc, 'still', 'yet', 8. 3. 2; with comparative, 5. 22. 9.

adjective, of number or quantity with sing. noun, 1. 70. 6; 3. 58. 7; 7. 36. 3–4; 7. 63. 8; 8. 3. 7; 9. 22. 4; distributive, in sing., 4. 64. 32; = adv., 1. 70. 15; 8. 50. 6; carries main idea, 9. 26. 7; 10. 23. 7; from proper names, 10. 30. 6.

ad lucernas, 10. 20. 18.

ad Pirum, 1. 117. 6.

adplicare, with dat., 6. 28. 8.

adserere, 1. 15. 9–10; 7. 63. 10; 10. 35. 5.

adsidere, of attending the sick, 2. 41. 19.

adtritus, 'shameless', 10. 72. 2.

adverb, used with noun, 3. 58. 51; with *sub*, 10. 50. 8; 12. 17. 9.

Advolans, 5. 24. 1, 6.

Aeacides = Achilles, 8. 6. 12.

Aeacus, 10. 5. 14.

Aedes Florae, 5. 22. 4.

fax, at funerals, 8. 43. 2.

fenerare (*aliquem*), 1. 76.6; 1. 85. 4.

fera, 'creature', 4. 59. 2.

fercula, 3. 50. 5.

ferre = *auferre*, 6. 70. 8; = *efferre*, 10. 5. 9; pun on, 2. 1. 2; *laudibus ferre*, 'extol', Lib. Spect. 1. 6.

ferre patique, 12. 29. 8.

ferrum = *ensis*, 1. 42.6; = *securis*, 9. 61. 20; 'knife', 10. 48. 15.

ferula, used in schools, 10. 62. 10.

fervens, 'resplendent', 10. 74. 6.

festinatus, 'forced', said of roses, 13. 127. 1.

festuca, 1. 15. 9–10.

fictitious names in M., § 38; 2. 41. 6; 5. 24. 1.

Fidenae, 4. 64. 15.

Fidentinus, plagiarist, 1. 29. Introd.; 1. 38; 1. 53.

fides, 1. 15. 2.

figs (Chian), 7. 25. 8.

figura = *imago*, 'portrait', 1. 53. 2.

final cl., after *facio*, *proficio*, 5. 76. 2.

fingere, of literary work, 12. 94. 9; work in clay, 8.·6. 2; 8. 24. 5; (10. 39. 4).

finger-rings, use of, 2. 29. 2; gold, worn by *equites*, 8. 5. Introd.; display of, 11. 59. Introd.

fire-insurance, unknown, 3. 52. 2.

fires in Rome, 3. 52.2; set, 3. 52. 4.

fishing, 3. 58. 25. See *calamus*; *linea*; *saeta*.

fish-ponds, 4. 30. Introd. See *piscina*; *stagna*; *vivaria*.

fistula, of Pan's pipe, 9. 61. 14.

Flaccus, 4. 49. 1; 8. 56. 5; 10. 48. 5; 11. 80. 3; of Patavium?, 1. 61. 4; 1. 76. Introd. See Horatius Flaccus.

Flaccilla, mother of M., § 6; 5. 34. Introd., 1, 7.

flagellare, 2. 30. 4; 5. 13. 6.

flagellum (*flagrum*), 8. 23. 3; 10. 62. 8.

flamingo, eaten, 3. 58. 14.

Flaminia Via, 3. 4. 2; 3. 14. 4; 4. 64. 18; 11. 13. 1.

Flavus, 10. 104. Introd.

flebilis, 10. 61. 5–6.

flere, with acc., 1. 33. 1; 6. 28. 10.

Flora, temple and worship of, 5. 22.4.

flumen, 'canal', 10. 58. 4.

focale, 4. 41. Introd.

focus, 8. 50. 4; 9. 61.20; 10. 96.8; 12. 18. 19; = *fornax*, 'crucible', 8. 50. 4; sacred to *lares*, 2. 90. 7; 3. 58. 22.

foedus, 1. 10. 3.

foliatum unguentum, 11. 18. 9.

follis, in game of ball, 12. 82. 5.

fools: see *morio*.

Formiae, 10. 30. 1.

formonsus, 5. 29. 2.

forms: in declension 1, dat. and abl. pl. in -*is* (not -*iis*), 1. 117. 17; 4. 18. 1; gen. pl. in -*um*, 12. 29. 6; in declension 2, gen. sing. in -*i* (not -*ii*), 1. 109. 5; dat. and abl. pl. in -*is* (not -*iis*), 1. 117. 17; in declension 4, gen. pl. in -*um* (not -*uum*), 2. 5. 3; of verb, *addixti*, 10. 31. 1. See also archaism; Greek; *here*.

foro abire, *cedere*, 5. 20. 6.

forsitan, with ind., 8. 32. 7–8; 10. 104. 7; 12. 18. 1.

fortis, of style, 8. 18. 8; of sound, 'loud', 3. 46. 10.

fortune-hunting: see *captatio*, *captatores*.

mordere, of cold, 8. 14. 2.
morio, at dinner, 8. 13. Introd.
morsus, 'pungency', 7. 25. 5.
morsus animi, 12. 34. 9.
morus, 1. 72. 5.
Mucius, story of, enacted by male-
    factor, 10. 25. Introd. See also
    Scaevola.
mucro, 4. 18. 6.
mule, as roadster, 9. 22. 13–14.
mulio, 10. 76. 9.
mullus, 2. 43. 11; 3. 45. 5; 10. 30. 24;
    10. 31. 3.
multa, 'many a', 3. 58. 7. .
Mulvius Pons, 3. 14. 4; 4. 64. 23.
municeps, 10. 65. 1.
murena, 10. 30. 22.
murex, 2. 16. 3; 13. 87.
murrina, 9. 59. 14.
Musae severiores, 9. 11. 17.
Muses, associated with Apollo, 1.
    70. 15; 7. 63. 11. See Camenae;
    Helicon; Pierides; *Pierius*; *Casta-
    lides sorores*.
music, Oriental, discordant, 11. 84.
    3–4.
mustum, 11. 18. 24.
mutuus, 2. 30. 1.
Myron, 8. 50. 1; 4. 39. 2.
myrtela, 3. 58. 2.
Mys, a *caelator*, 8. 50. 1.

names, κατ' ἀντίφρασιν, 10. 76. 9;
    freely treated in meter, 9. 11. 15.
    See fancy names; fictitious names;
    freedmen.
nanus, 8. 13. Introd.
nardinum, 11. 18. 9.
narrare, 'chatter', 'babble', 3. 46.
    7, 8; 3. 63. 13; as term of rhet-
    oric, 8. 17. 3.

Nasidianus, 7. 54. Introd.
Naso: see Ovid.
nasus rhinocerotis, 1. 3. 6.
natalis dies: see *dies natalis*; birth-
    day.
natare, trans., 4. 30. 3.
natus (*nemo natum te putat*), 10.
    27. 4.
Nausicaa, 12. 31. 9; *Nausicaā*, ibid.
navita = nauta, 6. 80. 3.
nec = ne . . . quidem, 1. 109. 20; 1.
    113. 2; 3. 2. 12; 4. 44. 8; 5. 69. 4;
    8. 14. 6; 9. 22. 12; 9. 48. 9–10;
    10. 2. 11; 10. 10. 7; 11. 52. 15; 12.
    18. 4; 12. 31. 3; = *neve, neu*, Lib.
    Spect. 1. 2; 1. 70. 6; 2. 36. 3; 5.
    34. 9; Critical Appendix on 7.
    91. 10; = *et tamen non*, 4. 69. 4;
    10. 29. 16; 10. 30. 12; 10. 31. 2;
    nec . . . et, 10. 2. 11; 10. 10. 7–8;
    nec . . . -que, 8. 50. 11.
nectar, 4. 32. 2; = *vinum*, 8. 50. 17;
    9. 11. 5; *nectare dulcius*, pro-
    verbial, 9. 11. 5.
necuter = neuter or *ne alteruter
    quidem*, 5. 20. 11.
negare, with inf., 7. 36. 1.
negative, double, 12. 51. 5–6; nega-
    tive sentences, condensation in,
    8. 50. 3–4.
Nemean lion, 4. 57. 5.
Nemesis, Tibullus's, 8. 73. 7.
nemus, 12. 31. 1–2; 8. 14. 1–2; 9.
    61. 9.
Nepos, friend of M., 10. 48. 5.
Neptune builds walls of Troy, 8.
    6. 6.
nequam, 'roguish', 1. 109. 1; 10.
    35. 11.
nequitiae, used of epigrams, 6. 82. 5.
Nereus, 10. 30. 19.

Prometheus, 10. 39. 3; 11.84. 9–10.

promulsis, 1. 43. 3–8; 3. 50. 3; olives served at, 1. 43. (3), 8; 1. 103.7; (11.52.11,12). See *gustus*.

prope, with *sum*, 10. 50. 8.

proper name, from adj., 10. 30. 6.

Propertius, § 33; 8. 73. Introd., 5; 14. 189. Introd., 1–2.

property rights of women, 4. 75. 3.

propinare, 8. 6. 13–14.

Proserpina, 3. 43. 3.

protasis, substitute for, 1. 79. 2; 3. 35. 2; 5. 56. 8; 6. 70. 7–10; in a command, 1. 107. 3; 2. 29. 10; in imv. subjv. clause, 11.84.9; in a question, 1. 70. 2; 3. 4. 5; in a statement, 3. 38. 8; 3. 46. 5; in a wish, 6. 70. 7–10; in a participle, 1. 12. 12; in abl. abs., 10. 35. 21.

prototomi, 10. 48. 16.

proverbs, 1. 3. 6; 1. 27. Introd., 7; 2. 43. 1; 2. 77. 2; 3. 43. 2; 5. 13. 3; 5. 37. 6; 5. 39. 9; 6. 11. 10; 6. 11. Introd.; 7. 88. 7; 8. 9. 3; 9. 11. 5; 10. 13. 7–8; 11. 5. 3; 12. 10. 2. See Greek.

provinces, Roman writers born in, § 1.

provincials, gravitation of, toward Rome, § 1; 3. 14. Introd.

Publilius Syrus: see Syrus.

Publius, 1. 109; 2. 57. 3.

pudor, 12. 94. 11.

puella = uxor, 7. 88. 4; 10. 35. 1, 3; 'lass', 10. 35. 20.

puer = servus, 1. 41. 8.

pueri molles, slaves, 9. 59. 3.

pueri virginesque, 9. 68. 2.

pugillares, 1. 2. 3.

pugnare, with inf., 10. 10. 8.

pulchre esse, with dat., 12. 17. 9.

pulpitum, at *recitatio*, 1. 76. 13.

pulsare ianuam, 10. 20. 12–13.

pulsare pectus, sign of grief, 2. 11. 5; 5. 37. 19.

pumex, used to smooth *frontes* of books, 1. 66. 10; 4. 57. 2.

pumiliones, fought in arena, 1. 43. (10)

Punica, of Silius Italicus, 4. 14. Introd., 2–5, 3–4.

Punica fides, 4. 14. 2.

Punica grana (mala), 1. 43. 6.

Punica spongea, 4. 10. 5–6.

purple, Tyrian, 2. 16. 3; (2. 43. 7); 6. 11. 7, 8; 10. 17. 7; 13. 87; smell of, 2. 16. 3. See *murex*; *Sidon*; *Tyrianthina*; *Tyros*.

purpura, 2. 16. 3; 'men of rank', 10. 5. 1; = *flabellum*, 10. 30. 15; = parchment cover of book, 3. 2. 10. See purple.

pusillus, 1. 9. 2.

pustulae, on silver, 7. 86. 7; 8. 50. 6.

pustulatum (argentum), 7. 86. 7; (8. 50. 6).

putator, 3. 58. 9.

pycta, pyctes, 11. 84. 14.

Pylades, 6. 11. 1.

Pyrrha, 5. 53. 4.

Pyrrhus, 11. 5. 8.

quacks, medical, 1. 47.

quadrantes centum, amount of *sportula*, 3. 7. Introd.; 4. 64. 1; 6.88.4.

quaero, with inf., 1. 2. 2; 11.84. 1.

quam, omission of, after *plus*, etc., 9. 100. 4.

quantity, variation in, § 54, b.

-que . . . -que, 5. 14. 5.

quercus = quercea corona, 4. 54. 1.